Power Without Responsibility

Press, Broadcasting and the Internet in Britain

Eighth edition

James Curran and Jean Seaton

LONDON AND NEW YORK

Eighth edition published 2018
by Routledge
2 Park Square, Milton Park, Abingdon, Oxon, OX14 4RN

and by Routledge
711 Third Avenue, New York, NY 10017

Routledge is an imprint of the Taylor & Francis Group, an informa business

First edition published by Fontana 1981
Second edition published by Methuen 1985
Third edition published by Routledge 1988
Seventh edition published by Routledge 2010

British Library Cataloguing-in-Publication Data
A catalogue record for this book is available from the British Library

Library of Congress Cataloging-in-Publication Data
Names: Curran, James, author. | Seaton, Jean, author.
Title: Power without responsibility: press, broadcasting and the internet in britain / James Curran and Jean Seaton.
Description: Eighth edition. | London; New York, NY: Routledge, 2018.
Identifiers: LCCN 2018001982 | ISBN 9780415706421 (hbk) | ISBN 9780415710428 (pbk) | ISBN 9781351212298 (ebk)
Subjects: LCSH: Press–Great Britain. | Broadcasting–Great Britain. | Digital media–Great Britain.
Classification: LCC PN5114.C84 2010 | DDC 072–dc23
LC record available at https://lccn.loc.gov/2018001982

ISBN: 978-0-415-70642-1 (hbk)
ISBN: 978-0-415-71042-8 (pbk)
ISBN: 978-1-351-21229-8 (ebk)

Typeset in Garamond
by Sunrise Setting Ltd, Brixham, UK

This book
offers
myth-
media
   It l
gone
of me
the ca

   Th
remal
declir
reforr
gram:
conte
to tal
Corby
It doe

Jame
Lond

Jean
and I

of progress;
; provides a
act of social
media.
t it has also
as 'a classic
has 'cracked
guages.
ess and the
, the moral
attempts to
etween pro-
n the wider
en updated
of Jeremy
ocial media.
a outcomes.

niversity of

estminster,

Praise for this book

'This is the book that changed everything in media studies.'

Sally Young, *University of Melbourne*

'This is a brilliant seminal history of broadcasting, press and the new media, vividly and insightfully told, with sharp vignettes of political interference and policy challenges. It is a powerful reminder of why public service broadcasting and truthful communication is vital to our democracy.'

Baroness Helena Kennedy,
President of Mansfield College, Oxford

'This skillfully revised and updated edition of Curran and Seaton's magnificent history is just as fresh and relevant now as it has been over the decades.'

David Hesmondhalgh, *Leeds University*

'The pleasure of a classic that just keeps redelivering. *Power Without Responsibility* proves itself yet again as the go-to source for analysis of the British media at their best and worst.'

Barbie Zelizer, *Annenberg School of Communication, University of Pennsylvania*

'If I was able to suggest one book about the history of journalism – whether to a student, a journalist or someone who simply wanted to know more about the role of the news media in our democracy – it would be *Power Without Responsibility*. Much of our understanding of the past is altered by the present, so we are all indebted to James Curran and Jean Seaton for this excellent new edition. There has been no shortage of controversies and debates about the news media in recent years: this book guides us through them with a sharp eye, a clear head, and the wisdom that comes from a formidable sense of history. Packed with eloquently delivered information, it is analytical but jargon-free, critical without ever being doctrinaire.'

Justin Lewis, *Cardiff University*

To our children and their partners: Kitty, Tristan, Cassie, Daniel, Margherita, Nathaniel, Seth and Pearl

Contents

About the authors

James Curran is Professor of Communications at Goldsmiths College, University of London, and Director, Goldsmiths Leverhulme Media Research Centre. He is the author or editor (some jointly) of *Mass Communication and Society*; *The British Press*; *Newspaper History*; *Culture, Society and the Media*; *British Cinema History*; *Media, Culture and Society: A Critical Reader*; *Bending Reality*; *Impacts and Influences*; *Mass Media and Society*; *Cultural Studies and Communications*; *Media, Ritual and Identity*; *Media Organisations in Society*; *De-Westernizing Media Studies*; *Media and Power*; *Contesting Media Power*; *Culture Wars*; *Media and Cultural Theory*; *Media and Democracy*; *How Media Inform Democracy: A Comparative Approach*; and *Misunderstanding the Internet*. He has been a weekly columnist for *The Times*, and a Visiting Professor at the Universities of California, Oslo, Pennsylvania, Stanford and Stockholm. In 2011, he won the Edwin C. Baker Award for his work on media, markets and democracy.

Jean Seaton is Professor of Media History at the University of Westminster and Director of the Orwell Foundation, which uses the work of George Orwell to help shape media and public understanding by celebrating honest writing and reporting and confronting uncomfortable truths. She is author, editor or joint editor of *Carnage and the Media: the Making and Breaking of News about Violence; The Media in British Politics; The Media of Conflict; The Prerogative of the Harlot: Politics and the Media; What is to be done? Making the Media and Politics Better* and her volume of the official history of the BBC *Pinkoes and Traitors: the BBC and the Nation 1974–87,* was published in 2015 and a much extended and amended paperback version in 2016. She was a founding member of the Board of Full Fact, and the Reuters Institute, and on the board of *The Political Quarterly*. She writes on a range of issues academically but also for the Guardian and other media and broadcasts regularly on contemporary history and current affairs.

Preface to the eighth edition

Since its first publication in 1981, this book has been cited in over 1600 academic publications, sold more than 90,000 copies and been translated into five languages. However, it has only flourished because the text has been periodically updated and revised. The book is often critical of the media: but in the hope of improving how we deal with them. It also shows how important reporting and the media are to our collective lives. As the photographer in Tom Stoppard's play *Night and Day* observes "People do terrible things to each other, but it's worse in the places where everybody is kept in the dark."

In this edition, a chapter covering the last seventy-odd years of press history has been retired and replaced with four new chapters. These focus on the role of the press in the making and remaking of Britain since 1945, concluding with a chapter on the moral decline of the press.

In addition, the public controversy generated by phone hacking and the Leveson Inquiry has prompted the writing of another new chapter in place of one that was showing its age. This new chapter examines different attempts to reform the press, and the reasons why these mostly failed. The rise of social media has also led to the introduction of a further new chapter which examines its impact.

The broadcasting history has been re-focused and enriched. Original archival material not previously available on pre-war reporting, Churchill's war time broadcasts, Poland, Suez and Hungary, the Coronation, the Cold War, the Cuban Missile Crisis, the Falklands War and security issues as well as more on the working of impartiality. There is a wider discussion based on original research of programmes such as *Civilisation*, the role of David Attenborough's work, arts programming and BBC Monitoring.

The book has also been updated and revised more generally. In response to peer reviews, a start has been made in providing full footnotes. This book took originally about four years to research and write, and we wanted then to present it in full academic dress. Detailed footnotes are a form of scholarly accountability. However, this book was originally aimed at a general public, and the publisher had other ideas. We compromised by having a general bibliography at the end, and a quota of ten footnotes per chapter. Reversing this decision made almost forty years ago is an arduous process: it has been confined to some parts of the book.

Over the years, family, friends and colleagues have helped in numerous ways (all acknowledged in previous editions). James Curran and Jean Seaton share a lifetime's passionate commitement to making discussion and policy about the media better but they do not always agree about how that is best done. In this edition, James Curran is grateful for the help of Eleftheria Lekakis who looked at newspaper responses to public enquiries on the press, a key input into chapter 25.

However, there is one debt we have shamefully never acknowledged. Two Welshmen were in different ways sponsors of this book. The eminent journalist, Hugh Cudlipp, arranged for the Mirror group (IPC) to make a donation to the Open University for a temporary fellowship to support press historical research. It enabled James Curran to extend his press history from 25 to 175 years, providing the foundation for Part I of this book. The other patron was Raymond Williams. He persuaded Fontana to commission this as the first book for a series he was editing. Without his championship, this book would probably have never seen the light of day.

Part 1

Press history

Chapter 1

Press history as political mythology

Pioneering Victorian studies portrayed the history of the British press as a story of progress in which newspapers became free from government and served the people.[1] This became an orthodoxy that lasted a hundred years.

According to this Whig account, the press became independent partly as a consequence of a heroic struggle against state censorship, inspired principally by a love of liberty. Key developments in this struggle are said to be the abolition of the Court of Star Chamber (1641), the end of newspaper licensing (1694), Fox's Libel Act (1792), and the repeal of newspaper taxes in the period 1853–61.[2]

The winning of freedom is also attributed, in this traditionalist view, to the capitalist development of the press. Indeed some Whig historians place greater emphasis on market liberation than on political struggle as the main driver of press freedom, especially in the eighteenth and early nineteenth centuries. 'The true censorship', John Roach writes of the press in the Hanoverian era, 'lay in the fact that the newspaper had not yet reached financial independence, and consequently depended on the administration or the parties'.[3] It was allegedly only when the press was established on an independent commercial footing that newspapers became 'the great organs of the public mind' free from both government and party tutelage.[4]

Advertisers are said to have played an especially important role in this process of liberation. As Ivon Asquith argues in relation to the press in the period 1780–1820:

> Since sales were inadequate to cover the costs of producing a paper, it was the growing income from advertising which provided the material base for the change of attitude from subservience to independence. It is perhaps no exaggeration to say that the growth of advertising revenue was the single most important factor in enabling the press to emerge as the Fourth Estate of the realm.[5]

The press, in this traditionalist account, became a representative institution by the mid-nineteenth century. Market competition, we are told, 'forced papers to echo the political views of their readers in order to thrive'.[6] As a consequence, the press became a great democratizing agency which 'helped to articulate, focus and formulate the growing force of public opinion'.[7] The press also contributed allegedly to the maturing of Britain's democracy in later Victorian Britain by reporting the news in a more responsible manner. This interpretation was once so hegemonic that even a Marxist like Raymond Williams wrote approvingly that 'most newspapers were able to drop their frantic pamphleteering' in the period after 1855.[8] Similarly, the progressive historian Alan Lee portrayed the later Victorian period as a near-golden age of journalism.[9]

Of course, Whig press history was never monolithic even during the period of its ascendancy. While most press historians in this tradition viewed the 1850s as the time when the British press became truly free, some revisionists argued that this happened later.[10] Foremost among these was Stephen Koss who argued, in a celebrated two-volume history, that the full emancipation of the press from authority did not take place until the later 1940s.[11] But while the date of the press's liberation was disputed, the storyline remained the same. The press progressed from being an instrument of government and party to becoming the voice of the people.

This book attacks this Whig narrative on three main counts. The period around the middle of the nineteenth century inaugurated, it is argued, not a new era of press freedom but a system of censorship more effective than anything that had gone before. Market forces succeeded where legal repression had failed in conscripting the press to the social order in mid-Victorian Britain. While market censorship softened in the subsequent period, it still rendered the press unrepresentative. Far from becoming the Fourth Estate of Whig legend, much of the press degenerated into 'rotten boroughs' dominated by oligarchs.

Secondly, the struggle against press censorship was not inspired solely by a love of liberty. This is to project contemporary sensibilities on to people with different mind-sets from our own. In fact, many leading parliamentary campaigners against press taxes in the nineteenth century were more preoccupied with indoctrinating the masses than with planting the tree of freedom. How they are remembered, in the Whig account, is different from how they were.

Above all, the Whig projection of press history as an unfolding story of popular empowerment is too simplistic. Of course, the dismantling of repressive state censorship was an historic advance; and up to the 1850s the theme of progress in the development of the press has some substance. But the press subsequently became ever more entangled in the coils of power: not just the influence of political parties that so concerned Whig revisionists but the bind-weeds of power in all its manifestations – economic, cultural, social and political. Much of the press chose to side with privilege, and in some cases to actively bully the vulnerable.

This counter-thesis was first published in 1981.[12] It contributed to a sea-change in the academic history of the press, reflected in recent overviews of the field.[13] Some thirty-five years and seven editions later, it is clear that

Whig press history is in retreat, with few adherents left.[14] No historian now narrates the development of the press 'up to the present day' as an unfolding story of progress in the way that Whig historians like Stephen Koss and their Victorian antecedents once did.

Afterlife

Yet if Whig press history has lost favour in universities, it lives on in the pages of the press. Hallowed Whig themes are reverently presented as established truths. 'It was advertising', proclaims the former *Guardian* editor, Alan Rusbridger, 'that set the British press free'.[15] 'Remember, advertisers guarantee press freedom', echoes John Bird, founder of the *Big Issue*.[16]

Another consecrated theme, the struggle against state censorship, gets a regular airing in a distorted form. Numerous newspaper articles and editorials in 2013 claimed that 'three hundred years of press freedom' would come to an end if Leveson-inspired reform was implemented.[17] This implied that the press was already free in 1750 when publication of fundamental criticism of the social order was a criminal offence, and when even the reporting of parliamentary debates was prohibited, and that this long entrenched freedom would be terminated if the press's self-regulatory system was audited by an independent panel established (like the BBC) by Royal Charter. This is not serious history but crude propaganda based on a total disregard of the evidence, in which the past is being misreported to influence the present.[18]

The empowerment theme of Whig press history is also often presented in the press in a simplistic way, stripped of any nuance. Thus, Trevor Kavanagh boasts in *The Sun* that 'a traditionally robust newspaper industry . . . for 300 years . . . has been the defender of the ordinary citizen against the rich and powerful'.[19] This is a view of press history in which imperialism, anti-semitism, hostility towards migrants, the persecution of gays and lesbians, the bullying of those on benefits, the adulation of 'wealth-creators' and cheerleading for right-wing governments has been conveniently airbrushed from the record.

These are all examples of the way in which Whig press history – now long repudiated by historians – lives on in the press. What follows is an alternative, evidence-based account informed by recent scholarship. For the sake of brevity, we will begin our account in the early nineteenth century when newspapers were displaying increasing signs of independence from government.

Notes

1 F. K. Hunt, *The Fourth Estate*, 2 vols. (London, David Bogue, 1850); A. Andrews, *The History of British Journalism*, 2 vols. (London, Richard Bentley, 1859); J. Grant, *The Newspaper Press*, 3 vols. (London, Tinsley, 1871); H. R. Fox Bourne, *English Newspapers*, 2 vols. (London, Chatto & Windus, 1887).

2 F. Siebert, *Freedom of the Press in England, 1476–1776* (Urbana, University of Illinois Press, 1956); H. Herd, *The March of Journalism* (London, Allen and Unwin, 1952).

3 J. Roach, 'Education and public opinion' in C. W. Crawley (ed.) *War and Peace in an Age of Upheaval (1793–1830)* (Cambridge, Cambridge University Press, 1965), p. 181.

4 Ibid., p. 180.

5 I. Asquith, 'Advertising and the press in the late eighteenth and nineteenth centuries: James Perry and the *Morning Chronicle* 1790-1821', *Historical Journal*, xviii (4), 1975, p. 721. This is an especially scholarly presentation of a once standard view, typified by R. Altick, *The English Common Reader* (Chicago, University of Chicago Press, 1957), and C. W. Crawley (ed.) *War and Peace in an Age of Upheaval (1793–1830)* (Cambridge, Cambridge University Press, 1965), p. 322.

6 H. Barker, *Newspapers, Politics and English Society, 1695–1855* (Harlow, Longman, 2000), p. 4.

7 Barker, *Newspapers, Politics and English Society*, p. 225.

8 R. Williams, *The Long Revolution* (Harmondsworth, Pelican, 1965), p. 218. He later modified his view in R. Williams, 'The press and popular culture: an historical perspective' in G. Boyce, J. Curran and P. Wingate (eds.) *Newspaper History* (London, Constable, 1978).

9 A. J. Lee, *The Origins of the Popular Press, 1855–1914* (London, Croom Helm, 1976).

10 For example G. Boyce, 'The fourth estate: the reappraisal of a concept' in Boyce et al. (eds.) *Newspaper History* (1978), documented the continuing influence of political parties on the press, extending into the twentieth century. Some historians in this tradition, such as F. Williams, *Dangerous Estate* (London, Arrow Books, 1959), were also concerned about the rise of press barons.

11 S. Koss, *The Rise and Fall of the Political Press in Britain*, 2 vols. (London, Hamish Hamilton, 1981 and 1984).

12 This book was preceded by two essays: J. Curran, 'Capitalism and control of the press, 1800–1975' in J. Curran, M. Gurevitch and J. Woollacott (eds.) *Mass Communication and Society* (London, Arnold, 1977); and J. Curran, 'The press as an agency of social control: an historical perspective' in Boyd et al. (eds.) *Newspaper History* (London, Constable, 1978).

13 K. Williams, *Read All About it: A History of the British Newspaper* (Abingdon, Routledge, 2009); K. Williams, *Get Me a Murder a Day!: A History of Media and Communication in Britain*, 2nd edition (London, Bloomsbury Academic, 2009); M. Conboy, *Journalism in Britain: A Historical Introduction* (London, Sage, 2011); M. Conboy, *Journalism: A Critical History* (London, Sage, 2004); M. Hampton, *Visions of the Press in Britain, 1850–1950* (Urbana, University of Illinois Press, 2004); J. Petley, 'What fourth estate?' in M. Bailey (ed.) *Narrating Media History* (Routledge, Abingdon, 2009), among others.

14 The most notable exceptions are Barker, *Newspapers, Politics and English Society* and H. Barker, *Newspapers, Politics and Public Opinion in Late Eighteenth Century England* (Oxford, Oxford University Press, 1998); and K. Schweizer, 'Newspapers, politics and public opinion in the later Hanoverian era' in K. Schweizer (ed.) *Parliament and the Press, 1689–c.1939* (Edinburgh, Edinburgh University Press, 2006). Had these historians researched the later period, it is likely that the Whig trajectory of their accounts views would have been modified. To this group should be added

M. Hewitt, *The Dawn of the Cheap Press in Victorian Britain* (London, Bloomsbury, 2014), an important new study which is addressed in Chapter 3.

15 'Q&A with Alan Rusbridger: The future of open journalism', *Guardian Online*, Comment is Free, 25 March 2012. Available at: www.guardian.co.uk/commentisfree/2012/mar/25/alan-rusbridger-open-journalism (last accessed 24 April 2013).

16 J. Bird, 'Remember, advertisers guarantee press freedom', *Big Issue*, 10–16 August 2009.

17 'Don't sacrifice our hard-won freedoms', *Daily Mail*, 18 March 2013; 'Press freedom: No longer made in Britain', *Sunday Times,* 24 March 2013; 'Free speech and revenge', *Sun,* 19 March 2013.

18 This is explored further in Chapter 26.

19 T. Kavanagh, 'If MPs seize the presses it is YOU who will lose out', *Sun*, 15 March 2013.

Chapter 2

The struggle for a free press

Like all persuasive mythologies, the Whig interpretation of press history contains a particle of truth. A section of the commercial press did become more independent of government in the period between 1760 and 1860, partly as a consequence of the growth of advertising. This additional revenue reduced dependence, in some cases, on party subsidy; encouraged papers to reject covert secret service grants (the last English newspaper to receive one was the *Observer* in 1840); improved the wages and security of employment of some journalists so that they became less biddable; and financed greater expenditure on news gathering, enabling newspapers to become less reliant on official sources and more reluctant to trade their independence in return for prior government briefing.[1] This last shift was symbolized by *The Times*'s magisterial declaration in 1834 that it would no longer accept early information from government offices since this was inconsistent with 'the pride and independence of our journal', and anyway its 'own information was earlier and surer'.[2]

However, this beguiling account has three limitations. Firstly, the independence of the commercial press was not sustained because numerous commercial newspapers became intertwined with political parties in the second half of the nineteenth century. Instead of functioning as a so-called Fourth Estate (an autonomous institution representing the public), much of the press became an extension of the party system during this period.[3]

Secondly, its portrayal of advertisers as the midwives of press independence is directly contradicted by the rise of the radical press. Early radical papers did not receive significant support from advertisers. Yet, they were totally independent of government and of the Westminster system.

More generally, this Whig account focuses attention on leading London commercial papers like *The Times* while downplaying the development of the radical press. If this selective perspective is shifted, a different understanding of the development of journalism emerges.

Rise of radical journalism

Governments in the eighteenth century sought to prevent the emergence of radical journalism through seditious libel and blasphemy law. This was framed in a catch-all way to make uncompromising criticism of the social order a criminal offence. However, the law became increasingly difficult to enforce once juries were empowered by Fox's Libel Act (1792) to determine guilt or innocence. This was brought home to the authorities by the sensational acquittals, in seditious libel trials, of Eaton, Hardy and Tooke in the 1790s, Wooler and Hone in 1817, and Cobbett in 1831. The sharp edge of the law was further blunted in 1843 when Lord Campbell's Libel Act made the statement of truth in the public interest a legitimate defence.

Yet even before the 1843 Act was passed, the authorities had come round reluctantly to the view that seditious libel prosecutions were often counter-productive. When the editor of *The Republican* was prosecuted in 1819, the paper's circulation soared.[4] Similarly disillusioning experiences prompted the Attorney General to conclude in 1832 that 'a libeller thirsted for nothing more than the valuable advertisement of a public trial in a Court of Justice'.[5] This disenchantment was reflected in a shift of government policy: there were only sixteen prosecutions for seditious and blasphemous libel in the period 1825–34, compared with 167 prosecutions during the preceding eight years.[6]

Instead, the authorities came to rely increasingly on the newspaper stamp duty and taxes on paper and advertisements as a way of muzzling critical journalism. The intention of these press taxes was twofold: to restrict the readership of newspapers to the well-to-do by raising cover prices; and to limit the ownership of newspapers to the propertied class by increasing publishing costs.

Successive governments increased the burden and scope of press taxation in order to make it a more effective safeguard against subversion. The newspaper stamp duty was doubled between 1712 and 1789, and doubled again between 1789 and 1815, while the advertisement duty more than trebled between 1712 and 1815.[7] Publications subject to the stamp duty were redefined in 1819 to include political periodicals. In the same year, a security system was introduced which, among other things, required publishers of weeklies to register their titles, and place financial bonds of between £200 and £300 with the authorities. Although the ostensible purpose of this requirement was to guarantee payment of libel fines, its real objective was to force up the cost of publishing and ensure, as Lord Castlereagh explained to the Commons, that 'persons exercising the power of the press should be men of some respectability and property'.[8] It is perhaps worth noting – in view of the subsequent soaring of publishing costs – that the government was persuaded that its initial proposed security of £500 was an undue limitation on the freedom of the press since it would have made the freedom to publish too costly.[9]

The government's reliance on press taxes seemingly worked for a time. The rise of radical journalism that had begun in the 1790s, and gathered momentum in 1816–17, subsided by the 1820s. However, the revival of radical agitation in the 1830s gave rise to a new phenomenon: an underground press which avoided the stamp duty, developed a well organised distribution system, and administered a hardship fund for the families of newspaper sellers who were imprisoned.

The authorities responded to this challenge by attempting to enforce the law more effectively. Unstamped newspapers were intercepted, and those involved in their production and distribution were jailed in increasing number. At least 1130 cases of selling unstamped newspapers were prosecuted in London alone during the period 1830–36.[10] Yet, despite these measures, the radical press continued to flourish. 'Prosecutions, fines and imprisonments were alike failures', the Minister in charge of the fight against the unstamped press later recalled.[11] In June 1836 the government was forced to concede defeat. The Commons was informed that the authorities 'had resorted to all means afforded by the existing law' but that it 'was altogether ineffectual to the purpose of putting an end to the unstamped papers'.[12]

By 1836 the unstamped press published in London had an aggregate readership of at least two million.[13] This probably exceeded that of its respectable, stamped counterpart. The fiscal system of press control seemed on the point of collapse, since leading publishers of stamped papers publicly warned that they would also evade the stamp duty unless more effective steps were taken to enforce it.

The Whig government responded to this crisis with a well-planned counter-offensive. New measures were passed which strengthened the government's search and confiscation powers. Penalties were also increased for being found in possession of an unstamped newspaper, and the stamp duty was reduced by 75 per cent in order to make 'smuggling' less attractive.[14] What has been viewed as a landmark in the advance of press freedom was in fact repressive. As Thomas Spring Rice, the Chancellor of the Exchequer, explained to the Commons, a strategic concession, combined with increased coercive powers, was necessary in order to enforce a system that had broken down. The intention, he stated candidly, was to 'put down the unstamped papers'.[15]

The government's new strategy succeeded in its immediate objective. 'No unstamped papers can be attempted with success', sardonically commented Henry Hetherington, a leading radical publisher, shortly after being released from prison, unless 'some means can be devised either to print the newspaper without types and presses, or render the premises . . . inaccessible to armed force'.[16] By 1837 the unstamped press had disappeared.

Compliance with the law forced radical newspapers to raise their prices, even though the stamp duty was much reduced. Whereas most had sold at 1d in the early 1830s, their successors in the 1840s charged 4d or 5d – a sum that was well beyond the means of the average worker. However, the government's attempt to destroy the radical press was thwarted through collective action. Informal groups of working people pooled their resources each week to purchase newspapers; union branches, clubs and political associations increasingly stocked radical titles; and publicans in radical neighbourhoods were encouraged to follow suit. Partly as a consequence of this concerted resistance, new radical papers emerged which gained even larger circulations than those of their predecessors.

Indeed, radical publications were the circulation pace setters throughout much of the period 1815–55, exceeding that of the respectable press. Cobbett's radical *Twopenny Trash* broke all circulation records in 1816–17.[17] This record was probably beaten in 1835–36 by the left-wing *Weekly Police Gazette*.[18] In 1838 the militant *Northern Star* gained the largest circulation of any newspaper published in the provinces and, in 1839, the largest circulation in Britain apart from the liberal-radical *Weekly Dispatch*.[19] The *Northern Star*'s circulation was later exceeded by that of the initially radical left *Reynolds's Newspaper*, which in the early 1850s had the second-largest circulation in Britain.[20] Along with the liberal-radical *Lloyds Weekly*, *Reynolds's* became the first newspaper to break through the 100,000 circulation barrier in 1856.[21]

Although newspaper circulations during the first half of the nineteenth century seem very small by contemporary standards, this is misleading because circulation is not a constant measure of 'audience'. The sharing of high-cost papers, together with the widespread practice of reading papers aloud for the benefit of the semi-literate and illiterate, inflated the number of 'readers' for each newspaper sold. Informed accounts estimate that radical newspapers had twenty or more readers per copy in the 1830s and 1840s,[22] compared with two to three readers per copy of a typical national newspaper today. Yet even if a *very* conservative estimate of ten readers per copy is adopted, this still means that the *Northern Star* and its successor, *Reynolds's Newspaper*, each reached at their peak, before the repeal of the stamp duty, half a million readers. In 1851 the total population of England and Wales was only 18 million. The emergent radical press was thus a genuinely popular force, reaching a large public.

The economic structure of the radical press

While the rise of the radical press was a direct consequence of the growth of trade union and working-class political organisations, it was also enabled by the prevailing economic structure of the press industry. Since this is an important aspect of the central argument that will follow, we will examine in some detail the finances of the early radical press.

The initial capital required to set up a radical paper in the early part of the nineteenth century was extremely small. Most radical unstamped papers were printed not on a steam press, but on hand presses, which cost as little as £10 to acquire. Metal type could be hired by the hour and print workers paid on a piecework basis.

After 1836 leading stamped radical papers were printed on more sophisticated machinery. The *London Dispatch*, for instance, was printed on a Napier machine, bought with the help of a wealthy well-wisher and the profits from Hetherington's other publications. The *Northern Star* had a printing press specially constructed for it in London. Even so, launch costs were extremely small in comparison with the subsequent period. The *Northern Star*, for instance, was launched in 1837 with a total capital of £690, mostly raised by public subscription.[23]

Financing a paper during its initial trading period could often cost more than setting it up. Even so, early losses were minimised by low operating costs. Radical unstamped papers paid no tax, relied heavily upon news reports filed by their readers on a voluntary basis, and had small newsprint costs because of their high readership per copy. Consequently they needed to attain only small circulations in order to be economically viable. Thus, the break-even circulation point for the *Poor Man's Guardian*, a leading newspaper of the early 1830s, was only 2500.[24]

Even after 1836, when a penny stamp duty had to be paid on each copy, the running costs of the radical press remained relatively low. The influential *London Dispatch* reported, for example, that 'the whole expense allowed for editing, reporting, reviewing, literary contributions etc., in fact, the entire cost of what is technically called "making up" the paper, is only six pounds per week'.[25] In the same issue it reported that, at its selling price of three pence, it could break even with a circulation of 16,000. Similarly the *Northern Star* which, unlike its predecessors, developed a substantial network of paid correspondents, spent about £14 a week on editorial costs in 1839–40.[26] Selling at four pence, its circulation break-even point was 6200 copies.[27] This meant that its run-in costs were small. Indeed the *Northern Star* almost certainly moved into profit within its first month of publication.[28]

Because publishing costs were low the ownership and control of newspapers could be in the hands of people committed, in the words of Joshua Hobson, an ex-handloom weaver and publisher of the *Voice of West Riding*, 'to support the rights and interests of the order and class to which it is my pride to belong'.[29] Some newspapers, such as the *Voice of the People*, the *Liberator* and the *Trades Newspaper*, were owned by political or trade union organisations. Other radical papers were owned by individual proprietors, such as Cleave, Watson and Hetherington, many of them people of humble origins who had risen to prominence through the working-class movement. While not lacking in ruthlessness or business acumen, these publishers tended to entrust the editing of their newspapers to former manual workers like William Hill and Joshua Hobson, or middle-class activists like Bronterre O'Brien and James Lorymer, whose attitudes had been shaped by long involvement in working-class politics. A substantial section of the popular newspaper press reaching a working-class audience was thus controlled by those who were committed to the working-class movement.

This influenced radical journalists' perception of their role. Unlike the institutionalized journalists of the later period, they tended to see themselves as political activists. Indeed, many of the paid correspondents of the *Poor Man's Guardian*, *Northern Star* and the early *Reynolds's Newspaper* doubled up as political organisers for the National Union of the Working Classes or the Chartist Movement. Instead of reporting the news as discrete events, they sought to understand the underlying dynamics of power and inequality shaping the news. Some also strived to have a reciprocal relationship with their readers. As the editor of the *Northern Star* wrote in its fifth anniversary issue:

> I have ever sought to make it [the paper] rather a reflex of your minds than a medium through which to exhibit any supposed talent or intelligence of my own. This is precisely my conception of what a people's organ should be.[30]

Another important feature of the radical press in the first half of the nineteenth century was that it was self-sufficient on the proceeds of sales alone. As mentioned earlier, the early radical press had limited advertising. The *London Dispatch* complained bitterly of the 'prosecutions, fines and the like et ceteras with which a paper of our principles is sure to be more largely honoured than by the lucrative patronage of advertisers'.[31] Its resentment, shared by other radical papers, was justified. There was a marked disparity in the amount of advertising duty per 1000 circulation paid by the radical press compared with its rivals. For example, in 1840, two middle-class papers published in Leeds (the *Leeds Mercury* and *Leeds Intelligence*) and the four leading mainstream, national daily papers (*The Times, Morning Post, Morning Chronicle* and *Morning Advertiser*) each paid over fifty times more advertisement duty per 1000 copies than the popular radical *Northern Star*, a Leeds-based paper with a national circulation.[32]

A similar pattern emerges in the case of other leading radical papers. Thus, Cobbett's widely read *Political Register* only obtained three advertisements in 1817, in sharp contrast to its principal rivals. Similarly, the radical *London Dispatch* paid less than half the advertisement duty per 1000 circulation compared with its principal respectable rivals.[33]

This limited advertising support meant that the radical press had less money for editorial development than the mainstream press. Yet, notwithstanding this, the radical press still prospered. While fortunes were not easily made, radical newspapers – both stamped and unstamped – could be highly profitable. Hetherington, the publisher of the stamped *London Dispatch*, was reported to be making £1000 a year from his business in 1837.[34] Similarly the stamped *Northern Star* was estimated to have produced a profit of £13,000 in 1839 and £6500 in 1840, which was generated very largely from sales revenue.[35]

This independence from advertising was a liberating force. Radical papers were not under pressure to steer towards an affluent audience, which advertisers would pay more to reach. Nor did radical editors have to worry about upsetting advertisers' political sensibilities. Indeed, by the 1830s, a growing number of radical papers were oriented primarily towards a working-class public, and became more uncompromisingly oppositional. They were free because they relied on their readers' pennies for their economic viability.

The impact of the radical press

The radical press did not merely reflect the growth of working-class organisations: it also extended their influence. It did this in a number of overlapping ways.

One of the least remarked upon, but most significant, aspects of the development of the radical press in the first half of the nineteenth century was that its leading publications developed a nationwide circulation. Even as early as the second decade, leading radical papers such as the *Political Register* and *Republican* were read as far afield as Yorkshire, Lancashire, the Midlands and East Anglia, as well as in the south of England. By the early 1830s the principal left newspapers like the *Weekly Police Gazette*, the *Poor Man's Guardian* and *Dispatch* had a distribution network extending on a north–south axis from Glasgow to Truro, and on an east–west axis from Norwich to Carmarthen.[36] Part of the impact of the radical press stemmed from the geographical extent of its circulation.

Leading radical publications fostered a collective sense of class identity because they provided a means of linking up local working-class communities. They also helped to knit together different groups within the highly stratified working class by demonstrating the common predicament of workers in different trades and occupations throughout the country. People seeking to establish a trade union organisation in their locality could read in the radical press in 1833–34, for instance, of similar struggles by glove workers in Yeovil, cabinet-makers and joiners in Glasgow and Carlisle, shoemakers and smiths in Northampton, bricklayers and masons in London, as well as of groups of workers in Belgium and Germany. Similarly, the radical press helped to reduce geographical isolation by showing that local agitation – whether against the administration of the Poor Law, long working hours or wage cuts – conformed to a common pattern elsewhere. Radical papers further expanded their readers' field of vision by publishing, particularly in the later phase from the 1830s onward, news that other respectable papers tended not to carry. In particular, they drew attention to growing support for the right to vote, and stressed that this was part of a wider struggle to transform society. The radical press was, in the words of the Chartist leader Feargus O'Connor, 'the link that binds the industrious classes together'.[37]

Radical papers also helped to foster the growth of progressive organisations, like the National Union of the Working Classes and the Chartist Movement, by giving them the oxygen of publicity. O'Connor recalled that before the emergence of Chartist newspapers, 'I found that the press was entirely mute, while I was working myself to death, and that a meeting in one town did nothing for another'.[38] Press publicity encouraged people to attend meetings, and to become involved. It also conferred prominence on leading activists, transforming for example six farm workers in the remote village of Tolpuddle who attempted to start a union in 1832, and who were jailed and transported to Australia, into national working-class martyrs. No less important, radical papers also helped to sustain activists' morale when, at times, it must have been tempting to give up. Without the *Northern Star*, declared one speaker at a local Chartist meeting, 'their own sounds might echo through the wilderness'.[39]

Leading radical publications were also a mobilizing force in their own right. We have become so accustomed to an individualized pattern of newspaper consumption amid a steady flow of information from a variety of media sources that it is difficult to comprehend the political significance of newspapers in the early nineteenth century. They were often the only regular source of information about what was happening outside the local community. They were important partly because there were few other diversions. Samuel Fielden recalls, for instance, 'on the day the newspaper, the *Northern Star* . . . was due, the people used to line the roadside waiting for its arrival'.[40] The impact of the radical press was further enhanced by the way in which newspapers read aloud in taverns, workshops, homes and public meetings triggered discussion. This social pattern of consumption continued on a diminished scale until late into the nineteenth century.[41]

The rise of the radical press also contributed to – as well as reflected – the radicalization of a section of British society. The first wave of radical papers from the 1790s through to the late 1820s raised expectations both by invoking a mythical past in which plenty and natural justice had prevailed, and by proclaiming the possibility of a future in which poverty could be relieved through political means. It was this raising of hopes, combined with a direct assault on the Anglican 'morality' legitimating social inequality, which especially alarmed parliamentarians at the time. As William Wilmot MP said in the Commons, after being informed that servants and common soldiers had been seen reading radical newspapers:

> Those infamous publications . . . inflame [working people's] passions and awaken their selfishness, contrasting their present conditions with what they contend to be their future condition – a condition incompatible with human nature, and with those immutable laws which Providence has established for the regulation of civil society.[42]

The radical press sought to erode political passivity, based on fatalistic acceptance of the social system as 'natural' and 'providential'. It also attempted to dispel class deference, and a limited sense of entitlement, by subverting the status hierarchy. 'The real strength and all the resources of the country', characteristically proclaimed the *Political Register*, 'ever have sprung from the *labour* of its people'.[43] This labour theory of worth reordered the social ranking of society. The highest in the land were deemed the lowest as idle parasites: working people, by contrast, were elevated to the top as the most productive and useful section of the community. The early radical press thus symbolically turned the world upside down. It also repeatedly emphasized the potential power of working people to effect change through the force of 'combination' and organised action.

Radical papers also developed a more critical political analysis. The first generation of radical papers tended to be trapped inside the intellectual universe of a standard liberal critique. Political attacks focused on corruption in high places and regressive, direct taxation that was said to impoverish the productive community. This critique implicitly promoted limited political reform in terms of ending corruption and burdensome taxes (and, sometimes, an extension of the franchise) rather than making the case for a far-reaching transformation of the social order. If an underlying conflict in society was depicted, it tended to be between the aristocracy and the 'productive classes' (usually defined to include working employers as well as their employees).

By the 1830s the more militant papers had shifted their focus of attack from 'old corruption' to the economic process which enabled the capitalist class to appropriate in profits the wealth created by labour. Conflict was redefined as a class struggle between labour and capital, between the working classes and a coalition of aristocrats, 'millocrats' and 'shopocrats', sustained by an undemocratic political system. This more radical analysis signposted the way forward towards a radical programme of social reconstruction in which, in the words of the *Poor Man's Guardian,* workers will 'be at the top instead of at the bottom of society – or rather that there should be no bottom or top at all'.[44]

This new analysis was sometimes conflated with the old liberal analysis in an uncertain synthesis. There was, moreover, an underlying continuity in the perspectives offered by the less militant sector of the radical press, which gained in influence during the early 1850s. But such continuity should come as no surprise. It was only natural that the political complexion of the broad left press should reflect the ebb and flow of militancy within the emergent working-class movement. Nor is it at all surprising that traditional political perspectives should have persisted in view of what we now know from communications research about the enduring resilience of belief systems.[45] But so long as the activist working class controlled its own popular press, it possessed the institutional means to explore and develop more radical understandings of society. It also had a collective resource for defining, expressing and maintaining a radical public opinion different from that proclaimed by the mainstream press. And it possessed a shield, however imperfect, to fend off the ideological assault mounted through schools, the Anglican Church, mechanics' institutes and useful knowledge magazines.

The rise of the militant press fostered the development of a radical subculture, posing a challenge to the undemocratic social order. Indeed, in 1842, a General Strike was called to secure universal suffrage through the force of industrial action. It received extensive support in industrial Lancashire, much of Yorkshire and parts of the Midlands.[46] While the strike was crushed, and some 1500 activist leaders were imprisoned, it was a sign of an increasingly unsettled society in which radical publications had become a disruptive force.

In short, the control system administered by the state had failed. Neither prosecutions for seditious libel nor a tax system designed to restrict newspaper readership had succeeded in preventing the rise of the radical press. As we shall see, this prompted thoughtful parliamentarians to consider whether there might be a better way to contain the threat posed by insurgent journalism.

Notes

1 A. Aspinall, *Politics and the Press, c. 1780–1850* (Brighton, Harvester, 1973 [1949]); I. Christie, *Myth and Reality in Late Eighteenth Century British Politics* (London, Macmillan, 1970); I. Asquith, 'Advertising and the press in the late eighteenth and nineteenth centuries: James Perry and the *Morning Chronicle* 1790–1821', *Historical Journal*, xviii (4), 1975, pp. 703–24; G. Cranfield, *The Press and Society* (London, Longman, 1978); S. Koss, *The Rise and Fall of the Political Press in Britain*, vol. 1 (London, Hamish Hamilton, 1981); H. Barker, *Newspapers, Politics and English Society, 1695–1855* (Harlow, Longman, 2000), among others.

2 Cited in Aspinall, *Politics and the Press*, p. 380.

3 See Chapter 4, p. 38 and Chapter 5, p. 50.

4 W. Wickwar, *The Struggle for the Freedom of the Press 1819–1832* (London, Allen and Unwin, 1928), p. 94.

5 Cited in J. Wiener, *The War of the Unstamped* (Ithaca, Cornell University Press, 1969), p. 196.

6 Derived from Wickwar, *The Struggle*, Appendix B, p. 315.

7 J. Black, *The English Press 1621–1861* (Stroud, Sutton, 2001), p. 166.

8 Castlereagh, *Parliamentary Debates*, vol. XCI (London, Hansard, 1819), col. 1177.

9 Castlereagh, ibid., col. 1177. The measure was fine-tuned, Lord Ellenborough also explained, not to undermine 'the respectable press' but to target the 'pauper press . . . administering to the prejudices and passions of the mob' (L. Ellenborough, *Parl. Deb.*, 1820, col. 1591).

10 P. Hollis, *The Pauper Press* (London, Oxford University Press, 1970), p. 171.

11 T. Spring. Rice, *Parl. Deb.*, vol. CXXXVIII (1855), col. 966.

12 T. Spring. Rice, *Parl. Deb.*, vol. XXIV (1836), col. 627–28.

13 This conservative estimate is based on the aggregate 200,000 circulation of six leading unstamped newspapers in 1836 (Hollis, *Pauper*, p. 124), assuming an average readership of ten per copy. In fact, there were many more than six unstamped newspapers (see Wiener, *War*, pp. 281–85), and per copy readership would have been higher.

14 T. Spring. Rice, *Parl. Deb.*, vol. XXIV (1836), col. 627–31.

15 T. Spring. Rice, *Parl. Deb.*, vol. XXXVII (1837), col. 1165.
16 *London Dispatch*, 17 September 1836.
17 Wickwar, *Struggle*, p. 54.
18 Wiener, *War*, p. 184.
19 *Report from the Select Committee on Newspaper Stamps* (SCNS), Parliamentary Papers XVII (London, Hansard, 1851), Appendix 4.
20 V. Berridge, 'Popular Sunday papers and mid-Victorian society' in Boyce et al. (eds.) *Newspaper History*, Fig. 1, p. 263.
21 Ibid.
22 Hollis (*Pauper*, p. 119) estimates perhaps twenty readers per copy for unstamped papers in the early 1830s, with supporting evidence. Readership per copy would probably have been greater for their higher priced successors between 1836 and 1855. Indeed, higher contemporary estimates of newspaper readership per copy are reported for the first half of the nineteenth century in D. Read, *Press and People* (London, Arnold, 1961), p. 202; and R. K. Webb, *The British Working Class Reader, 1790–1848* (London, Allen and Unwin, 1955), pp. 31–34.
23 Read, *Press*, p. 99. However, J. A. Epstein ('Feargus O'Connor and the *Northern Star*', *International Review of Social History*, xxi, 1976, p. 57) sifts through conflicting evidence to conclude that Feargus O'Connor donated a further £400 towards the paper's establishment.
24 See Hollis, *Pauper*, p. 132.
25 *London Dispatch*, 17 September 1836.
26 Epstein, 'Feargus O'Connor', p. 83.
27 Read, *Press*, p. 101.
28 Epstein, 'Feargus O'Connor', p. 56.
29 Cited Hollis, *Pauper*, p. 94.
30 *Northern Star*, 19 November 1842.
31 *London Dispatch*, 17 September 1836.
32 For this and other comparisons, see J. Curran, 'Capitalism and control of the press, 1800–1975' in J. Curran, M. Gurevitch and J. Woolacott (eds.) *Mass Communication and Society* (London, Edward Arnold, 1977), Table 1, p. 209.
33 Derived from *Parliamentary Accounts and Papers*, 1818 and 1838; and SCNS, 1851, Appendix 4 (consolidated stamp duty returns).
34 Hollis, *Pauper*, p. 135.
35 A. Schoyen, *The Chartist Challenge* (London, Heinemann, 1956), p. 133.
36 Hollis, *Pauper*, pp. 108–16.
37 *Northern Star*, 16 January 1841.
38 Ibid.
39 *Northern Star*, 18 August 1838.
40 S. Fielden, *Knights of Labour*, 1887 cited by Epstein, 'Feargus O'Connor', p. 72.
41 J. Rose, *The Intellectual Life of the British Working Classes* (New Haven, Yale University Press, 2002), Chapter 2.
42 W. Wilmot, *Parl. Deb.*, vol. XCI (1819), col. 1358. This quotation was wrongly attributed in previous editions to Dr. Joseph Phillimore, MP, due to a transcription error. Phillimore spoke shortly after William Wilmot, and said similar things, including the need to curb 'publications so destructive to the happiness of mankind in this life and hereafter' (col. 1363).

43 *Political Register*, 1816, cited by N. W. Thompson, *The People's Science* (Cambridge, Cambridge University Press, 1984), p. 112.
44 *Poor Man's Guardian*, 19 October 1833.
45 J. Curran, *Media and Power* (London, Routledge, 2002).
46 J. Foster, *Class Struggle and the Industrial Revolution* (London, Weidenfeld & Nicolson, 1976).

Chapter 3

Janus face of reform

The campaign against 'the taxes on knowledge' is generally portrayed as a triumphant struggle for press freedom, sustained by special interests but motivated largely by libertarian ideals in opposition to the authoritarian legacy of the past.[1] The only discordant note in this inspiring legend comes from the parliamentary campaigners it celebrates. Their aims and, indeed, their public utterances are difficult to reconcile with how they have been depicted in Whig history.

Dividing over social control

Press taxes became a recurrent subject of debate in parliament during the early 1830s, producing a sharp divergence of opinion. Defenders of the stamp duty argued that it limited the distribution of 'pernicious and mischievous' ideas by making newspapers more expensive.[2] They also pointed out that press taxes forced up the costs of publishing, and ensured that ownership of the press was restricted to the wealthy. As the Conservative MP, John Cresset Pelham, argued in 1832, press duties were:

> eminently useful in their effects, as newspapers were thus placed under the control of men of wealth and character who, for their own sakes, would conduct them in a more responsible manner than was likely to be the result of a pauper management'.[3]

All that needed to change, in his view, was that the government should be more vigorous in enforcing the law.

A minority group in parliament rejected this, arguing that the stamp duty had failed to 'prevent the circulation of the most dangerous doctrines',[4] and had become unenforceable. Radical publishers were not being silenced by ineffectual controls: instead they were being given a clear field without encountering competition in the form of a cheap reply from responsible publishers.[5]

This clash of opinion was often informed by a different approach to social control. Traditionalists tended to support a law-and-order approach, whereas opponents of press taxes tended to argue that public education was needed to stabilize the social system. Typical of this latter group was Edward Bulwer-Lytton who, when proposing the abolition of the stamp duty in 1832, declared cynically:

> At this moment when throughout so many nations we see the people at war with their institutions, the world presents to us two great, may they be impressive examples. In Denmark, a despotism without discontent – in America, a republic without change. The cause is the same in both: in both the people are universally educated.[6]

Abolition of the stamp duty would produce, he argued, a cheap press that would put to flight 'those superficial and dangerous notions of the injustice of the divisions of property, which men who are both poor and ignorant so naturally conceive . . .'.[7] This belief that popular journalism, in responsible hands, would defeat radicalism, rooted in ignorance, lay at the heart of the 1830s parliamentary campaign against the stamp duty. Francis Place, the organising secretary of the repeal campaign, told a Parliamentary Select Committee in 1832 that 'there would not have been a single trades union either in England or Scotland' if the stamp duty had been repealed earlier.[8] Similarly John Roebuck informed the Commons that, if the stamp duty had been lifted, agricultural workers at Tolpuddle would probably not have wanted to establish a trade union.[9] Another leading campaigner, George Grote, was even more sanguine about the benefits of an expanded, capitalist press: 'a great deal of the bad feeling that was at present abroad amongst the labouring classes on the subject of wages' was due, he believed, to 'the want of proper instruction and correct information as to their real interests' which the repeal of the stamp duty and the creation of a cheap, respectable press would rectify.[10]

The parliamentary clashes over the stamp duty in the 1830s were not about liberty. The two opposing sides in parliament were equally committed to conscripting the press to the social order: where they differed was how this should be done. As the Lord Chancellor, Lord Brougham, succinctly summarized in 1834:

> The only question to answer, and the only problem to solve, is how they [the people] shall read in the best manner; how they shall be instructed politically, and have habits formed the most safe for the constitution of the country.[11]

The majority of MPs concluded that the stamp duty should be retained because it provided a defence against radical subversion. The minority who disagreed was relatively small, never mustering during the 1830s more than 58 votes, even when the Commons was elected on an extended franchise.[12] Indeed, their opposition was sometimes hesitant, betraying anxiety that the time might not be ripe for repeal; and it subsided once the radical unstamped press was defeated in 1836.

Ambiguity was a continuing feature of the parliamentary campaign against press taxes. Collet Dobson Collet said of the 1836 reduction of the stamp duty, and assault on the unstamped press, that it was 'not a liberal, but it was, in some respects, a statesman-like measure'.[13] This was scarcely a ringing defence of press freedom. Yet, Collet was to become the principal organiser of the parliamentary campaign against press taxes, when it was re-established in 1848.[14]

Ambiguity of the renewed campaign

Martin Hewitt is the latest historian to bathe this revived campaign in a heroic light as being inspired essentially by a love of liberty, and to conclude that its success was wholly beneficent.[15] He does this, in a full-length monograph, by documenting with innovative scholarship the popular tail of the reform campaign, pointing to 'the more complicated and unruly tendencies of activists, supporters and fellow travellers'.[16] He also concludes that the cheap press that emerged after the abolition of press taxes lessened prejudice against popular journalism, and was a positive, integrative force.[17] His study ends with an exultant quotation from the veteran Manchester Liberal politician, John Bright, who looked back with pleasure in 1872 on how securing the 'freedom of the press' had the 'beneficial' impact which he and fellow campaigners had foretold.[18]

The trouble with this study, like others before it, is that it largely ignores what was being said at the time in parliament. It pays too little attention to changes in the wider context that made repeal acceptable. Above all, it is blind to the way in which press capitalism gave rise to a new form of censorship.

While the revived parliamentary campaign was presented at times as a people's crusade, it was led primarily by middle class Liberal politicians, mostly with business backgrounds. As Richard Cobden, a northern manufacturer and Liberal MP for Stockport – and one of the campaign's leading lights – confided privately, 'exclusively almost, we comprise steady, sober middle-class reformers'.[19] He and other like-minded colleagues created the Association for the Promotion of the Repeal of the Taxes on Knowledge (APRTOK), with the ubiquitous Collet as its organising Secretary. Significantly, this was established not as a national pressure group with branches and grassroots membership, but as a centralized lobbying organisation, which industrial Liberal MPs, and their close allies, sought to control.[20]

A powerful motivation for this revived campaign was the belief that the repeal of press taxes would give rise to a popular press propagating the principles of free trade and competitive capitalism. In particular, these Liberal MPs hoped that it would lead to the growth of a sympathetic local press, and the launch of a successful, national rival to the dominant but unreliable

The Times. They felt that the wind of change was behind them. They had recently run a triumphant campaign that had led, in 1846, to the abolition of the Corn Laws (tariffs and restrictions on imported grain that had artificially inflated bread prices in the interests of farmers). The political platform and mass meeting should now be supplemented, they believed, by cheap newspapers in order to spread the gospel of economic liberalism.

Some of the people involved in the renewed fight against press taxes were also engaged in the parliamentary struggle to establish free public libraries (secured in principle in 1850). Their belief was that enhanced access to knowledge would promote the advance of reason, and confound the forces of moral depravity and political subversion. In the words of the 1849 Select Committee on Public Libraries, free libraries would 'lessen or perhaps entirely destroy the influence of frivolous, unsound and dangerous works'.[21]

These reformers put together a broad-based coalition of interests to campaign against press taxes. This included educationalists, temperance campaigners and post-Chartist radicals; advocates of lower taxation and public retrenchment; and also a motley group of Conservative parliamentarians (including Whig Conservatives like Bulwer-Lytton, populist Conservatives like Disraeli who believed that the abolition of the advertisement duty would boost a popular conservative press, and opportunists chafing at *The Times'* repeated criticism of the Aberdeen coalition administration); and the press itself (though publishers were split over the stamp duty).[22] The composition of this coalition fluctuated, depending partly upon which press tax the campaign targeted.

But while backing came from diverse sources with different objectives, leading campaigners against press taxes *in parliament* had a shared vision. They believed that the social order would be rendered more secure if it was based on consent fostered by a cheap press. 'The larger we open the field of general instruction', declared Palmerston when speaking for the repeal of the stamp duty, 'the firmer the foundations on which the order, the loyalty and good conduct of the lower classes will rest'.[23] 'The freedom of the press', argued Gladstone, 'was not merely to be permitted and tolerated, but to be highly prized, for it tended to bring closer together all the national interests and preserve the institutions of the country'.[24] Repeal the taxes on knowledge, proclaimed the Irish politician John Maguire, and 'you render the people better citizens, more obedient to the laws, more faithful and loyal subjects, and more determined to stand up for the honour of the country'.[25] A cheap press, in other words, would strengthen the social system.

This was similar to the arguments aired in parliament during the 1830s. However, the rhetoric of the 1850s campaign was sometimes pitched in a more progressive register than before. Supporters of press taxes were stigmatized as enemies of liberty and the heirs of court censorship. Knowledge, it was proclaimed, should not be taxed; good publications would drive out the bad in open competition.[26]

This could give rise to a discourse in which libertarian and authoritarian themes mingled incongruously together. For example, Alexander Andrews, editor of the first journalists' trade journal, wrote that the great mission of a free press was to 'educate and enlighten those classes whose political knowledge has been hitherto so little, and by consequence so dangerous'. This stress on political indoctrination was combined with an invocation to liberty. 'The list of our public journals', Andrews continued, 'is a proud and noble list – the roll call of an army of liberty, with a rallying point in every town. It is a police of safety, and a sentinel of public morals'.[27]

This juxtaposition of 'freedom' and 'control' illuminated the ideological universe of many mid-nineteenth-century free press campaigners. It was tacitly assumed that there was no conflict of interest between classes: merely a conflict between ignorance and enlightenment, and between the individual and the state. Viewed from this perspective, an expanded capitalist press was to be welcomed because it would be both a guard-dog shepherding the people from radical heresy, and a watchdog restraining the state from encroaching on individual liberty.

Informing this approach was a conviction that the repeal of press taxes would enable a middle class version of enlightenment to prevail. The growth of a cheap press, explained William Hickson, a leading campaigner, would enlist journalists 'two or three degrees' above workers to instruct them.[28] To Gladstone, the principal attraction of repeal was that more men of 'quality' would be employed in an expanded press to educate the people.[29] 'A perfectly free press is one of the greatest safeguards of peace and order', wryly observed the lawyer, J. F. Stephen, because journalists come from 'the comfortable part of society, and will err rather on the side of making too much of their interests than on that of neglecting them'.[30]

Some senior campaigners also had close links to the local press, and understood how newspaper markets functioned. The repeal of press taxes, declared Thomas Milner Gibson, APRTOK President, would create 'a cheap press in the hands of men of good moral character, of respectability, and of capital'.[31] The free market, according to Sir George Lewis, the Liberal Chancellor of the Exchequer, would promote papers 'enjoying the preference of the advertising public'.[32] A cheap press in responsible hands, it was believed, would also educate demand. As one veteran campaigner put it, 'the appetite grows by what it feeds on'.[33]

But if one motivation behind reform was the conviction that an unfettered capitalist press would be in responsible hands, another was a growing sense – absent in the turbulent, early 1830s – that the public would be receptive to instruction. The campaign to repeal press taxes, though revived in 1848, only really took off in 1850–51 when it became increasingly apparent that the Chartist movement had failed. By then, a conservative reaction had also set in after the 1848 upheavals that had rocked much of Europe. There was, proclaimed Edward Bulwer-Lytton without a trace of irony, 'a great increase of intelligence among the people.'[34]

Changed times altered the calculation of risk. It was because the government was now confident of 'the loyalty and good disposition of the great body of the people', declared Sir George Lewis, Chancellor of the Exchequer in 1855, that he was proposing the abolition of the stamp duty.[35] This reassurance was repeated regularly by reformers. They urged those who were uncertain whether the working class would 'become the glory, or might prove greatly dangerous, to the peace of the country, and the prosperity of its industry' to seize this propitious moment to create a cheap press.[36]

However, those convinced that the lower orders were inherently susceptible to radical ideas stood firm. They included not only traditionalists but some who might have been thought to be natural allies of Manchester Liberals. Thus the liberal political economist, J. R. McCulloch, supported free trade in general but not in relation to the press. He refused to believe that 'circulation of low-priced journals can ever be of advantage' because 'the lower and poorer classes' were wedded, in his view, to 'prejudices' inconsistent with 'the interests of society in general'.[37] But the people who thought like this – though dominant in the 1830s – had ceased to be in the majority in parliament by the 1850s because working-class militancy had been defeated.[38]

The momentum for reform was skilfully exploited by the seasoned campaigners who led the struggle against press taxes. They initiated a Commons Select Committee on the Stamp Duty (and largely wrote its Report), won allies among civil servants, harried sometimes poorly briefed ministers, organised public meetings, petitions and deputations, wrote press articles and proposed Bills in parliament. Their virtuosity was rewarded with the abolition of the advertisement duty in 1853, the stamp duty in 1855, the paper duty in 1861 and the financial security system in 1869.[39]

In short, the campaign in parliament for a free press independent of state economic control was not inspired by a love of freedom, in a contemporary sense. Paradoxically, people supported the enforcement of the stamp duty in 1836 for much the same reason that they voted for its repeal in 1855. On both occasions, they were unwavering in their concern to ensure that the press underpinned the social order. But in the meantime public discontent had subsided, and there was a growing sense of security within the governing class. There was also a greater commitment to positive indoctrination of the lower orders through education and a cheap press, and an increasing conviction that free trade and normative controls were morally preferable and more efficient than coercive controls administered by the state.

In the event, reformers were vindicated. The radical press was eclipsed in the period after the repeal of press taxes. The reasons for this have never been properly explained, and will now be explored.

Notes

1 For example, G. A. Cranfield, *The Press and Society* (Harlow, Longman, 1978), p. 205.
2 L. Althorp, *Parliamentary Debates*, vol. XXIII (London, Hansard, 1834), col. 1212.
3 J. Cresset Pelham, *Parl. Deb.*, vol. XI (1832), col. 492.
4 E. Lytton Bulwer, *Parl. Deb.*, vol. XIII (1832), col. 624. He became known subsequently as Edward Bulwer-Lytton, and later Lord Lytton.
5 This sounded plausible but was misleading. In actual practice, the authorities harassed radical unstamped papers, while increasingly turning a blind eye to their more respectable, unstamped rivals.
6 E. Lytton Bulwer, *Parl. Deb.*, vol. XIII (1832), col. 633.
7 E. Lytton Bulwer, ibid., col. 621.
8 F. Place, Select Committee on Drunkenness, *Parliamentary Papers*, vol. viii (1834), question 2054.
9 J. Roebuck, *Parl. Deb.*, vol. XXIII (1834), col.1208.
10 G. Grote, *Parl. Deb.*, vol. XXIII (1834), col. 1221.
11 Cited in E. P. Thompson, *The Struggle for a Free Press* (People's Press, 1952 (April)), p. 14.
12 Their largest vote was on 22 May 1834 [*Parl. Deb.*, vol. XXIII (1834), col. 1222].
13 C. Collet, *History of the Taxes on Knowledge*, abridged edition (London, Watts, 1933), p. 29.
14 Collet was successively Secretary of the People's Charter Union, Newspaper Stamp Abolition Committee and the Association for the Promotion of the Repeal of the Taxes on Knowledge.
15 M. Hewitt, *The Dawn of the Cheap Press in Victorian Britain* (London, Bloomsbury Academic, 2014).
16 Ibid., p. 3.
17 Ibid., p. 127 and p. 171.
18 Ibid., p. 178.
19 Cited in C. Collet, *History of the Taxes on Knowledge*, vol. 2, 1st edition (London, T. Fisher Unwin, 1899), p. 207.
20 Hewitt, *The Dawn*, p. 42. He notes, however, that they lost control after 1855 (see pp. 171 ff.).
21 Select Committee on Public Libraries (1849), p. vii cited in A. Black, *A New History of the English Public Library* (London, Leicester University Press, 1996).
22 Different reasons for supporting repeal of specific press taxes are expressed for instance by A. Haywood, Select Committee on Newspaper Stamps (SCNS), *Parliamentary Papers*, vol. 17 (1851), paragraphs 658 ff: M. Whitty, *SCNS*, par. 688; B. Disraeli, *Parl. Deb.*, vol. CXXV (1853), col. 1178; E. Bulwer-Lytton, *Parl. Deb.,* vol. CXXXVII (1855), col. 1128; J. Bright, *Parl. Deb.*, vol. CXXV (1853), col. 1160; T. Milner Gibson, *Parl. Deb.*, vol. CXXV (1853), col. 1131–32; W. Ewart, *Parl. Deb.*, vol. CXXV (1853), col. 1145; among others.
23 Palmerston, *Parl. Deb.*, vol. CXXVI (1854), col. 459.
24 W. Gladstone, *Parl. Deb.*, vol. CXXXVII (1855), col. 794.
25 J. Maguire, *Parl. Deb.*, vol. CLVII (1860), col. 383.
26 For example, J. Bright, *Parl. Deb.*, vol. CXXV (1853), col. 1160; T. Milner Gibson, *Parl. Deb.*, vol. CXXV (1853), col. 1131–32; Marquess of Clanricarde, *Parl. Deb.*, vol. CLVII (1860), col. 1495.

27 A. Andrews, *The History of British Journalism to 1855*, vol. 2 (London, Richard Bentley, 1859), p. 347. The latent authoritarianism lurking within this 'progressive' championship of a free press and public education never really rose to the surface because predictions about the moderating effects of progressive reform were largely fulfilled in Britain. It was a different matter in India where the Viceroy, Lord Bulwer Lytton, reiterated his father's view that the spread of education and a free press would lead to political moderation, only to discover that the more educated the Indians were, the more critical they seemed to be of British rule. He then resorted to heavy-handed press censorship. See the classic pioneering study: A. Seal, *The Emergence of Indian Nationalism* (Cambridge, Cambridge University Press, 1968), pp. 143–46.

28 W. Hickson, Report of the Select Committee on Newspaper Stamps, *Parliamentary Papers*, vol. 17 (1851), par. 3197.

29 P. Magnus, *Gladstone* (London, Murray, 1963), p. 152.

30 Anon [J. F. Stephen], 'Journalism', *Cornhill Magazine*, 6, 1862, p. 58.

31 T. Milner Gibson, *Parl. Deb.*, vol. CXXVII (1854), col. 434.

32 Sir G. Lewis, *Parl. Deb.*, vol. CXXXVII (1855), col. 786.

33 M. Whitty, Report of the Select Committee on Newspaper Stamps, *Parliamentary Papers*, vol. XVII (1851), par. 600.

34 E. Bulwer-Lytton, *Parl. Deb.*, vol. CXXXVII (1855), col. 1118.

35 Sir G. Lewis, *Parl. Deb.*, vol. CXXXVII (1855), col. 782.

36 J. Bright, *Parl. Deb.*, vol. CXXVII (1853), col. 1118; cf. J. Roebuck, *Parl. Deb.*, vol. CXXVII (1853), col. 407.

37 J. R. McCulloch, *Dictionary of Commerce and Commercial Navigation* (London, Longman, Brown and Green, 1854), p. 893.

38 For an illuminating account of the subsequent evolution of this debate about whether the people could be trusted, see H. Cunningham, *The Challenge of Democracy* (Harlow, Pearson Education, 2001).

39 This drama is well told in Collet, *History*, vols. 1–2, and usefully rendered more complex by Hewitt, *The Dawn*.

Chapter 4

Industrialization of the press

During the half-century following the repeal of the 'taxes on knowledge', a number of radical newspapers closed down or were eventually incorporated into the mainstream of popular Liberal journalism. Militant journalism survived only in the etiolated form of small-circulation national periodicals and struggling local weeklies.[1] Yet this decline occurred during a period of rapid press expansion, when local daily papers were established in all the major urban centres of Britain and a new generation of predominantly right-wing national newspapers came into being. These included newspapers such as the *People* (1881), *Daily Mail* (1896), *Daily Express* (1900) and *Daily Mirror* (1903), which were to play a prominent role in British journalism.

Most historians attribute the decline of radical journalism to a change in the climate of public opinion.[2] The collapse of Chartism in the early 1850s produced a wave of disillusion. Some radical activists were absorbed into the Liberal Party or withdrew from the political scene. Some trade unions became more inward looking, seeking merely to improve wages and working conditions. Intensive proselytization of the working class through schools, churches, youth clubs, music hall and the press fostered patriotic and imperialist attitudes, and the spread of anti-socialist views.

Yet, even though the British state remained only quasi-democratic,[3] it introduced significant social reforms ranging from a major extension of workplace protection (1867) through to the introduction of free elementary education (1870) and legal support for women's rights (1870 and 1882). Crucially, the sustained growth of the British economy led also to the rise of workers' wages and a reduction of working hours.[4] In this context of social improvement, the Liberal and Conservative parties became mass political movements, marginalizing for a time the left.

These developments reduced consumer demand for militant journalism. They also had another consequence extending into the early twentieth century, which has tended to be overlooked. The decline of support for the left made it more difficult to raise money within the working-class movement for new radical publishing ventures. Liberal and Lib–Lab trade unionists were reluctant to invest their members' money in setting up new socialist publications, because they had become reconciled to the commercial press.[5]

However, while a 'zeitgeist' interpretation goes some way to explaining the fall of the radical press, it is an incomplete explanation. It is generally based on the over-simplistic assumption that market competition causes the press to reflect the views of the public. This is only partly the case. Thus, the radical press was still a force in popular journalism in 1860 when the radical movement had been decisively defeated. In sharp contrast, the radical press was dwarfed by its rivals in 1910, a time when the radical movement had made a comeback. The steady growth of general trade unionism, the radicalization of skilled workers, the spread of socialist and Labourist ideas, the rise of the suffragette movement and the revival of industrial militancy did not give rise to a substantial radical press in the early twentieth century, although it produced a few notable publications.[6] The absence of a close correspondence between press and public opinion is further underlined by subsequent voting figures. In the 1918 general election, the Labour Party gained 22 per cent of the vote but did not have the support of a single national daily newspaper.[7] So, while wider changes in politics and public attitudes go some way towards explaining the decline of radical journalism, other factors also need to be identified.

Lucy Brown advances a further explanation for the editorial realignment of the Victorian press. The political elite, she argues, became more adept at managing the press, and more influential in the sourcing and framing of news about public affairs. But while this helps to explain why the later Victorian press, in her words, 'declined in critical vigour',[8] it still does not account for the extent of the change that took place. The radical press's adversarial politics effectively inoculated it against the gentler arts of press management described by Brown. The defeat of militant journalism was more fundamental: its publications were eclipsed rather than seduced.

Virginia Berridge supplies another explanation of the decline of committed journalism. This was due, she argues, to the 'commercialisation' of the popular press. New popular papers came into being which were primarily business ventures, relying on sensationalist manipulation of popular sentiment rather than on what Berridge calls the 'genuine arousal' of authentic radical journalism.[9] In other words, they concentrated on populist entertainment rather than on political analysis, and consequently secured a much larger audience.

Berridge's pioneering analysis focuses attention upon *Reynolds's Newspaper* as an illustration of this shift. However, her general argument applies more widely to popular Sunday papers. The circulation of the quasi-radical press during the 1840s was swollen by the emergence of the *News of the World* and *Lloyd's Weekly*, both commercial papers whose initial radicalism was the product more of commercial expediency than of political commitment. As the *News of the World* frankly stated in its first issue, 'It is only by a very extensive circulation that the proprietors can be compensated for the outlay of a large capital in this novel and original undertaking'. Although the same issue contained an impassioned attack on conditions in some poor-houses, where inmates were forced to wear prison clothes, the paper also made clear that its general orientation was to please as many people as possible by serving 'the general utility of all classes'.[10] This led to the adoption of mainstream liberal politics, and an increasing stress on entertainment. Yet, not very surprisingly, Sunday papers like the *News of the World* and *Lloyd's Weekly*, with a professionally processed combination of news and entertainment, proved more appealing than the didactic journals that were the principal organs of the left in late Victorian Britain.

This explanation is persuasive as far as it goes. But it glosses over one striking feature of the development of the early radical press. During the first half of the nineteenth century left-wing papers evolved from being journals of opinion, based on a quarto format, into broadsheet newspapers carrying news as well as commentary. This change was particularly marked during the 1830s, and was accompanied by a significant broadening of editorial content. Some of these radical papers began to develop a wider audience appeal by drawing upon the popular street literature tradition of chapbooks, broadsheets, gallowsheets and almanacs.[11] Indeed, *Cleave's Weekly Police Gazette*, the *London Dispatch* and the early militant *Reynolds's Newspaper* were important partly because they started to rework this cultural tradition in ways that projected a radical perspective through entertainment (in particular crime reporting) not just through political coverage.

Why, then, did the committed radical press retreat increasingly in the second half of the nineteenth century into the ghetto of narrowly politicized journalism? Why did it leave the field of popular news coverage and entertainment to the commercial press? Thus the question that needs to be asked is not why Victorian working people should have preferred the *News of the World* to rather arid socialist journals such as *Justice* and *Commonweal*, but why the radical press should have failed to live up to its early promise (or, in Berridge's perspective, to its debased populism).

Her analysis is a historical version of a standard critique of mass culture. This assumes that communication processed commercially as a *commodity* for the mass market is inevitably impoverished because it relies on the manipulation of public tastes and attitudes for profit. This is based on an underlying premise that is open to question. In the context of Victorian Britain, it also obscures under the general heading of 'commercialisation' the complex system of controls institutionalized by the industrialization of the Victorian press.

The freedom of capital

One of the central objectives of state economic controls on the press – to exclude pauper management – was attained only by its repeal. The development of an unfettered free market raised publishing costs in a way that prevented groups of workers, or individuals with limited resources, from owning newspapers.

This was partly because an industrial system of production replaced a largely craft-based one. The lifting of press taxes set up a chain reaction: lower prices, increased sales and the development of new print technology to service an expanding market. Rotary presses, fed by hand, were introduced in the 1860s and 1870s and were gradually replaced by web rotary machines of increasing size and sophistication in late Victorian and Edwardian England. 'Craft' composing was mechanized by Hattersley's machine in the 1860s, and this was replaced by the linotype machine in the 1880s and 1890s. Numerous innovations were also made in graphic reproduction. These developments led to a sharp rise in fixed capital costs. For example, Northcliffe estimated half a million pounds as 'the initial cost of machinery, buildings, ink factories and the like, and this was altogether apart from the capital required for daily working expenses' in setting up the *Daily Mail* in 1896.[12]

The rise in fixed costs made it more difficult for people with limited funds to break into mass publishing. It also brought into play economies of scale and scope that favoured large publishers. Big circulation newspapers were able to spread their large 'first large copy' costs over a large print run. This reduced the unit cost of each copy, giving them a competitive advantage over their smaller rivals. In addition, some large groups gained the advantages of consolidation. Edward Lloyd led the way by both publishing multiple titles in the same site, and diversifying in the 1870s and 1880s into paper manufacture. However, while new technology raised the level of investment needed to start a paper, and tended to strengthen the position of major publishers, it did not in fact constitute an insuperable obstacle to the launch of new publications with limited capital, even in the national market. Newspapers such as the *Daily Herald*, launched in 1912, could still be started with only a limited outlay by being printed on a contract basis by an independent printer.

A more important financial consequence of the repeal of press taxes was to increase the *operating* costs of newspaper publishing. National newspapers became substantial enterprises, with growing newsprint bills and staff costs, during a period when cover prices were repeatedly cut. This forced up the circulation levels that newspapers needed to achieve in order to be profitable. This raised, in turn, the run-in costs of new ventures. New newspapers could be launched with limited funds and derelict newspapers could be bought relatively cheaply. It was increasingly the cost of funding trading losses before newspapers became established as profitable enterprises that required substantial capital (and the ability to access substantial credit).

Thus in 1855 Disraeli was advised that a capital of about £20,000 was needed to start a London daily paper.[13] In 1867 W. H. Smith estimated that about £50,000 was necessary to fund a new London morning paper.[14] By the 1870s Edward Lloyd needed to spend £150,000 to establish the *Daily Chronicle* (after buying it for £30,000).[15] During the period 1906 to 1908 Thomasson spent about £300,000 attempting to establish the Liberal daily, *Tribune*.[16] By the 1920s, Lord Cowdray spent about £750,000 attempting to convert the *Westminster Gazette* into a quality daily.[17] Even more was spent on developing mass-circulation papers during the same period.

Indeed, the full extent of the material transformation of the press is perhaps most clearly revealed by comparing the launch and establishment costs of newspapers before and after the introduction of mass production. As we have seen, the total cost of establishing the *Northern Star* as a leading national weekly newspaper on a profitable basis in 1837 was around £1000.[18] It broke even with a circulation of about 6200 copies, which was probably achieved in its first month. In contrast the *Sunday Express*, launched in 1918, had over £2 million spent on it before it broke even, and this needed a circulation of well over 250,000 to be profitable.[19] Thus, while a public subscription in northern towns was sufficient to launch a national weekly in the 1830s, it required the resources of an international conglomerate controlled by Beaverbrook to do the same thing nearly a century later.

These statistics illustrate the privileged position of capital in the creation of the modern press. Even when the cost of launching and establishing a popular paper was still relatively low in the 1860s, it exceeded the resources readily available to the organised working class. *The Bee-Hive*, for instance, was started in 1862 with capital of less than £250 raised by trade union organisations and a well-to-do sympathizer. Although its founders initially aspired to reach a wider audience by carrying both news and features, lack of funds forced them to create a low-cost weekly journal of opinion for a minority audience. Despite a small amount of additional capital put up by unions and other contributors, *the Bee-Hive* also had to sell at double the price of the large-circulation weeklies they had originally wanted to compete against. In effect, its under-capitalization confined it to the margins of national publishing as a specialist, if influential, weekly paper.[20]

The rise in publishing costs helps to explain why the committed left press in the late nineteenth century existed only as under-capitalized, low-budget, high-price specialist periodicals and as local community papers, an important but as yet relatively undocumented aspect of the residual survival of the radical press.[21] The operation of the free market had raised the cost of press ownership beyond the readily available resources of the working class.

As the resources of organised labour increased, so did the costs of publishing. It was not until 1912 that papers financed and controlled from within the working class made their first appearance in national daily journalism – long after popular national daily papers had become well established. The brief career of the *Daily Citizen* and the early history of the *Daily Herald* illustrate the economic obstacles to setting up papers under working-class control. The *Daily Citizen*, launched in 1912 with a capital of only £30,000 (provided mainly by trade unions), reached a circulation of 250,000 at its peak within two years and was only 50,000 short of overhauling the *Daily Express*.

But although the *Daily Citizen* almost certainly acquired more working-class readers than any other daily, it was still forced to close in 1915 for lack of funds.[22]

The more left-wing *Daily Herald*, starting with only £300 and sustained by public donations, lurched from one crisis to another despite reaching a circulation of over 250,000 at its meridian before 1914. On one occasion, when the *Daily Herald* could no longer afford to buy paper, it came out in pages of different sizes and shapes after old discarded paper supplies were 'found'. On another occasion, it acquired small quantities of paper under fictitious names from suppliers all over the country. Later it secured paper supplies without a guarantee by threatening to organise, through its trade union connections, industrial action against paper manufacturers.[23] While the *Daily Citizen* closed, the *Daily Herald* survived by switching from being a daily to becoming a weekly during the period 1914–19. Lack of sufficient capital prevented its continuation in any other form.

Market forces thus accomplished more than the most repressive measures of an aristocratic state. The security system introduced in 1819 to ensure that the press was controlled by men of 'respectability and capital' had fixed the financial qualifications of press ownership at a mere £200 to £300. This financial hurdle was raised over a hundredfold by the market system between 1850 and 1920.[24]

However, although the heavy capitalization of the British press was an important factor inhibiting the launch of new radical papers, it still does not explain the ideological absorption of radical papers already in existence before the repeal of the press taxes. Nor does it fully explain why small-circulation radical papers did not grow into profitable mass-circulation papers and accumulate sufficient capital, through retained profits, to finance new publications. For an answer to these questions we need to look elsewhere.

The new licensing system: advertising

The crucial element of the new control system was the strategic role acquired by advertisers after the repeal of the advertisement duty in 1853. Before then, the advertisement tax had made certain forms of advertising uneconomic. As John Cassell, the publisher of popular useful knowledge publications, argued before the Parliamentary Select Committee on Newspaper Stamps, the advertisement duty 'prevents a certain class of advertisements from appearing: it is only such as costly books and property sales by auction that really afford an opportunity of advertising and for paying the duty'.[25]

Cassell perhaps exaggerated the impact of the advertisement duty for political reasons. The growth of trade, and the reduction of the advertisement duty in 1833, had led to a substantial increase in press advertising in the 1830s and 1840s. Even before that, most commercial newspapers – but not the radical press – had been reliant on advertising. But it was only with the abolition of the advertisement duty in 1853 that popular press advertising came fully into its own. Between 1854 and 1858, for instance, *Reynolds's Newspaper* increased its advertising volume by over 50 per cent.[26] This surge in advertising expenditure, combined with the repeal of the stamp and paper duties, transformed the economic structure of the popular press. The modal price of popular papers was halved in the 1850s and halved again in the 1860s. At the new prevailing price structure, nearly all newspapers – including those with very large circulations such as *Reynolds's Newspaper*[27] – depended on advertising for their profits since their reduced cover prices no longer met their costs. Advertisers thus acquired a *de facto* licensing power because, without their support, newspapers ceased to be economically viable.

Rising circulations and the sharp fall in the price of newsprint between 1875 and 1895 did not diminish the central role of advertising in the press. Newspaper costs rose, due to increased paging, more staff and the introduction of sale-or-return arrangements with distributors. The prices of most popular papers again halved, dropping to ½d in the late Victorian period. These changes were funded in part by a large increase of advertising, which rose to an estimated £20 million in 1907.[28]

The political implications of newspapers' economic dependence on advertising have been ignored largely because it is assumed that advertisers bought space in newspapers on the basis of commercial rather than political criteria. But political considerations played a significant part in some advertisers' calculations during the Victorian period. In 1856 the principal advertising handbook detailed the political views of most London and local newspapers with the proud boast that 'till this Directory was published, the advertiser had no means of accurately determining which journal *might be best adapted to his views*, and most likely to forward his interests' (emphasis added).[29] Even non-socialist newspapers found that controversial editorial policies could lead to the loss of advertising. The *Pall Mall Gazette*'s advertising revenue dropped sharply in 1885 when the editor 'procured' a 13-year-old girl as part of the paper's campaign to raise the legal age of consent to sex.[30] The *Daily News* was boycotted by some advertisers in 1886 when it campaigned for Home Rule.[31] Government advertising long continued to be allocated on a partisan basis. As late as 1893 the incoming Home Secretary, Herbert Asquith, was told that generally 'it is the custom to transfer advertisements according to the politics of governments'.[32]

Political prejudice in advertising selection almost certainly declined during the latter part of the nineteenth century and early twentieth century, due to the rise of major national advertisers, the growth of advertising agencies and the greater availability of (still often unreliable) circulation statistics. But even when political partisanship played no part in advertising selection, left-wing publications still encountered discrimination on economic grounds. As a leading advertising guide counselled in 1856, 'some of the most widely circulated journals in the Empire are the worst possible to advertise in. Their readers are not purchasers; and any money spent on them is so much thrown away'.[33] Newspapers read by the well-to-do were assessed differently. 'Character is of more importance than number', advised an advertising handbook in 1851, adding that 'a journal that circulates a thousand among the upper or middle classes is a better medium than would be one circulating a hundred thousand among the lower classes'.[34] Similar, though usually more qualified, advice continued to be given for some time. For example, Sir Charles Higham, the head of a large advertising agency, wrote in 1925, 'A very limited circulation, but entirely among the wealthy . . . may be more valuable than if the circulation were quadrupled'.[35]

Some advertisers also made a key distinction between the skilled and poor working class. Indeed, the latter were often excluded from the early market research surveys in the 1920s on the grounds that they were not worth bothering about.[36] Once newspapers became identified with the poor, they found it difficult to attract advertising. As an advertising handbook cautioned in 1921, 'You cannot afford to place your advertisements in a paper which is read by the down-at-heels who buy it to see the "Situations Vacant" column'.[37]

This combination of economic and political discrimination by advertisers influenced the development of left-wing journalism. In the first place, it exerted pressure on the radical press to move upmarket in order to survive. A number of radical newspapers redefined their target audience, and moderated their radicalism, in an attempt to attract the more affluent readers that advertisers wanted to reach.

This process is well illustrated by *Reynolds's Newspaper*. It was founded in 1850 by George Reynolds, a member of the left-wing faction of the Chartist National Executive. Reynolds had urged a 'physical force' strategy in 1848 and opposed middle-class collaboration in the early 1850s. His paper was initially in the *Northern Star* tradition of class-conscious radicalism, and had close links to the working-class movement. Yet despite its radical origins, the paper changed under the impact of the new economic imperatives of newspaper publishing. The fact that *Reynolds's Newspaper* never provided, even at the outset, a consistent theoretical perspective doubtless made it vulnerable to ideological incorporation. Inevitably it was influenced by the decline of radicalism in the country during the 1850s and early 1860s, but an important factor in its absorption was also the need to attract advertising revenue. The change was symbolized by its inclusion of regular features on friendly societies in the year after the repeal of the advertisement duty, as a ploy to attract advertising. Enterprises which had been attacked in militant newspapers as 'a hoax' to persuade working-class people to identify with capitalism became a much-needed source of revenue for the paper.

Reynolds's Newspaper continued to take a radical democratic stand on most major issues of the day, but it also increasingly expressed the individualistic values of the more affluent readers whom it needed to attract.[38] It portrayed self-help rather than state activism as the way forward, endorsing 'prudent marriage' (i.e. sexual restraint) and emigration as the solutions to unemployment. Its radicalism increasingly took the form of stories about the vices of the aristocracy, corruption in high places, and the deficiencies of Anglican vicars. *Reynolds's Newspaper* became a paper that catered for the coalition of lower-middle-class and working-class readers necessary for its survival. Acquired by the Dicks family in 1879 and later by the Scottish Liberal MP James Dalziel, it gradually evolved into a conventional Liberal paper.

Reynolds was accused of commercial opportunism by contemporary critics (including Karl Marx); yet it is difficult to see what else he could have done if the paper was to survive the transition to an advertising-based system. Even the radical *People's Paper*, which Marx wrote for regularly between 1852 and 1856, boasted of its appeal to 'high paid trades and shopkeepers' in its promotion to advertisers.[39]

Radical newspapers could survive in the new economic environment only if they successfully moved upmarket or if they remained in a small working-class ghetto, with manageable losses which could be offset by donations. Once they moved out of that ghetto and sought a larger working-class audience, they became vulnerable. They were liable to find that their sales revenue did not cover costs due to insufficient advertising. If they increased their sales, they merely incurred greater losses.

This fate befell the London *Evening Echo*, which was taken over by wealthy radicals in 1901 and relaunched as a socialist paper, committed to 'the interests of labour as against the tyranny of organised capital'. In the period 1902 to 1904 its circulation rose by a remarkable 60 per cent, leading to its abrupt closure in 1905. The *Evening Echo*'s advertising had failed to keep pace with its growth of circulation, making its continuation impossible.[40]

The same thing almost happened to the *Daily Herald* when it was relaunched as a daily in 1919. It spent £10,000 on promotion – a small amount by comparison with its main rivals – but sufficient to boost its sales. 'Owing to the heavy price of paper, our success in circulation', recalled George Lansbury, 'was our undoing. The more copies we sold, the more money we lost'.[41] The situation became increasingly desperate when, aided by false accusations of being funded with Moscow gold, the paper's circulation continued to rise in 1920. 'Every copy we sold was sold at a loss', mourned Lansbury. 'The rise in circulation, following the government's attacks, brought us nearer and nearer to disaster'.[42] The money raised from whist drives, dances, draws and collections was not enough to offset the shortfall of advertising. The desperate expedient of doubling the paper's price in 1920 was not enough to secure its future. Money from the miners and the railwaymen prevented the paper from closing. But the only way the paper could be saved, in the long term, was by its being taken over as the official organ of the Labour Party and Trades Union Congress (TUC) in 1922. A paper that had been a freewheeling vehicle of the left, an important channel for the dissemination of syndicalist and socialist ideas in the early part of the twentieth century,[43] became the official mouthpiece of the moderate leadership of the labour movement. Lack of advertising forced it to become subservient to a new form of control.[44]

In short, one of four things happened to national radical papers that failed to meet the requirements of advertisers. Either they closed down; accommodated to advertising pressure by moving upmarket; stayed in a small-audience ghetto with manageable losses; or accepted an alternative source of institutional patronage.

Yet publications which conformed to the marketing requirements of advertisers obtained what were, in effect, large external subsidies which they could spend on increased editorial outlay and promotion to attract additional readers. Rising advertising expenditure also provided a strong incentive for entrepreneurs to launch publications directed at markets that advertisers particularly wanted to reach. Between 1866 and 1896 the number of magazines increased from an estimated 557 to 2097, many of which were trade, technical and professional journals aimed at specialized groups attractive to advertisers. The number of local dailies grew from under ten in 1850 to 196 in 1900, falling to 169 by 1920 (due mainly to the casualties caused by intense competition). There was also a substantial expansion in the number of local weekly papers from fewer than 400 in 1856 to 2072 in 1900, declining to 1700 by 1921. Above all, there was a substantial increase in the number of national daily and Sunday papers, mostly founded between 1880 and 1918.[45]

The growth in the number of publications was accompanied by an enormous increase in newspaper circulation. This was facilitated by rising incomes, improved reading skills (though mass basic literacy predated Foster's 1870 Education Act due to the impact of church schools) and reduced working hours. By 1920, total daily circulation had reached 14.67 million, while total Sunday circulation had soared to 20.32 million.[46]

In brief, the left press suffered a double defeat. It lost its leading position in popular journalism, and largely missed out on the major expansion of the press that took place between 1855 and 1920.

Impact of the industrialized press

At the turn of the nineteenth century, some traditional educationalists taught working-class children to read but not to write – as a way of containing the threat posed by literacy to the social order.[47] These children were to read what was good for them; not to write anything that might prove harmful. Something like this division of labour was achieved through the industrialization of the press. Workers became the consumers of newspapers; they no longer controlled its production.

Many of the new local dailies, founded after 1855, were started or bought by leading local industrialists. Both the *Northern Daily Express* and the *Northern Leader* were bought by colliery owners; the *South Shields Gazette* was acquired by Stevenson, a member of a local chemical manufacturing family; the *Bolton*

Evening News belonged to local industrialists, the Tillotsons; the *Yorkshire Post*'s principal shareholder was the Leeds banker Beckett-Denison; the *Ipswich Express* was owned by Colman, the mustard manufacturer, and so on.[48] These papers mostly offered a very different view of the world from that of the early radical press which they largely supplanted. Papers such as the *Northern Star* had amplified class conflicts in the local community ('to talk of reconciliation between the middle and working classes in Leicester will, henceforth, be a farce' was a typical lead-in to one of its news reports).[49] In contrast, the new local commercial press tended to block out conflict, minimise differences, and encourage positive identification with the local community and its middle-class leadership. Characteristic of this style of consensual journalism was a report in the *Leeds Mercury* (printed in the same city as the *Northern Star*) of a local dignitary addressing the annual public soirée of the Leeds Mechanics Institute on the subject of 'these popular institutions, sustained by the united efforts of all classes . . . thereby to promote the virtue, happiness and peace of the community'.[50]

The early militant press had fuelled suspicion of middle-class reformists with a barrage of criticism against 'sham-radical humbugs' and 'the merciful middle-class converts to half Chartism at half past the eleventh hour'.[51] In contrast, the industrialized press encouraged its readers to support the political establishment represented by the Conservative and Liberal parties. Indeed, the rise of the cheap press played an important part in the transformation of what had been in 1850 little more than aristocratic factions in parliament into political parties with a mass base. Between 1851 and 1887, the number of newspapers affiliated to the Conservative and Liberal parties increased from 189 to 707 (with most of the increase taking place in the 1860s).[52] And between 1857 and 1892, the number of newspaper proprietors elected to the House of Commons rose from four to thirty.[53] This marriage of journalism and party politics helped to integrate growing numbers of people into the political system, even though the majority did not gain the vote until 1918.

The new Liberal press, in particular, played a significant role in re-routing radical politics. Leading liberal papers, like the initially centre-left *Daily Telegraph* founded in 1855, adapted radical themes in ways that fundamentally changed their meaning. Thus, an earlier stress on co-operation based on common ownership was reincarnated as the partnership between employers and employees that would bring prosperity to all. A commitment to social reconstruction became transmuted into improvement through middle-class enlightenment. A view of education as a means of class resistance gave way to one that emphasized individual advancement. Admittedly these transformations drew upon a radical tradition that had contained contradictions within it. But by giving prominence to its liberal features, the industrial press diluted the radical inheritance of the Chartist era.

This is not to make light of the differences between liberal-radical newspapers and their rivals in the post-1855 period, not least in their reporting of trade unions, the emergent women's movement, Irish Home Rule, and state reform activism. But notwithstanding these important differences, all national newspapers launched between 1855 and 1910, and the overwhelming majority of new local daily papers, encouraged positive identification with the social system in contrast to their radical predecessors. This shift is perhaps best illustrated by the way in which Queen Victoria was portrayed. The radical press in the period 1837 to 1855 was aggressively republican: the Queen was vilified as being politically reactionary, the head of a system of organised corruption, the mother of a brood of royal cadgers, and the friend and relative of European tyrants. In contrast, the new press portrayed the Queen from the mid-1870s onward as a dutiful and benign matriarch who symbolized in an almost talismanic way the moral and material progress of her reign.[54] Projecting her as the living embodiment of national unity, the press also played a key role in transforming the royal jubilee celebrations of 1887 and 1897 into popular, mobilizing rites of national communion.[55]

Above all, the new popular press fostered the wave of imperialism that swept through all levels of society. Popular newspapers tended to portray Britain's colonial role as a civilizing mission to the heathen, underdeveloped world, or as an extended adventure story in which military triumphs were achieved through individual acts of courage rather than through superior military technology. Common to both themes was pride in Britain's ascendancy: as the *Daily Mail*, the most popular daily of late Victorian Britain, enthused:

> We send out a boy here and a boy there, and the boy takes hold of the savages of the part he comes to and teaches them to march and shoot as he tells them, to obey him and believe in him and die for him and the Queen. A plain, stupid, uninspired people they call us, and yet we are doing this with every kind of savage man there is.[56]

This celebration of Britain's dominion sometimes struck a more atavistic note, as in this report of the 1898 Sudan expedition in the *Westminster Gazette*:

> A large number of the Tommies had never been under fire before . . . and there was a curious look of suppressed excitement in some of the faces . . . Now and then I caught in a man's eye the curious gleam which, despite all the veneer of civilization, still holds its own in man's nature, whether he is killing rats with a terrier, rejoicing in a prize fight, playing a salmon or potting Dervishes. It was a fine day and we were out to kill something. Call it what you like, the experience is a big factor in the joy of living.[57]

The paper which celebrated 'potting Dervishes' was 'progressive' in terms of the narrow political arc represented by the contemporary London press. It was, for example, one of the few papers not to be in favour of the Boer War.

However, it subsequently joined other papers (with the notable exception of the *Daily Herald*) in providing Hun-hating support for Britain's involvement in the First World War.

The First World War had been preceded by regular press depictions of British military action as being necessary and desirable.[58] In part this stemmed from an imperialist mind-set in which colonial conflicts were likened to policing operations; in part from fashionable Social Darwinist thought which viewed war as a legitimate form of arbitration between competing nations; and, especially in the popular imperialist press, from what amounted almost to a cult of war.[59] This viewed military conflict as a purifying, redemptive process in which the ill-effects of over-civilization and racial degeneration could be exorcized. It was also bound up with a particular view of masculinity, in which war was viewed as something that men did. How men responded to war was a true test of their manhood: whether they reacted with the fear of a coward or, in the words of the *Daily Mail*, with the excitement of a young man 'responding to the blast [of the trumpet] as for his wedding bell'.[60]

This cult of war was especially evident in press responses to the Boer War (1899–1902) where the British experienced military reverses. The war was hailed by *Lloyd's Newspaper* as a cleansing purgative, restoring the nation to health after a period when the 'great heart' of empire had suffered 'from fatty degeneration'.[61] According to the *News of the World*, it had awakened Britain from its lethargy, rendering the country 'stronger and more fitted for the duties of Empire'.[62] In the *Daily Mirror*'s view, it revealed 'the elasticity of a great people'.[63] But the most eloquent tribute came in a *Daily Mail* editorial chillingly headed 'The Blessings of War'. The benefit of war, according to the paper, was that it provided an opportunity 'to re-examine the bases of our national life, ruthlessly digging away all that is decayed or doubtful' and at the same time enabled the Empire to emerge 'stronger, more fully prepared, amply equipped against the worst our foes can do to us'.[64]

The militarism of the British press helps to explain why, at the outbreak of the Great War, so many young men volunteered for the armed forces with excitement and enthusiasm, often egged on by the civilian population. The killing fields of the western front, and elsewhere, were to claim the lives of almost a million British soldiers. It was the bitter harvest of a press which had heedlessly preached for years the virtues of patriotism and valour in defending Britain's empire.[65]

Conclusion

The radical press was defeated decisively after the abolition of the 'taxes on knowledge'. Its defeat cannot be attributed solely to the changed climate of opinion, following the collapse of the Chartist Movement. This *Zeitgeist* or 'sovereign consumer' interpretation, though often invoked, fails to explain why the press, taken as a whole, moved further to the right than public opinion;

nor does it explain why the subsequent revival of the radical movement did not give rise to a stronger revival of radical journalism. The eclipse of the radical press as the dominant force in national popular journalism was also due to structural changes in the press industry. The industrialization of the press, with its accompanying rise in publishing costs, led to a progressive transfer of ownership and control of the popular press to wealthy businesspeople, while dependence on advertising encouraged the absorption or elimination of the early radical press and stunted its subsequent development before the First World War.

Notes

1 E. Miller, 'Literature and the late-Victorian radical press', *Literature Compass*, 7 (8), 2010, pp. 702–12; M. Tusan, *Women Making News* (Urbana, University of Illinois Press, 2005); D. Hopkin, 'The left-wing press and the new journalism' in J. Wiener (ed.) *Papers for the Millions: The New Journalism in Britain* (Westport, CT, Greenwood Press, 1988); and D. Hopkin, 'The socialist press in Britain, 1890–1910' in G. Boyce, J. Curran and P. Wingate (eds.) *Newspaper History* (London, Constable, 1978).

2 For example, L. Brown, *Victorian News and Newspapers* (Oxford, Clarendon Press, 1985), p. 276; S. Koss, *The Rise and Fall of the Political Press in Britain* (London, Hamish Hamilton, vol. 1, 1981), p. 414.

3 Despite three extensions of the franchise, only 60 per cent of adult men possessed the vote, while all women were disenfranchised, in 1914. See D. Cannandine, *The Undivided Past* (London, Allen Lane, 2013), p. 72.

4 H. Cunningham, *Time, Work and Leisure* (Manchester, Manchester University Press, 2014) summarises the latest evidence on increased leisure in Victorian Britain.

5 This is a key point documented in R. Holton, '*Daily Herald* v. *Daily Citizen* 1912–15', *International Review of Social History*, 19 (3), 1974, pp. 347–76.

6 For the relative weakness of the radical press in c. 1910, see A. Lee's 'The radical press' in A. Morris (ed.) *Edwardian Radicalism, 1900–1914* (London, Routledge and Kegan Paul, 1974).

7 D. Butler and G. Butler, *Twentieth-Century British Political Facts 1900–2000*, 8th edition (Basingstoke, Macmillan, 2000), p. 22. The *Daily Herald* did not resume daily production until 1919.

8 Brown, *Victorian News*, p. 276.

9 V. Berridge, 'Popular Sunday papers and mid-Victorian society' in G. Boyce, J. Curran and P. Wingate (eds.) *Newspaper History* (London, Constable, 1978), p. 264. This interpretation has been extended in divergent ways by J. Chalaby, *The Invention of Journalism* (London, Macmillan, 1998) and M. Conboy, *The Press and Popular Culture* (London, Sage, 2002).

10 *News of the World*, 1 October 1843.

11 B. Capp, *Astrology and the Popular Press* (London, Faber and Faber, 1979); L. Shepherd, *The History of Street Literature* (Newton Abbot, David and Charles, 1973).

12 R. Pound and G. Harmsworth, *Northcliffe* (London, Cassell, 1959), p. 206.

13 A. Lee, *The Origins of the Popular Press 1854–1914* (London, Croom Helm, 1976), p. 149.

14 Lee, *Origins*, p. 150.

15 H. Herd, *The March of Journalism* (London, Allen and Unwin, 1952), p. 185.
16 Lee, *Origins*, p. 167.
17 C. Seymour-Ure, 'The press and party system between the wars' in G. Peele and C. Cook (eds.) *The Politics of Reappraisal 1918–39* (London, Macmillan, 1975), p. 242.
18 See Chapter 2, note 23.
19 A. J. P. Taylor, *Beaverbrook* (London, Hamish Hamilton, 1972), p. 175.
20 S. Coltham, 'The *Bee-Hive* newspaper: its origins and early development' in A. Briggs and J. Saville (eds.) *Essays in Labour History* (London, Macmillan, 1960).
21 See in particular Hopkin, 'Socialist press'.
22 Holton, '*Daily Herald*', 1974.
23 G. Lansbury, *The Miracle of Fleet Street* (London, Victoria House, 1925).
24 Market entry costs were especially high in Britain due to the early emergence of a strong national press. They were lower in European countries with a dominant local press, such as Germany and Sweden, where it was easier for radical journalism to flourish.
25 Report of the Select Committee on Newspaper Stamps, *Parliamentary Papers*, 17, 1851, p. 236.
26 Berridge, 'Popular Sunday papers', Table 13.1, p. 250.
27 V. Berridge, 'Popular journalism and working class attitudes, 1854–86: A study of *Reynolds's Newspaper, Lloyd's Weekly Newspaper* and the *Weekly Times*', Unpublished Ph.D. thesis (University of London, 1976).
28 R. Critchley, *UK Advertising Statistics* (London, Advertising Association, 1974).
29 *Mitchell's Newspaper Press Directory*, 5th edition (London, Mitchell, 1856), p. 7.
30 L. Brown, *Victorian News and Newspapers* (Oxford, Clarendon Press, 1985), p. 23.
31 Brown, *Victorian News*, p. 23.
32 Brown, *Victorian News*, p. 57. This had also been true of the 1880s; see A. Aspinall, *Politics and the Press* (Brighton, Harvester, 1973 [1949]), p. 382.
33 C. Mitchell, *The Newspaper Press Directory and Advertisers' Guide* (London, Mitchell and Co, 1856), p. 15.
34 Anon, *Guide to Advertisers*, (London, 1851).
35 C. Higham, *Advertising* (London, Williams and Norgate, 1925), p. 166.
36 For example, the national survey on which *Press Circulations Analysed* (London, London Research Bureau, 1928) is based.
37 C. Freer, *The Inner Side of Advertising: A Practical Handbook for Advertisers* (London, Library Press, 1921), p. 203.
38 For a fuller analysis of the paper's editorial change, see Berridge, 'Popular journalism', 1976 and Berridge, 'Popular Sunday newspapers', 1978.
39 Advertisement placed in *Mitchell's Newspaper Directory 1857–8* (London, Mitchell, 1858).
40 F. Pethick-Lawrence, *Fate Has Been Kind* (London, Hutchinson, 1943), pp. 65 ff.
41 G. Lansbury, *The Miracle of Fleet Street* (Victoria House, London), p. 160.
42 Lansbury, *Miracle*, p. 161.
43 B. Holton, *British Syndicalism 1900–1914* (London, Pluto, 1976).
44 This is very well described in H. Richards, *The Bloody Circus: The* Daily Herald *and the Left* (London, Pluto, 1997).
45 Estimates derived from *Mitchell's Newspaper Press Directory* (London, Mitchell, 1850–1920).

46 N. Kaldor and R. Silverman, *A Statistical Analysis of Advertising Expenditure and of the Revenue of the Press* (Cambridge, Cambridge University Press, 1948), Table 45, p. 84.

47 B. Simon, *The Two Nations and the Educational Structure, 1780–1870* (London, Lawrence and Wishart, 1974), p. 133.

48 Lee, *Origins*, pp. 135 ff.

49 *Northern Star*, 7 May 1842.

50 *Leeds Mercury*, 14 June 1851.

51 *Northern Star*, 26 February 1842; cf. *Northern Star*, 11 June 1842.

52 Lee, *Origins*, Table 28, p. 290.

53 Lee, *Origins*, Table 34, p. 296.

54 J. Plunkett, *Queen Victoria: First Media Monarch* (Oxford, Oxford University Press, 2003); F. Prochaska, *Royal Bounty* (New Haven, Yale University Press, 1995). However, *Reynold's Newspaper* long remained a republican paper.

55 E. Hammond and D. Cannandine, 'Conflict and consensus on a ceremonial occasion: the diamond jubilee in Cambridge in 1887', *Historical Journal*, 24 (1), 1981, pp. 111–46.

56 *Daily Mail*, 23 June 1897.

57 Cited in P. Knightley, *The First Casualty* (London, Deutsch, 1975), p. 41.

58 G. Wilkinson, '"The blessings of war": the depiction of military force in Edwardian newspapers', *Journal of Contemporary History*, 33 (1), 1990, 97–115.

59 Press portrayals were part of a contemporary, literary cult of war, examined in P. Fussell, *The Great War and Modern Memory* (Oxford, Oxford University Press, 1975).

60 *Daily Mail*, 12 October 1912.

61 *Lloyd's Weekly Newspaper*, 28 January 1900.

62 *News of the World*, 1 June 1902.

63 *Daily Mirror*, 5 April 1904.

64 *Daily Mail*, 1 January 1900 cited in Wilkinson, 'Blessings'.

65 Remorse is movingly expressed by Rudyard Kipling (whose son was killed in the war) in the poem 'Epitaphs of the War 1914–1918'. Available at: www.kipling society.co.uk/poems_epitaphs.htm (accessed 8 February 2016). This reaction, shared by others of his generation, helps to explain the very different response of the inter-war press to the threat of war, described in the next chapter.

Chapter 5

Era of the press barons

The era of the press barons is often seen as a maverick interlude in the development of the press. According to this view, press barons gained an unprecedented hegemony over the press, and cynically manipulated their newspapers as engines of propaganda. The despotic rule of the press barons is contrasted with a preceding golden age when proprietors played an inactive role, and editors were 'sovereign'.[1] The press barons have thus become favourite bogeymen: censoring them has become a way of celebrating the former editorial integrity of the press.

But in reality the reign of the press barons did not constitute an exceptional pathology in the evolution of the press, but merely a continuation of tendencies already present before. Indeed, insofar as the barons may be said to have been innovators, it is not for the reasons that are generally given.

Creation of press empires

The large press groups built by the press barons did not represent a decisive break with the past. Newspaper chains had developed as early as the 1820s;[2] and continued to grow thereafter. Thus, the steel magnate, Andrew Carnegie owned eight British dailies and about ten weeklies in 1884.[3]

While the press barons were the beneficiaries of rising circulation, this was hardly new. Newspaper sales had been rising ever since 1695, and this growth greatly accelerated after 1855. Likewise, the leading position acquired by some titles owned by the press barons was not a novel phenomenon. Unequal competition between strong and weak papers had given rise repeatedly to market dominance. For example, *The Times* was especially dominant in the 1850s national daily press.[4]

In brief, the press empires created by the press barons merely continued three well-established trends – chain ownership, rising newspaper consumption and market ascendancy. All that happened was that, in some cases, these trends became more pronounced.

Thus, newspaper chains got bigger in terms of the percentage of titles they controlled. Between 1921 and 1939, the big five regional chains' share of local morning titles increased from 12 per cent to 44 per cent, while their share of local evening titles (excluding London) rose from 8 per cent to 40 per cent.[5] This was largely a consequence of newspaper acquisitions at a time of contraction in the number of titles.[6] This was organised partly through a series of cynical carve-ups in which press magnates – most notably, Lords Camrose, Kemsley and Rothermere – sold out in some areas and consolidated in others on the basis of tacit or explicit cartel deals with each other.[7] This facilitated the creation of local oligopolies where most local papers in the sub-region were owned by the same publisher, and contributed to a rise in the number of towns with no choice of local paper.[8] However, the rapid advance of the chains in the regional press took place mainly in the 1920s, and stalled in the 1930s.[9]

The press groups owned by the barons also benefited from an enormous increase in national daily newspaper reading between the wars. The Sunday press had already built a mass following in Victorian and Edwardian Britain, and consequently its gains – from 13.5 to 15.8 million between 1920 and 1939 – were relatively modest.[10] By contrast, national daily circulation almost doubled from 5.4 million to 10.6 million.[11] In 1932 national dailies outsold local dailies for the first time.[12]

A small number of national titles built mass circulations. Lord Northcliffe's *Daily Mail* was the first British daily to reach 1 million in 1915;[13] the *Daily Herald* was the first to notch up 2 million in 1933;[14] and the *Daily Express* was the first to break the 2.5 million barrier in 1939.[15] The prominence of Beaverbrook as a press baron was mainly due to the success of two titles: the *Daily* and *Sunday Express*.

But while the inter-war press barons commanded larger sales than before, they were in relative terms no more dominant in the national press than earlier in the century. Indeed, in 1937, the three leading national daily magnates (Beaverbrook, Rothermere and Southgate) controlled 58 per cent of national daily circulation,[16] significantly less than the estimated 67 per cent controlled by their counterparts (Pearson, Cadbury and Northcliffe) in 1910.[17] The market share of the three leading Sunday newspaper magnates (Beaverbrook, Carr and Kemsley) in 1937 was 55 per cent, again less than the 69 per cent share of their lesser known equivalents (Dalziel, Riddell and Lloyd) in 1910.[18]

Thus, the barons' hegemony over the national press waned during the inter-war period when their ascendancy became notorious. This reverse was partly due to the belated revival of a Labour movement press which was made possible, as we shall see, by changes in the market system. In addition one of the most powerful press barons, Lord Rothermere, overreached himself and was forced to sell major press assets during the Depression.

Press barons and proprietorial control

The two archetypal press barons, Northcliffe and Beaverbrook, had very different personal styles. While Northcliffe was notorious for personally haranguing his staff, Beaverbrook's remoteness was legendary. In *Scoop*, Evelyn Waugh satirized a visit to him:

> The carpets were thicker [as one approached Lord Copper's private office], the lights softer, the expressions of the inhabitants more careworn. The typewriters were of a special kind: their keys made no more sound than the drumming of a bishop's finger-tips on an upholstered prie-dieu. The telephone buzzers were muffled and purred like warm cats. The personal private secretaries padded through the ante-chambers and led them nearer and nearer to the presence.[19]

Yet despite their differences of personality, both men made sure that their wishes were followed. Beaverbrook sent 147 separate instructions to the *Daily Express* in one day. Northcliffe would ring up his staff as early as six in the morning, saying abruptly 'Wake up! Have you seen the papers yet?' When one weary editor explained that you could not get the papers so early where he lived, he was woken up at 5 AM the next day by papers being delivered to his home by a noisy pantechnicon.[20] Both proprietors generated terror as part of their managerial style, something that inspired anecdotes that were perhaps improved in the telling. 'Who is that?', Northcliffe said on the phone. 'Editor, Weekly Dispatch, Chief', came the reply. 'Ex-editor', responded Northcliffe, putting down the phone.[21] When a luckless sub-editor filled a lull in a meal-time conversation with the observation that he had been shipwrecked three times, Northcliffe said abruptly 'four times', and sacked him.[22] Beaverbrook also had a fearsome reputation for firing journalists.[23]

The barons combined terror with generosity. Their official histories and journalists' memoirs recount the sudden gifts, holidays and salary rises which were showered on staff. As a genre these stories could be called 'courageous underling gets his reward'. They usually take the form of the plucky journalist standing up for himself (or, more rarely, for what he believes) in the face of the baron's fury. They are clearly intended to enhance both the baron, who is revealed as discriminating and fundamentally right-minded in his judgements, and the journalist whose independence is demonstrated by his courage. But what they actually reveal is an almost continuous process of humiliation. Bernard Falk, usually rewarded with a cigar when he took down Northcliffe's dictated social column for the *Mail*, was once allowed to choose the one he wanted. 'What!' said Northcliffe, 'You have the nerve to pick on those cigars! Don't you know, young man, that they cost 3/6 each?' 'Yes', said the fearless reporter, 'but they're worth every penny'.[24] Another editor, who dared to disagree with Northcliffe, recorded gratefully the telegram he received: 'My dear Blackwood, you are grossly impertinent to your affectionate Chief'.[25]

Losing a battle with a press baron hardly made such a good story. George Buckle, the editor of *The Times* (whose editorial independence Northcliffe had promised to uphold), was eased out of the editorship when he failed to adapt to the political views and managerial strategy of the Chief.[26] Lewis Macleod, literary editor of the *Daily Mail*, received a communiqué from Northcliffe: 'This is the last occasion on which I can tolerate Macleod's gross neglect and carelessness. He will read this message out to the editorial conference on Monday'.[27] When Northcliffe was angered by what he thought were defects on the *Daily Mail*'s picture page, he lined up all those involved in its production and put the tallest man in charge.[28] Feeling dissatisfied with the *Mail*'s advertising department, he appointed the commissionaire to vet advertisements.[29] Beaverbrook was also unpredictable, though not on the scale of Northcliffe.[30] Yet behind both men's seemingly random acts of ferocity and generosity, there was often a careful regard for self-interest. Beaverbrook insisted, for instance, that some of his top journalists wrote under pseudonyms so that, if they left the *Express*, they could not take the goodwill generated by their copy with them.[31]

Northcliffe and Beaverbrook shaped every aspect of their favourite papers. Thus, Northcliffe instructed *Daily Mail* staff in 1912 to find striking miners 'enjoying themselves at the seaside or the dog races' in order to anger other workers suffering from the 'creeping paralysis' of the economy.[32] Beaverbrook maintained a notorious blacklist of people not to be reported favourably or at all.[33] The press barons' writ could extend to the smallest detail. When the weather report was repositioned, Northcliffe railed at a startled *Times* journalist: 'What have you done with the moon? Someone has moved the moon . . . Well, if it's moved again, whoever does it is fired!'.[34] He is also worried about the choice of pictures. 'Alfonso' (King of Spain), Northcliffe complained, 'is always smiling. His smile is not news. If you get a picture of Alfonso weeping, that would be news'.[35] Beaverbrook pestered journalists about the language and phrasing of their reports. 'To Eastbourne's balding, myopic, Edinburgh-trained physiotherapist, William John Snooks, 53, came last week news that . . . .', parodied Tom Driberg, a former *Express* journalist in the approved Beaverbrook style.[36]

The baron's personal foibles and predilections shaped the news values of the national press. Northcliffe had a lifelong obsession with torture and death: he even kept an aquarium containing goldfishes and a pike, with a dividing partition. When in need of diversion, he would lift the partition and watch the goldfishes being gobbled up.[37] His obsession was reflected in his first magazine, *Answers*, which dealt with such enquiries as 'what it felt like to be hanged' and 'how long a severed head might be conscious after beheading'.[38] His first article in the first evening newspaper he owned described the time he spent with a man accused of murder in Chelmsford Prison.[39] He later instructed his staff to 'get me a murder a day'.[40] Similarly Beaverbrook, a hypochondriac, told the editor of the *Daily Express* that 'the public like to know . . . what diseases men die of – and women too'.[41]

The two men's general outlooks also set the tone of their papers. The *Daily Express* aimed, in Beaverbrook's words, at 'the character and temperament which was bent on moving upwards and outward', reflecting Beaverbrook's admiration for self-made success.[42] The *Daily Mail*, on the other hand, projected a more static, hierarchical world in which, as the snobbish Lord Northcliffe put it, 'everyone likes reading about people in better circumstances than his or her own'.[43]

Not all newspaper proprietors in the inter-war period were interventionist. Major Astor, joint owner of *The Times* (after 1922), was teased by his friends for never reading his paper.[44] Even domineering press barons did not give the same amount of attention to all their papers. Thus, in the late 1930s Beaverbrook deluged the *Daily Express* with instructions to support appeasement ('No War Talk, NO MORE WAR TALK' read one telegram of the period).[45] But he did not fuss in the same way over the *Evening Standard*, his London evening paper edited by the radical but diplomatic Percy Cudlipp.

The editorial control exercised by the press barons did not represent a decisive break with the past. Indeed, Lucy Brown's revisionist account of the Victorian commercial press argues that 'what is an important and unvarying generalization is that the sovereign powers of decision were exercised by the proprietors and not by the editors'.[46] Many of the Victorian editors celebrated for their independence, such as C. P. Scott of the *Manchester Guardian* (1877 to 1929), were either owner-editors or members of the proprietorial family. Other leading editors prove, on close examination, to have been less than autonomous. Even John Delane of *The Times*, often seen as a model of the sovereign editor, was repeatedly excluded from key corporate decisions affecting the development of his paper.[47] Indeed, he was so convinced that he was going to be sacked at one stage that he started 'taking dinners' in order to become eligible to practise as a barrister. Others were less fortunate: Cook, Gardiner, Massingham, Greenwood, Annand, Watson and Donald were only some of the distinguished editors who were compelled to resign between 1880 and 1918 as a result of political disagreements with their proprietors.[48]

The tradition of editorial sovereignty which the press magnates allegedly destroyed was, to a large extent, a myth. The press barons were similar to their immediate predecessors in involving themselves in the editorial conduct of their papers. They differed only in that their editorial interventions mattered more because they commanded larger circulations.

Profits and politics

The press barons are often portrayed as journalist-politicians – a view of themselves which they cultivated. Beaverbrook, for instance, told the first Royal Commission on the Press that he ran the *Daily Express* 'purely for the purpose of making propaganda, and with no other motive'.[49] Yet this simple image of press barons as propagandists has tended to obscure another, more important aspect of their dominion over the press – their demotion of politics.

Intense competition led to a circulation war, triggered by the *Daily News'* innovative offer of reader insurance against Zeppelin air attacks during the First World War. The *Daily Mail,* the market leader, retaliated by spending approximately £1 million on reader insurance in the period up to 1928.[50] Its rivals countered with aggressive below-the-line promotion. Householders were offered anything from cameras and wristwatches to silk stockings and kettles in return for taking out a newspaper subscription. The promotion for the *Daily Herald* (which tended to take a more worthy form such as the offer of discounted Dickens' novels) is estimated to have amounted to £1 per new reader between 1930 and 1932.[51] In 1937, a typical morning newspaper employed five times as many door-to-door sales staff as journalists.[52]

Rivalry between newspapers also reconfigured newspaper content. Leading publishers used the new tool of market research to investigate what people read in newspapers. This included a massive survey, based on a national quota sample of over 20,000 adults, conducted for the *News Chronicle* in 1933. It revealed something that was to be found time and again in subsequent surveys, confirming contemporary Fleet Street folklore. The most read articles in popular national daily papers were stories about crime, divorce, accidents and human interest because they appealed to almost everyone.[53] Public affairs news had a sectional appeal, being read more by the old than the young and more by men than women.[54]

Between 1927 and 1937, the *Daily Mail* and the *Daily Mirror* – the two popular papers subject to a full content analysis by the first Royal Commission on the Press – halved or almost halved their proportion of news devoted to domestic public affairs in order to make room for other forms of news such as crime and court reporting.[55] The Commission's supplementary analysis, confined to the main news page, shows that there was a general movement from hard to soft news in most popular daily papers during this period.[56]

A separate quantitative analysis[57] offers a more detailed breakdown of newspapers in 1936. It reveals that by then the popular press was overwhelmingly dedicated to entertainment. Thus, Beaverbrook's *Daily Express* devoted 52 per cent of its editorial space to human interest and sport, compared to just 18 per cent to public affairs[58] – a very similar mix to Rothermere's *Daily Mail.* *The People,* then the second biggest selling Sunday paper in Britain, allocated 59 per cent of its editorial content to sport and human interest, compared to just 14 per cent to public affairs – proportions that were similar to those of the *Sunday Express.*[59] No sampled popular newspaper (save one) devoted more than 7 per cent of its editorial content to international public affairs news, despite the momentous foreign events of the 1930s that were to culminate in another cataclysmic world war.[60]

There were two exceptions to this general editorial reorientation. The topic distribution of the quality press changed relatively little during the inter-war period,[61] even though human interest stories appealed to its readers.[62] This sector's economic viability depended on charging high advertising rates for an affluent readership, and this discouraged the adoption of a popularizing editorial strategy. The other exception was the *Daily Herald* which devoted a third of its editorial content to public affairs news and comment, compared with less than a fifth in every other popular newspaper.[63] This reflected the political commitments of its editorial controllers, the Trades Union Congress (TUC).

By contrast, the press barons prioritized entertainment over public affairs. Paradoxically, their political eminence depended upon the huge circulations they controlled: yet to achieve these huge circulations, they had to steer their papers away from politics. Indeed, they speeded up the 'de-politicization' of the popular press which had begun in the mid-nineteenth century, but which gained increased momentum during the inter-war period.

Proprietors as politicians

The press barons are often accused of using their papers as instruments of political power, but they were hardly unique in this. What made the more notorious press magnates different from their immediate predecessors was that they used their papers not as levers of power within the political parties, but as instruments of power against them. The basis of the inter-war Establishment's objection to men like Rothermere and Beaverbrook was not that they were politically ambitious, but that they were politically independent.

In the early twentieth century the majority of London-based daily papers were owned by wealthy individuals, families or syndicates closely linked to a political party. Between 1911 and 1915, funds from the Unionist Central Office were secretly paid through respectable nominees to the *Standard*, *Globe*, *Observer* and *Pall Mall Gazette*.[64] A wealthy Conservative syndicate, headed by the Duke of Northumberland, bought the *Morning Post* in 1924. Similarly, Lloyd George engineered the purchase of the *Daily News* in 1901 by the Cadbury family in the Liberal interest, and arranged the purchase of the *Daily Chronicle* in 1918 through a syndicate headed by Dalziel, with money accumulated through the sale of honours and laundered through the Lloyd George Fund.[65]

However, the market development of the press eroded influence exerted through party finance. Between 1907 and 1938, total advertising expenditure (mainly on the press) rose from an estimated £20 to £59 million.[66] Increased advertising and also sales revenue funded fatter newspapers, employing more staff. Political parties and sponsors could not keep up with rising press costs. Pearson refused to dig deeper into his pocket to keep the *Westminster Gazette* going in the Liberal cause after 1928; Lloyd George and his associates were forced to sell the *Daily Chronicle* in 1928; the TUC relinquished financial control of the *Daily Herald* to the Odhams Group in 1929; no Conservative syndicate could be found to prevent the *Daily Graphic* from closing in 1926 or the *Morning Post* from folding in 1937.

The outriders of change were Northcliffe, Beaverbrook and Rothermere. Ironically, they all began as 'party' men. Beaverbrook was elected as a Conservative MP in 1910, and first acquired an interest in the *Daily Express* as a front man for Unionist party funds.[67] Both Beaverbrook and Rothermere were members of the coalition government headed by Lloyd George. When Lord Northcliffe played a significant part in deposing Asquith as Prime Minister in 1916, it was as a participant in an internal political revolt.[68]

These three press barons became more politically independent after the First World War. Rothermere led the way by openly breaking with the party system. Enraged by the coalition government's continuing high tax and spending policies (which his papers labelled 'squandermania'), Rothermere helped to found the Anti-Waste League in 1920. The League fielded 'independent' candidates who won three parliamentary by-elections (Dover, Westminster St. George and Hertford) in 1921. This demonstrated the extent of grassroots Conservative discontent, and gave increased impetus to a programme of deregulation in which three ministries were abolished, public assets were sold off, and numerous controls were lifted.

The Anti-Waste League disbanded with the breakup of the coalition government in 1922. The next maverick foray into politics took the form of the Empire Free Trade Crusade launched by the Beaverbrook press in 1929. Its objective was to establish the British Empire as a free trade bloc, which would be heavily protected by high tariffs against external imports. Failure to persuade the leadership of the Conservative Opposition to endorse this scheme led Beaverbrook (with the backing of fellow mogul Lord Rothermere) to set up the United Empire Party (UEP). This created political havoc. In parliamentary by-elections held in 1930–31, UEP-backed independent candidates split the Conservative vote in Bromley, took Paddington South, and forced the Conservative candidate into third place in East Islington.

This generated growing consternation within the Conservative Party, a section of which already had misgivings about Stanley Baldwin as leader. He was from an industrial rather than land-owning background, and had views that were thought by some to be insufficiently right-wing (especially on the emotive issue of colonial rule in India). Sir Robert Topping, the Conservative Party's Principal Agent, sent a memorandum reporting growing doubts about the leader's ability to carry the party to victory. Some of Baldwin's senior colleagues openly shared these doubts. Depressed and demoralized, Baldwin decided to resign. 'Very well, the sooner the better', he angrily declared. 'Let's have a meeting of my colleagues tomorrow when I can say goodbye'.[69] His wife looked on the bright side, saying that 'at long last, we will be able to spend a little time with our own people'.[70]

But under pressure from his close political friends, Baldwin changed his mind and decided to tough it out. He chose the imminent Westminster St. George's by-election as a battle ground in which to have a showdown with the press barons. All the resources of the Conservative party – its pool of talent, electoral experience, money, army of activists, class base and voter loyalty – were then pressed into service to defeat the rebel barons.

Westminster St. George, centred on Belgravia and Pimlico, was a perfect location for Baldwin since it was a dyed-in-the-wool Conservative constituency. An ideal Conservative parliamentary candidate, Duff Cooper, was drafted in, after being persuaded to stand down as a candidate for the safe Conservative seat of Winchester. He was a decorated war hero, personally charming and a good public speaker, with local ties (his father had been a society doctor). The Conservative party flooded the constituency with party activists, who discovered that many of the servants living in the constituency were as Conservative as their employers.[71] At meetings and on the doorstep, a loyalist appeal was made to Conservative voters not to 'hand over the fate of the party to irresponsible owners of newspapers'.[72] Leading families in the constituency did their bit by being generous hosts. Duff Cooper's aristocratic wife describes 'how Mayfair went mad' during the by-election, with parties every night after campaign work had been completed.[73]

Stanley Baldwin led from the front by making a speech, two days before the poll, which attacked press controllers with a ferocity that no British political leader has ever had the courage to match before or since.[74] Associating one section of the press with 'poison gas that poisoned men's souls', he declared:

> The papers conducted by Lord Rothermere and Lord Beaverbrook are not newspapers in the ordinary acceptance of the term. They are engines of propaganda for the constantly changing policies, desires, personal wishes, personal likes and dislikes of two men. What are their methods? Their methods are direct falsehood, misrepresentation, half-truths, the alteration of the speaker's meaning by publishing a sentence apart from the context . . .[75]

He went on to cite specific instances of misrepresentation and hypocrisy, based on careful research,[76] before, in the old-fashioned language of the time, calling the *Daily Mail* Editor 'a cad'. He concluded with a famous indictment (written by his cousin, Rudyard Kipling). 'What the proprietorship of these papers is aiming at is power, and power without responsibility – the prerogative of the harlot throughout the ages'.[77]

The by-election turned out to be an unequal contest. The Conservative party, able to draw upon extensive social, cultural and logistical resources, was more than a match for two press barons whose power was based ultimately on a consumer nexus. The Conservative candidate won 60 per cent of the vote.

Both Baldwin and Beaverbrook realized that it was not in their interests to continue warring with each other. A rapprochement was reached in 1931 when Baldwin endorsed some protectionist measures to support agricultural production. Beaverbrook put on a brave public face by calling this grandly the 'Stornoway Pact', although privately he told his mistress how disappointed he was with the outcome.[78] The United Empire crusade subsequently foundered because the Dominions concluded that imperial protectionism was not in their interests, and few Conservative politicians were persuaded that it was either desirable or feasible. Some imperial preference measures, and taxes on foreign food imports, were in fact implemented in the 1930s. But this was more a response to protectionist measures adopted by other countries than to pressure from Beaverbrook and Rothermere. These changes were also a long way short of what the press barons had hoped for.

Lord Rothermere proved to be less accommodating than Beaverbrook. In 1934 he backed another party against the Conservatives – the British Union of Fascists led by Sir Oswald Mosley. The *Daily Mail* announced its support on 8 January 1934 with the headline, 'Hurrah for the Blackshirts'.[79] The rest of the Rothermere press followed suit, with the *Daily Mirror* urging its readers to 'Give the Blackshirts a Helping hand', the *Evening News* offering free seats at a Fascist rally as prizes, and the *Sunday Dispatch* sponsoring a beauty contest for Blackshirt women.[80] This blaze of publicity boosted the membership of a relatively obscure organisation. Rothermere and Mosley then fell out (partly over a business deal), and the Rothermere press switched off its megaphone of support five months later. Britain's version of the Nazi Party was denied the sustained press support it needed to become 'respectable'.

These press insurgencies represented the beginnings of a shift. Although some press proprietors remained party loyalists,[81] three leading press barons – Northcliffe (who died in 1922), his brother Lord Rothermere and Lord Beaverbrook – broke ranks. Two backed new political parties (or stalking horse independents) and all three dealt with political leaders as if they were their equals. When determining whom to back at the forthcoming general election in 1918, Northcliffe demanded to know from Lloyd George who he was thinking of appointing in his post-election cabinet; and Rothermere made the same imperious request of Baldwin in 1930.[82] From being a satellite of the party system, the press was assuming the hauteur of an independent power centre which dispensed or withheld favours.

Fourth Estate myth

This has prompted some historians to view the press barons as maverick architects of a Fourth Estate, who established the press as an autonomous institution.[83] However, this claim glosses over the nature of the press barons' 'independence'. Their papers were in some ways pillars of the social order. This is illustrated by how they responded to a major royal scandal.

In 1936, King Edward VIII fell in love with Wallis Simpson, an American divorcee who was in the process of breaking up with her second husband. Divorce in the 1930s attracted strong social disapproval. The Church of England (of which the King was officially Supreme Governor) refused to marry any divorcee with a living former spouse. In addition, Wallis Simpson was not drawn from royal or aristocratic stock, into which British monarchs had traditionally married, but came from Baltimore.

None of this seemed to concern the bachelor King. In August, a month after Wallis's split with her second husband, she was a guest on the King's yacht in the Mediterranean. In September, the King installed Wallis in a house overlooking Regent's Park. In the autumn, the King was saying privately that he was serious. Meanwhile Wallis Simpson was getting a rushed divorce.

The Establishment's response was one of growing alarm. They had hoped that the King would become bored with his latest girlfriend, as he had done in the past, and would move on to someone more suitable. The less publicity the affair attracted, it was felt, the better. Pressure was applied behind the scenes to persuade the King to drop Wallis. He attempted to negotiate, mooting the idea of a 'morganatic' marriage in which Wallis would be recognized as Consort but not as Queen. In the end, Edward was given – through the threat of a mass Cabinet resignation – a simple choice: he could either drop the idea of marrying Wallis or abdicate. On 11 December, the King abdicated.

The bachelor King's romance, the drama of his undeviating love, the possibility of an American Queen, the issue of whether the King should marry a divorcee, and the simmering constitutional crisis that this created, was a great press story. It was reported around the world, from Shanghai to New York, with one notable exception – the country where it was all happening. Thus, Mrs Simpson's divorce hearing in October 1936 was either ignored or received only brief, formal reports in the British press[84] and went largely unnoticed by the British public unaware that she might become 'Queen Wally' (the American *Time* magazine's nickname for her).[85] This blanket self-censorship was only lifted on 3 December, just seven days before the King signed an Instrument of Abdication.[86]

The extended press cover-up was a response, in part, to pressure from government and Buckingham Palace.[87] But it was also authorized by press controllers (who communicated with each other)[88] and who, as Beaverbrook openly admitted, ordered that compromising news be suppressed.[89] The Wallis saga was viewed by those in authority – in government, in London's clubland, and by the press barons – as a threat to the monarchy. Their overriding concern was to protect the crown by keeping the King's subjects in the dark for as long as possible.[90]

This was a relatively minor matter compared with the prolonged press self-censorship that occurred in response to the rise of Nazi Germany. In the period 1934–39, Britain had a basic choice. It could either appease the growing militarism of Germany under Hitler's leadership, in the hope that diplomacy, conciliation and an appeal to a shared interest in peace would stave off an international war. Or it could pursue a policy of deterrence based on rapid rearmament, and the building of an international alliance against the Nazi regime (and its Italian ally), so that it would be in Germany's interests to avoid confrontation.

Successive administrations opted for a policy of appeasing Hitler, belatedly backed up by rearmament in case appeasement did not work. In this, they were strongly supported by the press. Newspapers played down criticism of Germany and Fascist Italy in order to avoid arousing public concern. They played up the prospects of appeasement succeeding. And they marginalized the growing body of opinion opposed to appeasement, not just in the Labour opposition (which switched from pro to anti-appeasement), but also in the Conservative party, the Foreign Office, and among the wider public.[91] In November 1938, the *News Chronicle* even suppressed the central finding of its opinion poll, which showed that 86 per cent of the public thought that Hitler had further territorial ambitions.[92] Less than a month before the outbreak of war, the *Daily Express* was still proclaiming that, in the view of ten out of twelve of its reporters in Europe, 'there will be no War'.[93]

This failure to scrutinise critically the case for appeasement was maintained in defiance of the evidence. Between 1936 and 1939 Germany annexed successively Rhineland, Austria, 'Sudetenland', and the rest of Czechoslovakia before invading Poland. Yet, only the *Daily Herald*, after equivocation and tense office politics,[94] and *Reynolds News* (now with an abbreviated title) were unequivocally opposed to the Munich 'peace with honour' pact with Hitler in 1938, followed shortly afterwards by the *Daily Mirror*. It was not until March 1939 that ardently pro-appeasement newspapers like the *Observer* had second thoughts. This awakening was a mere six months before the outbreak of war.

The coalition between press and government over appeasement was sustained in a variety of different ways. At its heart was the shared belief of ministers and press controllers that conciliation of Hitler was the best way to avoid war.[95] This conviction was reinforced through the personal friendship between Prime Minister Neville Chamberlain and the press baron Lord Kemsley, Home Secretary Samuel Hoare and Lord Beaverbrook, and Foreign Secretary Lord Halifax and Geoffrey Dawson (editor of *The Times*). These allies met on a regular basis, and developed almost a shared sense of responsibility for the success of British foreign policy. This alliance was accompanied by informal links between other press controllers and senior politicians, who favoured appeasement for a variety of reasons: an overriding fear of communism, sympathy for Hitler and Mussolini (in the case of Lord Rothermere), a sense of national duty, loyalty to the Conservative Party and strategic miscalculation influenced by the horrors of the First World War.

Informal interaction between leaders of the press and government was underpinned by the development of an efficient public relations machine.[96] This began with rebooting of the Prime Minister's communications office headed by John Steward (who forged a close relationship to the German Embassy); the neutering of the off-message Foreign Office News Office; the linked efforts of the Conservative Party's press office; and the already in-place rituals of managing the privileged 'lobby' group of journalists. On the press side, the benefits of conforming to what was wanted were combined with direct coercion. 'Write to orders', one editor, Arthur Mann, was bluntly instructed when he started criticizing Chamberlain's appeasement policy.[97]

Thus, it came about that a disastrous alliance was forged between government and press. It denied the public access to an open debate of a kind needed to make an informed, life-and-death decision about how best to respond to a resurgent Germany under Nazi leadership.

Press barons and social order

'No cause is really lost until we support it', joked the Beaverbrook editor, Percy Cudlipp.[98] Some historians, noting the tally of press barons' failed press campaigns, have reached a similar conclusion, and concluded that the press barons had very little power.[99] However, this mistakenly assumes that their influence can be assessed only in terms of changing public policy, as if they were the equivalent of a pressure group. In reality, the press barons' main influence lay in the way in which their newspapers reinforced conservative prejudices and strengthened opposition, particularly within the middle class, to progressive political change.

The press barons' papers projected imaginary folk devils, the most prominent of which were Marxists, allegedly controlled from Moscow, and their fellow-travelling Socialists. This 'red peril' campaign reached its height in the 1924 general election campaign, following the defeat of the minority Labour administration led by Ramsay MacDonald. The Labour government had recognized the Soviet government, as part of its negotiation for debt reparation, exposing it to the charge that it was controlled by Marxists, and their fellow-travellers, in league with Moscow. This smear was enhanced by a forged letter supposedly sent by Zinoviev (President of the Third International in Moscow) to the British Communist Party urging it to prepare for revolution in Britain. The *Daily Mail* reported the letter as 'Civil War Plot by Socialists' Masters',[100] a spin that was adopted in the rest of the right-wing press and maintained throughout the election campaign (with the partial exception of Beaverbrook papers). Thus the *Daily Mirror* used the forged letter to define the general election as a stark choice between centre-right politicians and Moscow control. 'Vote British, not Bolshie', it urged in its front page headline, printing underneath in heavy type: 'Do you Wish to Vote for Leaders of Law, Order, Peace and Prosperity or to Vote for the Overthrow of Society and Pave the Way to Bolshevism?' The question was accompanied by reassuring pictures of Conservative and Liberal politicians, and menacing images of Russian Politburo members (supposedly the puppet-masters controlling the Labour party).[101]

It is doubtful whether such crude propaganda deterred many would-be Labour voters, not least because many of them did not then read a national daily paper. In fact, Labour's share of the national vote increased by 3.2 percentage points in the 1924 general election, partly because it fielded sixty-four more parliamentary candidates.[102] The main effect of the 'red scare' was to drive Liberal voters into the Conservative camp. The centre vote collapsed, with the Liberal Party being reduced from 158 to 40 seats. Another effect was to boost turn-out which rose by over two million compared with the previous general election called only eleven months before.[103] The combination of Liberal defections and higher turn-out greatly increased the Conservatives' vote, giving them a landslide victory.

The Zinoviev 'red alert' was merely one example of the way in which the news was spun. The national press was prevented from publishing during the 1926 General Strike. Subsequently, many newspapers portrayed the Strike not as a class-based conflict between employers and workers but as the work of a minority inspired by red agitators. 'Trade unionists in this country', thundered the *Observer*, 'are and always will be in a minority, and if they seriously try to break the majority, they make it quite certain that the majority, if further provoked, will break them'.[104] 'The defeat of the General Strike', exulted the *Daily Mail*, 'will end the danger of Communist tyranny in Europe'.[105] A similarly persuasive framework was deployed to explain the Depression. It was portrayed as a product of the 1929–31 Labour government's mismanagement, and also as a natural phenomenon comparable to a flood. In this way, the appropriate response was defined as national unity in the face of calamity.

The press stigmatized activists who demanded far-reaching change. Thus, the communist-inspired Unemployed Workers Movement was anathematized when, following the 1929 crash, it organised marches of the jobless from Scotland, Wales and the north of England, all converging on the capital. *The Times* dismissed the protest as 'heartless, cruel and unnecessary'[106] while the *Daily Mail* dubbed it 'a weary tramp to advertise Reds'.[107] In common with most other papers, they defined the culminating march mainly in terms of the threat it posed to law and order rather than in terms of the protestors' demands. Significantly, the press provided relatively more sympathetic coverage of the 1936 Jarrow March, which had the support of both Conservative and Labour councillors. The press thus helped to police the boundaries of legitimate dissent.

However, the central core of the conservatism expressed by papers under the barons' control was a deep and emotional attachment to Britain and its empire. This intense patriotism sometimes shaded off into open racism and, particularly in the case of the papers controlled by Rothermere, aggressive anti-Semitism. Thus, the *Daily Mail* interpreted Hitler's rise as a response to 'Israelite' provocation, explaining that:

> The German nation was rapidly falling under the control of its alien elements. In the last days of the pre-Hitler regime there were twenty times as many Jewish government officials in Germany as had existed before the war. Israelites of international attachments were insinuating themselves into key positions in the German administrative machine.[108]

In line with these views, the Rothermere press opposed giving mass sanctuary to Jews fleeing Nazi Germany. A welcoming space was assured in the *Daily Mail* for bigots like local magistrate Herbert Metcalfe who complained that 'stateless Jews from Germany . . . pouring in from every port of this country is becoming an outrage'.[109] The Beaverbrook press was also unenthusiastic about mass Jewish immigration into Britain on the grounds that this could antagonize Germany, and undermine the search for peace. 'The Jews may drive us into war', warned Beaverbrook in a private letter to a friend.[110] The hostility of much of the press discouraged the liberalization of immigration rules, established in the 1919 Aliens Act and subsequent Alien Orders. It is estimated that as many ten times the number of European Jews were blocked as were granted asylum in Britain during the later 1930s, as a consequence of restrictive Whitehall regulation.[111] Some of those, made unwelcome in the popular press (with notable exceptions), were to die in death camps.

But if the inter-war press was politically reactionary, it also cautiously embraced some forms of social change. Most national popular dailies portrayed woman's increased freedom from confining social codes and dress in the 1920s as an advance, part of a generational shift that should be embraced as a necessary form of modernization. Successful women in public life were often portrayed in a favourable light. Most newspapers – though not those owned by Rothermere – also argued that young women should be allowed to vote (introduced in 1928). Yet, this opening to change was full of contradictions. The women's movement tended to be ignored or presented as superfluous. Women's pages were preoccupied with fashion, home-making and motherhood. And women, unlike men, came to be presented in more overtly sexualized ways in the inter-war press.[112]

Modification of market censorship

The press barons' ascendancy was underwritten by market censorship. The cost of publishing became so high that market entry to the national press was effectively blocked. Between 1919 and 1939, only one new national newspaper was successfully established: the *Communist Sunday Worker* in 1925, which was re-launched as the *Daily Worker* in 1930. The latter was boycotted by wholesalers for ideological reasons between 1930 and 1942,[113] helping to limit still further its very small circulation.

Despite the rise of the Labour movement, the *Daily Herald* also languished with a relatively modest circulation during the 1920s.[114] It was only when a major publishing company, Odhams, acquired in 1929 a 51 per cent stake in the paper (but leaving its editorial direction to the TUC) that the *Daily Herald*'s fortunes dramatically changed because it gained an enormous infusion of capital. Doubling in size, now with a northern as well as London printing plant, and very heavily promoted for the first time, the paper's circulation soared from little over 300,000 to two million between 1929 and 1933.[115]

Without this backing, Labour's official voice in the press probably would have remained muzzled by under-investment. *Reynolds News*, acquired by the Co-operative movement in 1929 but not benefiting from a large injection of cash, stayed marooned as the smallest circulation, national popular Sunday paper during the 1930s.[116]

However, one aspect of market censorship – press advertising selection – was modified during the inter-war period. The standard advertising textbook of the 1930s advised that 'the first test that must always be applied to a press advertising medium is the cost of placing the advertisement of a given size before a given number of suitable readers'.[117] This quantitative approach was enabled by the greater availability of relevant press data. From 1930 onwards, advertising industry bodies issued readership surveys, putting an official seal of approval on a development that had been pioneered, but not fully accepted, in the 1920s. These surveys provided detailed information about the social composition of the readership of all major newspapers. Circulation figures also became more reliable, with the establishment of the Audit Bureau of Circulation in 1931.

The adoption of a more quantitative approach to advertising selection reduced the significance of subjective judgement about the editorial ambience of a publication sometimes coloured by political prejudice. Readership research also caused advertisers to reassess a stereotypical image of left publications as being read by the 'down-at-heel'. For instance, an executive at the large advertising agency, London Press Exchange, advised in 1935 Farmer's Glory (a leading bread brand) to advertise in the *Daily Herald* because 'though primarily it caters for an artisan and lower middle class market, it also reaches a considerable percentage of the population of slightly higher earning capacity'.[118] This observation was based on the official readership survey of the previous year.[119]

The growth of market research in the 1920s also helped radical publications by underscoring the economic importance of the working-class market. It led the advertising agency, J. Walter Thompson (JWT), to advise clients such as Sun-Maid Raisins to switch from elite to mass media because, as one memo pointed out in 1929, research 'shows that 91.2 per cent of the families of Great Britain have incomes of under £400'.[120] This revalorization of the mass market was fostered further in the 1930s by the development of more sophisticated research. 'Inequalities of consumption', concluded the leading marketing handbook of the mid-1930s, 'are less than inequalities of income, and inequalities of income are less than inequalities of wealth'.[121] The same point was put less abstractly by Odhams, publisher of the *Daily Herald*, *John Bull* and other working-class publications:

> If the housewives who read *John Bull* put their purses together next year, they could buy the Golconda diamond or Da Vinci's 'Mona Lisa' hundreds of times over. Then they could spend the change on the richest treasures of Bond Street or the Rue de la Paix.[122]

Selling the working class to advertisers was also made easier by the growth of working-class purchasing power, and the related growth of consumption of mass-market goods. *Per capita* annual consumer expenditure at constant (1913) prices rose from £42 in 1921 to £54 in 1938, reflecting the continued increase of real wages among working people (with a job) during the Depression.[123] This led to a very large increase in the purchase of heavily advertised, branded products such as cosmetics, medicines, bicycles and electrical appliances.[124]

These changes did not bring to an end the economic disadvantages faced by radical journalism. *Reynolds News* received only 0.82 pence display advertising revenue per copy sold in 1936, less than half that of the *Sunday Express*. Likewise, in 1936, the advertising expenditure per copy on the hugely successful *Daily Herald* was less than half of that of the *Daily Mail*.[125] Even in 1933, when the *Daily Herald* became the largest circulation daily in the western world, it still traded at a loss.[126] However, its rise was not stalled by a massive advertising deficit (as in 1920 when the paper had been forced to double its price, while being half the size of its rivals). In 1936, the paper obtained over £1.5 million in advertising receipts, less per copy than its main competitors but still a substantial commercial subsidy.[127] The *Daily Herald* had ceased to be an advertising pariah – a prerequisite of its success in building a mass circulation.

Changing market perceptions also contributed to a key development in British journalism: the transformation of the *Daily Mirror* and its sister paper, the *Sunday Pictorial*. The over-extended Rothermere press empire offloaded the *Daily Mirror* because it seemed a doomed paper, with a steadily falling circulation. Although the paper reached an affluent audience, it did not reap the economic benefit of this because advertisers thought that, as a tabloid, it was only skimmed rather than read (a perception that was subsequently modified by readership research). Anticipating the *Daily Mirror*'s closure, Rothermere sold a substantial part of his stake in 1931, and disposed of most of his remaining shares by 1936.[128]

The shares were sold discreetly to multiple purchasers. This left no dominant shareholder with the result that effective control of the company devolved to senior executives. In 1934, the paper moved downmarket under Harry Bartholomew, the new editorial director. This was a commercial decision influenced by two things. Working class demand for dailies was increasing, yet publishers had neglected the bottom end of the market. And more advertisers wanted to reach this market. The commercial nature of this re-orientation was underlined by the extent of advertising agency JWT's involvement in the paper's relaunch. JWT carried out market research into readers' preferences; advised on lay-out; supplied (unintentionally) two key members of the new *Mirror* team; and, most important of all, encouraged clients to advertise in the rejuvenated paper.

The market repositioning of the *Daily Mirror* encouraged a shift in its politics, away from Rothermere's neo-fascism. As Cecil King, the paper's advertising director, put it:

Our best hope was, therefore, to appeal to young, working-class men and women . . . If this was the aim, the politics had to be made to match. In the depression of the 1930s, there was no future in preaching right-wing politics to young people in the lowest income bracket.[129]

However, the *Daily Mirror*'s make-over was more cautious than was recalled subsequently by those involved.[130] The paper backed the Conservative leader, Stanley Baldwin, in the 1935 general election. It adopted a non-interventionist stance on the Spanish Civil War until 1938 when it switched belatedly to the 'leftish' position of supporting a democratic government faced with a military coup. Even so, it held back from supporting the Labour Party until the paper was radicalized during the war.

This gradualist political shift was dictated partly by a desire to not alienate the paper's traditional readership. It also reflected a concern not to be typecast as a working-class tabloid. The *Daily Mirror* continued to emphasize its appeal to rich readers in its self-presentation to the advertising industry. Indeed, in 1938, it boasted in the trade press that 'only one of the six popular national papers can claim more "A" class circulation [the wealthiest readers]'.[131]

The really significant change represented by the *Daily Mirror*'s make-over was not its cautious, crablike movement towards the centre-left, but its prioritization of entertainment. It shifted further than its rivals in expanding human interest and sport content,[132] which by 1936 accounted for over five times its political coverage.[133] It also moved the goal posts by publishing revealing cheesecake photos of young women. The *Daily Mirror* was a taboo breaker, extending the boundaries of what was acceptable in a family newspaper.[134]

Between 1934 and 1939, the *Daily Mirror*'s circulation rose from around 850,000 to 1.57 million[135] and, after an initial period of difficulty, its advertising revenue also increased substantially. The *Daily Mirror*'s success inspired a similar make-over of its sister paper, the *Sunday Pictorial*, in 1937, under the aegis of Cecil King and Hugh Cudlipp. It, too, shifted downmarket, accentuated entertainment and moved away from right-wing politics.

In short, market censorship lessened during this period. The high costs of publishing ensured that the press was still largely controlled by right-wing millionaires. Nevertheless, a business partnership with a commercial publisher enabled the rise of a heavily capitalized, mass Labour movement daily. Advertising dependence still disadvantaged radical journalism but this was less of an obstacle than it had been before because workers had more money, and advertising agencies became more professional. Indeed, it was the pressure to respond to consumer demand that led two papers to seek out a more downscale readership, and shed their right-wing politics. The foundations had been laid for the mass social democratic press that was to develop in the different political and regulatory context of the Second World War.

Notes

1 Political and Economic Planning (PEP), *Report on the British Press* (London, PEP, 1938), pp. 179–80, among many others.
2 I. Asquith, 'The structure, ownership and control of the press, 1780–1850' in G. Boyce, J. Curran and P. Wingate (eds.) *Newspaper History* (London, Constable, 1978), p. 104.
3 A. Lee, *The Origins of the Popular Press in England 1855–1914* (London, Croom Helm, 1976), p. 168.
4 Anon, *History of the* Times: *The Tradition Established, 1841–1884*, vol. 2 (London, Times, 1939).
5 Derived from Table 1, Appendix 1 of *Royal Commission on the Press 1947–9 Report* (RCP 1949) (London, HMSO, 1949, p. 193). Most of this increase occurred between 1921 and 1929. The five leading regional chains' ownership of local weeklies – though increasing – remained relatively modest during this period (see RCP 1949, Table 1A, p. 194).
6 *Royal Commission 1949*, pp. 57–63 and Appendix 2, Table 2, p. 188.
7 *Royal Commission 1949*, p. 60.
8 *Royal Commission 1949*, Appendix 2, Table 1, p. 187.
9 *Royal Commission 1949*, p. 59; cf. Appendix 2, Table 2, p. 195.
10 N. Kaldor and R. Silverman, *A Statistical Analysis of Advertising Expenditure and of the Revenue of the Press* (Cambridge, Cambridge University Press, 1948), Table 45, p. 84.
11 Kaldor and Silverman, 1948, Table 45, p. 84. Sunday newspaper circulation includes both national and regional titles.
12 Kaldor and Silverman, *Statistical Analysis*, Table 45, p. 84. The circulation of London evenings have been added to that of regional ('provincial') dailies, both morning and evening, to obtain figures for local dailies.
13 According to convention, the *Daily Mail*'s circulation passed the landmark figure of one million at the end of the Boer War in 1902 (e.g. D. Griffiths, *Fleet Street: Five Hundred Years of the Press* (London, British Library, 2006), p. 132). However, the circulation table in H. Fyfe, *Northcliffe: An Intimate Biography* (London, Allen & Unwin, 1930), p. 113 shows that the *Daily Mail* did not reach that landmark until 1914, although it almost did in 1900. Fyfe's figures seem credible both because of their specificity and because he held senior positions in the Northcliffe empire, which would have given him access to internal records.
14 W. Belson, *The British Press*, vol. 3 (London, London Press Exchange Report, 1959), Table 1, p. 12.
15 Ibid.
16 Derived from *Royal Commission 1949*, Appendix 3, Table 1, p. 190.
17 Lee, *Origins*, Table 31, p. 293. Market share figures for 1910 are merely indicative since circulation data for this period were unreliable.
18 Derived from *Royal Commission 1949*, Appendix 3, Table 1, p. 192 (recording Sunday newspaper circulation in 1937) and *PEP Report*, pp. 96–108 (detailing Sunday newspaper ownership in 1937); compared with Lee, *Origins*, Table 31, p. 293. Regional Sunday papers in 1937 were excluded to maintain comparability with Lee's estimates for 1910.
19 E. Waugh, *Scoop* (Harmondsworth, Penguin, 1986[1938]), pp. 40–41.

20 T. Clarke, *Northcliffe In History* (London, Hutchinson, 1950).

21 B. Falk, *He Laughed in Fleet Street* (London, Hutchinson, 1933), p. 199. For a slightly different version of the same story, see R. Pound and G. Harmsworth, *Northcliffe* (London, Cassell, 1959), p. 341 in which Northcliffe says, 'You were the editor'.

22 P. Brendon, *Eminent Edwardians* (London, Secker & Warburg, 1979), p. 38.

23 T. Driberg, *Beaverbrook: A Study in Power and Persuasion* (London, Weidenfeld & Nicolson, 1956).

24 Falk, *He Laughed*, p. 163.

25 Falk, *He Laughed*, p. 153.

26 Anon, *History of* The Times*: The 150th Anniversary and Beyond, 1912–1948*, vol. 3, Part 2 (London, Times Publishing Company, 1952), pp. 748–72.

27 P. Ferris, *The House of Northcliffe* (London, Weidenfeld & Nicolson, 1971), p. 210.

28 Brendon, *Eminent Edwardians*, p. 33.

29 J. Hammerton, *With Northcliffe in Fleet Street* (London, Hutchinson, 1932), pp. 63–64.

30 Northcliffe became delusional in the last phase of his life when he was still running his press empire. See Ferris, *The House*; and J. L. Thompson, *Northcliffe* (London, Murray, 2000).

31 Driberg, *Beaverbrook*.

32 T. Clarke, *My Northcliffe Diary* (London, Victor Gollancz, 1931), p. 51.

33 For testimony by former Beaverbrook journalists, see *Royal Commission Report 1949*, pp. 125–27.

34 Brendon, *Eminent Edwardians*, p. 7.

35 Clarke, *Northcliffe*, p. 124.

36 Driberg, *Beaverbrook*, pp. 218–19.

37 Brendon, *Eminent Edwardians*, p. 8.

38 Ferris, *The House of Northcliffe*, pp. 36–37.

39 Pound and Harmsworth, *Northcliffe*, p. 176.

40 J. Rowbotham, K. Stevenson and S. Pegg, *Crime News in Modern Britain* (Palgrave Macmillan, Basingstoke, 2013), p. 103.

41 Taylor, *Beaverbrook*, p. 280.

42 Taylor, *Beaverbrook*, p. 175.

43 Cited in D. J. Taylor, *Bright Young Things* (London, Vintage, 2008), p. 12. For an account of the *Daily Mail*'s traditionalist perspective of society, see T. Jeffery and K. McClelland, 'A world fit to live in: the *Daily Mail* and the middle classes 1918–39' in Boyce et al. (eds.) *Newspaper History*, pp. 27–52.

44 M. Astor, *Tribal Feeling* (London, John Murray, 1963), p. 146.

45 For a detailed description of how Beaverbrook exerted pressure on his papers to follow an appeasement line, see A. Chisholm and M. Davie, *Beaverbrook: A Life* (London, Hutchinson, 1992), pp. 350–56.

46 L. Brown, *Victorian News and Newspapers* (Oxford, Clarendon Press, 1985), p. 89.

47 J. Tunstall, '"Editorial sovereignty" in the British press' in *Studies on the Press*, Royal Commission on the Press Working Paper Number 3 (London, HMSO, 1977); Anon, *History of* The Times*: The Tradition Established, 1841–1884*, vol. 2 (London, Times Publishing Company, 1939), p. 33, p. 36 *et passim*.

48 Lee, *Origins*; Brown, *Victorian News*; S. Koss, *The Rise and Fall of the Political Press*, vols. 1 and 2 (London, Hamish Hamilton 1981 and 1984).

49 *Royal Commission 1949*, p. 25.

50 *PEP Report*, p. 89.

51 Ibid.

52 Derived from *PEP Report*, p. 132.

53 *A Survey of Reader Interest in the National Morning and London Evening Press 1934* (London, London Press Exchange/News Chronicle). Despite the title, the survey was conducted in 1933.

54 Ibid.

55 *Royal Commission 1949*, Appendix 7, Table 4, p. 250. This relative reduction was partly offset by the increase in the size of newspapers.

56 *Royal Commission 1949*, Appendix 7, Table 14, pp. 257–58.

57 The summary results for 1936 and later years are presented in Table 4, p. 96–97 (Chapter 7). More detailed figures are provided in J. Curran, A. Douglas and G. Whannel, 'The political economy of the human-interest story' in A. Smith (ed.) *Newspapers and Democracy* (Cambridge, Mass., MIT Press, 1980), pp. 288–348.

58 Public affairs were defined as political, social, economic, industrial, scientific and medical affairs.

59 See Table 7.4, p. 96–97 (Chapter 7).

60 Curran et al., 'Political economy', Chapter 13 Appendix, Table 13.6.

61 *Royal Commission 1949*, Appendix 7, Table 4, p. 250 and Table 14, pp. 257–58.

62 *Survey of Reader Interest 1934*, London Press Exchange.

63 See Table 7.4, p. 96–97 (Chapter 7).

64 Taylor, *Beaverbrook*, p. 61.

65 C. Seymour-Ure, 'The press and the party system between the wars' in G. Peele and C. Cook (eds.) *The Politics of Reappraisal 1918–1939* (London, Macmillan, 1975), p. 241.

66 R. Critchley, *UK Advertising Statistics* (London, Advertising Assocation, 1974).

67 Taylor, *Beaverbrook*, p. 74.

68 J. L. Thompson, *Northcliffe: Press Baron in Politics 1865–1922* (London, Murray, 2000); Koss, *Rise and Fall*, vol. 2; S. Koss, *Asquith* (London, Allen Lane, 1976).

69 K. Middlemas and J. Barnes, *Baldwin* (London, Weidenfeld & Nicolson, 1969), p. 588.

70 Ibid.

71 D. [Duff] Cooper, *Old Men Forget* (London, Hart-Davis, 1953), p. 174.

72 Cooper, *Old Men*, p. 176.

73 D. [Diana] Cooper, *The Light of Common Day* (London, Hart-Davis, 1959), p. 99–100.

74 Lloyd George had previously attacked the press in general terms (see Koss, *Rise and Fall*, vol. 2, 294) while Baldwin had delivered a speech attacking Rothermere on 24 June 1930. But this last did not have the broad sweep, detailed research and fiery rhetoric of his 'power without responsibility' speech, delivered on 17 March 1931, which has secured it a place in history.

75 Middlemas and Barnes, *Baldwin*, p. 599.

76 Baldwin pointed out the contradictions between what the *Daily Mail* said to its British readers and to its American advertisers. Drawing on a private letter from a former *Daily Mail* editor, Baldwin also provided evidence that Rothermere had deliberately misled in a self-serving way. See Middlemas and Barnes, *Baldwin*, p. 600.

77 Middlemas and Barnes, *Baldwin*, p. 600.

78 A. Chisholm and M. Davie, *Beaverbrook: A Life* (London, Hutchinson, 1992), p. 306.

79 Cited in S. J. Taylor, *The Great Outsiders* (London, Weidenfeld & Nicolson, 1998), p. 281.

80 Ibid.

81 C. Seymour-Ure, 'The press and the party system between the wars' in G. Peele and C. Cook (eds.) *The Politics of Reappraisal 1918–1939* (London, Macmillan, 1975), p. 252.

82 Thompson, *Northcliffe*, p. 308; Middlemas and Barnes, *Baldwin*, pp. 573–74.

83 For example, Taylor, *Beaverbrook*, p. 136.

84 Taylor, *Beaverbrook*, p. 369; Chisholm and Davie, *Beaverbrook*, p. 336.

85 Cited in Middlemas and Barnes, *Baldwin*, p. 982.

86 The political elite split over the royal crisis, and this split was played out in the national press, once the news was out. The national press then went into overdrive promoting the new King, George VI, and contributed to making his coronation a great national celebration.

87 P. Ziegler, *King Edward VIII* (London, HarperCollins, 1991); Middlemas and Barnes, *Baldwin*.

88 Taylor, *Beaverbrook*, pp. 368–69.

89 Chisholm and Davie, *Beaverbrook*, p. 335.

90 The desire to protect the monarchy also led to self-censorship in the local press: see T. Luckhurst, 'Serving King and Country', *British Journalism Review*, 24 (3), 2013.

91 R. Cockitt, *Twilight of Truth* (London, Weidenfeld & Nicolson, 1989). This was a more tortuous process than Cockitt allows. For a sensitive analysis of *The Times* in this period, see C. Seymour-Ure, *The Political Impact of Mass Media* (London, Constable, 1974), Chapter 3; and for an account of the *Daily Mirror*'s gradual shift over appeasement, and the related issue of intervention in the Spanish civil war, see M. Edelman, *The Mirror: A Political History* (London, Hamish Hamilton, 1966), pp. 66 ff; and A. Bingham, 'Representing the people? The *Daily Mirror*, class and political culture in inter-war Britain' in L. Beers and G. Thomas (eds.), *Brave New World* (London, Institute of Historical Research, 2011), pp. 123 ff.

92 Cockitt, *Twilight*, p. 101.

93 *Daily Express*, 7 August 1939, cited in Chisholm and Davie, *Beaverbrook*, p. 356. War was declared on 3 September 1939.

94 H. Richards, *The Bloody Circus* (London, Pluto, 1997), pp. 156–57.

95 The trauma of the First World War changed the press. It was one reason why Fleet Street did not put its weight behind defeating insurgents in Ireland's War of Independence. See the illuminating study, Maurice Walsh, *The News from Ireland* (London, Tauris, 2008).

96 Cockitt, *Twilight*, p. 4, *et passim*.

97 Cockitt, *Twilight*, p. 98. Mann put up with this for a year before resigning.

98 In conversation with his brother, cited in H. Cudlipp, *The Prerogative of the Harlot* (London, Bodley Head, 1980), p. 256.

99 A. J. P. Taylor, *English History 1914–1945* (Harmondsworth, Pelican, 1970), pp. 355–57; cf. Ferris, *House*, p. 225–27; and D. G. Boyce, 'Crusaders without chains: Power and the press barons 1896–1951' in J. Curran, A. Smith and P. Wingate (eds.) *Impacts and Influences* (London, Methuen, 1987).

100 *Daily Mail*, 25 October 1924.
101 *Daily Mirror*, 29 October 1924.
102 D. Butler and G. Butler, *Twentieth-Century British Political Facts 1900–2000*, 8th edition (Basingstoke, Macmillan, 2000), p. 235.
103 Butler and Butler, *Twentieth-Century*, p. 235.
104 *Observer*, 16 May 1926.
105 *Daily Mail*, 14 May 1926.
106 *The Times*, 11 January 1929.
107 *Daily Mail*, 24 February 1929.
108 *Daily Mail*, 10 July 1933.
109 *Daily Mail*, 30 August 1938.
110 Cited in Taylor, *Beaverbrook*, p. 387.
111 L. London, *Whitehall and the Jews, 1933–48* (Cambridge, Cambridge University Press, 2000).
112 A. Bingham, *Gender, Modernity and the Popular Press in Inter-War Britain* (Oxford, Clarendon Press, 2004).
113 W. Rust, *The Story of the* Daily Worker (London, People's Press, 1949), p. 13.
114 H. Richards, *The Bloody Circus* (London, Pluto, 1997).
115 R. J. Minney, *Viscount Southwood* (London, Odhams, 1954), pp. 236 ff; Richards, *Bloody Circus*, pp. 144 ff.
116 Belson, *British Press*, pp. 14–15.
117 H. W. Eley, *Advertising Media* (London, Butterworth, 1932) p. 172.
118 'Farmer's Glory: Memorandum on an Advertising Policy', London Press Exchange 1935 (Leo Burnett Ltd. archives).
119 *An Analysis of Press Circulations* (London, Institute of Incorporated Practitioners in Advertising, 1934). In this transitional period, the words 'circulation' and 'readership' were treated as synonyms.
120 'Sun-Maid Plan 1929–30', 1929, J. Walter Thompson archives.
121 G. Harrison and F. Mitchell, *Home Market: A Handbook of Statistics* (London, Allen and Unwin, 1936), p. 6.
122 'Each week the shopping bills of "John Bull" families exceed three million pounds', [advertisement], *The Statistical Review of Press Advertising*, 1935, p. 2.
123 C. H. Feinstein, *Statistical Tables of National Income, Expenditure and Output of the U.K. 1855–65* (Cambridge University Press, Cambridge, 1976), p. 42.
124 R. Stone and D. Rowe, *The Measurement of Consumers' Expenditure and Behaviour in the United Kingdom 1920–38* (Cambridge, Cambridge University Press, 1966).
125 J. Curran, 'Advertising as a patronage system' in H. Christian (ed.) *The Sociology of Journalism and the Press* (Keele, Sociological Review Monograph (29), 1980), Table 3, p. 85.
126 Minney, *Southwood*, p. 243.
127 'A statistical survey of press advertising during 1936', London Press Exchange [Leo Burnett archives].
128 H. Cudlipp, *Publish and Be Damned* (London, Dakers, 1953), pp. 273–74.
129 C. King, *Strictly Personal* (London, Weidenfeld & Nicolson), p. 101.
130 Cudlipp, *Publish*; King, *Strictly*; H. Cudlipp, *At Your Peril* (London, Weidenfeld & Nicolson, 1962). For a useful corrective, see A. Bingham and M. Conboy, 'The *Daily Mirror* and the creation of a commercial popular language', *Journalism Studies*, 10 (5), 2009, pp. 639–54; and A. Bingham, 'Representing the people?

The *Daily Mirror*, class and political culture in inter-war Britain' in L. Beers and G. Thomas (eds.) *Brave New World* (London, Institute of Historical Research, 2011).

131 *The Statistical Review of Press Advertising*, 1938, 5 (3), p. 35 [advertisement]. Two years earlier, the *Daily Mirror* had claimed to reach 'the "A" class family most cheaply' in *The Statistical Review of Press Advertising*, 3 (4), p. 34 [advertisement].

132 *Royal Commission 1949*, Appendix 7, Table 4, p. 250 and Table 14, pp. 257–58.

133 See Chapter 7, Table 7.4, pp. 96–97.

134 A. Bingham, *Family Newspapers?* (Oxford, Oxford University Press, 2009), pp. 208 ff.

135 Belson, Table 1, p. 12.

Chapter 6

Press under public regulation

Nostalgia has encouraged the belief that the British people closed ranks with bulldog determination under the unchallenged leadership of Churchill during the Second World War. This mythical view obscures the political crisis of the early war years, leading to a major confrontation between the government and radical newspapers.

Many senior politicians and officials doubted the commitment of the British people to winning the war. A significantly named Home Morale Emergency Committee of the Ministry of Information reported in June 1940 on 'fear, confusion, suspicion, class feeling and defeatism'.[1] Another official report, in the same month, concluded that the 'chief weakness of home morale is a feeling that . . . we cannot hope to win'.[2] Even the Ministry's Parliamentary Secretary, Harold Nicolson, confided in his diary during this period: 'It will now be almost impossible to beat the Germans'.[3] For at least the first two-and-a-half years of the war, the relationship between the authorities and the press was dominated by a probably misplaced concern about the state of public morale.[4]

This was partly because the Second World War was different from previous wars in that the British people were in the front line. The strategic objective of the Blitz was to undermine the civilian population's willingness to support the war effort. Extensive censorship controls, some argued, were needed to combat the new, deadly technology of aerial warfare.

Anxiety about public morale was also exacerbated by concern about the growth of radicalism in Britain. In February 1942 the Home Intelligence Division reported a wave of admiration for Soviet Russia and a growing suspicion among sections of the working class that financial vested interests were hampering the war effort.[5] A month later it commented on what was to become a familiar theme – the flowering of 'home-made Socialism' of which important elements were 'a revulsion against "vested interests", "privilege", and . . . "the old gang"'.[6] France had fallen, it was believed, because the country had been divided. Yet here was evidence that divisions were deepening in Britain at a time when the country needed to be united against a common enemy.

Some ministers and officials argued that class hostility, stirred up by radical journalists, posed a threat to military resolve and efficient war production. Indeed, they came close to equating the maintenance of public morale with the need to suppress radical press criticism of any kind. This was bound up with the growing political difficulties of the government. In 1940 Neville Chamberlain was forced to resign as Prime Minister. The new coalition government, headed by Winston Churchill, came under growing attack as the military situation failed to improve. Criticism of the government was only partly defused by changes in the Cabinet and leadership of the armed forces in 1940, 1941 and 1942. The desire to censor the press was thus reinforced by an embattled administration's struggle to survive.

Yet, there was also a strong countervailing commitment to a free press in Britain. Early in the war, the Ministry of Information Censorship Division had proclaimed its desire 'to preserve maximum freedom for the press'.[7] This led to the establishment of a voluntary system of censorship in which the press continued to be free to publish, but could be prosecuted if it transmitted information of use to the enemy. This referred to information of military value, and did not apply to comment or opinion.[8]

But in the crisis summer of 1940, when there was fear of an imminent German invasion, the government issued regulations which gave the Home Secretary sweeping authority to control the press.[9] The most important of these was Regulation 2D, conferring on the Home Secretary the personal power to ban any publication which published material 'calculated to foment opposition to the prosecution to a successful issue of any war in which His Majesty is engaged'. The Regulation also denied the offending publication any automatic right of appeal or recourse to the law courts. As one angry MP declared: 'Its effect will be to put the Ministry of Home Security in a position by no means inferior, as regards the scope of its powers over newspapers, to that occupied by the distinguished Dr Goebbels in Germany'.[10]

The National Council for Civil Liberties responded by mobilizing a nationwide protest, which much of the press backed. Concerted opposition was also mounted in the Commons, with the result that the regulations were ratified by a majority of only 38 votes – the smallest majority on any issue gained by the new government. This opposition was important because it gave rise to a vital concession that limited the way in which the security regulations were interpreted subsequently. Sir John Anderson, the Home Secretary, said that they would only be directed against anti-war papers, and that Parliament would be consulted if they were amended.[11] In 1942, a move to close down a pro-war paper was blocked partly on the grounds that it contravened this undertaking.[12] Ministers felt that they needed first to redefine the scope of the regulations before enforcing them in an expanded form. As we shall see, this created a delay in which effective opposition was organised to prevent this from happening.

Silencing the communist press

The communist *Daily Worker* and the *Week* were closed on 21 January 1941. The *Daily Worker* had modified its anti-fascist editorial policy following the signing of the Nazi–Soviet pact in 1939, and attacked the war as a struggle between imperialist powers. The ostensible ground for banning the two publications was that they were impeding the war effort by setting people against the war. This was not borne out by research undertaken by the Ministry of Information, which indicated that they had little influence on public attitudes.[13] The *Daily Worker* accounted for less than 1 per cent of total national daily circulation, while the *Week* had even smaller sales.[14]

But if the two publications did not weaken public morale, they disturbed the peace of mind of government ministers. The *Daily Worker* campaigned against a number of shortcomings, such as the lack of deep underground shelters, which the government was not in a position to rectify in the short term. The paper also published vituperative attacks on ministers – including a cartoon portraying Ernest Bevin, the Minister of Production (and trade union leader), as being in the pay of captains of industry – which caused deep personal offence.[15]

The ban on the two papers was also part of a wider government campaign against communism in Britain which was being organised by the interdepartmental Committee on Communist Activities, including representatives from the Foreign Office and MI5, strongly supported by leading right-wing ministers. That the ban was motivated, in part, by political prejudice – and not simply by a concern about the papers' impact on public morale – is confirmed by the unwillingness of the authorities to allow the *Daily Worker* to begin republication when the British Communist Party came round to full-hearted support of the war.

The government chose to close down the two communist publications by ministerial decree rather than prosecute them through the law courts. Summary execution was preferred, partly because the government feared that it might lose the case and partly because, as a private memorandum from the Home Secretary explained, a law suit would provide the *Daily Worker* with 'a good opportunity for propaganda against what it would describe as the government's effort to "gag" the press'.[16] Although the government's actions clearly amounted to an attack on press freedom, it met with little opposition. When a group of senior journalists and publishers were informed of the decision, only one person objected.[17] In parliament, the best supported motion opposing closure garnered just 11 votes.[18]

The assault on the communist press was part of a wider move to curb criticism from left papers. The *Daily Herald*, which had been outspokenly critical during the early stages of the war, moderated its tone when the Labour Party joined the coalition government in response to pressure from the paper's Trades Union Congress (TUC)-nominated directors. Appeals to loyalty also helped to subdue criticism of the government in *Reynolds News*, the paper of the Co-operative Movement. But the *Daily Mirror* and *Sunday Pictorial*, which moved to the left during the war, were much more difficult to deal with. They were not controlled by the labour movement, nor were they answerable to a dominant shareholder (as the Cabinet discovered after authorizing an investigation into the share ownership of the two papers).[19]

At first, pressure was exerted informally through a series of meetings between senior members of the government and directors of the two papers.[20] When this failed, Churchill urged a more direct approach. Both papers, he argued in a Cabinet meeting on 7 October 1940, published articles that were subversive. He went on to suggest that a conspiracy lay behind this criticism. 'There was far more behind these articles', Churchill warned, 'than disgruntlement or frayed nerves. They stood for something most dangerous and sinister, namely an attempt to bring about a situation in which the country would be ready for a surrender peace'.[21]

The new Home Secretary, Herbert Morrison, asked for time to consider the issue. The next day he circulated a sharply worded memorandum to his Cabinet colleagues in which he suggested that 'there is much in the papers [*Daily Mirror* and *Sunday Pictorial*] which is calculated to promote a war spirit. They seem to be clearly anxious for the defeat of Hitlerism'. After arguing that government action would be counter-productive, he concluded: 'It is a tradition of the British people that they still remain obedient to the constituted authorities while retaining their liberty to ridicule and denounce the individuals who are actually in authority'.[22]

An unlikely struggle developed in which Morrison, the archetypal machine politician, vigorously defended freedom of expression against Churchill, a former journalist who, on numerous occasions, had extolled the virtues of having a free press. In the next Cabinet meeting, Churchill accused the *Daily Mirror* and *Sunday Pictorial* of 'trying to rock the boat', and demanded 'firm action to deal with this menace'. He was strongly supported by, among others, Sir John Anderson, who was in favour of issuing a warning to the two papers and then closing them down if they did not change. Morrison opposed this, arguing that such action would divide the Commons on party lines and amount to 'interference with the liberty of the press'.[23]

In the end the Cabinet agreed with the compromise plan proposed by Beaverbrook (now a Cabinet minister) of exerting pressure on the two papers through the Newspaper Proprietors Association (NPA). Beaverbrook and Attlee, representing the government, met the NPA, and told them that compulsory censorship of the press might have to be introduced if the *Daily Mirror* and *Sunday Pictorial* continued to be so irresponsible. The proprietors protested strongly, but subsequently urged the senior management of the *Daily Mirror* and *Sunday Pictorial* to restrain their staff. The effect of this intervention was limited. 'We shall pipe down for a few weeks', Cecil King, a director of both papers, noted in his diary.[24]

Churchill's allegations that the two papers were motivated by a desire to secure 'a surrender peace' were unjustified. Both papers were totally committed to winning the war. Indeed, they had opposed appeasement with Germany before anti-appeasement had become government policy; and they had backed Churchill for the premiership on the grounds that he would push for a more vigorous prosecution of the war. From the outset of the war, the *Daily Mirror* adopted a tone of patriotic defiance: 'We appeal to every worker and every employer to play the man . . . stick to your job unless it is foolhardy to do so'.[25] In the same vein, the *Daily Mirror* declared in 1940, 'Britain has risen to the height of heroism and resolution'[26] and shortly afterwards, 'Today, the world can only salute the heroism of London in her trial'.[27] The *Sunday Pictorial* was no different, pillorying Lloyd George as 'the marshal of the weak and terrorised' when he proposed a negotiated settlement with Germany.[28]

The real reason for the attack on the two papers was that they had become increasingly critical of the government. The *Sunday Pictorial* had called the failure of British forces to take Dakar, under Vichy control,[29] 'another blunder', while the *Daily Mirror* referred pointedly to 'futile dashes at remote strategic points'.[30] Both papers also argued that the retention of the pro-appeasement 'Old Gang' in the government was weakening the war effort.

Clashes between the government and the Mirror group escalated in 1941 and early 1942, largely because both sides had an irreconcilable view of how the national interest could best be served.[31] Leading Conservative ministers believed that criticism of officers in the *Daily Mirror* – including a reference to them as 'brass buttoned boneheads, socially prejudiced, arrogant and fussy'[32] – served to undermine the respect for rank that was the basis of good discipline in the army. They also felt that the *Daily Mirror*'s calls for post-war reconstruction were needlessly introducing political controversy, and dividing the nation, at a time of national emergency. In their view, the *Daily Mirror*, with a steadily rising circulation, had become an impediment to winning the war.

Mirror group journalists, on the other hand, saw themselves as contributing to the war effort. They argued that Britain, in its hour of need, could not afford the incompetence that arose from snobbery and privilege: responsible jobs should go to those selected on the basis of ability rather than of birth. Plans for a new deal after the war were not divisive in a society already divided by class inequalities; on the contrary, a programme for 'winning the peace' would help win the war by motivating people to contribute even more to the war effort.

These differences flared up into a full-scale confrontation in March 1942. The trigger, though not the cause, of the confrontation was a cartoon published in the *Daily Mirror* by Zec which showed a torpedoed sailor adrift on a raft in the open sea, with the caption: 'The price of petrol has been increased by one penny – official.'[33] This was interpreted by Churchill and many of his Cabinet colleagues as an irresponsible attack upon the government for sanctioning oil companies' profiteering at the expense of people's lives. Its real intention was quite different: Zec meant it as an attack upon the needless waste of petrol by dramatizing the human sacrifice involved in shipping oil to Britain.[34] This was how it was understood by most people, according to a Home Intelligence Report,[35] as well as by most MPs who commented on it in a subsequent Commons debate.[36]

Ministers' misunderstanding of the Zec cartoon was a symptom of their growing demoralization. In the previous three months, the allies had suffered defeats at Guam, Wake, Hong Kong, Manila, the Dutch East Indies, Rangoon, Benghazi and Singapore. In the embattled atmosphere of Cabinet discussions, the paper came to be held partly responsible for some of the things that were going wrong. The Labour Minister, Ernest Bevin, demanded in a highly emotional state, 'How was he to "press" people almost into the Merchant Navy if they were then to see the suggestion [in the Zec cartoon] that they were being "pressed" in order to put the price of petrol up for the owners?'[37] The *Daily Mirror*'s staff had become scapegoats for failure. 'We will flatten them', Churchill told his Information Minister, Brendan Bracken.[38]

The assault on the *Daily Mirror* was part of the government's struggle for political survival. At a time when some papers, like the *News Chronicle*, had become increasingly critical of the government, the *Mirror* went one step further publishing an editorial that came close to demanding the administration's resignation:

> The assumption that whatever blunders are committed, and whatever faults are plainly visible in organisation, we must still go on applauding men who muddle our lives away, is a travesty of history and a rhetorical defiance of all the bitter lessons of past wars.[39]

This indictment was published at a time when a number of insiders believed that the administration might be forced to resign.[40] Churchill himself believed that he could be ousted. 'My diary for 1942', writes a member of Churchill's personal entourage, 'has the same backcloth to every scene: Winston's conviction that his life as Prime Minister could be saved only by victory in the field'.[41] Even the general public, previously more loyal to the premier and his administration than the political elite, showed signs of turning against Churchill in early 1942.[42]

The attack on the *Daily Mirror* was thus a pre-emptive strike against the government's principal critic. Its purpose, as discussion among Cabinet ministers made clear, was not only to silence the *Daily Mirror* but also to intimidate the rest of the press into being less critical. Churchill demanded the immediate closure of the *Daily Mirror*, in a full Cabinet meeting on 9 March 1942.[43] The matter was referred to a Special Committee under the chairmanship of Sir John Anderson. The committee was advised by the law officers (rather surprisingly in view of the terms in which censorship regulations had been introduced) that it was legal to close down the *Daily Mirror* because, although it supported the war, it impeded its 'successful prosecution'. The Lord Chancellor also recalled cynically and inaccurately that: 'When the then Home Secretary quite illegally suppressed the Globe newspaper, there was a row in the House in one debate in which the government received overwhelming support, and nothing was ever heard of the Globe newspaper again'.[44]

The committee did not, however, endorse the closure of the *Daily Mirror* although it agreed that 'it would be helpful if an example could be made' to curb press criticism.[45] Those opposed to an immediate ban stressed that 'it was clear from the debates in parliament at the time when Regulation 2D had been enacted that it would be used to deal with Communist, Fascist or Pacifist Anti-War agitators' – but not, they pointed out, 'for the purposes now suggested'. There had to be a public redefinition of the government's censorship powers before anything could be done.[46]

At this stage a near consensus had been reached in favour of banning the *Daily Mirror*. The hawks, who wanted immediate suspension, had been strengthened by the recruitment of Bevin, the powerful Minister of Labour. The opposition of the doves, on the other hand, had weakened. They stood out for giving the *Daily Mirror* one last chance in which to reform itself, while at the same time seemingly consenting to the paper's suppression if it did not 'improve'.[47] Even Morrison, the principal dove and the minister who would be responsible for carrying out Cabinet policy, apparently agreed that if the *Daily Mirror* people 'did not amend I would suppress them'.[48]

Morrison announced that Defence Regulation 2D empowered the government to ban pro-war papers which undermined the war effort, even if the offence was not intentional but merely arose from a 'reckless and unpatriotic indifference' to the interests of the nation. He added that the *Daily Mirror* would be banned without further notice unless 'those concerned recognized their public responsibilities'.[49] The same warning was given personally to the *Daily Mirror*'s senior management, and a report of the meeting was released to the press.

Most government minsters did not anticipate the enormous storm of protest that followed. A large group of MPs demanded a special debate in the Commons. In a packed House the Liberal MP, Wilfred Roberts, tellingly quoted an article published in the USA by the Minister of Information, Brendan Bracken. In this Bracken had argued that 'the savage censorship imposed on the French press played no small part in the fall of France. It encouraged defeatism, and bred complacency. A blindfolded democracy is more likely to fall than to fight'.[50] The Labour MP, Frederick Bellenger, cited another embarrassing article, this one written by Herbert Morrison during the First World War in which he had urged all soldiers not to fight 'your German brother' in an imperialist struggle. Morrison was pointedly asked why he was not now extending the same freedom of expression to others.[51]

As the debate progressed, the government rather than the *Daily Mirror* became subject to sustained attack. While loyal Conservative MPs rallied to

Morrison's defence, the great majority of Labour and Liberal MPs who spoke were sharply critical. The coalition administration was confronted, as Morrison had feared, with an issue that divided the Commons along party political lines.

Newspaper proprietors and editors were also not as compliant as they had been over the closure of the *Daily Worker.* While many Sunday and local papers supported the government, the majority of national daily papers sided with the *Daily Mirror.* It thus became clear that closing the paper would lead to a major confrontation with a powerful section of the press.

The strength of opposition was such that, after March 1942, the *Daily Mirror* was never really in any danger of being banned. Thereafter official displeasure took the form of harassment, such as Churchill's personal request that Cecil King be conscripted into the armed forces.[52] However, the outcome was not entirely one sided. The *Daily Mirror*'s attacks on government became less belligerent, and William Connor (the paper's most outspoken columnist, writing as Cassandra) enrolled in the army.

The defence of the *Daily Mirror* overlapped with a major campaign to lift the ban on the *Daily Worker.* A mass rally was organised in Trafalgar Square and in London's Central Hall. The Labour Party Annual Conference voted for the ending of the ban, against its National Executive's recommendation. The Cooperative Congress and the Scottish TUC followed suit. In the face of this escalating pressure from the labour movement, the government backed down. The ban on the *Daily Worker* was lifted on 26 August 1942 – more than a year after the USSR had become one of Britain's closest allies.

The defeat of censorship

The *Daily Mirror* and *Daily Worker* campaigns were part of a wider victory. The government rejected general schemes for compulsory censorship of the press. It also turned down an insidious proposal for allocating rationed newsprint to publications according to their contribution to the war effort.[53] The notorious Regulation 2D was never invoked again after the closure of the *Daily Worker*.

The government drew back from more extensive censorship partly because the press proved, on the whole, to be co-operative. A leading editor even took the Ministry of Information to task for being too permissive in its advisory guidelines.[54] The press, including critical and independent-minded papers such as the *Daily Mirror*, consciously sought to bolster public morale. 'Bloody Marvellous' was how the paper hailed the evacuation of Britain's defeated troops from Dunkirk in 1940.[55] Coercive censorship was, to some extent, made unnecessary by voluntary co-option.

The authorities also refrained from exercising greater control over the press for purely pragmatic reasons. Military censorship of dispatches sent by war correspondents accompanying the armed forces provided a discreet means of filleting out bad news.[56] A number of senior Ministry of Information officials also became convinced that compulsory censorship was unnecessary, once they came round to the view that public morale was holding up. Some also believed that the credibility of a largely co-operative press would be undermined if it was seen to be directly controlled by the government. These arguments from the Ministry of Information helped to deflect those who wanted to exercise greater control over the press.[57] When the military situation improved after the summer of 1942, and the position of Churchill's administration became politically secure, ministers also became notably less sensitive to criticism.

However, active opposition also played an important part in curbing the extension of state censorship. Press freedom was one of the symbols of democracy that Britain was defending against Nazi Germany. This point was made repeatedly in anti-censorship campaigns, and was not something that the government could lightly dismiss. When a senior official in the Ministry of Information wrote that 'it would be improper to propose in this country either a moral or a political censorship of opinion, for that would be contrary to the last 300 years of English history', he added a significant postscript: 'It would also be perilous in view of the recent events surrounding the *Daily Mirror* and *Daily Worker* and the parliamentary and public attention that has been paid to them'.[58] In resisting the abuse of arbitrary censorship powers, relatively obscure politicians such as Bellenger and Roberts, along with a large number of now-forgotten labour movement activists, kept alive the tradition of an independent press. The political processes of a democratic society saved the government from itself.

Freedom from market censorship

The *Daily Mirror* became a Labour supporter in 1943.[59] By 1945, its soaring circulation reached two million, matching that of the *Daily Herald* which also prospered during the war.[60] The circulation of the now pro-Labour *Sunday Pictorial* rose still higher to 2.5 million by 1945.[61] Their rise was accompanied by the growth of liberal publications, notably the *News Chronicle*, *Manchester Guardian* and the popular news magazine, *Picture Post*.

Not since the 1850s had progressive journalism had such a strong presence in the press. The combined Labour and Liberal press had 48 per cent of national daily circulation in 1945, compared with 27 per cent in 1924.[62] Labour supporting national dailies accounted for 35 per cent of national daily circulation in 1945, greatly more than its 13 per cent share in 1931.[63]

The progressive press also became more left-wing during the war. The papers that changed most were the *Daily Mirror* and its sister paper, the *Sunday Pictorial*. In the case of the *Daily Mirror*, the language of its readers' letters and its 'Good Morning' interviews with ordinary people began to seep through the entire paper.[64] The *Daily Mirror* developed a boisterously colloquial style, and an 'us' and 'them' view of the world, that, combined with its continuing commitment to sex and entertainment, made it the favourite reading of young soldiers. It learnt to ventriloquize the thoughts and feelings of its readers. Its reduced size also compelled a reassessment of its priorities. The percentage of editorial space the paper devoted to public affairs in 1946 was more than double that in 1936.[65]

While this transformation was primarily a response to the radicalization of British society, it was facilitated by state regulation of the newspaper market. Newsprint rationing was introduced in 1940. This restricted the newspaper space available to advertisers (first on a voluntary basis, and then by regulation in 1942).[66] Advertisers queued up to advertise wherever they could,[67] leading to a redistribution of their expenditure across the press. This meant that the *Daily Mirror* and *Sunday Pictorial* no longer had to be concerned about retaining affluent readers who commanded an advertising premium. In the late 1930s, the *Daily Mirror* was a carefully judged middle market paper that was keen, as we have seen, to avoid being judged by advertisers as downscale. The official readership survey in 1939 revealed that the *Mirror* had the most classless appeal of any national daily, while the *Sunday Pictorial* still had a disproportionately middle class readership.[68] By 1947, both papers were read mainly by working-class readers.[69] They had been set free to target their natural constituency.

Newsprint rationing also inaugurated a period of general economic prosperity for the press.[70] Costs were reduced because newspapers became much smaller, but cover prices remained the same. The *Daily Mirror* and *Sunday Pictorial* became more politicized partly because there was greater interest in public affairs. But they also had freedom from financial pressure to publish what they thought was important.

Thus the *Daily Mirror* and *Sunday Pictorial* were able to shed the market constraints that had inhibited their pre-war development, and were free to cultivate a reciprocal relationship with working-class readers. The regulated economic environment of the press also enabled other papers to connect more freely to wartime changes in British society.

Radicalization of Britain

During the war, there was a conscious pulling together of the nation in a shared effort to defeat Germany. Increased solidarity strengthened the impetus towards collectivist politics. The Labour Party – which the Conservatives had rubbished for over a decade as totally inept – had a higher standing as a consequence of being full members of the wartime coalition government. Growing numbers of people thought that if an activist state was needed to win the war, it could also 'win the peace' and build a better post-war Britain. The war produced full employment, and a more confident, less deferential working class. It also exposed people to new places, ideas and experiences that led some to question inherited ideas.

The Ministry of Information's intelligence reports provide an insight into how this new mood spread around the country. They suggest that it began in 1940, and seemingly spread in a widening gyre – starting among the young and highly educated and in particular locations like London – and extended outwards.[71] It crystallized in 'general agreement that things were going to be better after the war'.[72]

This radicalization penetrated Britain's traditional elite. The Conservative Prime Minister, Neville Chamberlain, astonished by the poverty of evacuated families he encountered at first hand, wrote to his sister: 'I never knew that such conditions existed, and I feel ashamed of having been so ignorant of my neighbours. For the rest of my life I mean to make amends . . .'.[73] The Conservative Foreign Secretary, Lord Halifax, wrote to a colleague in July 1940: 'I am quite certain the human conscience in this country is not going to stand for a system that permits large numbers of unemployed . . .'.[74] This new mood found expression in a *Times* editorial which began: 'If we speak of democracy, we do not mean a democracy which maintains the right to vote but forgets the right to work and the right to live . . .'.[75] The editorial was published shortly after the German capture of Paris. It reflected an instinctive recognition that if Britain was to pull together in a defiant last stand against the Axis powers – now that all Britain's European allies had been defeated – the people had to be mobilized with the promise of a better tomorrow.

The Ministry of Information became the principal champion of this position within the government, believing that the formulation of 'peace aims' would neutralize defeatism and class resentment.[76] The progressive popular press also pressed early on for the clear formulation of post-war plans.[77] The potential thus existed for a new radical consensus to be established in wartime Britain.

Yet, large numbers of people were anti-party or politically disengaged, and many remained strongly individualistic – something that romantic views of wartime radicalization and collectivism overlook.[78] Although some within the traditional political elite responded to the progressive climate of the time, others were strongly opposed to the idea of a new post-war settlement (or even discussing it). Moreover, the desire to build a more secure, egalitarian Britain in peacetime initially took an unfocused form. This had been true of the First World War, and had resulted in very limited change.

Anchoring a public mood

In 1941, a committee of mid-level civil servants, under the chairmanship of an academic, Sir William Beveridge, was appointed to undertake 'a minor tidying up operation' in relation to social insurance benefits.[79] Departing from their brief, they produced in 1942 a report advocating the post-war reconstruction of Britain based on a policy of full employment, free health care and a comprehensive social security system, offering full protection, that would abolish poverty.

The government considered not publishing the report. Then Minister of Information, Brendan Bracken, instructed his staff to withhold 'official facilities' for publicizing it.[80] He only relented two days before the report's release on the grounds it would be useful in the propaganda war against Germany.

What could easily have been a little noticed government document was transformed by press publicity. The national daily press (and some Sunday papers) gave the Beveridge Report enormous prominence, and acclaimed it as the blueprint for the future. The Report was championed not only by left papers like the *Daily Herald* ('a massive achievement')[81] and the *Sunday Pictorial* (which compared it to the Magna Carta);[82] praised not only by liberal papers like the *Manchester Guardian* ('great piece of national reconstruction');[83] saluted not only by the voice of the Establishment, *The Times* ('great social measure');[84] but welcomed in the Conservative *Daily Mail* ('a big step forward in the long march of human progress')[85] and in a more lukewarm way in Beaverbrook's *Daily Express* ('security is a splendid social motive').[86] Beveridge also outlined his proposals on primetime radio (and these were given further prominence in the popular BBC Talks series, The World We Want).[87]

The media's agenda-setting power made this Report the cornerstone of a new consensus. Within a fortnight, a British Institute of Public Opinion poll recorded that 95 per cent had heard of the Beveridge Report.[88] Still more remarkable, 86 per cent believed that the report should be adopted, while only 6 per cent were opposed.[89] The Report, in summary form, even became a best seller.[90]

A pre-existing radical mood was given a programmatic focus. This made the pressure for reform more difficult to defuse since it was anchored to specific proposals rather than being just an unfocused aspiration. The Chancellor of the Exchequer, Sir Kingsley Wood, with support from the Prime Minister, did in fact try to avoid making policy commitments in relation to the Beveridge Report. But under pressure, the government was forced to do so.

In the event, the Beveridge Report was largely implemented by the first ever majority Labour government elected in 1945. It came to be accepted by a reformed, 'modernizing' Conservative Party in the later 1940s,[91] and became a cornerstone of the post-war political consensus.

In conclusion, the revival of radical journalism led to clashes with the government, culminating in a move to suppress the *Daily Mirror*. But the processes of democracy protected government from itself, while economic regulation created conditions in which radical journalism could thrive. The press helped to reinforce a radical public mood, and anchor it to a set of progressive policies. Indeed, the way in which newspapers championed the Beveridge Report in 1942 offers a tantalizing glimpse of how different Britain might have been if it had a different kind of press.

Notes

1 National Archive, Ministry of Information, INF 1/250, Report to the Policy Committee, 4 June 1940.
2 Ministry of Information, INF 1/533, Planning Committee Report, June 1940.
3 H. Nicholson, *Diaries and Letters 1939–45* (London, Collins, 1967), p. 96.
4 See in particular R. Mackay, *Half the Battle: Civilian Morale in Britain during the Second World War* (Manchester, Manchester University Press, 2002). For other assessments, see J. Gardiner, *The Blitz* (London, HarperCollins, 2010); P. Ziegler, *London at War 1939–1945* (London, Random House, 2002) and a breakthrough book, A. Calder, *The People's War: Britain, 1939–1945* (London, Panther, 1971).
5 Ministry of Information, INF 1/292, Home Intelligence Weekly Report no. 73, 16–23 February 1942.
6 Ministry of Information, INF 1/292, Home Intelligence Weekly Report no. 77, 16–23 March 1942, Appendix on 'Home-made Socialism'.
7 INF 1/187, internal memo, 6 September 1939.
8 For a detailed description of the chaotic restructuring of the Ministry of Information, and the machinery of consultation and censorship, see I. McLaine, *Ministry of Morale* (London, Allen and Unwin, 1979).
9 *Statutory Rules and Orders*, vol. 2 (London, Hansard, 1940), especially pp. 21–24, 36–38 and 55.
10 *House of Commons Debates*, vol. 363 (London, Hansard, 1940), 3 July 1940, col. 1307.
11 *HC Debs*, vol. 363, 3 July 1940, col. 1320.
12 National Archive, War Cabinet and Cabinet Office Papers [CAB], WM (42) 32, item 1, 9 March 1942.
13 Ministry of Information, INF 1/292, Home Intelligence Weekly Report, 22–29 January 1941.
14 However, *The Week* had made a valuable contribution to public debate (see P. Cockburn, *The Years of the* Week [Harmondsworth, Penguin, 1971]). It was never revived after its suppression.
15 CAB 65/8, WM 193 (40), 1940.
16 CAB 66/14, 23 December 1940.
17 W. Armstrong (ed.) *Cecil King, With Malice Toward None* (London, Sidgwick and Jackson, 1970), p. 93. The lone voice came from Frank Owen, Editor of the *Evening Standard*, who had been a Liberal MP.
18 *HC Debs.*, vol. 368, 28 January 1941, cols. 528–30.
19 CAB 65/9, WM 267 (40), 7 October 1940.
20 Reported in Armstrong, *With Malice*, pp. 47–54; 57–58 and 99–103; and in CAB 65/7, WM 170 (40), 17 June 1940.
21 CAB 65/9, WM 267 (40), 7 October 1940.
22 CAB 66/12, WP 402 (40), 8 October 1940.
23 CAB 65/9, WM 268 (40), 9 October 1940.
24 Armstrong, *With Malice*, p. 81.
25 *Daily Mirror*, 16 September 1940.
26 *Daily Mirror*, 21 September 1940.
27 *Daily Mirror*, 30 September 1940.
28 *Sunday Pictorial*, 18 October 1939.
29 *Sunday Pictorial*, 29 September 1940.

30 *Daily Mirror*, 2 October 1940.
31 For government perspectives, see notes 22–24; WM (41) 101, item 2, 9 October 1941; WM (41) 106, item 1, 27 October 1941; L. Macmillan, first Minister of Information, in CAB 65/2, WM 69 (39), 3 November 1939; and G. P. Thomson, *Blue Pencil Admiral* (London, Sampson, Low, and Marston, 1947). For the perspectives of Mirror group senior executives, see the exchanges in Armstrong, *With Malice*, pp. 94–99 and 103–7; and H. Cudlipp, *Walking on Water* (London, Bodley Head, 1976), pp. 115 ff. These mainly illuminate a left/right, and, to a lesser degree, a press/government split. But for an insight into intra-left differences, see the detailed report of an angry meeting between Home Secretary, Herbert Morrison, and *Sunday Pictorial* Editor, Stuart Campbell, with the former making a distinction between constructive and irresponsible press criticism, recorded in the National Archive, PREM 4/66-2, 21 November 1941.
32 Cited in *House of Commons Debates*, vol. 378 (London, Hansard), col. 2246, 26 March 1942.
33 *Daily Mirror*, 6 March 1942.
34 Cudlipp, *Walking*, p. 135.
35 INF 1/282, Home Intelligence Weekly Report 78, 23–30 March 1942.
36 *HC Debs.*, vol. 378, 26 March 1942, cols. 2233–308.
37 A. J. P. Taylor (ed.) *Off the Record: W. P. Crozier, Political Interviews 1933–43* (London, Hutchinson, 1973), p. 311.
38 Taylor, *Off the Record*, p. 325.
39 *Daily Mirror*, 16 February 1942.
40 J. Harvey (ed.) *The War Diaries of Oliver Harvey 1941–5* (London, Collins, 1978), pp. 94 ff. Likewise, Chips Channon wondered whether the forced resignation of Churchill would pave the way for the peerage that he craved (but never obtained). See R. R. James (ed.) *Chips: The Diaries of Sir Henry Channon* (London, Weidenfeld & Nicolson, 1978), p. 94.
41 L. Moran, *Winston Churchill* (London, Sphere, 1968), p. 63.
42 INF 1/292, Home Intelligence Weekly Report 72, February 1942.
43 CAB 65/25, NM (42) 32, 9 March 1942.
44 CAB 66/23, WP (42) 124, 17 March 1942, Appendix (Note by Lord Chancellor). In fact, the *Globe* was only briefly suspended in 1915, not suppressed. See C. Lovelace, 'British press censorship during the First World War' in G. Boyce, J. Curran and P. Wingate (eds.) *Newspaper History* (London, Constable, 1978), p. 313.
45 CAB 66/23, WP (42) 124, 17 March 1942.
46 CAB 65/25, NM (42) 35, 18 March 1942.
47 Ibid.
48 Armstrong, *With Malice*, p. 325
49 *HC Debs.*, vol. 378, cols. 1665–67, 19 March 1942.
50 *HC Debs.*, vol. 378, col. 2242, 26 March 1942.
51 *HC Debs.*, vol. 378, col. 2301, 26 March 1942.
52 Churchill to Minister of State for War (Prem. 4/66/4., 1942), cited in C. E. Lysaght, *Brendan Bracken* (London, Allen Lane, 1979), p. 200. In fact, King turned out to be medically unfit.
53 This had been piloted on a reserve allocation basis in May–December 1940 (see INF 1/239, 1940). It was proposed as a general scheme and rejected in 1942 (see INF 1/238, internal memo, 15 April 1942).

54 S. Carroll, Managing Editor of the *Daily Sketch* and *Sunday Graphic,* letter to Ministry of Information, 26 June 1940, INF 1/184.

55 *Daily Mirror*, 1 June 1940.

56 P. Knightley, *The First Casualty* (London, Deutsche, 1975).

57 McLaine, *Ministry,* pp. 88 ff.

58 Memorandum from R. H. Parker, INF 1/238, 15 April 1942.

59 A. Smith (with E. Immirzi and T. Blackwell), *Paper Voices* (London, Chatto & Windus, 1975), p. 111.

60 W. Belson, *The British Press* (London, London Press Exchange[mimeo], 1960), Part 3, Table 1, pp. 12–13.

61 Ibid., Table 3, p. 14.

62 J. Thomas, *Popular Newspapers, the Labour Party and British Politics* (Abingdon, Routledge, 2005), Table 1.1, p. 14.

63 Ibid.

64 Smith, *Paper Voices*, Chapter 3. For a different view, see A. Bingham and M. Conboy, 'The *Daily Mirror* and the creation of a commercial popular language: a people's war, a people's paper?', *Journalism Studies*, 10 (5), 2009, pp. 639–54, which questions how left-wing the paper became during the war.

65 See Chapter 7, Table 7.4, p. 96–97.

66 J. Gerald, *The British Press Under Economic Controls* (Minneapolis, University of Minnesota Press, 1956).

67 Ibid.

68 *Survey of Press Readership* (London, Institute of Incorporated Practitioners in Advertising, 1939).

69 *Hulton Readership Survey* (London, Hulton, 1947).

70 Royal Commission on the Press 1947–9 Report (London, HMSO, 1949), p. 81.

71 INF 1/250, Report to the Policy Committee, 4 June 1940; INF 1/292, Home Intelligence Weekly Report (HIWR) No. 10, 4–11 December 1940; INF 1/292, HIWR No. 11, 11–18 December 1940; INF 1/292, HIWR No. 15, 8–15 January 1941; INF 1/292, Home Intelligence Reports, 25 March 1942.

72 Ministry of Information, INF 1/292, Home Intelligence Weekly Report no. 77, 16–23 March 1942, Appendix on 'Home-made Socialism'.

73 P. Addison, *The Road to 1945* (London, Quartet, 1977), p. 72.

74 Ibid., p. 122.

75 *The Times* 1 July 1940, cited in R. McKibbin, *Parties and People: England 1914–1951* (Oxford, Oxford University Press, 2010), p. 118.

76 McLaine, *Ministry*, pp. 103 ff.

77 For example, *News Chronicle* 5 September 1940; *Daily Herald* 5 October 1940; *Sunday Pictorial* 15 December 1940.

78 S. Fielding, P. Thompson and N. Tiratsoo, *England Arise! The Labour Party and Popular Politics in 1940s Britain* (Manchester, Manchester University Press, 1995); S. Fielding, 'What did "the people" want? The meaning of the 1945 general election', *Historical Journal* 35 (3), 1992, pp. 623–39, among others. For the telling counter-argument that this revisionist tradition relies on too narrow an interpretation of 'what is political', see McKibbin, *Parties*, pp. 129 ff. Even so, this revisionism offers a useful redress to radical nostalgia, and has the merit of helping to explain what happened in the 1950s.

79 B. Abel-Smith, 'The Beveridge Report: its origins and outcomes', *International Social Security Review*, 45 (1–2), 1992, p. 9.

80 Addison, *The Road*, p. 217; cf. Abel-Smith, 'Beveridge Report', p. 12.
81 *Daily Herald*, 2 December 1942.
82 *Sunday Pictorial*, 6 December 1942
83 *Manchester Guardian*, 2 December 1942.
84 *The Times*, 2 December 1942.
85 *Daily Mail*, 2 December 1942. The first Lord Rothermere, who favoured small government, had died in 1940.
86 *Daily Express*, 2 December 1942.
87 D. Cardiff and P. Scannell, 'Radio in World War II' in *Open University Course, Popular Culture*, Block 2, Unit 82 (Milton Keynes, Open University, 1981), p. 59.
88 McKibbin, *Parties*, p. 133.
89 Addison, *The Road*, p. 217.
90 Ibid.
91 P. Hennessy, *Never Again: Britain 1945–51* (Harmondsworth, Penguin, 2006).

Chapter 7

Post-war press
Fable of progress

According to Stephen Koss, the post-war period marked the final instalment of an unfolding story of progress. 'By 1947', Koss writes, 'the party attachments of papers – as they had been understood to operate over the preceding hundred years – were effectively abandoned'.[1] By detaching themselves from political parties, newspapers allegedly became autonomous from the orbit of government. And by being oriented towards what sold rather than what furthered a party interest, newspapers supposedly became the servants of the public. 'The halting transition from official to popular control' of the press over a period of nearly two centuries was, in his view, now complete.[2]

Koss attributes this apotheosis not only to the ending of government and party control but also to the demise of propagandist proprietors. The press barons of the inter-war period gave way, he tells us, to a new type of proprietor who was 'a businessman first and foremost', concerned with profits rather than propaganda.[3] Newspapers became supposedly more truly the voice of the public because they were more fully responsive to the consumer.

This resulted, we are told, not only in popular control of the press but in better journalism. No longer in thrall to political parties, newspapers 'grew steadily more catholic and less partisan in their ordinary news coverage'.[4] They responded to events free from party loyalty. When confronted by a general election, Koss informs us, newspapers 'usually expressed a party preference' but 'often for a different party from the one that they had previously endorsed'.[5]

His account tallies with what senior journalists were saying shortly before he wrote his history. For example, Charles Wintour, London editor of the *Evening Standard*, argued in 1972 that a 'revolution in Fleet Street' had taken place in which proprietors had ceded control to editors and their staff, within broad budgetary limits.[6] Similarly John Whale, a prominent *Sunday Times* journalist, wrote in 1977 that in the post-war period 'proprietors disappeared from editorial conferences. The decision about what news to cover, and what to say about it in leaders, was left to staff journalists'.[7] The eclipse of the proprietor ensured, in his view, that 'the broad shape and nature of the press is ultimately determined by no one but its readers'.[8]

There is thus seemingly authoritative agreement about how journalism changed in the period 1945–79. The press, we are told, became fully detached from party influence; journalists were no longer subject to the whims of propagandist proprietors; the quality of journalism improved because it became less partisan; and control of the press was at last vested in the people.

There are small elements of fleeting truth in this account. However, it is fundamentally misleading because it inflates an incomplete change – which was reversed subsequently – into a permanent transformation. It ignores evidence that contradicts its thesis. And it is based on a very simplistic analysis of how the market operated, and how the press connected to power in Britain.

Myth of the disappearing proprietor

During the 1940s, some press barons claimed unconvincingly that they adopted a hands-off approach to running their newspapers. Beaverbrook told the first Royal Commission on the Press that his so-called 'directives' were 'really advice',[9] while Lord Kemsley proclaimed that his leadership style was based on team work in which all concerned pulled together.[10]

But if Beaverbrook professed that his role was confined to counselling, this is not what his editors remembered.[11] As Arthur Christiansen, his long-serving editor of the *Daily Express*, succinctly recalled: 'The policies were Lord Beaverbrook's job, the presentation was mine'.[12] Similarly, Lord Kemsley was remembered by his employees as being 'autocratic', having an 'overpowering personality', and fostering 'competitive tension' as a way of exercising control.[13] In the immediate post-war period, there were perhaps only two national papers – the *Manchester Guardian* and *The Times* – where staff enjoyed a high degree of autonomy.[14]

However, there was a shift towards greater devolution of editorial decision-making in the national press during the late 1950s and in the 1960s. This change was epitomized by the rise of Canadian businessman Roy Thomson who acquired much of Lord Kemsley's press empire in 1959. He proved to be an ideal proprietor, willing to both resource good journalism and to devolve editorial control to journalists. Harold Evans could recollect only one occasion in his fourteen years as editor of the *Sunday Times* when he received political guidance: the proprietor, he was told in 1974, would be unhappy if the *Sunday Times* supported the Labour Party in the forthcoming election.[15]

Reins of control slackened in other parts of Fleet Street. The second generation of press lords – the second Lord Rothermere and Sir Max Aitken (son of Lord Beaverbrook) – were less forceful and effective than their fathers. The *Daily Herald* was decoupled from its political masters, the Trades Union Congress (TUC), in 1964. Cecil King was deposed in 1968 as head of the Mirror group, after he commandeered the front pages of the *Daily Mirror, Sun* and *Daily Record* to demand the toppling of the Labour Prime Minister

Harold Wilson. The principal boardroom assassin was his friend and close colleague, Hugh Cudlipp, who replaced him as a less authoritarian boss.[16]

Under Lord Thomson's permissive regime, the *Sunday Times* became an independent voice of liberal conservatism. The *Daily Herald/Sun* ceased to be the organ of the labour movement, while the *Daily Mail* became a more liberal paper in the early 1960s under its editor William Hardcastle. Giving journalists more freedom seemed to encourage a more centrist style of journalism.

But the so-called managerial revolution, even at its zenith, did not reach all parts of Fleet Street. David Astor, proprietor-editor at the *Observer*, got his way without seeming to do so. In the sardonic (but affectionate) words of an employee, Astor was an 'an enlightened despot', who also 'liked his colleagues to agree with him which resulted in much discussion'.[17] The Telegraph group remained steeped in the past, something that was reflected in the ritual of the proprietor, Lord Hartwell's arrival at the office. Commissionaires would 'leap to attention before rushing to hold lifts for the great man', wrote a bemused underling, 'brushing lesser mortals aside like flies in paroxysms of deference . . . .'.[18]

A management consultancy report into how Fleet Street was run, commissioned by the Newspaper Proprietors Association in 1966, brought home the limits of change. 'When all allowances have been made for variations within the industry', the report concluded, 'its most striking feature, and possibly its greatest problem, is its dominance by a small number of highly individualistic proprietors . . . .'.[19]

Crucially, the trend towards greater devolution of editorial decision-making was reversed from the late 1960s onwards. A key change occurred in 1968–69, when Rupert Murdoch acquired the *News of the World* and the *Sun*. He immediately locked horns with the *News of the World* editor, Stafford Somerfield, who objected to the new proprietor giving direct instructions to staff, changing the lay-out and determining the content of a leader.[20] After twenty-five years in the job, Somerfield was sacked in a meeting lasting three minutes.[21] In conjunction with a hand-picked editor, Larry Lamb, Murdoch went on to transform the *Sun* from being a paper of the left to being a right-wing tabloid.[22] This was a cumulative transition, the key period of political transformation taking place in 1974–75. Murdoch subsequently subverted, as we shall see, the tradition of editorial autonomy that Lord Thomson had fostered in *The Times* and *Sunday Times*, forcing both papers to the right.[23] Murdoch was an old style press baron reincarnate.

In 1971, the third Lord Rothermere assumed control of the Mail group and installed David English as editor of the *Daily Mail*. For the next twenty-one years, English functioned as an authoritarian, surrogate proprietor.[24] In 1977, Lord Matthews became the head of the Express group. 'By and large the editors will have complete freedom', Matthews declared oxymoronically, 'as long as they agree with the policy I have laid down'.[25]

In brief, there was a partial and incomplete trend towards greater devolution of power in Feet Street during the 1950s and 1960s. This was reversed in the 1970s when a new generation of proprietors asserted a greater degree of control. As we shall see, this trend became still more pronounced in the 1980s, and was to persist thereafter.

This was not the only negative feature of the changing pattern of press control. During the 1960s and 1970s, Fleet Street ran into increasing financial difficulties. Loss-making press groups either diversified into more profitable sectors or were taken over by corporations centred outside the press industry. Ownership of the press became linked to core sectors of business most notably oil, engineering, travel, banking, insurance, leisure and construction.[26] This shift was so extensive that the third Royal Commission on the Press concluded in 1976 that 'rather than saying that the press has other business interests, it would be truer to argue that the press has become a subsidiary of other industries'.[27] In 1976–77, numerous directors of major concerns in other industries sat on the boards of newspaper groups.[28] At a time when there was a growing conflict between business and labour, the press was manifestly not an independent institution.

Myth of market democracy

Historians like Stephen Koss who extol the virtues of the free market rarely examine how markets operated in practice. The free market remains for them an abstraction, an idealized mechanism that is an engine of freedom and facilitator of popular control. That is the beginning and the end of their analysis: nothing more, in their view, needs to be said.[29]

In fact, the newspaper market during this period was imperfect due to restricted entry. Press costs rose dramatically in response to the end of newsprint rationing, and the dynamics of unequal competition in which strong papers, with large economies of scale, spent steadily more.[30] The only new national newspapers to be launched successfully in the post-war period were the *Sunday Telegraph* (1961) and the *Daily Star* (1978), both owned by large press groups. Market sclerosis thus weakened the power of the consumer by limiting choice, and entrenched the power of Conservative millionaires who owned most of the national press.

Consumer choice was further constrained by increased press concentration, driven mainly by newspaper acquisitions and mergers. Between 1947 and 1976, the big three groups' share of national Sunday circulation soared from 60 per cent to 86 per cent, while the big three's share of national daily circulation increased from 62 per cent to 72 per cent (though this last was less than in 1961). Concentration of total national newspaper circulation increased by twenty percentage points in thirty years (see Table 7.1).

In addition, the big five groups' share of local evening, local morning and local weekly circulation also increased significantly during 1947–76. But the

Table 7.1 Concentration of newspaper ownership, 1947–76

	National Daily	National Sunday	Total Daily and Sunday
Three leading groups' share of circulation[1]			
1947	62%	60%	46%
1961	89%	84%	65%
1976	72%	86%	64%
	Regional Evening	Regional Morning	Local Weekly
Five leading groups' share of circulation[2]			
1947	44%	65%	8%
1961	52%	70%	13%
1976	58%	69%	25%

Notes
1 Derived from *Royal Commission on the Press 1947–9 Report*, Appendices 3 and 5; *Royal Commission on the Press 1961–2 Report*, Appendices 2, 3 and 4; and *Royal Commission on the Press 1974–7 Final Report*, Annex 3. The three leading groups have been defined as those with the largest share in each category of publication.
2 Derived from *Royal Commission on the Press 1947–9 Report*, Appendices 4 and 5; *Royal Commission on the Press 1961–2 Report*, Appendices 2, 3 and 4; *Royal Commission on the Press 1974–7 Final Report*, Annex 3 and N Crafts, P. Gudgeon and R. Crafts, *Concentration of Ownership in the Provincial Press 1974–7*, Research Series 5. The five leading groups have been defined as those with the largest share in each category of publication.

national press was where the oligarchs' stranglehold was greatest and most problematic. Papers within their groups nearly all adopted the same political line.

The newspaper market was also distorted by having two sets of clients: advertisers and consumers. Some contended that only one of these two – the consumer – mattered. Advertisers merely follow, it was argued, where consumers lead. 'It is true', wrote John Whale, 'that advertising doubles the price on each new reader's head . . . But there is not much a newspaperman can do to differentiate a double from a single dose of zeal to attract new readers'.[31]

As before, this claim was misleading. During the post-war period, there was still some residual prejudice against radical publications. A small number of advertising agencies told the 1961–62 Royal Commission on the Press that they were reluctant to advertise in publications which, in their judgement, were 'against the national interest',[32] were of 'extremist outlook'[33] or 'unreasonably' pursued an editorial policy inimical to a particular industry.[34] A further small group of agencies said that the political concerns of their clients could influence media selection.[35] This is corroborated by anecdotal evidence. For example, in 1975, one businessman explained to a Press Association (PA) management consultant why he would never advertise in the short-lived *Scottish Daily News*: 'I'm not going to keep alive a newspaper which, the first time I have a strike, will back the strikers'.[36]

However, the advertising agencies that admitted overt political bias were, with one exception (S. H. Benson),[37] relatively small, old-fashioned companies. When political prejudice came into play, it was usually covert and legitimated by an assessment of impact. Some agencies explained to the 1947–49 Royal Commission on the Press that it could matter if editorial policy 'competes with the appeal of the product to be advertised'.[38] This was restated in a more general way in the 1960s by the top agency, Young and Rubicam, which declared that 'the "atmosphere" of a publication – which may include its leanings – is always taken into account'.[39]

Yet this backdoor form of bias, based on subjective assessments of impact, declined in the post-war period. The leading advertising textbook, sponsored by the Institute of the Practitioners of Advertising in 1955–68, included a short, speculative chapter about the 'intangible effects of accompanying editorial and advertising'.[40] Its official replacement, published in 1971, was openly scornful of this approach.[41] This shift reflected the increased importance given to optimizing cost-effective exposure of advertisements to a specific target group, reinforced by changes in market research and the computerization of media scheduling.[42] The press was increasingly viewed as a distribution system for advertisements rather than as an environment that conditioned reader responses.

But if advertising allocations were rarely guided by political prejudice, they were strongly influenced by income differences between readers. The main problem faced by radical publications was not that advertisers were bigots but, as we shall see, they spent more on papers read by people with more money.

In short, newspaper competition was rendered imperfect by restricted market entry, increasing concentration and unequal advertising subsidy. All this limited the capacity of the market to harmonize supply and demand, and to hold press controllers to account.

Newspaper epidemic

Other economic problems also became apparent that shaped the post-war press. The post-war newspaper industry had to cope with a contraction in consumer demand. National papers' circulation declined from 1958 onwards,[43] until there was a brief respite in the 1980s. The circulation decline was especially severe in the case of national Sundays, amounting to a 35 per cent drop between 1955 and 1976 (see Table 7.2). This reduction was caused initially by a decline in households' multiple purchase of newspapers – what the industry called 'duplication' – as consumers adapted to newspapers' increased size and cost after the end of newsprint rationing.[44] This decline then persisted as

Table 7.2 National newspaper circulation, 1950–76

	1950[1] '000	1955[1] '000	1961[2] '000	1966[2] '000	1971[2] '000	1976[2] '000
Dailies	16,680	16,224	15,823	15,591	14,176	14,006
Sundays	30,006	30,217	24,290	24,222	22,744	19,595

Notes
1 W. Belson, *The British Press*, Part 3 (London, London Press Exchange, 1960), Table 17, p. 29. The surge in the late 1940s was due to the temporary ending of pegged circulations in September 1946, enabling the release of pent-up demand.
2 *Royal Commission on the Press [1974–7] Final Report* (London, HMSO, 1977), Table 2, p. 272.

a consequence of the decline of newspaper reading from 1968 onwards in belated response to the rise of television and other sources of entertainment.[45]

The rise of press advertising did not fully compensate for this sales decline. Although total advertising expenditure increased, the press's relative share declined as a consequence of the launch of commercial TV in 1955.[46] The popular press, dependent on display advertising, was especially badly hit.[47] In an attempt to fend off competition from commercial television, the badly run press industry allowed its advertising profit margins to erode to a self-destructive degree in the later 1960s and 1970s.[48]

Still more problematic for the working-class press, the end of statutory newsprint rationing in 1956 led to a redistribution of advertising expenditure. Newsprint rationing had diverted advertising to weak and downscale publications because it created a shortage of advertising space. But with the resumption of normal competition, advertisers steered their spending towards newspapers whose readers had the most money. Table 7.3 charts the consequences of this over a thirty-year period: downscale papers obtained much less advertising per copy than midscale papers, and very much less than upscale papers.[49]

The centre-left press was greatly weakened. The *News Chronicle*, the heir to the liberal non-conformist tradition, died in 1960. This was followed in 1964 by the closure of the *Daily Herald*, and in 1967 by the demise of the *Sunday Citizen*, the only two mainstream national titles owned by the labour movement. Together, these three papers had a combined readership of 9.3 million people in, respectively, their last twelve months of publication.[50] Loss of these three titles removed important institutional props supporting a radical culture in Britain. Their demise was part of a more general pruning process that took place in 1960–71. The *Empire News* (1960), *Sunday Graphic* (1960), *Sunday Dispatch* (1961), and *Daily Sketch* (1971) also closed. Vehicles of popular conservatism, they too had supported a culture of democratic engagement.

All these papers – with the exception of the small-scale *Sunday Citizen*[51] – had substantial, but not massive, circulations. Sir Denis Hamilton, Chairman

Table 7.3 Advertising revenue per 1000 sales of selected national
newspapers, 1945–75[1]

	1945 £	1955 £	1965 £	1975 £
DAILIES				
Upscale: The Times	10.20	24.40	40.51	90.64
Midscale: Daily Express	0.38	4.61	10.05	16.25
Downscale: D. Herald/Sun	0.52	3.86	4.28	11.81
SUNDAYS				
Upscale: Sunday Times	4.18	22.83	116.38	232.90
Midscale: Sunday Express	0.91	7.60	24.77	53.56
Downscale: S. Pictorial/S. Mirror	1.14	3.69	9.28	19.92

Note
1 Advertising revenue figures are supplied from publishers, apart from that for the
Sun in 1975 which is estimated from information presented in Costs and Revenue of
National Daily Newspapers (London, HMSO, National Board for Prices and Incomes
Report no 43, 1967, Cmnd. 3435), Appendix F, p. 33 and Royal Commission on the
Press Interim Report, The National Newspaper Industry (London: HMSO, 1976,
Cmnd. 6433), Table E.7, p. 98. The advertising revenue figures relate to the financial
year but the circulation figures relate to the calendar year. All circulation figures
are derived from the Audit Bureau of Circulation, save for those for the Daily Herald
and Sunday Pictorial in 1945, which are based on publishers' estimates.

of Times Newspapers, sneeringly observed that the Daily Herald 'was beset by
the problem which has dogged every newspaper vowed to a political idea: not
enough people wanted to read it'.[52] He clearly had not grasped that the Daily
Herald's circulation (1.26 million), when it closed, was over four times that of
The Times.[53]

While these papers had different politics, they were the casualties of a dete-
riorating market environment in which costs were rising, circulations were
falling and advertising was being redistributed. They also had one further
thing in common: their circulations were smaller than those of mass papers,
and their readers were poorer than those of the quality press. There was to be
no room for 'minority' popular papers.

De-radicalization

The dynamics of the post-war newspaper market favoured two options: going
upmarket or going all out for a mass readership. The de-radicalizing consequences of these two alternatives will be illustrated by the evolution of the
two most important left papers of the post-war period: the Daily Herald and
Daily Mirror. One went upmarket, lost its way and died. The other sought
middle-of-the-road popularity, blunting its radical edge.

In the early 1950s, the Daily Herald's management responded to the paper's
growing shortfall in advertising not by modifying its editorial policy but by

seeking new and more imaginative ways of selling the paper to the advertising industry. Thus it undertook market research which showed that *Herald* readers were heavy spenders on certain products (such as canned meat, desserts, beer, sugar preservatives and cereals) in an attempt to demonstrate that the paper delivered a valuable advertising market.[54]

The diminishing success of these efforts led in 1955 to a review of the paper's editorial strategy and market position. Two clear alternatives emerged. One option, informed by internal market research, was to popularize the paper by having less political and industrial coverage and more human interest stories, cartoons and features like horoscopes. This would 'bring in women – vital to the advertising department'.[55]

The second option, and the one that was adopted, was to seek more advertising revenue by moving upmarket. This seemingly made not only economic sense but gelled with Gaitskellite revisionism (which was seeking to jettison the Labour Party's cloth cap image). In 1960, the TUC's editorial control of the paper was reduced. In the following year a new broom editor, John Beavan, was drafted in from the *Manchester Guardian*, and announced that he wanted to 'bring the *Daily Herald* into the drawing rooms of Britain'.[56] He pushed the paper upmarket, a shift symbolized by the introduction in 1962 of 'Music and Opera' and 'In the City' columns.

Yet, despite these changes, the *Daily Herald* remained obstinately proletarian. In 1963–64, only 13 per cent of its readers were middle class (ABCI).[57] In a deregulated advertising market, this was toxic. In 1955, the *Daily Herald* had an 11 per cent share of both national daily circulation and advertising revenue. By 1964, its share of national circulation had declined modestly to 8 per cent. But its share of advertising had plummeted to 3.5 per cent.[58]

The decision was taken to persist with the same upscale strategy but this time with more vigour. In 1964 the TUC was persuaded with great difficulty to sever its connection with the paper, which was relaunched as the *Sun*. 'The new paper', confided an internal memorandum, 'is to have the more representative make-up of readers essential to advertisers'.[59] This was to be achieved through building a coalition of *Herald* readers and the young, upwardly mobile. The new product would be attuned to the better educated, less ideological, more consumerist Britain unveiled by social research consultant, Mark Abrams.[60] It was to be 'the only newspaper born of the age we live in'.[61]

Management should have paid less attention to a fashionable guru, and more to its own in-house, survey-based research which revealed the enormity of the task faced by the *Sun*'s editorial team. Readers of the *Daily Herald* were economically radical but socially conservative: the target market was the reverse.[62] The implication of this research, headed by Bill McClelland, was that a popularizing strategy was more likely to succeed. But this was ruled out because it clashed with the interests of the parent group. 'Commercially, it would have been crazy', argued Editorial Director, Hugh Cudlipp, 'to set up a competitor to the *Mirror* within IPC [International Publishing Corporation]'.[63]

The paper's market research revealed the post-launch history of the *Sun* to be a slow motion car crash. The *Sun* failed to please *Herald* readers (who preferred their old paper), and failed also to attract young, affluent readers.[64] The paper then languished unloved and underfunded because an undertaking had been given in 1961 to keep the *Sun* going for seven years. In 1966, it had 77 per cent fewer reporters than its flagship sister paper, the *Daily Mirror*.[65] In 1969, the *Sun* was offloaded for £800,000 to Murdoch, and was transformed into a paper that stood for everything that the *Daily Herald* had opposed.

As late as 1958, research had showed that readers of the *Daily Herald* rated their paper more highly than other readers did their regular daily.[66] But over a million *Herald* consumers, mostly with low incomes, was not enough to keep their paper going as a viable enterprise. The paper was driven upmarket, then enfeebled, and finally sold off to a right-wing press baron.

However, the pursuit of a mass market strategy – as distinct from an upmarket one – could also lead to de-radicalization, as the post-war development of the *Daily Mirror* illustrates. In 1949, it became Britain's most popular national daily. Its success stemmed from the way in which it built a socially homogeneous readership, developed a colloquial voice, connected to the contemporary mood of radicalism, and combined progressive politics with entertainment (with the latter always receiving the most space).

However, sustaining a *mass* readership in the 1950s proved difficult, and led to editorial compromise. The 1951 general election inaugurated a long period of Conservative political ascendancy that lasted until 1964. The *Daily Mirror*'s circulation dipped in 1951, and bobbed up and down for the rest of the decade. The paper's management, sensing a change of mood, drifted towards the centre of gravity in the mass market. In the 1950s and early 1960s, the class divisiveness of the *Daily Mirror*'s 'us and them' view of the world softened into the more emollient rhetoric of 'the young at heart' against 'the old', the modern against the traditional, 'new ideas' instead of 'tired men'.[67] The rhetoric sounded forced and artificial, in contrast to the paper's wartime radicalism.

The *Daily Mirror* gained a new lease of life when it connected – rather belatedly – to the radical zeitgeist of the 1960s. By the mid-1960s, it had increased its circulation by appealing to a younger, cross-class audience. But this was viewed as a constraint by the paper's management. As Cecil King, the International Publishing Corporation [Mirror group] Chairman, explained in 1967:

> Today newspaper circulations are vast assemblies of people of all social classes and all varieties of political view. A controller who tried to campaign for causes profoundly distasteful, even to large minorities of his readers, would . . . put his business at risk.[68]

This commercial caution perhaps cloaked personal inclination. The politics of the Mirror group's management in the 1950s and early 1960s was reflected in their choice of paid political advisers, Alfred Robens, George Brown and Richard Marsh: all prominent Labour politicians who subsequently joined the breakaway Social Democratic Party or the Conservative Party. Cecil King's youthful radicalism waned as he grew older. In 1968 he even fantasized about replacing the Labour government with a national emergency administration headed by Earl Mountbatten of Burma,[69] and in 1970 he proudly voted Conservative.[70] King's successor, Hugh Cudlipp, subsequently joined the breakaway Social Democratic Party founded in 1981 by right-wing Labour politicians. The paper was not only disarmed by its concern to appease diverse readers but increasingly lacked a driving radicalism at its heart.

In the 1970s, the *Daily Mirror* was sucked into the right-wing slipstream generated by the populist right. Although still a Labour-supporting paper, it seemed increasingly hesitant about what it stood for, especially when it was outsold by the boisterously right-wing, hedonistic *Sun* from 1978 onwards. The *Daily Mirror*'s loss of sense of direction was symbolized by two changes. In 1959, it dropped its masthead slogan 'Forward with the People'.[71] In the 1984, the slogan was unfurled in a new form: 'Forward with Britain'.[72] The shift from radical populism to imitative patriotism captured the trajectory of a paper that had lost its progressive cutting edge and settled for following the market flow.

De-politicization

Popular newspapers emerged from their cocooned existence in the regulated market of the 1940s and early 1950s to battle with each other in an intensely competitive environment. The mounting pile of dead titles was a reminder of the consequences of failure.

How newspapers could stay ahead in the circulation battle was spelt out in extensive market research commissioned by increasingly anxious publishers. The most-read items were found to be human interest stories whose appeal transcended differences of age, class and gender. Sport was popular among men, while women's features appealed to women. However, public affairs coverage – as in the inter-war period – attracted generally low average readership scores because it appealed less to women than to men and less to the young than to the over-35s.[73]

The managements of popular newspapers responded by giving more space to content with a popular appeal. They expanded human interest content, entertainment features, sports and women's articles, and reduced public affairs coverage, as a percentage of editorial space (see Table 7.4).[74] This 'de-politicisation' was relative because the size of newspapers increased between 1936 and 1976.[75] Even so, in 1976, all seven popular papers in our sample gave less attention to public affairs than to sport.

In effect popular papers reverted to their pre-war character in response to market deregulation. However, popularization went one stage further in the post-war period. Public affairs accounted for a smaller percentage of editorial space in all seven popular papers in 1976 compared with 1936. In the case of the *Daily Herald/Sun*, it was down by over half, with a very large reduction also in the *People/Sunday People*.

A major investigation into what people read in popular national dailies in 1963 distinguished between different types of human interest story. It found that the most popular were celebrity stories and tragic stories about ordinary people, followed by 'light', romance/sex, and crime stories. These insights had long been part of the folklore of Fleet Street. The early post-war press was full of human interest stories about ordinary people, typified by 'I Took a Lorry Ride to Shame'[76] and 'I was a G.I.'s Slave Bride'.[77] This was accompanied by regular disclosures of social deviancy (such as intimacy between a Guide Mistress and Boy Scout),[78] and a staple of crime stories (including investigations into organised crime and prostitution, which were presented as a growing threat in the early 1950s).

In the later 1950s and 1960s, increased attention was given to 'confessional' celebrity stories. The *People* caused a sensation in 1959 by serializing the memoirs of the Hollywood film star, Errol Flynn, entitled 'My Wicked, Wicked Life'.[79] The *News of the World* successfully counter-attacked in 1960 by serializing the confessions of British film star Diana Dors. At her parties, Diana Dors said, 'it was a case of off with everything – except the light'.[80] In the 1970s, the popular press increasingly feasted off the private lives of TV stars.

However, popular newspapers had to walk a tightrope. They needed to be respectable family newspapers read by all ages, and also to titillate by reporting sex and crime in suggestive detail.[81] The way that Sunday newspapers in particular resolved this tension was to adopt a tone of Victorian rectitude. As the moral guardians of the nation, they had a duty to be shocked every week.

Conventions were also renegotiated. As noted earlier, the *Daily Mirror* and *Sunday Pictorial* moved the goal posts in the late 1930s by publishing pin-ups.[82] Other newspapers followed suit so that cheesecake pictures of women were commonplace in popular journalism by the 1950s. The re-launched *Sun* in 1969 moved the boundaries yet again, publishing topless photographs of women. By the 1970s, page 3 nipples became an institutionalized feature of the paper,[83] something that was presented as a refreshing repudiation of the sexual repression and prudishness of the past.[84] However, the *Sun*'s 'Cor! What a Scorcher!' objectification of half-naked women was accompanied, on other pages, by outbursts of old fashioned morality.

The trend towards more sexualized representations of women (but not of men) reflected the male domination of Fleet Street. Proprietors and national newspaper editors in the period 1945–79 were all men. Only 2 per cent of senior Fleet Street journalists were women in 1965;[85] and systemic discrimination was still keeping women down and largely confining them to the women's sections of national papers in the 1970s.[86]

Table 7.4 Content of selected national daily and Sunday newspapers, 1936–76[1]

Percentage of editorial space	Daily Express			Daily Herald/Sun			Daily Mail			Daily Mirror		
	1936	1946	1976	1936	1946	1976	1936	1946	1976	1936	1946	1976
Advertising (proportion of total space)	43	18	44	42	17	40	46	18	36	29	16	42
Editorial (proportion of total space)	57	82	56	58	83	60	54	82	64	71	84	58
Photographs[2]	13	7	13	9	5	16	15	7	14	21	8	18
Illustrations[2]	4	4	5	2	4	6	5	4	5	7	15	8
Public affairs news[3]	14	29	12	23	34	8	15	27	12	10	18	9
Public affairs features[3]	4	10	6	10	11	6	4	12	8	2	7	4
Finance	10	4	7	6	1	1	9	3	10	4	–	1
Sport	22	18	27	19	20	30	20	19	23	15	9	28
Human interest news	20	20	16	14	14	14	14	19	17	21	29	17
Human interest features	10	6	12	8	4	20	15	3	10	27	5	16
Consumer and women's features	7	2	4	5	3	2	8	2	5	6	4	2
Horoscopes, cartoon strips, quizzes and competitions	4	3	6	3	3	8	3	4	5	6	16	10
Arts and entertainment	6	4	7	6	4	7	5	5	9	4	1	8
Other features	5	5	4	6	4	7	7	6	3	7	10	5

Percentage of editorial space	Daily Telegraph			Sunday Express			People/Sunday People			Sunday Pictorial/ Sunday Mirror			Observer		
	1936	1946	1976	1936	1946	1976	1936	1946	1976	1936	1946	1976	1936	1946	1976
Advertising (proportion of total space)	47	35	48	51	16	56	38	22	44	24	25	46	46	36	49
Editorial (proportion of total space)	53	64	52	49	84	44	62	78	56	76	75	54	54	64	51
Photographs[2]	8	2	9	14	4	13	11	4	21	26	25	20	3	3	12
Illustrations[2]	1	1	1	4	6	9	2	2	2	6	6	6	1	–	3
Public affairs news[3]	19	40	26	8	20	5	10	15	2	7	10	5	20	28	16
Public affairs features[3]	3	9	4	10	19	12	4	11	6	10	16	6	6	19	14
Finance	20	8	20	5	2	2	1	1	1	2	–	2	7	2	10
Sport	14	11	15	21	20	25	25	28	30	18	20	27	17	12	16
Human interest news	14	12	13	15	11	12	18	15	13	11	14	13	7	5	5
Human interest features	10	10	2	23	9	17	23	17	22	15	26	28	6	7	8
Consumer and women's features	3	1	5	4	2	10	3	3	5	8	5	5	4	2	11
Horoscopes, cartoon strips, quizzes and competitions	1	1	1	4	6	6	8	8	6	14	3	5	3	5	1
Arts and entertainment	6	3	10	3	4	6	3	2	6	7	3	6	25	20	15
Other features	9	7	3	8	7	4	7	2	10	9	3	4	5	4	5

Source: 252 issues.

Notes
1 All figures have been rounded off to the nearest whole number.
2 Tabulated separately here but also included in relevant content category.
3 Defined as political, social, economic, industrial, scientific and medical affairs.

Growing gap

To a much greater degree than the popular press, the quality press maintained a commitment to serious political coverage. Between 1936 and 1976, both quality papers in our sample – the *Daily Telegraph* and the *Observer* – actually increased their relative coverage of public affairs, while reducing or merely maintaining their relative coverage of human interest content (see Table 7.4). A growing gap thus developed between a politicized elite press and an entertainment-oriented mass press.

Yet, a recurrent finding of post-war readership research is that quality paper readers had a strong preference for human interest content. Thus, in 1963 the most thoroughly read items in the *Daily Telegraph* were human interest stories – the same as for the four popular dailies that were also investigated.[87] Similarly, research undertaken for the Thomson Organisation revealed that human interest items were the most read articles in the *Sunday Times*, *Sunday Telegraph* and *Observer* in the period 1969–71[88] – precisely the most read content in the *Sunday Mirror* and *Sunday People* in 1968.[89]

The quality and popular sectors of the press diverged principally because of the way they were financed. Quality newspapers derived around three quarters of their revenue from advertising.[90] But in order to obtain this, they had to deliver an elite readership for which they charged high advertising rates. Popular newspapers obtained about 35–40 per cent of their revenue from advertising, and this revenue was linked to the size of their audience.[91]

This affected the way in which each sector related to the market. Quality papers privileged their public affairs oriented readers as a way of avoiding the indiscriminate expansion of their audiences. By contrast, popular papers catered for the common denominator of mass demand. Politicized *minorities* in the mass market (like numerous *Daily Herald* readers) were not catered for adequately because they generated insufficient advertising subsidy. Their money literally could not buy a paper of their choice.

Boundary lines were heavily policed during this period in a way that fostered a growing editorial gulf between the quality and popular press. This is illustrated by what happened at *The Times* when its able journalists, supported by Thomson's supportive regime, attracted a large number of new purchasers. In 1965–69, *The Times*'s circulation soared from 256,000 to 432,000. However, many of the paper's new readers were not drawn from the top social grade, prompting a revolt among advertisers who objected to paying high rates for 'wasted sales'. Perversely, *The Times*'s circulation success led to massive losses. A more sophisticated management then set about shedding unwanted readers by insisting on a change of editorial and promotional approach.[92] 'A reversal of policy changed the situation', recalled Michael Mander, Deputy Chief Executive of Times Newspapers, 'with a consequent dramatic improvement in profitability'. 'The circulation of *The Times*', he added proudly, 'is back down to just under 300,000'.[93]

Advertising also influenced the structure of the press. In 1970, approaching half the press – seven quality newspapers – catered for the top 14 per cent of the market.[94] The remainder of the press – nine popular newspapers – served the mass market. Large advertising subsidies were available for minority papers read by elites, but not for those read by the popular classes.

The economic inequality of society was thus reproduced in the structure of the press as a consequence of unequal advertising subsidies. Although this outcome was not sought by advertisers, it had profound political consequences. Nearly half the 'megaphones' afforded by the press served elite groups, and rendered their voices especially audible in public debate. These elite papers also offered more extensive news and commentary about public affairs than popular papers, enabling their readers to be better informed and better equipped to defend their interests. This is one reason why the 'chattering classes' had a disproportionate influence on the public life of post-war Britain.

Consumerisation

There was a very rapid growth of consumer-oriented features in the post-war press.[95] These were articles of interest to buyers of beauty, fashion, home-making, garden products, travel packages, properties, cars, and, most lucrative of all, investors and job seekers. The growth of these features was often linked to how much advertising they attracted.[96] Product-related advertisements were usually placed on the same or opposing page.[97] These advertising 'supported' pages were especially extensive in the quality and midscale popular press.[98]

The growth of consumer and business journalism was a way for publishers to organise readers into lucrative market categories, and herd them to particular parts of the paper, where their attention could be sold. Advertisers were not strong-arming the press. Quite the contrary, publishers were merely seeking to sell more advertising.

Critics (including journalists) complained that these consumer features were too uncritical.[99] But when this was the case, this was often the consequence of public relations rather than advertising influence.[100] The more serious problem generated by linked advertising is that it could have an agenda-setting effect. Women's pages often reflected the narrow horizons of related advertising. Business and financial pages focused on investment performance and management news, while paying little attention to the international and national economy. This narrow focus was encouraged by the domination of investment and management job advertising in the business sections of newspapers.[101]

In brief, the myth of market democracy fails to register the extent of market failure in the post-war press. It is silent about the unrepresentative nature of press ownership. It ignores the way in which the market was controlled through increasing concentration and high barriers to entry. It is blind to the way in which market change eliminated minority papers appealing to the popular classes but not to elites. It fails to comprehend also why market dynamics encouraged the de-radicalization and relative de-politicization of mass newspapers, but preserved the public purpose of elite newspapers. And it fails to grasp the way in which advertising influenced the editorial makeup of newspapers, and the agendas of advertising-supported features.

Myth of editorial renaissance

The case for thinking that the post-war period witnessed a great improvement in the quality of British journalism centres on the argument that journalism became less partisan.[102] But while partisanship became more muted, it did not disappear. Koss's claim[103] that national papers regularly switched support between parties in the post-war period is not true. With only two exceptions (*The Times* and *Guardian*), *every* national daily supported the same party with unwavering fidelity at *every* general election between 1945 and 1970.[104] The muting of partisanship was reversed in the 1970s: indeed partisanship returned with a vengeance in the 1979 general election.

The second grounds for thinking that journalism improved is that for a time proprietors became less important. Again, this argument is overstated. As we have seen, proprietors still mattered, and proprietorial control was reasserted in the 1970s.

However, there is substance to the claim that journalists, when they had greater autonomy, produced better journalism. This is exemplified by the *Sunday Times* under Harold Evans' editorship. He was not only free from proprietorial control, but also devolved considerable decision-making power to section heads and staff journalists.[105] The paper's best known, and often cited, campaign was on behalf of Thalidomide victims who were born disabled as a consequence of a sleeping pill, marketed by Distillers, which was taken by their pregnant mothers.[106] The paper mounted a campaign arguing that the victims were being offered inadequate compensation by Distillers; settlements were being delayed; and victims were being let down by the legal system. The paper kept up relentless pressure for something to be done, including a controversial article naming and shaming major Distillers shareholders. Despite a vigorous counter-attack from the company, with some right-wing press support, the *Sunday Times* won justice for Thalidomide victims. In 1973, Distillers paid £20 million in compensation, ten times the original offer. The *Sunday Times* also battled against the law of contempt which had been used to constrain its reporting of the Thalidomide scandal. This culminated in the law's liberalization through a European court judgement in 1982.

The Thalidomide story was only one of a number of remarkable investigations initiated by the *Sunday Times* insight team, founded in in 1962. This ranged from an expose of the slum landlord, Peter Rachman,[107] to the disclosure of the brutal interrogation techniques used by British armed forces in

Northern Ireland. Hooding, stress positions, sleep, food and drink deprivation, as well as beatings, were reported to be used in 'in depth' interrogations.[108] The paper excoriated in telling detail the limitations of the white-washing Report of the 1971 Compton Inquiry into allegations of brutality. This contributed to the hasty appointment of the 1972 Parker Committee, and the subsequent Directive issued by the Conservative Government in 1972 outlawing the use of five brutal interrogation techniques (which is still in force). This was great journalism, now largely forgotten.

The *Sunday Times* under Harold Evans was a transatlantic implant rather than part of the mainstream tradition of British national journalism. The paper's solemnity, the space it lavished on exposes (for example, the Thalidomide campaign began with three pages of reporting, and was accompanied by an editorial),[109] the extensive research that went into its investigations, the relentless way in which it returned time and again to the same campaign themes, its bi-partisan tone, its strong commitment to serving democracy, and its 'worthiness' were all traits of American metropolitan journalism.[110] This beacon of the American 'professional' style of journalism was to be extinguished, as we shall see, by a new regime at the *Sunday Times* in the 1980s when the paper returned to the top-down partisanship of the British journalistic tradition.[111]

But if the *Sunday Times* illustrates the way in which post-war journalism at its best championed the vulnerable, there is another darker side in which newspapers in the post-war era did the opposite. This is exemplified by the relentless way in which post-war popular newspapers persecuted gay men.[112] In 1952, the *Sunday Pictorial* (then Britain's second largest circulation Sunday newspaper) ran a three part series on 'Evil Men'.[113] Its central themes were that homosexuals preyed on children, and corrupted 'normal' people; their threat to society was underestimated because of their invisibility, and because of society's prudish reluctance to talk about the problem; and homosexuals needed to be cured through modern medicine or indefinitely detained 'until they threaten society no more'.[114] This series began a hue and cry that was joined by other papers. Prominence was given in 1952–53 to gay sex offences by well-known men, notably the aristocratic Lord Montagu and the actor John Gielgud. This fuelled in turn the demand for retribution. The *News of the World* called for protection against 'the evil in our midst';[115] John Gordon in the *Sunday Express* thought the answer was 'sharp and severe punishment';[116] while the *Daily Mirror* called vaguely for decisive government action.[117]

The anti-gay campaign gathered further momentum when it was revealed in 1955 that the Soviet spies, Guy Burgess and Donald Maclean, were, in the words of the *Sunday Pictorial*, 'sex perverts'.[118] The campaign culminated during the early 1960s, at the height of the Cold War, in press suggestions that there was a homosexual network in Whitehall providing cover for gay traitors, as well as complacent lapses in security vetting. This inspired

Lionel Crane in the *Sunday Mirror* (formerly *Pictorial*) to provide a checklist of 'How to Spot a Potential Homo'. Tell-tale signs, he warned, included being a 'fussy dresser', an 'over-clean man' or a man having 'an unnaturally strong affection for his mother'.[119]

Public persecution was accompanied by the outpouring of bile and ridicule. Thus Cassandra, a columnist in the *Daily Mirror*, summed up the American pianist Liberace (who was gay but professed not to be) as a 'deadly, winking, sniggering, snuggling, chromium plated, scent-impregnated, luminous, quivering, giggling, fruit-flavoured, mincing, ice-covered heap of mother-love'.[120] Cassandra combined cruelty with wit, making him the most admired bully in Fleet Street.

The press campaign against gay men abated in the 1960s only to be revived during the AIDS panic of the 1980s.[121] There was another aspect of British journalism that became more salient in the post-war period. As competition intensified, the pressure to cut corners increased. A top Fleet Street journalist, Harry Proctor, described his growing disillusion about being pressurized to stretch the truth,[122] inflate the danger posed by 'very small, very unimportant people'[123] and set aside norms of everyday decency. The final straw for him was taking a woman — whom he knew had probably killed her children — out shopping for the children's funeral. He got the exclusive, but felt cheapened when she was convicted of manslaughter.[124] Paying the intimates of criminals for insider information became widespread: friends and relations of the Moors Murderers in 1966, and of the Yorkshire Ripper in 1981, received money or gifts from newspapers.[125] Sensitivity was not regarded as a virtue. 'Anyone here been raped and speaks English?'[126] called out a journalist walking through a traumatized crowd of refugees in the Congo.

The post-war period was not the era of journalistic excellence that it is sometimes fondly remembered to be. The gap between the quality and popular press increased. The decline of extreme partisanship was not sustained. The press became more unrepresentative of public opinion, to judge from the growing gap between newspapers and election results during the 1970s. The press bullied as well as championed the vulnerable.

Yet, post-war journalism also included high points. Sadly, these high points were not sustained. The record of the post-war press was not the final chapter in an unfolding story of progress. On the contrary, it was the prelude to a precipitate moral decline.[127]

Myth of press independence

The final flaw in the Whig fable of progress is that it is based on a very simplified understanding of power. It assumes that when the press became free allegedly from party, it became 'independent'. What this fails to grasp is that the press was a pillar of the liberal corporatist Establishment in post-war Britain. When the press turned on this Establishment in the 1970s, it set out on a path that led ultimately to the press's integration into a new neo-liberal Establishment, consolidated in the 1990s.

This is a theme that we will develop over the next two chapters. But first it is necessary to start from the beginning in 1945. There was a brief period after the war when public life reverted to the political polarization of the inter-war period. In the 1945 general election, former colleagues in the wartime coalition government tore into each other, while newspapers reverted to being 'party' Rottweilers mauling their opponents. Thus, Winston Churchill claimed that a Labour government would 'fall back on some form of Gestapo' to supress discontent.[128] Conservative newspapers splashed Labour Party Chairman Harold Laski's unguarded response to a heckler in which he seemingly endorsed violence if fair, democratic means to secure socialist policies were denied.[129] Indeed, the *Daily Express* devoted nearly a quarter of its 1945 general election coverage to what it called the 'Laski affair'.[130] 'It was all-in wrestling, hand-to-hand fighting, commando stuff' gleefully recalled the paper's editor, Arthur Christiansen, who crowed that the Laski quote was 'as good as the Zinoviev letter'.[131] The Labour press countered with equal nastiness.

But by the late 1940s, warring political parties reached broad agreement about the direction that the country should take. This consensus was based on acceptance of Britain's equivalent of the New Deal: universal social security, free secondary education, the National Health Service, and the elevation of full employment as the central objective of government economic policy. It also included support for the Atlantic Alliance in the Cold War, and subsequently the dismantling of Britain's empire.

This consensus was underpinned by a liberal corporatist system of governance based on conciliation between the government, business and labour (and, to a lesser degree, other organised interests). This took the form of regular consultation in government decision making, the establishment of quasi-government agencies with corporate representation, numerous public enquiries to facilitate consensual policy shifts, informal communication between elites and the ceding of considerable influence to a neutral civil service.[132] Until the discord of the later 1970s, conciliatory industrial relations also gave rise to relative workplace harmony in which unions had an accepted role, and workers benefited substantially from productivity gains and increased prosperity.

Liberal corporatism was a progressive regime because it was based on pro-welfare principles and allowed trade union leaders to sit at the high table of policy-making. But it was nonetheless a structure of power, one that established the premises of public debate, and defined what was 'sensible' and 'reasonable'. Defenders of liberal corporatism argued that it sought to be inclusive, while opponents complained that it excluded voices outside its big tent. Both in a sense were right.

The press became a key means by which the post-war corporatist consensus was reproduced. General elections were generally fought by newspapers with less intensity than before, with guest spots sometimes being given in papers to party opponents to present their case.[133] While disagreements persisted in both politics and the press,[134] these were generally contained within the parameters of the post-war consensus until the 1970s.

However, there were moments before the 1970s when fundamental political differences broke out. This happened in 1956 when the Conservative government launched an attack on Egypt (with France, and in secret cahoots with Israel) in response to the nationalization of the Suez Canal. After initial equivocation, the Labour Opposition came out against the war. The resulting political schism gave rise to a sharp division in the press, with all centre-left national dailies opposing the Suez invasion, and the entire Conservative press supporting it (though sometimes critically).[135]

Deep fractures within the Conservative party could also be played out in the Conservative press. This occurred in 1968 when Enoch Powell advocated the effective ending of black and Commonwealth immigration, and the voluntary repatriation of immigrants living in Britain. Although Powell was promptly sacked as a shadow minister by Conservative Opposition leader Edward Heath, Powell's speech was given enormous prominence in the press (so much so that 96 per cent in an opinion poll conducted several days later said that they had read or heard about it).[136] The *Sunday Times* was strongly critical;[137] the *Daily Telegraph* and *Daily Express* were equivocal;[138] and the *News of the World* was wildly enthusiastic, proclaiming 'WE CAN TAKE NO MORE COLOURED PEOPLE. TO DO SO .... IS MADNESS'.[139] The large majority backed Powell in opinion polls in 1968, though support dropped to under half by 1970 in response to public debate about race.[140]

Less press support was available for those on the left who deviated from the political consensus. Thus the Campaign for Nuclear Disarmament (CND), formed in 1957, challenged the political consensus in favour of mutual nuclear deterrence in the Cold War. Such was CND's initial success among left activists and young people that unilateral nuclear disarmament was endorsed in 1960 by the Labour Party's annual conference, though not by its parliamentary leadership who got the decision reversed in the following year. Unilateralism found no friend in Fleet Street,[141] with one short-lived exception. In 1958 the *Daily Herald* published an enthusiastic editorial supporting unilateralism under the headline 'A Policy for Staying Alive'.[142] The paper was then brought to heel by its board of directors.[143]

However, Suez, CND and migration were exceptional flashpoints. In general, the press tended to reproduce a narrow arc of opinion represented by the modest differences between the Labour and the Conservative parties. This adherence to an Establishment consensus is perhaps best illustrated by the 1975 Referendum on the European Economic Community (then called colloquially the Common Market). The leadership of all the political parties, most business leaders, most union leaders, and most people in the professions, were in favour of staying. The press reflected this Establishment view: *every* national daily and Sunday newspaper backed the stay-in Europe position.

Yet, there were large numbers of people who held a different view. Those favouring leaving the Common Market were the plurality (41 per cent) in a January 1975 Gallup poll, and a still substantial 33 per cent in the actual 1975 Referendum vote itself.[144] Their voice was only heard in a muted form in the press. Only 15 per cent of popular newspaper coverage of the Referendum was hostile to continued Common Market membership.[145] The press megaphone belonged to the liberal corporatist Establishment.

Press support for the post-war consensus during the 1950s and 1960s reflected not just the views of press controllers but also of the journalists they employed. In the case of Labour quality and popular papers, all on the centre-left, only 2 per cent said that they were 'well to the left' of their papers in 1968. Similarly, a mere 4 per cent of specialist correspondents working for Conservative quality papers, and 11 per cent of specialists working for Conservative popular papers, said that they were to the right of their papers.[146] The politically centrist orientation of journalists was reinforced by the conventions and routines of newsgathering, which gave leading institutions privileged access to the media.[147]

Selling gossip and malice

But while the press was part of the liberal corporatist Establishment, it became in the 1960s a less restrained member of it. During the previous decade, the press had been willing, at times, to withhold information that powerful people wanted buried. Thus, in June 1953, the Prime Minister, Winston Churchill, had a massive stroke that caused his speech to become slurred and his walking to become unsteady. Churchill's entourage kept this secret, and issued a misleading press release which stated that: 'The Prime Minister has had no respite for a long time from his arduous duties and is need of a complete rest. We have therefore advised him to .... lighten his duties for at least a month'.[148] Churchill's close proprietor friends – Lords Beaverbrook, Bracken and Camrose – were in on the secret, and helped to suppress news about the true state of Churchill's health.[149] In the event, Churchill recovered sufficiently to chair a cabinet meeting in August 1953. But he never regained his old vigour and resigned in January 1955.

This cover-up was an extreme case arising in part from deep friendship between old colleagues. But it was indicative nonetheless of the press's willingness to withhold sensitive information about members of the Establishment. Thus, the wife of the Prime Minister, Harold Macmillan, had a longstanding love affair with the Conservative politician, Robert Boothby, while the leader of the Labour Opposition, Hugh Gaitskell, had a fling with Ann Fleming, wife of the novelist, Ian Fleming. Not a word of this was reported, even though it was widely known in the Westminster–Fleet Street village at the time.

This discretion gave way to a more inquisitorial approach during the 1960s, partly in response to pressure to arrest falling sales. Popular newspapers had allocated in the late 1950s more space to celebrity scandal, and political scandal was merely an extension of this development.[150] The shift was also a response to the decline of social deference during the war and post-war period.[151] Editor Hugh Cudlipp's disdain for the 'odious *obligato* of . . . snobbish flattery' and 'forelocking adulation' surrounding the monarchy[152] reflected the more irreverent attitude that had developed among some journalists towards authority. The press had reported fully the romance between Princess Margaret and divorced Group Captain Townsend in 1953, in contrast to its reticence about the romance between King Edward and divorcee Wallis Simpson in 1936. The more iconoclastic mood of the time found expression in *That Was the Week That Was,* a ground-breaking, political satire show which openly mocked the nation's rulers, first broadcast by BBC television in 1962.

In the same year, 1962, the press broke with post-war convention by investigating the private life of a government minister. The catalyst was twofold: a moral panic about homosexuality, and the intensification of the Cold War (due to the Cuban missile crisis in October 1962). This gave rise to the popular press's McCarthy-style witch-hunt of Thomas Galbraith, a junior minister in the government. He had, it was suggested, an 'improper' relationship with John Vassall, a gay junior civil servant who had been blackmailed into spying for the Soviet Union. Galbraith even had some responsibility, some newspapers implied, in making possible Vassall's traitorous activities and delaying his detection as a spy.

Galbraith resigned, and a formidable judge, Lord Radcliffe, was appointed to investigate the Vassall affair. During the tribunal's proceedings, top journalists were subjected to bruising cross-examination, and humiliated. The Radcliffe Report concluded that Thomas Galbraith had not been on holiday, as newspapers alleged, with the spy John Vassall; Galbraith had never invited Vassall to be a weekend guest at his country home; his dealings with Vassall had been entirely formal; and he had not connived in any way in Vassall's treachery.[153] The Report showed that manifest errors, once printed, had been uncritically repeated in the press. It was sharply critical of numerous papers but especially scathing about the *Daily Mail*.[154]

The *Daily Mail*'s sheepish response was that it had been 'wrong on detail' but 'not in instinct'.[155] Galbraith was exonerated and subsequently promoted to a more senior position. This public drubbing of the press by the Establishment was followed by short jail sentences for two journalists who refused to name their sources about Galbraith's alleged impropriety (because, it was suggested by some cynical colleagues, these sources did not exist).

Journalists blamed the Conservative government, led by Harold Macmillan, for their humiliation. In 1963, they got their revenge when it became known that the married War Minister, John Profumo, was having an affair with a young model, Christine Keeler. Newspapers portrayed this as both a moral issue since people 'of high breeding and grave responsibilities' should set an example[156] and also as a security issue since Christine Keeler, it emerged, had also had a sexual relationship with Yevgeny Ivanov, the naval attaché in the Soviet embassy. In addition, she was a close friend of Stephen Ward, an osteopath who, it was suggested, procured call girls for high society.

The press campaign resulted in the resignation of John Profumo, and the suicide of Stephen Ward. In retrospect, the national security dimension of press revelations was probably overblown since Keeler was *not* simultaneously having an affair with both Profumo and Ivanov. Stephen Ward was almost certainly not a pimp who received money for prostitution: merely a vulnerable man, driven to despair by press attacks and a public prosecution.[157]

This marked a resumption of the press's traditional role as a guardian scrutinising the morals of the governing class (as it had in late Victorian Britain). But now newspapers would not be content to rely on court cases but would undertake their own investigations. The press's next two scalps were Lord Lambton and Earl Jellicoe, who resigned as government ministers in 1973 after it was revealed that they had sex with prostitutes. No newspaper mentioned that the editor of the *News of the World*, Stafford Somerfield, also paid for sex, something that he openly talked about with his journalist colleagues.[158] The press window on the world was to be strictly one-way.

Breakdown of liberal corporatism

If the press was more iconoclastic in the 1960s, it played a prominent role in undermining liberal corporatism in the 1970s. This development needs to be briefly contextualized. Conciliation, the basis of corporatist governance, gave way to confrontation. The Conservative government introduced in 1971 new legislation curbing the power of trade unions. Seeking to break a long-running miners' strike, it called an election in February 1974 and was defeated.

Meanwhile, the post-war boom had come to an end in 1973, partly in response to the tripling of oil prices. This was followed by a period of economic turmoil in which inflation, the budget deficit and unemployment all increased. The Labour government, elected in 1974, imposed a prices and incomes policy that led to wage reductions in 1975–78 greater than at any time during the post-war period.[159] It lost the 1979 general election, leading to a new era dominated by a neo-liberal Conservative government led by Margaret Thatcher.

In this period of transition, the press functioned as a battering ram knocking down the decaying walls of liberal corporatism. This took the form partly of virulent anti-union reporting. Thus, in 1976, coverage of industrial relations tended to focus on strikes. These were reported overwhelmingly in terms of their harmful consequences rather than in terms of their causes. The three most frequent themes in reporting of industrial conflict were loss of output, loss of work by workers not involved in the dispute, and danger or inconvenience to the public.[160] In other words, the dominant news frame portrayed workers in industrial disputes as acting against the interests of the economy, other workers and the public. Unreasonable behaviour by employers rarely featured in press reports.[161] More generally, eight case studies revealed that points less favourable to trade unions were more often reported than those which were more favourable.[162] Perhaps the most striking revelation of this research (commissioned by the third Royal Commission on the Press) was that anti-union reporting extended across the entire national daily press (with the partial exception of the *Guardian*). The *Daily Mirror* emerged as being more hostile to trade unions in 1976 than the *Daily Express*.[163]

The press onslaught on trade unions was combined with a campaign against aspects of the welfare state. Reporting of social services in the mid-1970s tended to focus on benefit fraud. This centred on four themes. 'Scroungers', too idle to work, were abusing the system; they were living in luxury supported by the taxpayer; the poor were being turned into welfare junkies; and an over-generous welfare system was vulnerable to fraud.[164] These themes were illustrated by accounts of individual super scroungers, reported with a rich seasoning of indignation. 'PARASITES', screamed the *News of the World*, with the strapline 'The Scrounging Kinches cost you £500-a-week'.[165] The monstering of individual scroungers was accompanied by angry calls for action. 'GET THE SCROUNGERS' demanded the *Daily Express* in a front-page headline in huge capital letters.[166] These jeremiads were accompanied by sweeping indictments of the benefit system. 'Britain's welfare system is in chaos. It is too big .... ', thundered a *Daily Mirror* editorial.[167] Having a system 'in which it pays not to work' must be wrong, mused the *Daily Express*.[168] A 'Land Fit for Scroungers', warned the *Daily Telegraph*, encourages idleness and fraud, and damages the national character.[169]

What was striking in this coverage was the absence or weakness of the liberal voice. The fact that unclaimed benefits greatly exceeded benefit fraud or that tax evasion was a much more serious financial problem than social security abuse was little reported. The positive case for the benefit system was generally left unstated. Instead a campaign that drew on an age-old distinction between the deserving and undeserving poor (embedded in popular culture since at least the sixteenth century) and that tapped into growing resentment during the recession contributed to an erosion of welfare communality during the 1970s.[170]

Scroungers were only one of a number of public enemies identified by the press. In 1972, popular newspapers reported that a new wave of crime – mugging – was rising at an unprecedented rate. In fact the crime was not new, merely given a new label; and the incidence of mugging in 1972 was no greater than it had been in 1955–65.[171] Hall and his associates showed that by giving disproportionate attention to mugging, and associating it with black criminality, the popular press fuelled demands for a more authoritarian, law-and-order politics. Part of the potency of this press campaign, they argued, stemmed from the way it connected to pre-existing resentments arising from generational change, national decline and a sense of a loss of community. Anger was displaced on to an outsider group, giving it a greater impetus.

Black muggers and union militants were joined by other public enemies identified by newspapers as a threat to society. Moral panics were generated around youth gangs,[172] drug addicts,[173] football hooligans,[174] radical students[175] and other out groups.[176] In this way, an incremental impression was conveyed that Britain was gripped by a deep-seated malaise that was getting worse, and required a new kind of politics to cure.

These cumulative images of dysfunction and disorder were crystallized, and given a dramatic focus, in press reporting of the 'Winter of Discontent' in 1978–79.[177] A succession of mostly local disputes, generally involving low paid, public sector workers, was narrated increasingly by the press as a single coherent story. Its central themes were that union militants were holding society to ransom; strikes were the main cause of the country's economic crisis; the country was becoming ungovernable; the state was unable to cope because it was both over-extended and weak; and this inability was personified by the complacency of Prime Minister Jim Callaghan ('Inaction Man' as the *Daily Express* called him).[178] In the view of most newspapers, a new approach was needed: the tough, resolute, principled politics of Margaret Thatcher.

Thus, an industrial dispute in Liverpool involving gravediggers was reported by the *Daily Mail* as 'THEY WON'T EVEN LET US BURY OUR DEAD'.[179] Another dispute was reported by the same paper the next day as 'TARGET FOR TODAY – SICK CHILDREN', as if trade unions were fighting a national war against the public.[180] Other papers joined the hue and cry. 'STRIKE THREAT TO BONE BOY', proclaimed the *Daily Mirror*.[181] The main body of the article told a more complicated story than the one signalled in the headline. 'Anthony' turned out to be a patient at Westminster Children's Hospital, where there was no industrial dispute. But his plight was a national story because it was 'expected' that a strike would spread to his hospital from neighbouring Westminster Hospital where cleaners and porters were on strike. This extrapolation was indicative of how a preconceived narrative was in place, and was being imposed – and stretched – to explain what was happening.

Disputes that were mostly localized were portrayed as a national crisis. This was conveyed through headlines and captions such as 'Shutdown Britain', 'Britain Under Siege' and 'Crisis Britain'.[182] The government was then accused of failing to overcome this crisis through dithering and incompetence. 'WHAT THE BLOODY HELL'S GOING ON JIM?', demanded the *Sun* of the Prime Minister Jim Callaghan.[183] His alleged complacency was symbolized by the remark 'Crisis, what crisis?' which the *Sun* reported him as making shortly after his return to Britain after he had been 'sunning himself in the tropics'.[184] In fact, Callaghan had not been on holiday but attending an international summit meeting. He did not in fact make the comment attributed to him.[185] It was an ironic comment made in a *Daily Mail* feature article published a week before,[186] and cynically recycled by the *Sun* as a genuine quote.

The Winter of Discontent came to symbolize the bankruptcy of the old politics, and references to it appeared regularly in the press for over a decade. 'Crisis, what crisis?' became an iconic quotation signifying the need for a different approach: politics based on conviction rather than conciliation that would regenerate Britain. In 1979, a Conservative government under Margaret Thatcher swept to power.

In terms of its share of national daily circulation, the press was more lopsidedly Conservative in the 1979 general election than at any time since 1935.[187] This reversed the trend between 1945 and 1970, when the circulation gap between the Labour and Conservative press had tended to diminish.[188] The press was also more intensely partisan compared to recent general elections.[189] In the event, the historic Conservative victory in 1979 came about not because of a collapse of the Labour vote (which declined by only two percentage points) but because a large number of Liberal supporters defected to the Conservatives.[190] It marked the beginning of a new era in which Britain was to be remade.

Notes

1   S. Koss, *The Rise and Fall of the Political Press in Britain*, vol. 2 (London, Hamish Hamilton, 1984), p. 642; cf. S. Koss, *The Rise and Fall of the Political Press in Britain*, vol. 1 (London, Hamish Hamilton, 1981), p. 13.

2   Koss, *Rise and Fall*, vol. 1, p. 4.

3   Koss, *Rise and Fall*, vol. 2, pp. 667 and 674.

4   Koss, *Rise and Fall*, vol. 2, p. 658.

5   Ibid., p. 659.

6   C. Wintour, *Pressures on the Press* (London, Deutsch, 1972), p. 189.

7   J. Whale, *The Politics of the Media* (Glasgow, Fontana, 1977), p. 73

8   Whale, *Politics of Media*, p. 85.

9   R. Greenslade, *Press Gang* (London, Macmillan, 2003), p. 47.

10   *Report of Royal Commission on the Press 1947–9* (London, HMSO, 1949, Cmd. 7700), p. 48.

11   A. Christiansen, *Headlines All My Life* (London, Heinemann, 1961); P. Wintour, *Pressures on the Press* (London, Deutsch, 1972); R. Edwards, *Goodbye Fleet Street* (London, Cape, 1988).

12   Christiansen, *Headlines*, p. 144.

13   H. Hobson, P. Knightley and L. Russell, *The Pearl of Days* (London, Hamish Hamilton, 1972), pp. 247–49.

14   D. Ayerst, Guardian (London, Collins, 1971); *The History of The Times, 1939–1966*, vol. 5 (London, Times Books, 1984).

15   H. Evans, *Good Times, Bad Times* (London, Weidenfeld & Nicolson, 1983), p. 6.

16   H. Cudlipp, *Walking on the Water* (London, Bodley Head, 1976), pp. 348 ff.

17   J. Tunstall, '"Editorial sovereignty" in the British press: its past and present', *Studies on the Press*, Royal Commission on the Press Working Paper 3 (London, HMSO, 1977), p. 306.

18   Peregrine Worsthorne cited in Greenslade, *Press Gang*, p. 409.

19 *Survey of the National Newspaper Industry* (London, Economist Intelligence Unit, 1966), p. 52.
20 S. Somerfield, *Banner Headlines* (Shoreham, Scan, 1979).
21 C. Bainbridge and R. Stockdill, *The* News of the World *Story* (London, Harper Collins, 1993), p. 231.
22 L. Lamb, *Sunrise* (London, Papermac, 1989), pp. 160 ff.
23 See pp. 120–123.
24 Greenslade, *Press Gang*, p. 254.
25 S. Jenkins, *Newspapers* (London, Faber and Faber, 1979), p. 101.
26 J. Curran and J. Seaton, *Power Without Responsibility*, 1st edition (London, Fontana, 1981), Table 1, pp. 104–5.
27 *Royal Commission on the Press Final Report* (London, HMSO, 1977, Cmnd. 6810), p. 149.
28 G. Murdock, 'Class, power and the press: problems of conceptualisation and evidence', in H. Christian (ed.), *The Sociology of Journalism and the Press*, Sociological Review Monograph 29 (Keele, University of Keele, 1981), Table 3, p. 52.
29 Koss, *Rise and Fall*, vols. 1 and 2.
30 W. Reddaway, 'The economics of newspapers', *Economic Journal* (73), 1963; *RCP* 1962, pp. 65 ff.
31 Whale, *Politics of Media*, p. 93.
32 Notley Advertising Ltd., *Royal Commission on the Press: Documentary Evidence*, vol. 5 (London, HMSO, 1962), Cmnd. 1812–818, p. 100.
33 Central News Ltd., ibid., p. 15.
34 Service Advertising Ltd., ibid., p. 113.
35 Hobson Bates and Partners Ltd., ibid., p. 45; cf. Hirst Ltd., ibid., p. 41.
36 Cited in R. McKay and B. Barr, *The Story of the* Scottish Daily News (Edinburgh, Canongate, 1976), p. 108.
37 Benson Ltd., RCP 1962, vol. 5, p. 10.
38 Samson Jackson and Co. Ltd, evidence to the *Royal Commission on the Press, 1947–9, Memoranda of Evidence*, vol. 5 (London, HMSO, 1949); cf. Pritchard Wood and Partners Ltd., ibid., 1949.
39 Young and Rubicam Ltd., *RCP* 1962, vol. 5, p. 136.
40 J. Hobson, *The Selection of Advertising Media* (London, Business Publications, 1959), pp. 20–31; cf. Hobson, op. cit., revised edition, 1968, pp. 10–22.
41 J. Adams, *Media Planning* (London, Business Books, 1971), p. 69.
42 J. Curran, *Media and Democracy* (London, Routledge, 2010), pp. 160 ff.
43 W. Belson, *The British Press*, Part 3 (London, London Press Exchange, 1959), Tables 1 and 2, pp. 12–15.
44 J. Curran, 'The impact of television on the audience for national newspapers, 1945–68' in J. Tunstall (ed.) *Media Sociology* (London, Constable, 1970).
45 In the late 1960s, over 80 per cent still read a national daily newspaper (Curran, 'Impact of television', Table 10, p. 128). The downturn in 1968 is unintentionally concealed in this table by the construction of moving averages to compensate for a change of survey methodology in 1968. In fact, subsequent Joint Industry Committee for National Readership Surveys (JICNARS) revealed that the dip in readership registered in 1968 was the beginning of a sustained decline.
46 Curran, 'The impact of television'.

47 J. Curran, 'The impact of advertising on the British mass media', *Media, Culture and Society*, 1981 (3), pp. 47–50.

48 Ibid., Table 4, p. 50. For an analysis of managerial incompetence, see G. Cleverley, *The Fleet Street Disaster* (London, Constable, 1976).

49 Advertising distribution in the 1940s was distorted by the generous newsprint allocation deal secured by the quality press. See J. Gerald, *The British Press Under Economic Controls* (Minneapolis, University of Minnesota Press, 1956).

50 *National Readership Surveys* [NRS] (London, Institute of Practitioners in Advertising), January–December 1960, July 1963–June 1964, January–December 1966.

51 The *Sunday Citizen* was a quality newspaper in terms of its balance of content (and was classified as such in *RCP 1974–9 Final Report*, p. 272). It just lacked a 'quality' readership.

52 Sir D. Hamilton, *Who is to Own the British Press?* (Haldane Memorial Lecture) (London, Birkbeck College, 1976), p. 7.

53 D. Butler and G. Butler, *Twentieth Century British Political Facts, 1900–2000*, 8th edition (Basingstoke, Macmillan, 2000), p. 536.

54 Interview with William McLelland (a veteran of the 1950s Odhams research department, and subsequently its Head) in 1977.

55 '*Daily Herald* Reader Interest Recommendations', Research Department, Odhams, 9 May 1955, p. 8.

56 Cited in Greenslade, *Press Gang*, p. 154.

57 NRS, July 1963–June 1964, Table 18A.

58 Derived from Odhams Research Department records. Its estimates for advertising excluded classified advertisements.

59 'Attitudes to Newspapers and Newspaper Reading', Research Department, International Publishing Corporation, 1964, p. iii.

60 M. Abrams, *The Newspaper Reading Public of Tomorrow* (London, Odhams Press, 1964).

61 Cited in H. Richards, *Bloody Circus* (London, Pluto, 1997), p. 178.

62 'National Daily Newspaper Studies (2): Preliminary Report', Research Department, International Publishing Corporation (IPC), 1964.

63 Cudlipp, *Walking*, p. 251. IPC was the group owning both the *Daily Mirror* and *Daily Herald/Sun*.

64 'Report of an Investigation into the Transition from the *Daily Herald* to the *Sun*', Research Department, IPC, January 1968.

65 *National Newspaper Industry*, Part 1, p. 58.

66 'Report on a Survey to Study Attitudes to Daily Newspapers', Research Department, Odhams, July 1958.

67 A. C. H. Smith, *Paper Voices* (London, Chatto & Windus, 1975), pp. 161 ff.

68 C. King, *The Future of the Press* (London, MacGibbon and Kee, 1967), p. 88.

69 Cudlipp, *Walking*, pp. 324 ff.

70 C. King, *Without Fear or Favour* (London, Sidgwick & Jackson, 1971), p. 40.

71 J. Thomas, *Popular Newspapers, the Labour Party and British Politics* (Abingdon, Routledge, 2005), p. 36.

72 *Daily Mirror*, 14 July 1984.

73 'Feature readership in national dailies', Odhams Research Department, 1964. The results of this survey are summarized in table form in J. Curran, A. Douglas and G. Whannel, 'The political economy of the human-interest story' in A. Smith (ed.)

Newspapers and Democracy (Cambridge, Mass., MIT Press, 1980), Appendix, Table 13.9.

74 The sample was based on twelve issues of national dailies per title, and six issues per title in the case of Sunday papers, selected to be representative of the calendar year, with papers published on different days of the week, and different weeks of the month. A code-recode analysis revealed 83.5 per cent agreement.

75 However, there was a reduction in absolute terms in the case of some papers.

76 Cited in Greenslade, *Press Gang*, p. 26.

77 *Sunday Pictorial*, 19 January 1958.

78 The journalist, who wrote this story, was privately un-shocked since the 'boy scout' was aged 17. See H. Procter, *The Street of Disillusion* (Brighton, Revel Barker, 2010 [1958]), p. 202.

79 *People*, 18 October 1959 [continuing through to November].

80 *News of the World*, 31 January 1960.

81 A. Bingham, *Family Newspapers?* (Oxford, Oxford University Press, 2009).

82 See p. 61.

83 S. Taylor, *Shock! Horror!* (London, Bantam, 1991), pp. 29 ff.

84 P. Holland, 'The page three girl speaks to women, too: a sun-sational survey', *Screen*, 24 (3), pp. 84–102.

85 J. Tunstall, *Newspaper Power* (Oxford, Clarendon Press, 1996), p. 139.

86 R. Smith, 'Sex and occupational role on Fleet Street' in D. Barker and S. Allen (eds.) *Dependence and Exploitation in Work and Marriage* (London, Longman, 1976).

87 'Feature readership in national Sunday papers', Research Department, International Publishing Corporation (IPC), 1968.

88 Sunday Times Marketing Research, 1969–1971, based on a sample of 13 issues of the *Sunday Times*, *Observer* and *Sunday Telegraph*.

89 'Feature readership in national Sunday papers', Research Department, International Publishing Corporation (IPC), 1968.

90 This estimate is based on the average for quality daily and Sunday papers, for 1960–75, as reported in *Royal Commission on the Press Interim Report: The National Newspaper Industry* (London, HMSO, 1976, Cmnd. 6433), Table 2.9, p. 99.

91 Ibid., Table 2.9, p. 99.

92 F. Hirsch and D. Gordon, *Newspaper Money* (London, Hutchinson, 1975), pp. 78–80.

93 M. Mander, 'The integration of advertising and circulation sales policies' in H. Henry (ed.) *Behind the Headlines* (London, Associated Press, 1971), p. 75. This first-hand account corroborates Hirsch and Gordon's case study.

94 Derived from *Royal Commission on the Press Interim Report*, Table E.1, p. 92.

95 J. Curran, 'Advertising and the press' in J. Curran (ed.) *The British Press* (Basingstoke, Macmillan, 1978), Table 11.1, p. 234.

96 Curran, 'Advertising', Table 11.2, pp. 236–37.

97 E. Carter, *Tongue in Chic* (London, Michael Joseph, 1973).

98 Curran, 'Advertising', Table 11.1, p. 234.

99 I. Breach, 'Gentlemen of the road', *Sunday Times* colour magazine cited in Curran, 'Impact of advertising', p. 65.

100 Journalists' hostility to advertising influence is documented in J. Tunstall, *Journalists at Work* (London, Constable, 1971).

101 Curran, 'Advertising', Tables 11.3 and 11.4, pp. 242–43.

102 This is based on the assumption that journalistic partisanship is a bad thing. For an alternative view which argues that different kinds of journalism – including partisan journalism – make different inputs to the functioning of democracy, see J. Curran, *Media and Power* (London, Routledge, 2002), Chapter 8.

103 See footnote 5.

104 Butler and Butler, *Twentieth Century*, p. 536.

105 This comes through in Arnold Wesker's hostile ethnography of the *Sunday Times* (which is primarily objecting to the inherent limitations of journalism): A. Wesker, *The Journalists* (London, Cape, 1979), pp. 192–288. See also H. Hobson, P. Knightley and L. Russell, *The Pearl of Days* (London, Hamish Hamilton, 1972) and H. Evans, *Good Times, Bad Times* (London, Weidenfeld & Nicolson, 1983).

106 The campaign is documented in Evans, *Good Times*, pp. 58–79; Greenslade, *Press Gang*, pp. 275–78; and Sunday Times Insight Team, *Suffer the Children* (London, Deutsch, 1975).

107 Hobson, Knightley and Russell, *Pearl*, pp. 384 ff.

108 *Sunday Times*, 17 September 1971; 28 November 1971, *et passim*; Sunday Times Insight Team, *Ulster* (Harmondsworth, Penguin, 1972), pp. 291–97.

109 *Sunday Times*, 24 September 1972.

110 Harold Evans went on to have a leading role in American journalism.

111 Chapter 8, p. 120–123.

112 Bingham, *Family Newspapers?*; J. Bengry, 'Profit (f)or the public good? Sensationalism, homosexuality, and the postwar popular press', *Media History*, 20 (2), 2014, pp. 146–66.

113 *Sunday Pictorial*, 11 May 1952; *Sunday Pictorial*, 18 May 1952; *Sunday Pictorial*, 25 May 1952.

114 *Sunday Pictorial*, 25 May 1952.

115 *News of the World*, 1 November 1953.

116 *Sunday Express*, 25 October 1953.

117 *Daily Mirror*, 6 November 1953.

118 *Sunday Pictorial*, 25 September 1955.

119 *Sunday Mirror*, 28 April 1963.

120 *Daily Mirror*, 26 September 1956.

121 In 1987, during the AIDS panic, the *Sun* even offered gay men a one-way ticket to Norway, under the headline 'Fly Away Gays – and We Will Pay!', as an inducement to leave the country (cited in S. Watney, *Policing Desire* (London, Commedia, 1987), p. 147). The press hate campaign can be tracked through a good historical collection of newspaper cuttings in the Lesbian and Gay Newsmedia Archive at Bishopsgate Institute, London, also with an online index (www.lagna.org.uk/archive/cuttings).

122 Proctor, *Street*, p. 63.

123 Ibid., p. 202.

124 Ibid., p. 143. Proctor's confessional memoir caused him to be ostracized by many of his colleagues, and he died destitute in a Dagenham council estate.

125 Greenslade, *Press Gang*, pp. 435 ff.; Bingham, *Family Newspapers?* pp. 152–54.

126 E. Behr, *Anyone Here Been Raped and Speak English?* (London, New English Library, 1982), p. 136. The person quoted was a TV journalist.

127 See Chapter 10.

128 Cited in R. Toye, 'Winston Churchill's "crazy broadcast": party, nation and the 1945 Gestapo speech', *Journal of British Studies*, 49 (July 2010), p. 655.

129 J. Dean, *Hatred, Ridicule and Contempt* (Penguin, Harmondsworth, 1964).

130 C. Seymour-Ure, *The Political Impact of Mass Media* (Constable, London, 1974), p. 232.

131 A. Christiansen, *Headlines*, p. 240.

132 K. Middlemas, *Politics in Industrial Society* (London, Deutsch, 1979); L. Panitch, *Social Democracy and Industrial Militancy* (Cambridge, Cambridge University Press, 1976); P. Hennessy, *Having it So Good* (London, Penguin, 2007); J. Curran and C. Leys, 'Media and the decline of liberal corporatism in Britain' in J. Curran and M.-Y. Park (eds.) *De-Westernising Media Studies* (London, Routledge, 2000), among others.

133 Thomas, *Popular Newspapers*, pp. 48 ff.; Seymour-Ure, *Political Impact*, 1974, pp. 238 ff.

134 B. Pimlott, 'The myth of consensus' in L. Smith (ed.) *The Making of Britain* (Basingstoke, Macmillan, 1988) points, in a celebrated essay, to multiple policy differences.

135 G. Parmentier, 'The British press in the Suez crisis', *Historical Journal*, 23 (2), 1980, pp. 435–48.

136 Seymour-Ure, *Political Impact*, p. 105.

137 *Sunday Times*, 21 April 1968.

138 *Daily Telegraph*, 22 April 1968; *Daily Express*, 22 April 1968.

139 *News of the World*, 21 April 1968.

140 Seymour-Ure, *Political Impact*, Table 4.4, p. 124.

141 References to 'Fleet Street' or the 'national press' in this chapter, and hereafter, exclude the *Daily Worker* (renamed *Morning Star* in 1966) which accounted for around 0.5 per cent of national daily circulation during this period.

142 *Daily Herald*, 26 February 1958 cited in H. Richards, *The Bloody Circus* (London, Pluto, 1997), p. 172.

143 Richards, *Bloody Circus*, p. 174.

144 D. Butler and U. Kitzinger, *The 1975 Referendum* (London, Macmillan, 1975).

145 Derived from D. McQuail, *Analysis of Newspaper Content* (London, HMSO, 1977), Royal Commission on the Press Research Series 4, Appendix A 16, Table 1, p. 320.

146 Tunstall, *Journalists*, Table 4.1, p. 122.

147 J. Halloran, P. Elliott and G. Murdock, *Demonstrations and Communication* (Harmondsworth, Penguin, 1970); J. Tunstall, *The Westminster Lobby Correspondents* (London, Routledge, 1970); P. Golding and S. Middleton, *Images of Welfare* (Oxford, Oxford University Press, 1982).

148 L. Moran, *Winston Churchill* (London, Sphere Books, 1968), p. 434.

149 A. Chisholm and M. Davie, *Beaverbrook* (London, Hutchinson, 1992), p. 477. In due course, information about Churchill's health crisis leaked out. The *Daily Mirror* first got wind of it through the American press.

150 Bingham, *Family Newspapers?*; A. Bingham and M. Conboy, *Tabloid Century* (Oxford, Lang, 2015).

151 R. McKibbin, *Classes and Cultures* (Oxford, Oxford University Press, 1998).

152 H. Cudlipp, *At Your Peril* (London, Weidenfeld & Nicolson, 1962), p. 82.

153 *Report of the Tribunal Appointed to Inquire into the Vassall Case and Related Matters* (London, HMSO, 1963), pp. 64–77.

154 Ibid., pp. 67 ff.
155 *Daily Mail,* 26 April 1963, cited in Bingham, *Family Newspapers?*, p. 187.
156 *Daily Express*, 13 June 1963.
157 R. Davenport-Hines, *An English Affair* (London, Collins, 2013).
158 R. Greenslade, *Press Gang* (London, Macmillan, 2003), p. 129.
159 K. Middlemas, *Power, Competition and the State (vol. 3): The End of the Post-War Era: Britain Since 1974* (Basingstoke, Macmillan, 1991).
160 D. McQuail, *Analysis of Newspaper Content* (London, HMSO, 1977), Royal Commission on the Press Research Series 4, Table B14, p. 125.
161 McQuail, *Analysis*, Table B15, p. 127.
162 McQuail, *Analysis*, Table C33, p. 149–214.
163 Ibid., *Analysis*, Table B15, p. 127.
164 P. Golding and S. Middleton, *Images of Welfare* (Oxford, Martin Robertson, 1982).
165 *News of the World*, 17 October 1976.
166 *Daily Express*, 15 July 1976.
167 *Daily Mirror*, 16 September 1976.
168 *Daily Express*, 13 March 1978.
169 *Daily Telegraph*, 29 July 1976.
170 Golding and Middleton, *Images*.
171 S. Hall, C. Critcher, T. Jefferson, J. Clarke and B. Roberts, *Policing the Crisis* (Basingstoke, Macmillan, 1978), pp. 10–11.
172 S. Cohen, *Folk Devils and Moral Panics*, 2nd edition (Oxford, Martin Robertson, 1980).
173 J. Young, 'Mass media: drugs and deviance' in P. Rock and M. McIntosh (eds.) *Deviance and Social Control* (London, Tavistock, 1973).
174 G. Whannel, 'Football, crowd behaviour and the press', *Media, Culture and Society*, 1 (4), 1979.
175 S. Hall, 'Deviancy, politics and the media' in Rock and McIntosh (eds.) *Deviance*.
176 S. Cohen and J. Young (eds.) *Manufacture of News*, 2nd edition (London, Constable, 1981).
177 C. Hay, 'Narrating crisis: the discursive construction of the "winter of discontent"', *Sociology*, 30 (20), 1996.
178 *Daily Express*, 11 January 1979.
179 *Daily Mail*, 1 February 1979.
180 *Daily Mail*, 2 February 1979.
181 *Daily Mirror*, 30 January 1979.
182 *Daily Mail*, 13 January 1979, *et passim*.
183 *Sun*, 5 February 1979.
184 *Sun*, 13 January 1979.
185 What Callaghan actually said was: 'I don't think other people in the world would share the view [that] there is mounting chaos', BBC News/Politics, 12 September 2000. Available at: http://news.bbc.co.uk/1/hi/uk_politics/921524.stm (accessed 29 March 2016).
186 *Daily Mail*, 8 January 1979.
187 Thomas, *Popular Newspapers*, Table 1.1, p. 34.

188 D. Butler and G. Butler, *British Twentieth-Century Political Facts 1900–2000,* 8th edition (Basingstoke, Macmillan, 2000), p. 537.

189 Partisanship intensified in press reporting of the two 1974 general elections, but became still more pronounced in 1979. This became the new default position of the press: in effect a reversion to the past after a post-war interlude.

190 Butler and Butler, *Twentieth Century*, p. 238.

Chapter 8

Press and the remaking of Britain

The Conservative government elected in 1979 established a new political consensus based on the belief that the free market is more efficient and responsive than the public sector. This led to the privatization of major public enterprises like British Petroleum (1979), British Airways (1987) and British Steel (1988), of public utilities including telecommunications (1984), gas (1986), water (1989) and electricity (1990), and of leading public institutions like British Rail (1994) and the Royal Mail (2014).[1] It also gave rise to the outsourcing of public services to external contractors. This developed in earnest with local government services in the 1990s, and was extended to education and health in the 2000s. External contracting was greatly expanded in the 2010s to include more schools, a larger section of the National Health Service (NHS) and areas like probation and police support services.

The new consensus also held that government should not cramp market creativity. Keynesian interventionist policies, designed to sustain full employment, gave way to a stress on non-intervention, based on the view that the market should be free to generate wealth. This resulted in the ending of controls on capital movements out of Britain in 1979; the deregulation of banks in 1986; the easing of restrictions on foreign ownership in the 1990s; and the devolving of government powers over monetary policy to the Bank of England in 1998. Despite the 2007–08 financial meltdown, the structure and culture of the banking system remained relatively unchanged.

But if government was more passive in relation to the market, it also became more authoritarian. Changes in penal policy resulted in longer sentences, and more people being jailed.[2] The Thatcher government also weakened trade unions through incremental legislation, notably by outlawing negotiated agreements to hire union-only workers ('closed shop') and by banning strikes in support of other workers or a general cause ('secondary action'). These changes were never reversed.

The final part of the re-engineering of Britain was a change in its tax system designed to foster dynamic business leadership and foreign investment. The top rate of income tax was reduced, through successive cuts, from 83 per cent in 1979 to 45 per cent in 2013. Corporation tax decreased, while the burden of direct taxation (such as VAT) was increased. There was a sharp increase in inequality over the last forty years, with the rich getting richer and the poor getting poorer in relative terms. The wealthiest hundred people in Britain now have as much money as the poorest 18 million.[3]

This new approach was actively opposed during the 1980s, and was only accepted in Westminster when the Labour Party was rebranded as New Labour, under Tony Blair's leadership in 1994. In effect, the main opposition party concluded that it could only get elected if it accepted the terms of the social settlement established by Margaret Thatcher. However, this did not preclude continuing differences between the political parties, not least over the level of public spending.

Radical right-wing change was made easier by the evolution of a new way of governing Britain. The old regime of liberal corporatism – the inclusion and accommodation of organised interests within a conciliatory framework – gave way to a greater centralization of political power, a more politicized (and neutered) civil service, and a populist style of leadership relying heavily on public relations and media management.[4] The shift towards a neo-liberal settlement was also accompanied by greater social liberalism, especially under David Cameron. New legislation included the strengthening of anti-discrimination law (2010), gay civil partnership (2004) and same sex marriage (2013).

Despite the 2008 crash, the neo-liberal political consensus was only challenged belatedly from the margins. In 2015, the veteran left-wing backbencher, Jeremy Corbyn, was elected as Labour leader with strong support from young people who flocked to join the party. This insurgency was greeted with hostility by Corbyn's parliamentary colleagues, media incredulity and limited public support until the 2017 general election campaign.

What part did the press play in this remaking of Britain since 1979? One possible answer is that the press expressed the will of the British people in supporting the creation of a new social order. Another is that the press indoctrinated people into accepting the change. In fact, neither answer is correct. The truth is, as we shall see, a lot more complicated.

Centralization of press control

Proprietors strongly influenced the press in the post-1979 period. This claim goes against the grain of much academic thinking which sees an approach emphasizing ownership as part of a flawed media-centric view, a cliché of old fashioned leftism, which fails to grasp the way in which the media is shaped by external forces.[5] It is also runs counter to the thinking of some thoughtful journalists who see the shortcomings of the press as essentially a failure of journalistic professionalism, rooted in a surrender to the seduction of public relations.[6] So in advancing an unfashionable interpretation, let us begin with a case study of how press ownership mattered.

Fresh from imposing his authority on the *Sun* and *News of the World*, Rupert Murdoch acquired in 1981 *The Times* and *Sunday Times*. These were liberal Conservative papers, of an independent bent, which Murdoch wanted to make loyalist advocates of Thatcher's right-wing politics. However, he had given an undertaking not to interfere with their editorial content, as a condition of acquiring the two papers. This undertaking had been formally enshrined in articles of association and backed up by the appointment of independent directors. Murdoch thus found himself circumscribed by externally imposed constraints. In addition, journalists on both papers were used to having considerable autonomy, and had the confidence that came from being successful. They would not be easily cowed. Adding to Murdoch's difficulties, Margaret Thatcher's government was initially intensely unpopular, with the Conservative party even dropping to third place in the opinion polls during part of 1981–82.[7] Pushing Times Newspapers to the radical right meant going against the mood of the time.

Murdoch overcame all these obstacles with great finesse. He persuaded Harold Evans – the much loved editor of the *Sunday Times*, who would have been a formidable opponent of change – to accept the exciting challenge of editing *The Times*. Frank Giles, a malleable representative of the *Sunday Times*'s old regime, was installed as his replacement. Murdoch never issued a direct editorial instruction to Giles but made his views forcibly known. 'Murdoch, the paper spread out before him', Giles recollects, 'would jab his fingers at some article or contribution and snarl, "What do you want to print rubbish like that for?" or pointing to the by-line of a correspondent, assert that "that man's a Commie"'.[8] Further pressure was funnelled through Gerald Long, the new managing director appointed by Murdoch, prompting the editor to establish what he called the 'Long insult file'.[9] On one occasion, Murdoch fired mock pistol shots at his editor's back to signify to bystanders that Giles was on the way out.[10] Unable to bear constant humiliation any longer, Frank Giles retired early. A decent man, he left the *Sunday Times* both despised by his staff and scorned by his boss.

He was replaced by a new editor, Andrew Neil, who had previously worked for the Conservative Party and the *Economist*. Neil was more right-wing than Giles, and had the forceful personality needed to effect the political make-over Murdoch wanted. But to make sure, Murdoch bombarded the new editor with forcefully expressed views on current issues and politicians. 'Rupert expects his papers', Neil writes, 'to stand broadly for what he believes: a combination of right-wing republicanism from America mixed with undiluted Thatcherism from Britain'.[11] Neil also found himself anticipating what Murdoch might want. 'Rupert has an uncanny knack', he writes, 'of being there even when he is not. When I did not hear from him . . . he was still uppermost in my mind'.[12]

Neil replaced or intimidated section editors, in this way eroding the buffer that had previously insulated journalists from senior management pressure.

The new regime led, according to the paper's former literary editor, Claire Tomalin, to 'a reign of terror'. 'I was extremely aware' she remembers, 'of a great deal of misery and bullying'.[13] Her recollection of this period is echoed by other journalists. For example, Peter Wilby, the paper's former education correspondent, recalls: 'There was a tone of fear . . . a horrible, "totalitarian" atmosphere'.[14] 'A lot of people were being bullied', concurs Don Berry, the paper's former features editor. 'Life was deliberately made unpleasant for them in the hope that they would go'.[15]

What Neil called 'wet' or 'lefty' news stories were actively discouraged. Thus Donald Macintyre, the paper's labour correspondent, had a running battle over his reporting of the miners' strike (1984–85) in which he was regularly pressed by the editor to adopt a less critical attitude towards the National Coal Board and the government. Sometimes Macintyre felt that the editor's criticism was justified; sometimes he argued back; but at other times, he admitted, he censored himself 'to some extent'. The trouble with arguing back, Macintyre explained, is that it 'starts to become counter-productive and you get to the point where you either had to leave or you just become a sort of joke'.[16] Macintyre chose to leave.

At times the pressure on journalists was extremely abrasive. John Shirley (who described himself as 'right-wing Labour') was denounced by Neil as a 'Trotskyist' in a voice so loud that the newsroom fell into a shocked silence. Shirley was so outraged by the new regime at the *Sunday Times* that he refused to allow a copy of the paper – of which he was still chief reporter – to darken his home.[17] Joan Smith was also targeted when she complained about the way in which her report of the Greenham Common anti-nuclear protest had been altered. She was told by the news editor, Anthony Bambridge: 'The editor feels you have got in a rut on nuclear matters. He would like to see you broaden your range. He would like to see you in the paper more often'. Smith asked how often and was told every week, ideally. She then pointed out that she had had forty-six stories published in the past forty-four weeks. Bambridge replied, 'You are to be congratulated. I am having a terrible time. You are not the only one who is thinking of leaving'.[18] Two months later, Joan Smith left. Acrimonious encounters led to growing fear and insecurity in the office. 'It was like the Battle of the Somme', recalls Marjorie Wallace. 'You would come in on a Monday and find that another person had been taken out'.[19]

A further way in which the paper was propelled editorially to the right was through a cumulative process of attrition. This is graphically described by Isabel Hilton, the Latin American editor at the *Sunday Times*:

> What would happen is that you would write a story and it would disappear. The copy would vanish around the building and people would write little things into it and take out other things. It would eventually appear in a very truncated form with the emphases changed. It had all been done

at stages along the way. To try and make a fuss about this on a Saturday when everything was very busy was very difficult.

The accumulation of pressures led some journalists to internalize controls. 'The sense of intimidation', according to Hilton:

> was so strong that people actually started censoring themselves because it is very unpleasant to get into this kind of argument all the time. It is not just a collection of incidents; it's a collection of incidents *and* the atmosphere, which in the end is so depressing. You stop functioning as a journalist. There are things you just don't bother to pursue because you know you just won't get them into the paper.[20]

Hilton eventually left. Her example was followed by many others, although not all went for the same reasons. In early 1981, there were some 170 staff journalists on the *Sunday Times*. At least a hundred left the paper between February 1981 and March 1986. This exodus included most of the celebrated *Sunday Times* journalists from the pre-Murdoch era. During this process, independent directors did little to uphold the independence of the paper. Unlike their more effective counterparts at the *Observer*, they had not been elected by staff.

The *Sunday Times* shifted from the centre to becoming, in the words of its former political editor, Hugo Young, a 'hard-line paper of the Right'.[21] Its editorial agenda and stance increasingly followed during the 1980s that of the government, with predictable views on privatization, the shortcomings of the public sector, the need to curb trade unions and economic 'modernization'. By the time of Neil's departure, the editorial culture of the paper had been transformed. Murdoch subsequently intervened less often at the *Sunday Times* because he had less need to: the change in the culture and news agenda of the paper took the paper in the desired direction.

The Times followed a similar trajectory, though not without determined resistance from Harold Evans, the newly-appointed editor. Murdoch 'creates an aura', recollects Evans, that was deeply contemptuous of centrist and centre-right opponents of Thatcher.

> He did this by persistent derision of them at our press meetings and on the telephone, by sending me articles marked worth reading which espoused right-wing views, by jabbing a finger at headlines which he thought could have been more supportive of Mrs. Thatcher – 'You're always getting at her' – and through the agency of his managing director, Long.[22]

Long bombarded the editor with memos urging him to give the Thatcher government greater support.[23] Evans was not given a fixed budget allocation, and needed therefore to obtain financial permission for new editorial outlays. He also faced opposition from some *Times* staff, which Murdoch tacitly encouraged. In an atmosphere thick with intrigue, in which Evans' personal aide was secretly reporting to the opposition group, the editor became an increasingly beleaguered figure. He resigned in 1983 rather than 'be subjected to a thousand humiliations, challenged on every paperclip'.[24] He was followed by a succession of editors (some with exceptional ability like Sir Peter Stothard), who continued the paper's trajectory as an organ of the right.

When Murdoch's empire grew, he was able to give less detailed attention to his British newspapers. However, he developed a highly personalized management style in a corporation (subdivided in 2012) with weak formal processes and structures. Centralized control was maintained by moving senior executives around frequently, by fostering a sense of insecurity, by ruthlessly expelling those who stepped out of line, and by projecting a clear set of objectives and policy commitments.[25] 'When you work for Rupert Murdoch', writes Andrew Neil, 'you do not work for a company chairman or chief executive: you work for a Sun King . . . All authority comes from him . . . and he expects his remit to run everywhere, his word to be final'.[26]

These pressures encouraged senior Murdoch employees to internalize the Sun King's wishes. As the former *Sun* editor, David Yelland, wrote with disarming candour: 'Most Murdoch editors . . . think: what would Rupert think about this? It's like a mantra inside your head, it's like a prism. You look at the world through Rupert's eyes'.[27] Likewise, Bruce Guthrie, former editor of Murdoch's Melbourne *Herald Sun*, commented: 'most senior executives don't do anything without first asking themselves: "What would Rupert think about this?"'.[28] This serendipity does not come about by accident. According to Andrew Neil, 'Murdoch has the knack of picking people who know how to second-guess him'.[29]

In general Murdoch newspapers supported a pro-market, small government stance. They were also expected to heed what Murdoch said publicly on key issues. Thus, when Murdoch vocally supported the invasion of Iraq in the run-up period in 2002, only one of his newspapers – the *Hobart Mercury* – took a different view. But not for long: the *Hobart Mercury* supported the invasion of Iraq when it actually happened in 2003, as did all Murdoch's 172 other newspapers worldwide.[30] This unanimity demonstrates the falsity of the claim that Murdoch editors are entirely free to do what they want. However, conformity – at the level of leaders – did not preclude some degree of internal pluralism. Whereas feature articles in Murdoch's tabloid papers like the *Sun* and the *New York Post* followed the corporate line, his quality papers like *The Times* and the *Australian* gave some space to different points of view.[31]

There were also occasions when individual Murdoch papers were allowed to tack to the wind for regulatory or market reasons. Thus Murdoch allowed latitude to *Today*, acquired in 1987, because it seemed the best way to save the paper. It developed a green tinge, returned to the Conservative fold for the

1992 general election, strayed briefly to the centre-left and was then closed down in 1995. Murdoch's UK newspapers converted to New Labour in 1997, without deviating from the right, for reasons that will be outlined shortly. Similar pragmatism was on display when the Scottish edition of the *Sun* adopted a neutral stance about how to vote in the 2014 Scottish independence referendum, in contrast to the anti-independence reporting of the paper's London edition.

Interventionist press controllers

Murdoch was joined by other proprietors in pushing their papers to support the Thatcherite revolution. The construction and property tycoon, Victor Matthews, who acquired the Express group in 1977, not only urged the *Daily Express* to root for Margaret Thatcher but also made in 1979 a large corporate donation to the Conservative party. When his enthusiasm for Thatcher clashed with market logic, the former prevailed. His group launched the *Daily Star* in 1978 in order to utilise underemployed printing capacity, and directed the paper downmarket towards Labour supporters in order to avoid competing with the *Daily Express*. This prompted Peter Grimsditch, the editor of the new paper, to suggest that the paper should back Labour in the 1979 general election in keeping with its target readership. The proposal was vetoed by Matthews, and Grimsditch was sacked. His replacement, Lloyd Turner, was told explicitly that 'he must not attack Mrs. Thatcher'.[32] A loyalist to the core, Matthews confessed that if a Watergate-style scandal occurred in Britain, it would 'pose a dilemma for me' about whether it should be reported.[33]

After two subsequent takeovers, the ailing Express group was acquired in 2000 by Richard Desmond. His fortune was based initially on a porn empire that included the magazines *Asian Babes* and *Big Ones*, and the TV channels Red Hot and TV XXX (all subsequently sold). Desmond became notorious, even by the standards of the national press, for the demeaning way in which he treated his staff. At editorial meetings, Desmond would ring a bell or press a hooter to shut up speakers – even in mid-sentence – if he judged their contributions to be unhelpful.[34] In 2015, photos of his senior executives were placed on toy vehicles on a model race track, and moved forwards or backwards depending on their perceived contribution to the company.[35] Under Desmond's authoritarian rule, the papers in the Express group moved still further to the right. In 2014–15, Desmond gave £1.3 million to the right-wing UK Independence Party (UKIP).[36]

Conrad Black, a Canadian businessman, acquired the Telegraph group in 1987. He controlled it for nearly 19 years, during which time he aligned the *Daily* and *Sunday Telegraph* to the right of the Conservative party. According to his long-serving *Sunday Telegraph* editor, Dominic Lawson, 'Conrad adored Margaret Thatcher almost to the point of idolatry'.[37] After an initial period of disengagement, Black bombarded his editors with advice. He would even ring up the *Daily Telegraph* editor, Max Hastings, after midnight – usually from abroad – and expect him to engage in lively conversation. The editor's new wife would mutter at these moments: 'Think of the money, think of the money'.[38] However, Conrad Black's tenure ended ignominiously. He developed a Great Gatsby lifestyle, leading him to engage in corporate fraud.[39] In 2007 he was found guilty in the United States, and served three years in prison. His career as a press magnate – and champion of law and order – was over.

The Telegraph group passed into the hands of the Barclay brothers, retail and property billionaires, in 2004. Their approach to the Telegraph group was primarily commercial. They installed seven different editors in twelve years at the Telegraph group, in a maelstrom of cost-cutting and restructuring, which ensured that the group remained profitable. But while they were businesspeople first and foremost, they were also great admirers of Margaret Thatcher, whose low tax and deregulatory policies had helped to enrich them. In 2013, they installed Margaret Thatcher, by then critically ill, as a guest in a suite of the Ritz Hotel so that she could spend the last few months of her life in luxury. It was an act of homage by two admiring proprietors.

Robert Maxwell gained control of the Mirror group in 1984 – the first time that the company was subject to a dominant shareholder for over half a century. Maxwell, a successful business entrepreneur, treated the Mirror group as a toy train set in which, according to one exasperated editor, he 'attempted to play engine driver, signalman and station master'.[40] Initially, Maxwell would ring as many as six times in a day to staff at the *Daily Mirror*.[41] Senior executives were sometimes kept waiting for hours, like courtiers attending an eighteenth-century French monarch.[42] According to Tom Bower, 'everything revolved and depended upon' Maxwell.[43] Stories abound, testifying to Maxwell's monstrous ego, and the fear he inspired.[44] One journalist, working at his desk, received a sharp blow to the back of his head. Turning around, he saw the massive figure of his boss looming above him. Maxwell peered at him. 'Oh', he said, 'mistaken identity' before walking away without an apology.[45]

Maxwell pushed the Mirror group newspapers still further away from their moorings on the left. Maxwell had been a right-wing Labour MP (1964–70) who was influenced subsequently by the Thatcherite revolution. 'I will never vote for Mrs. Thatcher', Maxwell told Channel 4 News, 'but she has done some good things for Britain and she should be supported'.[46] In another television interview, he said that if his editor 'supported Labour's [left-wing] defence policy or attacked the royals', he would be fired.[47] Reading an article in proof alleging that Thatcher was pursuing a personal vendetta against striking miners, he rewrote it to remove its insulting imputation.[48] During Maxwell's reign, the *Daily Mirror* reported that the leaders of the Mineworkers Union had corruptly used money, donated by the Libyan dictatorship, to pay off personal loans on their homes. The story was subsequently demonstrated to be untrue, as the *Daily Mirror* editor at the time later (and contritely) acknowledged.[49]

Maxwell subsequently stole money from the *Mirror* staff pension fund in a desperate attempt to prevent his indebted company from going bankrupt. With his creditors closing in, and facing the prospect of prosecution and prison, Maxwell slipped overboard from his private yacht and drowned in 1991. It may have been an accident, though it seems more likely to have been suicide.[50] The Mirror group merged subsequently with a giant regional press group to become, in 1999, Trinity Mirror. The *Daily Mirror* became a victim of underinvestment, cost-cutting and erratic repositioning. No senior executive or editor emerged to give the paper a radical kiss of life. Its circulation was overtaken by the Conservative *Daily Mail* in 2000; and fell to little over half of that of the *Daily Mail* by 2015.[51]

The owners of the flourishing Mail group adopted a different strategy from their rivals. The third Lord Rothermere and his son (who took over in 1998) delegated editorial control of the *Daily Mail* to two successful editors. David English who reigned at the *Mail* between 1971 and 1992 was uncompromisingly right-wing. He provided covering fire for Margaret Thatcher in the early difficult part of her premiership between 1979 and 1982, and was consistently supportive of her mission to regenerate Britain. When Paul Dacre took over as the *Daily Mail* editor in 1992, his proprietors (both father and son) never sought to moderate his impassioned, angry brand of right-wing Conservatism (even though over a quarter of *Daily Mail* readers regularly voted Labour or Liberal).[52]

In short, a large part of the press – the papers controlled by Murdoch, Black/Barclays, Matthews/Desmond, and Rothermere (accounting for over three quarters of national daily sales) – were committed to remaking Britain.

Reinforcing influences

Top-down direction strongly influenced the press partly because editors accepted as legitimate the right of proprietors to determine the *broad* direction of their papers. As Max Hastings, editor of the *Daily Telegraph*, put it: 'I've never really believed in the notion of editorial independence as such. I would never imagine saying to Conrad [his proprietor], "you have no right to ask me to do this, I must observe my independence."'[53] Conflict was also minimised by the fact that the editor was usually chosen by the proprietor in the first place.

If ideological rifts between proprietors and editors were rare, it was rarer still for journalists to rebel in a sustained way against their line managers. Journalists were often recruited partly on the basis that they would 'fit in'. Accommodating to hierarchical requirements brought rewards in terms of good assignments, high exposure, peer-group esteem and promotion. Resistance invited escalating sanctions. As Anthony Bevins, a leading journalist who worked for both quality and popular newspapers, wrote in 1990:

> It is daft to suggest that individuals can buck the system, ignore the pre-set 'taste' of their newspapers, use their own news-sense in reporting the truth of any event, and survive. Dissident reporters who do not deliver the goods suffer professional death. They are ridden by news desks and back-bench executives, they have their stories spiked on a systematic basis . . . It is much easier to pander to what the editors want . . .[54]

The pressure to conform – illuminated by public enquiries into the press[55] – intensified during and after the 1980s. 'Bollockings' became an almost ritual-ized way of bullying journalists into submission in red top papers (something to which we shall return).[56] Regular downsizing encouraged greater confor-mity, with staff journalists becoming increasingly anxious to avoid 'the drop'. The growth in the number of journalists employed on a temporary or short-term basis also made for a more compliant workforce.

The influence exerted by the mainly right-wing leadership of the national press was reinforced by the external environment. News beats and diaries were organised around powerful institutions and groups because this was a quick, economic and uncontroversial way of gathering the news.[57] By the mid-1990s, elite political and economic sources were overwhelmingly advocates of market liberalism, including government spokespersons, opposition leaders, the Bank of England, organisations like the International Monetary Fund, leading Whitehall think tanks, the Confederation of British Industry and City finan-cial analysts.[58] Trade unions (one of the few major organisations opposed to the advance of market liberalism) were demoted as a news source because they were deemed to have become less important. Other dissenting civil society organisations, which challenged the neo-liberal consensus, also had difficulty in securing a press hearing.[59]

More generally, the elite political culture supported neo-liberalism. Its pollen was carried, so to speak, in the air that journalists breathed.[60] The back-grounds of many senior journalists also did not predispose them to be critics of inequality. In 2016, only 19 per cent of them had gone to a comprehensive, the type of school attended by the large majority of their readers. No less than 54 per cent had been educated at Oxbridge.[61] This made them more privileged than their immediate predecessors, though not by much. In 2016, around half senior journalists had attended a public school (which educated around 7 per cent) – the same as in 2006 and 1986.[62] Detailed information about the private views of journalists in general is not available. However, a recent study of business, economic and financial journalists found that they tended to accept the underlying premises of market liberalism.[63]

The state and big business also devoted more resources to spinning the news. Between 1979 and 1989, Whitehall press officers increased from

628 to 1163, a rapid expansion that continued under New Labour (1987–2010).[64] There was also an enormous increase in the number of publicists employed by large business corporations.[65] While journalists remained wary of public relations, their conditions of work made them more susceptible to its influence. Between 2001 and 2010, there was a sharp reduction in the number of journalists employed in Britain.[66] In some offices, journalists had to produce more copy because there were fewer of them. In addition, some staffers also had to work on both a newspaper and website in integrated newsrooms, and respond to a speeded up news cycle. This led to a more office-bound, shallow style of journalism dependent on public relations and news agency feeds.[67]

In brief, pressure from resurgent press controllers to support the Thatcher revolution was reinforced by the dominant political culture, the influence of elite sources, the backgrounds of senior journalists and, indirectly, by diminished press resources.

Countervailing influences

While editors accepted that it was legitimate for proprietors to demand editorial support for business-friendly policies in general, pandering to the *particular* commercial interests of their proprietors was a different matter. This could give rise to conflicts with management.

Conflicts surfaced at the *Observer* after it had been acquired in 1980 by Lonrho, headed by Tiny Rowland. In 1984, Rowland instructed the editor, Donald Trelford, to suppress an article reporting that the Mugabe government in Zimbabwe had been responsible for a massacre in the dissident Matabele province. Lonrho derived £15 million annual profit from its investments in Zimbabwe. Yet Lonrho had troubled relations with the Mugabe government, and the article seemed likely to make things worse. Trelford refused to spike the article, and offered to resign. The paper's staff and independent directors all rallied behind Trelford, forcing Rowland to back down.

Donald Telford was less courageous when he came under pressure to further a vendetta against the Al Fayed bothers (who had worsted Roland in a takeover battle for the House of Fraser group). The *Observer* published a succession of one-sided articles, culminating in the publication of an unprecedented, mid-week issue. This reproduced an official report critical of Mohamed Al Fayed under the headline 'Exposed: The Phoney Pharaoh'.[68] *Observer* journalists were appalled, and protested to their independent directors. After a formal enquiry, the directors condemned what had happened, declaring that the paper's reputation had been tarnished.

Undaunted, the Lonrho parent company exerted further pressure on *Observer* staff to pursue another corporate vendetta, this time against British Aerospace. This caused David Leigh, head of the *Observer*'s investigative team, to resign in 1989 in protest. The *Observer* was finally rescued from Lonrho's compromising ownership when it was acquired in 1993 by the Scott Trust.

Self-serving corporate demands gave rise to tensions even in the subjugated Times group. Journalists at *The Times* (but not at the *Sun*) objected in 1989 to the disproportionate editorial attention being given to the launch of Murdoch-owned Sky TV. *The Times'* ineffectual independent directors refused to take the matter up beyond having a private word with the editor.

An unexpected clash even occurred in 1994 in the *Sunday Times*. The paper published reports that British aid to Malaysia was linked to an arms deal, and that a British construction company, Wimpey, had authorized the payment of bribes to Malaysian politicians. This came at a sensitive time for Murdoch who was hoping that the Malaysian government would lift its embargo on his Star TV satellite network. Murdoch angrily remonstrated with his editor, Andrew Neil, saying 'You're boring people. You are doing far too much on Malaysia . . . They're all corrupt in that part of the world'.[69] Attempts to mollify Murdoch proved insufficient: Neil was moved to a News Corporation job in the United States, and was later squeezed out. After having served as Murdoch's hatchet man, Andrew Neil wrote ruefully: 'Rupert does not like anything to get in the way of business'.[70]

Another area of resistance was in relation to advertising pressure. The press's deepening financial crisis, exacerbated by loss of advertising to the internet, made this a more salient issue. In 2015, Peter Oborne, chief political commentator of the *Daily Telegraph* (and an impressive analyst of contemporary Britain),[71] resigned on the grounds that 'the Telegraph's recent coverage of HSBC amounts to a form of fraud on its readers'.[72] The paper had lost the valuable HSBC advertising account after it had published criticism of the bank. Oborne claims that, from 2013 onwards, 'stories critical of HSBC were discouraged' in a bid to win back the account.[73] The paper's management failed to offer a detailed rebuttal of Oborne's very specific account.

In resisting illegitimate corporate or advertising influence, journalists were seeking in effect to uphold quasi-professional norms. However, proprietorial pressure to support the broad precepts of the Thatcher revolution was less often contested by journalists because, in the partisan editorial culture of the British press, this pressure was viewed as legitimate.

There were other countervailing influences, in addition to professional norms: notably, source and consumer power, and wider cultural change. For example, source influence in the form of expert medical opinion dampened down, in the later 1980s, the AIDS moral panic initially spread by the press;[74] and the subsequent sea-change of public attitudes towards homosexuality contributed to a marked decline of press homophobia.[75] But the profound shifts that occurred in the cultural domain during this period did not extend, despite the 2008 crash, to reporting of government economic management. The dominant Conservative press remained constant in its support for the neo-liberal order.

Failed promise of the print revolution

This steadfastness was underpinned by the brute force of oligopoly. High costs had effectively closed Fleet Street to new entrants. The only new national papers to be established successfully during the post-war period – *Sunday Telegraph* (1961), *Daily Star* (1978) and *Mail on Sunday* (1982) – were all launched by big press groups. They were on the right, and merely amplified the dominant voices of Fleet Street. Although the Trades Union Congress (TUC) investigated the possibility of starting a new national daily, it concluded in 1984 that it lacked the funds to do so.

During the mid-1980s, numerous commentators argued that new computer-aided print technology would break the stranglehold of the big press groups. Thus *Observer* journalists Robert Taylor and Steve Vines proclaimed in 1985 that the new technology would lead to the rise of minority newspapers, undermining 'the tyranny of the mass circulation press, with its mindless formula journalism appealing to the lowest common denominator'.[76] Similarly, Ian Aitken, political editor of the *Guardian*, forecast that new print technology would enable the emergence of 'entirely new newspapers representing all points of view'.[77] They were part of a chorus proclaiming that a journalistic renaissance was imminent.

Most of these choristers were journalists with very little business knowledge of the industry they worked in. They were convinced that only restrictive print trade unions, and inflated print workers' wages, prevented the transformation of journalism. In fact, total production wages accounted for around 21 per cent of national daily costs before new print technology was installed.[78] Even when most print workers were sacked and the print unions broken, market entry was made only a little easier. New technology was expensive to install. Established newspapers cut advertising rates, reduced cover prices and advertised heavily, at strategic moments, to undermine new start-ups.[79] The savings achieved through new technology were also dissipated by a substantial increase in the size of newspapers.

New print technology was first introduced in the national press with ruthless duplicity. In 1985, Rupert Murdoch built a new technology plant in Wapping, East London, costing over £66 million, which was capable of printing all his newspapers. He told his Fleet Street printers that he intended merely to print a new local paper at Wapping, but secretly recruited and trained an alternative workforce. An independent distribution system was established through an Australian transport company to take advantage of new anti-union laws (1980 and 1982) which outlawed sympathy strikes. The old print workforce was then given an impossible ultimatum. This provoked a doomed strike in 1986. For a year production workers mounted a forlorn nightly vigil outside the coils of razor wire surrounding the Wapping plant, with occasional violent clashes with the police. In 1997, the strike collapsed amid bitter internal recrimination.[80]

The production of all national newspapers was transformed between 1986 and 1989. Computer processes replaced the manual casting of copy in metal type, and page makeup on boards. Powerful web-offset machines and full-colour offset printing was established. Facsimile transmission enabled newspapers to be printed simultaneously at different sites. This technical transformation was funded through the sale of prime Fleet Street premises and newspaper shares in the Reuters news agency. In 1989, the last national newspaper rolled off the last printing press in Fleet Street, bringing to an end a tradition that dated back to the dawn of British journalism.

Newspaper production became cheaper, cleaner and less noisy. But the larger transformation of journalism that was hoped for proved elusive. For a time, a shoal of minnows swam around the hulks of established titles. But most of these minnows did not last long. They included *News On Sunday* (1986), *Sunday Today* (1986–87), *Sunday Correspondent* (1989–90), *Today* (1986–95), *Post* (1998), *Sunday Business* (1996–2006) and *New Day* (2016).

Most of these papers had too little money and too little expertise. For example Eddy Shah launched *Today*, with capital of about £8.5 million, in 1986, only to run out of money in ten weeks.[81] His paper had to be sold hurriedly to the conglomerate, Lonrho. Similarly, a left-wing group launched *News on Sunday* with £6.5 million, and ran out of money in the first month.[82] The underfunding of these two ventures was matched by their lack of journalistic imagination.

Only three new ventures survived child birth and early adolescence. The most important of these was the *Independent*, launched in 1986 with £16 million capital,[83] which breathed new life into the tradition of independent, bi-partisan journalism. However, the paper's management mistakenly launched a sister paper, the *Independent on Sunday*, in 1990, shortly before a recession. This depleted the already strained finances of the group. The two titles ceased to be 'independent' when they were sold in 1996, and then resold in 2010 to the Russian oligarch, Alexander Lebdevev. The two titles ended print publication in 2016. They survive only in a residual form as a website with few staff; and as a compact edition, *the i*, sold to Johnston Press.

The *Sunday Sport* was launched in 1986, followed by the *Daily Sport* in 1991. The two papers published stories like 'World War Bomber Found on Moon'[84] and 'Marilyn Monroe is Alive and Working as a Nanny'[85] which, in the view of critics, parodied the excesses of tabloid journalism. The *Daily* and *Sunday Sport* also merged soft porn and celebrity story genres, epitomized by their 'upskirt' and nipple slip pictures. However, their narrow diet of sport, human interest and erotic content, without public affairs coverage, made them specialist publications rather than true national newspapers. They were also not very popular: their longevity was due mainly to their paring down of costs, with a skeletal staff and reliance on cheap, bought-in material. Even so, the *Daily Sport* ceased print publication in 2011, and now exists only as a website.

Table 8.1 Concentration of national newspaper circulation, 1976–2015[1]

Big Three % of national:				
	1976	1989	2002	2015
Daily circulation	72	73	70	70
Sunday circulation	86	80	79	79

Note
1 The big three have been defined as the three largest publishers within each class of publication. All figures are derived from the Audit Bureau of Circulation.

The third relative success was the *Daily Star Sunday*, launched in 2002 by the Express group as the sister paper of the *Daily Star*. However, this merely extended the pre-print revolution trend of large press groups expanding by launching a Sunday edition of a daily title.

Just how little had changed can be seen by the way in which the big groups continued to dominate newspaper consumption. The three largest groups' market share of the national daily market remained around 70 per cent over forty years (see Table 8.1). Although there was a small reduction of market share in the national Sunday market during the same period, the biggest three groups still accounted for a remarkable 79 per cent of national Sunday circulation in 2015.[86]

Second technological disruption

The print 'revolution' was a rainbow that came and went, though not before dazzling some impressionable journalists. However the hopes invested in computerized printing were resurrected, in a seemingly more persuasive form, in the internet. The new technology, it was proclaimed, would democratize journalism. 'Anyone with a computer and modem', explained Philip Elmer-Dewitt, 'can be his own reporter, editor and publisher – spreading news and views to millions of readers around the world'.[87] The overthrow of dominant press groups was once again said to be imminent.

The internet had wider transformative consequences for society that will be explored later.[88] But in terms of journalism, it had a less apocalyptic outcome than was anticipated. The internet led to a cumulative economic crisis in the press, which lost advertising to Facebook, Google and other sites. It led to a precipitate decline of print sales,[89] and young people increasingly obtained information from social media and other online sources.[90] But the internet did not bring to an end the old order of journalism. The major press groups became wounded leviathans: they lost copious blood but did not become extinct.

Indeed, they remained big beasts – hobbled but still dangerous – partly because they established, in the period 1999–2003, successful news websites whose content was mostly offered free. Indeed, their news websites became, with the BBC, the most popular news websites in Britain – a position they retained over a decade later.[91] The established press groups thus extended their reach across technologies, even if they haemorrhaged sales.

Their free offer proved to be an effective way of undermining new competition. Online news start-ups were deterred from charging a subscription because they feared that if they did so – in competition against heavily subsidised give-aways – they would fail to build a substantial audience. Yet without charging, it was very difficult for them to break even because prevailing online advertising rates were so low.[92] The newspaper groups' anti-competition strategy both discouraged the emergence of online news rivals, and weakened those who entered the market. By 2014, only one new start up (*Huffington Post*) had broken into the top ten news websites in Britain.[93]

The Murdoch group deviated from the free offer strategy for a time, though it relented by making the *Sun* free online in 2016. Consequently Murdoch publications lost ground in terms of their combined online and offline audience. This contributed to a reduction of news concentration. In 2015, the big four press groups accounted for 65 per cent of combined print, online and mobile readership – less than their combined print share (81 per cent).[94]

The online revolution thus diminished but did not dethrone the major press groups. How did they represent Britain? For the sake of brevity, our analysis will be confined in this chapter to issues relevant to the 'remaking of Britain', and give greater attention to the more recent period.

Market virtue

While most of the press regularly preached the virtues of the free market, the form of its apostrophizing varied over time. In the 1980s, the sale of public enterprise was celebrated as a way of establishing 'popular capitalism'. The people, it was proclaimed, were now stakeholders in the economic order. However this theme was played down in the 1990s, by which time most people had sold their shares. In the boom years of the early millennium, the press argued that business leaders should enjoy higher rewards as an incentive to create more wealth that would trickle down. However less was heard of this trickle-down theory during the post-2008 recession, when wealth bubbled upwards while most people's incomes stagnated. But if different arguments were emphasized at different times, the underlying message remained the same: the free market works for all.

This consistency is perhaps best illustrated by the way most newspapers responded to the 2008 crash since this seemingly called into question the efficacy of a deregulated market. Most academic economists argue that the economic meltdown was caused principally by the reckless lending of financial institutions.[95] The government incurred a large deficit principally because its tax income declined as a consequence of the ensuing recession. In this version of events, the crash arose from a systemic failure of the financial sector: a large budget deficit – and mounting public debt – was the consequence.

As Mike Berry's study of press coverage in 2009 shows, some Conservative newspapers reversed this sequence of causation. In their account a large budget deficit, and huge public debt, incurred by a profligate Labour government, was a major cause of the recession.[96] This tendentious interpretation of the crisis pre-defined its solution: an immediate reduction in public spending. While two left papers (*Guardian* and *Daily Mirror*) did not follow the pack in misinterpreting the cause of the recession, their alternative to austerity politics in 2009 appeared only in 'fragments' and lacked coherence.[97] In short, most of the press interpreted the crash in a way that sustained the neo-liberal consensus.

The press also helped to contain the resentments generated by the post-2008 slump by deflecting these resentments on to two out groups: the poor and migrants. But before considering this, it should be noted that from time to time the press also criticized the powerful.

Pulled punches

Between 2009 and 2016, newspapers attacked politicians fiddling expenses, ex-ministers peddling influence, bungling bankers, and judges accused of being too liberal and pro-European. Indeed, the Conservative press turned on the Conservative Prime Minister David Cameron in 2016, when the Panama Papers revealed that his father, Ian Cameron, had taken advantage of an offshore tax haven. This last example seemingly illustrates just how independent and critical the press was, regardless of affiliation.

The press demanded to know whether the Prime Minister had benefitted financially from his father's tax avoidance scheme. Pressure increased when it was revealed that Ian Cameron's investment fund, Blairemore Holdings, had a Vice-President who lived in a rundown shack in the Bahamas, and was employed as a front to avoid British tax. After stalling for four days, David Cameron admitted that he had owned £30,000 worth of shares in his father's investment fund before he became prime minister. But he declared that, in office, his hands were clean and he was happy to make available his recent tax declarations.

The *Sun* reproduced uncritically the Downing Street line. The paper's political editor, Tom Newton Dunn, wrote that Cameron had prevaricated about revealing his financial affairs because 'he was only protecting his mum'. 'The truth' was that his father's company, Blairemore Holdings, was just 'a boring investment fund set up in the Bahamas to buy things in dollars, as the Caribbean islands are within the dollar area'. Since Cameron was happy to publish his recent tax returns, everything would now be '100 per cent transparent'.

Alongside this article, an editorial warned how awful 'the pitiful Jeremy Corbyn' would be as an alternative to Cameron as prime minister.[98]

The *Daily Mail* and *Daily Telegraph* sought to defuse the story in a more sophisticated way. Most people, these papers argued, seek to limit tax: for example by owning an ISA or by making arrangements to avoid inheritance tax. 'The truth is that there are no parents in this country, of any income bracket, who do not want their children to do better than themselves and to give them a leg-up in life'.[99] The implication is that all are in the same boat. Furthermore, tax revenue is squandered on 'foreign aid to corrupt dictators, . . . lavish expenses for eurocrats, . . . and welfare benefits for terrorists . . .', whereas 'families and private businesses spend and invest their earnings far more wisely and productively than the state'.[100] Indeed tax avoidance, provided it is legal, can be viewed as positive in much the way that 'tax cuts create incentives to wealth creation, fuel aspiration and stimulate people to work harder, thereby generating income and extra revenues'.[101] Always remember, concluded the *Daily Mail*, that 'private property, the self-reliant family and the rule of law' are the 'foundation stones of liberty from state oppression' and the fount of 'wealth creation'.[102]

Most of the press defined the Cameron tax issue as a potential political scandal, concluded that it had 'no legs', and moved on. By contrast, the *Guardian* framed the Cameron story, and the wider Panama revelations, as an example of systemic abuse. It highlighted, the paper argued, 'the stark inequality between a system in which the richest pay so little tax when compared with the strictly enforced rules that govern the honest ordinary majority'. More generally, the Panama papers documented 'the enormity of the world's lightly taxed or untaxed offshore financial holdings'.[103] But as a press outrider with a very small circulation, the *Guardian* lacked the muscle needed to generate a public campaign on this issue.

The Cameron tax saga is part of a general pattern in which the press criticized powerful individuals but held back from urging systemic reform. In 2016, the press attacked Mike Ashley for allegedly mistreating his staff at Sports Direct, and Sir Philip Green and Dominic Chapell for allegedly plundering British Home Stores (BHS) when they were in control of the company. But most newspapers refrained from pressing for better business regulation.[104] One response was merely to demand greater individual responsibility. It is 'time', thundered the *Sun*, 'for the[se] billionaires to get their act together'.[105] Another was to downplay the significance of these scandals. Thus, the *Daily Telegraph* stressed that the BHS scandal is 'the ignoble exception to a successful rule: profit seeking businesses make us all richer and more free'. Always remember, the paper continued, that 'whatever the failings of particular companies or individuals, capitalism as an economic system works . . .'.[106]

In brief, these examples show that the press was not uncritical of contemporary capitalism. But, when attacking corporate abuse, newspapers tended to pull their punches because they were opposed to more state economic regulation.

War on the poor

Perhaps another reason why the press pulled its punches over corporate tax avoidance was that it came too close to home. The largest press group, News International, recorded profits of almost £1 billion between 1985 and 1995, yet paid only £11.74 million in corporation tax – a rate of 1.2 per cent.[107] The third Lord Rothermere, controller of the Mail group between 1981 and 1998, was 'non-domiciled' for tax purposes – an arrangement that enriched the fourth Viscount.[108] The Barclay Brothers, publishers of the Telegraph group since 2004, paid no corporation tax on the Ritz Hotel they had owned for seventeen years.[109]

By contrast, the abuse of social security gained much greater prominence than tax avoidance in newspapers, even though tax avoidance lost the Exchequer much more money.[110] Between 2010 and 2013, there was a deluge of newspaper articles conveying the impression that taxpayers were subsidizing a large, feckless and dishonest underclass. In this coverage, poverty tended to be portrayed as being the product of personal deficiency rather than external circumstance. Welfare benefits were discussed in terms of cost rather than of social justice. And the government's policing, trimming and capping of welfare benefits were welcomed – indeed celebrated – as a long overdue 'reform'.[111]

A central theme of this reporting was that most people on benefits were 'shirkers'. The *Daily Mail* reported that 'just one in six incapacity benefit claimants "is genuine" as tough new test reveals TWO MILLION could be cheating'.[112] The true picture was much worse, the paper claimed two years later. 'Time's up for the Shirking Classes' it crowed: 'Just one in 14 incapacity claimants is unfit for work'.[113] In a similar vein, the *Daily Express* reported that, of those claiming sickness benefit, '75% are faking'.[114]

A second theme was that welfare benefits harmed the people they were designed to help. The benefit system has given rise, mourned the *Sun*, to a 'lost generation of couch potatoes happy to live on state handouts and channel surf reality shows', which is why we should 'WAGE WAR ON SHIRKERS'.[115] Social benefits, concurred the *Daily Mail*, has fostered 'state-funded idleness'.[116] It is causing people, according to the *Daily Express*, 'to sink into a way of life which is not only unproductive but often pointless'. Furthermore, there is 'plenty of evidence that shirking is passed on from parents to children'.[117]

Above all, shirkers were denounced for imposing an intolerable burden on the rest of society. In an exclusive interview with Work and Pensions Minister, Iain Duncan Smith, the *Sun* reported: 'Britain's shirkers paradise shame with hordes of work shy claimants was blamed last night for much of our economic mess'.[118] The benefits system, raged the *Daily Express*, produces a moral deficit in which the 'worthy' support the 'unworthy'. This is why 'HARD WORKERS SHOULD NO LONGER SUPPORT SHIRKERS'.[119] When the government curbed the annual rises of state benefits in 2013, the *Daily Express* celebrated this 'as a massive victory for strivers over skivers'. The report was headlined 'Party is Over for Benefit Skivers', as if all those on jobseeker's allowance, income support and housing benefit could be lumped together as 'skivers'.[120]

The sustained press campaign against those on benefits entailed numerous claims that were revealed to be untrue.[121] However, its effect – as we shall see – was to channel anger generated by the recession towards people at the bottom of society. This was not of course the conscious intention of journalists. They were responding in the main to news initiatives from the Department of Work and Pensions. The Department, in turn, was seeking to justify cuts in public spending, and the rolling out of its programme of welfare reform.

Class contempt

However, the war on the poor did not derive only from the contingency of budget cuts. It had been prefigured by the press campaign against 'scroungers' in the 1970s, described earlier.[122] It was also preceded by a growing outpouring of scorn for 'non-respectable' working people.

In the late 1970s and 1980s, the right-wing press broke with the post-war tradition of one-nation, class conciliation by regularly disparaging the poor. This shift was typified by the *Sunday Times*'s angry complaint that football had become 'a slum sport played in slum stadiums increasingly watched by slum people, who deter decent folk from turning up'.[123] Similar class disdain led the *Sun* to report, under the headline 'THE TRUTH', that Liverpool football fans urinated on the police, and picked the pockets of people who were dead or dying as a consequence of being crushed in the Hillsborough football stadium.[124] This story had originated principally from anonymous police briefing,[125] and had been believed because, in the view of its editor, Kelvin MacKenzie, it had rung true. Indeed, his first choice of headline had been 'YOU SCUM'.[126] The Hillsborough Inquiry revealed subsequently that the *Sun*'s report was wholly inaccurate.[127]

Class scorn in the press intensified during the twenty-first century (until 2017). It gave rise to the label 'chav', first popularized in the early 2000s.[128] Newspapers defined chavs stereotypically as 'dole-scroungers, petty criminals, football hooligans and teenage pram-pushers';[129] 'pasty-faced, lard-gutted slappers who drop their knickers in the blink of an eye';[130] and the 'uber-chav children of single parents who are costing the taxpayer a fortune'.[131] This contemptuous depiction was reinforced by a number of contemporary reality and satirical TV shows (like *Little Britain* (2003–06)), and amplified in feature articles about these.[132] By the 2010s, the consumer taste and lifestyle of 'chavs' were routinely derided in articles of unabashed snobbery. Chavs were identified as people with bad hairdos, ugly clothes, eating unhealthy food, giving their children naff names, and going to cheap, foreign holiday resorts that should be avoided.[133] They also became the butt of everyday humour, notably in the form of punning jibes such as chavellers cheques (giro and benefit payments), chaving a laugh (laughter at chavs), and chavalier (chav car). This 'humour 'was also expressed as very unfunny acronyms of CHAV such as like Council Housed and Violent, and Council House Associated Vermin.[134]

There was thus a build-up of contempt for 'losers' amplified by the press. This created the conditions in which it became politically acceptable to turn on the poor, and seek to 'redeem' them. A programme of benefit caps and 'sanctions' made the poorest section of society still poorer, driving some into destitution and prompting charities to set up free food banks to prevent people from going hungry. This extended the Thatcherite revolution beyond anything attempted in the 1980s. The portrayal of the poor as being largely responsible for their own plight also offered a justification for the growing inequality of neo-liberal Britain.

Law and order

Redeeming the poor was bound up with a moral decline thesis popularized by the press. Throughout the 1980s, but especially in the aftermath of the riots in 1981 and 1985, Conservative politicians and journalists argued that the moral structure of the nation had been undermined by the permissive 1960s.[135] 'We are reaping what was sown in the 1960s', warned Prime Minister Margaret Thatcher in 1982, when 'the old virtues of discipline and self-restraint were denigrated'.[136] 'The demons of drugs, pornography, violence and permissiveness', lamented Christopher Booker in the *Daily Mail* in 1983, 'are now raging out of control' because of the forces unleashed in the 1960s.[137] This social pessimism drew on growing concern about youth, immigrants and the poor; and was fuelled by lurid press reports of football hooligans, drug addicts, violent pickets and urban riots inspired by criminality and outside agitators.[138] This helped to legitimate, in turn, the imposition of discipline through tougher sentencing.[139]

To glowing press approval, New Labour also developed a moral decline thesis. In a much publicized keynote speech, Tony Blair (then Opposition leader) lamented in 1995 'our broken society' with its 'drugs, violence, youngsters hanging around street corners with nothing to do'.[140] This thinking contributed to the thirty-three 'get tough' initiatives implemented by the New Labour government between 2001 and 2004.[141] When the government's energy on this front waned, the *Sun* took up the baton by launching a new law and order campaign against 'yob' culture, under the slogan 'Broken Britain'. This was endorsed by David Cameron as leader of the Conservative Opposition in 2009.[142] David Cameron returned to this theme as Prime Minister in the wake of the 2011 riots, when he called for the restoration of order and discipline. Britain, he lamented, was suffering from a 'moral collapse' caused by '. . . children without fathers, schools without discipline, reward without effort, crime without punishment, rights without responsibilities . . .'.[143]

The press not only endorsed these iterations of moral decline, but urged ever more coercive measures – more police, longer prison sentences, more traditional education – as a way of dealing with it. Newspapers also fed the politics of retribution by the way they reported crime. Robert Reiner argues that, by comparison with the immediate post-war period, crime stories gave less attention to the contexts that bred crime, while focusing in a more dramatic way on the suffering of the victim, and on 'the battle against one-dimensionally evil villains'.[144]

Swarm of migrants

From 2002 onwards, the popular press published an avalanche of anti-migrant stories. One central theme of this coverage was that Britain was being overwhelmed by the influx of too many migrants, conveyed through the use of metaphors such as 'swarm', 'wave', 'flood' and 'swamped'. The most frequent media image of a migrant, in 2002–03, was of that of a threatening young male attempting to enter Britain illegally.[145] The impression that Britain was under siege was also signalled more directly through front page headlines such as 'The Invaders', 'Migrant Seized Every Six Minutes', 'No End to Migrant Crisis'[146] and 'Migrants: How Many Can We Take?'.[147]

Migrants were depicted as a threat in a multiple ways. Firstly, they were said to be importing crime into Britain. According to the *Sun*, the first coach-load of Romanian migrants to Britain openly 'boast[ed] of plans to beg or steal'.[148] There are '4,000 Foreign Murderers and Rapists We Can't Throw Out', raged the *Daily Mail*.[149] 'Life for British women', lamented the *Daily Express*, had become 'less free and less safe' due to the migrants in our midst.[150] Indeed *'terrorists* are using the *migration* crisis', warned the *Daily Telegraph*, 'to enter Europe and plot atrocities across the continent'.[151] Secondly, migrants were said to be taking jobs from British workers. 'Millions of EU Migrants Grab our Jobs',[152] complained the *Daily Express* on a regular basis. The third, less frequent, allegation was that migrants posed a threat to national identity and social cohesion. They were said to have different cultural traditions, and to be reluctant to integrate. As an article in the *Daily Express* article put it, Britain was engaged in 'a grotesque form of assisted suicide' leading to 'the spread of sharia law', 'violent gangs in inner cities' and 'the rise of Islamic extremism'.[153]

Above all, migrants were said to be imposing an intolerable burden on already stretched public services, most notably on housing, schools, transport, medical and social care. The financial cost they represented was dramatized regularly through very selective statistics. '£17bn, the true cost of immigration to the UK every year', groaned the *Daily Mail*.[154] 'Migrant Mothers Cost £1.3bn', reported the *Daily Express*, followed by another front page headline: 'Soaring Cost of Teaching Migrant Children'.[155] Outrage was expressed for a time about health tourism (which only accounted for a tiny fraction of total

NHS costs). 'Throughout Britain a fortune in taxpayers' money', complained the *Daily Mail*, 'is being given in free maternity care, HIV drugs and the rest to foreign "health tourists"'. 'If this abuse is not stopped', the paper continued, 'then the NHS a key marker of British civilisation will be doomed'.[156] Migrants, it was also suggested, were receiving special favours from the authorities or were being over-indulged. In 'soft touch Britain', complained the *Sun*, migrants were seen 'tucking into takeaways and guzzling pop' at public expense.[157]

These negative portrayals were rendered more effective because migrants generally remained anonymous. Studies covering the period 2006–12 found that the popular press often used generic labels such as 'bogus asylum seekers', 'asylum cheats', and 'illegals' to describe *all* refugees and migrants.[158] While the more neutral word 'migrant' was later adopted by the press, different groups – refugees from war, economic migrants, students and others – continued to be lumped together in one undifferentiated mass. Migrants tended to be dehumanized because very little attention was given to who they were and why they had come to Britain. Indeed, a recurrent finding of research is that print journalists rarely quoted migrants when they wrote about them. In 2002–03, just 8 per cent of articles about migrants cited migrants as a primary source.[159] In 2015, only 15 per cent of articles about migrants contained a migrant voice or perspective.[160] More generally, the number of migrants dying in the Mediterranean was only fitfully reported, with more stress being given – for a time – to the inadequacy of attempts to stop them.[161] This prompted the *Sun* columnist, Katie Hopkins, to demand that the armed forces 'should force migrants back to their shores' because they 'are like cockroaches', comparable to a 'norovirus on a cruise ship'.[162]

Coverage of migrants was not always negative. There were two positive counter-narratives. One was that migrants brought both economic and cultural benefits. This was an argument more often aired in the broadsheet than in the popular press. The second counter-narrative was that of the migrant as victim. This gained ground for a time in 2015, when it was encapsulated by the image of a dead Syrian child, lying face downwards on a Turkish beach. The *Daily Mirror*, the only popular daily not to campaign against migrants, responded to this image with one word: 'Unbearable'.[163] But the moment passed. Coverage of migrants in the press was, overall, strongly negative in 2015.[164]

For over a decade, poison leaked into the cultural bloodstream of British society. The press in Britain was more hostile towards migrants than the press in Germany, Sweden, Italy and Spain.[165] Yet all these countries absorbed, as a percentage of their populations, many more migrants than Britain did. Interviews and focus groups suggest that some migrants in Britain felt threatened by this press hostility. This made them more inclined to retreat into their ethnic communities, and to feel alienated and resentful.[166]

Rallying behind the flag

Wars provided occasions for the press to rally behind the flag. The *Sun* reported the 1983 Falklands War with a degree of jingoism not matched by any British national daily since the Boer War. 'Stick it Up Your Junta' roared the *Sun* when peace negotiations with the Argentinian government broke down.[167] The paper scored the Falklands War like a football game, crowing: 'BRITAIN 6 (Georgia, two airships, three warplanes), ARGENTINA 0'.[168] 'Gotcha', exulted the *Sun* when an Argentinian ship was sunk with the loss of 368 lives.[169]

In the lead-up to the 2003 Iraq War, much of the press accepted uncritically the New Labour government's claim – subsequently revealed to be false – that Saddam Hussein had weapons of mass destruction. 'Brits 45 mins from doom', proclaimed the gullible *Sun*.[170] 'Mad Saddam ready to attack: 45 minutes from a chemical war', echoed the *Daily Star*.[171] Pro-Iraq war national dailies had 3.7 times greater circulation than anti-war dailies.[172] This was part of a recurring pattern. Most national newspapers backed in 2001 the failed occupation of Afghanistan. Most also supported the toppling of Colonel Gaddafi in 2001 that destabilized the country and spread terrorism. In all three conflicts, newspapers responded to the steer provided by the government, a simplistic 'good–bad' narrative and an underlying sense of national destiny.

National pride, sustained by memories of a glorious past, also found an outlet in the reporting of sport. England's defeat of Spain in the Euro 96 Football championship was reported by the *Observer* as 'Seaman [English goalkeeper] sinks Armada'.[173] The following day, the *Daily Mirror* trailed the forthcoming match against Germany with the front-page headline 'ACHTUNG! SURRENDER! For you Fritz, ze Euro 96 Championship is over'. It was accompanied by photos of two English football stars, Paul Gascoigne and Stuart Pearce, wearing superimposed Second World War helmets.[174] The *Sun* also invoked wartime memories, with the headline 'Let's Blitz the Fritz'.[175] When England duly lost, the *Sun* declared 'Every one of England's Euro '96 squad is a national hero . . . The team has raised national pride to new levels'.[176] In the 2012 Olympic Games, the British press rooted for 'Team GB', focused on events in which Britain did well, and celebrated Britain's hosting of the Games as an international triumph.

The version of nationalism invoked by much of the press in the immediate post-1979 period tended to be backward-looking and reactionary.[177] This blossomed into a sense of beleaguered nationhood in which Britain was portrayed as being subject to the growing tyranny of European institutions. This was conveyed through commentary, such as the angry claim in the *Daily Mail* that Germany was exploiting the financial crisis to build the 'Rise of the Fourth Reich'.[178] More potently it was furthered through regular reports over two decades featuring the European Union (EU) as bossing Britain in capricious, insulting and pettifogging ways. The British public read in leading newspapers that the EU was planning to ban barmaids from wearing low cut tops ('Hands off our barmaids' boobs')[179] instruct 'women to hand in worn-out sex toys' for health and safety reasons,[180] outlaw corgis ('the Queen's favourite dog'),[181] stop the weekday sale of booze by off-licences,[182] insist on the relabelling of yoghurt as 'fermented milk pudding',[183] 'rename Trafalgar Square and Waterloo Station'[184] and impose a quota of gypsy MPs on the UK.[185] Not one of these stories was true.[186]

The celebration of Britishness was not without complication, owing to the rise of nationalism in Wales and Scotland, and a reactive expression of Englishness. This last was fed by Our Island Story versions of the past, typified by the *Sun*'s eulogy to 'a land of heroes, inventors and explorers' under the headline 'This is Our England'.[187] A sense of imperilled nationhood, threatened by migration, also gave rise to popular newspaper attacks on 'failed multiculturalism', and an assertive championing of the need for ethnic and racial minorities to integrate into the national values, norms and identity.[188]

The 2016 European Referendum was the moment when the popular press drew upon cultural deposits built up over two decades, and cashed them in. Three strands of reporting – anti-migrant, anti-EU and patriotism – coalesced in the Brexit theme of 'taking back control'. Over a three-month period, only 27 per cent of articles concerned with the Referendum in nine national papers were pro-remain, whereas 41 per cent were in favour of leaving.[189] The true imbalance was even greater than this figure implies due to the circulation dominance of the Brexit press. Over 80 per cent of consumers who bought a daily newspaper read a title favouring British withdrawal from the EU.[190]

The outcome of the Referendum was a narrow vote in favour of leaving the EU. The popular press perhaps contributed to this result by channelling pre-existing resentments – about national decline, stagnant wages, de-industrialization and migrants – towards a vote for Brexit.

Communists, loonies and terrorists

The fall of the Berlin Wall in 1989, and subsequent collapse of the Soviet Union, was an occasion of press triumphalism. The defeat of Communism demonstrated, it was argued, that state planning was inefficient and oppressive, whereas unfettered capitalism delivered both prosperity and liberty. While this victory strengthened the political ascendancy of neo-liberalism, it also removed an ideological asset – a means to delegitimate the left.

Following the 2001 attacks on the Twin Towers in New York, Islamic terrorism became – in incremental stages – almost a surrogate for the Cold War. Terrorist attacks in Britain in 2013, 2015 and 2017 were portrayed, in some papers, as being part of a jihad against the British people, made more menacing by the presence of British Muslim communities incubating home-grown jihadis.[191] Sometimes, local terrorism and foreign conflicts were signified as being part of a Manichaean struggle between western enlightenment and

Islamic fundamentalism. As a *Daily Telegraph* article put it: 'In this war of civilisation, the West will prevail'.[192]

How the popular press portrayed radical politicians and activists was influenced by this changing context. During the dying phase of the Cold War, leading radicals in Britain were denounced in the popular press as Communist sympathizers. Tony Benn, leader of the parliamentary Labour left, was called 'Bolshevik Benn', 'Commissar Wedgie' and 'the Most Dangerous Man in Britain Today' in a stream of personalized invective.[193] Anti-Commie rhetoric was directed also at Ken Livingstone, the most prominent leader of the new municipal left. 'Where will you be?', the *Sun* asked Ken Livingstone, 'should the Russian Stormtroopers march through the streets of London . . . **In the streets** welcoming them with open arms?' (original emphasis).[194] The *Sun* later accused Livingstone of wanting to turn Britain into 'Cuba of the North Sea',[195] while the *Daily Express* urged him to settle in Communist Eastern Europe.[196]

Both politicians were in fact radical social democrats, little influenced by Marxist theory (or indeed by abstract theorizing in general). Tony Benn belonged to an ethical radical tradition that is a prominent strand of British social democracy.[197] Livingstone was strongly influenced by the radical counterculture, with its stress on social issues like racism, homophobia, women's liberation and the environment.[198] It was difficult to plausibly present either politician as a clone of Soviet Moscow.

Perhaps for this reason, some papers supplemented McCarthyite smears with the allegation that both politicians had mental issues. Benn was denounced as a 'wild-eyed political looney',[199] Livingstone as a 'crackpot'.[200] This line of attack was seemingly validated by medical expertise. The *Sun* obtained testimony from psychiatrists that Tony Benn had 'character disorders',[201] while the *Daily Mail* reported psychiatrists as saying that Ken Livingstone was emotionally damaged.[202] All these clinical assessments were anonymous, save for two – those of Dr. Hubbard and Dr. Mackay. Both doctors said subsequently that they had been misrepresented.[203]

Pathologizing the new urban left became the default position of most popular papers during the mid-1980s. The mostly young activists who were elected to run a succession of local councils in London and elsewhere were labelled 'crackpot', 'loopy', 'barmy', 'potty', 'fringe' and 'loony' (sometimes spelt with an e). Papers ranging from the *Daily Mail* to the *Daily Mirror* finally settled in 1986–87 on the alliterative phrase 'loony left'.[204]

This stigmatization was seemingly justified by numerous reports of manifestly absurd decisions taken by left-wing councils. An investigation into ten 'loony left' stories found all of them to be substantially or wholly inaccurate.[205] Two of these cases are worth citing briefly because they illustrate how stories could be distorted by a deeply partisan press.

In Haringey, a storeman joked to the effect that the council would soon be banning black bin liners as racist. This ironic comment was subsequently taken literally in a conversation between two council employees, one of whom complained to Councillor Brian Bullard. The Councillor spoke to a freelance journalist, who passed the story on to the *Mail on Sunday*. The paper duly reported that Haringey Council had banned black bin liners.[206] The journalist who wrote the story subsequently acknowledged that the report was not true. The evidence confirms that the council had not banned black bin liners, and indeed continued to use them.[207]

The second example relates to children in Beevers Nursery, Hackney. Although they sang 'Baa Baa Black Sheep', they sometimes sang 'Baa Baa White Sheep' as a humorous alternative, along with other lines added for humorous effect. A garbled version of what was happening at this nursery, run by parents, was relayed to the *Star* which reported 'toddlers have been ordered to stop singing Baa Baa Black Sheep . . . because it is racist'.[208] This story was then improved by the *Sun* which reported that 'loony left-wing councillors have banned children from reciting the nursery rhyme . . . because they claim it is racist'.[209] Neither version of the story was true but the latter was picked up by other papers not merely in Britain but around the world.[210]

'Loony left' stories were amplified through the media–political system. Conservative Central Office issued press releases relaying newspaper 'loony left' stories, supplemented by denunciations from government ministers. These were then reported in the press,[211] generating pressure on senior Labour politicians to publicly dissociate themselves from the 'loony left'. Condemnations from both Conservative and Labour politicians encouraged further press attacks on the 'loony left', leading to a perfect storm in which journalists and politicians reinforced each in a mutually reinforcing spiral of opprobrium.[212]

More recently, the left has been delegitimated not by being identified as closet commies or as loonies but as being friends of terrorists at a time when there was growing anxiety about the threat of terrorism in Britain. This was the popular right-wing press charge levelled against the Opposition Leader, Shadow Chancellor and Shadow Home Secretary in 2015–17. This strengthened the belief among some of their colleagues – duly reported in the media – that they were 'unelectable'. This assault reached a climax in the thirteen pages published by the *Daily Mail* on the day before the 2017 election 'proving' that these three were 'APOLOGISTS FOR TERROR'.[213]

Moderates and extremists

The degree of press hostility towards Labour party leaders depended on their politics. The two most left-wing leaders of the Labour Party during the post-1979 period were Michael Foot (1980–83) and Jeremy Corbyn (2015–). They were subjected to more sustained press abuse than any other post-1979 Labour leader. Foot was dismissed as 'pathetic, outdated and washed up', written off as 'half baked and half gone'[214] and even accused implausibly by the *Sunday*

Times of being Agent Boot paid by the Soviet KGB.[215] This last accusation was withdrawn following a libel suit.

Similarly, attacks rained down on Corbyn from the first week of his leadership,[216] typified by two sardonic obituaries: 'Bye Bye Labour' and 'Red and Buried'.[217] He was reviled as not only an ally of Islamic extremism but also of anti-semitism and Stalinism.[218] When Corbyn was re-elected as Labour leader in 2016 in the teeth of opposition from *every* national newspaper,[219] the result was portrayed as a disaster for Labour and the British people. 'An unelectable leader is about as much use', mourned the pro-Labour People, 'as an ice-cream in the desert'.[220] 'Mr Corbyn', muttered the pro-Labour *Sunday Mirror*, 'must get a grip on the trolls, racists and Trots . . .'.[221] The view from the Conservative press was a combination of contempt and disgust. 'Party will be Left for dead and buried', declared the *Sun on Sunday*.[222] 'Jeremy rides again, at head of walking dead', concurred *Sunday Times* columnist (and Sky TV presenter) Adam Boulton.[223] This derision culminated in the *Sun*, on the 2017 general election day, featuring a front-page montage of Corbyn with a rubbish bin on his head with the headline: 'Don't chuck Britain in the COR-BIN'. 'Vote Tory', it added, 'unless you want a friend of terrorists'.[224]

The next most reviled figures were Labour leaders on the centre-left: Neil Kinnock (1983–92), John Smith (1992–94)[225] and Ed Miliband (2010–15). The *Sun* published a typical burlesque article 'Why I'm Backing Kinnock, by Stalin',[226] and on the day of the 1992 general election ran a front-page headline, 'If Kinnock Wins Today Will the Last Person to Leave Britain Please Turn out the Lights?' beside a montage of Kinnock's head inside a light-bulb.[227] The image encapsulated the contemptuous Fleet Street view of Kinnock as a dangerous windbag. John Smith, although receiving strong support from the centre-left press, was denounced in right-wing papers as the 'dead loss' leader, who was 'even worse' than Kinnock, and would enable 'hard line socialists' to engulf the country in constant industrial strife.[228] Ed Miliband was attacked as '"loser" Red Ed',[229] a 'class war zealot',[230] the son of a Marxist who 'hated Britain',[231] and a walking disaster who would make as much a 'pig's ear' of Britain as he did his sarnie.[232]

The least attacked were Labour's most right-wing leaders, Tony Blair (1994–2007) and Gordon Brown (2007–10), the architects of New Labour. Indeed, New Labour obtained for a time unprecedented press support (peaking at 71 per cent of national daily circulation in the 2001 general election).[233] This did not reflect a sea-change in the press so much as a political realignment of the Labour party. Pro-Blair newspapers like the *Sun* and *Daily Express* remained strongly right-wing but warmed to Labour's Prodigal Son who had seen the light. The *Sun* commended Tony Blair in 1997 as the person who 'had pointed his party in the right way on the economy, unions and privatisation',[234] while Gordon Brown was lauded for ditching Labour's strongly redistributive tax policy. *The Times* urged its readers to vote Labour in 2001 on the grounds that the Blair government had 'consolidated many elements of

Thatcherism'.[235] The *Economist* supported Blair as the only credible conservative leader who had 'governed on the centre-right on most issues.'[236]

However, this press adjustment was also the product of other factors. Tony Blair's predecessor as Prime Minister, John Major, had come under press attack. New Labour established in the mid-1990s an effective PR operation. In addition, Richard Desmond temporarily converted Express newspapers to New Labour in order to frustrate a backbench attempt to block his proprietorship on the grounds that he was a pornographer. New Labour also seemed likely to be an electoral winner. But the main underlying reason for the press's conversion was that New Labour seemed unthreatening, and intent on perpetuating most of the Thatcherite legacy. With different politics, Labour would not have won so much press support.

This conversion did not last long. Desmond ditched New Labour shortly after 2001. In the 2005 general election, the *Sun* offered a grudging endorsement of New Labour under the headline 'One Last Chance'.[237] By 2009, the Murdoch press tired of Blair's successor, Gordon Brown, and mounted a sustained campaign against him. In the 2010 general election, Labour had minimal press support.[238] New Labour had not been conservative enough.

In short, most of the press became subject to the control of assertive, right-wing proprietors and editors. Their ascendancy was underpinned by oligopoly and restricted market entry. Their position was not destabilized by new print technology but was weakened by the internet. Under their direction, the press was virulently hostile to the radical left, and largely critical of the Labour party (save during the New Labour intermission). More generally, most popular newspapers hymned the virtues of the free market, displaced anger onto migrants and those on benefits, pressed for more coercive law and order policies, encouraged people in an increasingly unequal society to rally behind the flag, and to support the crusade against the Soviet Union and Islamic terror. Did any of this make any difference?

The answer should seem clear-cut. But as we shall see, it is far from being so.

Notes

1 The dates in parentheses refer to the principal year of implementation. In some cases, the transfer of ownership took several years.
2 R. Reiner, *Law and Order* (Cambridge, Polity, 2007).
3 'United Kingdom: Income Inequalities'. Available at: www.poverty.org.uk/09/index.shtml (accessed 25 April 2016). Cf. 'The Scale of Economic Inequality in the UK', Equality Trust. Available at: www.equalitytrust.org.uk/scale-economic-inequality-uk (accessed 25 April 2016).
4 D. Marquand, *Britain Since 1918* (London, Phoenix, 2009).
5 For a good account of writers scornful of the 'political economy' approach which attaches importance to ownership, see D. Hesmondhalgh, *The Cultural Industries*, 3rd edition (London, Sage, 2013). The case study in this chapter focuses on the broadsheet press; in the next chapter, more attention is paid to top-down pressures in the popular press.

6 N. Davies, *Flat Earth News* (London, Chatto & Windus, 2008).

7 D. Butler and G. Butler, *Twentieth-Century British Political Facts, 1900-2000*, 8th edition (Basingstoke, Macmillan, 2000), pp. 274–75.

8 F. Giles, *Sundry Times* (London, John Murray, 1986), pp. 202–3.

9 Giles, *Sundry*, p. 208.

10 Giles, *Sundry*, p. 206.

11 A. Neil, *Full Disclosure* (London, Macmillan, 1996), p. 165.

12 Neil, *Disclosure*, p. 165.

13 Interview with Claire Tomalin in 1986.

14 Interview with Peter Wilby in 1986.

15 Interview with Don Berry in 1986.

16 Interview with Donald Macintyre in 1986.

17 Interview with John Shirley in 1986.

18 Quoted in M. Hollingsworth, *The Press and Political Dissent* (London, Pluto, 1986), p. 204.

19 Conversation with Marjorie Wallace in May 2016.

20 Interview with Isabel Hilton in 1986.

21 H. Young, 'Rupert Murdoch and the *Sunday Times*: A Lamp Goes Out', *Political Quarterly*, 55 (4), 1984, p. 386.

22 H. Evans, *Good Times, Bad Times* (London, Weidenfeld & Nicolson, 1983), pp. 235–36.

23 Evans, *Good Times*, pp. 286–87.

24 Evans, *Good Times*, p. 371.

25 R. Tiffen, *Rupert Murdoch* (Sydney, NewSouth, 2014); M. Woolf, *The Man Who Owns the News* (London, Bodley Head, 2008); B. Page, *The Murdoch Archipelago* (London, Simon & Schuster, 2003).

26 Neil, *Disclosure*, p. 160.

27 Leveson Inquiry transcript (26 April 2012) cited in Tiffen, *Murdoch*, p. 294.

28 B. Guthrie, *Man Bites Murdoch* (Melbourne, Melbourne University Press, 2011), p. 18.

29 A. Neil, 'Lessons from a former Murdoch man'. *Portfolio.com*, 3 July 2007. Available at: www.upstart.bizjournals.com/views/columns/2007/07/30/Andrew-Neil-on-Murdoch.html?page=all (accessed 21 October 2016).

30 D. McKnight, *Murdoch's Politics* (London, Pluto, 2012), p. 187; *An Inquiry into the Culture, Practices and Ethics of the Press Report* [Leveson Report], vol. 3 (London, Stationery Office, 2012), p. 1148.

31 D. McKnight and B. McNair, 'The empire goes to war: News Corporation and Iraq', *Australian Journalism Review*, 34 (2), 2012.

32 Hollingsworth, *Press and Dissent*, pp. 233–34.

33 S. Jenkins, *Newspapers* (London, Faber and Faber, 1979), p. 101. To judge from this account, it is open to question how much detailed editorial influence Matthews – a newcomer to journalism – actually exercised.

34 *Financial Times*, 12 June 2015; *Guardian*, 19 June 2015.

35 Ibid.

36 In 2018, the giant Trinity Mirror group announced its intention to take over the Express group. If this goes ahead, Desmond's reign as a maverick press tycoon will come to an end.

37 *Daily Telegraph*, 25 January 2004.

38 M. Hastings (ed.), *Editor* (London, Macmillan, 2002), p. 235.

39 T. Bower, *Outrageous Fortune and Lady Black* (London, Harper Perennial, 2006).
40 Greenslade, *Press Gang*, p. 512.
41 A. Hetherington, *News, Newspapers and Television* (Basingstoke, Macmillan, 1985), pp. 28–29.
42 R. Greenslade, *Maxwell's Fall* (London, Simon & Schuster, 1992), p. 108.
43 T. Bower, *Maxwell: The Outsider* (London, Mandarin, 1991), p. 407.
44 On one occasion, Maxwell is said to have unzipped the front of his trousers, and relieved himself off the top of the *Mirror* building before stepping into his helicopter. The story has an eloquent symbolism. But I have yet to read or hear *first-hand* sources for this story. It is probably apocryphal.
45 J. Kelly, 'The strange allure of Robert Maxwell', BBC News, 4 May 2007. Available at: www.news.bbc.co.uk/1/hi/magazine/6620291.stm (accessed May 10, 2016).
46 Cited in Hollingsworth, *Press and Dissent*, p. 244.
47 Quoted in D. Campbell, 'The London legacy of Cap'n Bob', *Guardian*, 28 August 2006. Available at: www.theguardian.com/media/2006/aug/28/mondaymedia-section.pressandpublishing1 (accessed May 2016).
48 Bower, *Maxwell*, p. 385; Hollingsworth, *Press and Dissent*, p. 244.
49 R. Greenslade, 'Sorry, Arthur', *Guardian*, 27 May 2002. Available at: www.theguardian.com/media/2002/may/27/mondaymediasection.politicsandthemedia (accessed 10 May 2016). It is an exemplary apology which explains how the juggernaut of a 'good' story is difficult to stop.
50 Greenslade, *Maxwell's Fall*, p. 369.
51 Circulation figures derived from the Audit Bureau of Circulation.
52 Thus 32 per cent of regular readers of the *Daily Mail* voted Liberal or Labour in the 2010 general election, and 28 per cent did so in the 2005 general election (see D. Kavanagh and P. Cowley, *The British General Election of 2010* (Basingstoke, Palgrave Macmillan, 2010), Table 14.5, p. 293).
53 Cited in A. Bevins, 'The crippling of the scribes', *British Journalism Review*, 1 (2), 1990, pp. 13–14.
54 Bevins, 'Crippling', p. 15.
55 *An Inquiry into the Culture, Practices and Ethics of the Press Report* [Leveson Inquiry], vol. 2 (London, Stationery Office, 2012), pp. 493 ff.; House of Lords Select Committee on Communications, *The Ownership of the News*, vol. 2 (Evidence) (London, Stationery Office, 2008), pp. 338 ff.
56 See p. 176.
57 J. Curran, *Media and Power* (London, Routledge, 2002).
58 A. Davis, *The Mediation of Power* (London, Routledge, 2007); A. Davis, *Political Communication and Social Theory* (London, Routledge, 2010).
59 N. Fenton, 'NGOs, new media and mainstream news: news from nowhere' in N. Fenton (ed.) *New Media, Old News* (London, Sage, 2010). There were exceptions especially in the 1980s and early 1990: most notably green campaigners (P. Manning, *News and News Sources* (London, Sage, 2001)) and penal reformers (P. Schlesinger and H. Tumber, *Reporting Crime* (Oxford, Clarendon, 1994)).
60 The pervasive influence of the dominant political culture was brought home to me when I wrote a weekly op-ed column for *The Times*. Right-wing shorthand phrases like 'hard left' would appear unsummoned in what I wrote – and had to be weeded out when I revised my copy.

61 P. Kirby, *Leading People 2016: The Educational Backgrounds of the UK Professional Elite* (London, Sutton Trust, 2016), p. 2. Available at: www.suttontrust.com/wp-content/uploads/.../Leading-People_Feb16.pdf (accessed 3 June 2016). His definition of senior journalists included broadcasting as well as press journalists.

62 Anon, *The Educational Background of Leading Journalists* (London, Sutton Trust, 2006), p. 4. Available at: www.suttontrust.com/wp.../06/Journalists-backgrounds-final-report.pdf (accessed 3 June 2016).

63 G. Merrill, 'Convergence and divergence: a study of British economic, business and financial journalism', unpublished Ph.D. thesis (Goldsmiths, University of London, 2015).

64 Davies, *Flat Earth*, p. 86.

65 A. Davis, *Public Relations Democracy* (Manchester, Manchester University Press, 2002); D. Miller and W. Dinan, *A Century of Spin* (London, Pluto, 2008).

66 F. Nel, *Laid Off* (Preston, University of Lancashire, 2010). Available at: www.journalism.co.uk/uploads/laidoffreport.pdf (accessed 19 May 2016).

67 Davies, *Flat Earth*; N. Fenton (ed.) *New Media, Old News* (London, Sage, 2010); P. Lee-Wright, A. Phillips and T. Witschge, *Changing Journalism* (Abingdon, Routledge, 2010); A. Phillips, *Journalism in Context* (London, Routledge, 2014).

68 S. Lohr, 'British battle over Harrods: "Tiny" vs. "phoney pharaoh"', *New York Times*, 31 March 1989. Available at: www.nytimes.com/.../british-battle-over-harrods-tiny-vs-phoney-pharaoh.html (accessed 19 May 2016).

69 Neil, *Full Disclosure*, p. 426.

70 Ibid., p. 427.

71 P. Oborne, *The Triumph of the Political Class* (London, Pocket Books, 2008).

72 P. Oborne, 'Why I have resigned from the *Telegraph*', *Open Democracy*, 17 February 2015. Available at: www.opendemocracy.net/ourkingdom/peter-oborne/why-i-have-resigned-from-telegraph (accessed 3 June 2016).

73 Ibid.

74 C. Critcher, *Moral Panics and the Media* (Buckingham, Open University Press, 2003).

75 J. Curran, I. Gaber and J. Petley, *Culture Wars* (Edinburgh, Edinburgh University Press, 2005).

76 R. Taylor and S. Vines, 'Farewell to Fleet Street', *Observer*, 5 January 1985.

77 I. Aitken, 'Whose back against the wall?', *Guardian*, 25 November 1985.

78 *Royal Commission on the Press Interim Report: The National Newspaper Industry* (London, HMSO, 1976), Table E.11, p. 101.

79 J. Petley, 'A revolution that changed nothing', *British Journalism Review*, 27 (2), 2016.

80 L. Melvern, *The End of the Street* (London, Methuen, 1986).

81 D. Goodhart and P. Wintour, *Eddie Shah and the Newspaper Revolution* (London, Coronet, 1986).

82 P. Chippindale and C. Horrie, *Disaster! The Rise and Fall of* News on Sunday (London, Sphere, 1988), pp. 174 and 189.

83 S. Glover, *Paper Dreams*, rev. edition (London, Penguin, 1994), p. 73.

84 *Sunday Sport*, 14 August 1988.

85 *Sunday Sport*, 26 January 1988.

86 Since 1980, there has been a significant increase in local press concentration, following numerous mergers. But lack of comparable historical data (apart from the imperfect measure of share of titles) makes this difficult to document.

87 P. Elmer-Dewitt, 'Battle for the Soul of the Internet', *Time*, 25 July 1994.

88 See Part III of this book. This includes a more extended discussion of the impact of the net on journalism.

89 See Chapter 9.

90 *Digital News Report 2016* (Oxford, Reuters Institute for the Study of Journalism, 2016). Available at: www.digitalnewsreport.org/ (accessed 3 June 2017).

91 J. Curran, N. Fenton and D. Freedman, *Misunderstanding the Internet*, 2nd edition (Abingdon, 2016), pp. 23–24.

92 For a case study of a start-up, highlighting the financial obstacles it faced, see J. Curran, *Media and Democracy* (Abingdon, Routledge, 2011), Chapter 5.

93 Curran, Fenton and Freedman, *Misunderstanding*, p. 24.

94 National Readership Survey Print and Digital Data (NRS PADD), June 2015, reported in Media Reform Coalition (MRC), *Who Owns the UK Media?* (London, MRC, 2015), Table 4, p. 6.

95 J. Stiglitz, *Freefall: Free Markets and the Sinking of the Global Economy* (London, Penguin, 2010); J. Lybeck, *A Global History of the Financial Crash of 2007–8* (Cambridge, Cambridge University Press, 2011); A. Gamble, *Crisis Without End?* (Basingstoke, Macmillan, 2014), among others.

96 M. Berry, 'The UK press and the deficit debate', *Sociology*. Published online, May 2015 DOI:10.1177/0038038515582158 (pre-print), pp. 9 ff.

97 Berry, 'UK press', p. 14.

98 *Sun*, 9 April 2016.

99 *Daily Mail*, 11 April 2016.

100 Ibid.

101 *Daily Telegraph*, 11 April 2016.

102 *Daily Mail*, 11 April 2016.

103 *Guardian*, 11 April 2016.

104 R. Greenslade, 'Newspapers attack rogue capitalists but bridle at regulating them', *Guardian Online*, 9 June 2016. Available at: www.theguardian.com/media/greenslade/2016/jun/09/newspapers-attack-rogue-capitalists-but-bridle-at-regulating-them (accessed 20 June 2016).

105 *Sun*, 9 June 2016.

106 *Daily Telegraph*, 9 June 2016.

107 R. Greenslade, *Press Gang* (Biggleswade, Macmillan, 2003), pp. 673–74.

108 D. Leigh, 'A who's who of Britain's legal offshore tax avoidance', *Guardian Online*, 10 July 2014. Available at: www.theguardian.com/business/2014/jul/10 (accessed 21 May 2016).

109 'Barclay twins' RitzHotel pays no corporation tax', BBC News online, 17 December 2012. Available at www.bbc.co.uk/news/uk-20729430 (accessed 21 May 2016).

110 O. Jones, *The Establishment* (London, Allen Lane, 2014), pp. 64–65.

111 However, the *Sun* broke ranks by opposing in 2015 the shrinking of tax credits for the working poor (including numerous *Sun* readers). See, for example, www.thesun.co.uk/sol/homepage/news/politics/6763752/Osbornes-scraps-45bn-tax-credits-cut.html (accessed 21 May 2016).

112 *Daily Mail*, 20 October 2009.

113 *Daily Mail*, 11 July 2011.

114 *Daily Express*, 27 July 2011.

115 *Sun*, 9 February 2013.

116 *Daily Mail*, 28 December 2010.

117 *Daily Express*, 26 January 2011.

118 T. Newton Smith, 'Iain Duncan Smith on benefit Britain', *Sun Online* (n.d.). Available at: www.thesun.co.uk/sol/homepage/news/3254131/We-are-living-in-a-shirkers-paradise-in-the-UK.html (accessed 26 May 2016).

119 *Daily Express*, 26 January 2011.

120 *Daily Express*, 9 January 2013.

121 *Report of an Inquiry into the Culture, Practices and Ethics of the Press*, vol. 2 (Leveson Report) (London, Stationery Office, 2012), pp. 684–85.

122 See Chapter 7.

123 *Sunday Times*, 11 May 1985.

124 *Sun*, 19 April 1989.

125 'Hillsborough Independent Panel Disclosed Material and Report', 2016, Chapter 12. Available at: www.hillsborough.independent.gov.uk/report/ (accessed 28 May 2016).

126 P. Chippendale and C. Horrie, *Stick it up Your Punter* (London, Pocket Books, 1999), pp. 339 ff.

127 See note 125.

128 O. Jones, *Chavs* (London, Verso, 2011), p. 8.

129 *Daily Telegraph*, 1 February 2004.

130 *The Times*, 13 April 2006.

131 *Daily Mail*, 10 February 2009.

132 Jones, *Chavs*; I. Tyler, 'Chav mum chav scum', *Feminist Media Studies*, 8 (1), 2008.

133 *Daily Mail*, 19 June 2014, 3 March 2015, 25 March 2016; *Daily Express*, 27 January 2009, 4 February 2014, among many others.

134 Tyler, 'Chav mum', p. 21.

135 J. Curran, I. Gaber and J. Petley, *Culture Wars* (Edinburgh, Edinburgh University Press, 2005), pp. 23 ff.

136 *Guardian*, 28 March 1982.

137 *Daily Mail*, 10 November 1983.

138 G. Murdock, 'Reporting the riots: images and impacts' in J. Benyon (ed.) *Scarman and After* (Oxford, Pergamon, 1984); Hollingsworth, *Press and Dissent*.

139 S. Hall, *The Hard Road to Renewal* (London, Verso, 1988); Reiner, *Law and Order*.

140 Leader's Speech, Brighton 1995: Tony Blair. Available at: www.britishpolitical speech.org/speech-archive.htm?speech=201 (accessed 13 June 2016).

141 M. Dean, *Democracy Under Attack* (Bristol, Policy Press, 2013), p. 128.

142 'Cam: I'll mend broken Britain'. Available at www.thesun.co.uk/sol/homepage/ news/justice/741731/David-Cameron-Tory-leader-Plans-to-mend-broken-Britain. html (accessed 26 May 2016).

143 'PM's speech on the fightback after the riots', Cabinet Office, 15 August 2011. Available at: www.gov.uk/government/speeches/pms-speech-on-the-fightback-after-the-riots (accessed 26 May 2016).

144 Reiner, *Law and Order*, p. 148.

145 S. Buchanan, B. Grillo and T. Threadgold, What's the Story? Media Representation of Refugees and Asylum Seekers in the UK, *Article 19* (London, 2003). Available at: www.article19.org/data/files/pdfs/publications/refugees-what-s-the-story-.pdf (accessed 27 June 2016).

146 *Daily Express* front-page headlines, 2 June 2016; 10 June 2016; and 16 January 2016.

147 *Daily Mail*, 28 August 2015.

148 *Sun*, 31 December 2013.

149 *Daily Mail*, 2 January 2013.

150 *Daily Express*, 3 June 2011.

151 *Daily Telegraph*, 5 April 2016.

152 *Daily Express*, 18 February 2016.

153 *Daily Express*, 13 February 2011.

154 *Daily Mail*, 17 May 2016.

155 *Daily Express*, 20 April 2016 and 16 May 2016.

156 *Daily Mail*, 16 May 2006.

157 *Sun*, 6 December 2002 and 1 August 2015, *et passim*.

158 G. Philo, E. Briant and P. Donald, *Bad News for Refugees* (London, Pluto Press, 2013); S. Blinder and W. Allen, 'Constructing immigrants: portrayals of migrant groups in British national newspapers, 2010–2012', *International Migration Review* 50 (1), 2016.

159 Buchanan, *What's the Story?*, 2003.

160 H. Crawley, S. McMahon and K. Jones, *Victims and Villains: Migrant Voices in the British Media* (Centre for Trust, Peace and Social Relations, 2016). Available at: www.coventry.ac.uk/research/research-directories/research-news/2016/victims-and-villains/ (accessed 14 June 2016).

161 A. Balch and E. Balabanova, 'Ethics, politics and migration: public debates on the free movement of Romanians and Bulgarians in the UK, 2006–2013', *Politics*, 36 (1), 2014, 2016.

162 *Sun*, 17 April 1982.

163 *Daily Mirror*, 3 September 2015.

164 M. Berry, I. Garcia-Blanco and K. Moore, 'Press Coverage of the Refugee and Migrant Crisis in the EU: A Content Analysis of Five European Countries' (Report, United Nations High Commission for Refugees, 2015). Available at: www.unhcr.org/56bb369c9.html (accessed 13 April 2016).

165 Ibid.

166 Philo et al., *Bad News for Refugees*; Crawley et al., *Victims and Villains*.

167 *Sun*, 20 April 1982.

168 Cited in R. Greenslade, 'A new Britain, a new kind of newspaper', *Guardian Online*, 25 February 2002. Available at: www.theguardian.com/media/2002/feb/25/pressandpublishing.falklands (accessed 29 June 2016).

169 *Sun*, 4 May 1982.

170 *Sun*, 25 September 2003.

171 *Daily Star*, 25 September 2003.

172 The only anti-war national dailies were the *Daily Mirror*, *Independent* and *Guardian*. See C. Murray, K. Parry, P. Robinson and P. Goddard, 'Reporting dissent in wartime: British press, the anti-war movement and the 2003 Iraq War', *European Journal of Communication*, 23 (1), 2008.

173 *Observer*, 23 June 1996.

174 *Daily Mirror*, 24 June 1996.

175 *Sun*, 24 June 1996

176 *Sun*, 27 June 1996.

177 T. Nairn, *The Enchanted Glass,* 2nd edition (London, Verso, 2011).

178 *Daily Mail*, 17 August 2011.

179 *Sun*, 4 August 2005; cf. *Daily Telegraph*, 3 August 2005.

180 *Sun*, 4 February 2004.

181 *Daily Mail,* 30 April 2002.

182 *Sun*, 21 February 2005; cf. *Daily Star*, 21 February 2005.

183 *Sunday Mirror*, 5 March 2006.

184 *Daily Express*, 16 October 2003.

185 *Daily Express*, 30 September 2013.

186 These stories are anatomized in two anthologies: *Euromyths: A-Z Index of Euromyths 1992 to 2016* (European Commission), available at: www.blogs.ec.europa.eu/ECintheUK/euromyths-a-z-index/ (accessed 12 June 2017); and 'Guide to the best euromyths', *BBC 23*, March 2007, available at: www.news.bbc.co.uk/1/hi/world/europe/6481969.stm (accessed 11 June 2017). Those cited here are only a few examples from a very large number of fake news stories.

187 *Sun*, 12 June 2014.

188 J. Curran, I. Gaber and J. Petley, *Culture Wars*, 2nd edition (Abingdon, Routledge, 2018).

189 D. Levy, B. Aslan and D. Biron, 'The press and referendum campaign' in (Reuters Institute for the Study of Journalism, University of Oxford, 2016). Available at: www.referendumanalysis.eu/eu-referendum-analysis-2016/section-3-news/the-press-and-the-referendum-campaign/ (accessed 8 June 2017).

190 Ibid.

191 K. Sian, I. Law and S. Sayid, 'The Media and Muslims in the UK' (Leeds, Centre for Ethnicity and Racism Studies, University of Leeds, 2012).

192 *Daily Telegraph*, 18 October 2001.

193 *Sunday Telegraph*, 13 May 1973; *Sun*, 14 June 1974; *Daily Mail*, 5 May 1975.

194 *Sun*, 9 September 1982.

195 *Sun*, 10 July 1985.

196 *Daily Express*, 29 August 1983.

197 For an account placing Benn in a continuum of radical thought, see G. Foote, *The Labour Party's Political Thought*, 2nd edition (London, Croom Helm, 1986). See also R. Jenkins, *Tony Benn* (London, Writers and Readers Cooperative, 1980), and for Benn's own words, C. Mullin (ed.) *Tony Benn: Arguments for Democracy* (London, Cape, 1981).

198 J. Carvel, *Citizen Ken* (London, Chatto & Windus, 1984). For Livingstone's own words, see 'Local socialism: the way ahead. Interview with Ken Livingstone' in M. Body and C. Fudge (eds.) *Local Socialism?* (Basingstoke, Macmillan, 1984); and his latest memoirs, *Ken Livingstone: You Can't Say That* (London, Faber and Faber, 2011).

199 *Daily Mail*, 26 May 1981.

200 *Sun*, 27 July 1981.

201 *Sun*, 1 March 1984.

202 *Daily Mail*, 20 August 1981.

203 J. Curran, I. Gaber and J. Petley, *Culture Wars* (Edinburgh, Edinburgh University Press, 2005), p. 50; Hollingsworth, *Press and Political Dissent*, p. 72.

204 Curran, Gaber and Petley, *Culture Wars*, Chapter 2.

205 Curran, Gaber and Petley, *Culture Wars*, Chapter 4.

206 *Mail on Sunday*, 2 March 1986.
207 Curran, Gaber and Petley, *Culture Wars*, pp. 87–88.
208 *Star*, 15 February 1986
209 *Sun*, 20 February 1986.
210 Curran, Gaber and Petley, *Culture Wars*, pp. 97–105. The irony is that staff at Beacon Day Nursery, Islington believed the story, and did ban the nursery rhyme.
211 Goldsmiths College Media Group, *Media Coverage of London Councils: Final Report* (London, Goldsmiths, 1987).
212 Curran, Gaber and Petley, *Culture Wars*, Chapters 7 and 9.
213 *Daily Mail*, 7 June 2017.
214 *Daily Express*, 7 June 1983 cited in J. Thomas, *Popular Newspapers, the Labour Party and British Politics* (Abingdon, Routledge, 2005), p. 90.
215 *Sunday Times*, 19 February 1995.
216 Media Reform Coalition, 'Corbyn's first week: negative agenda setting in the press'. Available at: www.mediareform.org.uk/press-ethics-and-regulation/the-medias-attack-on-corbyn-research-shows-barrage-of-negative-coverage (accessed 1 July 2016). For an analysis of coverage over a longer time, see B. Cammaerts, B. DeCillia, J. Maghalhaes and C. Jimienez-Martinez, 'Journalistic Representations of Jeremy Corbyn in the British Press: From Watchdog to Attackdog', Media@LSE Report. Available at: www.lse.ac.uk/media@lse/research/pdf/JeremyCorbyn/Cobyn-Report-FINAL.pdf (accessed 15 July 2016).
217 *Sunday Express*, 13 September 2015 and *Mail on Sunday*, 13 September 2015.
218 *Daily Telegraph*, 2 May 2016; *Daily Mail*, 29 December 2015; *Independent*, 4 September 2015.
219 *The Morning Star* is not included since it no longer has a nationwide circulation.
220 *People*, 25 September 2016.
221 *Sunday Mirror*, 25 September 2016.
222 *Sun on Sunday*, 25 September 2016.
223 *Sunday Times*, 25 September 2016.
224 *Sun,* 8 June 2017.
225 John Smith was on the centre-right of his party but in the context of the New Labour era should be seen as being on the centre-left (see A. McSmith, *John Smith* (London, Mandarin, 1994)).
226 Cited in Thomas, *Popular Newspapers*, p. 103.
227 *Sun*, 9 April 1992.
228 Cited in Thomas, *Popular Newspapers*, p. 122.
229 *Mail on Sunday*, 8 February 2015.
230 *Daily Mail*, 6 May 2015.
231 *Daily Mail*, 27 September 2012.
232 *Sun*, 6 May 2015.
233 M. Scammell and C. Beckett, 'Labour no more: the press' in D. Kavanagh and P. Cowley (eds.) *The British General Election 2010* (Basingstoke, Palgrave Macmillan, 2010), p. 280.
234 Cited in Thomas, *Popular Newspapers*, p. 130.
235 *The Times*, 5 June 2001.
236 Cited in Thomas, *Popular Newspapers*, p. 143.

237 M. Scammell and M. Harrop, 'The press: still for Labour, despite Blair' in D. Kavanagh and P. Cowley (eds.) *The British General Election of 2005* (Basingstoke, Palgrave Macmillan, 2005), p. 125.

238 Scammell and Beckett, 'Labour no more', p. 280. This persisted: Labour only secured the support of two national dailies (*Daily Mirror* and *Guardian*) in the 2017 general election.

Chapter 9

Rise of the neo-liberal Establishment

Before assessing the impact of the press in the remaking of Britain, it is worth taking a quick look at the social science literature on media influence. This literature is not an infallible source of wisdom since it is beset with methodological problems. A cheap, one-off survey can be ambiguous about the direction of influence – for example whether the press influences opinion ('press effect') or whether readers choose a paper because they agree with it ('selection effect'). Experimental studies (for instance, exposing audiences to media content edited in different ways) address this issue of causation but raise two other issues: to what extent do laboratory conditions resemble real life situations, and how adequately does an analysis of short-term media effect measure the media's cumulative influence? This last issue is addressed by longitudinal studies (based typically on a large panel of respondents) which measure change over time. However the longer the period of time covered by the longitudinal study, the more respondents are exposed to varied, societal influences. This makes pinning down the media's role in contributing to change more difficult to assess. People are influenced by the conversations they have with other people: yet these conversations are influenced in turn by the media. Identifying the relative importance of non-media and media inputs in an interactive confluence of influence is hugely difficult.[1]

Ingenious research methods and statistical techniques have been developed to address these problems. Despite its limitations, this social science tradition offers insights that media history needs to take account of. Its most important argument is that people have prior values, opinions and understandings, formed by early socialization, membership of social networks and personal experience. This influences what media they consume; how they interpret information; and what they remember.[2]

People tend to read papers that accord with what they think already. For example, readers of the pro-Labour *Daily Mirror* are predominantly Labour supporters, while readers of the Conservative *Daily Telegraph* are overwhelmingly Conservative. The rise of Facebook as a means of accessing newspaper articles has reinforced, to some degree, this process of selective exposure. More generally, people can be exposed to the same communication, and understand it differently in line with what they thought beforehand. This is why researchers conclude that the media more often reinforce than change political attitudes.

However, the press can contribute to change, though sometimes in indirect or cumulative ways. The press can influence the political agenda: what people think about. It can channel pre-existing anxieties and resentments in a particular direction ('canalization'). It can influence public perceptions of society and levels of public knowledge. It can also affect how television reports and interprets the news. To judge from experimental research, television reporting can have a direct influence on attitudes and even frameworks of understanding – though only on some topics, among some audience members, in some contexts. In general people who are in two minds or have little interest in politics are the most susceptible to media influence, whereas those who have a strong ego involvement in holding an opinion, and are reinforced by congruent influences, are difficult to shift.[3]

In brief, social science research suggests two things. Media power is often less than it is widely assumed to be; and it is often exerted in circuitous ways in contrast to the simplistic, popular image of media 'brainwashing'. With these two provisos in mind, what influence did the post-1979 press have?

Central failure of press

The dominant right-wing press failed in one central respect. It did not succeed in generating *popular* consent for the Thatcherite revolution. Year after year, national papers extolled the virtues of moving towards a deregulated, free enterprise Britain. Yet, the British public clung obstinately to key tenets of the post-1945 social democratic consensus.

Survey research shows that, during the 1980s, the majority disapproved of important aspects of Margaret Thatcher's political programme, including privatization and lower taxes for the rich.[4] During the subsequent period, comparable surveys show that the majority of British people continued to support higher taxes on the rich, an activist government role in the creation of jobs, and collective provision of public services. Thus, throughout the period 1983–2002, over 70 per cent said that the income gap in Britain was too large.[5] In line with this, the majority wanted the rich to pay higher taxes in 2014, just as they had done in the 1980s.[6] The overwhelming majority continued to support the National Health Service (NHS) and BBC, institutions that are a product of Britain's collectivist past.[7] Indeed, in 2016, only 21 per cent supported even 'some degree of private sector involvement in the running of the NHS'.[8] Despite becoming more individualistic, the British public never converted to the neo-liberal vision of a low-cost, small-budget state. Throughout the period 1983–2012, less than 11 per cent favoured the radical right option of lower public spending and lower taxes.[9] And by 2016, a strong reaction had set in against austerity politics justified in terms of deficit reduction: just 13 per cent supported the level of cuts then imposed by the Conservative government.[10] This was also a time when support for an active state role in the economy – which never disappeared – became more pronounced. In 2013–15, the majority supported, among other measures, the renationalization of the railways and water companies, wanted the reintroduction of rent controls, and believed that large companies should be required to have staff representation on their boards.[11]

This then raises the question of how the 'Thatcherite revolution' had electoral support, if it did not have popular support. Part of the answer lies in Britain's majoritarian electoral system. The impression conveyed by the Thatcher's political ascendancy – in which she won three successive general elections (1979, 1983 and 1987) – is that the neo-liberal right had overwhelming electoral support. This was not the case. The Conservative party's share of the vote in its victorious 1983 and 1987 general elections was actually smaller than its share when it *lost* the 1964 general election.[12]

Thatcher was enormously helped by the launch, in 1981, of the Social Democratic Party (SDP), a centre-left breakaway group from the Labour Party. The SDP was initially very successful, gaining 24 per cent of the vote in the 1983 election and 21 per cent of the vote in the 1987 election.[13] But it failed to overtake and replace the Labour Party. Its effect was to split the progressive vote and enable the Conservative Party to win on the basis of a minority vote in a first-past-the-post electoral system.

Another part of the answer lies in the rise of New Labour which governed Britain from 1997 to 2010. Its political ascendancy for 13 years, and its domination of the Opposition for a time before and after this, meant that neo-liberalism – whether in a negotiated Labour or stronger Conservative version – defined the principal political choice available to the public.

A third part of the explanation is that while British society did not repudiate the post-1945 consensus, it did move to the right in some respects. Indeed, Conservatives 'won' the popular argument on a number of issues: on law and order, migrants, 'shirkers', defence and also support for austerity measures in the aftermath of the 2008 crash (until 2015).

But the post-1979 period was still not a time of neo-liberal hegemony. Growing numbers of voters had simultaneously left-wing and right-wing views.[14] Some voters swapped around, giving rise to the growth of minority parties from the 1980s onwards.[15] Others turned away from politics, giving rise to low electoral turnouts in the 1990s and 2000s.[16] Deep currents of anger and resentment – long flowing beneath the surface – became more pronounced following the 2008 crash. In 2015 72 per cent of British people agreed that politicians are 'protecting the interests of the already rich and powerful',[17] while another study found that only 16 per cent trusted politicians to tell the truth.[18] To invert a phrase from Herman and Chomsky,[19] the press did *not* 'manufacture consent' for the neo-liberal social order.

Public misperceptions

However, the press did have a significant influence. It affected behaviour (consider for example the effect of the measles, mumps and rubella (MMR) press scare in lowering take-up).[20] It also influenced public attitudes, not least through cultivating misperceptions about British society.

Thus, the press has long given prominence to crime, and in particular to untypical forms of crime (violent crime and sexual assaults). But in the 1990s and 2000s, right-wing popular newspapers combined this 'distortion' with a law and order campaign that attacked the authorities for not doing enough. This gave rise to the impression that crime was becoming more of a problem, when in fact the reverse was the case. Around two thirds of the population during the period 1998–2006 thought that crime was rising, when it was actually falling.[21] The public also overestimated the incidence of violent crime: for example, 79 per cent thought that the murder rate in Britain was higher than it actually was.[22] Exaggerated fear of crime, fanned by the press, fuelled the desire for greater retribution demanded by the press.

From 2002 onwards, most of the popular press also conveyed the impression that migrants were swamping Britain. This gave rise to an inflated view of migrant numbers. In 2009, the public estimated non-western migrants to amount to 25 per cent of the British population, whereas they accounted for around 5 per cent.[23] Even foreign-born migrants – that is *both* non-western and western migrants – accounted for no more than 11 per cent.[24] Most of the popular press also portrayed migrants as both a threat and a burden. This negative portrayal seems to have been especially persuasive in low migrant areas where migrants were encountered more through the media than in real life. By contrast, antipathy was often much less in high-immigration areas like London where migrants were known first hand.[25] Nevertheless, anti-migrant coverage sustained over more than a decade had a significant impact because it connected to underlying anxieties and concerns. In 2013, 77 per cent favoured a reduction of immigration, with 56 per cent saying that this should be 'by a lot'.[26]

Between 2010 and 2014, a torrent of newspaper articles conveyed the impression that the majority – still suffering the consequences of the 2008 crash – were supporting a large, workshy underclass. In 2012, the public thought that the share of the welfare budget going on unemployment benefit was 41 per cent whereas it was actually 4 per cent.[27] Respondents thought that, on average, 27 per cent of benefit claims were fraudulent, whereas the official estimate was 1 per cent.[28] Respondents also estimated, on average, that 50 per cent of new jobseekers were still signing on one year later:[29] the true figure in 2011 was 10 per cent.[30]

These misperceptions increased animosity towards the poor. In 2013, 54 per cent said that the unemployed could find work if they really tried, compared with 27 per cent who held the same view in 1993.[31] In 2014, 52 per cent thought that benefits for the unemployed were too high and discouraged them from working – much higher than the 30 per cent who agreed with this in 1995.[32] This shift encouraged a more critical attitude towards spending on the poor. Agreement with spending more on welfare benefits fell from 61 per cent in 1989 to 30 per cent in 2014.[33]

This anti-welfare reaction occurred at a time when the Conservative government argued that the first priority of the nation after the 2008 crash was to cut the deficit. The politics of austerity, backed by most of the national press, had for a time public support. Those favouring higher spending on health, education and social benefits, funded by higher taxes, decreased from 63 per cent in 2002 to 37 per cent in 2014.[34]

There is also a wide spectrum of press content, whose political significance has tended to be overlooked. The press's expanding sections concerned with travel, motoring, fashion, beauty, health, homes, personal finance and personal relations conveyed the powerful message that individuals can express themselves, and find fulfilment, through consumption. This content not only fostered consumerist values but carried the implication that shared access to consumer services constituted a form of 'market democracy' transcending the hierarchy of power. More generally, human interest stories tended to project an essentially conservative, individual-centred view of the world, shaped by elemental human motives and chance in which structural influences played little part.[35] The press's growing focus on celebrities drawn from the world of sport and entertainment shone a critical – even at times pitiless – light on a powerless elite. By contrast, economic elites escaped the same degree of critical scrutiny. This was part of a general pattern in which critical perspectives of society tended to be omitted or downplayed.

If the 'politics' of press entertainment has not received the attention it deserves, there are numerous studies of press influence on voting. The results of this research are sometimes contradictory or inconclusive. In general it suggests that the Conservative preponderance of the press – save in the New Labour era – gave the Conservative party an electoral advantage in successive general elections. However, the influence of the press, over and above other influences, on voting has been generally found to be relatively small.[36] This may be because most of these studies are confined to examining press influence during general election campaigns – typically four weeks. The main influence of the press on voting, it has been argued, can occur before the election campaign begins, and can be more significant than these studies suggest.[37]

Limits of popular press influence

However the central point remains: the press did not convert the public to full-hearted support for the neo-liberal order, even if it contributed to a rightwards shift on some issues. Why was the press not more persuasive? One part of the explanation has to do with the importance of socialization and social networks in shaping political attitudes, mentioned earlier. People are not easily persuaded to change their political orientations.

Second, the popular press is primarily in the entertainment business. While many readers read papers to be briefed about public affairs, some just wanted to be entertained. This was especially true of Britain's most popular daily, the *Sun*. Despite hectoring editorials and feature articles, the majority of its readers regularly rejected the paper's advice to vote Conservative: in 1979, 62 per cent of *Sun* readers did so; in 1987, 59 per cent; in 1992, 55 per cent and in 2010, 57 per cent.[38] If the majority of its readers finally voted Conservative in the 2017 general election,[39] this change was probably mainly due to the rapid decrease of its readership to a hard core.

Indeed, many *Sun* readers were unable for a long time to correctly identify which side their paper was on – illuminating just how little the political parts of the paper were read. In 1979, only 33 per cent of *Sun* readers registered the fact that the *Sun* had become a Conservative newspaper (for nearly four years).[40] Despite the vigorous support the paper gave to the Thatcher government, this rose to only 64 per cent of its readers by 1983.[41] Those correctly identifying the paper as Conservative was still only 63 per cent in 1987.[42]

Third, the press slipped down the media pecking order. By the early 1960s, the press had been displaced by television as the main source of news.[43] It was demoted again in the early 2010s when the internet overtook the press as a more widely used source of news.[44]

Fourth, the audience reached by the press contracted. In 1963–68, 83 per cent of the population read a national daily.[45] This fell to 59 per cent in 1992, and 45 per cent in 2006.[46] The extent of the decline in the subsequent period is difficult to measure because some readers transferred to the online edition of their paper (on which they generally spent less time). But this should not obscure the fact that the press continued to reach a shrinking audience. By 2013, large numbers of young people never or seldom read a newspaper.[47]

Fifth, the press had low credibility. We will present some arresting comparative data in the next chapter. It is sufficient to note here that, throughout the period 1983–2016, journalists were one of the most distrusted professional groups in Britain, while TV news readers were among the more trusted (reflecting the greater trust placed in TV news). Thus in 2015, only 25 per cent of the UK population trusted journalists to tell the truth – the same proportion as estate agents.[48] Some papers were notorious for being inaccurate and misleading. In 1992, the *Sun* was rated as less believable than even party political broadcasts.[49]

So, the failure of the press to successfully embed the Thatcher revolution is easily explained. The press was a declining institution, eclipsed by television and the internet, losing readers, commanding limited trust, and read sometimes more for its entertainment than its politics.

Nor did the press 'speak' for the public. In the 1979 general election, press support for the Conservative Party (79 per cent of national daily circulation) greatly exceeded its electoral support (44 per cent of the vote).[50] This disparity persisted until the New Labour interlude, and resumed thereafter. In the 2010 general election, press support for the Conservatives (72 per cent of national circulation) was almost double that of its electoral support (37 per cent of the vote). By contrast, Labour's support in the press (13.5 per cent of national daily circulation) was less than half of its electoral support (30 per cent).[51] This disparity became still greater in the 2017 general election.

Influence on broadcasters

Some argue that press influence is mediated through television. It is pointed out that some TV journalists are recruited from the world of print journalism, and many are voracious newspaper readers. The constraints of impartiality, it is also suggested, make TV journalists reluctant to initiate controversy, and dispose them to take their lead from unfettered newspapers. In this view, the press shapes attitudes in a two-step process – by influencing broadcasters who in turn influence the wider public.

A systematic study of inter-media influence confirms that there is something in this argument. In the 2015 general election, there was a close alignment of news agendas between TV and press; evening news sometimes followed the lead of morning newspapers; and broadcasters said in interviews that they would follow newspapers stories if these had sufficient news value.[52]

But a view of TV news and current affairs as being driven by the press is over-simplistic for two reasons. Firstly, it does not take account of change over time. During the 1980s there was a significant difference in the way in which television and the press interpreted the news. The BBC and ITV repeatedly clashed with the Thatcher government, unlike the mainly loyalist press.[53] The response of some newspapers was to attack TV programmes which questioned the official line.

For example, in 1988 ITV transmitted a programme, *Death on the Rock*, which suggested that an unarmed IRA unit had been executed by the British soldiers in Gibraltar.[54] 'IRA propaganda', snorted the *Sun*; 'TV slur on the SAS', complained the *Daily Star*; 'a woefully one-sided look at the killings', fulminated an article in the *Daily Mail*.[55] The strongest attack came from the government which had attempted to suppress the programme, and from the loyalist *Sunday Times*, which sought to discredit the witnesses who appeared in the programme.[56] In a collective act of defiance, the TV industry then snubbed both government and the press by giving *Death on the Rock* its top annual (British Academy of Film and Television Arts (BAFTA)) award.

In a similar vein, ITV broadcast in 1985 a programme, *In the Interests of Justice*, which suggested, on the basis of detailed evidence, that the six Irishmen convicted in 1975 of the Birmingham pub bombings could be innocent. It called into question the truthfulness and lawful behaviour of the police, and the reliability of the judicial system.[57] The initially sceptical press response turned into angry indignation when the Birmingham Six's appeal, authorized by Home Secretary Douglas Hurd, was dismissed in 1988. The *Sun* said of the Birmingham Six: 'If the *Sun* had its way, we would have been tempted to string 'em up years ago'.[58] The paper subsequently suggested that the principal investigative journalist working on the TV programme should take up residence in Russia.[59] In the event, critical TV journalism was vindicated: the Birmingham Six were acquitted in 1991.

Sometimes the divergence between press and TV was less clear-cut. In the early 1980s, numerous tabloid newspapers demanded that the Greater London Council (GLC) be closed down because its 'loony left' antics made it a public menace. By contrast, television scrupulously balanced the case for and against the GLC. However, television in the later 1980s gave to London's municipal left less airtime in which to defend itself, perhaps because it had become a political pariah denounced not only by the press but by Conservative government ministers and senior Labour politicians alike.[60]

This contrast between television and the press – not always sustained but still substantial in the polarized 1980s – became less pronounced in the subsequent period. The difference in the registers of the two media, one bi-partisan and the other partisan, remained. And there continued to be a variance between the two. Even so, research shows that on some issues reporting converged.

Thus, both television news and newspapers offered in 2009 very similar accounts of the origins of the budget deficit, its implications and potential remedies. Keynesian and radical interpretations of the deficit crisis, its scale and solutions were marginalized in both media.[61]

Similarly, implacable press hostility to Corbyn found an echo in the television news reporting, especially during the crisis in Corbyn's leadership of the Labour Party in 2016.[62] The crisis was defined in TV news bulletins as a conflict between moderates and the hard left – the latter sometimes described in explicitly pejorative language. What was at stake, TV journalists reported, was whether or not Corbyn was judged to be too divorced from mainstream opinion, and too lacking in authority, to continue as Labour leader. Balance was not always maintained. Unlike ITV, BBC News gave nearly twice as much airtime to sources critical of Corbyn compared to those who supported him. Even the tone of neutrality on occasion slipped. A BBC News at Six report concluded: 'This is a fight only one side can win. The others being carted off to irrelevance: the place for political losers'. The comment was accompanied by a shot of a moving rubbish truck on which was written in large letters 'Corbyn'.[63]

The second caveat is that when television and press coverage converge, this is not necessarily because newspapers influence TV. It can occur because both media are responding to the same political environment. Thus in the two instances cited above, convergence could be attributed to the fact that there *was* a large deficit, and a vote of no confidence in Corbyn by most of his colleagues. Both TV and newspaper journalists spoke to the same news sources – leading politicians, financial institutions and city analysts in the fiscal crisis story, and the same Labour MPs in the Corbyn crisis story. And to some extent both sets of journalists and their sources had shared assumptions about economic management and what constitutes effective political leadership.

Convergence was reinforced by the way in which TV reporting became embedded in Britain's Establishment. A comparative study of TV news in 2010 examined who was interviewed or cited in leading TV channel newscasts in ten countries. British TV emerged as being especially reliant on state spokespersons and experts, accounting for 62 per cent of sources for public affairs news. In this respect, it resembled TV reporting in countries like Japan and Berlusconi's Italy.[64] Social movements and interest group sources featured much less often in TV news in Britain compared with Norway, Greece and Canada.[65]

Political–media caste

Indeed, a narrow focus on inter-media influence misses the big picture: the development of an elite neo-liberal political culture which shaped both press and television. This development took decades to achieve.

Rupert Murdoch saw himself as being anti-Establishment. Yet, he was the son of a knighted Australian media tycoon, and educated at the same school as Prince Charles (Geelong). The fact that he went to Worcester College rather than Christchurch at Oxford University is hardly grounds for regarding him as a class rebel. Ironically, he was to become one of the principal architects of a new Establishment – opposed to the old one that he was born into.

While he and Margaret Thatcher admired and helped each other, they were never intimates. Thatcher kept herself relatively aloof from press magnates, and was notorious for only skimming newspapers. But Murdoch and like-minded press magnates backed her to the hilt, including siding with her against supporters of the post-1945 consensus within the Conservative party. The press, complained an enraged, leftish-Conservative Minister in Thatcher's first Cabinet, could 'scarcely have been more fawning if it had been state-controlled'.[66] This is not wholly true: some parts of the Conservative press were critical of the Thatcher administration during its initial period (1979–81); and were critical in the last months of her premiership, in 1990.[67] But it was broadly correct.

Yet, during the Thatcherite 1980s, the building of a neo-liberal Establishment was still a project in progress.[68] The Labour party had not yet converted to New Labour; the BBC was viewed by Thatcherites as 'pinko'; and there was still a substantial 'old guard' elite who clung to the post-1945 consensus. The alliance between the press and the Conservative government also broke down in the 1990s. Although the Conservative Prime Minister, John Major (1990–97) perpetuated Thatcher's legacy, he was attacked by the right-wing press because he was thought to have personally let down Thatcher, conceded too much to Brussels, mismanaged the economy and allowed the government to become mired in minor scandal. Labour's leader, Neil Kinnock, was monstered even though he moved his party away from the left. Both Kinnock and Major had a 'professional' relationship to the press – something that Major subsequently described as 'quixotic'.[69]

The period 1994–2016 witnessed the consolidation of the neo-liberal Westminster political consensus. The year 1994 marked the launch of New Labour under Tony Blair's leadership, first as opposition leader, and then as Prime Minister (1997–2007). It was a key moment when the two major political parties converged on a common course of privatization, deregulation and also financialization of the economy.[70] This legacy was extended under Gordon Brown (2007–10) and David Cameron (2010–16).

The forging of an elite political consensus was accompanied by the building of a closer social relationship between press and political leaders. Tony Blair courted Rupert Murdoch and became a personal friend, ending up as godfather to Murdoch's daughter, Grace. He also became a buddy of Rebekah Brooks (editor of the *Sun* and subsequently chief executive officer (CEO) of Murdoch's News UK), giving her worldly advice when she ran into trouble over phone hacking.[71] Gordon Brown found he had much in common with Paul Dacre, editor of the *Daily Mail*; Gordon Brown's wife gave a 40th birthday party for Rebekah Brooks at the Prime Minister's official residence at Chequers; and Brown's and Murdoch's children played together.[72] David Cameron also became a close friend of Rebekah Brooks, the Becky Sharp of British journalism. On one occasion, Brooks had to explain to Cameron that LOL means laugh out loud, not lots of love.[73] On another occasion, she sent this text to Cameron just before he gave a keynote to the Conservative Party Conference, revealing the collaborative nature of their relationship completely at odds with the ideal of the Fourth Estate:

> I am so rooting for you tomorrow not just as a proud friend but because professionally we're definitely in this together. Speech of your life. Yes he Cam![74]

At the suggestion of his spin doctor, Andy Coulson, David Cameron gave dinner parties with senior media executives and their wives so that he could get to know them socially.[75] Asked at the Leveson Inquiry to list his meetings with top journalists, Cameron had to exempt those who were at the centre of his overlapping family, social and professional circle. He met them so often that it was impossible to log.[76]

Social bonding was reinforced by an enormous outlay of energy in courting the press. Tony Blair, and his head of communications, Alastair Campbell, increased the politicization of the government information service. Policies were given more top spin; messages were orchestrated across departments; friendly journalists were cultivated and rewarded with exclusive briefings. Tony Blair himself admitted that 'we paid inordinate attention in the early days of New Labour in courting, assuaging and persuading the media'.[77] However, winning media support remained an obsessive preoccupation of New Labour throughout its period in office. No. 10 felt 'too much like a newsroom', recalled David Cameron when he moved in as Prime Minister.[78] But despite this implied criticism, not much changed. In the first fourteen months of the Cameron government, twenty cabinet ministers met senior Murdoch executives 130 times.[79]

Politicians also found that squaring the press meant not just becoming friends with powerful press magnates and journalists, asking them into their homes and family gatherings, spinning policies, and finding time for frequent professional meetings. They had also sometimes to anticipate or accommodate what the press wanted. In ten years, New Labour passed 53 Acts dealing with crime and punishment, greatly increasing the prison population, partly in a bid to placate right-wing tabloids.[80] When Tony Blair was told that the next release of statistics would register an increase of crime, he sent a hand-written note asking for a pre-emptive 'initiative, e.g. locking up street muggers. Something tough, with immediate bite . . . I, personally, should be associated with it'.[81] Murdoch, according to Lance Price, Deputy Director of Communications, was 'more influential on the Prime Minister [Tony Blair] and on the direction of government's policy' than most Cabinet ministers.[82]

But if the press made demands, it also helped to discourage apostasy. The press was especially useful to New Labour in policing internal dissent. Thus, when a centre-left minister, Peter Hain, suggested in 2003 that there should be a public debate about whether those at the very top of the income scale should pay more tax, the government publicity machine briefed against him to a receptive press. The *Sun* called Hain 'a backstabbing rat' who wanted to push 'Labour to the Red Flag days of Kinnock'; the *Daily Mail* denounced him as 'slithery and ambitious', intent on 'lurching back to the bad old days'; and the *Daily Express* reported that the suggestion of tax rises had caused an 'outcry'.[83] A penitent Peter Hain went round the television studios promising that there would be 'no going back to the old days of punitive rates to fund reckless spending'.[84]

The compact between politicians and journalists was not without tensions. The right-wing press eventually turned on New Labour because it was judged to be too manipulative and too wedded to high public spending. The Conservative press never really warmed to David Cameron because he was thought to be too pro-European, too socially liberal and too grand. The *Daily Telegraph* (where 'padding' was scarcely unknown) exposed in 2009 politicians' abuse of expenses. The BBC cleaved to the centre, prompting right-wing criticism. Even so, politicians across the political spectrum told the Leveson Inquiry that their relationship to the press had become 'too close'.[85]

But on fundamental issues (save, crucially, on Europe) there was broad agreement within the political and media elite about the direction that Britain should take. Many senior politicians and journalists had a similar educational background, similar views about the management of the economy, and were close friends with each other. To an even greater extent than in the post-war period, they constituted a narrow caste at the heart of British public life.[86]

Just how disconnected the media–political class had become by 2015 was apparent in its response to Jeremy Corbyn. He was an outsider who rejected the neo-liberal political consensus. He was a Polytechnic drop-out, not the product of Oxbridge. He lacked the nimble parliamentary debating skills honed by success in the Oxford Union. Most of his parliamentary colleagues and lobby correspondents dismissed him as a man of modest ability who had failed to make a mark after serving as an MP for over thirty years.

His election as leader of the Labour Party in 2015 was consequently viewed as a tsunami coming from nowhere. Once elected, Corbyn was rapidly written off as being not up to the job. It was not just his Conservative opponents who thought Corbyn was inadequate. The *Daily Mirror* and the *Guardian*, the only two pro-Labour dailies, called for his resignation;[87] some 80 per cent of Labour MPs passed a motion of no confidence in him; and there were mass resignations from his shadow cabinet. To growing elite perplexity, Corbyn was re-elected as Labour leader with an increased majority in 2016. But he was still dismissed as 'unelectable', a consensual elite view that encouraged Theresa May to call a general election in 2017 in the expectation of increasing her majority. Knowing experts anticipated a Labour melt-down.[88]

In fact the Corbyn-led Labour party increased its share of the vote from 31 per cent in 2015 to 40 per cent in 2017 – the largest percentage point increase between general elections since 1945 – causing the Conservative party to lose its majority. The result, like every step in the rise of Jeremy Corbyn, was greeted with amazement by the media–political class. They were so locked into a self-contained bubble, so immobilized by group-think, so removed from large swathes of society, that they had no understanding of the popular forces that had propelled Corbyn to rise above what they believed to be his natural station in life.

Notes

1 This is an historian's response to attempting to do this kind of research, as an intellectual break. I am struck by how rigorous this tradition is in seeking to pin down media influence.

2 J. Curran, *Media and Power* (London, Routledge, 2002).

3 For overviews, see S. Iyengar, *Media Politics*, 3rd edition (New York, Norton, 2015), especially Chapter 8; R. Nabi and M. Oliver (eds.) *Handbook of Media Processes and Effects* (Thousand Oaks, CA, Sage, 2009); R. Preiss et al. (eds.) *Mass Media Effects Research* (New York, Routledge, 2007).

4 This survey evidence is well summarized in I. Crewe, 'Has the electorate become Thatcherite?' in R. Skidelsky (ed.) *Thatcherism* (London, Chatto & Windus, 1988).

5 C. Bromley, 'Has Britain become immune to inequality?' in A. Park (ed.) *British Social Attitudes (20th Report)* (London, Sage, 2003), Table 4.4, p. 81.

6 W. Dahlgreen, 'Broad support for 50p tax', YouGov January 28, 2014. Available at: www.yougov.co.uk/news/2014/01/28/majority-support-50p-tax/ (accessed 27 October 2016); cf. Crewe 'Has the electorate', Table 6, p. 43.

7 'Public Attitudes to the NHS', The Health Foundation, 2015. Available at: www.health.org.uk/publication/public-attitudes-nhs?gclid=CLmCq7jx3swCFcFAG wodq7wKcQ (accessed 15 May 2016); 'Public perceptions of the impartiality and trustworthiness of the BBC', BBC Trust 2013 (PDF) (accessed 15 May 2016).

8 'Jeremy Corbyn's policies more popular than the Tories' [YouGov poll]. Available at: www.huffingtonpost.co.uk/entry/jeremy-corbyn-media-policies-labour_uk_57fe651be4b0010a7f3da76b (accessed 27 October 2016).

9 *British Social Attitudes*, 30th edition, 2012, Nat Cen Research, 'Government spending and welfare', Fig. 2.2. Available at: www.bsa.natcen.ac.uk/latest-report/british-social-attitudes-30/spending-and-welfare/introduction.aspx (accessed 16 May 2016).

10 See note 8.

11 W. Dahlgreen, 'Majority support for rail nationalisation – but also policies from the "radical" right', YouGov, 6 August 2015. Available at: www.yougov.co.uk/news/2015/08/06/support-radical-left-and-right/ (accessed 15 May 2016); Dahlgreen, 'Majority support', Table 1 and Dahlgreen 'Nationalisation debate: it's not about what works', YouGov, 12 March, 2015. Available at: www.yougov.co.uk/news/2015/03/12/nationalisation-ideology-beats-pragmatism/ (accessed 16 May 2016); N. Asinder, 'Public far to the left of Labour party finds poll', *International Business Times*, 5 November 2013. Available at: www.ibtimes.co.uk/left-wing-price-controls-nationalisation-yougov-poll-519684 (accessed 16 May 2016).

12 D. Butler and G. Butler, *Twentieth-Century British Political Facts 1900–2000*, 8th edition (Basingstoke, Macmillan, 2000), pp. 237–39.

13 Ibid., pp. 238–39.

14 R. Ford and M. Goodwin, *Revolt of the Right* (London, Routledge, 2014).

15 A. King, *Who Rules Britain?* (London, Pelican, 2015).

16 General election turn-out dropped from 76 per cent in 1979 to a low of 59 per cent in 2001 before partly recovering.

17 'Politics upside down', YouGov/University of Southampton, 2015. Available at: www.politicsupsidedown.files.wordpress.com/2013/06/university-of-southhampton-results-130606-disillusionment.pdf (accessed 15 May 2016).

18 'Politicians are still trusted less than estate agents, journalists and bankers', Ipsos Mori. Available at: www.ipsos-mori.com/researchpublications/researcharchive/3685/Politicians-are-still-trusted-less-than-estate-agents-journalists-and-bankers.aspx (accessed 27 October 2016).

19 E. Herman and N. Chomsky, *Manufacturing Consent* (New York, Pantheon, 1988).

20 See Chapter 10.

21 R. Reiner, *Law and Order* (Cambridge, Polity, 2007), Fig 3.8, p. 75 and Fig. 3.6, p. 71; M. Dean, *Democracy Under Attack* (Bristol, Policy Press, 2013), p. 129.

22 J. Curran et al., 'Crime, foreigners and hard news: a cross-national comparison of reporting and public perception', *Journalism*, 11 (1), 2010, Table 7, p. 11.

23 S. Blinder, 'UK public opinion toward immigration: overall attitudes and level of concern', Migration Observatory, Oxford University. Available at: www.migration observatory.ox.ac.uk/briefings/uk-public-opinion-toward-immigration-overall-attitudes-and-level-concern (accessed 17 July 2016).

24 Ibid.

25 This was true of non-migrant Londoners, not just Londoners in general, and so was not just a consequence of a higher migrant presence.

26 R. Ford and A. Heath, 'Immigration: a nation divided' in A. Park, C. Bryson and J. Curtice (eds.) *British Social Attitudes: 31st Report* (London, Nat Cen Social Research, 2014), p. 79.

27 J. Hills, *Good Times, Bad Times* (Bristol, Policy Press, 2015), pp. 259–60.

28 Hills, *Good Times*, pp. 263–64.

29 *Public Attitudes to Poverty, Inequality and Welfare in Scotland and Britain* (Edinburgh, Scottish Government, Communities Analytical Services, 2015), p. 5.

30 Hills, *Good Times*, Fig. 4.8, p. 91.

31 P. Taylor-Gooby and E. Taylor, 'Benefits and welfare' in R. Ormiston and J. Curtice (eds.) *British Social Attitudes: 32nd Report* (London, Nat Cen Social Research, 2015), p. 83.

32 Ibid., p. 91

33 Ibid., p. 74.

34 Ibid., p. 74.

35 J. Curran, A. Douglas and G. Whannel, 'The political economy of the human-interest story' in A. Smith (ed.) *Newspapers and Democracy* (Cambridge, MA, MIT Press, 1980).

36 W. Miller, *Media and Voters* (Oxford, Clarendon Press, 1991); K. Newton and M. Brynin, 'The national press and party voting in the UK', *Political Studies*, 49 (2), 2001; A. Reeves, M. McKee and D. Stuckler, '"It's the *Sun* wot won it": evidence of media influence on political attitudes and voting from a UK quasi-natural experiment', *Social Science Research*, 56, 2016, among others.

37 J. Curran, I. Gaber and J. Petley, *Culture Wars* (Edinburgh, Edinburgh University Press, 2005), Chapter 9.

38 Thomas, *Popular Newspapers*, 2005, Table 6.5, p. 157; M. Harrop, 'Press' in D. Butler and D. Kavanagh (eds.) *The British General Election of 1983* (London, Macmillan, 1984), Table 9.9, p. 215; M. Harrop, 'Press' in D. Butler and D. Kavanagh (eds.) *The British General Election of 1987* (Basingstoke, Macmillan, 1988), Table 8.7, p. 187; and M. Scammell and C. Beckett, 'Labour no more: the press' in D. Kavanagh and P. Cowley (eds.) *The British General Election of 2010* (Basingstoke, Palgrave Macmillan, 2010), Table 14.5, p. 293.

39 F. Mayhew, 'How daily newspaper readers voted by title in the 2017 general election', *PressGazette*, 14 June 2017. Available at: www.pressgazette.co.uk/murdoch-maclennan-replaced-as-telegraph-media-group-chief-executive-after-13-years-in-role/ (accessed 3 July 2017).

40 Harrop, 'Press', 1984, Table 9.9, p. 215.

41 Ibid.

42 Harrop, 'Press', 1988, Table 8.7, p. 187.

43 D. Butler and D. Stokes, *Political Change in Britain* (London, Macmillan, 1969), Table 10.3, p. 220.

44 J. Curran, S. Coen, T. Aalberg, et al., 'Internet revolution revisited: a comparative study of online news', *Media, Culture and Society*, 35 (7), 2013, Table 1, p. 884;

cf. N. Newman et al., *Digital News Report 2016* (Oxford, Reuters Institute for the Study of Journalism, 2016).

45 J. Curran, 'The impact of television on the audience for national newspapers, 1945–68' in J. Tunstall (ed.) *Media Sociology* (London, Constable), Table X, p. 128.

46 *The Ownership of the News*, vol. 1 (London, House of Lords, Stationery Office, 2008), Appendix 5, p. 140.

47 A. Durrani, 'YouGov study confirms young people abandoning newspapers', Campaign, 23 March 2013. Available at: www.campaignlive.co.uk/article/yougov-study-confirms-young-abandoning-newspapers/1174605?src_site=mediaweek (accessed 3 July 2017).

48 'Ipsos Mori Veracity Index 2015: Trust in Professions' (Ipsos Mori, 2016). Available at: www.ipsos-mori.com/researchpublications/researcharchive/3685/Politicians-are-still-trusted-less-than-estate-agents-journalists-and-bankers.aspx (accessed 30 September 2016).

49 Cited Thomas, *Popular Newspapers*, p. 152.

50 Butler and Butler, *Political Facts*, p. 536.

51 Kavanagh and Cowley, *General Election of 2010*, Table 16.3, p. 341; Scammell and Beckett, 'Labour no more', 2010, Table 14.1, p. 281.

52 S. Cushion et al., 'Newspapers, impartiality and television news', *Journalism Studies*, 19 (2), 2018.

53 J. Seaton, *Pinkoes and Traitors* (London, Profile, 2015); P. Holland, *Angry Buzz* (London, Tauris, 2006).

54 The full transcript of the programme is available in L. Windlesham and R. Rampton, *The Windlesham/Rampton Report* (London, Faber and Faber, 1989), pp. 28–68).

55 *Sun*, 29 April 1988; *Daily Star*, 29 April 1988; *Daily Mail*, 29 April 1988.

56 *Sunday Times*, 8 May 1988. *Sunday Times* journalists complained that their work had been distorted, prompting the paper's partial backtracking (see N. Davis, *Flat Earth News* (London, Chatto & Windus, 2008), pp. 303–10).

57 R. Fitzwalter, *The Dream that Died* (Matador, Leicester, 2008), pp. 28–30.

58 *Sun*, 29 January 1988.

59 *Sun*, 7 December 1988.

60 Curran et al., *Culture Wars*, Chapters 3, 6 and 9.

61 M. Berry, 'No alternative to austerity: how BBC broadcast news reported the deficit debate', *Media, Culture and Society*, 38 (6), 2016; M. Berry, 'The UK press and the deficit debate', *Sociology*, 50 (3), 2016.

62 J. Schlosberg, 'Should he stay or should he go? Television and online news coverage of the Labour Party in crisis', Media Reform Coalition. Available at: www.mediareform.org.uk/wp-content/uploads/2016/07/Corbynresearch.pdfmedia (accessed 20 June 2017).

63 BBC News at Six, 27 June 2016 cited in ibid., p. 15.

64 J. Curran et al., 'Reconsidering "virtuous circle" and "media malaise" theories of the media: an 11-nation study', *Journalism*, 15 (7), 2013, Table 4, p. 826.

65 R. Tiffen et al., 'Sources in the news', *Journalism Studies*, 15 (4), 2014, Table 10b, p. 386.

66 I. Gilmour, *Dancing with Dogma* (London, Simon & Schuster, 1993), p. 23.

67 For press criticism in the last phase of Thatcher's premiership, see in particular D. Deacon and P. Golding, *Taxation and Representation* (London, John Libbey, 1990).

68 For an eloquent evocation of just how politically beleaguered Thatcherites felt themselves to be in the early 1980s by the head of Thatcher's Policy Unit at No. 10, see F. Mount, *Cold Cream* (London, Bloomsbury, 2009).

69 *An Inquiry into the Culture, Practices and Ethics of the Press Report* [Leveson Report] (London, Stationery Office, 2012), vol. 3, p. 1126.

70 For a telling analysis of budget statements between 1976 and 2010 illuminating this shift, see A. Davis and C. Walsh, 'The role of the state in the financialisation of the UK economy', *Political Studies*, 64 (3), 2016.

71 Blair recommended among other things commissioning 'a Hutton style report', a reference to a report by a judge who found in favour of the government in its conflict with the BBC over reporting the Iraq war. BBC Online News, 'Phone-hacking trial: Blair "advised Brooks before arrest"', 19 February 2014. Available at: www.bbc.co.uk/news/uk-26259956 (accessed 4 July 2017).

72 Leveson, vol. 3, pp. 1152, 1153 and 1155.

73 Ibid., vol. 3, p. 1194.

74 Ibid.

75 Ibid., vol. 3, p. 1180.

76 Ibid., vol. 3, p. 1214.

77 Ibid., vol. 3, p. 1139.

78 Ibid., vol. 3, p 1209.

79 N. Fenton, *Digital, Political, Radical* (Cambridge, Polity, 2016), p. 182.

80 M. Dean, *Democracy Under Attack* (Bristol, Policy Press, 2013), p. 128.

81 Dean, *Democracy*, p. 140.

82 Cited in Dean, *Democracy*, p. 6.

83 *Sun*, 21 June 2003; *Daily Mail*, 21 June 2003; *Daily Express*, 21 June 2003.

84 J. Thomas, *Popular Newspapers, the Labour Party and British Politics* (London, Routledge, 2005), p. 145.

85 Leveson, vol. 3, p. 1181, p. 1439, *et passim*.

86 Brexit and the rise of Corbyn represent a break from the past. How much of a break will become clear by the time the 9th edition of this book is published.

87 Schlosberg, 'Should he stay', p. 4.

88 For example, J. Freedland, 'No more excuses: Jeremy Corbyn is to blame for this meltdown', *Guardian*, 6 May 2017.

Chapter 10

Moral decline of the press

Although phone hacking became a public scandal, it was only one of the dark arts practiced by the press.[1] Most national newspapers also engaged in blagging: accessing confidential data through deceit, usually from banks, police and government departments. By the early 2000s, newspapers increasingly outsourced this to private investigators skilled at impersonation and deceit. The top blaggers, Whittamore and associates, were commissioned by the press to investigate 13,343 cases. They were found guilty in 2005 of unlawful activity.[2]

Newspapers also gave bungs to public officials for story tip-offs. These sometimes entailed substantial payments that were a powerful inducement to abuse a position of public trust. Thirty public officials, bribed by the press, were jailed in 2013–16.

But whereas most papers were involved in bribery and blagging, phone hacking (the interception of telephone voice messages) was confined to red top papers owned by Murdoch and the Mirror group. Phone hacking provided a cheap, efficient way of gathering gossip – and dirt – on people in the public eye. It began in the late 1990s, and was carried out on an industrial scale by the early 2000s. The phone hacking specialist, Glen Mulcaire, targeted no less than 6349 people over a five-year period, principally on behalf of the *News of the World*.[3]

A sustained attempt was made to cover up the extent of phone hacking.[4] Murdoch's News International maintained that hacking was confined to just two rogue individuals when a journalist and private investigator were jailed in 2006. The *News of the World* and the *Sun* subsequently deleted a large volume of emails, and initially obstructed the police in its investigation. News International then sought to buy the silence of litigious phone hack victims by offering generous out of court settlements with confidentiality clauses.

For a time, it appeared as if all mechanisms of public accountability had been disabled. Senior police officers sat on a mountain of damning evidence about phone hacking without investigating it. They also made misleading statements – both in public and in private – seemingly designed to bury the issue. The Press Complaints Commission pretended that it had mounted a major investigation into phone hacking when it had done no such thing, and scoffed at the idea that hacking was extensive. Top politicians offered helpful covering fire: for example, the London Mayor, Boris Johnson, confidently dismissed allegations of widespread phone hacking as 'codswallop'.[5] Most newspapers (with the notable exception of the *Independent*) greeted with open scepticism or sepulchral silence the *Guardian*'s expose of phone hacking, and its cover-up. It took an American newspaper, the *New York Times*, to dig further and compensate for the failure of most of the British press.

The dam broke in 2011 when a local police force revealed that the phone messages of a murdered schoolgirl, Milly Dowler, had been hacked. There was an eruption of public anger that swept away further attempts at obfuscation. In 2011, the government set up the Leveson Inquiry into the press. The disgraced newspaper, *News of the World*, was closed, and replaced by the *Sun on Sunday*. Two senior police officers, Sir Paul Stephenson (head of the Metropolitan Police) and John Yates, resigned. Nine journalists, including the editor, news editor and features editor of the *News of the World*, were convicted for phone hacking in 2014–15.

Ethical decline

The phone hacking scandal was the culmination of changes that took place in Fleet Street during the 1980s. This is not to suggest that before the 1980s there had been a golden age, a prelapsarian period followed by a fall from grace. There had always been pressure to get results, and this had sometimes led to the cutting of corners.

But editorial standards declined markedly in the 1980s, something that was commented upon at the time. Writing in 1983, Henry Porter listed numerous inaccurate or misleading stories that had been recently published, including the invention of an overnight love tryst between Prince Charles and Lady Diana Spencer on a lonely railway siding in the royal train (*Sunday Mirror*);[6] the fabrication of an interview with Mrs Marica McKay, the widow of a Falklands VC hero (*Sun*); the touching up of a photograph of 'Lady Di' to give a hint of nipples in a low-cut dress (*Sun*); and pillorying a child as the 'Worst Brat in Britain' without mentioning that he was ill as a consequence of meningitis (*Sun*).[7] These were all examples, he argued, of a 'low regard for truth' that was spreading across different sections of leading newspapers.[8] Two years later Tom Baistow, the veteran commentator on Fleet Street, lamented 'the drift towards the gutter and the subordination of news content to sensation, scandal, jazzy packaging and million-pound bingo in the scramble for sales' in what had become the 'fourth-rate estate'.[9] The following year, Britain's best-selling newspaper cleared its front page for a story that symbolized the new ethos. 'Freddie Starr Ate My Hamster', announced the headline above a story claiming that the comic had devoured a live pet in a sandwich.[10] It transpired subsequently that Starr's publicist, Max Clifford, had colluded in the invention of this story in order to promote his client's forthcoming tour.[11] It was news reports like this which prompted the distinguished tabloid journalist, Geoffrey Goodman, to write in 1989 that the press had 'a crisis of standards, a crisis of credibility, a crisis of freedom itself'.[12]

Prominent proprietors set new ethical compass bearings in a way that is best illustrated by two telling incidents. In 1983, Murdoch's News International acquired Hitler's unpublished diaries, authenticated by the leading historian, Lord Dacre (Hugh Trevor-Roper). However, Dacre had second thoughts and rang to say that he now believed that the diaries were fraudulent. Panic ensued at the *Sunday Times*, prompting a senior executive, Brian MacArther, to ring Murdoch in America to ask what to do. 'Fuck Dacre', Murdoch replied. 'Publish'.[13]

What happened next was still more revealing. The diaries turned out to be a crude forgery, giving rise to dismay on the part of senior *Sunday Times* journalists who feared that the reputation of the paper had been irreparably damaged. But when they had a meeting to discuss the debacle with their visibly bored proprietor, he said: 'Look, I don't know why you are so worked up. We put on 60,000 in circulation last week, and there's every evidence we're hanging on to it'.[14] Subsequently he told a *New York Times* journalist enquiring into the fiasco: 'we are in the entertainment business'.[15]

The second telling incident is when Robert Maxwell, owner of the Mirror group, introduced a new competition in the *Daily Mirror* in 1990. Readers were offered £1 million if they could correctly identify from photos of football games where the out-of-shot ball was on the pitch. The offer ran for weeks offering the tantalizing prospect of becoming a millionaire. But it was all an illusion. Maxwell had taken aside the promotions manager and the paper's editor to ensure that the competition was rigged so that no one would win a £1 million prize.[16] Deceit was fostered by the boss.

The new direction at the top was in part a response to changes in the economic environment of Fleet Street. A circulation war broke out in the early 1980s, reminiscent of the inter-war period, leading to extravagant competitions and prizes. 'KILL AN ARGIE AND WIN A METRO' [car] mocked *Private Eye* in a spoof *Sun* headline.[17] By 1984, most papers (including *The Times*) were running some kind of game, with an estimated £30 million available from press competitions.[18]

New print technology intensified competition in the mid-1980s, when new national titles mushroomed in a way not seen since the late Victorian era. Although most of these new papers were short-lived, their demise was followed by a development that was to have a still greater impact: collapsing sales. National newspapers had temporarily arrested their decline during the 1980s. However, their sales decreased sharply in the 1990s, and this trend accelerated during the new millennium. By 2015, total national daily circulation was less than half of what it had been in 1980. The fall of national Sunday newspaper circulation was still more vertiginous. Total

Table 10.1 National newspaper circulation, 1980–2015[1]

1980	1985	1990	1994	2001	2005	2010	2015
National Daily ('000)							
14,886	14,731	14,225	13,585	11,586	10,804	9873	6794
National Sunday ('000)							
18,215	17,827	17,344	15,845	11,975	11,386	9404	6228

Note
1 Figures for 1980–94 are derived from C. Seymour-Ure, *The British Press and Broadcasting since 1945*, 2nd edition (Oxford, Blackwell, 1996), Tables 3.2 and 3.3, pp. 28–31. All figures derive from the Audit Bureau of Circulation. They exclude Scottish national papers and also 'bulks'.

national Sunday circulation in 2015 was little more than a third of its level in 1980 (see Table 10.1).

Falling circulation was partly offset by the launch of 'online editions' after 1999. But these latter proved to be poor earners since many online editions were offered free to users. In addition, the press's financial problems were confounded by their precipitate loss of advertising. 'Newsbrands' share of UK advertising more than halved between 2007 and 2016.[19] Within this category, even strong national papers' advertising revenue plummeted.[20]

The haemorrhaging of sales and advertising generated strong internal pressures within news organisations to stem the decline. Some journalists became ever more reckless – and indeed lawless – in their desire to win readers. The ethos of the Wild West, which had taken root in 1980s Fleet Street, became entrenched.

Institutional bullying

Intensified commercial pressures led to the browbeating of journalists to deliver results. An autocratic regime was established in the *Sun* under its authoritarian editor, Kelvin Mackenzie (1981–94). He would put his face close to an underperforming journalist and say: 'You still 'ere, then, eh? Haven't you gone yet?', creating terror that dismissal was imminent.[21] He would berate, on a regular basis, journalists in front of their colleagues in order to galvanize and motivate. When a reporter, Stuart Higgins, responded to his bollocking with a calm smile, Mackenzie roared: 'You smarmy cunt, Higgy, you take it all, don't you . . .'. Mackenzie then ordered a mugshot of Higgins, holding a telephone, to appear in the next issue of the paper, with the strapline: 'Want someone to yell at? Scream at? Fume at? RING HIGGY THE HUMAN SPONGE . . .' Printed in large type was the number of Higgins's direct line. The journalist had to endure insulting phone calls from the public in Mackenzie's version of the medieval stocks.[22]

A tyrannical regime was also established at the *News of the World*. An official tribunal investigating a case of unfair dismissal at the paper concluded that the paper had a 'culture of bullying'.[23] Testimony from journalists to the Leveson Inquiry corroborated this claim.[24] The favourite method for getting results was again a 'bollocking', the ritualized humiliation of journalists in front of their peers. Journalist bylines were also monitored as performance indicators. As one senior executive explained, 'if your byline count was low, then obviously your job would be in jeopardy'.[25]

Similar pressures were exerted across the popular national press. The long-serving editor of the *Daily Mail*, Paul Dacre, was notoriously bullying. His intemperate railing at subordinates, beginning with his pet phrase 'You cunt', became the stuff of legend. It was nicknamed – after a well-known play – as his 'Vagina Monologues'.[26]

However, top-down pressure was greatest in red top newspapers because this was where economic insecurity was most acute.[27] The lowest of the low at red top papers were the 'shifters': journalists who did not know whether they would be working the next day. A winnowing process took place in which only some shifters were asked back, thus creating a strong incentive for young, ambitious journalists to get stories by, if necessary, bending the rules. A natural career progression beckoned: short-term contract, well paid staff job and subsequent promotion. Meanwhile some middle-aged staffers saw energetic, young journalists climbing the ladder and felt threatened, at a time when declining circulations and advertising receipts were leading to successive waves of redundancy. Senior journalists were expensive: it made economic sense to let them go if they lost their youthful edge.

Senior managements pressed for results, and journalists had to find ways of delivering. This was the institutional context that gave rise to the phone hacking scandal. Intercepting voicemail was an easy way to get good stories, like plucking low-lying fruit. It gave young journalists a leg-up; it offered beleaguered, middle-aged journalists a chance to save their careers;[28] and it provided a way for section heads to manage a manic system that demanded great stories.[29]

However, the rise of phone hacking was not just the culmination of increased institutional bullying and economic insecurity. It also reflected the wider culture of the industry.

Trade identity

Phone hacking took place in a sector of the press where truth-stretching and veiled blackmail had become increasingly acceptable. Tabloids found that a good way of generating copy was for a journalist to talk to a public relations executive (PR), and jointly come up with a story that might be fictitious but worked well for both client and paper.[30] Fabrication could also be instigated from the news desk. Sharon Marshall (who worked for the *Daily Star*, *Sun* and

News of the World in the late 1990s and early 2000s) recalls that 'sometimes the quotes were written before we even left the office. Before we even knew who we were interviewing'. Thus, at the time when the Steps song '5, 6, 7, 8' was a hit, she was told to get a story that fitted the headline 'My 5, 6, 7, 8 Times Every Night with Steps Girl'. Being resourceful, she found a man who was willing to say, for a fee, all the right things about his ex-girlfriend, Lisa, a member of the Steps group.[31]

At the tougher end of the news trade, journalists sometimes coerced their sources. This could take the form of horse-trading: for example, saying to a celebrity 'We'll take out the cocaine bit if you cough to the shagging'.[32] If well managed, the victim would be positively grateful while providing the right quotes. Alternatively, an informant would be offered the choice of co-operation or humiliation. As one witness to the Leveson Inquiry explained: 'you say to the girl, "we're going to make you look tawdry and awful and sluttish, but if you talk to us, . . . we'll make you lovely and we'll give you some money as well"'.[33] The informant was rarely paid what was offered before publication: it became the starting point for subsequent negotiation.[34] The most extreme form of coercion, described by Graham Johnson, a seasoned investigative tabloid journalist (who worked for the *News of the World* and *Sunday Mirror*) was to stage a 'swarm'. Colleagues and helpful paparazzi banged on the door, and hosed down the property with flashlights. A friendly journalist then offered the victim protection on signing an exclusive agreement.[35]

Cynicism was built into the DNA of tabloid journalism. The shocked tone with which red top journalists revealed transgressions was not their true voice, and bore no relationship to how they actually led their lives. The married editors of the *News of the World* and *Sun*, Andy Coulson and Rebekah Brooks, were having an adulterous affair, starting in 2008, when their papers ran scandalized stories about 'love cheats', 'love rats', 'torrid romps', 'lust-fuelled sessions' and 'illicit sex'.[36] Drug-taking was also widespread in some papers that published articles about the 'drug shame' of celebrities.[37]

The view that journalism is 'all a game' is part of the tradition of Fleet Street. Most British national newspaper journalists see themselves as belonging to a trade rather than a profession. They embrace a trade identity because they associate it with *not* being part of the Establishment: with belonging instead to a rumbustious, competitive, irreverent, rule-breaking, untameable *industry*. Unlike the professionally oriented American press corps, British tabloid journalists are inclined to stress craft skills, to see themselves as having one foot in the entertainment industry, and to relish some of the outrageous things done by colleagues.

This celebration of transgression became institutionalized in the Shafta awards, launched in 1987, which honoured the best of the worst in journalism in an ironic but also indulgent and affectionate way. In the early 2000s, when phone hacking was at its peak, the Shafta awards ceremony was a well-attended annual event held in glamorous locations like London's Café de Paris. The

Wing Commander award went to the biggest 'flyer' in print – the most obviously invented story that was brought safely to land with no legal comeback. The 'Princess Margaret' award (commemorating a report that Princess Margaret was about to appear in the TV series, *Crossroads*) was given to the most ludicrous story printed that year. Lifetime awards went to top chancers, like the former *Daily Mirror* editor, Piers Morgan.

Cynicism was combined with hubris. Senior journalists regularly sang their own praises. For example, the *Daily Mirror* editor Richard Wallace told the Leveson Inquiry that the British press is 'the envy of the world'.[38] Numerous politicians also paid homage to the press. In a speech to the Society of Editors in 2014, Sajid Javid, Minster for Culture, Media and Sport, lauded 'the hardworking, highly skilled' journalists who, 'time and again, help to change the world for the better'. 'Britain's newspapers', he purred, 'remain the best in the world'.[39] Mazher Mahmood, the maestro of sting journalism, told a court with great pride that his work had been 'praised by two Home Secretaries'.[40] In 2016, he was jailed for perverting the course of justice when he was found to be suppressing evidence – in court – in his stitch-up of the pop star Tulisa Contostavlos.

The combination of collective self-regard, praise from government ministers and also a cosy relationship with the police encouraged a sense of impunity among journalists. As a tabloid journalist recalls in relation to blagging:

> I never stopped to think whether any of this was illegal. To tell you the truth, I didn't care. There was definitely a feeling that we, the *News of the World*, were above the law, and we could do anything we wanted. Who was going to turn us over? No one. Why? Because that was our job. We turned people over. Not the other way round. Anyway, the police looked upon us as the good guys . . .[41]

There were counter-currents opposed to this vainglorious righteousness. One was a professionalizing shift that occurred during the 1960s and 1970s, when journalists on some newspapers gained greater autonomy. The flagship of this 'professional' approach was the much admired *Sunday Times* under Harold Evans' editorship (1967–81). This tradition shrivelled with the renewal of press partisanship in the 1980s, although its legacy was perpetuated for a time by the now defunct (in print form) *Independent*.

Another counter-current came from the National Union of Journalists (NUJ). In the 1970s, the union was a significant force. It had a long history of attacking press controllers for lowering editorial standards, and of criticizing the Press Council as inadequate.[42] It even set up in 1985 its own Ethics Council which took action against members who behaved unethically – something that proved to be deeply controversial within the union. But the NUJ lost members and influence during the later 1980s and early 1990s, when a large number of newspaper groups de-recognized the union and imposed personal contracts on staff. The NUJ's Ethics Council became increasingly ineffectual.

In brief, economic failure – reflected in falling sales – led managements to exert greater pressure on journalists to get results. This pressure was intensified by competition with social media in the last decade. Fear of falling down on the job at a time of increasing economic insecurity, and sometimes driving ambition, led some journalists to engage in unethical, and even criminal, activity. The absence of a professional culture among British journalists made them especially vulnerable to managerial pressure. Collective self-regard and courtship by politicians fostered a reckless, hubristic culture in the press industry, which an inadequate self-regulatory system did little to constrain.[43] This resulted in popular newspapers becoming increasingly heedless of the harm they inflicted on innocent members of the public.

Wrecking lives

Madeleine McCann, a three-year-old girl, was abducted from an apartment in Portugal on 3 May 2007 where the McCann family were staying on holiday. At first, press coverage was deeply sympathetic to the parents. But intense public interest persisted, and journalists had to find new ways to report the same story. On 7 September 2007 the Portuguese police gave the McCanns the status of 'arguidos' (persons of interest for the investigation, not a synonym for accused), and this provided the cue for the construction of a new narrative. A series of seemingly authoritative reports suggested that the McCanns were responsible for the death of their daughter, and were involved in covering up the crime. 'Police believe Mother killed Maddy' reported the *Evening Standard*.[44] 'Blood found in McCanns' hire car "DID come from Madeleine"', according to the *Daily Mail*.[45] The story was untrue[46] – indeed the car was hired after the abduction – but it had the ring of truth. These damning reports were made more persuasive by newspaper accounts that blackened the character of the McCanns. The most damning was the *Daily Star*'s headline 'Maddie "sold" by hard-up McCanns' above a story alleging that they had sold their child into white slavery.[47] On another occasion, the inventive *Daily Star* reported that the McCanns were involved in a 'sleazy wife-swapping ring'.[48]

The McCanns had to cope both with the heartbreak of their child's abduction, and also the accusation in newspapers that they were involved in the killing of their child. Their suffering was exacerbated by the constant harassment they were subjected to. Journalists and photographers camped close to their house for almost four months. Photographers banged on the windows of their car or jumped out from behind a hedge to catch a 'startled' look. This led Amelie, their daughter, to say on several occasions: 'Mummy, I'm scared'.[49] The *News of the World* also published excerpts from Kate McCann's private diary – which her husband had not even seen – after the paper acquired it for a substantial payment indirectly through the Portuguese police.[50]

The McCanns were lied about, vilified and their wellbeing utterly disregarded in order to boost flagging newspaper sales. Yet, what happened to them was mild compared to the crucifixion of Christopher Jefferies, following the murder of Joanna Yates in 2010. The popular press's first response was to speculate about who the murderer was, with police help. Was the killer someone Joanna Yates had cooked for since she had bought a large, ready-made meal enough for two people, just before her murder?[51] Did a Facebook friend kill her?[52] Was she the victim of an obsessed prowler?[53] Was it the work of a 'rogue cop'?[54] Comparisons were made with the murder of another blonde (Melanie Road) in Bath, and another woman (Glenis Carruthers) strangled in Bristol in 1974, with the suggestion that somehow the murders were connected.[55] Or maybe there was an accomplice, which meant that more than one sexual predator was on the loose?[56] Like writers of crime fiction, journalists were looking for a storyline.

They found it in Christopher Jefferies, a retired school teacher who lived in the same building as Joanna Yates and was her landlord. When he was detained and questioned by the police for three days, there was a feeding frenzy. According to the *Sun*, *Express* and *Mail* respectively, Jefferies was 'a creepy oddball', 'a sort of Nutty Professor' and 'an eccentric loner'.[57] Journalists questioned acquaintances, dug for dirt and fictionalized his life. Jefferies allegedly bought a flat from a paedophile (in fact there had been two other intervening purchasers);[58] he had an unhealthy interest in blonde women;[59] and he was obsessed by death.[60] A strong impression was conveyed that the police had found the murderer. But in fact Christopher Jefferies was entirely innocent. A neighbour, Vincent Tabak, had strangled Joanna Yates and was convicted in October 2011.

There were other victims of the press's desperate desire to hold readers' attention. For example, press reporting of murders at the Stepping Hill Hospital, Stockport in 2011 had a strong resemblance to the reporting of Joanna Yates' murder.[61] As before, the press speculated about the identity of the murderer, with help from the police. Was the killer who injected saline bags with insulin 'a warped mercy killer'?[62] Or a cruel psycho who got a kick out of playing Russian roulette with peoples' lives?[63] Or perhaps someone similar to the 'Angel of Death' Beverley Allitt who had murdered four children in 1991?[64] Once again, journalists were storytellers casting around for a plot.

And then they got the cue they needed when Nurse Rebecca Leighton was taken into questioning, and subsequently charged. Some newspapers reported her arrest in a way that implied her guilt. The *Daily Star* ran a headline that included the phrase 'Angel of Death', accompanied by a pointed photo of Rebecca Leighton.[65] The *Daily Mail* asked 'How many more poison victims? . . .', with an inset picture of Rebecca Leighton dressed as a cowboy with a suggestive toy gun in her mouth.[66] Leighton's character was blackened, though not in as dark a hue as Jefferies.[67] Articles, some drawing on Rebecca Leighton's Facebook profile, portrayed the nurse as dissolute, averse to work, and fond of booze.[68] Perhaps she had acted out of revenge, it was suggested, because she had been rejected for promotion.[69] Pictures of her partying, 'days' after a poisoned patient had died, were published to highlight her supposed heartlessness.[70] But once again, the person fitted up by the press as the killer was innocent. The true murderer turned out to be the male nurse Victorino Chua, who was convicted in 2015.

Leighton was collateral damage in the battle to staunch falling sales. So were the Dowler parents who attracted public sympathy when their private lives were picked over, and their murdered daughter's phone was hacked. However, the plight of the Watson parents was worse. Newspapers published articles suggesting that their murdered daughter had been a bully, with the implication that she had brought her tragedy upon herself. This seemingly tipped their vulnerable 15-year-old son over the edge. He killed himself: his body was found with the attack articles in his hands.[71]

Of course, words can have unintended consequences, and errors inevitably occur when working against the clock. Yet, during the Leveson Inquiry, some senior journalists in charge of papers which traduced innocent people displayed – apart from the occasional piety – little real concern for their victims. What came through more strongly was their righteous libertarianism, their determination not be to be beaten by their rivals, and their preoccupation with what was legal rather than what was ethical.[72]

Perhaps the most revealing testimony came from Richard Desmond, proprietor of the Express media group (Northern and Shell). He went through the motions by declaring that 'we would not run a story if we thought that it would damage that [our paper's reputation] or seriously affect someone's life'.[73] This was not entirely convincing from the proprietor of the *Daily Star* which suggested, as we have seen, that the McCanns sold their child into white slavery. But he also expressed with candour his underlying approach:

> I think that we are in a business to give readers/viewers what they want to read and watch and as long as it is legal that is what we aim to do. We do not talk about ethics or morals because it is a very fine line and everybody's ethics are different.[74]

Nothing could make clearer the moral vacuum at the heart of his media group, unless it was his earlier response: 'Ethical – I don't know what the word means . . .'.[75]

Others shared his flexibility. As the much admired Press Association journalist, Chris Moncrieff, put it wryly on an earlier occasion:

> For myself I have never yet been able to locate a conscience even if I had wanted to struggle with it. If a story is on offer it seems to me it doesn't matter how it is imparted so long as it is within the law.[76]

Threat to public health

If one strategy for grabbing attention was to embellish crime reports, another was to make readers afraid. This was why the press published a growing volume of medical scare stories.[77] The irresponsibility of some of this reporting is best illustrated by press coverage of the MMR (one-in-three, mumps, measles and rubella) vaccine.

In 1998, Dr. Andrew Wakefield and associates published an article which argued that the MMR vaccine was linked to autism. At a subsequent press conference, he suggested that the link could be causal. This triggered a story that received extensive press coverage for over a decade. The suggestion that parents were causing irreparable damage to their children by taking them to the doctor's surgery for a triple jab was likely to generate reader interest. It was the reason why the scare was sustained for so long.

In January 2001, the *Sun* published an article about the vaccine, on average, every other day for the entire month.[78] Its style of reporting is typified by its story that 'anguished mother Mary Robinson' is 'convinced' that the MMR jab 'caused autism in four of her kids and behaviour problems in another'.[79] The article offered no evidence to support Mary Robinson's conviction, but quoted her as saying that 'they withdraw a hairdryer if there is a problem – why aren't they withdrawing this drug [meaning the MMR vaccine]'? Celebrities were also mobilized in the cause. 'TV star Carol Vorderman led calls for a safe measles jab last night', reported the *Sun*, adding that the Countdown star had 'talked to many people' with children who had been damaged by the MMR vaccine.[80]

Other parents were quoted as saying that the triple vaccine had caused their children to become autistic. The story gained further impetus when the Prime Minister, Tony Blair, declined to say in 2002 whether his youngest son, Leo, had received the MMR vaccine. By then, the *Sun* and the *Daily Mail* had moved into campaign mode. They gave prominence to maverick doctors who warned against the vaccine but whose research was not published in leading, peer-reviewed journals – and sometimes never published at all.[81] It was only in the 2010s that the press campaign against the MMR petered out. In 2015, the *Daily Mail* published a face-saving article: 'There is NO link between MMR and autism . . . landmark study declares'.[82] In fact, the conclusions of this supposed 'landmark' study merely corroborated what authoritative research had been demonstrating for years.

The Wakefield paper, which had triggered the MMR scare, was based on just twelve, non-randomly selected subjects referred to one hospital.[83] Andrew Wakefield failed to declare a financial interest in the outcome of his research (which received funding from litigants against the vaccine), and concealed how the subjects were recruited, among other shortcomings. The article was subsequently disowned by the journal which published it, and retracted by most of its co-authors.[84] Serious charges, on multiple counts, caused Dr. Wakefield to be struck off the medical register by the British General Medical Council in 2010.

While the testimony of parents of autistic children made good copy, it was not scientifically based. Autism often becomes apparent at around the age of two when children are given the first dose of the triple MMR vaccine. This is not causally connected, but the timing naturally gives rise to the suspicion that it is. In fact, scientific research conducted in the UK, USA, Finland, Denmark, Japan and elsewhere repeatedly showed that the MMR vaccine was safe.[85] Unlike the discredited 1998 Wakefield study, this research included studies which used rigorous methods: namely case control studies which compared autistic with comparable non-autistic subjects, and cohort studies based on large samples which compared the incidence of autism among those receiving and those not receiving the triple vaccination.[86]

Newspapers employ science and medical correspondents with the relevant training enabling them to distinguish between good and bad research. But, significantly, they were largely sidelined in the reporting of the MMR vaccine.[87] Most MMR scare stories were written by general reporters and feature writers. While it was legitimate for them to question medical orthodoxy, it was irresponsible to fail to represent the balance of scientific evidence, or the limitations of non-expert, parental anguish. This is because the sustained MMR scare led to a serious reduction in those taking the MMR vaccine.[88] Even by 2009, the MMR uptake had not recovered to the pre-scare level before 1998.[89]

This increased individual vulnerability to infection, and also diminished collective 'herd' immunity. Before the scare, both mumps and measles had been in sharp decline. After the scare, mumps reached epidemic proportions by 2004.[90] Measles also spread rapidly, registering the highest incidence level for two decades in 2012.[91] It was concentrated among those who were not vaccinated during the height of the MMR scare, and in those areas where vaccination had been low.[92]

Mumps and measles are significant illnesses which can give rise to serious complications. Measles can lead to encephalitis, brain damage and even death (with one British child dying in 2005), while mumps can lead to meningitis and hearing loss. A number of newspapers carry a heavy responsibility for what happened. Their drive to sell copies, at whatever cost, led to the revival of avoidable diseases.

Spreading hatred

Another way of winning reader attention was to arouse indignation. 'We must make the readers cross', instructed an internal memo at the *Sunday Express* in 2003.[93] As we have seen, there was a large number of newspapers stories from 2002 onwards about migrants committing crimes, taking jobs, importing terrorism, receiving special favours or behaving in an alien way.[94] Popular papers (with the notable exception of papers in the Mirror group) looked for these stories because they elicited a strong reader reaction.

However, newspaper demand for these stories outstripped supply. Some journalists, under intense pressure to deliver, looked for ways make up for this shortfall. Thus, a number of stories appeared in 2003 about migrant eating habits. Migrants were said to be eating donkeys,[95] guzzling fish ('Now They are Eating Our Fish!'),[96] and barbecuing swans. This last story was designed to raise eyebrows since killing swans – legally protected since Norman times – was a symbolic affront to Britain's cultural heritage. It was judged to be so important that the *Sun* made it a front-page story, under the headline 'SWAN BAKE. Asylum Seekers Steal the Queen's Birds for Barbecues'. The paper announced that 'an official Metropolitan Police report' had found that 'East European poachers lure the protected royal birds into baited traps'. The *Sun* also revealed that 'the police swooped on a gang of East Europeans and caught them red-handed about to cook a pair of royal swans . . . . The discovery last weekend confirmed fears that immigrants are regularly scoffing the Queen's birds'.[97]

Although this report had all the ingredients of a 'make readers cross' story, it had one major defect. It was made up from beginning to end. There was, in fact, no Metropolitan Police Report about East Europeans laying traps for swans, merely an internal, one-page memo clarifying the nature of the law in relation to poaching. There were no police arrests of any immigrant 'gang' about to roast swans.[98] The *Sun*, concluded the Press Complaints Commission, 'was unable to provide any evidence for the story'.[99]

In a similar vein, in 2010 the *Daily Star* ran a front-page story reporting that Rochdale Council 'wastes YOUR money' by funding 'Muslim-only Public Loos'.[100] In fact these loos were not funded by the local council but by a developer who was building a new shopping centre. And they were not 'Muslim-only': the squat-down loos that so riled the paper are widely used in Asian countries regardless of a person's religion.[101]

These reports were unusual in being total distortions. The more frequent practice was to spin a story. For example, the *Daily Express* reported that, in Lubeck, 'children as young as 13 have been told to cook and clean for migrants' as part of their work experience programme. A 'furious mother' was quoted as saying that it represented a new form of 'servitude', while the UK Independence Party (UKIP) deputy leader Paul Nuttall expressed concern about the children's safety. This story was headlined 'Children Told to Cook and Clean for Migrants', with the sub-head 'No Wonder Germans are Fed up with the EU'.[102]

What the paper omitted to mention was that the idea of cooking and cleaning came from pupils themselves, after migrant children had sat in on a class. The authorities did not compel children to do this. On the contrary, parents had to give permission in a written form of consent, issued by the Kiel Ministry of Education, before their children were allowed to participate in the scheme.[103] Volunteering to be nice to migrants was not a *Daily Express* story, so it was given a twist to fit the paper's news agenda.

Another way of making up for the shortfall of anti-migrant stories was to commission a spurious poll or spin its results. For example, the *Sunday Express* reported on its front page a 'shock new poll' revealing that '12m Turks say they'll come to the UK' once the proposed European Union (EU) deal with Turkey is signed.[104] In fact, the question put to Turkish respondents was 'would you, or any members of your family, *consider* relocating to Britain?' (emphasis added).[105] The phrase 'any members of your family' was clearly intended to inflate the number saying yes. Considering is not the same as *intending* to relocate. So the report was manifestly misleading. It is also unlikely that Turkey will join the EU. However, the poll provided a cue for a dire warning from the leading Conservative politician, David Davis, that a new wave of migration will 'threaten our security'.[106]

Similarly, the *Sun* published in 2015 a 'shock poll' revealing that 'nearly one in five British Muslims has some sympathy with those who had fled the UK to fight for IS in Syria'. This report was published shortly after terrorist attacks had killed 130 people in Paris. It was the front-page story, illustrated by a picture of 'Brit Jihadi John' – the IS fighter who had executed western captives – in a threatening pose, holding a long dagger. Coverage extended to other pages, including an outraged article by a columnist who expressed her 'shock, horror, bewilderment, anger and disbelief' that so many Muslims harbour sympathy for 'such a murderous twisted ideology'.[107]

There were two problems with this report. First, the question was ambiguous. The word 'sympathy' could mean understanding, at an emotional level, the feelings and motives of those volunteering to fight in Syria without agreeing with their decision – or it could denote outright support. The phrase 'join fighters in Syria' could be interpreted to mean joining IS *or* joining other groups fighting IS. So, it is not clear what the answer to the question revealed.

Second, the same question had been put to non-Muslims earlier in the year. Those expressing sympathy among this group (14 per cent) was similar to the proportion among Muslims (19 per cent).[108] This undermined the central thrust of the *Sun*'s coverage. As Patrick Brione, Director of Research for Survation, the polling company that carried out the survey for the *Sun*, acknowledged: 'attitudes [to joining the fight in Syria] held by the Muslim and non-Muslim populations are not that different'.[109]

Changing norms

In the period after 1979, there was an increased blurring of the distinction between facts and opinions. It was accompanied by the weakening of a stress on accuracy.

This last is exemplified by the alacrity with which leading popular newspapers published fake news supplied by the documentary film-maker Chris

Atkins in 2009. The project began with his researcher, Jen Richardson, ringing up the *Daily Mirror* posing as Gigi, a French party girl, to report that the Canadian singer, Avril Lavigne, had fallen asleep in the fashionable nightclub Bungalow 8 and started snoring. The fabricated story duly appeared in the paper the next day.

The next fake story was an elaborate tale about how the singer Amy Winehouse and her friend changed a fuse in the dark, at her party, when the power went out. In this made-up account, they both got an electric shock, knocking her friend out and causing Amy Winehouse's famous hair to start smouldering. Even though the story was presented as coming from a second-hand source, it duly appeared without checks in the *Daily Mirror* and *Daily Star*. The latter added a fictional element to the story: 'a friend was called in and ending up punching Flamey Amy's head to put out the blaze'.

The next concoction proved irresistible. The *Sun* was told that Sarah Harding, from the group Girls Aloud, was a fan of quantum physics. It was duly published in the paper, and embellished with a fabricated quote: 'There is a lot more going on under that blonde barnet than Sarah is given credit for. She's a smart cookie and does read an awful lot'.

Newspapers fell for further fake stories: Russell Brand, the radical comedian, aspiring to be a banker when he was young (*Daily Express*); Guy Ritchie, the film-maker, injuring himself juggling cutlery in a restaurant (*Sun*); and Pixie Geldof, the model and singer, padding her bra with sweets (*Daily Mirror*). In total, six out of seven fictional stories presented to national papers in a two-week period in March 2009 were published. Only one about the famously litigious tycoon, Sir Alan Sugar, was rejected.[110] The cavalier attitude towards checking stories that this project revealed shows how bad things had got by the new millennium.

If one normative shift was a more relaxed attitude towards accuracy, another was seemingly a repudiation of sexism. Page 3 topless women, introduced as a regular feature in the *Sun* in 1970, was discontinued in 2015. This appeared to be a response to the feminist campaign against it, and perhaps the increased number of women journalists employed by the national press.

However, this adjustment was less than it seemed. The *Sun* compensated by publishing more standard cheesecake pictures. It also introduced occasional body part inspections. 'Quiz of the rear: try to name cheeky stars', urged the paper above a display of twenty naked or almost bottoms of well-known women.[111] This was a re-tread of its previous 'Booty Contest', in which readers had been asked if they could 'match the fit celebs to their shapely assets' from photos of ten semi-nude bottoms.[112] Another variant of this formula was to invite female readers to compete in the 'Are you the breast of the bunch?' contest, leading to a 'Booby Wonderland' double spread featuring twenty-three sets of breasts.[113]

Moreover, the cancellation of page 3 in the *Sun* was compensated by its reincarnation in the *Daily Star*. The paper also featured semi-naked women in numbers not seen before in a national newspaper. A not untypical issue of the *Daily Star* in 2017 had fourteen images of semi-clad women.[114]

The red tops' use of 'cheeky' language, puns and *double entendres* was designed to defuse criticism, conveying the message that only prudes would disapprove. But these papers' repetitive depiction of women as sex objects was dehumanizing and degrading. It showed that a patriarchal culture still dominated the tabloid press.

Public verdict

The press at its best holds power to account. In the 1960s, 1970s and 1980s, great journalism championed the vulnerable in need of protection, from Thalidomide victims to the Birmingham Six imprisoned for crimes they did not commit. Individual papers continued to break important stories such as, in the last decade, politicians' abuse of expenses (*Daily Telegraph*), the sexual grooming of underage girls in Rotherham (*The Times*), phone hacking (*Guardian*) and the hidden homeless (*Hackney Gazette*). However, it is noticeable that most of these important investigative stories came from the broadsheet and local press. Very few originated in popular national papers.

The moral decline of the press was largely confined to the popular press, although it probably coloured public attitudes to the press as a whole. This moral decline was caused by a new generation of cynical controllers, managerial bullying, a corporate culture of impunity and above all falling revenue. This led to the use of the 'dark arts' on an unprecedented scale, culminating in the phone hacking scandal. It also gave rise to increasing disregard for the damage that newspapers could inflict on innocent people in the public eye. And it resulted in sustained distortion, exemplified here by anti-migrant stories, a medical scare campaign, and fake news.

There were also other subsidiary causes at work. The shrinkage of the national press corps[115] made it more vulnerable to manipulative public relations. There is probably something in the 'old guard' explanation that fewer national paper journalists have done a proper apprenticeship in the regional press, where accuracy and good faith are instilled as journalistic virtues.[116] The increase of national press partisanship from the late 1970s also encouraged a more cynical and strategic orientation to news reporting. But in essence the moral decline of the popular press was a response to precipitate institutional decline. Managements and journalists resorted to increasingly desperate attempts to limit collapsing sales and advertising.

Yet, senior journalists continued to boast that the British press is the envy of the world, and is cherished by the British public. Since the British public is always spoken for in this self-regarding discourse, it is worth examining what surveys of public attitudes reveal. In 2016, only 18 per cent of British adults said that they trusted national newspaper journalists to tell the truth.[117] This was a fall from 37 per cent in 2006, registering growing public distrust.[118] Yet, this sharp decrease was merely the culmination of a trend that had begun in the 1980s. Those believing that journalists tell the truth nearly halved between 1983 and 1993, making journalists in 1993 the most distrusted group – out of 15 – in Britain.[119]

Even these figures do not fully convey just how low the British public's estimation of its press had sunk. In 2016, distrust of the press was greater in Britain than in 31 other European countries. The British press was an outlier, commanding *much* less credibility among its national population than the press elsewhere in Europe. The British press's net trust rating was –51 per cent, lower even than the Serbian press with a net trust rating of –36 per cent.[120] The low comparative ranking was consistent with previous surveys extending back to 2002.[121]

This is what the British public actually thinks about 'the finest press in the world'.

Notes

1 My thanks to members of the Goldsmiths Leverhulme Journalism Research Group who read and commented on this chapter.

2 N. Davies, *Hack Attack* (London, Chatto & Windus, 2014), p. 14.

3 Davies, *Hack Attack*, pp. 137–38.

4 This is well described in *Hack Attack*, and in the *Report of an Inquiry into the Culture, Practices and Ethics of the Press* (Leveson Report) (London, Stationery Office, 2012) especially volume 2.

5 *Guardian*, 15 September 2010.

6 For a rueful account of this story's origins by its author, see W. Clarkson, *Dog Eat Dog* (London, Fourth Estate, 1990), Chapter 1.

7 H. Porter, *Lies, Damned Lies and Some Exclusives* (London, Chatto & Windus, 1984), Chapters 2 and 3.

8 Ibid., p. 5.

9 T. Baistow, *Fourth-Rate Estate* (London, Commedia, 1985), p. 57.

10 *Sun*, 13 March 1986.

11 Testimony to the Leveson Inquiry, reported in the *Telegraph Online*, 9 February 2012. Available at: www.telegraph.co.uk/news/uknews/leveson-inquiry/9072308/ Leveson-Inquiry-the-truth-behind-Freddie-Starr-ate-my-hamster.html.

12 G. Goodman, 'Why we are here', *British Journalism Review*, 1 (1), 1989, p. 2.

13 R. Harris, *Selling Hitler* (London, Arrow, 2009), p. 315.

14 M. Linklater, 'Murdoch's bravado forced through the publication of the Hitler diaries', *Guardian Online*, 25 April 2012. Available at: www.theguardian.com/ commentisfree/2012/apr/25/rupert-murdoch-bravado-publication-hitler-diaries (accessed 1 December 2016).

15 Harris, *Selling Hitler*, p. 368.

16 R. Greenslade, *Maxwell's Fall* (London, Simon & Schuster, 1992), pp. 113–16.

17 Cited in R. Greenslade, 'A new Britain, a new kind of newspaper', *Guardian Online*, 25 February 2002. Available at: www.theguardian.com/media/2002/feb/25/ pressandpublishing.falklands.

18 R. Greenslade, *Press Gang* (Biggleswade, 2003), p. 408.
19 Advertising Association/Warc, *Expenditure Report* (London, Advertising Association, 2017 (April)).
20 R. Greenslade, 'Suddenly, national newspapers are heading for that cliff edge', *Guardian*, 27 May 2016. Available at: www.theguardian.com/media/green slade/2016/may/27/suddenly-national-newspapers-are-heading-for-that-print-cliff-fall (accessed 26 July 2017).
21 P. Chippindale and C. Horrie, *Stick It Up Your Punter* (London, Pocket Books, 2005), p. 247.
22 Ibid., pp. 247–48.
23 Leveson, vol. 2, p. 498.
24 Ibid., pp. 497–501.
25 Ibid., p. 497.
26 A. Addison, *Mail Men* (London, Atlantic Books, 2017), p. 266.
27 Leveson, vol. 2; G. Jackson, *Hack* (London, Simon & Schuster, 2013); S. Marshall, *Tabloid Girl* (London, Sphere, 2010); Bill Coles, *Red Top* (London, Paper Books, 2013); W. Clarkson, 'Confessions of a tabloid hack', *Guardian Online*, 11 July 2009. Available at: www.theguardian.com/media/2009/jul/11/notw-phone-hacking-private-investigators (accessed 14 December 2016); P. Gilfeather, 'Confessions of a (former) *News of the World* man', S G Links, 16 July 2011. Available at: www.sglinks.com/pages/1108785-sunday-special-confessions-former-news-world-man (accessed 14 December 2016), among others.
28 N. Davies, *Hack Attack* (London, Chatto & Windus, 2014), pp. 49 ff. argues that Clive Goodman, the first senior journalist to be jailed for phone hacking, was 'well past his prime', and used hacking as a job saver.
29 A former *News of the World* senior journalist, with whom I had dinner a couple of days before he was jailed, responded to my suggestion that he was, in a sense, a management victim by saying – in a self-reflective way – that he was 'part of the pressure' that was exerted on journalists.
30 Marshall, *Tabloid Girl*, p. 231; cf. the witness statement of Richard Peppiatt to the Leveson Inquiry. Available at: www.webarchive.nationalarchives.gov.uk/2014012 2145147/http://www.levesoninquiry.org.uk/evidence/?witness=richard-peppiatt (accessed 24 November 2016).
31 Marshall, *Tabloid Girl*, p. 226.
32 Johnson, *Hack*, p. 264.
33 Leveson, vol. 2, p. 522.
34 Johnson, *Hack*, p. 96.
35 Ibid., p. 63.
36 BBC News Online, 31 October 2013, 'Rebekah Brooks and Andy Coulson had affair, phone-hacking trial hears'. Available at: www.bbc.co.uk/news/uk-24762474 (accessed 15 October 2016).
37 Johnson, *Hack*, p. 93; Marshall, *Tabloid Girl*, p. 138.
38 Leveson Report, vol. 2, p. 563. See also the self-congratulatory comments of senior journalists, responding to the papers presented in the Leveson Inquiry Seminars on 6 and 12 October 2011. Available at: www.webarchive.national archives.gov.uk/20140122145147/http://www.levesoninquiry.org.uk/ (accessed 15 December 2016).

39 'Speech: Society of Editors Conference 2014', Gov.UK. Available at: www.gov.uk/government/speeches/society-of-editors-conference-2014 (accessed 15 December 2016).

40 Trial transcript excerpts reproduced on *Guardian Online*, 4 October 1999. Available at: www.theguardian.com/media/1999/oct/04/newsoftheworld.mondaymedia section (accessed 15 December 2016).

41 Johnson, *Hack*, p. 32.

42 T. Gopsill and G. Neale, *Journalists: 100 Years of the NUJ* (London, Profile, 2007), pp. 245 ff.

43 The shortcomings of this self-regulatory system are examined in Chapter 26.

44 *Evening Standard*, 7 September 2007 cited in *Press Gazette*, 23 November 2011.

45 *Daily Mail*, 8 January 2008.

46 See cross-examination of Dr. Gerry McCann, Leveson Inquiry. Available at: www.webarchive.nationalarchives.gov.uk/20140122145147/http://www.levesoninquiry.org.uk/wp-content/uploads/2011/11/Transcript-of-Afternoon-Hearing-23-November-20111.txt (accessed 8 December 2016).

47 *Daily Star*, 26 November 2007.

48 *Daily Star*, 5 November 2017.

49 Cited in Leveson, vol. 2, p. 548.

50 For the cynical duplicity involved in its publication, see Leveson, vol. 2, pp. 555–58.

51 *Daily Mail*, 8 January 2011.

52 *Daily Mail*, 7 January 2011.

53 *Daily Star*, 7 January 2011.

54 *Daily Star*, 16 January 2011.

55 *Sun*, 15 January 2011.

56 *Daily Mail*, 4 January 2011.

57 *Sun*, 31 December 2010; *Daily Express*, 31 December 2010; *Daily Mail*, 31 December 2010.

58 *Sun*, 31 December 2010.

59 *Sun*, 1 January 2010.

60 Ibid.; *Daily Mail*, 31 December 2010.

61 K. Syzmnik, 'Between facts and fiction', Political Communication MA dissertation, Goldsmiths, University of London, 2012.

62 *Sun*, 18 July 2011.

63 *Daily Mail*, 18 July 2011.

64 *Sun*, 16 July 2011.

65 *Daily Star*, 23 July 2011.

66 *Daily Mail*, 22 July 2011.

67 The newspaper narrative of Leighton as a 'bad' person was flipped subsequently to that of a 'good' person but by then serious reputational damage had been done.

68 *Sun*, 21 July 2011; *Daily Mail*, 21 July 2011.

69 *Daily Mirror*, 21 July 2011.

70 *Sun*, 21 July 2011; *Daily Mail*, 21 July 2011.

71 Evidence submitted by Margaret Watson to Leveson Inquiry, 22 November 2011. Available at: www.webarchive.nationalarchives.gov.uk/20140122145147/http://www.levesoninquiry.org.uk/evidence/?witness=margaret-watson (accessed 23 December 2016).

72 Among others, Peter Hill (*Daily Express*), 12 January 2012; Richard Wallace (*Daily Mirror*), 16 January 2012; and Stephen Waring (*Sun*), 24 January 2012.

These are available at: www.webarchive.nationalarchives.gov.uk/2014012 2145147/http://www.levesoninquiry.org.uk/hearing/2012-01-12pm/ (accessed 28December2016);www.webarchive.nationalarchives.gov.uk/20140122145147/ http://www.levesoninquiry.org.uk/hearing/2012-01-16am/ (accessed 28 December 2016); www.webarchive.nationalarchives.gov.uk/20140122145147/levesoninquiry. org.uk/hearing/2012-01-24pm (accessed 29 December 2016).

73 Leveson, vol. 2, p. 732.

74 Ibid.

75 Ibid.

76 C. Moncrieff writing in *The House Magazine* (5 June 1989), cited in Goodman, 'Why We are Here', p. 4.

77 This became so pronounced that it became the subject of satire. See Dan and Dan, 'The *Daily Mail* Song'. Available at: www.youtube.com/watch?v=5eBT6OS r1TI (accessed 10 November 2016).

78 Seventeen out of the 27 publishing days in January 2001.

79 *Sun*, 26 January 2001.

80 *Sun*, 8 January 2001.

81 B. Goldacre, *Bad Science* (London, Fourth Estate, 2009) pp. 318 ff.

82 *MailOnline*, 21 April 2015. Available at: www.dailymail.co.uk/health/article-3049044/Another-study-finds-no-link-vaccine-autism.html (accessed 14 December 2016).

83 A. Wakefield, S. Murch, A. Anthony et al., 'Ileal-lymphoid-nodular hyperplasia, non-specific colitis, and pervasive developmental disorder in children', *Lancet,* 351 (9103), 1998. The journal's online version now has 'retracted' in red letters stamped across it.

84 'Journal regrets running MMR study', BBC News Online, 20 February 2004. Available at: www.news.bbc.co.uk/1/hi/health/3508167.stm (accessed 15 July 2006).

85 'MRC Autism Review', Medical Research Council, 2006; 'MRC Review of Autism Research: Epidemiology and Causes', Medical Research Council, 2001. Available at: www.mrc.ac.uk/index/public-interest/public-topical_issues/public-autism_main (accessed 15 July 2006).

86 Goldacre, *Bad Science*, pp. 313–14.

87 Ibid., p. 308.

88 T. Boyce, *Health, Risk and News* (New York, Lang, 2007).

89 'Rise in measles "very worrying"', BBC News Online, 2 June 2009. Available at: www.news.bbc.co.uk/1/hi/health/7872541.stm (accessed 1 March 2010).

90 Goldacre, *Bad Science*, p. 329.

91 'Measles outbreak in maps and graphics', BBC News Online, 2 May 2013. Available at: www.bbc.co.uk/news/health-22277186 (accessed 30 December 2016).

92 Ibid.

93 Quoted in N. Cohen, 'Going nowhere fast', *Observer*, 12 October 2003. This internal memo made no explicit reference to migrants.

94 See Chapter 8, p. 139–140.

95 *Daily Star*, 31 August 2003.

96 *Sun*, 7 July 2003.

97 *Sun*, 4 July 2003.

98 N. Medic, 'Swan bake: making a meal of a myth' in R. Cookson and M. Jempson (eds.) *The RAM Report* (Bristol, MediaWise, 2005), p. 56.

99 Letter from the Press Complaints Commission cited in N. Medic, 'Making a meal of a myth' in M. Jempson and R. Cookson (eds.) *Satisfaction Guaranteed?* (Bristol, MediaWise, 2005), p. 29.

100 *Daily Star*, 15 July 2010.

101 'PCC: Star story on "Muslim-only public loos" inaccurate', *Press Gazette*, 27 September 2010.

102 *Daily Express*, 16 October 2015.

103 Clarke V *Daily Express*, IPSO 065593-15. Available at: www.ipso.co.uk/rulings-and-resolution-statements/ruling/?id=06593-15 (accessed 5 January 2016).

104 *Sunday Express*, 22 May 2016.

105 Cited in Wyper V *Sunday Express*, IPSO 03069-16, 2016. Available at: www.ipso.co.uk/rulings-and-resolution-statements/ruling/?id=03069-16 (accessed 5 January 2016).

106 *Sunday Express*, 22 May 2016.

107 *Sun*, 23 November 2015.

108 P. Brione, 'New polling of British Muslims', Survation Blog, 2015. Available at: www.survation.com/new-polling-of-british-muslims/ (accessed 6 January 2017).

109 Ibid.

110 C. Atkins, 'How to fool the tabloids over and over again . . .' in R. Keeble and J. Mair (eds.) *The Phone Hacking Scandal* (Bury St. Edmunds, Abramis, 2012). His documentary film, released in 2009, is called *Starsuckers*.

111 *Sun*, 6 January 2017.

112 *Sun*, 25 February 2016.

113 *Sun*, 30 March 2016.

114 *Daily Star*, 6 January 2017.

115 F. Nel, *Laid Off: What do UK Journalists Do Next?* (Preston, University of Central Lancashire, 2010). Available at: www.journalism.co.uk/uploads/laidoffreport.pdf (accessed 20 August 2011).

116 There are no historical data on changes in the careers of journalists to sustain this argument, though this does not mean that it is incorrect.

117 'Trust in journalism sinks to all-time low', IMPRESS News, 5 December 2016 (YouGov poll). Available at: www.impress.press/news/yougov-poll.html (accessed 4 January 2017).

118 Ibid.

119 R. Worcester, 'Demographics and values: what the British public reads and what it thinks about its newspapers' in H. Stephenson and M. Bromley (eds.) *Sex, Lies and Democracy* (London, Longman, 1998), Table 3.5, p. 47.

120 'Trust in Media', European Broadcasting Union, 2016. Available at: www.press-gazette.co.uk/survey-finds-that-uk-written-press-is-by-some-way-the-least-trusted-in-europe/ (accessed 16 January 2017).

121 2015 results reported in ibid.; 2011 results (*Public Opinion in the European Union* (European Commission, Brussels, 2011)); and the 2002 Eurobarometer survey results reported in the *Guardian*, 24 April 2002.

Part 11

Broadcasting history

Chapter 11

Reith and the denial of politics

How was a great democratic institution invented? The British Broadcasting Corporation (BBC) – and the whole tradition of broadcasting it influenced – that of the management of communications in the public interest has been a staggeringly important and visionary addition to democratic life. The 'public interest' (despite the limitations it could be subject to) was a far more hopeful and broad idea than that of what the 'public were interested in'.

The BBC emerged out of a period of terrible anxiety: would the public vote responsibly and have the information they needed to make up their minds as voting was extended to everyone over 21? Would commercial interests be able – unfairly and behind the scenes – to influence democratic outcomes by 'buying' opinion? Would propaganda, as the Bolshevik revolution raged and right-wing forces gathered distort and inflame public life? Would public discussion and democratic decisions be based on truth? Or would voters' choices be distorted by propaganda? People felt that they had been misled by the stories they had been told – and not told – about the First World War and were mistrustful of authority and the media. Meanwhile, governments were anxious about the effectiveness of propaganda and revolutions. The 1920s were alarming and unsettled times. One solution came to be the BBC.

The BBC became an institution that represented the British public – in all of its uncomfortable diversity – to itself. It helped it understand and confront difficult things. But that capacity was based on the way in which the BBC offered the public diversions that delighted, amused and infuriated the public. It addressed the audiences not as consumers to be sold things, not as dupes or propaganda fodder, not as partial bigots who could only hear what they already agreed with, but as equal citizens capable of reflection and growth. In time it developed the priceless values of impartiality and independence. Of course, it often got things wrong – veered too far in one way or another – but as it belonged to the people in a way no other communication ever has – they could always demand it to change. Sceptical, interrogative, it developed an image of a common project towards progress to educate, inform and entertain. But it was by no means inevitable that broadcasting should be so generous and grand – both nationally and in time internationally.

Beginnings

There are two accounts of the origins of the BBC. The first is that the Corporation was the personal achievement of John Reith. The second is that its emergence was accidental. According to the first view, the BBC's monopoly of broadcasting was an inevitable consequence of the Corporation's cultural mission shaped by a unique and prophetic leader. This is partly true. Without Reith there would have been no BBC. For the second, as R. H. Coase the economist wrote, 'The problem, to which the monopoly was seen as a solution by the Post Office, was one of Civil Service administration. The view that a monopoly in broadcasting was better for the listener was only to come later'. Coase, a Nobel prize-winning economist was ideologically opposed to the BBC's monopoly. But he was not in possession of the whole story.

The two theories appear to conflict. According to one view, Reith made history fit his vision. According to the other, a great institution took a particular form because no one appreciated its future importance. Both, however, have a central flaw in common: they disregard political and social change in the world outside broadcasting.

Indeed Reith's creation of the BBC came, at least in part from his capacity to mobilize support for the idea because it called on shared assumptions, anxieties and emerging beliefs. The Corporation was the product of a moment in which many were hostile to propaganda and the political control of information. The First World War had instilled a horror of misleading information and what was widely seen as a dissembling, jingoistic, press. The papers domestically had been abjectly willing to promote Government propaganda, their reporters turning their faces away from the reality of slaughter on the battlefields of the war. Hugh Dalton, later a prominent Labour politician, wrote in his diary from the Italian front 'The press have not been to the front, do not care about ordinary soldiers, have no grasp of the international situation, they bluster and lie'. Clement Attlee – later Labour leader – profoundly altered by the experience of the resilience of working men at the front thought they were 'betrayed by a baying press'.

But there was also, in the 1920s a new hostility to commercial exploitation and a concern with public service and collective interests. Public service was seen as modern and efficient. These ideals were combined with a deep anxiety about how the newly enfranchised electorate could be adequately informed to make responsible electoral decisions. There was a belief that planning and centralized control of utilities was the efficient – modern – way to run organisations.

Discovering an audience, a director and the money

Broadcasting – the transmitting of programmes to be heard simultaneously by an indefinitely large number of people – is a social invention, not a technical one. The capacity to broadcast existed long before it was recognized. 'Wireless telegraphy' was developed during the First World War for military purposes. It was used as a substitute for the telephone, but one with the perceived disadvantage that it was impossible to specify the audience which heard the message. An American engineer, David Sarnoff, first saw the possibilities of radio in 1916. 'I have in mind a plan of development which would make radio a "household utility" like the piano or electricity', he wrote. 'The idea is to bring music into the house by wireless'.

Yet for some time after popular broadcasting had started in the 1920s, wireless was regarded as little more than an experimental toy. It took Northcliffe, a pioneer in the commercialisation of leisure, to demonstrate the potential audience for the new invention. He arranged a promotion stunt for the *Daily Mail*. Dame Nellie Melba was to be broadcast singing from Chelmsford. This event, which began 'with a long silvery trill' and ended with *God Save the King*, attracted a much larger audience than had been expected. It made the wireless manufacturers aware for the first time of a potentially huge market for them to supply. It is also clear that had the press barons – Northcliffe and Beaverbrooke – understood what a powerful institution broadcasting and the BBC were to become they would have strangled it at birth. They saw it as something 'experimental' that they could use, not as a political or commercial challenge. So there was indeed an aspect of happenchance in the BBC's creation and survival.

In 1922 there were nearly a hundred applications to the Post Office from manufacturers who wanted to set up 'broadcasting' stations. This demand created the need for control. As Peter Eckersley, one of the company's first employees, wrote later, 'The BBC was formed as an expedient solution to a technical problem. It owes its existence to the scarcity of air waves'. The Postmaster General solved the problems of radio interference by persuading rival manufacturers to invest jointly in one small and initially speculative broadcasting station: the British Broadcasting Company. John Reith was made its Managing Director.

How would the BBC have developed if its first director had been a career civil servant, a businessman keen to make a profit for shareholders, or a Bloomsbury intellectual? Many of the features of broadcasting which have made the BBC so central to British society would certainly be absent. Reith's domination of the Corporation in its early days was massive, overwhelming and idiosyncratic, and for many decades the traditions of the BBC seemed to flow directly from his personality. The British Broadcasting Company was set up as a business. Reith turned it into a crusade. 'Scotch engineer, Calvinist by upbringing, harsh and ruthless in character', as A. J. P. Taylor has described him, Reith used 'the brute force of monopoly to stamp Christian morality on the British people'. While waiting to find out whether his application for the directorship had been successful Reith wrote in his memoirs, 'I kept my faith alive night and morning and encouraged myself with the text "Commit thy way unto the Lord, trust also Him and He shall bring it to pass"'. Later he was to exhort his staff to dedicate themselves to 'humility in the service of higher pursuits. The desire for notoriety and recognition', he warned, 'sterilizes the seeds from which greatness might spring'.

He was the son of the manse – his father was a minister in the Free Church of Scotland. The intense, puritanical faith he was raised in however helped form the BBC in quite different ways from the commitment to Christianity. Based on the interrogation of the bible and belief in the value of the sermon it provided him with a deeply felt belief in the power of words to transform and save people.[1] The vision of the BBC's role in democratic society was formed (and is still formed) by this passionate commitment to improvement. It also provided him with a sense of a mission that he instilled in the Corporation. 'Public Service' broadcasting was to become a vocation and a calling. Reith had been wounded in the First World War – and was sent to America to improve the quality of American mass small arms production. This experience too – the practical experience of the value of mass production and that it could be improved and held to a high standard – also influenced how Reith formed the BBC.

This ability to impose his will on staff was helped by his size. Churchill nicknamed him 'Wuthering Heights' and senior staff would stand on the stairs to argue with him, 'so that I can see you eye to eye, Sir'. His administrative style, and indeed his private diary, were characterized by self-laceration and abuse. Memoranda sent to Reith would return peppered with 'rubbish', 'stupid', 'soft minded idiocy', 'he lies'. Frequently he saw his life in nautical terms: the Corporation was a ship and he was at the helm. He was pompous, humourless, arrogant and, like most megalomaniacs, paranoid and self-pitying. He was also inspiring, effective and ambitious. He was overbearing and depressive. The near absurdity of his vision enabled him to foresee the power of the new service.

Broadcasting was to be financed partly by a tariff on wireless sets, and partly by a licence fee. These sources soon proved inadequate for the rapidly expanding station. Listeners evaded the tariff by building their own sets with cheap foreign components. They then evaded the full licence fee by applying for experimental licences. The BBC complained, and the manufacturers were angry that the monopoly of wireless production was not proving as profitable as they had hoped. In 1923 the Sykes Committee was set up by the Post Office to inquire into the Company's finances. This rejected advertising as a source of revenue because 'The time devoted to it . . . would be very small and therefore exceedingly valuable'. Radio advertising would interfere with market competition by favouring large firms. Instead the report recommended that a simple licence fee (for the right to hear broadcasts) should be raised to finance the service.

The Crawford Committee, two-and-a-half years later, unquestioningly accepted the necessity of a broadcasting monopoly, and recommended that the private company be replaced by a 'Public Commission operating in the National Interest'. The service was felt to have outgrown the petty limits of a business enterprise. 'Formed at a moment when broadcasting was still embryonic – regarded by many as a toy, a fantasy, even a joke', the report argued, 'the company by strenuous application to its duties aided by the loyalty of its staff has raised the service to a degree which reflects high credit on British efficiency and enterprise'.

In 1926 the British Broadcasting Company closed, and the new British Broadcasting Corporation opened. Reith was delighted that the unique status of his organisation was recognized. 'The Royal Academy and the Bank of England function under Royal Charter', proclaimed the 1927 *Handbook*. 'So does the BBC. It is no Department of State'.

The BBC as a public corporation

The BBC came to be seen, in the words of William Robson the reforming economist, as a 'sociological invention of immense significance', and a 'breathtaking administrative innovation'. Hilda Matheson, the first head of the Talks Department, one of the gifted and significant women who dominated the early BBC,[2] wrote in 1933 that the Corporation was 'wholly in keeping with the British constitution, and it is more and more common to find it quoted as a possible model for the management of other national services for which private control and direct state management are equally unsuitable'. What, then, was the novelty of the BBC's organisation and to what extent was Reith responsible for it?

Reith did not invent the notion of a public corporation. Neither did the Corporation simply emerge accidentally. Reith exploited a theory because it was convenient to do so. The Post Office, which played a critical role in the BBC's development, was itself an early example of a nationally run business – but also one that re-distributed in the pursuit of efficiency and the national interest. The invention of the pre-paid 'penny post' that charged the same for wherever the item was sent naturally seemed like a model for the new service. William Beveridge had commented in 1905 that the General Post Office (GPO) was the 'one socialist experiment . . . that now works well'. Forestry, water and electricity were all important public corporations set up in the years before the BBC was even thought of. Lincoln Gorden, the economist, wrote that by the 1920s, 'Public boards had become all the rage, politicians of every creed when confronted with an industry or a social service which was giving trouble or failing to operate efficiently – create a board'.

The First World War had been critical in establishing the conditions for the acceptance of a 'Public Service Utility'. Despite bitter opposition, the centralized control of health, insurance, coal, and ultimately the rationing of food had been introduced. These were seen as exceptional wartime measures. By the 1920s, however, a generation of reformers who had been civil servants during the war were experienced in organising the centralized distribution of resources. Indeed for a brief period after the war even the government accepted a more interventionist role. The BBC was formed in this period.

The development of the public corporation depended on the rejection of both market forces and politics in favour of efficiency and planned growth controlled by experts. Briggs has pointed out that the acceptance of the BBC and its monopoly was a consequence of the 'substantial and influential support' the Company received between 1924 and 1925. The monopoly remained in Reith's keeping because 'a large number of important people and a large section of the interested public felt that it was right that this should be so'. These influential people were those who were personally impressed by Reith: the Post Office officials; the director of the wireless manufacturers' association; even the Prime Minister, Baldwin. Reith was adroit at making the BBC central to national life: from police notices and emergencies, to the weather forecast and most of all programmes, he wound the tiny organisation into a prominent role.

However, there was another interest that helped determine that the BBC became a monopoly – that Briggs mentioned but did not accord full weight to – not least because the full details could only be recently pieced together. The BBC's monopoly was also created because the government were concerned that the new medium might interfere with the security and military use of the airwaves. This was a technical anxiety about securing a range within the spectrum for defence use. This was matched by another political worry: the use of radio for subversion. Radio had been used as an instrument in the recent 1917 Russian revolution, and the Bolshevists had on several occasions attempted to run amateur propaganda stations in Britain. The BBC – as a singular, regulated broadcaster – was seen as a solution to both of these problems.[3]

However, the idea of the BBC also had more general support. There was a widespread dissatisfaction with the *ad hoc* nature of industrial competition. Even in the 1920s, during the first post-war slump, there was a sense that there must be alternative ways to manage the distribution of resources. Men like Beveridge, who had demonstrated the justice of centralized control in the arrangements for social security and in the rationing of food during the First World War, were opposed to the social consequences of industrial competition. In 1934 Beveridge was to argue:

> In a free market economy consumers can buy only that which is offered to them, and that which is offered is not necessarily that which is most advantageous. It is that which appears to give the best prospect of profit to the producer.

This kind of attitude, which Beveridge later developed and popularized in his broadcasts, was surprisingly widely held in the early 1920s. For example, Sir Stephen Tallents, who was to play a prominent role in the BBC as well as in the British documentary movement, had advanced views on the use of advertising, had worked on rationing with Beveridge, and held very similar opinions.

Reith's view that capitalist competition was not wrong but could be inefficient was not original and tapped into a modernizing and progressive set of ideas.

The BBC was to be used repeatedly as a prototype of the public corporation, especially by Herbert Morrison – later the visionary leader of the London County Council and an important minister in wartime coalition and then the reforming Labour Government. Perhaps the feature which particularly attracted socialist writers was the BBC's distance from the world of capitalist industry. The Corporation made no profits. But in addition the goods it made, programmes, were in theory accessible to an infinite number of consumers. It was also a completely new enterprise with no capitalist inheritance to weigh it down. As Robson wrote, 'The BBC is an engine of the mind . . . it represents socialized control not encumbered with compensation'.

It was this aspect of broadcasting which Reith, with tremendous prescience, grasped. He argued that it was in the very nature of the medium that it should be available for all, for it 'ran as a reversal of the natural law that the more one takes, the less there is left for others'. In broadcasting, he wrote, 'There is no limit to the amount which may be drawn off. It does not matter how many thousands there may be listening; there is always enough for others'.[4] In order to exploit broadcasting fully, Reith had argued, it must be governed by social and not financial priorities.

Thus considerations of profit would have restricted the service to the populous urban areas. Reith was determined that the BBC must serve the whole nation. However, Reith also saw that a national service was vital for the defence of the Corporation's monopoly. 'About a week ago', he wrote in 1923, 'we got wind of a projected attack'. This was to be:

> based on the grounds that under the present system we had already reached the limits of our expansion. The deduction to be drawn was that the British people would never be supplied with adequate services unless the principle of competitive commercialism were admitted.

Reith rejected commerce because it would have diminished his empire and lowered its status. But he also believed it to be inefficient in the management of national resources: utilities, and he wanted broadcasting to be seen as a national utility, were (and many would argue continue to be) natural monopolies. Many shared this view.

Even the government had come to see some kinds of goods as exceptional. In 1927 the film industry, suffering from foreign competition, was protected by import controls, because films were of 'outstanding national importance'. The BBC had been established because the government was anxious not to exercise unfair patronage by granting a monopoly to any one commercial company. But it had also been considerably affected by the report of a Post Office official, F. J. Brown, who was appalled to find on a visit to the USA 'an epidemic of broadcasting was raging'. Thousands of American companies had started broadcasting and President Hoover had demanded central control over the new technology, claiming that it was as if '10,000 telephone subscribers were crying through the air for their mates'. As a result of interference, Hoover declared, 'the ether will be filled with frantic chaos'.[5] The British government realized, on the basis of the American experience, that broadcasting was a new kind of resource whose management demanded a new form of administration.

However, the BBC was also founded on a rejection of politics. From the start of broadcasting there had been anxieties that the service would become an agency of government propaganda. Sir Charles Trevelyan, a Labour representative on the Sykes Committee, asked the Company's lawyer whether 'for public reasons a government could intervene to prevent anything it regarded as undesirable being broadcast'. He was told that there might be control of the news, but that a government was unlikely to bother with concerts, lectures, speeches or the weather. There was a real anxiety that any monopoly might be used for propaganda.

While Reith believed that the BBC should be above politics, politicians at first believed the BBC to be beneath them. Direct public ownership was rejected because it was felt 'A Member might well shrink from the prospect of having to defend in Parliament the various items in a government concert'.

Reith despised politicians and disliked party politics. Although at various times he had political ambitions, he hated the 'toadying, the cringing pursuit of popularity' which he believed characterized politics. 'It is pathetic', he wrote, 'how apprehensive Labour leaders are of their followers and how little control they seem to have over them'. Reith often misjudged the significance of political events (he felt that the split and collapse of the Labour government in 1931 was unimportant, 'Silly, over money'). 'The whole horrid technique of politics should be abolished', he wrote in his diary. 'Government of a country is a matter of proper administration, in other words efficiency. It need not be different in nature from the government of a business – only in degree' (29 November 1936). But he was also mobilizing a post-First World War hostility to the press – which was felt to have substituted jingoism and propaganda for a proper interrogation of the conduct of the war.

Perhaps the most significant feature of Reith's distaste was the sense that politics led to vacillation and compromise when firm government was needed. Reith was not alone in this view. Indeed an interest developed during the late 1920s and early 1930s, from the extreme right to the fellow travelling left – and including the Keynesian centre – in the benefit of planning.

'The Next Five Years Group' and Political and Economic Planning (known then as PEP!) were groups involving members with different political allegiances but who were agreed on the need for more social planning. 'It may be', wrote one reformer in *The New Outlook*, 'that the Party structures will act for some time as an obstacle in the way of new developments'. Harold Macmillan, later to be Prime Minister, summed up this position:

Most of us recognize that the old system of free unplanned Capitalism has passed away. Most of us agree that a leap forward to complete state planning is politically impossible. But . . . our search is for some practical scheme of social organisation . . . which is neither.[6]

On the left, the XYZ club and the New Fabian Research Bureau soon became the natural home for planners and economists.

It has been argued by Cardiff and Scannell that the BBC legitimized its model of broadcasting not by the huge audience the service soon attracted but by reference to the elite of 'the great and the good who trooped into studios to educate and inform on every subject from unemployment to the Origin of the Species: Shaw, Wells, the Webbs, Beveridge, Keynes and Huxley – the roll call is endless'. Broadcasting, they argue, was dominated by a specific, reforming, fraction of the middle class. 'They saw themselves as superior to the aristocracy, for they were efficient and uncorrupt, and claiming to act for the general good, they presumed (naturally) to speak and act on behalf of the working classes'. Robert Skidelsky has argued that Keynes's economic theories provided the basis for a new liberal politics in the 1940s, which avoided class struggle and yet implied 'Keynes's most characteristic belief: that public affairs should and could be managed by an elite of clever and disinterested public servants' (*Encounter*, April 1979). The BBC provided a cultural institution which performed the same function. Indeed the economic and political structure of the BBC was also a product of the experience and beliefs of this reforming intelligentsia. Reith's view of what he intended the BBC to be, those pressures he perceived as threatening, and the alternatives he rejected, were typical of what has been seen as a 'middle opinion'. Indeed it might be claimed that the success of the BBC vindicated the view that a strong middle-class consensus lay beneath the dissent and turmoil of the 1930s.

However, this view can be questioned. Arthur Marwick early on argued, in an article called 'Middle opinion in the thirties', that 'they did not in their own day achieve much, these advocates of political agreement, the "soft centre" as they were not unjustly called'. Indeed, the 'great and the good' were, as Hugh Dalton wrote in 1936, 'more or less eminent persons who are disinclined to join any existing political party, but who are prepared to collaborate with others in writing joint letters to the Press, and in such organisations as the Next Five Years Group'. They were a band of leaders – but they had no followers. As Pimlott has argued in *Labour and the Left in the 1930s*, their policies might have developed 'into the basis of a powerful campaign for a British New Deal as a frontal assault on mass unemployment'.[7] But in fact the supporters of middle opinion were politically isolated. Keynes and Beveridge had to wait until the Second World War to see their ideas implemented.

Yet the BBC was not merely a dream or a plan for reform. It was a rapidly growing institution. By the middle of the 1930s it had become an established and central component of British culture.

Perhaps pressures other than those of the liberal intelligentsia were at work in the making of the BBC? Certainly, unlike Beveridge's plans for insurance, the BBC cost the government no money. The personal connections of the BBC producers were with Bloomsbury literati rather than with liberal reformers. Reith (who temperamentally was more like one of the Victorians Lytton Stratchey, the Bloomsbury writer, satirised) was more an evangelist than a liberal. 'Anything in the nature of a dictatorship is the subject of much resentment these days', Reith wrote in 1924. 'Well somebody has to give decisions'. While liberals planned, Reith bullied, wheedled and built an empire. 'It is occasionally indicated to us that we are apparently setting out to give the public what we think they need and not what they want – but few know what they want, and very few what they need'.

Reith was authoritarian and successful. In the 1930s the new liberals were neither. Moreover, although they dominated broadcast talks, this category hardly dominated the BBC's output. Despite Reith's preoccupation with culture, contemporary critics most frequently accused the Corporation of philistinism. 'The company undoubtedly saw itself as a cultural force', wrote R. S. Lambert, 'by which it meant something constituted to avoid the postures of vulgarity'. Perhaps the BBC was less dominated by the concerns of the liberal intelligentsia and more successful in the 1930s because it was paternalist. Perhaps, also, it gave the public what it wanted rather more than Reith was prepared to admit. For, as the BBC *Handbook* shows, by 1934 the BBC was broadcasting more light music, comedy and vaudeville than any other European station. It was hardly the stuff of social revolution. The BBC was also competitive, and intended to be popular.

The BBC and political independence

How was the BBC's independence from partisan political pressure to be achieved? The directors of the private company were replaced by publicly-appointed Governors in 1926. These were to be the trustees of the public interest. At first the Governors and Reith disagreed about how the responsibility should be divided between them.

Thus Philip Snowden's wife Ethel – described in Beatrice Webb's diaries as having 'caricatured social climbing' (19 March 1932) – arrived at the BBC expecting an office, a secretariat and a full-time job. Appointed a Governor as a 'convenient representative of both Labour and Women', she believed the Director General should play an administrative role, and that the Governors should make all policy decisions. Reith detested her, and commented that she thought that 'there ought to be a board meeting every day . . . an abominable exhibition by her. A truly terrible creature, ignorant, stupid and horrid'. He saw her as a threat to his own position. Indeed he was quite correct to do so. Hugh Dalton, the Labour politician, recorded in his diary (3 August 1930) that Ethel Snowden had asked G. D. H. Cole – another Governor – to help her get rid of Reith. 'Who would she suggest as his successor?' Cole had asked. 'I would gladly take it on myself', Ethel had replied.

Governing the BBC was a project – and far more important than its audiences recognized. But it was never a perfect mechanism – rather one in evolution.

Herbert Morrison wrote in his important work on nationalization, *Socialization and Transport*, 'It is a matter of argument whether the Director General of Broadcasting should, or should not, be a strong personality'. Reith's views were quite straightforward: he wanted to be in control, and he wanted the Governors to back up his decisions.

The Corporation was supposed to be independent and non-partisan: in practice it was not even indirectly accountable to parliament. In a Report on the Machinery of Government written in 1918, the Webbs had opposed the increased use of public corporations because 'when a board is set up without explicit status provided for ministerial responsibility to parliament – the situation is obviously unsatisfactory. Only ministerial responsibility provides safeguard for the citizen . . . and consumer'.

However, these objections were not understood. The government had felt in 1925 that: 'The progress of science and the harmony of art would be hampered by too rigid rules and too constant supervision by the state'. So, between Reith, anxious to avoid having the content of broadcasting politically manipulated, and therefore determined to evade political control, and the government, anxious to avoid responsibility for trivia, the BBC was left with no effective accountability. This omission came to be treated as though it were a principle. Herbert Morrison later claimed to have invented it. Robson wrote in 1935 that it was:

> in strict conformity with the English tradition . . . derived as a practical expedient to perform a particular function, without any concern for general principles – or indeed any awareness that questions of principle were involved.

It is perhaps better seen as the elevation of an uneasy compromise into an ideal type.

The BBC and the General Strike

The BBC's practical interpretation of impartiality was soon tested during the General Strike in 1926. The strike, which had been provoked by the slashing of coal miner's wages in the post-war recession (when one in eleven of all male workers were miners) divided the nation and brought it to a standstill. Some of the strikers wanted political revolution – most of them were suffering economically. Later in the twenties, after the 1929 banking crash there were hunger marches as more workers were unemployed. Meanwhile 'strike breakers' organised transport and opposition to the strike. The bitter memory of the betrayal of the generation who had fought the war and the organised opposition to the strike divided the nation. Reith knew that the survival of the Corporation (whose constitution had not yet been formally accepted) depended on its conduct during the crisis.

One effect of the strike was to create a national audience for broadcasting. At the end of 1926 Hilda Matheson was able to write, 'The public and wireless listeners are now nearly synonymous terms'. Beatrice Webb noted in her diary that 'The sensation of the General Strike centres around the headphones of the wireless set'. Although there were only two million licence holders these represented a far greater number of listeners, and 'communal listening' was a feature of the crisis as people gathered in halls and outside shops to hear the news.

The BBC seemed more important because of the absence of all other sources of information. An old-age pensioner in the 1950s told Julian Symons that he still had 'the little homemade crystal set which worked lovely with the iron bedstead for an aerial . . . and which told me what was *really happening*'. Despite the inadequacy of its news, the Corporation emerged from the strike with a national audience and increased authority.

Another effect of the General Strike was that the BBC invented modern propaganda in its British form. During the First World War persuasive techniques had been crude. All Germans were characterized as vicious beasts intent on murdering children and raping nuns. Meanwhile the scale of casualties, and the military dogmas that led to them were not revealed or questioned. The rejection of the propagandists of the First World War, the widespread belief that was both elite and popular – that the press had misled the public about the causes and the catastrophic conduct of the war – was one of the profoundest influences on the men who came to lay the foundations of broadcasting in the early 1920s.

However, the First World War view of propaganda was still accepted by many during the strike. Its main proponent was Churchill and its main instrument the *British Gazette*. This was a daily news-sheet that few took seriously, so evidently biased were its contents. Churchill wanted to commandeer the BBC, as the government had the right to do. Reith argued that if the BBC was taken over the strikers would merely close the service down. Apart from destroying 'the pioneer work of over three years', by shattering public confidence in broadcasting, 'It was no time for dope, even if the people could have been doped'. He argued that to suppress information was likely to exacerbate the crisis. His most telling point was that by gaining the trust of both strikers and the government the BBC could positively facilitate a resolution of the crisis:

> In the end conciliations of some kind must supervene and . . . the BBC could act as a link to draw together the contending parties by creating an atmosphere of good will towards its service on both sides.

Reith argued that the trust gained by 'authentic impartial news' could then be used. It was not necessarily an end in itself. He stated, however, that 'Since the BBC was a national institution and since the Government in this crisis was acting for the people . . . *the BBC was for the Government in the Crisis too*'.

Indeed it was Reith's own political judgement which controlled policy throughout the strike. Briggs has pointed out:

> He preferred mediation to showdown. If his views had coincided with those of the sponsors of the *British Gazette* he would have had fewer qualms about allowing the BBC to fall directly into the hands of the government. As it was, his personal conviction gave strength to his resistance on constitutional principles.

Reith, as another writer, Patrick Renshaw, has argued, 'would have supported the union against the owners. But he was certainly not prepared to support the TUC against the Government'. However, Reith's 'distinct' view seems very close to that of the most implacable opponent of the strike, Churchill. Martin Gilbert argues that Churchill was quite prepared to accept a conciliatory policy towards the resolution of the coal-miners' dispute with the owners; it was only the general and political strike he was opposed to.

Until 1926 the press had prohibited the BBC from collecting any news. The strike allowed the Company to develop a news service of its own. This reported statements by the strikers as well as the strike-breakers. One of the bulletins on 4 May started with the Trades Union Congress (TUC) statement, 'We have from Land's End to John O'Groats reports of support that have surpassed our expectations'.

During the strike no representative of organised labour was allowed to broadcast, and the Leader of the Opposition, Ramsay MacDonald, was also banned. These restrictions were imposed by the government. Reith thought them wrong, but said he could do nothing about them. Willie Graham, one of the strike leaders, wrote angrily to him:

> The Government emphatically deny that they interfere with the BBC in any way. On the other hand the company states that it was not a free agent. I am sure that you will agree that it is impossible to make any sense of these two statements.

Called by some workers the 'British Falsehood Corporation', the BBC learnt how to censor itself during the strike in order to forestall government intervention. Nevertheless, the General Strike marks the end of propaganda based on lies and the start of a more subtle tradition of selection and presentation.

Throughout the strike the government had emphasized that the strikers were politically motivated and hence unconstitutional. The BBC emerged from the crisis with an ethic of political neutrality, which was expressed as much in the tone of its broadcasts as in any formal regulations. This was to have consequences for politics and the conduct of political life.

Governments and the BBC in the 1930s

The General Strike initiated a pattern that was to recur throughout the 1930s: the BBC was forced to pass off government intervention as its own decision. In 1935 it was proposed to include talks by a communist and a fascist – Harry Pollitt and Sir Oswald Mosley, respectively – in a series on the British constitution. The Foreign Office protested, arguing that Pollitt could not be allowed to broadcast, as he had recently made a speech supporting armed revolution. The BBC responded by referring the matter to the Governors, who declared that, 'More harm than good could be done if a policy were adopted of muzzling speeches'. A BBC official told the Foreign Office, 'We can't chuck Pollitt unless, under our charter, we are given instruction from government that he is not to broadcast'.

The Foreign Office remained adamant that Pollitt should not broadcast. They suggested, however, that the question could resolve itself into the undesirability of *Mosley* speaking.[8] The matter was finally brought to an end when the Postmaster General wrote to Reith pointing out that, as the Corporation licence was due for renewal, it would be wiser to comply with government demands. The BBC then asked for permission to say why the programmes had been banned.

The government reacted sharply. According to a Cabinet minute:

> It would be neither true nor desirable to state publicly that the talks would be an 'embarrassment to the Government' at the present time. But it would be true to say that 'they would not be in the national interest'.

Despite the feeling of Corporation officials like Tallents and Graves that the BBC's chances of survival were better if it were seen to be acting in strict accordance with the Charter, the series was dropped and no mention made of government pressure. But lessons were being learnt.

However, when in 1937 Mosley, backed by fascist money, proposed to set up a 'cable broadcasting station' – that would broadcast popular music into Britain from the Channel Islands – the government and the BBC worked together. By 1937 – although the policy of 'appeasing' German demands was at its height – behind the scenes there was cautious preparation for conflict. Mosley's interest in the cable station was hidden behind a tangle of commercial companies. It was not immediately apparent that the station was to be controlled by Mosley. It was the BBC who established his interest, and consequently alerted the government to the potential political threat of a fascist cable station pretending to be the commercial broadcaster of amusing music. The idea for 'popular music' that would break the 'gloomy monopoly' of the

BBC was a 'Trojan horse' for introducing foreign propaganda into British homes, said Tallents. At the time the answer (which was in the BBC's interest) was to argue that the BBC's monopoly ought not be broken. It was this argument that Coase took at its face value and disagreed with. But behind the scenes the argument was quite different – it was a political decision about protecting the nation in a time of war.[9]

An even more peculiar damaging example of the BBC's relationship with the government occurred in the period immediately before the outbreak of the Second World War. On 25 August 1939 the Labour leaders Hugh Dalton and Harold Laski, together with the General Secretary of the TUC, Walter Citrine, wanted to broadcast a direct personal message and warning to the German people. In an interview with them, the Director General of the BBC, Ogilvie (who had replaced Reith in 1938), refused to tell them whether their request would be granted. In the event, news that a 'statement' had been made was broadcast, but nothing whatsoever was mentioned about its contents.

Ogilvie, Dalton pointed out, clearly wanted to consult the Foreign Office but refused to admit this. The next day the Labour leaders complained to the Foreign Secretary, Halifax, of the way in which the BBC had treated them. By this time Ogilvie apparently claimed that he had told Dalton and Citrine that he was going to consult the Foreign Office.

Walter Citrine complained to Halifax that 'Our people are getting pretty fed up with being expected to shout with the government one day and being treated like a lot of children or nobodies the next'. He went on to say that Ogilvie (who had been a Conservative MP) 'might be good enough to help them [the Tories] collect material to rag Lloyd George with – but that doesn't satisfy me that he is fit to be Director General of the BBC'.[10] As war appeared increasingly unavoidable the Labour Party spent the last week of peace debating whether this incident demonstrated the continuous and insidious dependence of the Corporation on the government. It is not merely that the decision whether to broadcast the message was referred to the Foreign Office. In addition, Ogilvie was predicting Foreign Office policy, and indeed covering for it. Earlier, the BBC had been concerned to make government pressure on its decisions public. In 1939 it was protecting the Foreign Office, and passing off Foreign Office demands as its own policy.

Since 1927 the BBC had been strenuously courting government departments in an attempt to evade press restrictions on its reporting. 'We ought to be the arbiters of what Government news goes out', wrote a Corporation official, 'not a commercial company like Reuters'.[11] A close relationship with civil servants grew up and government pressure was often exercised informally and personally. 'Vansittart' (the Head of the Foreign office – privately a strong anti-appeaser) 'would like the BBC to get pro-France in our news and stop using words like insurgent', Reith wrote in his diary in 1937. The Corporation was most concerned that disputes with government should not be resolved by the emergence of any official regulations.

This cautious self-protection was shrewd, and may have been the only strategy available. However, it potentially made the BBC vulnerable to bullying. As a result, the most important constraint came to be the Corporation's anxiety to pre-empt the threats. Yet the BBC was accumulating cultural power, authority and affection with audiences which was also perhaps the best defence.

The BBC, society and programmes

During a decade of depression and industrial decline, the BBC grew, quadrupled its staff, raised salaries and acquired vast buildings. Its audiences grew so fast and so widely that they became synonymous with the nation. One writer, D. G. Bridson, recalled his shock at being asked to work for the BBC. 'In 1935 I mentally bracketed it with Parliament, the Monarch, the Church and the Holy Ghost', he wrote.

However, the Corporation also intended to become part of the Establishment. Its development into an authoritative institution was a complex process. This was expressed in the choice of outside broadcasters, and what they were allowed to say. It was also expressed in how the Corporation treated them, and its own staff. It was expressed in the distance between what it claimed to do and what it did.

In a decade of hunger marches and 'red united fighting fronts', the BBC regarded a succession of royal broadcasts as the triumph of outside broadcasting and actuality reporting. Broadcasting in the 1930s was dominated by state openings, royal anniversaries, visits, deaths and births, and by the Coronation. 'The floral decorations for His Majesty's broadcast', ran one press release, 'will be one bowl of hiskura (mauve) and a small vase of grape hyacinths'. In 1923 Reith had exercised a servile cunning in his attempt to persuade the Dean of Westminster to allow the Duke of York's wedding to be broadcast. It would, he suggested, even have advantages 'from the devotional point of view'. Many who 'by sheer force of circumstance, or negligence had little to do with the Church' would hear the 'measured cadence of the sacred words'.[12] The experience, Reith implied, might change their hearts.

Reith's greatest *coup* was the annual Christmas message delivered by the monarch. These events were usually preceded by an 'Empire programme', making contact with far-flung colonial stations. 'Goodbye Wilmington', ran one, 'and a Happy Christmas to you all . . . behind us the mountains which encircle Vancouver are still lost in darkness . . . though a faint radiance announces that dawn is on its way'.[13] In turn this led to the more regular Empire Service, launched in 1932 which was aimed at colonial administrators and English speaking colonies of the empire. But the Royal Christmas message became a part of the Christmas celebrations. George V's funeral resulted in an eighty-page BBC policy document, 'Procedures on the death of a sovereign'. The first televised outside broadcast was of King

George VI and Queen Elizabeth attending a state opening of Parliament. The BBC producer delicately asked whether the royal couple could *possibly* wave and smile to the left as they came around a corner (there was a camera there).[14]

Reith and the Corporation did not merely present traditional pageantry to a wider audience. They established a new manner for royalty which was more appropriate to the twentieth century. Reith made suggestions for what royalty should say, and how they should say it. He recognized what kinds of occasion a royal presence would grace – and benefit from. One of the bitterest complaints of Reith's old age was his omission from royal Garden Party invitation lists. He felt he had 'done much to serve the House'. Indeed the BBC was responsible, at least in part, for moulding a new domestic and populist image for the monarchy.

The BBC in the thirties placed itself firmly as part of the Establishment. It was liberal and staffed by creative and curious staff. One of the clearest aspects of what came to be known as the 'William Ferrie incident' was the incomprehension of the Corporation's *bourgeois* but liberal-minded staff, when confronted with a worker.[15] Ferrie, a communist trade unionist, was invited to reply to a talk given by Sir Herbert Austin, who had spoken on the immense improvement of working-class conditions during the twentieth century. This was in 1932. It must have rung a little hollow in Jarrow and Glasgow. Ferrie committed the Corporation equivalent of original sin by departing from his written script when he reached the microphone. He began to tell the public how the BBC had censored him, and how he had meant to give a rousing speech. Horrified Corporation officials rushed to fade out the programme. Ferrie later wrote:

> I was particularly incensed at their demand that I should put across that the slogan 'Workers of the World Unite' is not a revolutionary slogan. I also refused to drop my h's and talk as they imagine a worker does.

His talk had quite clearly been altered to make it more politically acceptable. But the way in which it was done is even more revealing. The BBC censored him in ways that the officials would hardly have recognized as such. Mary Adams was one of the formidable and intelligent women who had such influence in this period of the BBC, and she told Ferrie 'Your language was too literary and impersonal'. Ferrie, to her surprise, came 'in an agitated state' to see her at her Chelsea home. He arrived at the studio with three colleagues 'for support'. All of this seemed odd to middle-class BBC producers, even though Adams was sympathetic to the union case. It seems in retrospect a perfectly regular way for a working-class trade unionist to deal with an institution that seemed bent on intimidating him. But the BBC was in a wider way inventing programmes that would bring the political world to life in the nation. *This Week in Parliament* began in November 1929. Hilda Matheson invented it to help inform women about political affairs. The 1929 election was known as the 'flapper' election as it was the first where women between the ages of 21 and 29 were allowed to vote. The idea was that a woman MP or politician would give a short talk to women at home. The first presenter was the pioneering Margaret Bondfield – who was the first woman Cabinet Minister. Other programmes – talks and discussions – and even drama brought political and social topics into the studio.

The Corporation began to use radio for drama in new and experimental ways, music programmes rapidly developed their own broadcast manner, children were carefully attended to, gardeners, drivers, ornithologists, the ill and the 'working man', the old and the 'housewife', the 'women in an office' and the 'anxious mother', the categories of how the BBC thought of its audiences burgeoned. Above all imaginative programme-makers found new ways of fascinating audiences. The real story of the 1930s is that radio listening – BBC listening – became synonymous with the nation.

Yet visionary as Reith was he was also difficult and tyrannical. Reith would banish rebels from the centre of the empire to the periphery. 'You're a very dangerous man Harding', Bridson recalls Reith telling one, 'I think you'd better go up North where you can't do so much damage'. Indeed, by 1937 the only doubts about the Corporation's monopoly were centred on the rights of its staff. There was the forced resignation of P. P. Eckersley, an engineer and programme innovator of enormous talent who had worked for the Corporation since 1926. Eckersley wrote his own epitaph, 'He had ideas: We stopped them'. He was obliged to resign because he was cited in a divorce case. There was a difficult libel case, and there were rumbling discontent.

Reith's view was succinct. 'It's a mug's game', he wrote in a book called *Personality and Career*, 'to pull contrary to your boss'. In 1937 the Ullswater Report recommended, under pressure from Clement Attlee, the Labour MP, that a Staff Association should be set up, and for the first time the BBC's workers had organised representation. Attlee later observed that having staff who had rights made the BBC stronger.

The BBC saw itself as a humane and enlightened employer, which had always pursued strictly egalitarian and meritocratic appointment procedures. In 1934 an internal report commented complacently that there was 'a good proportion of women to men on the staff'. Hilda Matheson and Mary Somerville had set up the key Talks Department and the Education Service when the Company started. It was a woman's initiative which had started the Sound Archive. Women, however, were never announcers, rarely presenters, and the proportion of women in administrative and creative posts declined. Between 1926 and 1936 the Corporation's staff had increased fourfold, yet, as the BBC's annual reports show, the number of women in creative jobs had risen by little more than one third, and in senior administrative positions by barely one quarter. The early heady days of creating a new service had been good for women – as the BBC became more established men took over.

Nevertheless, the atmosphere in the BBC, a new, exciting, glamorous place where it was better, as Peter Eckersley remarked, 'to have discreet affairs than to remarry', is summed up by Maurice Gorham:

> The BBC secretaries were beginning to bloom though they reached full flower later. By that time many of them were pin money girls. It was a great sight to see them going out at lunch, high heeled, sheer stockinged, beautifully made up, talking disdainfully in high clear voices.

By the 1930s the BBC had become an august institution. It was not a crude agent of the *status quo*, rather it advocated acceptable change, in some areas, in certain circumstances, sometimes.

The BBC and journalism

Indeed, by the end of the decade the sheer amount of news that broadcasting and the press were flooded with was so large that, had it wished to, a government could hardly have pre-censored it all. However, a new tradition in reporting imposed new criteria of selection on the news. Journalists stopped being passionate advocates, saw themselves rather as independent professionals, and their writing as a negotiated product of conflict between partisan views. This self-image and its practical consequences were most fully developed in the BBC. Reith was not opposed to conflict. On the contrary, he fought the press for the right to broadcast on contentious issues. But the BBC and the new 'professional journalist' retained a monopoly over deciding its limits.

The BBC and appeasement

The BBC's brokerage was subject to pressure. In the eyes of the BBC's programme-makers, politics was an activity which only happened between major political parties. Two kinds of political dispute never reached the air waves: divisions within parties and the expressive politics of the streets. Winston Churchill, repeatedly excluded from broadcasting because his views were seen as eccentric, wrote to Reith saying he wished he could buy broadcasting time. He preferred the American commercial system 'to the present British method of debarring public men from access to a public who wish to hear'. In 1933 Churchill and Austen Chamberlain complained that the BBC 'had introduced an entirely new principle of discrimination into British public life, namely the elimination from broadcasting of any Members of Parliament who were not nominated by the Party leaders or the Party Whip'. Such a crucial innovation, they protested, should be decided by parliament, not arbitrarily imposed by the BBC.[16]

The most important dispute the BBC ignored, and one which cut across party loyalties, was that of the government's policy of appeasing German territorial ambitions. Churchill claimed that the BBC conspired with the press to exclude all opponents of this policy from any access to the public. Gilbert and Gott have suggested that appeasers were effective for so long mainly because of their success in keeping the opponents of German rearmament out of public office.

However, the control of public knowledge and opinion was also crucial. An early reference to Polish rearmament lost a producer his job in 1932. Speakers were banned because of their hostility to the Fascist states. Later, the BBC was to apologize for its attitude during the 1930s by explaining that, while mistaken, it was merely following the trend of opinion of the times. Was this the case? Certainly the press was overwhelmingly pro appeasement and in the case of the *Daily Mail* overwhelmingly in favour of fascism (whether German, Italian, Spanish or British).

Hugh Carleton Greene, later a brilliant Director General of the Corporation, worked for the *Daily Telegraph* reporting from Berlin as a young man from 1932. He spoke German and was quite clear about the way in which fascism was developing. He wrote to his mother (understanding that his letters would be opened) that 'if the BBC would take a stronger, better informed line then it would change everything'.[17]

Reith's diary first mentions preparations for war in 1933: plans for the physical protection of transmitters and broadcasting stations were in hand by 1935; Reith was involved in discussions over the organisation of a Ministry of Information in the event of war by 1936; details of trains in which to send personnel from London were established by 1937. Thus the BBC was secretly preparing for a war which it did not officially expect, while the public were kept in ignorance of these cautious foresights.

The BBC at the end of the decade

Reith resigned in 1937, restless and dissatisfied. The BBC no longer stretched him, and he hoped for something better, which never came. Increasingly, as the prospect of high office receded, he regarded the Corporation which he had created with resentment. It had not, he came to feel, treated him well.

By the end of the 1930s the BBC seemed a natural and inevitable solution to the problem of administering a national broadcasting system. It had won the right to discuss controversial politics against the determined opposition of suspicious governments and a jealous press. But it developed unnecessary conventions, and had become too defensive. The real test of the Corporation's independence was to come during the Second World War. It had invented what broadcasting might be – delighted audiences, enthralled children, become a necessary part of every day life. It was stuffy in places. Straight laced and pompous – like Reith. But it was also full of new comedy, new ways of learning and many ingenious and intelligent things. Its programmes had taken it close to how the British people understood themselves. It served its audiences and honoured them.

Notes

1 C. Higgins, *This New Noise* (London, Fourth Estate, 2016).
2 K. Murphy, *Behind the Wireless: An Early History of Women at the BBC* (Basingstoke, Palgrave, 2016).
3 J. Seaton, 'The BBC and the "hidden wiring" of the British Constitution: the imposition of the "broadcasting ban" in 1988', *Twentieth Century British History*, 24 (3), pp. 448–71. ISSN 0955-2359.
4 J. W. C. Reith, *Broadcast Over Britain* (London, Hodder & Stoughton, 1924), p. 52.
5 F. J. Brown, 'Broadcasting in Britain', *London Quarterly Review*, 145, 3 (January 1926).
6 H. Macmillan, 'Looking forward', in the Next Five Years Group, *The New Outlook*, 1 (8 May 1937).
7 B. Pimlott, *Labour and the Left in the 1930s* (Cambridge, Cambridge University Press, 1977).
8 'The citizen and his government' (1935–36), *BBC Written Archives*.
9 J. Seaton, *Pinkoes and Traitors: The BBC and the Nation 1974–87* (Profile Books, expanded paperback edition, 2016).
10 The unpublished diary of Hugh Dalton (25–29 August 1939). For a further development of this affair, see J. Seaton and B. Pimlott, 'The struggle for balance: the BBC and the Labour Movement 1920–45', in J. Seaton and B. Pimlott (eds.) *Politics and the Media in Britain* (Aldershot, Gower, 1987).
11 'Relationship between the government and the BBC: the Foreign Office', *BBC Written Archives*.
12 Duke of York's wedding, *BBC Written Archives* (Royalty).
13 Christmas broadcasts, *BBC Written Archives* (Royalty).
14 J. Seaton, 'The media and the monarchy', *The Political Quarterly*, 2002.
15 The William Ferrie incident, *BBC Written Archives*.
16 The Churchill and Chamberlain complaint, *BBC Written Archives* (Churchill).
17 Hugh Carleton Greene papers, 23 May 1934. The Bodleian Library, TS 02.

Chapter 12

Broadcasting and the Blitz

The Second World War was the first and only war ever declared together with the majority of the British people: live, on air, on the BBC. Just after 11.15 on Sunday 3 September 1939 the anxious British public heard Prime Minister Chamberlain say:

> This morning the British Ambassador in Berlin handed the German Government a final note stating that, unless we heard from them by 11 o'clock that they were prepared at once to withdraw their troops from Poland, a state of war would exist between us. I have to tell you now that no such undertaking has been received, and that consequently this country is at war with Germany.[1]

At that moment, with audiences tense around their radios, the war began. The Prime Minister's announcement had led to some hurried re-scheduling of programmes. At 10.30 the first of a four-part lecture series on the 'Modern Idea of Death' was hastily replaced with a programme on the uses for canned fruit.[2]

After the speech, the corridors of the Corporation were full of the sound of the ripping of envelopes. As the sirens wailed (it turned out to be a false air raid alarm as a French plane had blundered into Britain) BBC staff opened their 'Top Secret' instructions for what to do if war came. Some were told where to catch the buses for evacuation to secret locations for new broadcasting facilities (the 24 bus stop was one). Some were told to report to the regional stations. Some were given orders about safety, alternatively told to go to the roof to fire fight in event of a raid, to go to the basement shelter, while others told firmly to stay where they were. But mostly the instructions were about new bureaucratic controls. The mood was apprehensive and surreal.[3]

But there was also relief. 'Can you give me any hope?' Hugh Dalton, the Labour anti-appeaser had asked Lord Halifax the Conservative Foreign Secretary the day before – who had told him that he believed war would be declared on the Sunday. 'Thank God' said Dalton.[4] What had been feared for so long was better than another round of betrayal and submission in appeasement.

Yet, by 1939 BBC engineers had already saved the BBC – and in a broader way freedom of speech – from direct take-over by the government. In 1938 (after Chamberlain's return from Germany with the promise of Peace in our Time and appeasement) government had planned to take over the BBC in the event of war because broadcast transmissions from fixed transmitters could be used by enemy bombers to pin-point targets during raids. In the intervening year the engineers developed an ingenious way of switching broadcast signals between transmitters. It was a technical solution – but – as so often with engineering, it was as much an answer to a political problem as a practical one. The BBC's relationship with government during the total war that followed was complicated – but the Corporation was never – because of the creativity of the engineers – a 'state' broadcaster.[5] The BBC's independent control over editorial matters, always compromised in a total war for national survival, nevertheless mattered.

As Penelope Fitzgerald – a young and insignificant producer in the BBC in 1940 – wrote in her novel about the Corporation during the war *Human Voices* of an organisation that was full of maddening acronyms, bureaucracy and men. But she also wrote:

> Broadcasting house was also dedicated to the strangest project of the war, or of any war, that is telling the truth. Without prompting, the BBC had decided that truth was more important than consolation, and in the long run would be more effective.[6]

The 'Dunkirk spirit' and the comradeship of the air-raid shelter during the Blitz have long been part of our national self-image. How much was this myth and how much reality? Officials concerned with civilian morale in the Ministry of Information and the Home Office who had seen ordinary people as unintelligent and weak during the 'phony' war in 1939 – when war had been declared but little happened on the home front – came to see them as dependable, shrewd and courageous by 1940. There was always a deep anxiety about public mood and this made audience research and public opinion polling vitally important. What was the mood of the people? How could it be improved and what was bad for it were urgent not casual questions. But there was a shift in how the public was conceived of. What was the cause of this change?

It is clear that the BBC, the most important instrument of domestic propaganda during the war, conducted a campaign intended to convince the public of its own endurance and solidarity. This 'image' also convinced anxious policy makers of the reliability of the British public. It was all also undercut (but oddly ultimately re-enforced) by a grumbling, sceptical public mood. The 'everyday' British public, and their efforts, had never mattered more and they were also in the front-line of much of the war. All of these aspects of public opinion were reflected in the BBC's output: from news to comedy, from documentaries to drama, from speeches to talks, BBC producers invented new forms of broadcasting. In her novel *Human Voices*, Fitzgerald wrote of the BBC at the start: 'The corridors were full of talks producers without speakers, speakers without scripts, scripts which by clerical error contained the wrong words or no words at all. The air seemed alive with urgency and worry'.[7] The BBC emerged from the war as both a symbol and an agent of the victory. More than at any other time, the BBC was part of, and seen to be part of, the history of the nation.

'The people will break'

When war was declared in 1939 most people expected a cataclysm. Pre-war pessimism about popular morale had largely been forgotten, yet it had been common to many groups who were otherwise opposed to each other.

During the 1930s another war was felt to be imminent. The main aim of many politicians was to avert the repetition of a disaster like that of the First World War. Even pacifists organising peace pledges came to feel, like Vera Brittain, that they were trying 'Canute-like to reverse the inexorable'. Indeed, memories of the First World War dominated the British as they entered the Second.

The success of the fascist dictatorships had led to a growing distrust and fatalism about the political will of the 'masses'. J. A. Hobson argued in the left-wing *Political Quarterly*:

> No one could have predicted the possibility of the collapse of all codes of decent conduct, all standards of justice, truth, and honour, not only in international affairs but in the revealed nationalism of the brutalitarian state, the facile acquiescence of whole peoples in the absolute domination of self-appointed masters, and the amazing credulity of the educated classes under the spells of the crudest propaganda.
>
> (January 1938)

Many on the left believed that the organisation of the resistance to fascism would lead to totalitarianism at home. 'If you go to war to save democracy', Kingsley Martin wrote in the *New Statesman* (1 September 1939), 'you will give up democracy in doing so, and find that you are fighting for the overseas investment of your own capitalist classes'. Even after the outbreak of war Sir Charles Trevelyan, a former Labour Minister of Education, wrote privately, 'I have a deep-seated feeling that none of the people want to fight, and that the war will collapse'. It was thus felt by some on the left either that the workers would refuse to fight a war against fascism abroad, because it would only lead to fascism at home, or that they would not fight anyway, because of the iniquitous lack of justice in Britain. The left was wrong.

The marches and demonstrations of the 1930s had led the right to believe that British workers were too anarchistic and socialist to be trusted to fight. Those in authority were also anxious about the effects of class division on morale. As early as 1926 a pioneering social scientist, Lasswell, had written, 'Governments of Western Europe can never be perfectly certain that a class-conscious proletariat will rally to the clarion of war'. The right was also wrong.

Indeed the whole concept of 'public morale', which so preoccupied the government during the war, originated in the 1930s. It was a concept originally based on naïve psychological and sociological assumptions; in particular, that individuals' attitudes and behaviour were peculiarly susceptible to manipulation in the conditions of modern 'mass' society. 'Morale' was seen as single and malleable and individuals subsumed in the whole. The success of the fascist dictators had confirmed these views, and demonstrated that the urban masses acted in response to crowd psychology and not according to rational political calculation. One reason for this view of the masses, as Bruntz indicated, was the widespread belief that superior allied propaganda had helped to shorten the First World War. *The Times* in 1918 had argued that effective propaganda had hastened victory by a year, and consequently saved a million lives. Indeed, as Shils pointed out, the Nazis may have overestimated the effect of propaganda, because they concluded that 'If Germans failed to be tricked by propaganda this time, success was assured'. In addition, the decades between the two wars had seen the dramatic success of commercial propaganda in advertising. The people, then, were thought to be persuadable.

Parallel to this anxiety was the belief that the new technology of destruction, the bombing attack on cities, would lead to a collapse of civilian society. These fears were based on exaggerated projections of the number of deaths which could be expected for each ton of explosives dropped, and on the biased intuitions of military 'experts' about how civilian populations would respond to bombing. 'In simple terms', Richard Titmuss, the pioneering social reformer, wrote, 'the experts foretold a mass outbreak of hysterical neurosis among the civilian population'. His own work on the history of social organisation during the war would disprove that – and form a foundation for the new post-war Labour Welfare state. Meanwhile, pre-war psychoanalysts argued that, under the strain of bombing, people would 'regress', and behave like frightened and unsatisfied children. A group of eminent psychologists reported to the government that 'The utter helplessness of the urban civilian today when confronted with the simplest task outside his ordinary work is likely to be a potent factor . . . in the war effort'. Experts confidently predicted that for every survivor injured by bombs at least three others would be driven mad.

It was therefore widely believed that the British worker would be devastated by an attack from the air. Perhaps this fear explains the curious official ambivalence about the approaching war during the late 1930s. Detailed preparations were made for war, indeed the BBC was planning how to broadcast during a conflict – yet rearmers were still banned from the microphone. Left-wing realists who had battled the honourable pacifist tradition within the Labour Party and swung the party around to the un-avoidable necessity of fighting fascism like Hugh Dalton and Ernest Bevin were banned from broadcasting but so were the right wing anti-appeasers like Churchill. Rather an atmosphere of dignity, gloom and appeasement dominated broadcasting even after the declaration of war. Harmon Grisewood recalled that at the end of September 1939 the new Director General, Ogilvie, suggested that a lady cellist, playing a duet with a nightingale in a wood, should be broadcast to Germany. Ogilvie believed that the sound would induce peaceful and harmonious thoughts in the belligerent fascists.

The first months of war

When the war started normal programmes were replaced by news bulletins interspersed with portentous, glum and what was believed to be appropriate music. 'Almost everything is obscured at present', the *New Statesman* commented on 9 September.

> For the first days of the war the BBC monotonously repeated news which was in the morning papers and which it had itself repeated an hour earlier. While each edition of the papers repeated what had already been heard on the wireless.

The news black-out was as complete as the black-out of the streets. During the phony war the BBC paid for nominal independence by doing exactly what the government wanted. Jack Payne noted that the music department was 'deep in memos', one of which listed the eighty banned German and Italian composers, including Monteverdi, who had died in 1643 (this was rapidly overturned and German music remained central to the repertoire). Another BBC employee claimed that the only explanation for the failure of the Germans to devastate Bush House was that 'no BBC administrator had remembered to send Hitler the memo reminding him to have it done'.[8]

When more varied programmes started from new provincial centres in unlikely country houses, at first they were dire. Basil Deane, who ran the Entertainment National Service Association (ENSA), the organisation responsible for the entertainment of the troops, wrote, 'Public anxiety was not lessened by the forced gaiety of variety artists whose personal jokes and excessive use of each other's Christian names – syndicated familiarity – savoured of self-advancement and was out of key with the national mood'. Many early propaganda broadcasts had a peevish, hectoring tone. A month after the outbreak of war a British Institute of Public Opinion poll showed that 35 per cent of the public were dissatisfied with the BBC and 10 per cent did not listen to it. In the winter of 1939 to 1940 Mass Observation reported that rumours were rife; the people apparently did not believe the newspapers, the Ministry of Information or the BBC. They trusted only their friends.

The 'phony war' forced the BBC to regionalise and extemporise. Young producers and directors poured into the Corporation, were galvanized and began to take serving the public seriously with ingenious ideas. The Corporation grew dramatically. In 1939 the BBC had 4000 staff, by the beginning of 1940, 6000, and by November of that year nearly 11,000. Roger Eckersley, the staid brother of Peter Eckersley, wrote, 'I knew directly or indirectly most of the senior staff up to the outbreak of war. Now, I shared lifts with complete strangers'. It became increasingly difficult to control the hordes of new staff and this in itself led to a period of anarchy and change. The new employees were quite different from the regular Corporation men. George Orwell, the anti-imperialist, ran influential broadcasts to India and Burma. His broadcasts gave a national platform to a generation of writers from the sub-continent. He complained that he had no idea who was listening. But recent research has shown that there were large audiences especially in Burma and India.[9] Despite his reservations about the BBC – he wrote his two great books, *Animal Farm* and *1984*, after he had worked for the great popularizer. He learnt something about pared down economy and perhaps something about appealing to wide audiences from the Corporation (as well as finding models for absurd bureaucracy and Room 101 there). William Empson the poet broadcast to China, he organised engineers like Bernard Crowther and economists like William Beveridge to broadcast helpful advice.[10] Herbert Read organised poetry readings, Edward Blunden arranged talks, and Basil Wright and the lyrical British surrealist Humphrey Jennings made programmes on the principles of documentary. According to Orwell:

> The British Government started the present war with the more or less openly declared intention of keeping the literary intelligentsia out of it, yet after three years almost every writer, however undesirable his political history or opinions, had been sucked into the various ministries or the BBC . . . No one acquainted with Government pamphlets, the Army Bureau of Current Affairs lectures, documentary films and broadcasts to occupied countries . . . can believe that our rulers would sponsor this kind of thing if they could help it.[11]

Indeed, as the war effort depended on continuous communication between the government and the public it was in many ways a war of words. Consequently, most of the new staff in the Ministry of Information and the BBC were writers. As Paul Addison wrote 'Although the War Coalition was predominantly Tory in composition, Government propaganda owed more to the Fabians or the Workers' Education Association than any Conservative organisation'.[12] The notion of a Corporation converted from philistine reaction to progressive culture became part of the fable of the BBC at war. But all over Britain conservative administrative authorities were forced to work with creative intellectuals. Scientific 'boffins' invented curious bombs for the military; literary and artistic 'boffins' did intelligence work. The Ministry of Information was notorious for the strange collection of dilettantes, anthropologists and advertising copy writers which it employed. Duff Cooper, who directed the Ministry, wrote that a monster had been created, 'so large, so voluminous, so amorphous, that no single man could cope with it'.[13] 'Frustrated' was the word he came to hate most: the plaintive cry of brilliant amateurs thwarted by bureaucracy. Yet the intellectuals were more prepared to take risks, as they had no careers to jeopardize. The *Radio Times* became filled with pictures of distinguished chemists putting bicycle power to strange purposes, and professors of literature 'thinking' about future programmes; the image of 'boffin' at least provided an accommodation and role for experts. For a brief period it was respectable, and even useful, to be serious. Nevertheless the BBC, wrote Orwell, felt 'halfway between a girls' school and a lunatic asylum'.

Programme changes

The first radio personality of the war was not a patriotic politician or a staunch common man, but Lord Haw Haw. By 1940 William Joyce dominated German propaganda to England. His voice was rich, apparently upper class, 'Cholmondeley-Plantagenet out of Christ Church',[14] and caused much speculation. It was difficult to avoid Joyce's wavelength when tuning into British stations, as Rebecca West recalled. 'There was an arresting quality about his voice which made it a sacrifice not to go on listening'.

Everyone in Gosport knew that Haw Haw knew that their town hall clock was two minutes slow. In Oxford everyone knew when the Germans were going to bomb the Morris works; Lord Haw Haw had told them. The myth of the English aristocrat with inside knowledge of the German High Command – a kind of diabolical Peter Wimsey – was powerful. What Lord Haw Haw said was less important than what the British came to believe he had said.

It has been argued that Haw Haw was ineptly used by the Germans, who failed to keep him adequately informed about military developments. However, both the government and the BBC were seriously worried about the broadcasts. Robert Silvey of the Audience Research Department was commissioned to conduct a survey of Joyce listeners for the BBC. 'It produced highly reassuring results', he wrote in the BBC *Handbook*. 'It showed that the British welcomed the new guest to the fireside as a diverting entertainment in the first bleak wartime winter'. But the survey included some less comfortable findings: by the end of 1939 over 30 per cent of the population was listening to Joyce regularly. The BBC's Home Broadcasting Board had sneered that only 'adolescents, and middle-aged women' listened to him. Silvey's work revealed that every kind of person heard the programmes. The reassuring feature of the audience, little understood at the time, was that Haw Haw's listeners were particularly discriminating ones. Most read one or more newspapers; 34 per cent of the listeners were *Times* readers. Those most exposed to enemy propaganda were those least likely to be taken in by it: they were well informed and curious.

The fall of France in 1940 demonstrated the potential power of enemy propaganda. It was widely believed that German broadcasts were responsible for the failure of the French civilians to resist the German invasion, and for the strength of the French 'fifth column' of collaborators. British officials felt that radio was crucial, yet the BBC was too solemn, aloof and boring. The problem was urgent.

1940 and cheerful patriotism

Dunkirk has been seen by most historians as a key turning point in the war. A massive defeat was turned into triumph, and the British, curiously relieved to be without allies, found a new determination to win the war. Calder sees Dunkirk as the point at which the 'old gang' of pre-war reactionaries was finally exposed. Found to be guilty, they were thrown aside. After Dunkirk, he argues, people were concerned with winning the war, and ensuring a 'New Deal' for the peace. Mass Observation noted a steady growth of left-wing opinion from this period.

What is remarkable is the absence of any evidence of popular pressure for a negotiated peace. Rationally, invasion seemed certain, and defeat, accompanied by appalling devastation, seemed likely. Yet where, during the 'phony war' period, there had been a degree of indifference, now there was a closing of ranks. It was not that morale was high, nor that anybody believed Britain was likely to win the war: rather, the war was accepted. The public decided to try to survive it as best it could.

Broadcasting contributed to this shift in mood. The tone changed. It ceased to be exhortative. It became more sensitive to popular feeling and, in consequence, more successful in moulding or at least channelling public opinion. It did it by allowing its young producers to get on with creating original programmes. The BBC never *talked* about 'independence' or even made a decision to be as truthful as it could. More remarkably up and down the BBC, in small and large arguments and practical decisions made by important senior people and unimportant minor people, the Corporation saw as its prime task the struggle to be truthful.

Dunkirk meant that the war changed from being an affair of soldiers abroad to one of civilians at home. It was quickly followed by the Battle of Britain and then the Blitz. The kind of war that people had expected had arrived. Yet, though devastating, the catastrophic effects widely predicted in the 1930s did not occur. Survivors went on with what Churchill called 'their job of living through the blitz'. Even Mass Observation, which documented the panic and virtual disintegration of civilian life in the worst-hit towns at some times during the winter, noted the remarkable capacity of the public to adapt to new conditions. In London, Tom Harrisson wrote, 'the unfailing regularity' of German attacks 'greatly raised the ability to adjust, and created the best organised centre in the country'.

The First World War was traumatic partly because the horror of a large-scale modern conflict had been far greater than anybody had ever imagined. The Second World War – especially on the civilian front – was bearable precisely because literature, memory and rhetoric had led everybody to expect a repetition. Yet civilians in cities, like men in trenches, were prisoners. In the First World War the troops called trenches on the Western front by familiar names, Piccadilly, Liverpool Street, Elephant and Castle, Penny Lane. Then, soldiers brought literary and popular cultural references to understanding their circumstances. The 'Great War' (now recalled almost exclusively and narrowly through the prism of suffering and trauma) set the conditions a generation later for a kind of endurance.[15] In 1940 it was the real places in Britain which suffered. In effect although people could not escape there were civilian 'front' and 'relief' lines. In the First World War men would be regularly moved back from the front to security behind the lines. In the Second World War (as Titmuss argued) the underprivileged survived the stress of attack partly because there was a variety of 'safety valves' they could use. The government never stopped the nightly 'trekking' out of the city centres, nor did it resist the take-over of tube stations as deep shelters. On any one night of the Blitz seven out of ten Londoners slept in their beds. But in any single week during the Blitz nearly everyone spent at least a night in the shelters or the equivalent. Civilians thus survived the stress partly because – like the soldiers in the First World War – they took some relief from the front. But some of the tension and some of the relief found expression in more sensitive and imaginative BBC programming.

The prevailing atmosphere in 1940 among the civilian ranks was, as in the 1914 army, one of 'us' against 'them'. However, the opposition was as much to the petty bureaucracy of British administration as to the Nazis themselves. Strachey expressed this mood when he wrote:

> There is no public record of the labour of the interdepartmental committee, of the coordinating committee, the Board of Enquiry, or of the Treasury minute, or indeed of the final Cabinet minute which settled upon the word 'incident' as the designation of what takes place when a bomb falls on a street.

One way of dealing with the Second World War was to refer firmly to the First. Like many of his listeners, the broadcaster J. B. Priestley's own image of fighting was based on memories of 1914–18, and he particularly liked to draw parallels between trench life in the First World War and civilian mores in this one.

In his memoirs, Priestley referred to a folksong of the Great War:

> 'It's hanging on the old barbed wire
> I've seen 'em, I've seen 'em'.

. . . [E]ven the devilish enemy, that death-trap the wire, has somehow been accepted, recognized, acknowledged, almost with affection.

A similar point about public attitudes in the Second World War was made by John Strachey:

No the people didn't call Germans Huns . . . or dirty bastards. No one knows in what region of the unconscious the English people decided that their formidable enemy were best called Jerry . . . There is in it an acceptance of destiny; of a destiny to resist. There is a refusal to take the panoply of the German might at its own evaluation.

Both writers are pointing to an attitude of familiarity, though not of contempt, for the enemy. This had first developed among soldiers in the proximity of the trenches. In the First World War it had separated them both from those who lived in the security of high commands, and from everyone in the safety of home. In the Second, such irony was an appropriate attitude for civilians' nightly encounters with bombers.

To what extent did the BBC lead, follow or play a part in the creation of a new rhetoric to handle the experience of being bombed nightly?

The war brought the blue joke and an anarchistic, almost surreal, assault on authority to the radio. Shows like *ITMA (It's That Man Again)* never challenged the basis of authority; rather, they consolidated it by making a joke of its misuse. In the 1930s radio comics had been warned that there were to be 'no gags on Scotsmen, Welshmen, clergymen, drink or medical matters'. *ITMA* thrived on innuendo, and on a skilful nudging at the previously taboo.

The programme was based on a formula. It had a repertoire of characters with stock phrases. Funf, 'the enemy agent with the feet of sauerkraut', made a joke of the spy panic of 1940. 'This is Funf speaking', he would intone, muffled by a glass. 'After you Claude – No, after you Cyril', Royal Air Force (RAF) pilots would quip as they queued to begin the attack, using another *ITMA* catch-phrase. Each programme had eighteen-and-a-half minutes of talk into which an attempt was made to pack 'at least one hundred laughs'.[16]

The strength of the show was its topicality. The writers visited factories and army camps to pick up current slang – but also jokes, discontents, the tone and manner of grumbling and wit. The programme would be rewritten up to the hour before it was broadcast in order to include jokes on the latest news. *ITMA* summed up public frustration and gave it vent. In an early show transmitted from Bush House, itself next door to the Ministry of Works, Tommy Handley issued a memo. 'To all concerned in the Office of Twerps. Take notice that from today, September the twenty-fourth, I the Minister of Aggravation, have power to confiscate, complicate and commandeer'. In 1940 there was a period of remorseless exhortation of the public by the government. Frank Owen noted in the literary magazine *Horizon* that he was obliged to pass thirty-seven government posters on the way from his house to the Post Office. The Ministry of Food was particularly active in impressing on the public the virtues of the carrot. An *ITMA* sketch took note:

> *Door opens.* Voice: Do you know what you can do with a carrot?
> Tommy Handley: Yer.
> *Door closes.*

Frank Worsley, the producer, thought that the humour of *ITMA* was 'the closest radio had come to the everyday jokes that ordinary people have always made . . . The characters were not trying to be funny in themselves, they were only funny in relation to the situation'.

Women

One of *ITMA*'s most popular characters was 'Mrs. Mopp, the vamping vassal with the tousled tassel', a charlady who worked for a pompous civic dignitary. 'Can I do you now, sir?' she would ask. Mrs Mopp was perhaps the most famous version of a familiar figure of the period. She glares at German bombers during an attack in an *Express* cartoon by Giles (20 November 1940). 'Never mind about it not being arf wot we're giving them – let's git 'ome', demands her husband. The same figure – phlegmatic and grumpily imperturbable – was dug out of ruins. She was a mythical figure, and real people were frequently credited with her well-known characteristics. 'Mrs. Wells is an obstinate woman', John Strachey wrote about one lady who survived an air raid. 'You may drop big bombs on her, you may kill her dearly loved husband before her eyes, you may bury herself and her daughter under her home: but you do not alter her'. People who signed themselves 'Mrs. Mopp' sent letters to the *Listener* and the *Radio Times*; she was discussed in the *New Statesman* and she asked the Brains Trust questions.

Mrs Mopp was an image of the working-class woman at war. Her characteristics were an indefatigable appetite for work, and stubbornness. She did not mean to be heroic, but simply to get on with things. Titmuss saw her in 'a certain Mrs. B., a beetrootseller by trade', who brings order and comfort to a shelter in Islington but who returns daily to her stall.

When 'charladies' had first been mentioned in a broadcast in 1938 by John Hilton, the programme received hundreds of letters correcting his language. He should have called them 'charwomen' for, wrote the aggrieved listeners, they were hardly ladies.[17] By 1942 charladies were featuring regularly in BBC programmes – recognition of a kind of the importance and power of working-class women. 'Kitchen front' programmes were broadcast 'for the busy working woman – the charlady'. 'Mrs. Mopp', said Priestley on the radio, 'could easily believe there weren't any women in Germany . . . just tramping, bragging, swaggering males, silly little boys'. 'When I think of the country now', said another speaker on the Home Service at the height of the Blitz (*Listener*, 9 September 1941), 'I see representing the country an embattled Mrs. Mopp shaking her fist at the sky. "I'll do yer," she says, "I'll do yer"'.

The other woman the BBC gave the nation was 'the girl next door', Vera Lynn. She sang sweet but not sexy songs. The typical 'crooning' style implied an intimate relationship between the singer and her listener. This was hardly appropriate, and possibly embarrassing, to the communal listeners of the *Forces Programme*. Vera Lynn was the solution. A Vera Lynn song was a cross between a hymn and a pub song: feminized and personalized but not sexualized, men and women both took comfort in her songs.

Yet nostalgia and sentiment were not thought by the BBC to be proper fare for fighting men. 'Why should we hear so much from Vera Lynn?' Joint Director General Cecil Graves wrote: 'How can men fit themselves for battle with these debilitating tunes in their ears?' The BBC Board of Governors remarked testily, 'Sincerely Yours deplored – but popularity noted'.[18] Military authorities demanded something more martial, yet the show survived, simply because it had such a vast and enthusiastic audience. 'The girl next door' was loyal, sincere, faithful, ordinary and unsophisticated. She was 'the mainstay of most war fiction', Tom Harrisson noted in a review of war literature written in *Horizon* (December 1941) and was the heroine of a number of films.

However, there was also a change within the BBC (as there was in the Civil Service and throughout the nation): the war provided opportunities for a new and formidably able group of women to stream into the BBC. The BBC had been an exceptionally progressive employer early on – with prominent women in leading roles, but by the late thirties men were taking over. The war saw women flooding in and they became producers and directors: not least because as one Ministry of Information memo put it:

> Women are the target group as they are replacing men in industry. Women are vital to our effort to save waste and keep the nation healthy at home under rationing, and their morale sets the mood . . . the BBC must serve and monitor them in all of these roles.[19]

Programmes for women, *The Kitchen Front, How to Bring up Baby*, but also music and drama all turned towards women. Isabel Quigly began a ground-breaking series of programmes on child care that brought together experts and the real problems women faced: having to bring up children with no men around, in the face of real shortages, or feeling bereft when children had been evacuated, of dealing with evacuated children, of losing everything to bombs.

'The people are changing'

According to contemporary commentators, the war made the public more serious minded. Yet Robert Silvey certainly felt in 1946 that there was no evidence that public taste had 'deepened'. But there was undoubtedly a shift in interest. The public appetite for news broadcasts became insatiable. Less predictably, the audiences for serious music increased sharply, and drama ratings doubled between 1939 and 1941. At the start of hostilities the BBC had assumed that the people would be 'too tired for much heavy stuff', and in too sombre a mood to appreciate variety. Both assumptions were revealing – and wrong.

It was generally believed that the masses were becoming more informed, and the success of programmes like the *Brains Trust* was seen as evidence of this. 'One of the surprises of wartime radio', wrote Howard Thomas, the programme's producer, 'is that five men discussing philosophy, art and science, should have a regular audience of ten million listeners'. As many people listened to the *Brains Trust* as to the most popular variety shows. Such was the influence of current affairs and discussion broadcasting that the *Brains Trust* formula replaced orthodox debating in innumerable social clubs and societies. It was particularly popular with local Conservative Associations.

The *Brains Trust* panel consisted of three regular members and two visiting guests. The original trio were Julian Huxley, the scientist, the philosopher Cyril Joad, and Commander A.B. Campbell, a retired soldier. In retrospect Campbell seems like a character from Evelyn Waugh, or perhaps Captain W. E. Johns – an enjoyable, overdrawn caricature with a background of exotic experience: he claimed to be able to sleep with his eyes open, to have solved the mystery of the *Marie Celeste*, to have seen and smelt sea serpents, and to have 'married' a South Sea Island girl by eating some fish with her.

Brains Trust questions were wide ranging. 'Why should we learn algebra?' asked a class of Manchester schoolgirls. 'Why can you tickle other people but not yourself?' asked a bus conductor. 'What is hate?' enquired a schoolmistress. A group of RAF pilots who asked why flies could land on ceilings started a dispute which lasted months. To be mentioned on the *Brains Trust* was fame indeed. A week after *War and Peace* had been recommended by the panel it had gone out of print. This kind of impact was hard to ignore. In 1941 the Ministry of Food was exhorting women to make the new, economical, soya 'Joad in the Hole'.

The importance of the show was recognized by Whitehall in other ways. There was concern about the programme straying into delicate political areas, highlighted by the fact that Joad and Huxley were socialists. In 1942 questions on religion were banned because the churches complained that the programme had an agnostic bias. In 1943 the government banned the discussion of politics, and MPs were excluded from the panel. When Huxley attacked patent medicines and called for a National Health Service the Tories complained. After a period of increasing restriction the original panel were forbidden to appear together. From 1943 each was allowed to broadcast only one programme in three.

The *Brains Trust* was somewhere between a culture and an institution. Like other programmes, it provided a new currency of conversation. Women in shelters discussed Campbell's views on hypnosis. (He claimed it could be beneficial: 'I knew a man who put his wife to sleep with it at weekends'.) In 1940 the *Listener* reported that Gilbert Murray's jokes were swapped in bus queues. 'Veni, Vidi, Vichy', he had said. 'I came, I saw, I concurred'.

The success of the *Brains Trust* was the basis for many theories about public opinion during the war: left-wingers felt that a population interested in the panel's views on social justice would also be susceptible to socialism. Whether or not this was right, the programme presented to the listener an image of himself as engaged, participant and capable of confounding experts. Perhaps the real significance of the *Brains Trust* was that it represented a shift not just in public attitudes, but in the Corporation's willingness to cater for them. Despite restrictions and political interference, the *Trust* provided for and encouraged an immense public curiosity about the natural world, the world of affairs, and about questions of ethics, philosophy and psychology, and in so doing it began to foster a less aloof and distant image of the Corporation.

Yet the most dramatic image of the radio at war is of families clustered around their sets, listening with reverence to speeches by Churchill, the news, or J. B. Priestley's Sunday night talks. These commanded some of the largest audiences ever known. 'By 1941 over 50 per cent of the adult population listened to them', reported Silvey.

Churchill had long been an opponent of the BBC. His crude approach to propaganda during the First World War was one impetus for the founding of the Corporation. He had led the calls for the direct censorship of the BBC during the General Strike. During the thirties as an outsider to all parties and an anti-appeaser he had rarely been allowed to broadcast. Reith loathed him. The Corporation even censored him after the war had begun. At the beginning before he became PM he was considered too anti-German. In 1940 at a War Cabinet he bitterly complained that the BBC was an 'enemy within the gate'.[20]

Yet his speeches as Prime Minister, always delivered first to parliament, were perhaps the most dramatic events of wartime broadcasting. He claimed that he merely gave words to what people felt: 'The people's will was resolute and remorseless, I only expressed it, I had the luck to be called upon to give the roar'. Churchill believed that military success, rather than propaganda, was the only way to win a war. 'If words could kill', he broadcast in 1939, 'we would all be dead already'. Despite his claim to the contrary, Churchill was of course an expert propagandist, and the government, whatever it said in public, remained desperately concerned with the public opinion throughout the war. For the first time it and the BBC strained to understand shifts in public mood with every contemporary instrument they could find.

If Churchill expressed confidence in the people, J. B. Priestley claimed to represent them. His first series of 'Postscripts' started after Dunkirk, at the peak listening time after the Sunday evening news. The series turned him into a household name. 'I found myself', he wrote, 'tied like a man to a gigantic balloon — to one of those bogus reputations that only the media know how to inflate'.

Churchill combined an appreciation of practical problems with a deep, almost metaphysical romanticism, based on an appeal to honour, national pride and a sense of history. Priestley was just as practical but looked to the future. He helped to give the war an aim beyond military victory by focusing attention on the world to be built in the aftermath. Priestley talked about a level of society with which Churchill had had little contact and of which he understood less. While Churchill talked of Henry V and quoted Macaulay, Priestley's examples were Falstaff and Sam Weller. George Orwell loathed Priestley's sentimental 'hokum' – the public loved it.

Priestley's success, however, had essentially the same foundation as that of Churchill. It was based on an appeal to traditional values; indeed, on an appeal to a traditional social order. Priestley's Postscripts make a virtue of getting on with the job in hand, even when there were no alternatives. Like Churchill, Priestley linked current events with the past. He reminded listeners after Dunkirk of Hardy's descriptions of the Napoleonic wars, and described it as another English epic. 'So typical of us, so absurd, yet so grand and gallant that you hardly know whether to laugh or cry'. Official propaganda, Priestley claimed, encouraged people to see the war as an interruption. It was, he said, rather 'a chapter in a tremendous history'.

Postscripts continually emphasized the rural nature of Britain. In the First World War officers read *The Field* and *Country Life* in the trenches, and war poets contrasted the seasons and images of nature with the war. Priestley, broadcasting to the most urbanized population in the world, referred in ten out of his seventeen talks to the country and nature. 'I don't think that there has ever been a lovelier English spring than this last one', he said at the start of the Battle of Britain, 'now melting into full summer'. Later, after the news that the British had been obliged to sink the French fleet, he started the broadcast by saying that he had seen two heartening things that week. 'The first was a duck and the second was a dig in the ribs'. The duck swimming with her ducklings, 'triumphant little parcels of light', was in a country pond; the dig in the ribs was given by Churchill to Bevin in parliament before the grim announcement. Priestley talked about factories and the Blitz, British restaurants and London humour, but the village or the Welsh hills were more frequently the setting for his talks. Priestley provided his listeners with a way of handling their experiences. 'I don't like danger', he said in November 1940, when Londoners were facing their twenty-eighth consecutive night of bombing, 'but the fact that we are all at least within reach of danger seems to me a better, not a worse, feature of the war'. In the First World War men in the trenches, and the writers who recorded their lives, had survived its horrors by rejecting romantic heroism. In the Second, Priestley made the everyday and commonplace heroic.

Priestley demanded 'more flags and less red tape, hard work and high jinks'. He challenged the old order and called for more social justice. He praised the courage of individuals and criticized their leaders for ineptitude. In his second series of Postscripts he proposed to talk about money, class and equality.

'I received', he wrote, 'two letters'. One was from the Ministry of Information, telling him 'that the BBC was responsible for the decision to take me off the air'. The other was from the BBC saying 'that a directive had come from the Ministry of Information to end my broadcasting'. They were both anxious to make it clear that 'the order to shut me up had come from elsewhere'. It had come from Churchill. The Minister of Information, Brendan Bracken, had seen Priestley earlier and warned him to say more about Dickens and less about the government. As with the Brains Trust, there had been complaints in parliament about Priestley's socialism. Churchill felt it intolerable that the BBC should broadcast criticism of the government. Already, within the Corporation, the Controller of Talks had written to Ryan, the Controller of News:

> Priestley has definite social and political views which he puts over in his broadcasts . . . The question which I want to raise is one of principle, whether any single person should be given the opportunity of acquiring such influence . . . merely on the grounds of his merits as a broadcaster, which are, of course, very great.[21]

Priestley's removal was widely greeted – rightly – as a sign of government censorship. The *New Statesman* printed a selection of the letters of protest, 'representative of the many others we have received'. Even the *Radio Times* printed letters of complaint for several weeks.

The removal of Priestley showed how limited was the official concern for reform. Priestley's programmes proposed different priorities from the war aims laid down by Churchill. To talk of new orders and redistribution was, in the view of the government, merely to distract the public from the urgent business of winning the war. Yet it was at precisely this point in the war that even the officials in the Ministry of Information were beginning to urge the government to plan post-war reconstruction. The public, they argued, needed the prospect of a better future to enable them to cope with the rigorous present. Priestley had merely started the shift in propaganda a little early. Later it was to be taken up with growing enthusiasm by the government itself.

Harold Nicolson dismissed the talks as 'sentimental banalities'. Priestley himself was puzzled by their success. Subsequently they have been seen as a major contribution to a change in public mood. Yet the most notable feature of Priestley's talks was that a concern for ordinary people and their future emerged and was expressed by very traditional images of rural England, village communities and nature. This was hardly the rhetoric of a revolutionary.

The news

The most important wartime programme was the news. Information about the conduct of the war was the main determinant of morale on the Home Front. However, complaining about the war was part of a realism that was also a profoundly important aspect of the way this war was conducted. Knowing as much as was possible about the enemy and recognizing as much as you could about the impact of the war in Britain were related. Indeed the BBC's claim to accuracy and objectivity was, in itself, a propaganda weapon – a demonstration of the superiority of democracy over totalitarianism. This was particularly true because the BBC – much more than the press – was the 'voice of Britain'. Unlike newspapers, its messages reached a wide foreign audience in neutral and occupied countries. Broadcast news also seemed to be an authoritative reflection of official policy and opinion. There were allegations on the left that the real facts of the situation were kept from the people; these were particularly relevant during the period of the 'phony war', when many on the left expected imminent defeat. The Service Ministries, on the other hand, viewed radio news with suspicion for a different reason: they saw it as a threat to morale, as a dangerous source of news for the enemy, as a distraction.

News, like everything else for the duration, was determined by the necessity of winning the war. The Corporation's sense of priorities was often inevitably close to the government: checked with government departments. It was a battle for national survival. The BBC needed to know what was happening.

At the beginning of the conflict, such was the demand for news that when little of the real thing was available because of military inactivity, the public created its own. Rumours acquired a special influence. The Ministry of Information waged a relentless and unsuccessful campaign against them. Mass Observation divided them into three categories: impressive, informative and inhibited. The first were a compensation for non-involvement in the war; the second were based on an attempt to improve the teller's prestige, and the third kind, the inquiry claimed, were based on fear. Mass Observation argued that rumours arose from a general distrust of published and broadcast sources, and so were a product of official censorship. But they may also have been a simple reflection of anxiety, a context in which to talk about the war. The BBC always argued that rumours could be stopped only by more comprehensive news.

Several departments fought each other as well as the BBC for the right to control the Corporation. Even more believed that they deserved it. The Ministry of Information was concerned to encourage morale at home; the Political Intelligence Department to scavenge information from abroad; the Foreign Office to maintain friendly relations with allies and neutral countries; while the Ministry of Economic Warfare was interested in the immediate effects on the enemy's industry and morale, even if this involved ignoring the interests of the neutrals. They had competing objectives – and fought each other.

At the start of the war an official wrote that the Ministry of Information 'recognized that for the purpose of war activities the BBC is to be regarded as a Government Department'. He added: 'I wouldn't put it quite like this in any public statement'.[22] This implies a rather different relationship between broadcasting and the government than that which the BBC claimed. Yet the control by the Ministries was often irregular and contradictory. For a time, even the BBC's Director Generalship was divided: one Director to say yes to the Ministry (broadcasters joked) and the other to say no to the staff.[23]

The Ministry of Information, which had most direct control over broadcasts, had been the butt of much humour when it was formed: the inefficiency of its organisation seemed to be surpassed only by the scale of its notional operation. It was lampooned by novelists (several of whom were employed within it) like Evelyn Waugh and one of the models for Orwell's sinister Ministry of Truth in *1984*.[24] It was believed to be staffed by brilliant but dotty amateurs. Nigel Riley (who resigned from the Ministry) pointed out that in 1940, of 999 Ministry employees only 47 were journalists. Stories about the department's gentlemanly eccentricities were legion. One incident involved a Ministry official dispatched to lecture in the provinces on the wickedness of gossip. Complaints came back that his speech had been almost entirely composed of long quotations in Latin. 'Oh', replied the department, 'Latin? It's usually Greek with him'.

Reith, who was appointed Minister of the department in 1940, was deeply depressed by its pointlessness. Nevertheless, before Churchill dismissed him later in the same year he had begun to define the work of the Ministry and to discipline its staff. Reith believed that it was essential to have news and propaganda controlled by the same authority. By the end of the war historians now argue that the much maligned Ministry was less damaging than it was felt to be at the time and was often actively defending the press and broadcasting from the Service Ministries. But the BBC gained confidence and became the expert. News and propaganda were different but the success of the latter (both at home and abroad) depended on the accuracy, reliability and trustworthiness of the news. If people believed the news because it seemed true to their experience, then this was the stable basis for morale and indeed propaganda.

Indeed many future BBC leaders – and great public servants – worked in the strange hybrid world between government and public information. Alan Bullock, a Yorkshire born historian, was plucked by the war to work in information; it changed him into a great historian and a great reformer. Ian Jacob, a soldier – later a Director General – worked with Churchill, Hugh Carleton Greene and journalists running propaganda into Germany. The intersection between government, information and the public was so important it changed a generation. Indeed the Second World War was a modern war in which influence and persuasion were more important than ever.

Broadcasting and the press

Which did people believe more, the newspapers or broadcasting? Intellectuals certainly did not trust the Corporation. They recalled its role during the General Strike. 'What could possibly take the place of newspapers?' wrote the editor of the *Picture Post* (1 December 1940). 'There surely cannot be any sane man or woman who would argue that the Ministry of Information, or its near relation the BBC, have so far offered a serious alternative to the newspapers in conveying information?' Yet there were also grounds for distrusting the press. Newspapers had deceived the public in the interest of the Establishment over the abdication crisis and over appeasement. The *Daily Mail* had backed Mosley and British Fascism – and been an appeasing paper.

The war heightened a long-standing rivalry between press and radio. The *Listener* was voicing a widely held BBC view in 1941 when it claimed that while radio was concerned to report events as they occurred, news in the press was regarded as entertainment. A Home Service talk in March 1941 maintained that newspaper stories might have come 'from a report from a Mexican correspondent of a Portuguese journal quoted in a Roman paper'. The public had little idea of the tricks employed by the press in presenting events.

Mass Observation reported that radio was the most important medium of information in 1941, and that by the end of the war it had replaced the newspapers for some kinds of news, particularly immediate accounts of battles.[25] When more systematic surveys asked people to rank the media on which they based their opinions, radio came far below personal experience and several points below newspapers. Yet between January 1940 and the end of the war in Europe the authority of the press fell steadily, from third to sixth place in people's ranking. In contrast, the position of broadcasting remained constant throughout this period, between fifth and sixth place. By the end of the war people had come to trust broadcasting more – at least in comparison with other sources of information.

Topicality and the BBC

The Second World War made topicality the dominant news value: getting accurate news out fast before German propaganda became a furious battle. The BBC learnt that bad news was best told fastest. Trying to scavenge every scrap of information and assess it became the core of the BBC's purpose. German scoops had shocked the public and done much to discredit the Corporation at the start of the war: the public were sceptical. But the BBC learnt that news, even bad news, in a time of anxiety was more settling than uncertainty.

Topicality then became the key weapon in the BBC's defence against the expansionist censorship of the Service Ministries. Indeed, as the first years of the war offered many defeats, the loss of Europe, and swift German victory – the BBC and indeed the government learnt the necessity of getting terrible news out fast. In the battle for attention and trust, the truth – even a tinted version like Dunkirk – was the best weapon. A memorandum ordered 'Action to strengthen confidence in BBC news. Confirmed items to be included in earliest available bulletins, even at the expense of friction with the Press'.[26]

From 1939 the BBC's news section grew rapidly, gathering material from an increasingly wide range of sources. One extraordinary new source was the BBC Monitoring Service which was set up in 1939. The idea was simple – BBC 'monitors' listened to and translated all the broadcasts made everywhere – what the Germans were saying in Germany and what they were saying in France, what the Russians and Czech radio were saying, what Canadian, Moroccan, Algerian, Polish and Dutch broadcasts said. Although information was the focus of monitors' reports – the tone and voices of broadcasters, and other aspects of programming were poured over for direct information and what they might – inadvertently – give away. This information – gathered slowly and reliably – establishing normal broadcasting and consequently being able to pin-point subtle shifts – informed both the BBC news services and government. It became a vital source for BBC broadcasts into occupied Europe and the world. It nuanced the BBC's broadcasting abroad by direct, in depth understanding of what was going on behind enemy lines.[27] BBC Monitoring became one of the great institutions of the BBC. It informed the BBC's broadcasts into occupied Europe, it informed government and military calculation, it was highly refined and nuanced. It provided direct information of the situation under Nazi Europe.

Domestically the BBC also developed the ultimate 'topical' news, the 'on the spot' or 'outside' broadcast. If one source of this was sports reporting another was America. As Deborah Cohen has shown, American reporters were celebrities and mostly deeply hostile to Britain – which they saw as a backward and repressive imperial power.[28] But then a set of American broadcasters, especially Ed Murrow, reported their direct experience of London under bombing attack in the Blitz, and these vivid first hand accounts helped swing American public opinion towards entry into the war. The American ambassador to the UK – a young, handsome Roosevelt New Deal reformer John Winant – worked tirelessly to help bring America into the war and argued that the broadcasts from the Blitz were one element 'that took the reality of bombs to homes in America'. He talked from personal experience as the American Embassy was destroyed and he describes looking out over Mayfair with smoke and ruined churches 'and the smell of charring and cinders' everywhere.[29]

Winant was dining with Churchill and Averell Harriman, the American envoy to Europe, on 7 December 1941. They were despondent and Churchill darkly depressed. The British situation was perilous – it was alone, a tightening blockade made morale at home as Britain faced a lack of basic foodstuff uncertain – and any chance of taking the battle back to Europe had become increasingly remote. At the end of a gloomy meal the butler brought in the radio for the guests to hear the nine o'clock news on the BBC. The Japanese raid on Pearl Harbour was the first item of the news. Remarkably no one had phoned the British Prime Minister – and again like his people he heard the momentous news from the BBC. According to the official account, Churchill had to be dissuaded from immediately declaring war on Japan. According to the family account Winant, Harrimen and Churchill danced around the room in exultation – America would enter the war.[30] Churchill wrote he slept the 'sleep of the saved and thankful'. But few have noticed what this revealed of BBC news and BBC monitoring – who had broadcast the news in a kind of real time.

Yet everything broadcast on the BBC was also deeply considered. The BBC had been campaigning to do an outside broadcast from a bomber and the Air Ministry had repeatedly refused. But in 1943 – on the fourth anniversary of the start of the war – when there was considerable official anxiety about public resolution, suddenly there was a switch in policy. The people were war-weary and the Government wanted to show that they were 'taking the war back to Germany'. Suddenly, permission was granted for the BBC's Wynford Vaughan-Thomas to go on a raid in a Lancaster bomber. The decision to allow the broadcast went, astonishingly, up to Cabinet. It was not an exultant broadcast but the terror inflicted by the bombs is hardly considered though the terror of flying through flak is vividly experienced.[31] Yet the report of the attack on Hamburg was angrily compared by a *Radio Times* correspondent to 'someone at a Welsh Rugby International – not a person watching death and destruction'.[32] The pilot had been carefully selected – he had beaten the odds many times over and had flown eighty raids. The relief as they return home is palpable: and there is no triumph in the raid. It is a programme about fear.

By late 1944 teams of broadcasters were regularly accompanying British units both in France and in the Far East. Commentators developed a way of reporting conditions at the front which related the soldiers' experience more closely to their families at home. 'If you've got a brother or a husband or a sweetheart in Normandy today', started one famous report from the war zone in 1944, 'there's a fair chance you might see your name riding along the dusty roads, your name on a truck, on a lorry, on a bulldozer, on a tank, somewhere in France'.

The war led to a victory for those who believed in the superiority of the scientific assessment of public opinion. At the start of the war the government believed that this could be tested by consulting elite pressure groups and opinion leaders. By the end of the war the public was being polled, probed and assessed by a multitude of official surveys. These new sources of information made it clear that, in everyday matters of which the public had experience, it was essential that news should be given quickly and accurately. If people had been bombed out of their homes and their towns devastated, it was imperative that the BBC should be able to say so. Knowledge of the extent of destruction was an important factor in coming to terms with it. At the start of the Blitz Maurice Gorham had written, 'The news sounded all the more alarming for being so vague'. But by November 1940, although scrupulously censored for information which might be useful to the Germans, it had become fast and precise. In Britain, at least, 'topicality' became the dominant news value as a consequence of the war.

The 'manner' of the news

Before the war, the BBC's announcers had been anonymous: Reith felt this to represent the Olympian independence of the BBC. However, from the start of the war they were named, and this innovation excited considerable comment at the time. The change was introduced in order that, in the case of invasion, the public would not be taken in by orders issued by the enemy. After the war it was discovered that the Germans had carefully trained substitute announcers to sound like Alvar Lidell and Stuart Hibberd to be used during the proposed invasion of England. However, the BBC maintained some pre-war standards. The announcers, despite sleeping in a lavatory adjoining the studio, and living for days underground, continued to present the news in dress suits. When the BBC received a direct hit which made an audible thump in the middle of a bulletin, the announcer paused, a whispered 'Are you all right?' was heard, and then he continued, with Corporation-bred aplomb, to read the news without comment.

Before 1939 style had often seemed more important than comprehensibility in BBC news broadcasting; during the war ease of understanding became paramount. There was a new anxiety about syntax and vocabulary, and scripts were scrutinised for difficult words and constructions. The Corporation also became more sensitive about the voices of its news-readers. Clement Attlee, Deputy Prime Minister as well as leader of the Labour Party, complained that the monopoly of upper-class voices was likely to offend workers. Indeed this anxiety was shared, and a Home Morale Emergency Committee in the Ministry of Information suggested that 'something might be done to diminish the present predominance of the cultured voice upon the wireless. Every effort should be made to bring working-class people to the microphone'. The Corporation responded by employing Wilfred Pickles, whose voice combined the properties of being both working class and northern.

Broadcasting had developed a unique pitch of speech in the 1930s and 1940s, a high and hard voice. One news-reader, Joseph Macleod, wrote that he had two voices. One was low, gruff and Scottish. The other, which he always used when broadcasting, was 'young, suave, rather pedantic and intolerant, a voice in a higher register'. The war also made the tone of voice a more sensitive matter than before. Macleod lost his job, ostensibly because his style of announcing was too 'tendentious'. He was accused of putting too much emphasis on certain words, and apparently sneering at the government. He was dismissed, according to Harold Nicolson, soon after Bracken had 'spoken openly about the left-wing fanaticism of certain members of the BBC, especially in the news room'. Another news-reader wrote of the problems posed, for example, by announcing the suicide of the Commander of the *Graf Spee* after the ship had been lost. If the announcer sounded pleased the item 'would sound gloating. While if he sounded sympathetic it would sound fifth column'. The BBC's solution to this problem was that announcers should sound as 'official, neutral, and unaffected as possible'.

Another, more urgent, reason why announcers became so careful of their words and their timing was the problem of the sarcastic comments which German propagandists had at first managed to slip in during pauses in bulletins. The only way to stop this was to read the news smoothly and unhesitatingly.

By the last months of 1940 the only comment a German commentator managed to intrude was an exasperated, 'Oh that's not fair!'

The Holocaust

In a broader way the BBC's reporting of what came to be known after the war as the Holocaust – the unique, industrialized extermination of Jews by the Nazi state (and also of Sinta people, the disabled, political opponents, homosexuals, Jehovah's witnesses) – showed the way in which domestic and foreign news interacted: the problem of understanding some of what was happening behind enemy lines, and the impact of prejudice and ignorance. At the beginning of the war the BBC was concerned not to inflame hatred of the German people – only of their Nazi rulers. The British public saw things rather differently and Robert Vansittart's BBC series on *The Germans* (which dwelt on such stereotypes as 'the German professor' and the 'German housewife' – and concluded that the Germans were a 'war-loving irrational race') was hugely popular; so popular that the BBC did not commission another series because it was thought to be propagandist. Then the fear was that describing what was known about the fate of European Jewry as a specifically Jewish problem would legitimate Nazi claims that the war was about Jews. After 1942 – when the Nazi intention to exterminate Jews was explicitly recognized in Parliament in a silent vigil on 17 December – the Ministry of Information and the BBC were alarmed by public opinion polling evidence that the more the fate of the Jewish population abroad was discussed the more domestic anti-Semitism rose. But the ambiguity of 'deportation' and the notion of 'ghettos' also obscured the reality of extermination.

Meanwhile the Polish Service and BBC Monitoring were reporting back to the Foreign Office and the BBC reports that described the destruction of Polish Jewish communities.[33] Nevertheless, the true nature of the Holocaust was not accepted or perhaps understood.

A policy established early in the war by the BBC was never properly reconsidered. The BBC resisted pleas that it should intervene (by broadcasting the known names of police and officials involved) to save the Hungarian Jewish community as late as 1944. This had survived largely intact despite restrictions because the Hungarian government had protected it. By 1944 when the mood about the outcome of the war was altering, such a policy of naming individual criminals might well have had an effect. It had been an article of faith that the system was to be held to account – but naming might have worked. Indeed, more recent documents show that information about what had happened to other Jewish communities (which might have warned Hungarian Jews – although there was nowhere safe to flee) was deliberately held back, and that in 1944 warnings were held back because of the belief that the Hungarian population was anti-semitic and so might resist the German invasion less fiercely. More significantly Carlile McCartney – the most influential advisor in the BBC on Hungarian affairs, an Oxford academic and MI6 official (this was not unusual and was widely known) – had longer-term links with the Hungarian right.[34]

Hugh Carleton Greene had reported for the *Daily Telegraph* all through the late 1930s warning of the dangers of fascism. He was one of the last reporters to leave Berlin in 1939, and then worked alongside Richard Crossman in running propaganda and broadcasting into Germany throughout the war. A fluent German speaker he was as close to understanding what went on in Germany as anyone. He later reported that he had been taken to Belsen as the Allies swept through Europe in 1945. He admitted that even he had not understood what the extermination programme meant until he saw the camp.[35] Later, as a great, reforming and inspiring Director General of the BBC he was passionately opposed to racism: he argued that some voices were so opposed to democracy in principle they could not be afforded the rights of freedom of speech.

The news, enemies, allies and neutrals

Another, more romantic image of the Corporation at war was of the BBC as provocateur, spy and supporter of resistance movements. The Corporation recruited many refugees to staff the foreign broadcasts, and these formed a new and exotic element within the Corporation's staid departments. 'The Hungarian Unit', read a dry memo of the period, 'a duel averted by Duckworth'. A recurring tension in all of these sections was between the demands of the centrally controlled news service and the interests of individual nations. The Danish section complained that they were not allowed to deal with events in Denmark itself in sufficient detail. Correspondents who supplied the service with its information from neutral Sweden even organised a news strike in an attempt to change the BBC's policy.[36]

Other countries complained that the broadcasts implicitly criticized the occupied countries. Listeners who took risks to hear the BBC felt that they should be complimented on their resilience, rather than condemned for their failure to do more. Indeed, like home broadcasting, the Foreign Service suffered from a tendency to exhort rather than inform or support in the first year of the war. Richard Crossman argued that too many of those employed in directing propaganda had come from the advertising world. 'Do you suffer from National Socialism?' was their line. 'Then buy British Democracy!'

Another tension was the extent to which the broadcasts should encourage (as one BBC administrator put it) 'listeners to *do* something rather than *feel* something'. It seemed presumptuous to instruct foreigners in sabotage when the British had little experience of it, and were themselves safe. More significantly, the dramatic success of the 'V' campaign, when in 1941 Dutch, French, Belgians and Scandinavians in occupied Europe were asked to use the letter 'V' as a rallying sign, revealed the dangers of such a strategy. In one Vichy town, Moulins, graffiti Vs for 'victoire' were so numerous that the Germans imposed fines and penalties on the whole town. In Prague 'multitudes of little Vs had appeared on all sides'. From Belgium it was reported that 'never had so much chalk been sold so quickly'. The campaign, initiated almost accidentally, was evidently a success. Its effects, however, were disastrous. It merely exposed those who were prepared to be active resisters to the Germans at a time when there was no possibility of any allied invasion. Men lost their lives in a campaign with no practical goal. In addition, the BBC was in effect making foreign policy. The campaign was stopped. Similarly in the desperate struggles of the Polish opposition against the Nazis the news they gleaned from the BBC (repeated in underground papers) may have caused them to rise against the occupation – when they had little chance of success. This has become a bitterly contested episode in Polish history. Crossman later argued that it was a great mistake for those involved in psychological warfare to suggest that they have 'a mystical substitute for military action'. Broadcasting had to be as concerned with preventing resisters from acting unwisely as with prompting them to action when the right moment came.

It is not easy to assess the effect of the BBC's foreign broadcasts. Indeed it is difficult enough to decide what the overall impact of resistance was on the German war effort. Every clandestine listener, however, had already committed an act of resistance in their minds, and the BBC's service provided information – even if of a selective kind – to populations who were starved of news. The BBC's bulletins provided most of the material for the underground press in occupied Europe. People did take extraordinary risks to listen to it – because they believed what the BBC told them; this itself was an incalculable part of the battle for freedom. Recent and original research in Germany by Nicholas Stagardt has shown, using the evidence of diaries and letters, that contrary to much that has been claimed, ordinary Germans knew for example more about the conduct of the war than had previously been understood and they especially knew about what their nation had done to the Jews – they saw bombing as retribution for it – so knowledge and information certainly influenced morale.[37] M. R. D. Foot concluded that the role of broadcasting was to 'keep the mechanism of the canal gates of freedom oiled and in decent order, till the water levels of fluctuating public opinion could move up and down again'.

This image of the heroic BBC was not, however, shared in the USA. 'To Americans, not very enthusiastic about British cooking, the warmed up remnants of the original meal were not very palatable. News bulletins – one half an hour long – often contained items from yesterday's American press', wrote an academic, Emmanuel Katz, in 1944. The constant stress on the collapse of social barriers in Britain only emphasized how tenacious they had been, and to what extent they still survived. However, American public opinion was never wholly pro-British, and the attitudes towards broadcasting were part of a wider feeling about the war.

In matters concerning the allies, the BBC's policy was dictated by government. When the Russians started to fight the Nazis, the cover of the *Listener* was devoted to a pageant in honour of Russia, while the *Radio Times* was packed with tributes to Russian workers. This was a period of extraordinary enthusiasm for Russia and all things Russian. As Elizabeth Bowen wrote of a character in her wartime novel, *The Heat of the Day*, 'The effect of her was, at first glance, that of a predominating number of London girls this summer when the idealization of Russia was at its height – that of a flying try at the Soviet comrade type'. However, the BBC was told not to include the 'Internationale' in the popular Sunday evening concert of allied national anthems. The Corporation abandoned the series rather than be embarrassed by the sound of the communist song.

Conclusion: 'my country true or false?'

In 1939 the Home News Service editor had said that in the event of war the BBC would 'tell the truth and nothing but the truth, even if the news was horrid'. By the end of the war the Corporation was arguing that the pursuit of truth had been victorious. 'Today', the 1946 *Handbook* proclaimed, 'we can point to the history of broadcasting in Europe and say that certain good principles in broadcasting have defeated the worst possible principles'. During the war the BBC seldom lied if it could avoid doing so. Indeed, as the war began with a series of devastating defeats for the allies it might have been difficult to disguise the situation. However, that the BBC could claim independence was at least partly because it suited the government that it should do so. For the government continually intervened in the conduct of the Corporation. This was inevitable. What was not inevitable was the degree of authority and freedom the BBC developed.

Veracity, however, was perhaps the only acceptable aim for a democratic news policy. More practically, telling the truth was probably the most effective propaganda with which to face a sustained war. 'You must hate propaganda to do it well', Richard Crossman wrote, 'and we British did hate it and therefore took more trouble to conceal what we were doing'.

The contemporary judgement of the BBC's performance was enthusiastic. 'In a world of poison the BBC became the great antiseptic', said Léon Blum, the French socialist leader. Recently the claims of broadcasters that they have independence have been challenged. 'Bias' and opinion are fundamental conditions of the production of news, not accidental pathologies. Hence the work of the BBC during the war has been viewed with greater scepticism. A belief in its independence is little more than a self-adulatory part of the British myth.

The BBC cannot simply be distinguished from its totalitarian opponents in terms of its intentions. In both Britain and Germany broadcasting was seen as a crucial instrument in the war effort. Indeed both countries even shared practical concerns: hopes should never be raised unless they could be met; controversy between enemy allies was, as Goebbels claimed, 'a small plant which thrives best when it is left to its natural growth'. He continued that 'News policy is a weapon of war. Its purpose is to wage war and not to give out information'. The BBC also viewed news as part of propaganda. However, the use of the 'news' weapon was determined by quite different constraints and pressures in a democratic society.

British home propaganda depended on an informed public. The BBC remained a civilian institution, whose employees saw themselves as broadcast-ers: as people doggedly determined to serve the British public according to their own judgement and principles. Once committed to a policy of inform-ing the public, the war acted as an extraordinary accelerator for an improve-ment in the news services. Although the BBC broadcast optimistic official figures for enemy fighters shot down in the Battle of Britain, tended to treat raids on Germany as victories, cut, edited and censored news, its main pur-pose remained that of telling people what was happening.

In Britain, Asa Briggs has observed, the mystique of radio meant little. In Germany, the new medium had been credited with almost magical powers of suggestion. These views affected the way in which broadcasting was used in both countries. The dominating image of the BBC during the war (indeed the dominating image of the war in Britain) was one of relentless domesticity. 'Every time I listen to these programmes I cry', a factory worker told Mass Observation about a radio link-up between soldiers and their families. 'You hear the women giving the men their messages . . . they can hardly get through sometimes'. Another describes her day. She gets back from work 'about nine o'clock, and they've got the wireless on. Dad's asleep in the chair – the kiddies are in bed'. Families were united around the radio; 52 per cent of respondents to one survey always listened to the news with their families, 76 per cent preferred to do so if possible. In Titmuss's classic account of the development of welfare policy during the war, he saw the security of the family as the crucial guarantor of good morale. By 1945 the radio had become an essential element of the image of the family in its home.

Before the war the BBC had regarded the regular expectation of particular kinds of programmes as 'lazy listening'. In contrast, during the war the BBC made considerable efforts to develop such habits. Regular programmes pro-duced predictable audiences. The knowledge of these could be used in pro-paganda appeals and information campaigns. Indeed the predictability of the daily broadcasts was a kind of security in itself. 'At the moment, all similes for safety are slipping', wrote C. A. Hudson in 1941. 'How can one say as safe as houses?' But the BBC at least seemed dependable. Modern programme planning, a matter of inducing habit, was at least in part a consequence of the war.

By 1945 the Corporation had apparently become less aloof. Programmes like *ITMA*, *Hi Gang*, and *Worker's Playtime* introduced a more vigorous tradition of speech and humour to broadcasting, one that was closer to the music hall tradition than the well-mannered 'variety' of pre-war programmes. They were part of a feeling that the British war, unlike that of the prudish Germans, was taken seriously, but never solemnly. Even government propaganda came to appreciate the 'common man's sense of humour':

> Those who have the will to win
> Eat potatoes in their skin,
> Knowing that the sight of peelings
> Deeply hurts Lord Woolton's feelings

exhorted the Ministry of Food. Humour was part of the protective self-image with which the British faced air attacks and the possibility of invasion. It was an image that the BBC helped to create, and was determined to encourage. Harold Nicolson even broadcast talks on the subtle superiority of British humour to that of the status-conscious Germans (*Listener*, December 1942).

There was, of course, another war which did not get much broadcasting time. This was one of apathy, and dingy making-do rather than cheerful resilience. Life in shelters was not a protracted East End party; it was squalid, with inadequate sanitary arrangements, little food and chaotic overcrowding. Novels of the period document the dreariness and austerity of life in Britain after several years of war, and newspapers campaigned against the petty-mindedness of official regulations and bureaucracy. The BBC did not campaign for the public on any of these issues.

However, the Corporation succeeded in producing a dignified but humorous image of what kind of people the British were. It was not that the BBC 'came closer to the people'. Rather it represented them as a liberal, compassionate, reforming administrator might have seen them. The BBC innovated within a repertoire of very traditional ideas. Subsequently it has been argued that there was a significant change in public mood during the war. The people became determined that there would be greater social justice after it. The huge success of the Beveridge Report in 1942, and the emphasis in BBC broadcasting on the equality of effort during the war, were just symptoms of a collective will to remake Britain that took shape in the 1945 Labour Government's welfare state. Certainly the war changed the BBC, which had turned to pay urgent attention to the public and its wants and moods – and it changed public taste.

Yet the day after the war in Europe ended, the public changed again. The audience for the news dropped by half, and never returned to wartime levels.

Notes

1 BBC: Available at: www.bbc.co.uk/archive/ww2outbreak/7957.
2 Daily schedule, T34, RS 4, 3 September 1939, *BBC Written Archives*.

3 The Announcement of World War, T34, RS 4, Notes, 4 September 1939, *BBC Written Archives*.
4 The Earl of Halifax, *The Fullness of Days* (London, Dodd Mead, 1957), p. 270.
5 BBC Engineering: see A. Briggs, *The War of Word* (Oxford, Oxford University Press, 1970).
6 P. Fitzgerald, *Human Voices* (London, Fourth Estate, 2014), p. 24.
7 Fitzgerald, *Human Voices*, p. 65.
8 D. G. Bridson, *Prospero and Ariel: The Rise and Fall of Radio* (London, Gollancz, 1971), p. 269.
9 See D. J. Taylor and BBC archive, 'Who was the Real George Orwell?' 2013/2017. Available at: www.bbc.co.uk/programmes/p013qs8w
10 Bernard Crowther's personal papers by kind permission of the Crowther family.
11 G. Orwell, *The Lion and the Unicorn: Socialism and the English Genius*, 1941 (London, Penguin, 2015), p. 33.
12 P. Addison, *Churchill on the Home Front* (London, Jonathan Cape, 2011), p. 344.
13 D. Cooper, *Old Men Forget* (London, Hart-Davis, 1953), p. 79.
14 H. Hobson, *Daily Express* (14 January 1940).
15 See P. Fussell, *The Great War and Modern Memory* (Oxford, Oxford University Press, 2013), and the subsequent literary and historical debate.
16 T. Kavanagh, *Tommy Handley* (London, Hodder & Stoughton, 1949), p. 73.
17 *Listener* correspondence, *BBC Written Archives* (John Hilton).
18 Board of Governors' Minutes (5 July 1941), *BBC Written Archives*.
19 Ministry of Information, Directorate 231/12, Rp to BBC co-ord. 43, 10 January 1940.
20 CAB 65/9, War Cabinet 267 (40), 6 November 1940. Prime Minister Personal Minute M96/1, 29 January 1941, PREM 4/57/7.
21 Maconachie to Ryan, 6 September 1940, *BBC Written Archives*.
22 A. P. Waterfield to W. Palmer, *Ministry of Information Files*, INF 1/238.
23 A. S. Hibberd, *This is London* (London, Macdonald & Evans, 1950), p. 307.
24 See '1984: Live', the first ever reading aloud of the novel in Senate House, which housed the Ministry of Information, The Orwell Foundation, 6 June 2017.
25 Mass Observation, *The Press and Its Readers* (London, Art & Technics, 1949), p. 41.
26 *Ministry of Information*, INF 1/250, Home Morale Emergency Committee, Item 13 (22 May 1940).
27 BBC Monitoring Collection: AHRC and the Imperial War Museum; S. Bardgett and J. Seaton, *Listening to the World*; R. Hughes, J. Seaton and A. Webb, 'BBC Monitoring as an Institution'. Available at: www.iwm.org.uk/research/research-projects/bbc-monitoring-collection/BBC-Monitoring-as-an-Institution
28 D. Cohen, Ben Pimlott Memorial Lecture, *What Marriages do to People*, 2017, *20th Century British History*. 7 July 2017. Available at: www.academic.oup.com/tcbh/pages/pimlott.
29 L. Ison, *Citizens of London: The Americans Who Stood with Britain in Its Darkest, Finest Hour* (London, Random House, 2010), p. 496.
30 Author's interview.
31 Listen to BBC Radio 4, *Archive on 4*, 14/09/2013. Available at: www.bbc.co.uk/programmes/b039lmkg (Steve Evans with Jean Seaton).
32 *Radio Times*, 30 September 1944.

33 J. Seaton, 'Reporting atrocities: the BBC and the Holocaust' in J. Seaton and B. Pimlott (eds.) *The Media and Politics* (London, Longmans, 1984), pp. 46–57.
34 'Could the BBC Have Done More to Save Hungarian Jews?' Available at: www. bbc.co.uk/news/world-europe-20267659.
35 Author's interview with Hugh Carleton Greene.
36 PP 34, 4751, 23 June 1943, *BBC Written Archives*.
37 N. Stagardt, *The German War* (London, Bodley Head, 2015).

Chapter 13

Public service commerce
ITV, new audiences and new revenue

If 1956 brought the BBC into conflict with Government over the Suez crisis – it brought another existential challenge to the Corporation: the arrival of Independent Television (ITV). This was to be financed by advertising, make new kinds of programmes for new audiences and yet also be held to public service standards (not that any of these high-minded outcomes were inevitable). It was to become a tremendous spur to innovation as the two stations competed to make better programmes. Together the TV industry became a huge source of growth and became the most desirable place for the ambitious young to work. Yet how had the Corporation's monopoly been shattered?

The tiny BBC television station had been shut down for the war. By the time the new-fangled invention began broadcasting again in 1946 the BBC's popularity at home and prestige abroad were even greater than ever before. The Corporation had become part of the national story. Because of the war, and in the immediate aftermath the period of bleak austerity (bread which had never been rationed during the war was rationed after it) radio felt necessary – serious – and television seemed a frippery: at least to BBC Mandarins.

Yet barely a decade later, the BBC's much protected monopoly of the air waves was destroyed and television came to characterize an age. Television – and perhaps commercial television, (and then radio) in particular – seemed synonymous with a new era of consumption and leisure.

The change was not brought about by public pressure or demand but by a small group within the ruling Conservative Party: it was a coup. Opposed by bishops, vice-chancellors, peers, trade unions, the Labour Party and most national newspapers the market outsiders outwitted them all. Reith compared the introduction of commercial broadcasting into Britain with that of dog racing, smallpox and bubonic plague.[1] The objections to commercial broadcasting were diverse, but most were anti-American, anti-commercial and opposed the encouragement of crude materialist desires. Criticisms of this kind were particularly vehement on the left. The British Communist Party ran a variety of effective campaigns against American comics, American films and American commercial culture. This anti-Americanism was something they shared with very right-wing 'moral re-armament' groups, parts of the British Establishment and Enoch Powell. Of course it was legitimate to resent America – which had quite deliberately sought to reduce British power by imposing draconian repayments for the loans that had propped Britain up during the Second World War. But this was a wider hostility focused on culture and especially TV and popular culture.

Austerity, monopoly and the Beveridge Report

The BBC's prestige contributed to its undoing. The Corporation had assumed that it was invulnerable, and so had the 1945 Labour government, which consequently did not hurry to renew its licence. In 1947 Beveridge was asked to conduct an inquiry into the BBC's affairs: after the success of his 1942 report that laid the basis for the welfare state he was an Olympian and distinguished choice. He might have been expected to sympathize with Reith's legacy of benevolent, high-minded despotism at the BBC, for Beveridge had once claimed that his ideal society would be run by neither parliament nor dictators, but by professional administrators – 'social doctors' – who would organise society 'to adapt the social and economic relations of clients so as to produce the maximum economic health'.[2] However, as a liberal, Beveridge was in fact, highly critical of the Corporation.

He distrusted the tone and character of the BBC, which, 'beginning with Londonization, going on to secretiveness and self-satisfaction, and ending up with a dangerous sense of mission became a sense of divine right'. He was constantly on the watch for 'the four scandals of monopoly: bureaucracy, complacency, favouritism and inefficiency'. Written in Beveridge's inimitable style, the report nevertheless finally recommended that the Corporation's licence be renewed, because the alternative, American-style commercial television, seemed far worse.

The recommendations of the Beveridge Report were ignored by the Conservatives after they beat the Labour Party in the 1951 general election. Instead, the Conservative politician Selwyn Lloyd's dissenting minority report, which was in favour of commercial broadcasting, became the basis for the commercial lobby. But Beveridge's findings influenced the form of British commercial broadcasting. First, the report preferred spot adverts to sponsored programmes because they gave advertisers less control over programme content. 'A public broadcasting service', the report commented, 'might have its controlled and limited advertisement hour, as every newspaper had in its advertising columns, without sacrificing the independence of standards of broadcasting'. Second, the report advocated the regionalisation of broadcasting and the decentralisation of the BBC. These arguments were fundamental to the organisation of the commercial system when it was introduced.

The commercial television lobby has been seen by some writers as a tiny group of back-bench MPs, 'who worked night and day on the project'. This is conveniently democratic. However, they were backed by the immense power of the great entertainment industries. Pye Radio, the largest West End theatre management, and J. Walter Thompson, the advertising agency, were all involved in the campaign. Although a member of the group declared in the House of Commons that 'Any suggestion that the Bill was fostered by commercial interests is a complete figment of the imagination of the Party opposite', the speaker at the time was a director of various electronics firms who expected to profit out of an increase in the market for televisions.[3] 'At what point', H. H. Wilson asked, 'were the members speaking as MPs representing their constituencies, and when were they speaking as directors, managers or employees of advertising agencies, market research organisations or radio and television manufacturers?'

However, the most important organiser of the lobby *was* a broadcaster, Norman Collins. He had been director of the *Light Programme*, and controller of BBC Television. When he was not appointed Chief Executive of Television, Collins resigned from the BBC. He told *The Times* that he had left:

> because of a clash of principle . . . whether the new medium of TV shall be allowed to develop at this, the most crucial stage of its existence, along its own lines and by its own methods, or whether it shall be merged into the colossus of sound broadcasting.

He was a visionary man and as concerned in his way with 'the way in which television could reflect Britain better'.[4] The commercial lobby fought a hard and frequently unscrupulous battle. It was successful because important members of the government, including the Prime Minister, Churchill, were not prepared to defend the BBC. Significantly, the campaign also had the active support of Lord Woolton. He had modernized the Conservative Party organisation before the 1951 election and brought a new kind of candidate into parliament. This group represented industry and advertising rather than law or hereditary wealth.

Woolton wanted free enterprise to dominate the 'new age of post-war prosperity'. 'Our individual lives today', he complained in a broadcast, 'are hemmed in by no less than 25,000 controls'. He wanted to associate the party with the long-term material aspirations of the people, and believed that commercial television would help to do this.

The opposition to commercial television was organised by the National Television Council with Christopher Mayhew as its secretary. Support came from surprising quarters. 'The Establishment', wrote Henry Fairlie, 'came as near as it has ever done to organising a conspiracy against the government of the day – a Conservative Government'.[5] This group objected to the cultural consequences of commercial television: it would 'vulgarize, bowdlerize, and coarsen', wrote one critic.

Coronation

Yet barely three years before the Coronation broadcast had shown the BBC at its innovative, ambitious best. It transformed television and the monarchy. When George VI had died even *Listen with Mother* (the programme of stories and music for pre-school children that had become a national institution) had been interrupted by the dreadful news. It was replaced much to the perplexity of the nation's tots by appropriately momentous music. However very soon the same tots were busy in a frenzy of Coronation excitement – cutting out pictures of carriages and crowns: and learning to identify the flags of the Commonwealth. The BBC made special programmes for the under fives to explain the meaning of the day.

For the very first time cameras were allowed inside the Abbey. This made everyone who watched a participant. As Briggs observed: 'In the majestic drama of the Coronation . . . with cameras on the inside of the Abbey . . . new meaning was given to the ancient rubric as the young Queen was the first monarch to be "crowned in the sight of the people"'.[6] Ben Pimlott wrote that:

> If the Coronation was a burial service for the Empire whose passing took away one of the main roles of the Monarchy, it was also a baptism for a new kind of mass participation in national events, which changed forever the way royalty would be perceived.[7]

There was already much talk of a 'new Elizabethan Age'. Richard Dimbleby, the BBC reporter and presenter of *Panorama* – a dominant current affairs programme that set the agenda – had argued within the BBC that television (rather than radio) ought to be the most important broadcast vehicle.

The trouble was that apparently the Queen did not want to be televised. The ceremonial procession was one thing, the crowning another. She was allegedly anxious that any mistake would be amplified (and the Palace worried that people would not watch the ceremony with the due respect). 'Live Television' reported her Private Secretary to the Prime Minister 'would add considerably to the strain on the Queen'.[8] However, pressure on the Cabinet and perhaps pressure at home (Prince Philip, who the Prime Minister had observed 'is insupportable when idle', had been given the job of organising the Coronation, and Philip was a modernizing force within the Palace) led to a change of mind. The particular concern was the close up of the Queen so these were not permitted and there were several months of argument about the siting of the cameras (one vital camera ended up in a kind of pit in the Abbey, and the cameraman 'Bud' Flanagan was chosen because he was the smallest and so would be least obtrusive). Yet these restrictions added to the ceremonial solemnity.

People were moved especially by the ritual anointing – an ancient and profound moment shared for the first time with millions. But the solemnity was experienced not merely observed, partly because many were seeing such an event for the very first time, partly because there had been such a build up to the event, partly because in some way the event embodied a collective hope. But also, perhaps it was seeing, as Pimlott argued 'the divestment, by the sense of exposure and the simplicity of the anointing dress – as though the sacrifice were a physical one and the rite performed under the Canopy an act of violation'.[9] One observer said 'I thought how young she looked and how vulnerable, how resolved and how steadfast'.

An estimated twenty-seven million people watched the event on TV. Many people bought or rented television sets especially for the Coronation. Only 12 per cent of the British public neither saw nor listened to the service. Millions of people flooded into London to see the decorations and the nation erupted into a blaze of red, white and blue. There was a transformative breakthrough in international broadcasting – with coverage all over Europe and the event was filmed and flown to America (where eighty-five million people watched the event) and Canada and Australia. The Commonwealth had its own commentators (and of course Commonwealth leaders played a large role in the ceremony). The French and Germans were entranced as they peered at the procession – with thousands of spectators along the route apparently undimmed in the driving rain. Indeed, the world was riveted by the strange ceremony. The Corporation had innovated technically, created a spectacle that enhanced the ritual, created an audience for television, helped project a new image of Britain all over the world, created a new international model for broadcasting and in Richard Dimbleby had a key commentator who brought a gravity and compassion to the ritual. As one of the BBC officials said afterwards, 'it was a long road that lead to the Coronation theatre, but we got there and then a miracle happened and we seem to have achieved something beyond most people's dreams'.[10] The BBC thought that it had beaten off the idea of a commercial opposition. They were wrong.

The Coronation certainly played a part in arguments about the introduction of commercial television. When it was learnt that in the USA the Coronation had been shown interspersed with NBC's television chimp, J. Fred Muggs, selling tea and that deodorant had been advertised just before the ritual anointment it seemed to confirm the vulgarity of advertising-funded broadcasting. Horrified MPs suggested that if a commercial system were started here, royal tours would be interrupted by commercial breaks extolling the makers of the Queen's chairs and carpets.

Nevertheless the Act introducing commercial television was passed in 1954 because most Tories believed that in some way it would promote industry, commerce and the free market. The new service was named, by some genius of euphemism, 'Independent Television'.

Commercial television and the new world

'A whole new world has come', proclaimed the first commercial television *Yearbook* in 1955. 'We've won, and now we can really get going', said Norman

Collins. 'The importance of the introduction of commercial TV goes far beyond any question of the merits of commercial versus public service broadcasting', wrote Wilson, 'for it may also seem to symbolize a change within the Conservative Party, and give expression to an accumulation of influences which are securing the future of British society'. ITV brought about a revolution, it has been claimed, because it challenged the complacent pre-war conservatism of the BBC. The allegation was that the Corporation was staffed by narrow-minded, middle-class professional bureaucrats who had little sympathy for working-class interests. Collins complained of the 'apathy, disinterest and often open hostility towards the new medium' that existed within the BBC (certainly pioneering BBC television producers found themselves despised by the austere radio side of the Corporation). Indeed in 1946 when Haley, the Director General, was shown a television demonstration he had remarked that he would not have one in his house.

The BBC, one producer wrote, regarded radio as 'the father figure, established and responsible', while television was seen as a 'spendthrift tiresome adolescent'.[11] The BBC bureaucrats, secure in the imperial comforts of Broadcasting House, deluged television producers in the unheated wastes of north London with memos. These detailed the proper procedures for the purchase of books and why it was outrageous to suggest that book covers should be cut up, even to be shown on the screen. The tensions were exacerbated by the influx into television of cameramen, technicians and directors who were used to the high living which characterized the precarious film world. 'Disorder has been repeatedly reported from the television studios . . . new employees do not seem to have become one with the Corporation', read one ominous memo of the period. 'Perhaps', another memo replied, 'a brief course on the history of the Corporation might be of assistance?'[12]

Indeed, during the 1950s the Corporation appointments policy was apparently designed to keep the new service in order, rather than accelerate its development. Gerald Beadle was an amicable BBC administrator, quietly approaching retirement in the Western Region, when the call came. 'About 1953', he remarked, 'every BBC directorship in London was filled by younger men than me . . . but then in 1956 something quite unexpected happened . . . at the age of fifty-seven I was appointed Director of TV'. Beadle was to hold this post during the critical early years of commercial television.

Beadle was a typical example of the BBC administrator of this period. The Corporation man, as the sociologist Tom Burns later argued, did not work for the BBC, he worked *in* it – as a secular church of professional excellence. One writer noted that a Corporation producer 'breathes the BBC ritual welcome to eminent persons as they arrive' (to have their personalities 'brought out', rather than be put on the spot), 'How good of you to come!' (*Encounter*, October 1960).

Nevertheless, a remarkable generation of television producers and directors started work during this period. They were to dominate the entire output of British television, on both channels, for the next twenty years. From David

Attenborough to Donald Baverstock, from Grace Wyndham Goldie and Alasdair Milne to Paul Fox, they made up television forms. Goldie was to be a formidable creator of political television – and a rather terrifying mentor of young men like Baverstock and Milne.

The BBC also pursued a policy of national transmitter coverage and, extraordinarily, by 1956, 98 per cent of the country was able to receive television. This was achieved only by a massive redistribution of resources away from the rich south-east, where there were many television owners, to the more remote regions. A national service was an investment which could not at first have been made by the commercial companies.

Competition new and old

It has been argued that commercial competition changed the BBC. Competition forced the Corporation to consider public wants more seriously. 'The BBC will have to abandon the ivory towers for the beaches! People prefer fun', wrote one critic (*Daily Mail*, 15 February 1957). Peter Black comments that a kind of myth developed, based on an image of:

> the energetic thrusting showbiz visionaries elbowing aside the compla-
> cent bureaucrats of the BBC, by presenting a series of audacious novelties
> that blew the stale air of monopoly out of television and sent the invigo-
> rating breezes of free enterprise whistling through it.[13]

Yet competition came to the BBC long before Independent Television was thought of. The decisive break with Reithian paternalism occurred during the war, when the General Forces Network was established. Similarly, the BBC had always been obliged to prove that the size of its audience legitimized its receipt of the licence fee. Indeed, the BBC had been subject to competition from foreign commercial stations since the 1930s. It was the challenge of Luxembourg which had broken the dismal Reithian Sunday on the radio. However unctuously it was defended, the BBC had abandoned the concept of planned programming considerably before the introduction of Independent Television, while programme-makers have always been most sensitive to the competition offered by colleagues. Anthony Smith has argued in *British Broadcasting* that 'Producers within the BBC were more often conscious of an internal competition within the different sections of the BBC'. This, he claimed, led in the 1960s to 'an enormous flowering of talent and inventiveness'. Such internal pressure had the greatest effect on standards and innovation within both stations.

From the introduction of ITV there was a bitter ratings war: as this was constrained by public service values this was at least in part about scoops, about quality, about making better programmes. Both the BBC and ITV soon discovered that the public would watch anything in preference to a party political programme. (The parties reacted swiftly and ensured that these broadcasts were shown simultaneously on both channels.) When ITV offered the audience the Hallé Orchestra, the BBC's share of the audience rose. When the BBC offered the people *La Bohème*, the numbers watching fell to 2 per cent. However, both soon discovered the comforts of competition and the security provided by the dependability of the enemy's programming. It was found that documentaries and current events programmes achieved their maximum audience only if they were shown at the same time. Indeed, it could be said that a rigidly conventional use of time and categories of programmes was reinforced by competition.

Commerce and the audience

At first ITV struggled to acquire an audience. Howard Thomas wrote that by January 1957, 'The situation was very grim. The costs of running commercial television were enormous for the audience was simply not large enough to attract advertising revenue'.

However, the situation improved. In a well-publicized campaign in 1957 Sir Kenneth Clark was claiming a 79:21 preference for the commercial channel. In December of the same year, out of 539 programmes listed by Television Audience Measurement (TAM) in the top ten ratings, 536 were from ITV and only three produced by the BBC. 'Once they had a choice', Black wrote, 'the working-class audience left the BBC at a pace that suggested ill will was more deeply entrenched than good'. The first *ATV Showbook* put the point more jubilantly: 'We've got the audience', it proclaimed. Norman Collins said that the BBC would soon 'grind to a halt'.

Certainly the BBC panicked. *Ariel*, the staff magazine, became full of war-like metaphors about 'beating back the enemy' and getting into 'fighting formation'. As large numbers of staff left the Corporation for the higher salaries and more makeshift offices of the commercial companies, Sir Ian Jacob wrote, 'I doubt whether any organisation in peacetime has been subject to comparable strain'. The apparent collapse of the audience posed a dilemma. The BBC might be destroyed because its share of the audience would no longer justify the collection of a licence fee from all viewers. Or the BBC might be destroyed because it would be forced to emulate the commercial programmes.

However, the argument about which service had won the largest audience was confused, in the first place because the two authorities counted their audience in different ways. 'For us', wrote Robert Silvey, the head of the BBC's audience research, 'it meant people, and for ITV it meant TV sets. Our method was based on questioning samples of the population about their previous day's viewing; ITV's on metered records of when TV sets in a sample of homes had been switched on'. Although both methods showed trends in viewing behaviour, they could not be directly compared.

Indeed the commercial companies had not 'won' a 70 per cent share of the total viewing audience as Clark had implied (he was after all desperately trying to keep ITV afloat). Rather, this was the proportion of those viewers who had purchased a new television set which could receive both channels. At first this was a tiny fraction of the total audience. Even as late as 1960 the Independent Television Authority (ITA) estimated in its annual report that fewer than 60 per cent of licence holders had two-channel sets. Given their considerable financial investment, it was hardly surprising that viewers with new sets at first preferred the novelty of commercial television. Nevertheless, throughout the period the BBC's total audience was over twice that of ITV.

Indeed, the introduction of commercial television had no independent effect on the overall growth of the television audience.

Public service: private enterprise

Commercial television in Britain was hardly revolutionary. Indeed, it was carefully modelled on the BBC. The traditions of public service were inherited by the new authority – the way ITV was governed really mattered.

The ITA was responsible for regulating the commercial stations and made no programmes. Like the BBC, ITV was licensed only for a limited period, a system which ensured that the whole of British broadcasting came under periodic review. Like the BBC, it had a publicly appointed controlling board. 'The BBC triumphed', Peter Black wrote, 'because all of those chosen as members of the IBA [Independent Broadcasting Authority] might equally well have been BBC Governors'.

The new service was more limited than the BBC. It was banned from broadcasting its own opinions, and the injunction that it should observe 'impartiality in the treatment of all controversial issues' has been interpreted narrowly to imply a balance of views within each programme. Hence ITV had been given less political independence than the BBC.

Thus, Independent Television was made in the image of the BBC. Introduced after a controversy which the *Economist* called 'a soufflé of high principles and politics' (15 June 1954), which disguised a simple profit motive, commercial television was nevertheless formed as a public service.

New programmes and the new style

Perhaps the most important innovation which ITV introduced was the change of mood which it brought to broadcasting. The atmosphere of the new companies, owned and run by showmen like Val Parnell and the Grade brothers, was quite different from the stifling solemnity of the BBC bureaucracy. 'It was more like Klondyke than Maida Vale', wrote Howard Thomas. Parnell and the Grades were successful, ebullient showmen. They were also Jewish outsiders who were hugely successful. When Thomas went to see Lew Grade at ATV about new programme ideas he would be met by a cloud of cigar smoke, and Grade who was a tremendous enthusiast for programmes and showmanship would start to extemporize. Describing Parnell and Grade negotiating a new contract for ATV Thomas wrote, 'They sat like boxers pausing between the rounds of a heavyweight championship'.

Once ITV had begun broadcasting, it no longer had to fight the moral scruples of the Establishment and its first priority was to capture an audience. 'Variety', claimed the first *ATV Showbook*, 'although accumulating the largest number of viewers, has been taken to task by critics of commercial television who have asked for "more cultural programmes and less airy frolics"'. The article continued, 'Many will agree with ATV chief executive Val Parnell when he says there is a lot of culture to be gained from watching a great clown performing'. However, it was not the big top or the *Commedia Dell'Arte* which drew the ATV audience, but rather the giveaway shows, Double your Money, Take your Pick, and Beat the Clock. The Labour MP Tom Driberg compared the audience's howl of laughter at one of these shows to that of the circus crowd in ancient Rome (*New Statesman*, 25 December 1959).

ITV's most important contribution to television was to develop a format for the news. The BBC bulletin had been read by an unseen newscaster accompanied by still photographs. Cardiff and Scannell argue that this failure left a gaping hole in the very centre of television programme output. The function of a daily news service is not simply the continuous up-to-the-minute monitoring, processing and defining of immediate national and international news events. It also serves to define the currency and topicality of events and issues for current affairs programmes.[14]

Vital to the ambition and achievement of the new commercial news service was the way in which it was organised, financed and run. Its independence was buttressed at every point: a separate company distanced from the other regional television producers, financed by a levy on the other companies (not directly exposed to advertising demands), run by a new and independent group of tremendous journalists. Independent Television News (ITN) attracted an immense audience. It used journalists as news-readers, allowed them to write their own scripts, and showed them on the screen. ITN led to a proliferation of commercial news stations on radio as well all doing investigative, serious news and using a new demotic voice.

Robin Day, one of ITN's first newscasters, commented in his memoirs that 'The man on the screen had a further task, to win the professional confidence of his colleagues'. ITN developed television journalism in new directions. The obligation to exercise balance proved particularly difficult. 'Any problems?' Day once asked the news director. 'Yes', Cox replied bitterly, 'a call from a chap called Pontius Pilate who says his case has not been properly put'. The success of the ITN approach in turn provoked the BBC into improving its own news services.

However, ITV also inherited many traditions from the BBC. One disgruntled critic claimed, 'The BBC has precedents for everything, for handling a monarch's abdication, a State Opening of Parliament or a boy scouts' jamboree'.[15] More significantly, the BBC solved many of the political and social dilemmas that confronted television. The BBC showed the first televised election, and established the rules governing politicians' access to television, while the practical consequences of 'neutrality' and 'balance' in a visual medium were developed by a new generation of BBC producers and presenters. Goldie employed several young Labour ex-MPs defeated in the 1951 general election to make current events programmes. Later she claimed her choice was vindicated because Mayhew, Taverne and Wyatt moved from the left to the middle and right of the political spectrum. These shifts in attitude might also demonstrate the power of the ethic of consensus which came to dominate television journalism. The commercial companies simply took over the conventions developed within the BBC. Both, wrote Stuart Hood, 'interpreted impartiality as the acceptance of that segment of opinion which constitutes parliamentary consensus. Opinion that falls outside that consensus has difficulty in finding expression'.

The BBC had also set precedents for the solution of technical dilemmas in television journalism before ITV started. New rhetorics of documentary and current affairs coverage were established. At first most cameramen had been trained in the cinema, and had little experience of journalism. 'In those early days', Goldie wrote, 'I often discarded glamorous pictures of cherry orchards, or flocks of bleating lambs, or children dancing in playgrounds because, though improbably useful in a travelogue, they did nothing to a study of, say, the relationship of Yugoslavia to the USSR'.[16] She concluded that, as pictures would always override words, a style had to be found which ensured that they would reinforce rather than distract from the meaning of a piece. It was also recognized that the use of film raised problems of authenticity. Viewers could easily be led to believe that a film taken in the past actually portrayed events happening in the present. One solution was to use someone who had helped to make the film as the programme presenter. Reviewing the BBC magazine series *Foreign Correspondent* in the *Listener* (May 1959), Goldie had written that they:

> were using film but we were not trying to make films. We wanted the programmes to be dominated by the personality of the commentator . . . We were all feeling our way but when the series finished we felt that we had hit on a new form that had come to stay in television. The key to the new form is the use of film to illustrate a personal experience.

This form was quite opposed to the style of the British documentary movement, in which the film purported to represent an authoritative reality, rather than any personal view.

These innovations and cautious explorations of the specific properties and opportunities of televised politics and current affairs were made well before ITV started. They solved dilemmas that were common to any television service.

End of a monopoly: vulgar new world

The introduction of Independent Television did not mark such a decisive break with the BBC. Rather, the brash new companies owed more to the Corporation than has usually been recognized. The BBC had already begun to change in fundamental ways before ITV was started. The commercial station provided a stimulus for the maturing of a national television service. Sir Hugh Carleton Greene claimed that dramatic changes were to come later in the 1960s, and these were as much to do with a shift in the political and social climate as with any administrative innovations.

This is not to deny that the BBC had a radically different manner and organisation from Independent Television. Like the British Raj, the BBC combined privilege and moral purpose. It was a world in which 'unsoundness' was a major crime. Independent Television provided an alternative source of employment for dissidents and had no deadweight of custom or dignity. Personnel moved continually and freely between the two authorities by the 1960s. The competition for talent and imagination made television one of the most exciting (and glamorous) places for young and really able people to work.

It has often been claimed that ITV was a vulgar debaucher of cultural standards. In the pursuit of profit it merely pandered to the lowest common denominator of public taste. More recently a far more subtle case has been advanced which is not so crudely anti-commercial. This claims that ITV was, rather, an energizing, populist force which gave expression to working-class culture.

Notes

1 J. C. W. Reith, *House of Lords* (22 May 1952), H. L. 176: 1293–1451.
2 Quoted in J. Harris, *William Beveridge* (Oxford, Clarendon, 1977), p. 311.
3 Captain L. P. S. Orr MP, *House of Commons Debates* (22 June 1951), 529: 327.
4 Author's interview.
5 H. Fairlie, 'The BBC' in H. Swynnerton Thomas (ed.) *The Establishment: A Symposium* (London, New English Library, 1962).
6 A. Briggs, *Competition: The History of Broadcasting*, vol. 4 (Oxford, Oxford University Press, 1990).
7 B. Pimlott, *The Queen* (London, HarperCollins, 2006), p. 205.
8 Government papers. PRO PREM (11/34), 30/10/52.
9 Pimlott, *The Queen*, p. 213.
10 WAC R34/, Coronation/EII, Y/24, 3321, *BBC Written Archives*.
11 G. Wyndham Goldie, *Facing the Nation: Television and Politics 1936–1976* (London, Bodley Head, 1977), p. 45.
12 'Television staff policy', *BBC Written Archives* (1955).
13 P. Black, *The Mirror in the Corner* (London, Hutchinson, 1972), p. 115.
14 P. Scannell, 'The social eye of television', *Media, Culture and Society*, 1 (1), 1979.
15 H. Fairlie, 'TV: idiot box', *Encounter* (August 1959).
16 G. Wyndham Goldie, 'TV report', *Listener* (23 October 1968).

Chapter 14

Foreign affairs

The BBC, the world and the government

In 1956 the British invasion of Suez – as major national crises do – created a secondary BBC crisis. It came to a head in the same ten days at the end of October and beginning of November as the Hungarian Revolution. In this Hungarians rose against the tyranny of Russian rule. Broadcasting was central to the evolution of the tragedy; the BBC close to every shift in affairs. For a moment it looked as if the Soviet system might liberalize. But both Suez and the Hungarian uprising happened as the BBC grappled with the arrival of ITV – the breaking of the Corporation's monopoly and the emergence of commercial broadcasting financed by advertising. It was a tempestuous year but all these events national and international, British values and place in the world, had consequences for the BBC. The Corporation was a player in all of them.

Suez was a crisis about British position in the post-war world: the BBC was perhaps the most powerful tool for projecting British influence. For the government and the BBC it was a domestic crisis, in that it was about the rights of the government to demand to broadcast on the BBC and to deny a reply to opponents – because the British public were divided about the military action. It was also foreign: both in the sense that the BBC was in the frontline of communicating British views abroad and that it was a crisis about world power. Hungary was a terrifying demonstration of the impregnability of the Iron Curtain and represented a turning point in the Cold War. Commercial TV was about a shift in mores and values at home.

Every political emergency had issues of communication and political pressure that were central, not peripheral, to the course of huge, consequential events. The BBC had tough challenges. It had a reputation for fairness and this gave it a kind of separate power in the nation and internationally from governments. Politicians wanted to harness this power for what they perceived as the national good. But the BBC also had a responsibility to the nation that was wider. But how far in a crisis should it comply with government? What resources, understanding and principles could it apply to making decisions? How right was it to challenge government and how far could it become an interlocutor in policy? These issues had become central to all political crises. Politics and communications were indivisible.

The Hungarian and Suez crises, intimately connected by world politics and happening in the same short time span, one ending in tragic repression and failure in Hungary and the other in Suez marking the emergence of a new power in the Middle East, involved two great BBC institutions: the External Services and BBC Monitoring. The External Services broadcast all over the world (they were later re-named the World Service.). They had emerged out of the Empire Service – which had communicated with British colonies and colonial administrators during the 1930s. During the Second World War it had turned into a service that brought information and indeed hope to occupied Europe. At the end of the war there had been a proposal that it should be greatly reduced, as it was somehow believed that foreign threats had been dispatched. But the emergence of the Iron Curtain and the Cold War – with Eastern and Central Europe and Russia shut away from freedom and from much information and cultural exchange – it had a new and significant role in the battle for minds and ideas. It was funded by a 'grant-in-aid' from the Foreign Office – which had the right to determine which countries the BBC broadcast into. But the BBC was in charge of determining programmes and news agendas; it was editorially independent. Preserving this separate view was helped because – unlike other foreign broadcasting stations – it had what John Tusa (later an inspiring leader of the service) called 'the mother ship' of the larger domestic BBC that bulwarked that independence.[1]

They broadcast international news into places starved of outside information and carefully sourced any reliable news about the countries they broadcast into. They were often the only reliable information available. But because the services were so attuned to the nations they broadcast into they also understood them very well. The External Services were the basis of an international reporting organisation within the BBC that had a unique capacity to report world affairs. The External Services were always clearly based in London – they put over the British point of view and never deceived their listeners about where they were coming from (London Calling was the sign). Broadcasting into foreign nations was always determined by what audiences needed and wanted – and was respectful of local views and sensitivities. They also broadcast cultural and social and entertaining programmes, always carefully tailored to local tastes as well as sporting and musical events. Yet they did it in the context of providing news, discussion and information that was unavailable within the nations they broadcast into.

In turn the External Services were alerted to and kept intimately in contact with developments all over the world by the material BBC Monitoring produced – by listening to, translating and interpreting the world's broadcasts. BBC Monitoring 'patrolled the ether' roving across wavebands listening to all of the official and unofficial broadcasts from all over the world. 'Monitors', many of them refugees, many multi-lingual, worked from Caversham Park, a grand country house near Reading. They were listening to and translating and transcribing about 1.5 million words a day in 37 different languages.[2] There were carefully developed protocols about translating – so that 'product' was comparable. BBC Monitoring often picked up news of foreign events before any other source and on several occasions this was so significant that it changed the course of events. BBC Monitoring 'firsts' included the first news of the end of the Bay of Pigs nuclear crisis in 1963, the first news of the imprisonment of the Solidarity leader in Poland in 1981, and the first news of the Argentinian invasion of the Falklands in 1982.

From Russia and Eastern and Central Europe, to Angola and South Africa, and China and Korea, Latin America and Western Europe – Monitoring and the External Services together produced delicately nuanced and forensically examined information about the world. It was urgent – the Cold War felt very threatening at many points. It was subtle – understanding the intentions and capacities of other countries was necessary. It was continuous. This meant that Monitoring could detect and understand the meaning of quite small deviations or changes from the 'normal' either in content or tone. If there was a crisis unfolding abroad there would be a sense of urgency and Monitors would gather round and work extra shifts – often sleeping overnight in Caversham.

The interpretation of the meaning of this extraordinary wealth of cultural and political information informed the External Services and they both informed the BBC's domestic news agenda. Monitoring material was also shared with the Foreign Office and the Government Communications Headquarters (GCHQ) and the security services – this was how Monitoring had been set up at the start of the Second World War. Indeed BBC Monitoring was an important source for the Foreign Office Information and Research Department – which had been set up to counter communist propaganda and influence, as well as routinely translating and assessing news developments. Monitoring often picked up and correlated events across the world that were linked but not otherwise understood.[3] It was the range that provided the additional value.

The BBC was in a unique position to understand the development of world affairs: it thought 'globally' and was located deeply in domestic British life and public opinion. The events of 1956 were traumatic for the nation – but also for the BBC, which found itself simultaneously in conflict with the Conservative Government and working closely with it.

Suez

Abdel Gamal Nasser had nationalized the Suez Canal in July 1956, partly in response to American refusal to fund the Aswan Dam. In doing so Egypt took over access to the vital shipping lane from the Mediterranean to the Red Sea (the main route for bringing oil to Europe). Meanwhile, supported by Russian money and arms he was believed to be assisting Algerian rebels against France and was determined to reduce the power of the new state of Israel on his border. In 1953 Egypt had launched a highly effective radio station Voice of the Arabs (VOTA) from Cairo that voiced growing pan-Arab nationalism. To combat this the British had both a British radio station in Aden and a 'music' Arabic language station broadcast from Cyprus.[4] Meanwhile the BBC External Services had a regular, open, Arabic station that was well trusted. Much of the information for the political analysis of what was happening came from the BBC Monitoring Service. The Israelis, followed by the French and British invaded the canal area in 1956.[5] Almost immediately petrol rationing was imposed in Britain as vital supplies were under threat.[6]

At the height of the invasion Anthony Eden, the new Prime Minister who had been a campaigning conservative 'anti-appeaser' and saw the conflict in Egypt as a dangerous repetition of the rise of a tyrant as in the Second World War, called on the governmental right to make a BBC broadcast to the nation in a time of crisis. Eden was fevered with an infection – and in constant pain. The young, up-and-coming BBC producer who was sent to Number 10 to run the broadcast – Alistair Milne – thought that the Prime Minister was dangerously ill and indeed deranged by a combination of the symptoms and the medication he was taking. It was to have a long-term impact on how Milne, later a BBC Director General, viewed politicians – as in a wider way – irresponsible.[7] Milne was shocked by what he had seen, and it altered and in a way damaged his relationship to politics.

However, there was significant national opposition to the invasion – which many saw as provocative, likely to be unsuccessful – and, as the Americans had not been informed, international opinion was hostile. Hugh Gaitskell, the leader of the Opposition, after the initial shock of the nationalization of the Canal when he at first supported Eden, opposed the invasion. He asked that the BBC allow him to broadcast his party's opposition and reply to the Prime Minister's broadcast. Eden claimed that as it was a 'war' different rules were in place and that Gaitskell did not have the normal 'political' right to reply. Eden also wondered – was the BBC being obstructive because it was full of 'enemies or just socialists?'[8]

This put the BBC Governors in a delicate quandary. By making a decision about who had rights to broadcast they were determining the nature of the crisis. Was it a national war or was it a contestable political action? How should the BBC represent the divisions of domestic and international opinion? This all in the face of a government that was apparently prepared to slash BBC funds.

During the 1940s the BBC had not been led especially well by its Director Generals, yet had responded to a total war by creating a service both at home and all over the world that had put truth first. It was the men and women on the shop floor of the BBC who had been creative and developed the principles. But the BBC Director General who was in charge during Suez – Sir Ian Jacob – was a canny politician and familiar with the working of the civil service and government. He had been born in Quetta (later in Pakistan), the son of a British General. He had worked closely with Churchill throughout the war, organising and accompanying the Prime Minister on thirteen vital foreign diplomatic trips. So he understood the development of the Cold War and the world order from the inside. Then he had been Head of the BBC's External Services. This experience gave him a special understanding of the interaction of foreign opinion, national standing and the BBC. But, as he put it, Suez was a new kind of emergency for the BBC:

> The procedures which govern political broadcasting were designed for domestic controversy of the kind that normally accompanies public life; a national emergency when government action has international consequences and during which the national interest is in question is different . . . It must be governed by the appropriate principles and cannot be smuggled under the rules of normal, domestic, politics.

The government threatened to take over the BBC (something it had not formally – let alone aggressively – done during the Second World War) as it had a right to do. But such a provision had been designed for the eventuality of a total war – not a foreign invasion by Britain.[9] First the BBC was threatened with a cut in the licence fee. Indeed, just before the climactic events of the Autumn – the fortnight when the Suez invasion and the Hungarian uprising coincided – there was a dramatic government proposal to slash the funding for BBC external services and impose a closer governmental control on content by imposing a foreign office official in the BBC 'to advise on the content and direction of BBC overseas programmes'. Because, it was argued, the 'Corporation had not been contributing greatly to our anti-communist work'.[10] This was a financial and ideological attack on the Corporation's editorial independence. From the BBC's perspective it was a grave national error.

The Corporation also believed that it understood the national interest better than the government. For BBC mandarins telling the truth – in as far as it could be ascertained – demonstrated British, democratic, values in action.

Meanwhile the British government took over the BBC's local Arabic station (and all of the locally employed Arab staff walked out in protest at the propaganda they were going to be obliged to broadcast). It was run as a propaganda station, The Voice of Britain, VOB (although wits called it the Voice of Government), an inept propaganda station attempting to change Egyptian public opinion. It was crude, obvious, bungled and did not work. Worse – it used some BBC material and so confused the output and compromised the BBC. When Anthony Wedgwood Benn (whose brother David Wedgwood Benn was a gifted External Services producer) saw the transcripts of the British government station, he demanded an inquiry as the output was 'so crude'. Indeed, as Barbara Castle argued in a *New Statesman* article, the government 'had seriously weakened – "by contamination" – the authority of the BBC' by its actions.

Eden was incensed that the BBC continued to report the hostile local reaction to the British bombardment and demonstrations and opposition at home. In fact the External Services had been careful not only to make the British position clear throughout the crisis – but they also included reactions from the region to it. The situation was tense but the BBC stood, uncomfortably, firm.

There were a number of principles at stake. One was that the BBC had to tell the same story at home and abroad – and not moderate stories for political convenience. Another was that it would tell the truth in as far as it could be discerned. Jacob wrote:

> If the BBC is found for the first time to be suppressing significant items of news, its reputation would rapidly vanish and the harm to the national interest would enormously outweigh any damage caused by displaying to the world the workings of a free democracy.[11]

Trust in the BBC had been built through the decades. It depended on news that was accurate and felt reliable to the listeners. If what they heard accorded with their personal experience this reliability meant that they could believe the Corporation when it told them of things they did not know. Yet this precious trust – the very basis of what had become the fight for minds in the Cold War – could be squandered. The government wanted short-term expediency – the BBC was in it for the long game.

At first the BBC Governors, rattled by the Government, said that the BBC must do nothing to underline the division within the nation. This was absurd. To ignore the demonstrations that began in London against Suez or the dissent in Parliament would have been censorship. Then Jacob braced them. The BBC Governors decided that Gaitskell had indeed the right to broadcast a reply to Eden.[12] In effect that it was a party political decision. Douglas Dodds-Parker – who had been fighting the BBC from Whitehall, and as a distinguished Special Operations Executive (SOE) administrator during the war dealing with information and policy was intimate to the problems and who was an MP – nevertheless wrote that the Corporation had 'in the last instance done what had to be done and was right.'[13] Yet the BBC was punished: revealingly the bizarre decision to cut the External Services wrote one official 'might administer a psychological shock to the BBC'.[14]

Hungarian uprising

Meanwhile as the Suez crisis came to a head in late October and November 1956 on the 23 October the Hungarian revolution suddenly erupted. What started as a student protest swiftly turned into a national movement as Hungarians rose up to overthrow the oppressive communist government imposed by Russia. The uprising had been prompted by Kruschev's speech recognizing at least in part some of the terrible crimes of the Stalin era which had suggested that the Russian regime would soften. In contrast to Suez during the Hungarian crisis the BBC and British officials and politicians worked closely and collaboratively together. As the Cold War had come down over Eastern Europe, Hungary had seemed unimaginably distant. Alban Webb, the official historian of the External Services wrote 'There is no doubt with whom the sympathies of the BBC lay in Hungary . . . the fight of the Hungarian people for freedom against their soviet oppressors was a common cause'.[15]

The Iron Curtain and the Cold War were information battles: in which the Communist authorities attempted to hermetically seal their public in an information world they controlled. They spent very large amounts of money and ingenuity in the attempt to jam the BBC and other western stations. In 1950 the passing of the Defence of Peace Acts all over Eastern and Central Europe meant that listening to the BBC and the American Voice of America, (VOA), or Radio Free Europe, (RFE), became serious offences.[16] Jamming, a kind of audible prison and surveillance, was in itself obvious and an intrusion into it had become what the Hungarian historian Istvan Rev called 'the private sphere of the secret listener'.[17] In Hungary there were many illicit listeners to the BBC and as the uprising unfolded radio and the radio station itself became the focus of the events.

Earlier the BBC Hungarian service had given prominence to the 'Writer's Revolt', which focused on the opposition to the regime by poets and scholars, then as Gregory Macdonald, the BBC Head of Central European Services, remarked just before the uprising took place that:

> the most important single development . . . is the way in which criticism of Stalin in Hungary developed into a full scale attack (on the Hungarian government) . . . and the readiness of party members to criticize rationally rather than dogmatically not only the past misdeeds but the present situation.[18]

The BBC carefully coordinated programmes in the late summer – offering Hungarians contrasting pictures of the freedoms developing in Austria since the war, and carefully reporting and analysing the significance of the emergence of the Petofi Circle – a national debating club which raised issues about censorship and press freedoms – often to audiences of many thousands. Talks entitled 'Rumblings in Hungary' and 'Hungarian Alarms' left listeners in no doubt that appeals for greater freedom of expression were widely popular in Hungary.

George Tarjan, a BBC Hungarian Monitor, recalled listening to the early broadcasts on the 24 October as the uprising burst out: 'there were untrained voices making uncertain hasty statements . . . we knew then that the Communist Government had lost control . . .'. Later, there was a battle for control of Budapest broadcasting station in which hundreds died. BBC Monitors listening to foreign events 'could interpret minor developments such as delays in incidental music and what it might mean' and the changes in the fortunes of government and revolutionaries was clear from the announcements, their tone, and the speakers as much as the direct words. Tarjan said evocatively 'we felt that only by listening ourselves to Radio Budapest could we get near enough to the atmosphere in the Hungarian capital to gauge what events really meant'.[19]

The Hungarian uprising was a momentous moment in the Cold War. At first it looked as if a heroic and widespread revolt against Russian communists (in favour not of 'capitalism' but local, national, communism) – a battle for freedom of expression and rights – might be won against overwhelming odds. Radio was a lifeline to the outside world for those who were part of the uprising. News was relayed to the British public through news and commentary and the BBC was very close to unfolding events. In the end the West was not prepared to materially help the Hungarians (and radio was criticized for not making this sufficiently clear). Indeed, there was also an American Election taking place and some have argued that it inhibited American assistance. But it would have ended in a direct confrontation with the Soviet Government.

Meanwhile, as the uprising progressed, BBC Hungarian Unit staff attended Foreign Office meetings and were kept closely informed by the British legation in Budapest of developments. On the 30 October the Soviets announced that they were withdrawing troops from Hungary. But then a combination of increasingly radical Hungarian proposals, the pressure of China, and Soviet dismay at the revolt led to a change of policy.

In the end first Hungarian and then Soviet forces put down the revolt brutally. But every step and the final re-taking of the broadcasting station was heard and reported in Britain. Over 2700 people died, nearly 200,000 escaped over borders into free Western Europe. It became a defining reference point for understanding the nature of Soviet rule for many people: the sound of the uprising and the final pleas for help were radio events. Maurice Latey, in a BBC commentary broadcast on the day the Soviet army retook Budapest, said 'And now must we stand by impotent and guilty watching the destruction of the Hungarian nation? I think the feeling must be one of shame'.[20]

All the way through the BBC and the government had informed each other of developments: the Consulate in Budapest sending direct first-hand information to the BBC and political assessments flowing between them. There was no suggestion that there had been any divisions between them about interpreting events or how they would handle them. Western Governments were criticized for not assisting the Hungarian opposition and the BBC was valued because unlike other international broadcasters it had remained objective and cautious. Tarjan wrote later:

> It was our job to follow the uprising not to lead it, but at the same time it was not for us in the BBC to set limits to the aims of the Hungarian uprising, and certainly not to underbid them from London in their fight for freedom and national independence.[21]

Security

The BBC's relationship to government was complicated. The Corporation's governance and what it did sat between any British government and the rest of the world. If BBC Monitors found out about the world – they were only noting and translating what regimes and broadcasters said about themselves in public in broadcasts – this 'product' had many consumers – some in GCHQ and the security services and some in BBC news rooms. The 'product' was never changed for any particular consumer. The Corporation's analysts were dedicated to accuracy and not to any ideology.

In addition the BBC had a special relationship to necessary government planning for wars and indeed, in the case of a nuclear attack, armageddon. BBC engineers were at the cutting edge of transmission and broadcasting technology. The same systems as broadcast the Light Programme to the British public would have been used to warn them of a nuclear attack. Peter Hennessy, the historian of the 'secret state', observed that when he visited the British Government's nuclear bunker – the place where government would carry on after an attack – 'the only part of the large underground facility that was furnished, wired up, ready at a moment's notice to start work' was the Broadcasting Studio – to be staffed by the BBC.[22]

As the Second World War approached, the capacity of people who worked for the BBC – either as engineers or as programme-makers and presenters – to subvert the British effort and their proximity to sensitive thinking and information meant that an informal 'vetting process' was in 1937 replaced by a formal one.[23] Vetting in the British system was essentially positive – to rule people out of being a risk. It meant establishing that there were no reasons *not* to trust a person fully. Many people in the External Services and Monitoring were refugees from regimes that would punish their families and try to bring pressure on them. They routinely were not passed for vetting – and knew and were pleased about it. It meant that they were more immune from threats to relatives because there were some aspects of British policy and information they had no access to. Indeed, vetting was enhanced after a series of spies, including Guy Burgess who had worked for the BBC twice, defected to Russia – where information he provided led to the deaths of many pro-western agents, particularly in East Germany.

Many people in the media were vetted by the security services without them knowing anything about it. Many in the press were very close to the security services. However only the BBC had its own internal and special vetting procedure. 'It made working more secure, it ruled out risks, it was essentially positive and helpful' said Mike Hodder, one of the security experts in the BBC much later.[24] Yet vetting happened across the Corporation (the BBC argued that it needed to know about risks as it was not large enough to give people jobs in less sensitive areas of work – which was the common civil service practice). In many ways the British system was consciously in opposition to the American (and in the 1950s Macarthy-ite) process. It did not ask people to affirm anything about their beliefs. But nevertheless many people across the BBC were vetted – and some did not pass the process and their careers were altered. Nor was the system perfect: Isabel Hilton, the impeccable Chinese scholar and journalist – a woman of distinction – was found later in the eighties to have not been 'passed' by the process in a terrible error.

Aftermath

The reporting of the Hungarian uprising and its terrifying denouement was kept alive by a series of BBC programmes both on the external services and the BBC at home. Listeners all over eastern Europe were reminded both of the heroic ambition and its suppression. It reinforced the BBC's caution and reputation. It was a turning point as the Cold War became implacable and grimmer. The trauma of the government's punitive attack on the BBC during Suez had another impact. It did not chill BBC reporting or ambition. But it meant that the Corporation was concerned to handle governments more adroitly. When Hugh Carleton Greene became the DG after a remarkable foreign career – the last reporter out of Germany in 1939, handling propaganda into Germany during the Second World War, de-Nazifying German broadcasting after the war and being head of the External Services – he knew that avoiding head-to-head conflict with government if possible was necessary.

The Cuban Missile Crisis in 1962, when it seemed as if America and Russia might engage in nuclear war, was his first major test. The BBC Monitors (who picked up the Russian stand-down first) were important in it. The BBC also put on a *Panorama* (edited by the same Alasdair Milne who had interviewed Eden and the acutely able Paul Fox) which attempted to calmly explain to the British public the causes of the events that might result in a nuclear war. It was guided by a belief in the rationality of the public.

There were to be many further crises. In extreme moments governments wanted the BBC to comply with their policies and support their views. During the Iranian Revolution in 1979, Iranian government supporters in London brought pressure to bear on the BBC – and Anthony Parsons, the British Ambassador in Tehran, demanded that the BBC Iranian service be shut down because its reporting was stoking – he claimed – the violence of the supporters of Ayatollah Khomeni. The Head of the External Services, Gerard Mansell, was called into the Foreign Office and asked whether the material they were reporting was 'inflammatory'. Mansell replied that the BBC was reporting what was happening and that they had checked every event as fully and carefully as they could.[25]

Understanding the enemy, not preaching at it, was one aspect of the BBC's contribution. To Mansell, understanding alien regimes and the states of mind they induce was a matter of 'sitting quietly':

It means reviewing known facts sorting out the significant form the insignificant, assessing them severally and jointly and arriving at a conclusion by the exercise of judgement. Absolute intellectual honesty is essential. The process must not be muddled by emotion or prejudice, or by a desire to please.[26]

John Tusa explained that the External Services saw themselves as the independent guardian of the national interest abroad: 'Self-appointed but not arbitrarily appointed'. Every programme, he said, 'smelt of pluralism'. They sounded different because the mechanism was different. Other international broadcasting services were the voice of their governments. The BBC External and then World Service 'was the voice of the people it broadcast to'.[27] This was true abroad but had to be remade at home.

Notes

1 Author's interview with Sir John Tusa.
2 See 'BBC Monitoring as an Institution: 1939–1982' – Imperial War Museum. Available at: www.iwm.org.uk.
3 See www.iwm.org.uk/research/research-projects/listening-to-the-world-bbc-monitoring-collection-ahrc-research-network for papers on BBC Monitoring.
4 A. Webb, *London Calling: Britain, the BBC World Service and the Cold War* (London, Bloomsbury, 2014).
5 BBC WAC R34/1580/2 Policy Suez Crisis Historical II Nov & Dec 1956.
6 My father, a disabled butcher, had a special ration to collect meat from market and one of my earliest memories is sitting beside him in the van as we went through a quite aggressive crowd at Smithfield meat market to collect meat – it meant that the delivery drivers were on short time.
7 Author's interview with Alasdair Milne, 2011.
8 A. Briggs, *Competition: The History of Broadcasting*, vol. 4 (Oxford, Oxford University Press, 1990), p. 87.
9 BBC WAC R34/1580/2 Policy Suez Crisis Historical II Nov & Dec 1956.
10 TNA:PRO, FO953/161, BBC External Services, 20 February 1956.
11 Sir Ian Jacob, BBC BOG, R12/22, 6 November 1956, *BBC Written Archives*.
12 See www.bbc.co.uk/worldservice/history/story/2007/01/070124_suez.shtml to hear both of the speeches.
13 BBC WAC R1/92/6,G73, 18 September 1956, *BBC Written Archives*.
14 National Archives: Inf. 2/33 Suez. 15 October 1956.
15 Webb, *London Calling*, p. 192.
16 BBC WAC E3/279/1, 'Hostility to western broadcasts', *BBC Written Archives*.
17 I. Rev, 'Just Noise? Cold War Broadcasting: Impact on the Soviet Union and Eastern Europe'. Available at: www.jstor.org/stable/10.7829/j.ctt1282v9.
18 BBC WAC E35/50/1 H.C.Eur. 19 July 1956, *BBC Written Archives*.
19 BBC WAC Pas,b, V1, 'The BBC and the Hungarian Revolution', 23 January 1957, *BBC Written Archives*.
20 BBC WAC E2/81/1, Macdonald to DXB, 6 July 1965, *BBC Written Archives*.
21 BBC WAC Pas,b, V2, 'The BBC and the Hungarian Revolution', 23 January 1957, *BBC Written Archives*.

22 P. Hennessy, *The Secret State: Preparing for the Worst 1945–2010* (Penguin Books, 2010), p. 146.
23 For a fuller and original discussion of this based on previously unseen papers see J. Seaton, *Pinkoes and Traitors: The BBC and the Nation 1974–1987* (Profile Books, 2015), Chapter 12.
24 Author's interview.
25 Seaton, *Pinkoes and Traitors*, pp. 295–97.
26 G. Mansell, *BBC Oral History*.
27 Author's interview with Sir John Tusa.

Chapter 15

Class, taste and profit

Post-war affluence was measured in 'white goods' – consumer durables. Particularly for women refrigerators, hoovers and washing machines made it easier to do what had always been done. It was a worldwide movement. At a 1959 major exhibition of American culture and society in Moscow at the height of the Cold War, a BBC *Panorama* reported long, patient queues of Russians; it caused the reformists in the Kremlin to understand that Soviet industrial production was failing and had be changed: the exhibit everybody wanted to see was the miracle of an American 'labour saving kitchen'.[1] It was this affluence that ITV seemed to be in-tune with. Television, it was believed, changed people's social life and habits. Commercial television was believed to alter their aspirations and values as well.

In the late 1950s and early 1960s television was central to a debate about supposed changes in the British class structure. The growth of a mass television audience and the setting up of a commercial service were seen as agents of a revolution that was eroding class distinction and increasing social mobility. Television has more often been seen as a destructive than as a creative force. In the 1950s many regarded it as a threat to traditional ways of life, and hence to the basis of traditional political loyalties.

In 1962 the Pilkington Report summed up this debate. The Director General, Sir Hugh Carleton Greene, later called the report 'the most important piece of work on the purposes of broadcasting which has appeared in this or any other country'.[2] In fact Greene lobbied tirelessly behind the scenes to get the second channel that Pilkington was going to recommend allocated to the BBC. He lobbied to get the right people on the Committee, the right person in charge of writing the Report and to make sure that it was shown the right evidence. The report was drafted by the 'public intellectual' of the moment – Richard Hoggart, who had written widely about culture and the working class in his book *The Uses of Literacy*, but who frequently appeared on the BBC as an expert commentator. 'Professor Hoggart' observed a BBC producer 'seems to have his finger on the pulse of the moment.'[3] Greene saw him as a 'progressive but culturally acute man with a gift to communicate'.

Asa Briggs, the pioneering social historian, former Bletchley Park decoder, had been appointed the first Official Historian of the BBC in 1956. But when asked if the BBC had ever brought any pressure to bear on his work – he said no with one exception. Hugh Carleton Greene (who Briggs perhaps understandably did not rate as highly as everyone else as a Director General) had, he said, tried to influence his work to make it more hostile to ITV.[4] Pilkington attempted to establish the criteria for producing – and judging – good broadcasting.

The myth of the disappearing working class

Broadcasting was seen as an instrument of changing values and the worry was that 'advertising' would change more than individual wants: it would persuade people that material gain was the only value. During the 1950s it was argued that affluence was 'destroying' the working class. The general elections of 1955 and 1959 seemed to support the view that there were no longer two nations: fewer and fewer people were prepared to back the Labour Party. Two complementary explanations were put forward. According to the first, as the working class had become richer it was actually disappearing through assimilation into the middle class. According to the second, a working class had continued to exist but prosperity had undermined an awareness of its own interests: capitalism was successfully eradicating the consciousness (though not the reality) of class.

In fact, something dramatic was happening to 'class'. A series of important books, and television and radio programmes put working-class life into the broadcasting frame in a new way. A discussion of the 'value of regional accents' at a BBC advisory board made the point that 'The BBC has to reflect how the nation speaks and working class tone and life better'. Alan Bennett said that 'reading Hoggart made me feel that my life, dull though it was, might be the stuff of literature'.[5] David Lodge – the novelist who combined acute social observation with great wit – said that *The Uses of Literacy*, was 'In those days a kind of a bible for first generation university students and teachers who had been promoted by education from working class backgrounds'. The book was discussed extensively on the BBC: 'for the first time working class experience is seen from the inside in this moving book' . . . 'It dissolved any middle-class persons' idea of superiority' agreed a panel discussion on 'Class and Literature' on the third programme. Was this true, queried one critic, after all D.H. Lawrence had done it thirty years before? *Panorama* produced a programme that asked 'Questions about Class'. Then there were a series of sociological inquiries – most significantly Peter Willmott and Michael Young's *Family and Kinship in East London*. Yet what all of these books shared was a strange nostalgia and indeed sentimentality about a working-class formation that was indeed disappearing: the 'traditional' working class – dependent on heavy industry. Hoggart relativized experience but was overwhelmingly hostile to modern, mass, media.

That the working class was actually changing was more directly understood and perhaps more anxiously attended to among Labour politicians (who used it to justify an attempt to remove socialism from the party's constitution). 'The steady upgrading of the working class', wrote Anthony Crosland in his book *The Future of Socialism*, 'both occupationally and still more in terms of political and social aspirations, renders Labour's one-class image increasingly inappropriate'. It was also widely held by social scientists, who invented the inelegant term 'embourgeoisement', to describe the alleged process. As Butler and Rose wrote after the 1959 general election, 'It is more than ever possible to speak of the Conservatives as the country's usual majority party . . . the Labour Party has to face the fact that its support is being eroded by the impact of age and social change'.

Between 1951 and 1958 real wages rose by 20 per cent. The proportion of manual workers who owned their own homes rose from 32 per cent to 39 per cent in the four years before 1962.[6] Between 1951 and 1964 the number of television sets rose from one million to thirteen million. Indeed, as televisions were clearly not useful, the widespread ownership of sets merely appeared to confirm what Crosland called (dismissively – he was criticizing sentimental and condescending views) the 'pubs, pools and prostitutes' view of the working class, which was seen to 'waste all its higher income on alcohol, tobacco, gambling and fun . . . if not actually women'.[7]

During the same period, working-class habits also changed. People went on more holidays, went to the cinema less frequently, began drinking more at home and less at pubs. As these goods and habits had previously been the prerogative of higher social classes, it was assumed that their use also entailed middle- and upper-class views and beliefs.

The second explanation of the decay of the working class depended on the centrality of culture. The rituals which were a source of strength to working-class life were disappearing, partly (so it was argued) because of the homogenizing influence of television. Paradoxically, working-class culture was celebrated just as it seemed to be about to vanish. Indeed, its condition was detailed by a generation of academics whose origins were working class, but all of whom had been upwardly mobile.

'To live in the working class', Hoggart had written, 'is to belong to an all-pervading culture, one in some ways as formalized and stylized as any that is attributed to the upper classes'.[8] Jackson and Marsden, in their book on working-class life, argued that two-and-a-half centuries of urban life 'have established distinct working-class styles of living with very real values of their own. Values which are perhaps essential to society and which do not flourish that strongly in other reaches of society'.[9] In a chapter headed 'An acceptance of the working-class life', they remarked that obliterating these values and way of life 'can be so quick in a technological society . . . the mass media, the central planning office, the bulldozers are all characteristic instruments of change'. Wilmott and Young compared the warm closeness of a Bethnal Green working-class community with the more isolated life of a new suburb. In the East End the emphasis was on the informal collective life and the extended family, the pubs and the open-air market. 'There is a sort of bantering warmth in public', they claimed, which in the new suburb, Woodford, was reserved for the family home. There seemed to be more uniformity in gardens, attitudes and behaviour in Woodford than in the East End. 'Maybe uniformity is one of the prices we have to pay for sociability in a more mobile society', they concluded.[10]

In a waspish review in the *Listener* Kingsley Amis observed there was an awful lot about 'mums' in the book – apparently working-class women wanted to be closer to their 'mums'. Television was in these books seen as replacing old communal forms of leisure with isolated and standardized entertainment.

Hoggart applied F. R. Leavis's concern with the moral quality of elite literary culture to a broader problem of working-class life. For Leavis, Annan wrote, 'The analysis of the text is only important in so far as it reveals the profundity or morality of the writer's moral consciousness'.[11] Leavis was concerned to evaluate the purpose of literature. 'Where there is not in the literary critical sense a significant contemporary culture', he wrote, '*the mind* is not fully alive'.[12] Hoggart was concerned to judge modern working-class culture. He concluded that 'Most mass entertainments are in the end what D. H. Lawrence described as "anti-life". They are full of corrupt brightness and improper appeals and moral evasions'. Progress had been reduced to material improvement: 'It only offered an infinite perspective of increasingly good times. Technicolour TV, all smelling, all touching, all tasting TV'.

Thus the Pilkington Report was the product of two contemporary concerns: that the working class was being absorbed into the middle class, and that working-class culture was decaying because of the industrialization of leisure.[13] The committee had been asked to review the development of television. In fact they did much more, producing a report which judged the nation's culture. Television, the report argued, was 'one of the major long-term factors that would shape the moral and mental attitudes, and the values of our society'.

Yet the working class did not disappear, and neither did working-class culture. There is little evidence that people lose a sense of their social identity simply because they become comparatively better off. Indeed the really remarkable feature of the period was not affluence – the rise in living standards looks far less impressive when it is compared with the growth in other European countries – but full employment. For the first time there was work for everyone, and it gave working-class culture, taste and life a confidence which it had rarely had before.

The Pilkington Report depended on a sentimentalization of an earlier 'golden age', just as Hoggart and Willmott and Young had before it. Indeed it demonstrates a puritanical distaste for the effects of improved material conditions. Although its concern with the influence of television on social and cultural behaviour is important, the standards by which it judged the mass media were based on false premises about the nature of working-class life.

The power of the media

The Pilkington Report mobilized a view of the power of the media to influence individual behaviour. If the media had an independent capacity to change people's attitudes then that 'socializing' capacity had to be managed in the interest of the society not just profit and indeed in order to preclude propaganda. The BBC and public service were seen in the front line of another larger battle. Advertising, and in particular its newest and most dramatic form, the television commercial, was regarded as immensely persuasive. After all people flooded out to buy things that had been advertised: it demonstrably affected behaviour. In this context, the post-austerity explosion of advertising amazed the public, and academics and politicians became very sensitive to its effects.

Television advertising in particular was regarded as potentially sinister. It was often equated with 'brain-washing' techniques which had been exposed during the Korean War. 'It may well be', wrote Daniel Bell in the *Listener* (December 1956), 'that our fears are excessive, that the pliability of the consumer, like that of the "indoctrinated" communist youth, is an exaggerated fact'. The fashion for 'motivation research' seemed to suggest that advertisements relied on an appeal to people's irrational and subconscious feelings in order to sell goods. The model of the consumer as a rational hedonist was replaced by another in which many goods were purchased not for their intrinsic worth or usefulness, but in an attempt to assuage anxieties. Marketing, dependent on the 'eight hidden needs' (most of which could be reduced to one – sex), was claimed to have dramatic effects. 'The ability of advertisers to contact millions of us simultaneously through television has given them the power to do good or evil on a scale never before possible', one persuader put it.[14] Leavis wrote that 'a new brand of applied psychology . . . and a highly specialized profession' had been developed. 'Years of carefully recorded and tabulated experiment [led advertisers] to develop their appeal in the confidence that the average member of the public will respond like an automaton'.[15] Television advertising, which reached people in the defenceless privacy of their own homes, seemed to assume that consumers were unable to introspect sufficiently to understand their own motives.

The working class were felt to be the group most vulnerable to the ambitions of advertisers. 'There is one kind of person who seems particularly responsive to advertising: the man or woman who is moving up from one class to another', Mark Abrams argued in a broadcast in 1956. 'These people – and there are an incredible number in Britain – have to shed their old buying habits and acquire new ones. The class-destroying function of modern advertising is cumulative', he suggested:

> The initial effect is to encourage people to want to buy consumer goods formerly enjoyed by their social betters. As they achieve this and become more socially mobile, advertising and television provide them with knowledge that enables them to fill their new role.[16]

Indeed, the first television commercials seemed to confirm this view of the direct impact of the media on behaviour. Shops almost immediately sold out of the advertised goods, and jubilant market researchers discovered that the public recalled the commercials long after they had first been shown.

Later research seemed to show how complex the relationship between media message and audience behaviour is. The public is not a passive, empty box merely waiting to be filled with the injunctions of advertisers. How people react to what they see is determined by their class, age and the beliefs they already hold. Nor is the public subconscious so easily manipulated as many assumed. As one contemporary market researcher pointed out, surveys which concluded that housewives did not like macaroni which cooked to a wet sticky mass because wet sticky masses aroused sexual guilt in them were not treated with the scepticism they deserved.[17] Some critics reacted cautiously to the power of advertisements: 'I cannot think so poorly of British Fathers', wrote Tom Driberg in the *New Statesman* (20 December 1958), 'as to accept the diagnosis proclaimed by one ITV advertiser last week, "Every daddy *deserves* a Brylcreem home dispenser for Christmas"'. However, most critics believed it to be overwhelming. Advertising executives were credited with a power they would have been delighted to exercise, but which was far in excess of their rather unpredictable performance.

This overestimation of the manipulative power of the media influenced the Pilkington Report. It led to a somewhat crude view of the public – particularly the working-class audience – as passive, gullible and misled.

Real and false wants

The Pilkington Report dismissed expressed public preferences as unreal and the product of commercial manipulation. A Labour Party report on advertising written in 1962 developed some of these arguments. Advertising, it claimed, could not be defended by the assertion that it merely reflected the times. For, in order to make advertisements, individuals were obliged to make decisions. Insofar as advertisers determined what was shown they were responsible for their choices. Some people, the report argued, had claimed that advertising 'reinforces attitudes of materialism, only too prevalent in society'. In the committee's opinion:

> This charge is probably the opposite of the truth: for it seems more likely that what advertising does is to interfere with the appreciation of material goods to the extent that it substitutes for a genuine assessment or perception of their qualities, vague sentiments and fantasies.

The choices that were expressed under these conditions were consequently not 'real'.

The report's attitude towards cultural choice was particularly clear in its discussion of entertainment. ITV defended itself by arguing that its programmes were popular. Pilkington replied that:

> to give the public what it wants is a misleading phrase . . . it has the appearance of an appeal to democratic principle, but the appearance is deceptive. It is in fact patronizing and arrogant, in that it claims to know what the public is but defines it as no more than the mass audience, and it claims to know what it wants, but limits its choice to the average of experience.

The commercial companies suggested that there was no need to consider entertainment as it was so unimportant. However, for Pilkington, the individual programme was analogous to the text for the literary critic. As such, it was as essential to judge 'trivial entertainment' as more serious programmes. This was all grist to the larger argument about who should be allocated another station. In this sense, it was an agile argument and raised enduringly significant issues.

However, as Crosland pointed out, it was patronizing and perhaps unwise to dismiss expressed public wants as irrelevant. He argued that the range of newspapers and television programmes was 'still considerable, certainly wide enough to offer genuine comparison'. Indeed, most people, for most of the time, chose the escapist, the diverting or the trivial. Policy should not ignore these needs, but should also seek to encourage minority interests.

The Pilkington Committee's fears that the public was passive led it to consider audience preferences as little more than the expression of commercial manipulation. Consequently, the report became insensitive to public taste. Indeed, it endorsed the BBC's popular music policy when this was clearly out of touch with what people wanted to hear, as the success of the pirate stations soon demonstrated.

Entertainment, politics and advertising

The Pilkington Committee was romantically committed to a concept of folk culture. Its emphasis on the importance of the 'authenticity' of cultural products meant that many other considerations were ignored. For instance, television entertainment programmes often implicitly supported particular political values. These long-term values – great shifts in humour and what values are advanced or impeded – are an important question.

Indeed, the report's[18] identification of programmes as the central focus for any assessment of broadcasting is crucial. Moreover, its recognition of the structural effects of advertising on the quality of programmes is original and shrewd, and still pertinent.

Indeed, the allocation of the third channel to the BBC, and by strengthening the power of the Independent Television Authority (ITA) over the companies all improved the service to the public. In particular, the report, which had been wonderfully orchestrated by Sir Hugh Carleton Greene, also gave the BBC the *élan* and confidence which were the basis for its most exciting expansion in the 1960s.[19] For the first time, the Corporation attempted to make broadcasting something like a quality popular newspaper. This is perhaps the most challenging model for a national broadcasting service.

The BBC – with almost no time – managed an engineering coup. The new station (called BBC2) opened in 1964. The first night was a catastrophe as there was a London-wide power cut and the first night's programme could not be shown. Michael Peacock, the gifted administrator and programme-maker was the first Director. He ensured that the new channel had an almost immediate 'hit' with a long running 'Edwardian' drama serial *The Forsyte Saga*. The nation was gripped. But more dramatically colour television was introduced into Britain for the first time on this channel in 1967. Colour TV set new problems and opened up new possibilities for what television could do; David Attenborough – who became the second Head of the new service – immediately understood the opportunities. Colour TV in America was seen as vulgar. His idea was to launch a series that was up-market, clever and 'used colour to show pretty things'. He commissioned the first spectacular series of *Civilisation*, a thirteen-part series which changed the reputation of colour broadcasting. It would capture the watching public, exploit colour and identify the new channel as 'adventurous, thinking, important – new *and* good'. Presented by Sir Kenneth Clark, *Civilisation* was an Olympian, highly personal exposition by a great communicator and scholar.

Under Greene – and after Pilkington – the BBC invented new drama, employing Ken Loach and David Hare, new arts programmes, new forms like satire and *That Was the Week That Was*, *Panorama* became more adventurous as reporting was made possible from abroad and the BBC news operation (close to Greene's heart and understanding) reported on Vietnam and South Africa, Russia and American convulsions with greater authority. Pilkington had made the BBC more confident and, in turn (while always hunted by an ever more adventurous ITV), this meant that it served different audiences better. It represented them more fairly and it gave them delights and insights, fun and improvement.

Notes

1 See www.vam.ac.uk/content/articles/c/crisis-and-fear-in-cold-war-design/ for a number of interesting discussions of Cold War cultural competition. Also see M. Moore, *The Origins of Modern Spin: Democratic Government and the Media in Britain, 1945–51* (London, Palgrave, 2006).

2 Sir H. Carleton Greene, 'The future of broadcasting in Britain', Granada Guildhall Lecture (1972), p. 24.

3 R22, P 1, Programme Board and discussion, July 1959, *BBC Written Archives*.

4 Author's interview with Lord Briggs.

5 A. Bennett, *The History Boys* (New York, Farrar, Straus and Giroux, 2004), p. 3.
6 M. Pinto Duschinsky, 'Bread and circuses: the Conservatives in office 1951–64' in V. Bogdanor and R. Skidelsky (eds.) *The Age of Affluence* (Harmondsworth, Penguin, 1970), p. 55.
7 C. A. R. Crosland, 'The mass media', *Encounter* (November 1962).
8 R. Hoggart, *The Uses of Literacy* (London, Chatto & Windus, 1957), p. 16.
9 B. Jackson and D. Marsden, *Education and the Working Class* (London, Routledge & Kegan Paul, 1962), p. 223.
10 P. Willmott and M. D. Young, *Family and Class in a London Suburb* (London, Routledge & Kegan Paul, 1960), p. 129.
11 N. Annan, 'Love among the moralists', *Encounter* (February 1960), p. 37.
12 F. R. Leavis, *The Common Pursuit* (London, Chatto & Windus, 1952), p. 192.
13 R. Williams, *Communications*, revised edition (London, Chatto & Windus, 1966), p. 10.
14 Fougasse (pseud. C. K. Bird), *The Changing Face of Britain* (London, Methuen, 1950), p. 15.
15 F. R. Leavis and D. Thompson, *Culture and Environment* (London, Chatto & Windus, 1953), p. 48.
16 M. Abrams, 'Advertising', *Listener* (15 December 1956), p. 1089.
17 M. Abrams, 'Motivation research', *Advertising Quarterly* (November 1959), p. 311.
18 Author's interview with David Attenborough.
19 See M. Tracey, *A Variety of Lives: The Biography of Sir Hugh Greene* (London, Bodley Head, 1983).

Chapter 16

Managers, regulators and broadcasters

Commercial television produces audiences, not programmes. Advertisers, in purchasing a few seconds of television time, are actually buying viewers by the thousand. The price they pay is determined by the number of people who can be expected to be watching when their advert is shown. Hence, advertisers regard programmes merely as the means by which audiences are delivered to them. The sequence of programmes in any evening, week or season reflects the quest of commercial customers to get the largest or most appropriate public they can. 'The spot is the packaging', wrote a market researcher in *Advertising Quarterly*, 'the product inside the package is an audience'. These are the realities that help to determine what kinds of programmes are made, when they are shown and who sees them.

Commercial television was introduced in the 1950s because it was claimed that it would bring competition into broadcasting and make the service more responsive to popular demands. The Independent Television channel was supposed to break the narrow elitism of the BBC's cultural policy. Indeed, once it had been given a regional structure, it was also supposed to promote provincial culture and oppose the BBC's metropolitan bias. Finally, commercial television, its advocates claimed, would be less vulnerable to political pressure. Unlike the BBC, its finances would be independent of official control.

Few of these hopes were fully realised. The allocation of the franchise areas in which commercial companies were given the right to broadcast was designed to produce a system in which four (later five) of the largest and wealthiest regions made most of the programmes for the national network. The smaller companies made most of their programmes for local consumption; only a few of their products were to be shown nationally.

The first commitment of the commercial companies was to make a profit. Hence, they were concerned to minimise the financial risks involved in making programmes. The smaller regions, whose audiences were not so attractive to advertisers, could not afford to invest in expensive programmes unless they were guaranteed a national showing. Similarly, the large networking companies needed to be able to show their programmes in every region in order to cover their costs. Consequently, decisions about which programmes were to be networked became centralized.

This centralisation was formalised when the Independent Television Companies Association (ITCA) was set up in 1971. Yet British 'commercial' television was not merely a product of market forces. If financial pressures were the only influence, the programme makers' aim would always be simply to reach the largest possible audience for the smallest amount of money.

In practice this would have meant a diet of American soap opera, variety shows, filmed series, quizzes and chat shows, based on proven formulae, endlessly repeated. 'Minority' programming would cater only for groups defined by consumption patterns. Current affairs might have been confined to news bulletins, and advertising spots would have been longer, more frequent and more intrusive. In addition, even more programmes would have been bought from abroad – particularly the USA – and fewer programmes made in Britain or directed at a British audience. Commercial broadcasting did not develop these features in Britain because of the framework of public regulations within which it was obliged to operate. Nevertheless, these pressures remain the dominant features of a commercial service.

The Independent Broadcasting Authority (IBA) exerted a major influence on commercial television. The powers of the authority were widened following the report of the Pilkington Committee (1962), but the most public job of the IBA was to license television franchises and to reallocate these periodically. The authority was also required to ensure 'balanced programming', 'due impartiality' in the treatment of controversial issues and a high quality in programme production as a whole. To enforce its recommendations, the IBA could determine the broadcasting schedule, prohibit the transmission of particular programmes or even revoke the franchises of offending companies. In addition, the IBA monitored and controlled the amount, timing, quality and content of advertisements shown on commercial television.

When commercial television started in Britain in 1956, there was little idea of what form it would take. 'All we had in the beginning', recalled Sir Robert Fraser, the first Director General of the ITA, 'was an Act of Parliament, an untested authority, a little prefab in a mews by Marble Arch, and a bit of money we had to pay back'.[1] Nevertheless, the new controlling authority quickly developed a commitment to public service. Thus, in the first months of broadcasting, as Sir Kenneth Clark recalled, the IBA threatened to make current affairs programmes itself to counter a proposal to abandon such programmes by the commercial companies. The determination of the authority to maintain minority programming in peak viewing time was similarly demonstrated when it came to reallocate franchises. In 1967, some of the original commercial franchises were not renewed. As a result, programme scheduling on ITV had an important though secondary goal, that of securing the reallocation of franchises. 'Advertisers understand that current affairs and n ews programming is a condition of the survival of the commercial television companies', wrote one advertising executive. 'It is no good complaining about them'.[2]

The IBA also intervened in the construction of programme schedules, requiring that one third of all material broadcast by commercial TV companies should be 'serious non-fiction, sensibly distributed over the week as a whole in appropriate times'.[3] Without this intervention, a service that many people relied on as their primary source of news might have carried very little current affairs coverage.

The IBA's intervention also helped to maintain a wider range of cultural output than would otherwise have been the case. In 1956, 'serious programming' accounted for 19 per cent of the companies' schedules. This rose to 26 per cent in 1959, and 36 per cent in 1965, a proportion that was maintained. However, official figures were inflated by the growing number of programmes that were classed as serious documentaries, but which were on entertainment topics (such as Alan Whicker's series). In addition, there were an increasing number of consumer-oriented programmes (on cars, holidays and gardening, for example), some of which scarcely qualified for their official classification as 'serious and informative'. Nevertheless, programming on commercial television undoubtedly included more serious material because of the IBA's influence, and many of these programmes gained large audiences. The most striking example was ITN's News at Ten, innovative in its presentation of news and which regularly featured in the IBA's yearly 'Top Twenty' popularity ratings.

The Authority was also important in maintaining the standards of entertainment on commercial television. It limited the number of cheap American imports and the frequency with which programmes were repeated. The IBA also assisted the smaller regional companies by charging the more profitable regions a higher rent for the use of the television transmitter that it owned, and thus made them subsidise the rental of the poorer companies. In addition, through its position on the committee, which decided which programmes were shown on the central network, it ensured that some of the regional programmes were shown nationally.

Regions and audiences

The Television Act of 1954 had not specified how commercial television was to be organized. It had laid down no principles to guide the allocation of contracts. When commercial companies began to submit proposals to the ITA they suggested many different ways of dividing commercial broadcasting between competitors. Thus, some contractors offered to provide particular kinds of programmes, for instance, all the light entertainment or all the music; others proposed to make the programmes for particular times of day, for example, 6 pm to 9 pm or 3 pm to 7 pm. However, Sir Robert Fraser decided that the system should be based on regional companies. In this way, he intended to prohibit the growth of a centralized monopoly based on London, and to 'give real creative power to the regions'.

Yet the principle of the federal structure seemed threatened from the very start. During the first two years, commercial television was so expensive to run, reached such a small audience and was so unprofitable that there was little interest in the smaller regions. It was during this disastrous period that Roy Thomson acquired Scottish Television at a very low cost. It was only when this company overcame its initial difficulties that the other regional services began to develop. Thomson, famous for having said that owning a commercial station was like having a licence to print money, soon made Scottish Television profitable. 'I like monopolies', he said, 'when I operate them'.[4]

Regional commercial broadcasting has survived, but in a form that makes sense in economic rather than cultural terms. Thus, Tyneside and Teesside have little in common apart from geographical proximity. Yet they were given a combined television station because only the joint purchasing power of their audience was sufficient to make up a marketing unit. A more serious case was that of Harlech Television, supposedly a Welsh station, but actually required, for commercial reasons, to cater for a large English audience as well. It has been argued that some regional television stations, for example, Border Television, may have strengthened, or even created, a sense of local identity. However, most of the regions have no real justification except in marketing terms. Apart from London, television regions have not even approximately coincided with local authority areas. This has inhibited the discussions of local political issues.

The regionalism of commercial television appears less firmly rooted in popular needs than in the convenience of the market.

Indeed, the most important response by the commercial companies to regional differences within Britain was to identify and sell distinctive characteristics in marketing terms. 'Granada has the skilled workers: surveys prove it!' read an advertisement in a 1959 trade magazine. 'Westward where women cook', read another in *Campaign* in 1962. In 1979, Southern Television was pointing out that its A, B and C1 housewives cook and have time to be *femmes fatales* afterwards (*Campaign*, 5 July 1979). The differences between the habits and tastes of the various regional audiences became an essential feature of sales campaigns. In 1962, one writer claimed that 'The television regions made scientific selling more possible than ever before'.[5] New products could be launched in regions where they were most likely to be successful and advertising campaigns could be tested by pilot surveys in a particular region. In the same way, regional television meant that additional advertising pressure could be applied in any area where sales were slumping. The most important effect of the regional structure of commercial television was to change the marketing map of Britain.

Franchises and owners

The cost of developing commercial television was at first so great that franchises had to be given to syndicates that had the resources to undertake the necessary capital investment. This brought an important change in the kind of people who controlled broadcasting. Hitherto in the BBC, responsibility had been vested in professional administrators whose social origins, training and attitudes reflected the 'public service' philosophy of the Corporation. Independent television introduced a new type of executive, business-oriented and entrepreneurial, geared to the commercial criteria of the sponsors. Thus, while the BBC was directed by Sir William Haley, who had started his career as a journalist on the *Manchester Guardian*, and who became editor of *The Times*, Associated Television's first director was Lew Grade, a show business and theatre impresario.

By the time that the franchises were reallocated in 1967, commercial television had become highly profitable, and consequently, the justification for allowing it to be controlled by speculative capital no longer held good. Indeed, such vast profits had been made from a publicly owned asset, the air waves, that the prospect of their reallocation created a flood of applications. There was an atmosphere reminiscent of Klondike gold fever. Many of Britain's major corporations financed 'prospecting' companies composed of theatre managers and entertainment moguls, spiced with a few peers or eminent members of the BBC. Although changes were made in the new franchises, instead of widening control, the redistribution, in practice, merely consolidated the power of the great media empires.

This pattern continued until the 1980s; the government encouraged the oligopolistic tendencies of the broadcasting industry itself – in the name, of course, of freedom. If one contradiction of this period was that free market rhetoric was accompanied by interventionist practice, another was that talk about a media marketplace was accompanied by its virtual eradication. Technological change, with its requirement of long-term investment and large-scale capitalization, produced a bureaucratic jungle of profit-taking conglomerates that now own huge shares in all the media which the public consumes.

By 1990, the small number of corporate owners were not competitive in a sense that could be conceivably expected to produce an improved product: but their financial rivalry undoubtedly imposed pressure to produce a cheaper one. That meant an almost inevitable lowering of standards: it is cheaper to buy in agency news than to send a reporter to the scene, it is cheaper to buy in internationalised soap opera than to make your own drama and so on.

The victims of media concentration are variety, creativity and quality, while the future proliferation of broadcasting channels in the hands of a shrinking band of operators is certain to make matters worse.

However, the control of commercial television companies could not simply be equated with ownership. Those who actually produced commercial television programmes enjoyed a significant degree of autonomy. But, most important of all, the pressure of market forces imposed powerful constraints on what could and could not be broadcast. These operated irrespective of the formal ownership of commercial television. In a study of the way in which programming is determined in the USA, Wolf argued that ownership does not explain the differences in programming between stations. 'It may be', he suggested,

> that those who saw such influences labored under a false analogy between the small town newspaper editor who may have shaped every word in his paper, and the television corporate executive, who according to the analogy controlled what was shown on the air.[6]

Indeed, he concluded that in the USA the more diversely owned companies were less likely to take the networked programmes, particularly the news, current affairs and documentaries, and more likely to broadcast a diet of old movies, old quiz shows or old operas. They did this simply because of the pressure to attract the largest possible audience.

The economic and social organization of broadcasting is very different in Britain from that described by Wolf in the USA. There, the more diversely owned companies were the smaller and less successful ones, which were more vulnerable to market pressures. Nevertheless, the inevitable pursuit of profit within a commercial system must have some similar consequences for the programming decisions that can be made in any country. Market forces operate as a continual limiting pressure on any commercial broadcasting system. Yet it is also clear that more socially diverse patterns of ownership could be an important factor in creating the conditions for more adventurous and varied programming.

The audience that advertisers want

The most important pressure on television scheduling and programme making is that of advertising expenditure. If television companies sell audiences, what kinds of audiences do advertisers want and how are they packaged to attract sales? Indeed, how does the real purpose of producing audiences for advertisers affect the apparent purpose of producing programmes for audience consumption?

The American system of programme sponsorship, in which advertisers pay for individual programmes, was rejected when commercial television started in Britain on the grounds that it gave advertisers direct power over programme content. Instead, only 'spot advertising' was permitted, time slots only between or within programmes, initially limited to an average of six minutes per hour. Later, when it was seen that this led to an accumulation of advertisements in peak viewing times, it was decided to limit advertisements to no more than seven minutes in any one hour.

The decision to adopt restricted spot advertising had been hailed as a victory for public service broadcasting. 'The prohibition of sponsorship was an inspiration of the Television Act', declared Fraser, 'since it established the supremacy of the editorial principle'.[7] Spot advertisements were compared with newspaper advertising. They were seen as guaranteeing the independence of programme making from the influence of advertisers: no rational person, it was argued, supposes that what newspapers publish in their editorial columns is determined by advertisers. Spot advertising would protect the editorial integrity of commercial television. 'Advertising will be an asset worn as a bright feather in the cap of free TV', Sir Robert Fraser wrote, 'not as a soiled choker around the throat'.

Sponsorship of all programmes except news and current events was finally permitted in 1988. However, on the ITV channels there continued to be a fierce battle about who could sponsor what – and considerable anxiety about potential commercial abuses of the authority of some programmes. Such niceties, of course, were not part of the satellite broadcasting regime. Here, there were few restrictions on sponsorship and far more advertising was allowed. Indeed, one of the oddities of the intense political campaigns of the period was the BBC's failure to point out, in its own defence, that while the British public enjoys some adverts, repeated research has shown how irritating they have been found to be to many people. Historically, the British public has enjoyed and endured less advertising per hour of viewing than any American or European viewer. It may be appalled when the full commercial diet of adverts reaches it.

However, during the 1980s, powerful interests complained to a sympathetic government that the ITV companies and the IBA were using their monopoly too effectively. Between 1981 and 1989, the advertising revenue of commercial television doubled in real terms, fierce competition for air time raised the price of advertising and increased the discretionary power of companies. Thus, there was great commercial pressure to create alternative sources of air time: cable, satellite and a competing commercial terrestrial Channel 5 were proposed in order to bring down advertising costs. Advertisers believed they had a strong interest in breaking the economic basis of the existing ITV companies' cultural power.

Hostile critics argued that the IBA had become too closely identified with the ITV companies. A new body, the Independent Television Commission (ITC), was set up to preside over the 'deregulated' commercial system, but with far more limited powers than its predecessor. Thus, franchises for ITV (which after 1993 became known as Channel 3) were to be auctioned. Auction winners will hold franchises for ten years and the ITC has little authority to demand changes in programme performance. Thus, while the Commission is obliged to ensure that public sensibilities about images of sex or violence are not offended, it has limited authority with which to perform the more critical task of ensuring that good programmes continue to be made and shown by companies desperately trying to recoup the huge capital expense of their franchise bid.

The IBA's powers, however imperfectly exercised, stemmed from its economic sanctions within the ITV system. Since its inception, the ITC has developed imperialist ambitions. Clearly, it would like to use its controls to bring traditional public service criteria to bear on the enlarged commercial sector. Indeed, the ITC is probably responsible for a profound metaphorical change in ministers' language. In 1986, guarantees of programme quality were to be a 'factor' in allowing applicants to enter the auction for Channel 3 franchises; by 1987, they were being discussed as a 'hurdle'; they rose during 1988 to a 'fence'; and by 1990, they were confidently described as 'a barrier to the inferior'. But metaphors alone will not control commercial pressures to maximise profits and it remains to be seen how far the ITC can realise its ambitions.

Yet many of the pressures exercised by advertisers on the content of programmes have remained remarkably consistent since the start of commercial broadcasting. The extent to which they affect programmes and schedules depends on the ways in which they are balanced and regulated.

Thus, it is clear that even spot advertising does not preclude advertisers from calculating how the editorial content of programmes affects the impact of their advertising message. 'After all', as an advertiser wrote as early as the 1950s, 'an advert is seen as part of a programme' (*Campaign*, 14 March 1956). Advertisers have prior knowledge of programme schedules, which are published each quarter in advance of their transmission. They thus know the general character, if not the precise content, of the programmes with which their advertisements will be shown. There have been cases in which advertisers have avoided certain programmes on the grounds that their content is unlikely to dispose viewers to respond favourably to their advertisements. This is most common when the content of the programme clashes directly with the appeal of the advertisement (for example, airlines have withdrawn advertisements from appearing in documentaries about air disasters). However, it has also occurred when a programme is thought to have associations that detract from the broad image of the product.

In contrast, some programmes may be preferred because they provide an editorial environment conducive to a favourable response to particular advertisements or because their prestige is thought likely to enhance that of the product or service advertised within them. Thus, advertisements for newspapers appear near the news and those for beer are often placed close to programmes on sport. The very fact that such intuitive judgements associated with programme content can influence how advertising time is bought must affect the decisions made by the companies about scheduling.

This pressure is, however, marginal. The main consideration of advertisers is not the programme environment of their advertisements, but the size and composition of the audience that the programmes will attract. Advertisers buy television time in two ways. Sometimes they buy a 'guaranteed audience', that is, a fixed number of viewers. This may be made up of many small sections of the audience and spread over a whole range of programmes with low ratings. Alternatively, it may be composed of a few large audiences during peak viewing times. In either case, what is bought is viewers. However, advertisers may also purchase particular advertising slots. The television companies may oblige advertisers to buy a 'package' of slots, composed of some of the peak viewing times the advertisers want, but combining other, less attractive slots. Nevertheless, advertisers are more in control of the kinds of audiences their campaigns will reach if they buy specific slots.

Commercial television rapidly became the leading advertising medium for mass consumer products and so was under pressure to put on programmes with an appeal to a mass audience. However, many patrons of commercial television have sought to reach particular constituents within the mass market, in particular women (who are the key decision makers in many consumer purchases) and young people. As commercial television derives its revenue from advertisers and not from viewers, the commercial system is thus led towards catering for these groups. Thus, the success of commercial breakfast television depends almost entirely on its capacity to attract an audience rich in housewives that are consumers.

Market research can provide a detailed breakdown of the audience profile for particular programmes. A massive investment is made in monitoring how many and what categories of people watch each programme. This research assists the television companies to produce programmes that will deliver the required audiences and provides them with an accurate measurement of the audiences that they have sold.

Research also helps advertisers predict from advance programme schedules what audiences they can expect to buy. This research takes the form of continuous monitoring of a representative sample of viewers, providing detailed figures for programme viewing analysed in terms of the size and class of audience. It is supplemented by additional surveys that analyse other, more specialised characteristics of viewers. This research has established that certain types of programmes – soap operas, situation comedies, the main news bulletin and variety programmes – have a generalised appeal that transcends differences in social class, age and sex. It also reveals that other types of programmes – most notably political documentary programmes and serious drama – are not watched as much by women and young people. The results have shown a remarkable stability of viewing preferences since the introduction of commercial television. There has been little change in the pattern of mass viewing, apart from a small shift away from variety and sport.

The way in which commercial television time is sold generates pressure for the quantity of audience, rather than the quality of audience appreciation. It has even been suggested that some advertisers prefer television programmes not to be too involving, for fear of detracting from the impact of their advertisements. This has been called the 'Let's-give-the-public-the-shows-they-*least*-like-so-they'll-watch-the-ads' theory.[8]

The IBA attempted to offset the pressure for quantity of audience by circulating the companies with a weekly Audience Appreciation Index, which monitors the quality of audience response to individual programmes. This index has consistently shown that information programmes are more highly appreciated than those concerned with entertainment. There seems to be an inverse relationship between audience size and audience enjoyment.

However, it is doubtful whether this intervention had much influence on the time-buying decisions of advertisers, as no connection has yet been established between the audience's enjoyment or involvement in programmes and their responsiveness to advertisements shown at the same time. The implications of audience appreciation research have only lately begun to be developed. It has been argued that within the two categories of information and entertainment programmes, those with large audiences tend to have higher appreciation scores than those with small audiences. Indeed, some market researchers have come up with the less-than-remarkable finding that the more demanding a programme is, the better it has to be before people will watch it.[9]

The pressure on commercial television to maximise audiences naturally leads to a preference for 'entertainment' as opposed to 'serious' programmes. Within the broad category of entertainment there is a preference for programmes that have previously demonstrated their appeal to women and young people. Hence there is a bias against showing sport at particular times of the day, as it mainly appeals to men. Commercial pressures have also led programme makers to emphasise the personal and human interest aspects of documentary stories. Thus, structural social problems are treated in the form of individual case studies. This kind of programme reaches a wider audience, particularly among women, than other documentary styles. The prominence given to certain types of programmes on commercial television is a direct consequence of the pressures generated by advertising for the production of certain types of audiences.

Advertising also generates a strong pressure for television companies to produce predictable and regular audiences, as well as to maximize them. While the ratings for any particular programme may be hard to predict, because they depend so much on factors outside the control of any commercial company (in particular what the BBC is showing), viewing patterns over a year, as well as the categories and sequences of programmes, have been easy to predict.

Advertisers rely on programme schedules to produce the audiences that they pay for. This has encouraged attempts to use the sequence of programmes in order to manipulate the size of an audience over an evening. Consequently, programmes with a broad audience appeal are shown early in the evening, in an attempt to capture viewing families for a particular channel for the rest of the night's programmes. Scheduling attempts to expand and consolidate the mass audience throughout the evening. It is this pressure that leads to the screening of 'minority' information programmes outside peak viewing times and to the 'twinning' of BBC and ITV schedules for current affairs programmes. By doing this, the companies may minimize choice, but they also minimize the loss of audience from programmes that get low ratings. In addition, current events programmes are thus seen by a far larger general audience than would otherwise be the case.

The proliferation of broadcasting channels, which was so enthusiastically advocated by advertisers, will, however, make many of these calculations increasingly insecure. Accelerating fragmentation of the great national audiences previously enjoyed by the duopoly may provide, as some have argued, many new specialised concentrations of consumers or it may provide nothing more than smaller, more unpredictable audiences. Indeed, the most enthusiastic advocates of 'deregulation', the advertisers, have begun to be anxious about the future effectiveness of advertising on TV at all, particularly in the iPlayer age of viewing on demand.

Whatever happens, there is evidence that these commercial attempts to manipulate the audience are only partly successful. Goodhardt has argued that most families watch television sporadically. The 'inheritance factor' (or the likelihood of watching the programme that comes next) seems effective for only one programme, not the whole evening's viewing. Nor would it seem that people become loyal to a channel because they are addicts of particular series. Out of forty serials screened in the spring of one year, only 54 per cent of people who saw one episode of any serial also saw the next. Most of the people watching the second half of the story were different from those who had seen its beginning.[10]

Nevertheless, the commercial companies necessarily continue to try to maximise their audiences. The pursuit of the largest possible audience is not in itself harmful. But if it is narrowly interpreted, it may lead to schedules that are cautious, conservative and that very rarely break established patterns.

The needs of all advertisers using commercial television are not the same. Some have sought more specialised groups within the mass audience and the financial significance of this kind of advertising is growing. This is indicated by the growth of corporate advertising, in which giant companies are merely concerned to project an image of their activities rather than any specific product. In addition, there has been an increase in consumer durables and motor advertising. These categories have risen as a proportion of total television advertising expenditure from 7 per cent in 1968 to 30 per cent in 1988.[11] This has been accompanied by a fall in food, drink and household advertising directed at the mass market. Furthermore, there has been a growing tendency even among mass market-oriented advertisers towards directing their campaigns at particular segments of the market.

The impact of this shift, however, has been muted by the difficulties involved in translating the aims of marketing strategies into buying television time. There have been fashions in market research that determine how the audience is offered to the advertiser. In the 1950s and 1960s, motivational research was dominant. 'Beecham's buyers are a little more likely to strive, and are a little more neurotic', stressed an Associated Rediffusion survey in 1962. 'Compared, that is with Aspro, Anadin and Disprin buyers, however, they are noticeably more extrovert'. Increasingly, though, there was a trend towards pilot studies of particular products and towards attempts to segment target markets with a fine precision.

However, despite attempts (by Leo Burnett and the British Bureau of Market Research in particular) to develop 'psychographic' profiles of television viewers, such methods remain impressionistic. No satisfactory method has been developed that enables advertising men or women to select time slots in a way that allows them to reach the types of personalities believed to be particularly susceptible to their advertising campaigns. Consequently, commercial television companies have not been obliged to cater for particular groups (at least those defined by psychological categories) to any great extent.

Advertisers have been most interested in reaching 'light viewers', who are like the 'floating' voters in election studies. The success of a campaign may depend on the proportion of light viewers, who might not otherwise know about the product, that it can reach. For a time, light viewers were regarded as being particularly selective in their television watching habits. This was partly because a large proportion of light viewers were middle class and were believed to be discriminating.

However, this view has now been challenged. Goodhardt has suggested that light viewers tend not to watch particular types of programmes, nor do they prefer low-rating minority programmes. They tend to be as unselective as heavy viewers, but merely watch less television. Hence, support of minority programmes does not seem to be a means of reaching the light viewer. On the contrary, it appears that advertising on high-rating programmes represents the most efficient way of reaching light viewers. Another study suggests, furthermore, that the pursuit of light viewers is in itself misguided. What matters is not how many advertisements of a particular product are seen, but how many in relation to the number of advertisements of a competing product.[12] The light viewer sees less than the heavy viewer of *all* the competing products on television. It may, therefore, be better to reach him or her through other advertising media.

A further problem for the advertiser is that neither minority programmes nor particular genres of programmes can be relied on to deliver specialised audiences. Goodhardt's analysis of the housewife audience for twenty different categories of programme showed that only Westerns are positively sought out by any viewers. Westerns were the only kind of programme with a slightly higher level of 'duplication viewing' – that is, the likelihood of a viewer seeing more than one programme within this category – than could be explained by channel loyalty or overall rating figures. Most people, Goodhardt's work suggests, see further programmes of any particular genre only because they prefer one channel or because the programme has a high rating, not because they are specifically interested in its content. 'People who watched one arts programme', according to Goodhardt, 'had no more tendency to see another arts programme than to see, say, a Western or a religious programme, or a sports programme with a comparable weighting'.

This characterisation of television audiences as indiscriminate and promiscuous in their viewing habits has been challenged. Sue Stoessel argued that the results of Goodhardt's research were misleading because they aggregated behaviour over several weeks. This obscured major changes in viewing behaviour from week to week. It is only by examining these detailed changes in viewing behaviour, she suggested, that preferences for individual programmes could be revealed. An analysis of changes in viewing figures over successive weeks reveals the effects of positive choice and preference, as does an analysis that distinguishes between audience behaviour in the different regions. In London, she argued, light viewers are more heavily concentrated among the audiences of some specific programme types. There are significant groups of viewers, at least in the London area, who do choose to watch programmes because of their content.[13]

This debate is likely to continue. The apparent failure of different categories of programmes to divide audiences into conveniently specialised groups has important implications. It may reduce the potential for commercial television to create new patterns of programmes. A low-rating current affairs programme has little to offer advertisers if it does not deliver a discriminating elite (like a 'quality' national newspaper), but large numbers of heavy viewers so hypnotised that they cannot even summon the energy to switch off the ballet or Third World poverty programme offered at the margins of peak viewing times.

Indeed, the audiences for specialized programmes do not necessarily share other characteristics that would make them marketable packages for sale to advertisers. A shared interest in Westerns does not imply, for instance, a propensity to trade in a new car each year or a tendency to be a young couple setting up home for the first time. On the other hand, if Stoessel is correct, there is a market for élite and quality advertising in television, but it may not be most efficiently reached through this medium.

Indeed, insofar as advertising has promoted minority programming hitherto, it has tended to be in a form that produces groups of viewers that are marketable. Travel programmes, and those about cars and cooking, have all developed partly because they cater for audiences with a shared interest in buying certain sorts of products. The advertising for cable and satellite television depends on the development of this commodity-based 'narrowcasting'. The greater choice of channels will, it is suggested, offer advertisers more refined groups of audience interest. However, those with fewer material interests in common have been, and will continue to be, less favoured.[14]

Public regulation and the public interest

In its time, the IBA played an important role in mitigating the adverse effects of advertising on broadcasting. Nevertheless, at times, the Authority was passive. For example, it was reluctant to ensure that companies adhered to the programme policies on which they won franchises. It was difficult for the Authority to be more active in its surveillance, partly because its statutory obligations were imprecise in many areas. However, political realities limited its power more fundamentally. The commercial television lobby is highly organised and politically effective. It employs public relations officers and cultivates an able group of MPs. In addition, many newspapers are sympathetic to the commercial television lobby. Its interests are also protected by an extensive network of contacts based on the interlocking directorships linking commercial television companies to other banking and industrial organisations. In contrast, the IBA was less effectively organised as a political lobby, and its powers of supervision – which were inevitably the product of political negotiation – were consequently constrained. Finally, the IBA would be 'punished' for its interventions into schedules or programme decisions. Thus, having been required to present more balanced programming over Christmas, the companies could retaliate by showing programmes that only received very low ratings.

However, the aims of the IBA were furthered by the presence of the BBC as a 'public service' institution, committed to broad social and political objectives rather than to the maximisation of profit. There was in Britain a great convergence between public and commercial broadcasting in which the two systems influenced each other.

In addition, for much of its history, commercial television was in a strong bargaining position in relation to advertisers. ITV was able in the past to resist some advertising pressure precisely because it was in a seller's market. Companies sold advertising time in ways that reduced the pressures to maximise audiences. The high profits and monopolistic position of commercial television created an environment in which the IBA could be more effective.

Swinging sixties and sober seventies

In the 1960s and 1970s, television came of age. Since 1970, there has been a remarkable revolution not in the technology but in the content of broadcasting. In this period, television rapidly developed its own forms – in the treatment of politics, interviews, documentaries and plays – that were quite different from the earlier styles of radio or film. During the 1960s, television humour began to take the form of satirising itself – an indication of how widely the conventions of the new medium had been publicly absorbed.

This was partly a product of a more generally liberal mood, which made a wider range of possibilities available for broadcasters. After the Pilkington review of 1962, the BBC became a more adventurous organisation. At the same time, the independent television companies became more secure and more profitable. By the 1960s, moreover, television had taken over from the cinema for a mass working-class audience.

In many ways, the vast size of the television audience has posed problems for the medium. There is a continual pressure to screen programmes that will attract the largest audiences and cause offence to the smallest numbers of viewers. Yet the attempt to reach a big audience while meeting 'public service' criteria has been a creative tension.

Some commentators, such as Stuart Hood, Michael Tracey, Anthony Smith and even Sir Hugh Carleton Greene, have seen the period since the early 1970s as one of increasing caution in television. Not only did the reporting of the troubles in Northern Ireland provide many problems for the broadcasting institutions, but the BBC and ITV also became more vulnerable to government threats over a broad range of issues.

Notes

1 Sir Robert Fraser, *ITA Notes* (October 1970).
2 P. Todd, 'Scarcity of TV time!', *Campaign* (26 January 1979).
3 IBA, *IBA Annual Report* (1978).
4 R. Thomson, *Contrast: Television Quarterly* (Winter 1961), p. 107.
5 Associated Rediffusion, 'Cold and flu remedies', *Market Profiles*, 6 (1962).
6 F. Wolf, *Television Programming for News and Current Affairs* (New York, Praeger, 1972).
7 Sir Robert Fraser, *ITA Notes* (January 1970).
8 C. E. Setlow, 'TV Rating, there just might be a better way', *New York Times* (31 December 1978).
9 T. P. Barwise, A. S. C. Ehrenberg and G. J. Goodhardt, 'Audience appreciation and audience size', *Journal of the Market Research Society*, 21, 4 (October 1979), p. 269.
10 G. J. Goodhardt, A. S. C. Ehrenberg and M. A. Collins, *The Television Audience: Patterns of Viewing* (Farnborough, Saxon House, 1975).
11 Tables of advertising expenditure in *Admap*, No. 2, 1988.
12 A. Roberts and S. Prentice, 'Reaching light TV viewers', *Admap* (March 1979).
13 S. Stoessel, reply to Roberts and Price, 'The real weight of light viewers', *Admap* (June 1979), p. 277.
14 M. Johnson, 'Narrow-casting – problems and opportunities', *Admap* (June 1983).

Chapter 17

Public service under attack

The BBC had often annoyed politicians. ITV prided itself on following suit. Channel 4 did it too. Public service broadcasters were there to be impartial – not the official Opposition – not merely opposed to Governments – often to explain government. But, on occasions all of this required a steady head.

In some places and situations, for example during the conflict in Northern Ireland that raged from 1968–97, the BBC was more exposed than the commercial broadcasters because in Northern Ireland it was seen as 'British'. This meant that the protestant community thought it ought to be closer to their interests and the republicans and nationalists identified it as opposed to them. The BBC was blown up more frequently, its reporters attacked more when out on the street and it was also subject to greater pressure from the government than the commercial broadcasters. Yet much of this tension was inevitable as governments struggled with resolving a desperate conflict that spiralled dangerously close to a civil war. It forged a remarkable news and reporting machine within the BBC in Northern Ireland.

Independent Television News (ITN) (which in the 1980s was far more lean and mean than the BBC) and the BBC – competing fiercely as they did – also respected and understood each other. The independence and the glorious impartiality of the broadcasters was not a weak or a mealy mouthed compromise. Impartiality was intellectually demanding and could be exhausting to try and exercise – but it was also satisfying. It was a strong, bold and important thing. Of course it was not perfect: broadcasters often judged things wrongly, they were there to try as best as they could to tell the truth and ask hard questions.

Public service broadcasters believed that they were there to entertain and that losing the public's attention or boring them was the cardinal sin. Yet such broadcasters also believed that they were there to serve and educate a public which was capable of discrimination and reason.

Perhaps the single most important thing about public service broadcasting was its image of the audience as people who would make up their own minds when presented with proper evidence.

Broadcasters knew they had a duty to represent the nation to itself: including and hunting out less powerful or attractive voices and putting them into the national conversation. Impartiality was not a mask for absolving responsibility: views in a democracy had to find expression, holders of views deserved respect as people but they had to be challenged and, if wrong, then the public had to be clear about the facts. Broadcasters also had a duty to situate the nation in the world, exploring for better and worse our condition at home and abroad. Telling the nation uncomfortable things. Public service values were different from commercial ones. The ends were different – because for public service the audience is not consumers (though it may address their consuming interests) nor the commodities that advertisers actually buy, but citizens. Or – in the case of children – as sentient citizens-in-waiting. By the late eighties the BBC's magnificent Editorial Guidelines had become a world-class resource.[1] But writing down principles is one thing – it is their breathing life that matters.

Independence, impartiality and all that stuff

How was the editorial and political independence maintained? It was linked to impartiality, the crown jewel that kept the public informed so that they could make up their own minds and hold power to account. It was a top-down *and* a bottom-up business. It is especially hard to understand because it involved a relationship *with* the state but also involved policing the lines of independent editorial control and telling governments and the wider state what they could not have. The idea was simple – the broadcasters had a duty to set the questions they asked, the programmes they made, the news agendas they broadcast, in ways they best saw fit and in ways that best served the public interest. Did the BBC and the other public service broadcasters get it right? Not all the time. But, like democracy, independence cannot be owned and the threats take new forms as circumstances throw up new challenges. Foreign affairs were one constant source of irritation, but domestic crises even worse.

Of course the structures that guarded the values had to be supported and lived out – they too were subject to pressure. Running a delicate and important bit of the constitution takes care, attention and serious understanding – together with good will and efficiency. British institutions – like the British constitution – work in practice not on paper.[2] Although there is more and more pressure to write down the constitution (and many campaigns to suggest this will improve rights) the disconcerting verity is that a written set of values guarantee little or nothing: practice is the place where citizens live. So one uncomfortable reality for social scientists is that individuals, their character, their formation, their principles, their capacities and outlook are of real significance in institutions. Given the circumstances of the Cold War, which blew hot in the early eighties before ending with the fall of the Berlin Wall, there were large international as well as turbulent national pressures on the system.

Political independence was a top-down affair because the structure of how the broadcasters were held to account and the nature of political power at the top really mattered. Money mattered. In the case of the BBC although governments could set the level of the licence fee, and could ask the Corporation to set out in its Charter (which usually lasted about a decade – and was carefully timed as far as possible not to coincide with elections so that it was de-politicized) what ambitions it set for itself and mandate other mechanisms for holding the BBC to financial account, they had absolutely no right to set schedules of set agendas or interfere in editorial decisions. Although the finances of commercial broadcasting – making profits out of advertising – were different, nevertheless after the financial accountability was in place the regulator had the same role: to set targets and police public service delivery. Governments were similarly constrained. So the broadcasters got money and might of course make mistakes with it, commission programmes that did not work or invest in the wrong technology – and although these would be matters of public scrutiny nevertheless choosing which items went where in the news was forbidden to governments. It looks a small thing – but it is in practice one of the largest bulwarks of democracy. The free and independent choice of content in the public interest.

Independence was also a top-down affair because the BBC was founded by a Royal Charter (and so was technically above any particular government). The velum and gold lettering (and the handsome scarlet ribbon) and the Queen's signature look like flummery – but had given the Corporation a special status. Did this protect it? It is perhaps fair to say that it was one factor. Building robust institutions is like a complex, three-dimensional jigsaw. Another factor was that impartiality and independence have, at least historically, been the prized values of the civil service – so sometimes, but not always, officials have sought to protect the BBC quite simply because they appreciate and are governed by similar principles.[3] The regulators (and we will come back to their evolution) that have governed commercial television – the ITA, the IBA, and more recently The Office of Communications (Ofcom) – have also been independent.

Then there are ministers. Protecting independent institutions that affect social and political life is also a governmental task. Broadcasting policy issues were until 1992 'held' in the Home Office. Douglas Hurd, a Conservative home secretary who did much to protect broadcasting from the worst ideas of Mrs Thatcher, said that 'in the bran-tub of the Home Office the broadcasters were the occasionally fascinating and quite often troublesome parcel that when it came to the top often meant an unpleasant row'.[4] In many ways being a small part of a wide ranging and jumbled collection of responsibilities in a very large office of state helped: it meant that the ministers in charge of broadcasting were big beasts in the Cabinet jungle (like Hurd) who was more than willing to go into battle with the Prime Minister. So although *bad* government policy was a threat *good* policy protected it.

Later, responsibility was moved to a new Department of Culture, Media and Sport (DCMS; originally called 'Heritage' which had the effect of making culture an issue of the past not the present or future). The ministers in this have been more junior – but the department itself perhaps more expert. The canniness and principles of both the civil service and ministers, and the immediate communication problems they encounter, change. But there are real problems: digital policy as it evolved (or failed to keep pace in any meaningful way with developments) was also held in the DCMS. It was, observed one critic, 'Like running world football from an amateur Under-11 club in Cleethorpes'. Something central to all government and commerce, all private life and national delivery was held in a minor department of state with junior ministers.

Public service communications depends on well made governmental policy. It does not in this way survive outside the political system although at times it has to duck and weave through badly made or badly intentioned policy. However, its duty is to reflect on it. This is another fragment of the top-down view of what builds independence.

Governing

The BBC's ultimate authority was the BBC Governors: they 'were' the BBC and their Chair was the key appointment. In theory if a government attacked the BBC improperly they could all resign and that would stop any political aggression in its tracks. They never have resigned but they have considered doing so on a few, but important, occasions. Fashions changed about how governors were to be chosen and whether they were representative (and of what). For most of their existence they did balance left and right-wingers, men and women, people from the regions and from the central metropolitan classes. There was usually a Scottish, Welsh and Northern Irish Governor – who were to bring the particular flavour of their nations to the table. The general idea was to get people of capacity and common sense with a wider experience. Sometimes they represented culture (like the poet Roy Fuller) or good works and politics (like Peggy Jay) or journalism (like William Rees-Mogg) or business (like Stuart Young) or a particular community, or a grasp of world affairs (like Edward Forde). Someone like Richard Eyre – who had run the National Theatre – would also bring a wider variety of contemporary values to the room. The important thing about the Governors was that they were neither BBC editors or censors but they were there to set a vision, and to oversee the service. They were also there to stand up to governments if they were being unreasonable. This was often a fraught business.

The Chair of the Governors was key. It was their shrewd appraisal of what the Corporation needed, the Director Generals they appointed and values and issues that the BBC needed to be concerned with that maintained independence and growth. When the Chair and the Director General worked as a team – challenging each other – but supportive – astringent when needed – canny and proper: then the BBC flourished.

The Chair is appointed separately and usually the Corporation tried to negotiate a suitable candidate. Although there is an independent procedure in practice it is such an important appointment that Prime Ministers want some say. Harold Wilson annoyed the BBC when he appointed Charles Hill to be Chair (Hill had been the 'radio doctor' during the war and then Chair of ITV so it was felt an insulting imposition). Hill could have been a good appointment but was heavy-handed. Then Mrs Thatcher, as Education Minister, who believed he was too confrontational and secured the appointment of Michael Swan to replace him. This was a wise appointment. Nevertheless as Mrs Thatcher believed that the Board ought not 'represent' interests but be there to 'do' things, so she appointed some people who were positively hostile to the Corporation (like William Rees-Mogg). This was alarming, damaging, hard to manage. But not necessarily terminal.

However, independence was also a bottom-up affair because every decision, every day, about every item of every kind of programme involved a question – was this balanced, fair and was it in some ineffable way 'public service'? This was most obvious in news, documentaries and current affairs, but was important in comedy and drama. From the mandarins commissioning programmes that gave shape and flavour to the schedules – through the producers and directors making programmes – through the news editors and directors – down to the journalists and researchers – the choices had to be impartial and proper. Any specific programme would seek out alternative views but independence had to be exercised across the schedules. Nevertheless, the most junior person making a decision about who to invite onto a programme to discuss an important topical event was also exercising editorial independence (and could compromise it by ill-judged decisions). There was a separate issue that became critical by the eighties – how the broadcasters managed the ways in which they challenged authorities.

In news rooms the broadcasting values of fairness were also embodied in balance and if it was working a restless self-scrutiny. In an ideologically committed newspaper the question would be 'Does this story fit our agenda?' In a public service news room it ought to have been 'Does this story matter and are we covering it fairly?' At first television news had been the domain of ex-newspaper journalists, but by the eighties ways of putting more background into stories were developing and a different generation of broadcasting journalists were emerging. Indeed, 'current affairs' programmes – like *Panorama* or *The World in Action* – had originally developed to carry the foreign news; that took time in the pre-satellite era to arrive as it had to be flown in. They had developed a more argumentative and complex style. Yet as the technology changed 'news' got further access to foreign stories. The clear division between the two genres began to dissolve and this caused political problems. Nevertheless, editors could be fierce and tensions could be high in public service news rooms – but the battles had an additional set of values. Of course no public service broadcaster always made the 'correct' judgement. But they ought not make decisions because they would please or mollify politicians.

As John Tusa, Director of the World Service, said, 'the proper job of people at the top was to keep politics and the important people away from interfering in the work of the journalists'.[5] Meanwhile, Baquer Moin – a young Iranian refugee working in the World Service, broadcasting into Iran – said, 'The shared BBC editorial guidelines were a wall of protection for journalists. If you met them then you had done your job. It was other people's job to manage the consequences'.[6]

Independence and impartiality were also bottom-up affairs because they depended on initiative, creativity, surprise, having a challenging view of the issues of the moment. It depended on the public (who often complained and disagreed) over all seeing their lives and voices reflected (in comedy and discussion and drama).

These are grand principles – but they came under the most intense pressure (although ultimately adapted, survived and flourished) in one of the most challenging periods of the BBC's existence – the 1970s and 1980s. Indeed, by the end of the time in the 1990 Broadcasting Act, it was the ITV (and especially the regulator the IBA) which were effectively de-constructed while legislation made exemptions from 'public service' commitments for a new enterprise: Sky TV. This weakening of public service commitments was damaging to the BBC and to the offer to the public. The legislation was to herald the transformation of football into a great global enterprise – as Sky invested in it. It was also to eventually take football away from the working class, local, roots. It was a cultural loss that was global. The mating of football and television would create an economic behemoth. While many would say that it created economic value and made the game immensely competitive, it also made the rewards irrational, the game more subject to corruption, made it a vehicle for betting, and stripped local fans of a meaningful relationship to local teams. Another loss perhaps from globalization.

1979: Ideology takes command

The 1970s were difficult for the nation. There was rocketing inflation and widespread industrial unrest as the real value of wages collapsed. In 1976 the country had to – humiliatingly – go to the International Monetary Fund for a loan. It was argued that the pictures from the Vietnam War had shifted American public support for the war – (and armies all over the world controlled media access ever after) but much less discussed is the impact of consequences of images of domestic news stories. These were, as one BBC audience report suggested during the 'winter of discontent' of 1979, when for the first time badly paid public sector workers, especially rubbish-collectors, struck 'shocking for most respondents. They said they were ashamed of the state the country seemed to be in'.[7] The images of a polity out of control were re-enforced on screens all over the world by images of conflagration in Northern Ireland and large and increasingly tense demonstrations

The utopian left-wing movements of the sixties hardened into narrower, conspiratorial organisations; meanwhile there was the emergence of both extreme right-wing popular movements and the rumour of right wing coups. Indeed, in 1975 *Panorama* made a breezily sinister programme exploring what a coup might look like, presented by Michael Cockerell.

Yet through all of this period in many ways public service broadcasters were at the height of their reach, commanding vast national audiences. Their influence was enhanced because these audiences watched programmes collectively. The commercial television sector was also an unusual industry for the period (when industry was struggling) that was making huge profits and so was flush with money to spend on programmes – which brilliant public service obligations forced it to do. Yet in 1979, when a new Conservative Government was elected with a new ideological conservative leader – Mrs Thatcher – for the first time ever there seemed as if there was a challenge to the very existence of public service broadcasting and especially the BBC.

Social revolution?

The notion of public-service broadcasting had developed from the high-minded dirigisme of Lord Reith, but management structures had not developed with it, and in the 1970s, it had hardly changed since the Second World War. It is a commonplace of twentieth-century social history that world war has been the agent, or at least the catalyst, of major change. What has been less noticed is the extent to which wartime forms of organisation – born of the unusual conditions and needs of the moment – created structural fossils in important areas of policy, surviving immutably in peacetime, but with no particular relevance to the post-war world.

Broadcasting and education provide interesting examples of this process. Both were drastically reorganised at the end of the Second World War. In each case, the most striking feature of the reforms was the imposition of a 'tripartite' division, based on a supposed hierarchy of talent. The changes represented a sharp move away from a view of society as an aggregate of individuals and towards an official concept of particular groups with separate needs.

Reith's programme policy depended on an assumption of cultural homogeneity: not that everybody was the same, but that culture was single and undifferentiated. He had been determined to avoid the mediocrity that he believed would accompany freedom of choice. 'It is occasionally indicated to us that we are apparently setting out to give the public what we think they need and not what they want', he wrote in 1924. '[B]ut few know what they want, and very few what they need'. Advisory panels of 'experts' were established to lay down canons of taste in music and to adjudicate correct pronunciation. Their purpose was to give authority to cultural values, not to represent listeners' interests.

Reith believed that the function of broadcasting was primarily educational: its purpose was to train 'character'. According to this view, your class of origin and what you learnt mattered less than how you lived and how you learnt. This principle was the basis for his programming policy. Men might be unequal, but they could all try equally. Hence the Corporation defended a policy of mixed programming, in which talks, light music, chamber music, quizzes, vaudeville and plays succeeded each other. The service was not planned to provide appropriate listening for different interests or to allow people to avoid what was serious in favour of the trivial. Reith was determined that the audience should encounter everything that broadcasting could offer.

Mixed programming determined many aspects of the Corporation's policy between the wars. In 1934, a BBC administrator wrote that 'the most advantageous single extension or change in programme policy'[8] would be to stop broadcasting programmes at regular times and so break the audience's conservative listening habits. This was part of the Corporation's campaign against what was contemptuously known as the 'tap' listener 'who wants to have one or more very light programmes available at all hours between breakfast and bedtime'.[9] 'The BBC definitely aims at having an interval of four or five minutes between programmes', the 1932 *Yearbook* claimed, and 'it is obviously irritating for a listener who, switching on his set to hear, say, the news, finds himself listening to the last minute of an opera or vaudeville turn'. Listening was a serious business.

The BBC's belief in cultural homogeneity was a useful weapon in the defence of its broadcasting monopoly, particularly against the commercial wireless exchanges. These retransmitted a selection of BBC and continental programmes to simple home 'speakers', improving reception and making it cheaper. The number of such stations had risen from 34 in 1929 to 343 by 1935. The BBC argued, in the 1931 *Handbook*, that the relay system contains within it forces which, uncontrolled, might be disruptive of the spirit and intention of the BBC charter. The people in charge of wireless exchanges have power, by replacing selected items of the Corporation's programmes with transmission from abroad, to alter entirely the general drift of the BBC's programme policy.

The BBC was defending its own position and what it assumed was a generally recognisable set of cultural values. Reith's objection to audience research was also based on the principle of cultural homogeneity. He did not want to know popular preference, because of the danger that programme organisers would pander to it.

The BBC had a distinctive model of the listener. 'Broadcasting is not mass projection, though it seems to be so, it is an individual intimate business', wrote Hilda Matheson, the first head of the Talks Department in the *Sociological Review* (no. 3, 1935). The personal relationship between listener and programme was elevated into a principle. The class and tastes of groups of listeners were irrelevant. Any variety in programmes was justified by the changing moods of the average listener and not by reference to the interests of different groups. In this way, 'entertainment' had its appropriate place: it was meant to provide periods of relaxation in the broadcasting diet of the Reithian 'average' listener.

The Reithian approach was paralleled during the 1920s and 1930s by similarly 'unitary' assumptions in state education. The content of state education between the wars was common to all schools: children merely received more or less of it. At the top of the ladder, children had access to 'the whole world of learning', while at the bottom, they had 'the hems of learning only'.[10] The curriculum was governed by notions of a 'general liberal education', a direct legacy of Matthew Arnold's philosophy of education.

State education, like state broadcasting, was (in theory) designed to enable the hard-working and to be able to develop those faculties that were regarded as common to all. In education there was also emphasis on the development of 'character', a nebulous and undefined moral concept, taken undiluted from the 'muscular Christian' ethos of leadership training that governed public schools. Until Cyril Burt's ideas on scientific intelligence testing were accepted during the 1940s and 1950s, the ideology of 'character' pervaded educational policy as well as broadcasting.

In many ways, of course, education and broadcasting are not comparable: for one thing, state education hardly grew at all during the 1930s, while broadcasting developed very quickly. For another, broadcasting was centrally controlled with a national monopoly, while education was administered locally and alongside (rather than in competition with) a prestigious private sector. Nevertheless, broadcasting and schooling as communicators of accepted values have enough in common for the similarity to be striking. The similarities in the organisational changes, which occurred as a result of the impulse for reform created by the Second World War, are more remarkable still.

Reform, the war and education

The needs of war radically altered education and broadcasting. The Education Act of 1944 recommended that schools be reorganised 'firstly to provide opportunities for a special cast of mind to manifest itself . . . indeed to develop specialised interests and aptitudes'.[11] The Act was not the result of radical political pressure, but of official initiatives within the Board of Education itself. In 1938, the Spens Report had suggested that 'it is becoming more and more evident that a simple liberal education for all is impractical'. It drew a distinction between those children 'who work with hands, work with tongue, or work with pen' and suggested that 'one child differs from another far more than is generally supposed'. The Norwood Report and the 1944 Act went further and distinguished between three kinds of children. First, the child 'who is interested in learning for its own sake, who is interested in causes and who can grasp an argument' and 'is sensitive . . . he is interested in the relatedness of related things . . . he will have some capacity to enjoy from an aesthetic point of view'.

A child of this kind was to go to a grammar school, the distinct feature of which 'lies in the intellectual ideal which it upholds'. This category of school was to retain the values that had been intended for all schools before the war and was to produce the new professional and managerial élite.

The second kind of child 'often has an uncanny insight into the intricacies of mechanisms, whereas the subtleties of language construction are too delicate for him. To justify itself to his mind, knowledge must be capable of immediate application'. These children would 'go into industry' and were to attend the new technical schools (which never in fact emerged).

The third kind of child 'may have much ability but it will be in the realm of facts. He is interested in things as they are . . . he must have immediate return for his effort'. These residual children were to attend the new secondary modern schools. These schools were to be separate but equal and were, according to the report (incredibly) to have 'parity of prestige'. It was implicit in the Norwood Report and the Act that there were children who could think, children who could do and the rest.

More strikingly, the proportions of children that it was projected would attend each kind of school closely approximated to Burt's 'normal curve' of the distribution of intelligence within the population. Indeed, in an article devoted to 'the psychology of listeners', Burt wrote: 'Politically no doubt all men are born equal. Mentally however, as the results of surveys incontestably show, the range of individual differences is far wider than had ever been suspected'.[12]

Reform, the war and the BBC

The war also revolutionised the BBC. During the war, Reith's 'cultural unity' was abandoned. After a visit to the troops in France, Ogilvie, Reith's successor as Director General, had come back convinced that the morale of the forces would be improved by knowing that their families at home were listening to the same programmes with them, but also that the Corporation's whole programming would have to change. Ian Hay, a BBC comptroller, had written in 1939, 'We shall need a lot of entertainment before this business is over'. It was recognised that the new forces service would have to be quite different from a 'watered-down version of our peacetime programmes', for 'if we give them serious music, long plays, or peacetime programme talks they will not listen'.[13] The lure of the continental stations could not be ignored during the war and programme changes would inevitably have more long-term consequences. An official wrote ominously, 'We shall not be able to return to our Sunday policy when the war ends'.

More light music, comedy, crooning and jazz were justified not only by the immediacy of wartime demands, but also, crucially, by a new model of the psychology of the listener. The first step argued that the service had to be changed because troops were listening to it communally in the mess or in camps. Then it was suggested that different programmes were appropriate to different occupations. Very quickly the audience research department was trying to establish which kinds of music had the best effect on factory production.

Modern wars change the status of entertainment: leisure is seen as an aspect of 'public morale'. This was particularly true in Britain after 1940. Nevertheless, the Corporation was anxious not to be accused of producing 'programmes fit for morons', and the *Listener* printed many letters on this subject. 'I think you will find this army more highbrow than you suppose', wrote one officer (15 February 1941).

What had first been seen as a temporary expedient became a permanent feature when the General Forces Programme was changed to the Light Programme in 1946. Grace Wyndham Goldie commented on the consequences of this innovation for the internal structure of the Corporation. 'It is not only that this is lighter, more gay, fresher in its approach; but for good or evil it is more closely related to the box office than any broadcasting in England has ever been before' (*Listener*, 26 December 1940). Competition was introduced between various parts of the Corporation. It meant the recognition of distinct groups whose tastes the BBC was obliged to identify rather than to change. This internal reform was of more fundamental importance than the competition later offered by commercial television. An editorial in the *Listener* claimed that 'the position is that the Forces Programme is carefully planned and not a casual proliferation of high jinks for low brows' (13 March 1941). Yet providing the public with what it wanted had become central to the Corporation's plans.

The introduction of a 'Light' Programme inevitably had implications for the Home Service. As early as 1940, the Home Service Board had decided that the 'barometer of listeners' preferences' should be a regular item on its agenda. However, the Home Service also broadcast the main news bulletins, and came to be seen as the part of the BBC that was most concerned with 'citizenship, family and home'.

The final and most revealing innovation was the introduction of the Third Programme. An internal memorandum in 1944 had suggested that the BBC should provide three competing services. Programme A 'should be of the highest possible cultural level, devoted to artistic endeavour, serious documentary, educational broadcasting, and the deeper investigation of the news, corresponding in outlook to a *Times* of the air'. Programme B, 'the real home programme of the people of the United Kingdom', would 'give talks which would inform the whole democracy rather than an already informed section, and be generally so designed that it will steadily, but imperceptibly, raise the standard of taste, entertainment, outlook and citizenship'.[14] Programme C was to divert and needed little detailing.

The Third Programme was a survival of the Reithian ethic of 'mixed' programming. It emphasised that it should be judged by the whole programming of the service rather than individual items.

The daily broadcasting schedules rush by the listener like the scenery past the windows of an express train . . . The Third Programme from the beginning has arrived at a standard which has brought it into conflict with this ephemeral characteristic of broadcasting.[15]

Elsewhere, Harold Nicolson wrote, 'Every cultural pill is coated with sugar; and an item which it is felt might be unpalatable is tendered with a tone of apology, or with the horrid cheeriness of the scoutmaster, the padre, or the matron'. The Third regarded broadcasting as an art.

The 1950 White Paper on the future of broadcasting argued that 'listeners will now normally have a wider choice of contrasting programmes', while Nicolson, who had been involved in the creation of the Third, was at pains to point out that 'at no time, I am glad to say, did we entertain the doctrine that the listening public should be segregated between sheep or goats'. Sir William Haley, the Director General who had originally thought of the Third, put the classification clearly in a lecture given in 1948:

Before the war the system was to confront [the listener] with pendulum-like leaps. The devotees of [Irving] Berlin were suddenly confronted with Bach . . . Since the war we have been feeling our way along a more indirect approach. It rests on the conception of the community as a broadly based cultural pyramid, slowly aspiring upwards.

This concept resembled the hierarchy of ability now being pioneered in education.

Progress or rationalisation?

By the end of the war, British broadcasting and education had been radically reformed. Is it a coincidence that the two most important vehicles of national culture were reorganized almost simultaneously and in each case along very similar lines?

Listeners and children are not obviously analogous. Yet what is striking is the similarity in the proportions of people assigned, quite independently, by education and broadcasting authorities to three categories. It is as though in the natural order of things there were three types of children and three types of listeners reflecting a three-way divide in society as a whole. It was expected that the population would divide as follows:[16]

Grammar schools 5%	Third Programme 6%
Technical schools 15%	Home Service 20%
Modern schools 80%	Light Programme 74%

In both cases, the figures were based more on a hunch than on statistics, and in both cases, they proved wholly unrealistic. In education, the technical schools barely got off the ground and completely failed to produce the technical administrators that had been expected; instead, the grammar school section expanded. The estimate of the Third Programme audience of serious listeners was wildly optimistic; it never attracted more than 1 per cent to 2 per cent of listeners. Neither projection was officially justified in terms of social class; yet in both cases what seems to have occurred is the imposition on social policy of official assumptions based on military and administrative experience.

The war had one undeniable impact in delivering a substantial and permanent increase in the power and scope of government. Whitehall's view of society and human nature, essentially meritocratic and hierarchical, pervaded policies which in normal times would have been fought out in the political arena. The reforms in both broadcasting and education reflected an approach to organisation that had more to do with a civil service conception of the world as itself writ large, than with the reality of the world as it existed. Thus, in Whitehall there were administrative, executive and clerical grades (and in the services there were officers, NCOs and privates). Officials found their own tripartite system natural and efficient. In creating new structures for the public, they assumed a similar pattern of talent and need. In broadcasting, as in education, reforms contained a contradiction. On the one hand, they were progressive in that they sought to cater for the whole society; but on the other, they reinforced class divisions by giving new life to old hierarchical assumptions.

And the management structure that emerged survived into the 1970s, even if the social upheaval of the 1960s had tested the stratified deference of traditional hierarchies to destruction. The notion of public service broadcasting had survived, even if altered from Olympian Reithian ideals. So while the Light Programme may have been replaced by Radio 2 in 1967, and at the same time a new station, Radio 1, delivered pop music, both still adhered to public service traditions, and ran news, religious programming, and campaigns on subjects such as AIDS and teenage pregnancies. But the corporate structure that surrounded them would have been identifiable to a BBC executive from the 1950s – and would face the chill wind of change from the incoming Conservative government in 1979, like so much of the British industrial and institutional landscape that had not kept up with the times.

The prime minister Margaret Thatcher would demand fundamental reform that threatened the existence of the BBC, but first had to preside over the extension of public service broadcasting with the introduction of Channel 4 in 1982, whose inception had been decided in principle before her election in 1979.

Channel 4, minorities and money

The idea behind the creation of this new channel was a product of the tensions identified during television's most creative and expansionist years. However, by the time the station opened in 1982, there had been a change not only in the general economic climate but also, more damagingly, in the conditions of competition for television audiences.

Channel 4 'publishes' programmes made by independent production companies. It does not make any programmes of its own, although it does commission them. Originally, it was financed by the existing commercial companies who supplied much of its material. As it did not sell its own advertising time, it was somewhat removed from the direct pressures experienced by the rest of the commercial sector. The 1990 Broadcasting Act changed this: the channel was now to be made more vulnerable to advertisers' interests. However, it is still obliged to screen programmes for the various 'minority' interests that are not well served elsewhere in the television system.

The minority-based rationale of Channel 4 had a number of origins. Perhaps the most important was the experience of even the most distinguished and 'marketable' producers and directors, that it was impossible to work, in Britain, outside the BBC or ITV companies.[15] Those who wanted to make programmes that did not conveniently fit into the patterns of viewing developed by the duopoly, or those who simply wanted a greater control over their own material, found it difficult to raise the necessary finance or find buyers for what they made. It was argued that there evidently were audiences within the mass of viewers with more distinctive tastes and needs, but the existing channels allowed these consumers little opportunity to demonstrate their preferences. A new pattern of differently organised production companies, liberated from the limitations of the ITV or BBC systems, would be able to find and develop these more specialised audiences. Therefore, any innovation in the television service ought to make it possible for 'independent' producers to explore the interests of these minorities.

It was also strongly argued that television had failed to reflect Britain's contemporary cultural diversity. Reformers emphasised the needs of emerging Black, Asian and minority ethnic communities, as well as those of the young and the old, for programmes that dealt with their concerns and ways of life. Any new service, it was suggested, should produce material for these social and ethnic groups.

Finally, some market researchers believed that the blunt instrument of television advertising could, by the 1980s, be refined. A new channel could offer programme incentives that attracted discriminating 'minorities' of selective television viewers and could sell them the things they had particular interests in. For the first time, television would be able to deliver higher concentrations of the more affluent consumers that advertisers wanted.

The logic of Channel 4 looked appealingly neat. It would offer greater freedom of choice, and serve minorities neglected elsewhere. Unfortunately, the minorities that producers, social reformers and advertisers were interested in were somewhat different.

Channel 4 represents an important (and perhaps the last) reinterpretation of the public service role of broadcasting. In this version, the freedom of creative individuals to risk making the programmes they want to make is seen as the guarantor of public good. It was a Labour government that decided to back the new channel (although a Conservative one presided over its birth). Labour support was based on a feeling that the political consensus developed by the existing broadcasting services was too restrictive. Consequently, the channel was given the opportunity to create new conventions for dealing with controversial and political issues. It is not obliged to balance views within a programme, but only over the whole schedule and over time. It can, therefore, broadcast more clearly partisan material.

However, the channel's capacity to innovate depends on the politics of money. The only ultimate defence Channel 4 has for its style and programmes is their ability to attract advertising revenue. By the 1980s, the Conservative government was using the success of Channel 4 to attack public service broadcasting by demanding that greater numbers of programmes should be produced by 'independent' companies. Yet Channel 4's innovations had been completely dependent on the development of public service ideals.

In the late 1980s, both the BBC and ITV companies were obliged to take an increasing proportion of their programmes from the 'independent' sector; by 1993, this was expected to account for 25 per cent of their output. This has led to the emergence of some culturally important and commercially successful companies – and of innovative programmes. 'The Media Show', the astutely topical series on Stalin and many others were made by production companies outside the duopoly. However, whether such companies are actually independent, except in the formal sense, is dubious. A survey by the London Business School showed that they were all financially precarious, with low profit margins.[16] People set up independent television companies because they want to make programmes – not because they want to make money. The study also showed how completely dependent these companies were on the patronage of the established channels. The new satellite companies were, as yet, hardly interested in their quality products.

The limitations of commercial broadcasting are largely the result of the economic pressures to which it is exposed. That British commercial television has been in some ways superior to others is due to the public service traditions and institutions that have so far determined its development. Nevertheless, the implications of a comment by Sidney Bernstein, the television industrialist, should always be borne in mind. 'Commercial television is a very unusual business', he said, 'you don't necessarily make more money if you provide a better product'.

Yet the market and the audience for television programmes is altering dramatically under the impact of a whole series of technological changes. Whether the advantage of increased variety will be enough to offset the dilution of resources remains to be seen. Indeed, this period may yet be regarded, in television terms, as a lost golden age.

Disorder

Omnibus was bold. It put challenging programmes about the arts onto BBC1, the home of the mass audience and the most brutal and competitive channel, from 1967 to 2003. In doing so, it was offering the great British public (not the niche, already culture consuming, more educated public) the very best of British and foreign music and writing, painting and sculpture: because on BBC1 it would find large and unexpected audiences. It specialized in concentrating a programme on a subject or even a thing: Van Gogh's Sunflowers or The Trumpet. It interrogated artists and musicians – Lucian Freud gave his first (and almost unique) interview to Jake Auerbach for *Omnibus*. It also elevated contemporary culture and approached modern cultural icons equally; there was an early programme on David Bowie, another on The Thriller. Humphrey Burton, who started the programme, brought in what he called 'a boisterous and bolshie crowd'[17] of young directors and producers. Burton was a distinguished scholar – and this omnivorous and scrupulous taste forged great alliances. Burton had the most fruitful collaborative relationship with Leonard Bernstein – the whirlwind of American classical music who shared a passion for what music could do.[18]

Yet despite this wonderful creative impetus, the BBC was by the late 1970s in trouble. There was rampant inflation that damaged broadcasting because it was a skills heavy industry. Most of its costs were in wages and the costs of production were at the top of the inflationary spiral. Broadcasting unions became militant – and those that wielded most power were those, like the electricians and scene shifters, who were not close to the creative process. Then governments bore down on the BBC as a public example. Meanwhile, ITV was raking in very large profits – and was quite prepared to damage the BBC by paying larger wages. But as well as this internal upheaval, there was a loud, continuous, not well-handled set of political irritants.

Notes

1 www.bbc.co.uk/editorialguidelines/
2 P. Hennessy, *The Hidden Wiring: Unearthing the British Constitution* (Phoenix, 1996).
3 J. Mair and R. Keeble (eds.), *Is the BBC in Crisis?* (Abramis, 2014).
4 Author's interview with Douglas Hurd.
5 Author's interview with John Tusa.
6 Author's interview with Baqer Moin.
7 BBC Written Archive, WAC, R23.1 Audience Research Report, V11, November 1979.
8 Filson Young to Dawney, BBC Internal Memorandum, 'Programme policy', *BBC Written Archives* (3 March 1934).
9 'Programme revision committee', *BBC Written Archives* (June 1934).
10 Board of Education, *Inspectors' Report*, Cmnd 4068, 1932, 12, para. 7.

11 *The Nation's Schools: Their Plans and Purposes*, Ministry of Education Pamphlet 1 (London, HMSO, 1945).
12 Sir Cyril Burt, 'The psychology of listeners', *BBC Quarterly*, IV, 1 (April 1949), p. 7.
13 Ryan to Nicolson, BBC Internal Memorandum, *BBC Written Archives* (17 January 1940).
14 'Programme development', BBC Internal Memorandum, *BBC Written Archives* (14 February 1944).
15 See S. Lambert, Channel 4 (London, British Film Institute, 1982).
16 *Independent Television Production: Finance and Dependency*, London Business School Report (December 1989).
17 Author's interviews with Humphrey Burton and Lesley Megahey.
18 See BBC clips of Bernstein rehearsing for *Omnibus*. Available at: www.youtube.com/watch?v=NlmSqKBPuQ0.

Chapter 18

Broadcasting roller-coaster

For most of the BBC's existence, the principle of 'public service' embodied in the 1926 Charter had not been the special preserve of the Corporation. Indeed, the idea that some organisations should operate for the public good and at the public expense was shared by all political parties, as well as the leaders of private industry and commerce, and ordinary voters. In the 1980s, however, the idea was strongly challenged for the first time. For broadcasters who had taken 'public service' for granted, life suddenly became uncomfortable. One problem was the issue of political independence. Institutions like the BBC, whose *raison d'être* included the principle of impartiality, are never at ease with very ideological governments. Their distress becomes acute when there is only one party in office for a protracted period. In the case of public service broadcasting, it needs the threat of potential opposition power as a sabre to rattle warningly at governments. Yet, as the Conservative Party won one election after another from 1979 onwards, British politics became increasingly one-party rule. Indeed, the emergence of a coherent, highly ideological project for the transformation of British politics and society after 1982 put the BBC even more under threat.

The new Thatcherite project was highly individualistic: it argued that public interest could only be secured by maximising the capacity of individuals to choose; and that government should seek to abandon controls, not exercise them. 'Deregulating', however, often had an ironic effect: a policy supposed to get government off people's backs often turned out, in practice, to be highly centralizing. Frequently, fiercely *dirigiste* measures of deregulation became instruments for delegitimizing, eradicating and diminishing any institution or organisation that had alternative views. In addition, the project could be a politicizing one. The fashionable neo-liberal creed often ignored cultural constraints: like scientific socialism in a different era, it was over-rational.

'The New Right', as John Gray points out, 'failed to perceive the dependence of individualistic civil society on a dwindling but real patrimony of common ideas, beliefs and values'. In other words, the possibility of extreme individualism depended on the cultural, educational structures that formed active, independently-minded individuals. Public service broadcasting had been founded precisely to shore up and improve the common store of ideas, values and knowledge. Thus, the story of public service broadcasting in the 1980s and 1990s had a far wider resonance than the question of whether people watch one chat show or another. It is a story of whether a plurality of voices can survive – and at what cost – in monolithic times.

Of course, the BBC and all responsible broadcasters always are, always have been, and always will be, worried about how to deal with politicians. The problem is that recently, handling politicians has become more important than making programmes, thinking of new programmes, relating creatively to audiences, or expressing what is going on within the nation. On the other hand, only if broadcasters abandon trying to provide a comprehensive and objective schedule, and opt instead for entertainment, will the pressures cease. In turn, all politicians seek to influence, cajole, bully, manipulate and prejudice, if they can, how broadcasters deal with their affairs. Broadcasting is far too important to them for seemly good manners. Indeed, consideration of how the media will react is playing a larger part in political calculation than before. Policy, not just its presentation, is increasingly tuned to media reaction – despite, or perhaps because of, the declining capacity of media news organisations to interpret and process sophisticated news. In a sense, nobbling the media, however you do it, is just politics.

However, what marked out the 1980s was that political pressure assumed a new form. For the very first time since British broadcasting started in 1926, the issue became not merely what the BBC did, but whether it would survive at all. Indeed, to some members of the Conservative government, the BBC as an institution, and public service as an ideal, began to be seen as key obstacles to its attempt to revolutionize how Britain was run, and its ways of thinking. Public service was seen as the inefficient self-serving camouflage of groups who wanted to protect their own interests from the correcting force of competition. Mrs Thatcher put the case inimitably in her memoirs: 'Broadcasting was one of those areas – the professions, such as teaching, medicine and the law were others – in which special pleading by powerful interest groups was disguised as high minded commitment to some common good'.[1]

Regarding the BBC as an irritatingly arrogant, cosily protected Establishment dinosaur, Thatcherites marked it down for eradication in the radical right cultural revolution. At first, Mrs Thatcher merely sought to harness two quite contradictory pressures to cure the BBC of the tendencies she objected to. The first consisted of the self-appointed moral regulators, such as Mrs Whitehouse's Viewers' and Listeners' Association, with vociferous support in the middlebrow press, who argued that television was to blame for a decline in morals in the country. Public service broadcasters, the Prime Minister put it, rephrasing the words of Adam Smith, 'were claiming the rights of poetry, but providing us with a push pin'. The second consisted of the commercial interests of her most influential supporters in the press, particularly those of Rupert Murdoch (whose name and organisation, significantly, received no mention in her memoirs). Murdoch was interested in the profits that could be made if British television was 'deregulated'. This would make it easier for his present or future chances to succeed. As his deal with Tony Blair and the Labour Party showed in the run-up to the 1997 election, Murdoch liked to extract maximum commercial interest from his newspapers' political power. Mrs Thatcher, however, argued that increasing competition would lead to an improvement, 'raising' standards of taste and decency. This was an odd position, because everywhere else unregulated competition had tabloidized, coarsened and vulgarized broadcasting. Indeed, the Premiere showed a touching faith in Murdoch's capacity to raise standards – his previous contribution to halting moral decline having been the relaunch of the *Sun*.

Mrs Thatcher never saw much television, except when she was on it. However, her husband, who watched a lot, was widely reported to have given her daily resumés of its iniquities. But broadcasting happens to be almost the only industry which politicians ever see much of at work, as they slip in and out of studios. During Mrs Thatcher's premiership, College Green, a windswept triangle of grass with good shots of the Houses of Parliament behind it, virtually became part of the British, as yet unwritten constitution. College Green, and Millbank next to it, where the television stations broadcast much of their political reporting, increasingly took over from Parliament itself as the most critical area of public life, especially at times of crisis, the place where politicians hunt for attention, and journalists hunt for someone with an angle. Mrs Thatcher's observation of the television industry at work, 'too many men, too much waste!' fuelled her conviction that television embodied the hydra-headed enemy of British laxity: archaic union practices that preserved unnecessary jobs, and smug management. In contrast, print journalism caused the Conservative government few problems in the 1980s. In her first term of office, the Prime Minister gave knighthoods to the editors of the *Sun*, *Sunday Express* and *Daily Mail*. In return, these and other newspapers softened their criticism of the government and concentrated their attacks on its enemies – a novel interpretation of the duties of the Fourth Estate. One minister asked Mrs Thatcher about her favourable press, and she replied guilelessly, 'That's because I've been so kind to them'.[2] She did not think broadcasters treated her fairly, nor did she set out to be nice to them.

However, there were many other aspects of broadcasting that increased tension between broadcasters and politicians during the 1980s. The Prime Minister was angered by the sceptical ways in which some broadcasters dealt with her, and she believed they were promoting an out-of-date view of the contemporary world. Bernard Ingham, her abrasive No. 10 Press Secretary, called them (the broadcasters) – the Dimblebys and Elsteins – the unelected princelings of broadcasting. Less personally, but more provocatively, in practice, public service broadcasting was not merely any one organisation – it was the product of a regulated market. In the regulated market the worst economic pressures to produce the cheapest programmes for the most viewers can be counterbalanced by the requirements to be impartial, to inform, to entertain and to educate, to match the audience share of the competition, and to secure licences to broadcast. Yet the guiding idea of the 1980s, and one that has survived Mrs Thatcher's departure, was that any market regulation impeded the proper outcome of market choice. The more sophisticated interpretation of choice, according to which regulation provides a wider variety of programmes for a wider variety of audiences, was anathema to governments for whom deregulation, privatization and the efficacy of market choice were the main instruments of reform and which had become, by the 1990s, ends in themselves. Thus the very basis of public service broadcasting made it peculiarly vulnerable to government attention.

However, it was inevitably politics that most inflamed the relationship. Sweeping government denunciations of the BBC's left-wing bias, and of alleged misreporting, and allegations against journalists, became routine. Individual presenters, television executives, journalists, particular items and whole strands of coverage were targeted. The cumulative effects of such intimidation were profound. 'If the television of the western world uses its freedom continually to show all that is worst in our society', said Mrs Thatcher after the reporting of the riots of 1981, 'how can the uncommitted judge?'[3] As Hugo Young, in his biography of Mrs Thatcher, *One of Us*, argued: 'The less formal, but no less purposeful attacks, led by Mrs. Thatcher herself, on the BBC and other television broadcasters who threatened to loosen ministers' control over the agenda of the nation were ferocious'.

The Prime Minister's determination to reform broadcasting was given an added twist by the political challenges her government faced. First, she regarded much of the BBC's reporting of the Falklands War (particularly the use, on news broadcasts, of the term 'the British troops', rather than 'our troops') as almost treasonable. She was incensed by a 1983 election phone-in which included tough questions by members of the public – as she wrote 'put up, not properly edited out' – about the conduct of the war, especially the sinking of the *Belgrano* (an Argentinian cruiser, sunk, controversially, within the exclusion zone around the Falklands while it was apparently attempting to leave the area). Above all there was the reporting of Northern Ireland.

Brian Wenham, an influential BBC programme maker and bureaucrat, contemplating the evidence about one programme, *Real Lives*, which caused an early prime-ministerial explosion, later observed that 'It was usually Ireland, it was usually the BBC, it was usually a row bigger, with more heads rolling, than you'd ever think possible'.[4] Eddie Mirzeoff, a senior BBC producer, talked about the pervasive self-censorship to which the rows led: 'the cost was always in programmes we did not make, ideas we dare not have'.

Certainly, the government's reaction to the BBC's handling of Northern Ireland was a major factor in the growing sense of panic within the BBC during the 1980s. It was, in part, a battle about unspecified constitutional rights. The BBC claimed, on the basis of its obligation to be impartial and to inform, the right to include Sinn Fein, the Protestant extremists and sometimes the IRA, as voices that needed to be heard, while the government claimed the political right to exclude from the BBC voices which they thought had to change in order to win a right to a voice. The government always interpreted exposure as endorsement. 'Publicity', said Mrs Thatcher famously, 'is the oxygen of terrorism'.

Mrs Thatcher often gave the impression that broadcasters existed to support her, correct, views. If they gave air time to other points of view they were, in effect, opposing her. As she had been elected and they had not, her views were legitimate, those of others were not. Impartiality – even over as intractable and complex an issue as Northern Ireland – was seen as a mischievous disguise for disloyalty. Time and again, broadcasters offended her over their handling of the issue: indeed, they were bound to. Mrs Thatcher's feelings on this issue need exploring, for they ran high. That they did so was understandable. Shortly after she was elected, the MP Airey Neave, a close friend and confidant since Mrs Thatcher had been an aspiring, unmarried young lawyer in the 1940s, was blown up by the Irish National Liberation Army (INLA), a splinter faction of the IRA. The BBC screened an interview with an INLA representative, who triumphantly boasted of the achievement. Many found the interview offensive, but revealing. Mrs Thatcher, mistakenly, saw it as support for INLA views. Later, in 1984, she and her husband survived an IRA bomb in the hotel in Brighton where she was staying for the Conservative Party conference. Perhaps not surprisingly, an intolerance of argument over Northern Ireland ossified into a narrow-minded zeal. Many observed that the bombing had profoundly changed her.

Thereafter, almost any television reporting in this area seemed to add to her fury. A number of incidents were interpreted as further evidence of subversion. There was the initial refusal of the BBC to hand over its film of the terrible mob lynching of two plain-clothes policemen; there were interviews with members of the IRA; there were attempts to include IRA and Protestant community political representatives in studio discussions; there were conflicts over a series of programmes – Real Lives, A Question of Ulster, Death on the Rock – which increased tension between broadcasters and politicians. After the Prime Minister had seen, and been enraged by, Real Lives, a programme which showed the 'everyday' lives and families of a Protestant and a Sinn Fein extremist, the Broadcasting Ban was imposed. This meant that when members of terrorist groups appeared on television, their voices could not be heard and actors had to read their words. This ban did nothing to reduce public interest in paramilitary personalities. It did, however, constitute a humiliation to the public service broadcasters, as it was little more than a visible badge of government power. It also meant that television executives did not make programmes about Northern Ireland if they could help it. However, the long-running Ulster saga did not go away, and its existence meant that government hostility to public service broadcasting continued to be underpinned by the Prime Minister's fierce passion about the issue.

In addition to this, the war on the 'complacent' public service tradition was ardently supported by a range of newspapers. The *News of the World* called the BBC 'The Boring Bonkers Corporation', the *Mail* said it was '(utterly) Biased (morally) Bankrupt and (politically) Corrupt'. The lead, however, in BBC bashing was provided by the *Sun*, *The Times* and the *Sunday Times*, shock troops of Thatcherism in its Maoist phase. The *Sun* described the BBC on one day as being 'Boring Old Auntie', and on the very next day accused it of 'Sleaze and Sluttery'. Broadcasting was attacked for loose morals, extravagance, fifth columnism and offending against public taste. *The Times*, for the first time since the abdication crisis, ran editorials on three consecutive days to the same theme: the inadequacy of the BBC. However, as newspapers, unlike MPs, are not required to declare an interest, none of these scions of Murdoch's News International felt called upon to mention that their proprietor happened to have growing ambitions for his satellite television stations. In every sphere, from the domestic British to the international market, the BBC and its World Service, and more generally the constraints of public service programming, with its emphasis on programme diversity and impartiality, stood in the way of News International. And indeed, anyone who stood in the way of the party most likely to deliver policies friendly to News International was also an enemy. As William Shawcross shows in his biography, Rupert Murdoch has little or no interest in news or programming, and while he routinely 'asset strips' news rooms, he has seldom invested in media content. His interest in politics tended to reflect the needs of his businesses: beyond that he was apolitical. Thus the News International campaigns against the existing broadcasting arrangements increased in parallel with the Corporation's interest in satellite. The *Sun*'s shrill demand that 'Aunty Must Go' was a pragmatic piece of commercial lobbying.

As if this fetid brew of political and economic hostility were not enough to seal the fate of the BBC, technological and social developments in satellite and cable broadcasting would have meant that any administration would have had to consider how to handle changes to what had been a relatively stable competition which had developed between ITV and the BBC over thirty years. Whatever happened, the 'duopoly' of public service broadcasters would have been bound to face considerable competitive challenge for audiences by the end of the decade. The adjustment, the possibilities, the role of 'public service' advantages in these changes were not inevitable. Different policies would have different outcomes, but a period of rapid and potentially difficult change was unavoidable.

Moreover, the era of public service broadcasting also seemed to have passed throughout the world. In many countries it appeared that 'public service' channels, of varying strengths and success, were being obliged to take on advertising, faced rapidly declining audience shares and suffered a loss of authority. Even in sympathetic political climates, like those of Scandinavia and the old Commonwealth, public service broadcasters found it difficult to maintain distinctive broadcasting values. The sense of a regulated diet of programmes, even the sense of a scheduled progression of programmes and predictable audiences, looked as if it might fray or even disappear once the public had a larger choice of channels to choose from, and more things to do with their television sets.

All over the world in the 1980s, public service channels were being deregulated, and as a result saw their audiences collapse. Some even began to suggest that in any case the heyday of television had passed. The very peculiar capacity of the medium to assemble, address and touch the emotions of huge national audiences simultaneously seemed to be disappearing. Television had become one component of a huge entertainment industry that now included music, films, videos and the rapidly expanding computer market. Commentators began to suggest that television had lost its dominating cultural role. However, most people continued to watch television regularly. It was perhaps more accurate to say it was the power of the television corporations, the programmes and schedules which were changing.

Thus the alliance of political and commercial interests, arraigned against public service broadcasting in the mid-1980s, looked overwhelming. The radical ideas of right-wing think-tanks such as the Institute of Economic Affairs and the Adam Smith Institute, criticized for their extremism and impracticability in the early part of the decade, seemed positively mainstream and cautious later. In particular, they advocated the break-up of the BBC, the superiority of advertising revenue over licensing revenue, and the benefit of consumer 'choice' through increased channel availability. They argued that regulation was unnecessary, and praised the role of auctions in allocating commercial broadcasting licences. It was not just that the political climate had changed; everything that had previously been a source of protection for public service broadcasting suddenly made it vulnerable. The BBC was, as the decade progressed, under sustained commercial and political threat as never before.

Government attacks

How did the government go about 'dealing with the problem of the BBC' – the issue that Mrs Thatcher was so determined to address? The first line of attack was political. Part of the 'consensus' that Mrs Thatcher's administration set out to change was the idea that appointments to public bodies, such as the BBC's Board of Governors, should be more or less bipartisan. Prime ministers and home secretaries had, of course, liked to exercise choice in these appointments in the past. Thus, Harold Wilson had appointed the ITV Chairman, Charles Hill, as BBC Chairman in 1971 to bring the Corporation to heel. However, even Hill could not be regarded as a party political placement; he had been a Conservative, not a Labour minister.

The Conservative government believed that such delicacy on such a point was unnecessary, and indeed inefficient. If the BBC was to be encouraged to be friendly towards the government's project, you needed to be sure of the loyalty of those who ran it. Hence, during the 1980s, appointments to the BBC's Board of Governors became increasingly politicized. Qualified but unsympathetic candidates were not appointed, while ill-qualified ones were – a process of committee management which indeed applied to many other public bodies as well. Hugo Young, in his biography of Mrs Thatcher, quotes a colleague: 'Margaret usually asked "Is he one of us?" before approving an appointment'. It was the appointment of sympathetic chairmen of the Governors that gave the government its real power over the BBC. The first Chairman appointed by the new administration was Stuart Young, who happened to be the brother of a Conservative government minister. However, he showed signs of going native on the BBC. His successor, Marmaduke Hussey, was made of sterner stuff. Hussey, an ebullient Second World War veteran, had no background in broadcasting, had come straight from being the Chairman of Times Newspapers, where his confrontation with the unions had helped to change Fleet Street but had also led to the papers being closed for a year. One of his qualifications may have been that he had worked for Murdoch and, in a sense, was unlikely therefore to cause Murdoch problems. A charming, forceful man, he saw his chairmanship as a full-time job to 'sort out the BBC'. Over the next decade, he oversaw all the major changes in the Corporation, brutally dismissed one Director General, shabbily pushed aside the next, and appointed the third, John Birt, without even advertising the job or considering other candidates. Coming from newspapers, he treated the BBC, one critic remarked, 'rather as if he had owned it'. He was treated with a fearful deference by the Corporation until the end of his reign.

Hussey's influence was supposedly balanced by that of his deputy, Lord Joel Barnet, a former Labour Treasury minister who also chose to work at the BBC on a full-time basis. Barnet, however, accepted much of the Hussey diagnosis, and once even acknowledged that he did not, in practice, represent any difference in view from Hussey. Meanwhile, the Board of Governors, one critic commented, came to represent 'an unfortunate combination of low calibre and high prejudice'.

Of course, the 'packing' of boards, and in turn the administration of increasingly large tracts of contemporary life by committees and quangos rather than by elected government, had been an article of faith of the Conservative reforms. One argument was that there should be a move from 'representative' boards of directors, chosen because, however loosely, they stood for specific interests (in the BBC this might mean the regions, or writers, or women or educators) to so-called 'corporate boards', where individuals were selected on their merits. Well managed, this could be a useful development. In practice, however, it was taken to mean that members should be chosen for their adherence to an agenda. Indeed, against a background of mounting unease about the impact of some of these ideas on the quality of services, in 1994 the Nolan Committee on Standards in Public Life was asked to address the problem of whether the perceived bias in public appointments was a media-induced mirage – or a real issue. Nolan concluded that there was clear evidence of a political bias in those who had been appointed: '[I]ndividuals who are Conservative Party supporters, or whose companies donate to the Conservative Party, are more likely to be found on appointed boards, than those who support Labour or the Liberal Democrats'.[5] The report also recommended that when 'individuals had political interests they ought always to be declared'. The Committee recommended that an independent commissioner should oversee all such appointments. Nolan's 'public service' ethic incorporated the values of selflessness, integrity, objectivity, accountability, openness, honesty and leadership. In the case of the BBC there was evidence of direct interference in appointments to the Board of Governors and, perhaps more importantly than Nolan's virtuous criteria, individuals were nearly always selected for their compliance, and never for their independence.

With the Chairmanship in a safe pair of hands, and a politically packed Board of Governors, the government had a Trojan horse to take its policies right to the centre of the Corporation. There was a dramatic shift of power inside the BBC, with the Chairmen and the Board of Governors extending their power and interfering over an increasingly wide area. The Board of Governors is, constitutionally, the BBC, and as such has an immense authority within the Corporation: to have a Board that was hostile to everything the Corporation had done was deeply demoralizing. The first casualty was the independent-minded representative of an Olympian BBC tradition and elegant draughtsman of memoranda, the Director General, Alisdair Milne. In his memoirs Milne laid down his battle credits: a succession of brilliant, innovative programmes, whose object had been first, in *Tonight*, a hugely successful news magazine, to get on a level of conversation with viewers, and famously, in *TW3*, the pioneering satire show, 'to address, late on a Saturday night, people who are more aware of being persons and more aware of being citizens than at any other time of the week'. He had defined the job of Director General as being to engineer a harmonious relationship with the Chairman and, above all, 'to provide a climate of confidence in which programme makers can do their best work'.[6] Milne was certainly not able to achieve harmony with Hussey, nor was he able to control a sense of mounting hysteria in the BBC. Personality always plays a part in appointments and dismissals, and Milne and Hussey did not get on, partly for the good reason that Hussey regarded Milne as part of 'the problem' he had been sent in to sort out. Milne was peremptorily sacked. The first he knew of his departure was when, in a lunch break between meetings, Patricia Hodgson, the BBC's Secretary ('carved from deep frozen Oil of Ulay', according to one wit) used his Christian name – not the usual DG – in asking him to see Hussey, who disposed of him and told him to leave the building, in which he had worked for over thirty years, by teatime. Milne was succeeded as Director General by Michael Checkland – an accountant who had never made a programme but who had nevertheless worked for the BBC for many years, and who was known for his prudent capacity to save money, and more interestingly, to save it to spend wisely on important projects. Checkland was finally replaced by John Birt, first as Deputy Director General, and then as his replacement. Mrs Thatcher's memoirs icily assert that 'the appointment of Duke Hussey, and later of John Birt, as Director General represented an improvement in every respect'. At last she apparently had her men in place. During the late 1980s and 1990s it was widely believed that the Governors of the BBC were working behind the scenes to make programme makers not so much yield to government pressure as make it unnecessary. In many ways this was part of the new managerialism: managers and boards were not merely required to take hard decisions, but there was a macho pride to be taken in making these decisions as unpleasant as possible. In part, of course, this was merely an attempt to browbeat groups of people with values, or indeed the social capital of respect, into compliance. It was part of a far wider plan to limit the authority of professionals. However, it was also, in itself, an expression of the new orthodoxy: to manage properly, it had to hurt.

The second line of Conservative attack on the BBC was, of course, the licence fee. When there are periods of 'natural' revenue expansion, as when television ownership was increasing, or there was a switch to colour licences, when the BBC's funds increase because of a change in demand for its services, the Corporation has greater independence. There was no such natural increase in the 1980s, and television production costs were rising faster than general inflation. Thus, simply by not raising the licence fee, the government could impose savage cuts on the Corporation. Most prime ministers have probably warned the BBC's Director Generals that the licence fee would be cut. Most have not, in the end, meant it. During the 1980s and 1990s, the fee was eroded by a government that was intent on changing the nature of the BBC. Having abandoned its original ambition simply to abolish the Corporation, the government determined to exert its power, not only by interfering with the licence fee, but also by changing expectations, and radically altering the ecology of broadcasting institutions within which the BBC works. The aim was to change the kind of institution that the BBC aspired to be. Death by beheading was to be replaced by death by salami cuts. There had been no doubt, among politicians on both sides and in pressure groups, that the object of the 1990 Broadcasting Act had been intended to be the destruction of the BBC. The Peacock Report had not, much to Mrs Thatcher's chagrin, put advertisements on the BBC screens. By the late 1980s, as the next recession hit, the last thing any commercial station, or indeed even any advertiser, wanted was more broadcast advertising time; by the great recession of 2009–10 commercial television was in considerable difficulty as advertising revenue leaked away to other media. Ironically, the loss of public service restraints had probably made it less, not more, attractive to audiences as well. Nevertheless, having been thwarted once, 'this time the feeling was', commented one politician, 'we'll get them'. The likelihood that the Corporation would disappear seemed high.

Survival or sea-change?

Yet the BBC, despite the most determined onslaught it has ever faced, survived. The BBC was understandably reluctant to point out that it had won. It would not have been tactful. Yet, as Anthony Smith, one architect of Channel 4, remarked afterwards: 'It was a miracle. All the fire was deflected from the BBC on to ITV – the opposition got it'. And when the Broadcasting Act was finally passed it was indeed commercial television – the partner in a public service duopoly – that undoubtedly took the brunt of assault. Lord Thomson – a previous Chairman of the IBA – ruefully pointed out: 'When the BBC needed help, we gave it. But they kept their head down when we were under attack'. The campaign had been started by Brian Wenham's masterly organisation of the BBC's evidence to the Peacock Committee. It developed through Extending Choice (that characteristic product of managerialism, the BBC's mission statement), through Producer Choice (the introduction of internal markets) and a continued process of management reorganisation. The BBC ducked and weaved in every way it could, using reform both as an expedient political face saver, and sometimes as a real agent of necessary change. Thus, despite the strong pro-government bias on the Board of Governors (who seemed to dislike much of what the Corporation did, and who beguilingly claimed to be 'often too busy actually to watch television'), despite the animus of a very directed Prime Minister, and despite the pressure on revenue, the BBC survived. In this light, Hussey, Birt and all the rest are not villains but, on the contrary, heroes, doing what had to be done, or doing what had to be seen to be done, and radically propelling the BBC along the road to a real future.

But what BBC, for what purposes, and at what cost, survived? Most popular accounts of the reforms emphasize their costs and consequences. In two powerfully argued and sharply contrasting books, Chris Horrie and S. Clarke's *Fear and Loathing at the BBC*, and Steve Barnett and Andrew Curry's *The Battle for the BBC*,[7] it is suggested that at the very least the process of reform in the BBC was awkward, ruthless, inefficient, unhappy and self-destructive – and that, in the end, the Corporation only survived by voluntarily and lavishly doing to itself almost everything a hostile government wanted. Indeed, the debate is similar to one that recently raged among art historians, discussing the fate of much great medieval painting and sculpture during the Reformation, when previously sacred images were seen as idolatrous and attacked. It has been suggested that many great works were saved from the image breakers by being *slightly* defaced. A nose or an eye was sacrificed, say some, to save the whole. Others argue that, on the contrary, the sense and purpose of the whole was lost by the defacement and that afterwards the images simply decayed and fell apart. Is that what has happened at the BBC?

Another version of this account is that the quite horrible means by which the BBC secured change, the ruthless exclusion of alternative voices in the process, the application of management and production targets, the process by which, far from becoming less bureaucratic it has become (like many other institutions), it was asserted, far more top heavy, were all instituted not to make better programmes, but to deal with politics. Dissent, argument, creativity, such an account suggests, are the source of vigorous and creative programmes. Most people who have left the BBC now have little good to say for it. But then, on the other hand, their accounts may be biased.

Managers and the media

There is, first of all, no doubt that the organisation needed an overhaul. A British Steel manager invited to talk to the BBC in the early 1980s said that he came away convinced that something had to change. The Corporation was over-bureaucratic, too large, too cumbersome. It did not, he added, feel like a modern, slim, confident organisation.[8] Management was the big 1980s idea, and institutions, businesses and services throughout the nation were adjured to 'manage' themselves better.

However, the BBC had, in the past, been rather good at 'management'; indeed, when the Corporation was first set up, 'public service management' had itself been a huge innovation and was much praised and copied as a valuable new way of running an enterprise. Indeed, Ian MacIntyre in his biography points out that the first Director General, Reith, came to the BBC precisely as a manager, one with the highly relevant experience acquired on active service in the First World War, where his job had been to improve the quality of the hugely increased productivity of mass-produced American armaments factories. The BBC had grown fast, and gone on growing, because it was always an organisation that took management seriously. On the other hand, 'management' within the Corporation was originally carefully separated from 'programmes'. 'Good Management', wrote Reith, 'is what is necessary to provide the conditions in which good programmes – far more important – can be made'.

During the early post-Second World War period, the BBC's response, both to staff shortages and to production problems, had been increasingly to assimilate wider aspects of the production process into the organisation. The BBC had grown. Of course, the trend had been present since the BBC began, when, in order to have sound engineers or to build adequate transmitters, the Corporation had found that it had to train them itself: its problems were too specialized for the general level of technical training provided by the market.

However, with the emergence of television, the process accelerated. The BBC instigated make-up and make-up training, set-building, lighting, costume design, studio design, studio space and more and more engineering within the Corporation as it found it needed them. In so doing, the BBC both established production standards and became the main provider of training for the entire broadcasting industry. Although it could be argued that this had been an important infrastructure for broadcasting in Britain and that the industry was a vital one, nevertheless, as money got tighter, it became harder for the BBC to continue to be such a generous patron. The sense of an over-staffed, over-protected, over-bureaucratic corporation made the BBC vulnerable to calls for reform. But something had to change; it had become increasingly difficult to innovate – resources and money were used efficiently, but inflexibly.

However, one of the difficulties in analysing the impact of 1980s manage-rialism on the purpose and function of institutions like the BBC is that quite separate problems and solutions were deliberately confused in the project 'to manage better'. The first aim was to make sure that resources were used effi-ciently: this was often genuinely urgent. However, the second aim was to reduce dissent within organisations, while the third was to demonstrate that organisations were willing to be 'managed' better. In a rite of passage, it became a ritual of the Thatcherite cultural revolution that organisations like the BBC should admit their guilt, and perform acts of contrition and expia-tion before finally emerging, to use the fashionable managerial jargon, 're-tooled'. It was not merely that the BBC required direction and change, but that it was necessary that these should be seen to be difficult and that the end result should be a 'new' BBC.

The real problem, of course, is how you measure improvement in manage-ment in an organisation like the BBC. As John Harvey-Jones, the former Chairman of ICI and a prominent management 'guru' of the 1980s, pointed out, organisations have to change continually, and better management should mean greater scope for entrepreneurial innovation. But who are the 'entrepre-neurs' in a broadcasting empire – the managers or the programme makers? Moreover, the BBC, like any large and old organisation, has been perpetually reorganised ever since it was founded. In the early 1970s it had already under-gone four major organisational changes in forty years. In the beginning, 'administration' had been firmly separated from programme making and out-put, and indeed the separation had become 'an article of faith', remaining as a convenient fiction as late as the 1970s. When Tom Burns talked to the top levels of the BBC hierarchy in the late 1960s for his book, several complained that 'Managers were seen by everyone else as lepers'. Managers and adminis-tration were still far less important than programmes. It was still the roll-call of good, innovative, successful programmes that really ambitious broadcast-ing careers were made from. Burns reported one respondent as saying, 'Everybody in the Corporation, I suspect, sneakingly wants to get nearer and nearer to programmes, and I think, too, that one is always frightened as an administrator of stopping something'.[9] For the ambitious and driven, the pull, the gravitas in broadcasting was through making programmes, and remained so until the late 1980s. Yet the reality was changing. By then, the people who made programmes were far less important than the people who did the accounting for programmes.

Running a modern broadcasting organisation almost inevitably develops a tension between industrialization and craft production. A great deal of television is in effect mass produced, falling into a narrow range of categories – sit-coms, game shows, chat shows, soap operas and so on. There are also other, more idiosyncratic kinds of programme. However, there is always pressure to reduce costs and standardize production. As we have seen, this became more acute during the 1980s. Nevertheless, within these constraints the challenge is to produce novel, intriguing, stimulating, fun, serious, enlightening programmes. Such creative products will always in part be a product of a culture, ways of thinking, a rewards system – what actually gets you on, and ultimately the kinds of personality that survive best in a system. Thus the question of creativity is never simply one of resources – although television is costly, in terms of both money and organisational needs. Nevertheless, the difference between good and indifferent programmes is one of giving permission and receiving encouragement.

However, one mounting pressure as the 1980s moved on was a sense not so much of permanent revolution as of permanent hysteria within the BBC. One young current affairs journalist, just down from Oxford, described it as 'a very volatile panicky place', where crises were always breaking out. Birt and Hussey calmed everything down.[10]

The BBC entered the process of being reformed with a naturally articulate and vociferous staff. The journalist recalled meetings in the BBC canteen at Lime Grove, an old labyrinthine building where news and current events were produced, ripe with corners for conspiracies, 'where producers screamed and management cowered'. Indeed, John Birt's initiation into the Lime Grove experience, confronting angry producers assembled to hear his plans, is said to have rocked him by its unrestrained hostility. He returned from the meeting determined to change the culture, no doubt to change the people and, while he was about it, to pull down the building – and to call in the management consultants.

Managers and management

The BBC called in four different firms of management consultants to oversee its reform during the late 1980s and 1990s. Such advice is not cheap. Such people do not make programmes. What do management consultants do? Ideally, they enable an organisation to do what it does better, or they may help it to change what it does. This may be all very desirable and, as we have seen, the BBC may have needed something like it. However, management consultants tend, on the whole, to accentuate the role of managers. In a widget industry, managers, not workers, may be the people who create new opportunities for the firm. This is only partly true in broadcasting, where the people who make things make the opportunities. There was a radical shift in power within the BBC: what had been a producers' programme-led hierarchy became a management-led power structure.

Titles and salaries illustrate this trend. Thus, when an outstanding head of radio drama resigned, his job was replaced by that of a drama business unit manager. The change in title reflected a change in priorities, and a shift in the kinds of talents apparently required. Another indicator was that the salaries paid to the exhausting front-line current events and news personnel, who in a real sense are the BBC's 'face to the world', between 1980 and 1995 fell from having been equal to those of comparable managers to being less than one third. Inevitably, management-led organisations recruit people who want to be managers.

The consultants, apart from harassing liberal-minded producers into line for the government, were also widely believed to be there less 'to make the organisation run more efficiently', and more to increase the Director General's control over unruly troops. Certainly, one of the things management consultants can do is describe in apparently uncontestable, neutral and pseudo-technocratic terms, the apparently inevitable necessity of doing what those who call on them want. Yet, in order to meet the government's onslaught, greater discipline was necessary.

Management became increasingly fashionable and important during the 1980s. Many believed that better management was an instrument which could reform ailing British institutions and habits. Those in apparently radical think-tanks – such as Demos – endorsed the desirability of wholesale changes to the organisation of institutions, and a steady stream of political pamphlets discussed efficiency, and how to measure outcomes. Indeed, for those organisations that were wealthy enough to measure what their impact was, it was a useful tool. 'Modernization' became synonymous with change brought in from outside an organisation. The emphasis in whole rafts of social thinking moved from what kind of services were desirable to how they were to be delivered. Under this there was also – as is usual – a political change in emphasis. The 'new managerialism' substituted a legitimate concern for the efficiency of the process of production for an older and perhaps also legitimate question about distribution.

One of the problems in assessing the effect of these ideas was that there was an element of genuine utopianism in some of the thinking. Thus Charles Handy, a humane and liberal management guru, produced a series of ideas for the reform of organisations which he saw as both desirable for management and liberating for individuals. Later he was to ruefully acknowledge that their outcome – in practice – was often disastrous.

Some new principles of management were enthusiastically applied to enterprises everywhere. The first was the 'death of organisation'. Handy had written that 'the telephone makes it possible for people to work together without being in the same place'.[11] He went on to consider the impact of communication changes and said that organisations, institutions, offices, careers, were all fast becoming irrelevant. It was not merely that commerce would become leaner – a new, radical division of labour should be developed.

You could be liberated from the inflexible institution because its work would change more rapidly. Businesses should become increasingly 'federal', buying in and commissioning specialized work as they needed it: 'Life in more and more organisations is going to resemble a consultancy firm', he claimed. Handy's optimistic utopian vision of a new social order, with individuals freed from jobs and companies, and in charge of their own work destiny as never before, included a claim that in future hierarchies would be old hat, organisations would be 'flat'; workers, he claimed, would:

> have a right to do their own things in their own way as long as it is in the common interest, that people need to be well informed, well intentioned and well educated in order to interpret their common interest.

Handy's ideas suited the BBC well. The Corporation faced savage financial cuts, and the consequences of the 1990 Broadcasting Act – that it eventually commission 25 per cent of its programmes from outside the Corporation in the independent producers' sector. A plan for forcing through some drastic reorganisation was needed and the new managerialism appeared to be one way forward. Such reform was also, no doubt, seductive, because, despite Handy's vision, delayering, federalist, re-tooled organisation also happened to provide the upper of the hierarchies that survived with hugely increased powers.

W hy did the BBC bother with all the management hoo-ha, and not just cut bits off? The benign interpretation is that management wanted to make sure it got rid of the right – that is, the worst – bits. The more sceptical view is that it wanted to legitimate what it did. The least attractive view is that, although there were endless meetings, guidelines, mission statements and flow charts, it had no clear vision of what a streamlined 'better' BBC would be like – except that it should be more docile and smaller; but perhaps it was trying to find out.

The process began slowly but gathered speed. Indeed, when Mrs Thatcher was replaced by decent Mr Major, the BBC juggernaut of reform went right on rolling. Part of the incentive for reform came from the need to cut production costs and to use plant and people more efficiently. This led to the 'TV Resource Study', which started from the assumption that regional BBC plant was under used and should be 'reorganised', i.e. that some of it should be shut down and that expensive London plant ought to be better used or disposed of. More to the point, perhaps, the management consultants suggested that 'plant', television studios and the resources and people should be utilised on a twenty-four hour-a-day, seven-day-a-week schedule. This plan, jauntily entitled 'The Twenty Four Hour Rolling News Day', claimed to be about a 'new concept in news readiness'. In fact, one critic claimed that its primary target was the rewriting of staff contracts. In the past, long hours had meant overtime payment; in the future they meant just that, long hours. The structural supports now seen as 'irrelevant' or surplus were lopped wholesale.

However, the problem was whether the way in which cuts were made was rational or even cost-effective. Expensive new Manchester studios were 'disposed' of before they even opened. Elstree Studios, tatty but fertile in programmes, were deemed to have the wrong image, and sold. But the 'TV Resource Study' was the place where the real motor of BBC reforms was invented. At first it was called the 'internal market', but a public relations alarm bell rang, and a special brainstorming session was set up to think of something better. It came up with 'Producers' Choice'.

This title, instantly recognizable as another example of 'Newspeak', sounded positive, programme-centred, something you'd like to have. It did not sound like lots of meetings, lots of invoices and the 'wholesale transformation of perfectly good programme makers into second rate accountants', which is how one producer described it.[12]

'Producers' Choice' was intended, like the other artificial internal markets of the 1990s, to make costs transparent. In the past, not only had there been a good deal of cross-subsidization within budgets, but also many of the resources used in making programmes – studios, training and so on – had been paid for centrally. The new, stern philosophy in public affairs argued that this led to waste and extravagance because the true costs of using any resource were disguised. 'Producers' Choice' was supposed to make the real costs of making programmes apparent. However, it was also intended as a mechanism that would discreetly dispose of parts of the organisation. So producers, having been allocated budgets, had to buy in the services they needed as cheaply as they could. That the real purpose of the exercise was to shut departments was made clear by the simple diktat that, while producers were encouraged to look outside the BBC for services, production departments were prohibited from trying to sell their services beyond the Corporation.

The trouble with artificially constructed internal markets – in all institutions – is that while they may drive down the costs of the central activity of the institution (replacing hips, teaching students, making programmes), they also require much of their resources to be spent on accounting and on monitoring financial systems. They redistribute resources away from the central activity. Producers (like teachers, nurses, doctors and so on) spent more of their time than was congenial, possibly a great deal more than was efficient, filling in forms and sending out invoices. Power usually flows from where the money is used – and so there was a further shift in power within the organisation. In the early 1990s the staff magazine and the national press were full of BBC job advertisements: 'financial assistants', 'accountants', 'financial controllers' were much in demand. Many of the management consultants brought in from outside jumped ship and became BBC managers instead, not programme makers. Nevertheless, the reforms did deliver far greater resources back to programme makers in the end.

The second part of the agenda was to make the BBC more orderly. Was this a necessity in order to bring the Corporation into line with Conservative ideology so that it might survive, or did it, as some have claimed, bring about a collapse of traditional BBC values? John Harvey-Jones, the great industrialist, in his gospel of management *Making It Happen*, comments:

> our forebears have given our companies a tradition of open speaking and respect for differences of opinion which is, in my view, the most precious single inheritance we have. There is no way in which a vision of the future can be developed among a group of people unless they have a very high degree of toleration, and indeed enthusiasm for argument.[13]

Toleration was not a word that many felt characterized discussions in the BBC in the 1990s.

A guiding tenet of the new managerialism was that long-term careers within organisations are bad: not so much for people, but for organisations. Anyone who actually stays with an organisation must be a dullard. People were supposed to hop from job to job. Indeed, there is now almost a cult of the 'outsider'. In the late 1960s, when Tom Burns was writing his book, most people within the BBC could think of their own long-term interests and those of the Corporation together. Although competition with ITV, and then Channel 4, gave individuals real freedom and flexibility, nevertheless they could focus ambition, groom experience, have expectations and calculate. During the 1990s, the BBC became a rich source of baroque fables about the impact of 'managerialism' on an articulate and competitive group of people and, moreover, a group well able to mobilize publicity on their own behalf. The conflict between the managers and staff often represented a battle about words. Language and the problems of its use had always taken a concrete form in broadcasting. Indeed, the early history of the medium was of the slow, cautious licensing of spoken ad-libbed speech, as opposed to scripted language. The use of scripts had been both a means of social and political control, ensuring that dangerous, untoward or offensive things did not get said, and also a way of refining and attending to the impact of speech. Only very gradually were people's own voices and words permitted on air, legitimizing new points of view in public debate. Today, there is more unscripted broadcasting than ever. Nevertheless, the meaning and impact of language remains a vital and delicate part of broadcasting culture.

Words matter to journalists, and are what their work depends upon. As BBC journalists are not yet at the tabloid end of the market, they use words to describe, identify and discriminate.

Yet, one of the consequences of the new managerialism is the use of words for obfuscation rather than clarification. The use of words to disguise intention rather than to reveal it. It seemed to many that everything had to be translated into a new vocabulary: long-winded, tedious, pompous, technocratic. Journalists loathed the corrosion of words. A disgruntled wit called the new language 'Birtspeak'. It was easy to assume it had a purpose.

The management revolution at the BBC, as everywhere else, meant interminable meetings. It also created many examples of that newly fashionable ritual, the management 'away day'. This was accompanied by enforced '*joie d'esprit*' involving strange settings (once in a marquee, disconcertingly like a big top) which disguised the reality that real jobs, futures, the nature of the BBC, were all on the line. What gave rise to bitter jokes was the perverse distance between the ostensible intent and the manner of these events – the supposed 'open' discussion, 'exchange of views', jolly team-spirit building, and what was seen to be their real purpose, the identification and exclusion of opponents. Indeed, what journalists felt they reacted to was the undermining of language as a means of describing. Nevertheless, attention reality was refocused. If the first part of the project had been to save the Corporation from the government, the second was to re-engineer the BBC from within.

History and managers

Another aspect of 1980s managerialism was a contempt for history, and a cavalier rewriting of it. Of course, this may, in part, be necessary. The world changes: concern for how things were done may be an impediment to how they must now be done. On the other hand, institutions only really function at their best if people working in them want to do more rather than less than is necessary. Tradition and history – values even – and a pride in what has been done well can be invaluable stimulants to ambition. Institutions also have to remember their history so that they do not repeat their mistakes. The past can be a resource for the future, not just a hindrance to it.

Yet, within the BBC, 'looking back' was seen as being a characteristic of the 'old guard', the people who had run the Corporation in the inefficient past. To say why things had been done as they had, or to query the logic of innovation (for example, of spending a lot of time and money attempting to create a 'price' for studio time, when there was in no real sense a market for it) was to 'mark you down as a doomed, old-speak person', recalled one veteran. 'The past was a very dangerous place to mention', maintained another.[14]

But perhaps all the hostility to change was just part of a recurring romanticism about the past? Or perhaps the myth of a golden history is necessary to organisations like the BBC, where, unlike many industries, people ought not to be consensus minded. Being difficult (up to a point) may indeed be a very important part of good journalism.

Indeed, an organisation like the BBC that has endured, and developed, always at the very edge of rapidly evolving technology, has a peculiar relationship with its own past. It is made all the more strange by the way in which it can *use* its past. Old programmes are continually reshown, readapted. The 'past' of the BBC is more visible than that of most firms, and the BBC's involvement in its audience's past is also complex. People remember events and themselves through what they saw or heard broadcast. Elaborating conservative tradition has been one way of handling dramatic technological change. Indeed, the fatigued sense that there has recently been too much change, which seems to characterize people working for the BBC, is a product not only of change – which the Corporation has always had to do – but of having to produce rationales as well as action.

The BBC shared this sense of 'too much change' with several other institutions. Indeed, those working in the Health Service, for example, just like those in the BBC, naturally have to deal with constant change because treatment is altering all the time. On the other hand, the core activity of other institutions, like education, that also complain of 'too much change' remains remarkably constant over time. But perhaps what all these services share is that they provide goods which cannot easily and perhaps ought not to be assessed by profitability. 'Good' broadcasting and 'good' education are not easy to measure – though we may feel quite secure about identifying them when we see them.

Nevertheless, the past's superiority is a recurring theme in the BBC's self- perception. When the Corporation moved out of its original, cramped offices on Savoy Hill in 1926, one broadcaster asserted that the old offices 'had been quite the most pleasant club in London'; before, he went on, 'all was intimacy and harmony. After, all was bureaucracy and conflict'. During the Second World War, one broadcasting official recalled 'the old, intimate, close days of pre-war broadcasting'; after it, others repined 'the urgent, close sense of purpose the war produced in the BBC'. Grace Wyndham Goldie, a doyenne of a whole generation of broadcasters and a stern innovator in political broadcasting, nevertheless said that 'the smaller BBC of the early 1950s meant that ideas flowed more freely'. Tom Burns pointed out that by the mid-1970s everyone he talked to in the BBC complained that it had recently become 'too big', yet in fact the Corporation had grown far less quickly than in the previous decade. By the 1990s, BBC employees were still saying that it was far too big, even though it had recently got much smaller. But, above all, they said that, in the past, working for the BBC had felt like a vocation; people were sometimes infuriated by it, but also proud of it as an idea and as a standard. Argument, they also claimed, had been allowed, encouraged and was not stoppable.

In the early 1990s, some distinguished voices expressed deep anxiety about the kind of place the Corporation was becoming. They were all the more impressive because none of them was under any threat: they mattered too much. Indeed, in different ways, they summed up, in the programmes they had made, the independence of their views, the accumulated concessions and stands they had taken and, in a creative authority, why public service broadcasting had been an important and exciting part of public and private life. David Attenborough, a great programme maker, and in his time a very distinguished BBC administrator, and Mark Tully, a legend in India, on which he had reported for years, argued that the BBC had become a hostile, demoralized, over-managed and secretive place. The dramatist Dennis Potter, in a scathing attack on Rupert Murdoch and the BBC at the Edinburgh Tele-vision Festival (1987), lamented the retreat of all television from innovative programme making.

Of course, the BBC culture is wordy, sarcastic, urbane, discontented, sometimes fashionable – and perhaps, properly, always likely to be disgruntled. Sniping, gossiping and griping are part of the atmosphere. Yet, in this period, the BBC, like many other managerialized institutions, became a feverish place, with the political pressure from outside transmuted into intense internal pressure. Perhaps again because, ultimately, the BBC makes ideas, trades in images, the impact of managers and their 'correct' and 'incorrect' ideas is felt more personally. 'I don't mind being told what to do by some chap in a suit who's never edited a programme', complained one BBC producer, 'but I'm buggered if I'm going to be told what to think'.[15]

Leaders

Part of the new managerialism of the 1980s was an importing of a kind of posturing ruthlessness. Everywhere, passengers, patients and those out on parole were renamed 'clients' in the public services. If Hussey was sent into the BBC by the Conservative government to bring it into line, John Birt was widely seen as his agent in the new tough mode.

Birt had been a very successful and innovative programme maker in the smaller but hugely fertile LWT. Trained as a scientist, one observer claimed that he thought in structures, and then tried to make the organisation fit the ideas. He was, commented another, 'a facts and figures man'. Asked to speak about quality drama, he wanted evidence about numbers of plays shown, hours broadcast, percentages of viewers. Those who worked with him also commented that he was 'a rules man – his plan was always to decide on a "rule" and keep to it'. Privately energetic and charming, in public meetings, although always well prepared, he could, in the early days, be wooden, an odd mixture of shyness and bombast. He became more relaxed and confident as his tenure moved on. Yet arguably, the two previous, indisputably great Directors General – John Reith, and Hugh Carleton Greene in the 1960s – had both also often been accused of being overbearing and dictatorial. Greene was also a mischievous person. Both men combined aggressive style with a widely recognized – if not always approved of – image of what the BBC should do. Birt began his career at the BBC in the most difficult times the Corporation had ever experienced, but he did have a vision. He was subjected to a furious, unrestrained barrage of press opposition. At first, some sensed that he didn't particularly like the BBC. Roger Bolton, a former BBC producer and respected programme maker, wrote in the *Guardian*: 'The BBC has a deep and abiding hold on those who have worked for the Corporation'; he went on, 'The overwhelming impression given by those who now run the BBC is that they have no affection for it and for its past achievements, and no respect for its programme makers'. But then, some saw Bolton as a critic, in turn, with an axe to grind. Birt was, he would argue, focused on the future. Simmering internal resentment, combined with a hawkish press, meant that Birt's every action was under media scrutiny. It didn't help that the twelfth Director General of the BBC got his job almost by fiat, and that able, respected competitors, like John Tusa, who had recently successfully reformed the prestigious World Service (and carried an enthusiastic staff with him), were told by Hussey that there was no point in applying. How he was appointed was not Birt's fault, but it made him look like the product of the kowtowing politics of the 1980s. What became known as 'Armani-Gate' also did damage. The title came from the Director General's preference for stylish designer suits. However, it shocked BBC employees (many of whom were now on short-term contracts and had recently been sternly warned by the rectitudinous Corporation that they must pay their taxes properly) when they discovered that the Director General himself apparently did not actually work for the Corporation. Instead, he was paid his salary through a holding company which permitted him to make a small – and indeed in the rest of broadcasting, routine – tax advantage. At the time it was as if a great British institution had been so undermined by the Conservative onslaught that those who were supposed to hold its future dearest were not committed to it.

Birt was saved as influential and objective commentators rallied to support him. Particularly important was a letter sent by senior journalists to the *Independent*, publicly backing him. 'Old axes are grinding', Polly Toynbee, Peter Jay and others wrote, and 'old scores are being settled in the attack on the Director General'. He was certainly helped by distinguished and, on the whole, left-wing members of the general committee. It was a delicate moment; Michael Checkland, the previous Director General, reduced a meeting to roars of appreciative laughter when he began a speech by quoting his BBC employee number. The problem was not whether Birt was or was not venal, but what people thought it meant for the BBC. Indeed, the incident may have been a turning point in showing that the public still cared quite passionately about the Corporation.

As the 1990s progressed the BBC calmed down. Perhaps this was because all the opposing voices had been shunted off, retired, or were too busy. Perhaps it was because political pressure from government and opposition had changed from volatile hysteria to a steady pressure of objections, attempts to arrange favourable news running order, lunches and telephone calls. Or perhaps it was because the BBC had been reformed and was more in control of its own agenda of change than in the volatile 1980s.

There was also a shift of power within the Corporation; Birt was even prepared to humiliate Hussey – soon to retire anyway. The Chairman, married to a lady-in-waiting to the Queen, was given no prior warning and was hugely embarrassed that the BBC had conducted a secret, and constitutionally damaging, deal with the Princess of Wales for a revenge interview to put her case against Prince Charles. It was seen by the BBC as a scoop – and it netted the Corporation a huge world audience. Whether it was proper, or properly conducted, or not, seemed to matter little. Certainly Hussey was ruthlessly side-lined as his influence waned.

By the 1990s, the BBC was undoubtedly more disciplined. Most important of all, it was producing some outstanding programmes. However, above all, under John Birt the BBC had, against all the odds, survived.

Who saved the BBC?

How was Mrs Thatcher thwarted? Part of the answer was just politics. There was an important element in her Cabinet who were determined to protect the BBC. Of these William Whitelaw was undoubtedly the most influential: no one could have been closer to her, making his determined opposition all the more effective. Whitelaw pointed out that when the Conservatives were in opposition in 1965 the BBC's Director General had been very determined to protect Conservative opposition interests against the then Labour government. It was a debt that was amply repaid. Whitelaw saw it as important evidence of the benefits of independent, impartial public service broadcasting.

'In a difficult field', he was to write, 'we should be most careful not to endanger what we have achieved'. Early on in government Whitelaw oversaw the implementation of a Labour plan, and introduced Channel 4. He remained a resourceful Cabinet player. Whitelaw had said, 'It's committee work and behind the door work, and respect that gets you what you want' and, almost in direct contradiction to his leader, concluded that 'I am always disturbed by talk of achieving higher standards in programmes at the same time as proposals are introduced leading to deregulation, and financial competition because I do not believe that they are basically compatible'.[16] Whitelaw knew what he didn't want, and traded his indispensability to the Prime Minister for it. After the early, lunatic faith that the Prime Minister held, that a technological transformation of Britain could be carried out on the backs of people's appetites for old movies, and after Rupert Murdoch had got everything he could wish for in terms of favourable policies for his new satellite station, Mrs Thatcher's attention also turned elsewhere.

The second factor was that, despite growing competition, people still liked watching BBC programmes. Popularity – and a sense that programmes reflect and shape viewers' and listeners' interests, that there are some programmes at the edge of public opinion and pleasure – proves the most solid defence for broadcasters. Yet, in the beginning, programmes seemed so very removed from the heart of the new regime – and the fertile argument, and sense of ideas flowing that encourage creativity, seemed so alien to the new, neatly managed structure – that there was a fear that the Corporation had been saved, but that quality broadcasting had not. There were continuous and growing anxieties about radio, which worsened with the departure of one of Birt's most respected appointees, Liz Forgan, from the post of Head of Radio. She had left because the next stage in rationalization was to be the creation of 'bi-medial departments', serving both radio and television. It was feared that the specialized culture of, for example, children's television, or the alternative news agenda of the World Service, would be lost. However, at least by the mid-1990s, the argument was again about programmes.

One effect of the Broadcasting Act had been to create new opportunities for all the people who could not bear the old broadcasting sector any more – in the independent sector. Indeed, for at least one generation public service broadcasting values (that you made programmes because they were important and interesting and necessary) survived in the best of the independent companies. So the BBC exported values – and could import back programmes made by its own kind of broadcaster.

The third factor was that the reforms cut costs at the BBC. However, huge sums were wasted on the way. Early on, the producer's choice system was discovered to be paying some costs twice, and money was 'lost' in the system (malcontents grumbled that at least under the old scheme transferred funds were spent on programmes, not 'lost'). Money was also mishandled in setting up BBC Enterprises. This was a typical 1990s venture. The idea was that it earned the BBC 'extra' revenue by exploiting BBC programmes. It cost more than it ever brought in. Nevertheless, however ramshackle the process, a leaner, more cost-conscious BBC did emerge.

Perhaps Birt was more in debt to all the dissidents than he realized. So vociferous was the campaign, as successive waves of reorganisation cut swathes through what journalists saw as the central BBC ways of doing things, it certainly seemed that the process was very painful. Loud complaints may, ironically, have served to placate the government that the BBC was being reformed as it would wish.

Birt, and his team, managed to steer the Corporation through the greatest-ever challenge to its existence. By the mid-1990s the BBC felt as if it was, slightly grimly, on a course it understood. It is a story which may show how flexible British Establishment institutions can be. The BBC remained a national and international institution; it had not, in the end, been fatally politically compromised. It made good programmes. The public also actually cared about it. It was Birt's particular capacity, in a way, to look forward, and the Corporation began to prepare for how it might give a 'public service' interpretation to the opportunities of digital television.

Public service can perhaps only be measured by what it is institutions agonize over. If you are only there to make a profit, everything is far simpler. Questions like *what do children need?*, *how ought the public to be informed about the election?*, *what new dramatists should be developed?*, *how do we reflect the debate about contemporary society?* and many others are simply not relevant in a commercial system. But they continue to be relevant in the BBC.[17]

Broadcasting in the twenty-first century

Indeed, by the beginning of the new millennium, the unthinkable had happened. The BBC emerged from two decades of political and technological (if not creative) turmoil as the strongest player on the British broadcasting scene and with an enhanced international presence.

At the start of the 1990s it had seemed possible that the Corporation was doomed to a twilight life of decreasing revenue, declining and fragmented audiences and enfeebled performance. At best it might expect a reduced role making programmes for elite minorities or worthy causes that commercial broadcasters would not touch because of their narrow appeal. The BBC, whose whole history has been one of combining popular and quality programming, would fade into insignificant mediocrity.

That this was its likely fate was all the clearer when what was happening elsewhere was taken into account. Other public service broadcasters all over the world had become pale shadows of their former selves. They had lost finance and clout. Even great national broadcasters like NBC in America had been eviscerated by a combination of deregulation, and a collapse in the will to protect information as a public good. Canadian public service broadcasting had lost monopoly rights, finance, and swiftly lost audience share: it was reduced to appealing for charitable funds from viewers to continue to make programmes. Australian public service broadcasting suffered a similar fate. A previously robust element of a broader commercial programme-making culture, public service barely survived either as an institution or as a set of values. Similarly RAI in Italy was reduced to a small, apologetic organisation. Almost everywhere the story was the same. These precipitous declines were not inevitable but the predictable outcomes of broadcasting policy. On a more positive note, novel news services like CNN swiftly gained authority and reach in their reporting – yet CNN was more widely watched in the rest of the world than it was in America. All over the world, traditional public service broadcasters were in trouble – how could they survive here?

Meanwhile, throughout the 1990s, it was argued that 'broadcasting', or terrestrial broadcasting at least, was doomed by inexorable technological change (actually this was always talked about as if it were good; technology would promote progress). Experts confidently predicted that people would stop watching old-fashioned steam television, and that if they did watch it they would customize their programme choice from the huge range of new channels available. In any case, they would not be watching television or listening to the radio, because they would be too busy buying products and services off the net – or 'interacting' with it. The theorists of interactivity were very clear that this was absolutely novel, engrossing – and very superior to old, passive spectatorship. They dismissed any idea that when you look at a picture and are delighted by it, or read a novel and find yourself transported into the mind and understanding of characters within it, watch a drama and feel involved in the outcome of the story, or contemplate news with apprehension, you are altered by the experience. 'Interactivity' was, it was claimed, revolutionary.

Indeed, the main concern throughout the 1990s was the means of delivery of new services and not their content. Indeed, content delivery was changing; by 2002 nearly 40 per cent of British homes had access to cable or satellite television. Meanwhile sports, especially football, had been transformed as money was pumped into them in order, at least in part, to develop exclusive access to attract viewers to the new services. Of course, there were profound changes in audiences' behaviour. People spent time in the new sociabilities of the net, they spent time on videogames and watched videos. Indeed, many movies began to look increasingly like videogames, and were often made as much for the home video market as for public display. Evidence from the Independent Television Commission showed that multi-channel households watched a variety of offers, and browsed through entertainment opportunities more freely. There was some evidence that the multi-channel homes (that might soon be in the majority) did not watch television collectively, and watched television slightly less, overall, than previous generations. Younger people in a period of great affluence went to the cinema more.

Yet people went on watching television in far greater numbers and for far more of the time than had been predicted at the start of the new technological revolution. Moreover, the majority of them continued to watch terrestrial channels (however they received them) more than any other channels. Channel 5 – originally given very light regulation because it was not expected to last more than a few years – grew into a serious competitor for ITV. (The light-touch regulation made it attractive to buyers who saw it as a way to tabloidize the television market.) Channel 4 went from strength to strength in the 1990s. ITV, saddled with huge auction bids to pay off, lacking the regional tension that had once made it so creative, and having made many mistakes on its way to the new digital channels, began to have more acute problems. When the long boom of the 1990s stuttered to a halt, all the commercial broadcasters faced severe adjustments as advertising revenues collapsed. But these problems were trivial in comparison to a stark and unexpected reality: people still liked watching television for the same kinds of reasons that they had liked watching it in the past. Most startling of all, the BBC survived, flourished and became (for the moment at least) the dominant player. It was a remarkable outcome.

Partly it was the product of a frequently ignored problem – that of content. Despite the huge attractions of sports channels, which soon bought up all sorts of events and privatized them (and outpriced the terrestrial stations), and children's channels that offered a reliable diet of cartoons, steam television still made new programmes that people wanted to see – and imported the best of foreign production. In the case of the BBC the outcome was largely a vindication of the Birt–Hussey reforms. Together with an astute, well-prepared move into digital, the BBC offered new services that led people into a new era of broadcasting and information. BBC World, from a shaky and unconvincing start, improved and began to grow into an authoritative new international presence. The BBC website received more hits than any other in the UK: the BBC was again a persuasive representative of the nation all over the world. Ultimately, broadcasting services confounded the pessimists because they were still able to touch audience tastes, pleasures and hopes.

Yet broadcasters were also able to exploit a political and regulatory regime which – in the end – supported them. The public takes its leisure for granted, yet even fans enjoying their passion depend on structures of broadcasting that are politically determined. This is as true of wholly commercial systems of broadcasting as of those with a public service component. These political realities cannot alter the terms of international broadcasting trade – but they can modify their impact if there is the will to do so.

Nevertheless, the ideals of public service broadcasting were under powerful new strains. News, especially, suffered from many challenges. Rolling 'live' news is more vulnerable to unsubstantiated rumour than the old, slower kind. 'Representing' the nation is more complex, for you must find, for example, the 'representative' Muslim voices (not just the excitingly newsworthy extremist ones) – and broadcasters have to be acutely aware across a whole landscape of political interest. Audiences, through the long, comfortable boom years perhaps felt little to threaten them, and were less interested in threats to other people's safety, in the new, complicated international disorder of the post-Cold War world. As the press reacted to the dominance of broadcasting and became more campaigning and opinionated (and less concerned with news as such, which the broadcasters could do better), this in turn reflected back on broadcasters – who, despite their dominance, still seem to find it hard to establish independent news agendas. In America broadcast news has become more like the press: more partisan, less impartial. It is rather disturbing to watch – but many argue that it is the way forward for news. In addition, much political coverage seems to operate in a simple – and misleading – moral universe of rights and wrongs. As successful political negotiation always deals with making painful concession about strongly felt interests, the very basis of democratic politics is all too often traduced. In particular, the idea of politics as a discussion about genuinely difficult-to-resolve issues is being lost.

Legislation, technological change and evolving audience habits could swiftly alter the broadcasting landscape again. There is no divine right to broadcast. Yet, despite the threats and the problems – and the alternatives – we still seem to like it. Perhaps, grudgingly and almost unconsciously, we value broadcasting as part of a national conversation: it still remains a mirror we hold up to our increasingly diverse selves.

The BBC: an imperfect beauty

The problem with all of the media industries is that they are politically and socially very important indeed and economically of the middling rank. The asymmetry is more threatening now that they are all so international. If they are doing their work properly they act like a kind of antibiotic in public life – keeping the system clean. But this is in the public interest – not necessarily of any concern to the businesses that run them. The media are also like the canary that used to be kept in a cage in the mines – sensitive to foulness, they and their condition offer an early-warning system of political dangers. 'Broadcasting' driven by public service values has been an especial feature of the British media ecology. But it is in some ways under the most serious threat since the challenges of the 1980s. Increasingly, it is clear that many of the valuable producers of media content all over the world depend on some kind of 'gift'. Al-Jazeera was launched with one, the BBC has the licence fee. But they also have to be forged by intense competition. In the digital world, when – for example – research shows that the consumption of news programmes drops by almost 40 per cent, keeping the public attention is about as difficult as it gets.

For the first sixty years of its existence the threat to the BBC was political. Now it faces even more formidable foes: huge, rapacious, rich, multinational information/entertainment empires that see it as an inconvenient competitor which they would simply like out of the way. These are able to wield greater power because governments are more economically 'liberal', less willing and less able to protect public services. Behind closed government doors, and in the corridors of the regulators, in international regulatory venues, beyond the public eye, these commercial interests argue – often successfully – for their own interests. Indeed, while it is possible to have a clear battle with a political party, commercial interests are far harder for the Corporation (and those who seek to support public service values) to fight against: the public often does not like the pressure a government exercises on a broadcaster, but hardly thinks of the media conglomerates.

In America, there are public service ideals in the media – but no institutions to put them into practice. 'Public' values reside more in the press in the states – yet the newspaper industry is in severe collapse. President Reagan's abolition of the 'fairness doctrine' in 1988 (which had required political balance of broadcasters) led directly to this emaciation of public discussion in broadcasting. It has led to an American public ignorance that has squandered the authority of its 'soft' power, with consequences for the whole world. In Britain and Europe we have the institutions (although we barely value them or their practitioners), but will we permit them to innovate sufficiently to survive, if they can?

The BBC is an institution: it has been a broadcaster, it generates all kinds of content, it is many other practical things (the inventor, for example, of well-informed and expert helplines). But, most importantly, it is a set of values embodied in considered and evolving practices which it can use to re-engineer public life in the interests of the public. In this way content and public service content (which is not just a rump of glum, improving material, but the whole

range of 'information, education and entertainment') is a habit of mind that
has done much to change and mould – largely for the better in British life.
David Hendy's funny, witty, wise and gloriously imaginative account of Radio
4, *Life on Air*,[18] answers the question of why the audience for a unique radio
station found it 'stitched into the very fabric of their being', but in a larger
way the BBC is part of the British unwritten constitution.

The BBC was not and never has been a 'state' broadcaster (although its
relationship to the state is more complex than it looks at first sight). The
'licence fee' (a regressive poll tax, or a hypothecated tax of the kind most people resent) on the right to receive radio signals, gave it an income separate
from a state grant. It was a brilliant invention because the BBC has never been
like a department of state, precisely because of its separate finances. Like many
British constitutional arrangements, this independence is a fuzzy, indistinct
notion. Governments set the level of the licence fee. However, whatever its
imperfections, the licence fee has been a real constitutional prop. The BBC
had its own income. Indeed, as technological innovation and audiences grew
there have been times when the income has grown quite separately from government control. Of course, now we have an institution – the BBC – the
means of financing of which, new technology may make impossible.

In addition to an income, there were other constitutional niceties that
protected the BBC from undue political pressure, up to a point. That politicians have sought to bring pressure onto the BBC is not the issue: how the
BBC, and indeed politicians, have handled the pressure is what has mattered.
The BBC is independent from any particular government – and indeed has
particularly onerous responsibilities – because it outlives them all. But the
BBC is an institution which, in some sense, has to pursue the same objectives
as the state, and it has undoubtedly been one of the mechanisms that has kept
politics decent. In turn, of course, it has been bullied, harassed, charmed,
wheedled, chivvied, threatened and argued with by all governments. While
there is little or no public discussion as to whether the press is reasonable or
how it spends money, there is a heated debate, over all of these matters, about
the BBC, and this in itself is a public good (even if the overwhelming hostility
of the press increasingly represents the interests of commercial competitors).

However, the BBC time and time again has also negotiated with the British
state – on the basis that there were some things it understood better than the
political classes. This is most apparent in news and foreign broadcasting,
when the Corporation has often felt that it has an especial expertise in understanding the 'hearts and minds' of audiences. Time and again the World
Service has gone out and brought its understanding of the temper and views
of foreign audiences to bear on government attempts to influence those
audiences – not, it has to be said, always successfully. Nevertheless, the BBC
has behaved as an expert and influential co-worker. On many domestic issues
as well, from how to tackle teenage pregnancy (in soap operas or dramas), to
how to approach great, state public crises, terrorist attacks, and Princess

Diana's funeral, the BBC has brought a special expertise to the task. The BBC has not been a client of the state but an independent dealer with it.

This is one reason why we argue our mores and principles out in public over it. The *Daily Mail* (which has a higher proportion of BBC consumers in its readership than any other newspaper) quite often rails against it. But then the BBC is a place where the colliding morality of young and old fight it out. It often gets things wrong – sometimes casually, sometimes it makes the wrong choices carefully, but at least we can interrogate those decisions in public.

Ever since John Birt and his team made the counter-intuitive but visionary choice to put BBC content out on all platforms, the Corporation has been a leading market maker in technological innovation. The British public has taken to downloading, iPlaying, 'watching again' with enthusiasm. Conventional watching and scheduling are evaporating – but once the BBC has made a market, other commercial players want a slice of it. Although some have argued that the licence fee is peculiarly vulnerable in a multi-channel digital world, nevertheless the notion of content free at the point of consumption (which is what the licence fee provides) is actually very contemporary. In any case, the licence fee was never rational, it just worked, and has been preserved by political will. If the BBC goes, then that will have been a political, not a commercial decision. One attempt to answer the 'accountability' problem that some argued was the Corporation's weakness was to replace the BBC Governors – a mysteriously British institution – in 2007 with the BBC Trust. This body was set up to articulate more clearly the interest of the public. Actually, it has worked rather more flexibly and intelligently than many critics thought that it would, yet it too finds it difficult to speak 'for' the BBC. So the BBC combines a large, powerful, at times overwhelming voice with an incapacity to speak for itself. This may become more of a problem.

The BBC has become a world exporter of 'impartiality' and, more importantly, 'objectivity'. This is a very simple principle, important in news but with a wide, cultural reach: the ambition is to describe the world as it is, not through pre-set ideological blinkers of any kind. In news, you do it through attending to all sides, in culture you do it by creatively permitting a variety of truths to be expressed with all the fluency that can be mustered. In the old days, you were being impartial if you 'balanced' a 'left'-wing point of view with a 'right'-wing one, and the BBC could (and did) often argue that if both 'sides' complained, it was doing its job. If the nation is uncomfortable, then that makes things more demanding for the Corporation. As one BBC Chairman put it, 'A Nation on the rack puts the BBC on the rack'. Now, on almost any issue, there are many more varied opinions, and Britain is a more diverse society – with powerful, globally-linked communities.

A recent BBC report attempting to grapple with multi-ethnic, multi-world connected audiences argued that now there was a 'wagon wheel' of contemporary, contending views. 'Impartiality', however, is testing work and not about being in the 'centre'. Thus, for example, one BBC news executive added a useful idea – that of 'hard impartiality', a robust determination to report what is happening, not what audiences or authorities are comfortable with. Thus, there should be no impediment to exploring and displaying the most alien of views, including those of our 'enemies' (or, one might say, especially our enemies) in any conflict. Thus, a report by David Loyn on the Taliban's changing tactics, from inside the group, by an 'embedded' reporter, which showed the Taliban as a group with political intelligence and indeed developing policy, was a perfect example of proper journalism in this tradition: despite some cries of treason, it told citizens what they needed to know, in the classic public service tradition. Yet 'impartiality' is often treated as if it were a thing, or a goal. It is neither: it is merely a tool, a sceptical injunction to avoid *a priori* assumptions. It also means that audiences trust a source which they know is not lecturing them for its own purposes, in which they can see their own views, but in which they are also exposed to other views and may come to appreciate them. 'Objectivity' is more important, as it demands judgement, not a weak 'balancing' of views. A proper journalist in a hard place has to come to a judgement of what is going on there. But, in turn, judgement does not mean campaigning. These are vital arguments and delicate decisions to make in a very opinionated but not very informed world. So we can demand that the BBC is impartial but that it uses this on the way to better judgements. Freedom of speech is a lovely, buxom, bountiful idea about holding the court of opinion open: and this is also an issue for the BBC. Thus, another duty of public service news and other kinds of content is to provide a forum for the wide variety of views that exist. It is especially important in contemporary societies. You are bound into a society where your views and position are given a hearing. However, while public service ought to report and respect the sincerity of views, neither the strength of the belief, nor the authenticity of the believers, nor the fashionableness of the ideas are sufficient grounds for a capitulation of judgement. An objective report is likely to have been tempered by and adjusted to the widest possible range of views, yet reporting is not excused, by the process of consulting a variety of views, from the obligation to account for the world as accurately as it can. Creationists ardently believe what they claim to be the origins of the world, there are a lot of them about, they have all sorts of consequences in schools, we all need to know what they are saying and why. They certainly have a right to say what they want to. But the BBC does not fulfil its obligations if it is 'impartial' between the well-founded scientific evidence of evolutionists and the sincere beliefs of creationists. Nor is the formulation that it often seems to use, 'creationists believe' and 'scientists believe', acceptable. Scientists do not 'believe' their findings – their relationship to them depends on several thousand years of rational enquiry. Of course, sometimes scientists hold misunderstandings – but these are correctable by their own processes. Thus, the BBC must apply objectivity. But it must also hold the forum open to views that many find unpalatable.

In a rather direct way, the BBC is the inheritor of a great British pragmatic philosophical tradition – that of the utilitarian John Stuart Mill. Mill's elegant thought is simple, the argument is organic and it improves and grows. Arguments do not arrive at the table as fully formed, as they can be formed by interaction with other arguments. Arguments are not 'commodities' to be 'bought', nor are they armies that 'win' because they are the strongest. Rather, they are creative instruments of exploring and developing improved solutions. The BBC's respect for its audience and place in the analysis and interrogation of the world requires it to have and implement just such a view of ideas and solutions: that the cauldron of argument is the place to grow discussion.

The BBC is an engine of the mind. It has become a national treasure and world resource because it has been given the creative freedom and political responsibility to attract audiences, tell the truth and be playful. Even if it sometimes fails to adhere perfectly to its principles, at the very least we can argue that it should try harder. That it is 'ours', it belongs to us all, not its shareholders, is also part of its glory. Indeed, not only has it lasted longer than many media organisations, more significantly, it has constantly changed, yet in doing so has reimagined enduring social and political values and made them sparklingly relevant to shifting history. In doing so it has become a world by-word for reliability. Moreover, it has, over time, got it more right (and worried about getting it right) than most other organisations – and the public understand this. Indeed, the BBC is possibly more famous than Britain, more accepted all over the world, and as vulnerable as it has ever been.

Thus, in shanty suburbs of Addis Ababa and out in Ethiopia's rural villages, where there is a café there is a television which people pay small sums to watch. Standing in the smoky haze of freshly roasting coffee, one journalist recently saw the locals watching the war in Afghanistan on the BBC. In the middle of a refugee camp in the horror of war in Southern Sudan, an anthropologist friend saw a television powered by a generator, Ethiopians enthusiastically engaged in watching an Arsenal game on the BBC. Meanwhile, in America this summer, in Williamsburg in Brooklyn, New York, while sitting in the café with my cappuccino, I realized that two adjacent lap-tops (each accessorized by an achingly fashionable youth) were checking the news on the BBC website. This is simply because the BBC has become one of the world's great objectivity traders. Such assets are very precious, very few in number, and are endangered in any number of ways.

How has the BBC survived? The Corporation has been repeatedly saved by three allies. First and most important, paradoxically, have been governments. They have often had rows and threatened the BBC, but nevertheless, in the last instance, governments of all political complexions have recognized something in the BBC which operated in the interests of public life. Politicians and politics are more beleaguered now than ever before. For nearly twenty years, governments all over the western world have been outsourcing political decisions: finding themselves unpopular, they have sought to divest themselves of power.

However, it is probably to politicians that we must look still for engineering the solutions to the survival of values.

Second, public service broadcasting has been protected by a network of impartial institutions: impartiality is highly valued yet under tremendous threat. The British civil service has, time after time, gone out and adjusted the machinery appropriately to do its best to protect a service that it has understood is based on compatible principles. The regulatory bodies that we now have in place, both nationally and internationally, do not always interpret their job properly. In America, the regulator is part of the problem. It has collaborated with the impoverishment of public discussion. Regulators today often have marvellously clean and tidy economic objectives; they have aims and principles, targets and standards by the cartload – yet running a creative institution is about independence to get on with the difficult job of inventiveness. Are the regulators working? They have taken over the nasty political work and turned it into the clean laundry of economic models. But, given the technological and social challenges, are they adequate?

Then there is the public. Being popular and valued has been the best political strategy for survival. However, this is more difficult to achieve, and when it is achieved, as we have often seen, the opposition ignores it. Technology is like a whirlwind, remaking public life and public expression (as well as overturning economic models for information and cultural creativity at a break-neck speed) in magnificent new ways. The BBC will survive – or not – if it continues to weave itself into our everyday lives and our aspirations – and if, we the public, value it.

Notes

1 M. Thatcher, *The Downing Street Years* (London, HarperCollins, 1995), p. 210.
2 H. Young, *One of Us* (London, Cape, 1992), p. 510.
3 BBC WAC, R213, Mrs Thatcher General. Mrs Thatcher, speech to the Parliamentary Press Gallery, 11 July 1981.
4 Institute of Contemporary British History, 'Witness Seminar', *Real Lives* (February 1995).
5 *The Nolan Report on Standards in Public Life*, Cmnd 2850, 1995, 1, para. 70.
6 A. Milne, *DG: The Memoirs of a British Broadcaster* (London, Hodder & Stoughton, 1988), p. 74.
7 S. Barnett and A. Curry, *The Battle for the BBC: A British Broadcasting Conspiracy* (London, The Aurum Press, 1994); C. Horrie and S. Clarke, *Fuzzy Monsters: Fear and Loathing at the BBC* (London, Heinemann, 1994).
8 Interview with Chris Beauman.
9 T. Burns, *The BBC: Public Institution and Private World* (Basingstoke, Macmillan, 1977), p. 43.
10 Author interview.
11 C. Handy, 'Balancing corporate power: a new Federalist paper', *Harvard Business Review*, 1992, p. 572.
12 Author interview.

13 J. Harvey-Jones, *Making it Happen* (London, HarperCollins, 1991).
14 Author interview.
15 Quoted in Barnett and Curry, *The Battle for the BBC*, p. 219.
16 W. Whitelaw, *The Whitelaw Memoirs* (London, The Aurum Press, 1989), p. 285.
17 This chapter is based on a number of confidential interviews with policy makers, broadcasters and politicians.
18 D. Hendy, *Life on Air* (Oxford, Oxford University Press, 2007).

Part III

Rise of new media

Chapter 19

New media in Britain

Introduction

The rhythm of change in the media does not resemble the regularity of the seasons. Thus the period 1900 to 1940 was a time of rapid transformation, when the hegemony of print, music-hall and piano was undermined by the rise of film, radio and gramophone (to say nothing of television, which first broadcast in Britain in 1936). By contrast, the following forty-year period was an era of relative stability, marked by a reshuffling of the media pack. Between 1940 and 1980, television became the principal mass medium, other media were demoted, and the transistor radio, Walkman and video recorder became popular media accessories. However, after 1980, the pace of change again quickened. The desktop computer became a mass medium; the internet and web came into their own; television channels – satellite, cable and digital – mushroomed; production techniques changed across the media; and computer games won a mass following. This was followed by the rise of social media, the take-off of the smartphone, and the rapid diffusion of on-demand and streaming services.

This acceleration of change was fuelled by new communications technology. The invention of microprocessors brought into being powerful, compact computers and facilitated the rise of the internet. Satellites orbiting in space and relaying information between terminals on earth, and fibre-optic cable systems transmitting coded impulses of light down hair-like strands of glass, transformed the carriage of communications. Above all, the digitization of communications (the conversion of words, numbers, sounds and images into electronic binary digits) initiated a chain reaction of innovation that continues to this day. Digitization reduced production costs in many media industries. It offered enormous advantages in terms of compressing, storing, editing, copying and distributing communications. It enabled more digital television channels to be transmitted on the same spectrum. It became possible to watch a film or TV programme on a computer, tablet or smartphone.

New media, we are told, are remaking the world. According to the New Labour government, in 2000, 'The explosion of information has fuelled a democratic revolution of knowledge and active citizenship. If information is power, power can now be within the grasp of everyone'.[1] Its cheerleading White Paper *A New Future for Communications* descanted eloquently on the way in which new communications technology was expanding choice, extending media diversity, and increasing pluralism of media ownership. Future developments, it concluded, will move us towards 'full and sustainable competition' in the broadcasting industry. The government's positive reading of technology-driven media expansion provided the main rationale for its decision to accelerate deregulation through its 2003 Communications Act.

However, New Labour's justification for change had a suspiciously familiar ring. Both the Thatcher and Major governments had invoked similar arguments when they had pressed ahead with media deregulation. Yet, the pace and impact of media change did not seem to match the forecasts they made. Ironically, when the pace of change really did pick up, the Cameron government was much more cautious.[2]

The wisdom of hindsight is a useful corrective to uncritical acceptance of seemingly authoritative opinion, especially when this is summoned to justify important changes of public policy. Hindsight also highlights how fallible technology gurus, in smart suits, have been. Time and again, custard pie has dribbled down their cheeks, and down those of people who uncritically believed what they said.

Cable television

In 1982, few people were better placed to discern the future of the media in Britain than Kenneth Baker, the newly appointed Information Technology Minister. A rising star destined to become a long-serving member of Conservative cabinets, he had been briefed by civil servants and leading industry experts. His considered judgement, delivered in a Commons speech, was that the advent of cable television 'will have more far-reaching effects on our society than the Industrial Revolution 200 years ago'.[3]

His assessment was part of a euphoric moment of anticipation. Leading industrial experts had predicted that cable TV would be a great engine of economic growth.[4] The *Times Educational Supplement* compared the advent of cable TV to the coming of public libraries,[5] while the *Economist* concluded that the decision to green-light cable TV was 'the most important industrial decision' of the Thatcher administration.[6]

This optimism was based on the conviction that cable television was going to be unlike anything that had been seen before. 'Off-air cable television sets' would deliver new services such as banking, shopping, meter reading, domestic security systems and even visits from the doctor. Cable TV would provide narrowcasting: numerous channels for minorities, including the elderly, deaf and those seeking adult education. Above all, it would be immensely popular, generating an entertainment-driven information revolution. Its most compelling feature would be 'film-on-request', a service that would enable viewers to select the film they wanted to see from an electronic film library.

Successive governments leant over backwards to ensure that cable television was a triumph. Interim cable TV franchises were awarded in 1983, before the cable TV regulator had even been established, in order to take advantage of the commercial momentum building up among investors. While an initial tax break was not sustained indefinitely, cable TV was exempted from the high-cost, public service requirements imposed on its competitors. In 1987, cable television operators were given permission to compete in the telephone market. In 1990, the prohibition on non-European ownership of cable television was lifted. Restrictions on the growth of a cable TV oligopoly were also rescinded. By 1999, all but six of the country's 136 operational franchises were owned by just two companies: NTL and Telewest.[7] These were allowed to merge in 2005 to form a giant cable TV monopoly that was renamed Virgin Media in 2008.

However, we now know that what was foretold did not happen. The advent of cable TV did not change Britain more than had the Industrial Revolution. Indeed, even Kenneth Baker's (now Lord Baker) more precise and low-key pronouncements were way off the mark. He had predicted in 1982 that 'by the end of the decade [1980s], multi-channel cable television will be common-place countrywide', and that cable TV 'will be used for armchair shopping, banking, calling emergency and many other services'.[8] In fact, far from becoming 'commonplace', cable TV was adopted in just 1 per cent of homes by the end of the 1980s,[9] and by only 13 per cent in 2008.[10] Many of cable TV's much-vaunted new services, such as home banking, calling emergency services and domestic security systems, either never materialized or were short lived.

Cable TV was also a let-down in terms of content. The availability of films, on its delayed film-on-request scheme, was limited. The legion of worthy channels (i.e. adult education) that had been promised was not much in evidence. In fact, most of the programmes shown on cable TV were recycled; and a good many of them had been made originally for large audiences.

But if the output of cable TV was a disappointment, this was nothing compared to the prolonged agony of its long-drawn-out failure. Cable TV had great difficulty in attracting both investors and customers in the 1980s. It obtained a new lease of life during the 1990s, when there was massive inward investment, mostly from the US. All over Britain, roads were dug up to install fibre-optic cable, and hopes in the industry rose. Yet, even during the high point of expansion, 1993–99, the underlying participation rate – that is, the proportion of households passed by cable which subscribed to cable TV – remained almost static.[11] NTL and Telewest duly ran into financial difficulty, and were forced to cancel their ambitious investment plans, limiting access to their services.

In the event, the private, unregulated development of cable TV in Britain did not become an engine of growth, because its off-air services largely failed.

Instead, cable TV led to massive losses, and almost bankrupted the giant corporation NTL.

Satellite television

Satellite television began in Britain as a feed to cable television in 1984, but only really came into its own with the launch of a direct broadcasting service to homes in 1989. Murdoch's Sky TV gained 'first mover' advantage by launching fourteen months ahead of its rival, British Satellite Broadcasting. There was then an extended period of bloodletting, marked by heavy discounting and promotion, that resulted in the two companies making a combined estimated loss of £1.4 billion.[12] Murdoch emerged as the victor, in effective control of the merged company, BSkyB. Despite being based in Britain, and becoming in effect the British satellite monopoly broadcaster, BSkyB was exempted from burdensome public service obligations, initially on the dubious grounds that it was a 'non-domestic' broadcaster.

This enabled BSkyB to dodge an obligation to originate programmes – a key dispensation that has been central to its parasitic existence. Unlike HBO in the US, or Canal Plus in France, BSkyB (now Sky TV) makes little drama of distinction. Most of its programmes are imported, primarily from the USA.

This makes Sky TV no different from cable TV companies. But it had one key advantage over cable TV: it had lower costs. This enabled Sky TV to buy better programme rights over a longer period. It rapidly overtook Virgin in terms of the number of households which subscribed to its services. Even so, Sky TV's staple of films, cartoons, music channels and live sport accounted for only 8 per cent of viewing time in 2016.[13] However, being exempt from cost-bearing regulation, it made enormous profits. In 2015–16, its revenue was £7.8 billion, compared to the £4.8 billion revenue of the more popular and creative BBC.[14]

However, Sky TV's history was part of a bigger drama than becoming a money-making machine. It was a pioneer of interactive digital TV, launching Sky Digital in 1997. This realized a dream that had been eagerly awaited for years.

Interactive digital television

From 1994 through to the early 2000s, there was a steady flow of articles in the national press about the wonders of interactive TV. Essentially the same forecasts that had been made for cable TV in the early 1980s were reprised for interactive digital TV, only sometimes with different jargon. 'Two-way television' was now called 'iTV'; 'film-on-request' was renamed 'video-on-demand'. This last was to be even better than anything promised before. According to the *Independent*, 'video-on-demand, once fully operational, will allow us to call up almost any film in the world, to watch any TV programmes, and to compile "dream schedules" – our own perfect evening's viewing'.[15] Once again, new services, including banking, shopping and visits from the doctor, were trumpeted. And once again, it was foretold that the society would be significantly changed by new technology. '"Interactive TV"', according to the *Sunday Times*, 'is poised to revolutionise the way information, education, media, commerce and entertainment are channelled into the 21st century home'.[16]

But, in one important respect, this good-news message was pitched in a higher rhetorical register, with much greater emphasis on user empowerment than before. Readers of the broadsheet press learnt that viewers of iTV would be able to 'vote on key issues';[17] 'be able to choose the storyline for a drama and [specify] whether they want a sad or happy ending';[18] instruct their TV sets to scan and select from hundreds of channels of information overnight to report whatever news they were interested in;[19] have 'elaborate conversations' through their TV sets with travel companies about the kind of holidays they wanted;[20] try out new clothes on a virtual cat walk;[21] and saunter down a shopping mall, walk into virtual shops, and buy whatever they liked, without ever moving from their sofas.[22] In short, interactive digital TV meant the kiss of death for the couch potato, and would lead to a 'fundamental shift in power from the TV director to the consumer in the home'.[23]

In fact, the iTV that was developed in the late 1990s and early 2000s bore very little relation to the hype. Shopping on TV meant choosing between a limited range of heavily promoted products; video-on-demand offered a restricted number of often not very good films; home visits by the doctor amounted in the end to NHS Direct, in effect the accessing of a glorified medical dictionary; NatWest pioneered an interactive TV banking service in 1995, only to close it down in 2003;[24] there was a restricted choice of camera angles for some football games on certain subscription channels; and iTV provided an alternative way of placing bets.

Yet, despite the fanfare of press publicity, viewers were mostly unimpressed. A mere 20 per cent, in a 2003 Ofcom survey, indicated a willingness in principle to pay for interactive television services.[25] Indeed, these services accounted for only 36 per cent of British television's *non*-broadcast revenue in 2006,[26] and most of this was attributable to premium-rate phone calls.[27]

The most important form of commercial TV interaction was probably mass voting in the *Big Brother* series. However, the principal way that votes were registered was through the nineteenth-century technology of the telephone. This became the only mode of interaction after the option of red-button voting was discontinued in 2004, and that of SMS voting in 2006.[28] This outcome was not what the transformation of 'dumb' television sets into 'intelligent machines' had been intended to achieve.

Indeed, according to a number of market research studies, only a minority with red-button facilities actually used them.[29] Yet, still the true gospel was proclaimed from press pulpits. For example, the distinguished journalist

Emily Bell proclaimed in 2001 that 'iTV is threatening to be the hot platform of tomorrow'.[30] Seven years later, and now promoted to be the *Guardian*'s Director of Digital Content, she was still writing enthusiastically about the power of 'red button interactivism'.[31]

Going digital

In November 1998, the two giants of ITV joined forces to launch OnDigital, Britain's first digital terrestrial television channels. Part of their pitch had been that digital television would provide better clarity of sound and image. Yet, to general surprise, the picture and sound quality of these new digital channels was sometimes greatly inferior to that of conventional television. Indeed, in some parts of the country the sound simply disappeared. This technical failure was due to packing too many channels into the available frequencies, causing transmission power to be curtailed in order to prevent interference with existing analogue signals. With the incompetence that characterized the entire history of OnDigital, the new venture was launched before the new technology had been mastered.

OnDigital's conception was also flawed. It went head-to-head against BSkyB, a company with more money, more subscribers (built up over years), more channels and a smarter management. BSkyB did the obvious thing. It hit OnDigital as hard as it could before the new pretender found its feet. First, BSkyB's installation charges were cut, and then its set-top boxes were given away free. OnDigital's launch funds drained away, as it was forced to match this promotion. Only inspirational programming, at this stage, could have saved it. OnDigital's inspiration was League football, attracting fewer viewers (and smaller match crowds) than BSkyB's Premiership football. Observers watched with horrified fascination as ITV's finest presided over OnDigital's slow-motion death. Attempted mouth-to-mouth resuscitation, in the form of a belated relaunch as ITV Digital, failed. The company collapsed in 2002, with an estimated £1.2 billion loss.[32]

The victor in this contest did not have it all its own way. BSkyB joined BT and others to launch the Open Channel on Sky Digital in 1989. It was a state-of-the-art digital shopping channel which, it was hoped, would revolutionize shopping. Open Channel received a fanfare of publicity, not least in newspapers owned by Murdoch (also controller of BSkyB). *The Times*, for example, reported that Open Channel was valued at £1.4 billion before it had even started trading, in anticipation of the profits that it would generate.[33] In the event, the Open Channel was an ignominious failure and closed in 2001.

At this stage, national conversion to digital television was running into difficulties. The key breakthrough occurred when the BBC, with junior partners BSkyB and the transmitter company Crown Castle, launched a 'Freeview' service of digital channels in 2002. Once a £99 set-top adapter had been installed, these digital channels were available without subscription.

Others (including ITV and Channel 4) subsequently joined the scheme after it had proved to be a popular success. Thus, what drove the digitizing project forward was not interactivity but 'free' content. The new licence fee settlement had funded the BBC to develop new digital channels and develop the 'freeview' package. This time round, technical problems were minimised by opting for fewer channels in return for stronger transmission power.

Freeview contributed to a sharp reduction in the number of analogue TV users, as did the increasing success of satellite TV. Even so, the government had been forced to delay its planned conversion from analogue to digital broadcasting, which had originally been scheduled for 2006–10. The digital switchover was completed in 2012.

Dotcom bubble

During the 1990s, articles about the marvels of interactive television had been accompanied by another story, mostly confined to the business pages of the press. This reported that the internet was about to transform buying and selling, and was already making fortunes for techno-savvy entrepreneurs. Thus, the *Independent on Sunday* recorded, under the headline 'Web Whiz-Kids Count Their Cool Millions', that 'the precocious and proliferating breed of "dot com" millionaires are fabulously rich and ludicrously young. Their fortunes reduce national Lottery jackpots to peanuts . . . '.[34] The implication was that readers could also share in this market jackpot. The *Sunday Times* reported that 'the mania for investing, to hitch a ride on the road to wealth, is reflected in the cover of the current *Forbes* magazine, which proclaims that: "Everyone Ought to Be Rich"'.[35] The *Sunday Mirror*'s advice was characteristically more direct: 'Your Wealth: Get on the Net to Get Ahead'.[36] Wildly overoptimistic forecasts, widely reported in the press, fuelled the dotcom bubble. For example, the *Independent* reported Silicon Valley venture capitalist Joel Schoendorf as saying in 1999: 'I wouldn't be surprised if we saw a 5 per cent increase in investment next year, and every year for the next five to ten years'.[37]

In fact, the dotcom boom came to an end less than twelve months after this pronouncement was made. Yet, very few British publications – with the notable exceptions of the *Financial Times* and the *Economist* – clearly foresaw the bust before it happened (resembling in this respect the American press, which was no less gullible).[38] For the most part, British newspapers were content to chronicle the accumulation of wealth during the dotcom boom without properly investigating whether it was based on a secure foundation. There was little informed discussion about the extent of cost reductions secured through net retailing (which varied widely between different market sectors), or analysis of which consumer groups were most accessible to net retailing. Indeed, there was very little awareness of just how low home internet penetration was in Britain in 1999.

In the event, a large number of dotcom companies went bankrupt during 2000–02 without ever making a profit. Pension funds were seriously depleted, and Britain only narrowly missed following the US into recession.

Seismic change

Yet, the irony was that the mass adoption of the internet only occurred towards the end of the dotcom bubble, and persisted *long after* it had burst. The take-off moment was the summer of 1999. Between early 1999 and 2002, the proportion of UK households with internet access soared from 13 per cent to 46 per cent.[39] This grew to 65 per cent by 2008.[40] By 2016, 89 per cent of adults had recently used the internet.[41]

Thus, in just under a decade, those with ready internet access had grown from a small minority to two thirds of the nation – a shift comparable in scale and significance to the growth of television ownership during the 1950s. Underpinning this quiet revolution was the rapid diffusion of household computers (in just over half of homes in 2002, and in 70 per cent by 2007).[42] The rise of the internet was so momentous a development that it will be examined separately in the next two chapters, concerned with its history and impact.

The rise of the internet was accompanied by another development that changed everyday life: the rise of the mobile phone. Mobile phones first came into use in 1973. They weighed over a kilo, were shaped like bricks and had to be frequently charged. Over time, they became smaller and easier to use. They also gained a key new function – SMS messaging (texting) – first introduced in 1992. Most people in Britain acquired a mobile phone during the later 1990s and early 2000s. By 2015, 93 per cent of adults possessed one.[43]

The standard mobile was 'superseded' by the smartphone (in effect a miniature computer that doubled up as a mobile phone and camera). This was the 'killer application' that apostles of digital convergence had been predicting. The smartphone became available in an elegant, easy-to-use form in 2007. By 2017, more than seven in ten adults in Britain owned a smartphone. Four in ten said that it was their principal way of accessing the internet.[44]

Another key development was the rise of a new entertainment industry. Videogames first became popular in the 1970s, with the introduction of gaming consoles. Online gaming, and later mobile gaming, took off in the 1980s. Games became increasingly sophisticated, and acquired higher production values. By 2013, the revenue of the videogames industry in the US greatly exceeded that of the film industry (excluding DVD and TV rights).[45] Britain became a major games producer (with creative hubs in locations like Cambridge, Guildford and Dundee, with links to local universities).

The third key development is the breakthrough of online on-demand services, delivered through the computer, tablet, smartphone and smart TV sets. Netflix began as a DVD mail rental business but introduced in 2007 a streaming service enabling people to access selected films and TV programmes.

In 2013, it moved into film and TV production, and greatly increased its investment in 2017, following a number of hits and booming subscriptions. Amazon Prime launched a similar service, combining original content with a back catalogue of films and TV series. In 2017, Ofcom reported that 'subscription libraries like Netflex and Amazon Prime' were used by 45 per cent of adults in Britain.[46]

The significance of this development is that two large American companies, operating outside the regulatory framework of public service broadcasting, are making major inroads into the British market and indeed markets around the world. They command enormous resources. Thus, Netflix's series *The Crown* (2016) cost over £100 million to make, enough to fund the BBC2 channel for three months.[47] The television landscape seems set to change in the internet age.

Threads of continuity

Amidst all this flux and change, there is also continuity. Television remains very popular. In 2016, 91 per cent in Britain watched television at least once a week.[48] Indeed, the average person over the age of four spent three hours and thirty-two minutes watching *broadcast* television every day in 2016. This is only six minutes less than in 2006.[49] Radio still has a devoted following. In 2016, nine out of ten listened to the radio at least once a week, listening for three hours three minutes a day on average.[50]

The internet has also become a major source of recreation and pleasure, with many people checking social media first thing in the morning and last thing at night. In 2016, 72 per cent said that they turned to the net for news, compared with 70 per cent citing TV, marking the first time in Britain that the internet had overtaken TV.[51] Forty-one per cent also said in 2016 that they used social media for accessing the news,[52] a significant increase on the recent past.[53]

A clear picture is beginning to emerge. New media have not displaced old media but supplemented them. Television remains central. However, the pecking order – the hierarchy within the media – is shifting, with the internet becoming more important.

The only rider to this is that young people use the media very differently from old people. Thus, those aged over sixty-four watched five hours forty-four minutes of television a day in 2016, whereas sixteen to twenty-four-year-olds watched an average of one hour fifty-four minutes a day.[54] This difference between young and old is not new. In the past, the young watched more television as they grew older. But it is possible that this gap between old and young – which is increasing – may mark the beginning of a larger shift in which television will be demoted.

More generally, the fact that the media system has been restructured – with many more TV channels, many more ways of accessing TV content, many more alternatives – also has wider social and political consequences.

Fragmentation and social cohesion

In the 1960s, families regularly gathered in the same room and watched one of the three available TV channels: BBC1, BBC2 (launched in 1964) and ITV. Television was a strongly unifying force, providing a shared experience for both the family and for the nation.

This has been modified by the proliferation of devices for watching TV: smartphones, tablets, multiple TV sets in the home, play-back systems, DVD box sets and on-demand services. In 2016, 45 per cent said that they watched programmes or films by themselves every day. A further 31 per cent said that while members of the household came together at least once a week to watch TV in the same room, they watched on different screens. These tended to be households with younger members who wanted to watch something different. But despite this shift towards individualized consumption, 30 per cent of people say that they sit together with family members to watch the same TV programme or film every day.[55] Television is still a cohering force within the household, although not to the same extent as before.

The centripetal power of TV to bind the nation has also been diminished by the proliferation in the number of channels. Instead of the three-channel ration of the 1960s, Sky TV offers around 600, Freesat 140 and Freeview 60 channels. This expansion of the TV system, it is argued, is eroding communication between social groups in a shared public space; subdividing the public sphere into 'sphericules'; encouraging individuals and sectional groups to assert their values and interests without regard to others; and more generally, undermining a shared sense of common purpose.[56]

But in a British context, this argument overstates the extent of change. The dominance of the five leading channels has declined in response to rapidly widening choice, falling from 76 per cent to a 53 per cent share of viewing between 2001 and 2016. Even so, leading television channels like BBC1 still account for a substantial share of total viewing each day (see Table 19.1). Their primetime share is still higher. Individual programmes on these leading

Table 19.1 TV channels' share of viewing time

	BBC1	BBC2	ITV1	Ch4	Ch5	All others
	% all viewing time					
2016	22	6	15	6	4	47
2008	22	8	18	8	5	39
2006	23	9	20	10	6	32
2001	27	11	22	10	6	24

Sources: BARB (2016 and 2008); European Audiovisual Observatory Yearbook 2007, vol. 1 (2006); European Audiovisual Observatory Yearbook 2002, vol. 2 (2001). All figures are rounded off to the nearest whole figure.

channels can attract very large audiences. For example, the final of the BBC's *The Great British Bake Off* – a cooking competition which implicitly celebrates social unity – was watched by 14.8 million people in 2016, and 13.4 million in 2015.[57]

The national community still comes together on a regular basis, laughs together, shares a sense of outrage, and is drawn into a debate about common social processes, through mass television channels during peak viewing hours. These constitute the primary public sphere of contemporary Britain which has shrunk but not disappeared.

Globalization and the nation

The transformation of the media, it is argued, has eroded a sense of nationhood. Satellite television and the internet transcend national boundaries. Television has also become more integrated into the global economy and is increasingly showing, it is claimed, the same programmes around the world. In this view, the rise of transnational media and media globalization is weakening identification with the nation. It is also said to be eroding engagement in national politics, since this derives ultimately from a sense of national belonging.[58]

Again, this argument is not true of a British context. Although cable and satellite television channels transmit a large number of foreign (mostly American) programmes, they have a minority share of the market. Public service TV channels (channels publicly owned or regulated) accounted in 2016 for 70 per cent of total TV viewing time in Britain.[59] The BBC originates the majority of its programmes from the UK, while commercial public service TV has long been subject to import quotas. As late as 1998, ITV was required to generate 60 per cent of its programmes from Europe (in effect, mostly the UK), while Channels 4 and 5 had to fulfil a 55 per cent quota.[60] Although these quotas were lightened in the subsequent period, 52 per cent of *total* public service broadcast hours in 2016 were still first-run UK originations.[61]

Indeed, the argument that globalization is hollowing out British media should be turned upside down. The British media are strongly insular. In 2010, only 23 per cent of national press news, 32 per cent of TV news, and 33 per cent of news in leading news websites was international. A significant part of this international news was explicitly related to domestic issues. The remainder was concentrated on the US, neighbouring countries and nations with which Britain has strong ties. Whole tracts of the world are rendered relatively invisible by this selective British media gaze.[62] More generally, the British popular press is strongly anti-migrant and anti-European.[63]

Opening up British television to American programmes meant that British viewers gained access to great TV drama, the product of the renaissance generated by a new business model – premier subscription TV in the US. The regret is that British TV does not provide greater access to the TV drama of other countries.

Retrospect

The media are going through a process of rapid change. Bookshops are closing, and newspapers are in decline. Videogames are overtaking films, and social media have come into their own. Smartphones are modifying, along with other devices, the way we watch television.

But change is balanced by continuity. People still love television, and listen in great numbers to the radio. While audiences are subdividing and filter bubbles are multiplying, the media still bring large numbers into communion with each other. Although the media system is now more exposed to international influences, it is still anchored to the nation.

Indeed, some things seem almost constant. The logic of profit and power has not been subverted. Media moguls like Murdoch have not been dethroned. Public service broadcasting remains dominant, assisted by the licence fee, prominence on electronic programme guides (EPGs), and its expansion of minority channels.

Insofar as an argument can be made that there has been a fundamental change in the media system, and that this is having transformative consequences for society, it comes down to one thing: the internet. It is this to which we now turn.

Notes

1 *A New Future for Communications* (London, Stationery Office, 2000), p. 8.
2 'Digital Communications Infrastructure Strategy: Consultation', Department of Culture, Media and Sport, August 2014. Available at: www.gov.uk/government/consultations/digital-communications-infrastructure-strategy-consultation. Accessed 3 August 2017.
3 K. Baker, *Parliamentary Debates*, 6th series, Vol. 22, 20 April 1982 (London, Hansard, 1982), p. 230.
4 Information Technology Advisory Panel, *Cable Systems* (London, Cabinet Office, HMSO, 1982).
5 *Times Educational Supplement*, 28 October 1983.
6 *Economist*, 6 March 1982.
7 C. Leys, *Market-Driven Politics* (London, Verso, 2001), p. 127.
8 P. Goodwin, *Television Under the Tories* (London, British Film Institute, 1998), p. 68.
9 D. Goldberg, T. Prosser and S. Verhulst, *Regulating the Media* (Oxford, Clarendon Press, 1998), p. 10.
10 *Communications Market Report* (London, Ofcom, 2008), p. 21. Available at: www.ofcom.org.uk/research/cm/cmr08/cmr08_1.pdf. Accessed 12 February 2009.
11 S. Lax, 'The Internet and democracy' in D. Gauntlet (ed.) *Web Studies* (London, Arnold, 2000), p. 166.
12 N. Chenoweth, *Virtual Murdoch* (London, Secker & Warburg, 2001), p. 98.
13 'Share by broadcaster', BARB, 2016. Available at: www.barb.co.uk/trendspotting/analysis/share-by-channel-2/. Accessed 3 August 2017.
14 *Daily Telegraph*, 28 April 2016.

15 *Independent*, 12 January 1996.
16 *Sunday Times*, 4 October 1998.
17 *Guardian*, 21 June 1994.
18 *Independent*, 9 September 1996.
19 *Sunday Times*, 30 April 1995.
20 *Independent*, 24 October 1994.
21 *The Times*, 27 November 1994.
22 *Independent*, 6 October 1994.
23 *Sunday Times*, 30 April 1995.
24 Information derived from *Daily Telegraph*, 6 September 1995, and NatWest Customer Services.
25 Ofcom (2004).
26 Ofcom (2007).
27 Information obtained from interview with Ofcom executive, 2008.
28 Information provided by Nikki O'Shea, Factual Entertainment, Channel 4, 2008.
29 *New Media Age*, 27 April 2006.
30 *Guardian*, 7 May 2001.
31 *Guardian*, 24 November 2008.
32 T. Lennon, 'Digital TV: a phoenix risen from the ashes', *Free Press*, 129, 2002, p. 2.
33 *The Times*, 15 April 1999.
34 *Independent on Sunday*, 25 July 1999.
35 *Sunday Times*, 26 December 1999.
36 *Sunday Mirror*, 17 October 1999.
37 *Independent*, 14 July 1999.
38 J. Cassidy, *Dot.Con* (London, Penguin Books, 2003).
39 'Family Expenditure Survey (1998–2002)'. Available at: www.statistics.gov.uk.
40 Office for National Statistics. Available at: www.statistics.gov.uk/cci/nugget.asp?id=8. Accessed 14 February 2009.
41 'Internet Users in the UK: 2017', Office for National Statistics, 2017. Available at: www.ons.gov.uk/businessindustryandtrade/itandinternetindustry/bulletins/internet users/2017. Accessed 4 August 2017.
42 'Family Expenditure Survey 2002', Office for National Statistics. Available at: www.statistics.gov.uk/cci/nugget.asp?id=868. Accessed 14 February 2008.
43 'Mobile Phone Ownership in UK', Office for National Statistics, 2017. Available at: www.google.co.uk/search?q=mobile+phone+statistics+uk&sa=X&ved=0ahUKE wj2u_LDir7VAhVDDcAKHcR7Cy0Q1QIIfygA&biw=1024&bih=659. Accessed 4 August 2017.
44 *Communications Market 2017* (London, Office of Communications (Ofcom), 2017), p. 1.
45 Theatrical Market Statistics 2013, Motion Picture Association of America and Global Games Report 2013 cited in D. Mullich, 'Who makes more money: Hollywood or the video games industry?', *Quora*. Available at: www.quora.com/Who-makes-more-money-Hollywood-or-the-video-game-industry. Accessed 4 August 2010.
46 *Communications Market 2017*, p. 1.
47 N. Purnell, 'Future of broadcasting', 1 March 2017, Speaker's House, UK Parliament (unpub.).
48 *Communications Market 2017*, p. 6.
49 Ibid., p. 82.

50 Ibid., p. 1.
51 *Daily Telegraph*, 14 June 2016.
52 N. Newman et al., *Digital News Report 2017* (Reuters Institute, University of Oxford), p. 55.
53 R. Nielsen and K. Schroder, 'The relative importance of social media for accessing, finding and engaging with the news', *Digital Journalism*, 2 (4), 2014.
54 *Communications Market 2017*, p. 1.
55 Ibid., p. 12.
56 For example, T. Gitlin, 'Public sphere or sphericules?' in T. Liebes and J. Curran (eds.) *Media, Ritual and Identity* (London, Routledge, 1998).
57 BBC News Online, 27 October 2016. Available at: www.bbc.co.uk/news/entertainment-arts-37786108. Accessed 7 August 2017.
58 E. Katz, 'And deliver us from segmentation', *Annals of the American Academy of Political and Social Science*, 546, 1996.
59 *Communications Market 2017*, Figure 2.45, p. 86.
60 Information derived from the Independent Television Commission in 1999.
61 *Communications Market 2017*, p. 62.
62 J. Curran et al., 'Internet revolution revisited: a comparative study', *Media, Culture and Society*, 35 (7), 2013, Table 7, p. 891: cf. T. Aalberg et al., 'International TV news, foreign affairs interest and public knowledge: a comparative study of foreign news coverage and public opinion in 11 countries', *Journalism Studies*, 14 (3), 2013, p. 63.
63 See Chapter 8.

Chapter 20

History of the internet

Introduction

The internet began as an American invention, and developed subsequently into a worldwide phenomenon. The internet's history cannot be written therefore as a national story, like the history of the press or broadcasting.

The development of the internet can be briefly summarized. The internet began as a small, publicly-owned American computer network in 1969. It expanded with the development of a shared computer language and set of protocols. Email (or network mail, as it was first called) was introduced in 1972. The term 'internet' emerged in 1974 as a simple abbreviation for *internetworking* between multiple computers. The modern internet dates from 1983, with the establishment of a network of networks wholly independent of the US armed forces.

A US-centred network expanded into a fully international network during the 1980s. A key moment of transition was when CERN, the European Organisation for Nuclear Research, adopted Internet Protocol (IP) for its internal network of computers in 1985, and opened its first external IP connections in 1989. The internet reached Asia by the late 1980s, but it was not until 1995 that Africa established its first home-grown internet services. By 1998 the internet reached every populated country in the world.

The internationalization of the internet was accompanied by its popularization. The first key applications of the internet were emails, bulletin boards and listservs deployed during the pioneer phase of 1970–90. This was followed by the breakthrough application of the 1990s: the world wide web publicly launched in 1991. The introduction of a graphical browser in 1993, and the development of search engines in the late 1990s, encouraged mass use of the web. The subsequent period saw the rise of social media, a trend marked by the launch of Facebook in 2004. The internet's different uses and applications fostered its rapid diffusion. In 2017, an estimated 49.7 per cent of the world's population were internet users.[1]

Underpinning this remarkable rise were four distinct strands of technical innovation. One was the transformation of the computer from a vast, complex machine into a small, compact artefact that was crucially assisted by the development of the microprocessor. Another was the development of computer networking, facilitated by the invention of shared codes for transporting and addressing communications and of packet-switching. A third was the transformation of connective software that facilitated the accessing, linking, storage and generation of information from the read-only technology of the world wide web to the read-write technology that made possible the rise of social media. A fourth strand was the development of communications infrastructure. The internet was able to 'piggy back' on phone lines and cable that had already been established to enable interoperability between countries. The internet's subsequent massive expansion was enabled by the development of high bandwidth cable and the growth of wireless networks.

Underlying science

Histories focusing on the technological development of the internet emphasize that its innovations usually had a clear intellectual bloodline.[2] They were the product not of a flash of insight coming from nowhere but of an incremental progression of thought and practice. The invention of packet-switching provides a case in point. Packet-switching disaggregates messages into units (*packets*) before dispatch; sends them through different routes, depending on the flow of communications traffic; and reassembles them on arrival. Each packet is wrapped in a kind of digital envelope containing transport and content specifications. It was a breakthrough technology, central to the development of computer networking and the functioning of the internet. It was conceptualized by Paul Baran in 1964; developed and implemented by Donald Davies and Lawrence Roberts in the later 1960s; revised significantly by Vinton Cerf and Robert Kahn in 1974; and refined thereafter. The 'auteur' theory of the creative process, to be found in some versions of film history, gets short shrift in academic histories of the net (and in the history of science more generally).

While this approach is broadly correct, it tends to downplay the excitement of discovery, at least as it is experienced in the low-key register of academic life. Yet the birth pangs of the web were not free of drama. The inventor of the web, Tim Berners-Lee, was low down in the food chain of academic grants when he began work on the web. He was a scientist, without a Ph.D., on a temporary fellowship in the European physics laboratory, CERN. His repeated requests for additional resources all met with polite refusals. Indeed, he began to fear that his web project – justified on the less-than-straightforward grounds that it would facilitate information sharing between scientists *within* the CERN laboratory, rather than around the world – might be cancelled. When he first unveiled his visionary work it met with a lukewarm response from his colleagues, with the exception of Robert Cailliau.

The future of the web thus seemed to depend upon winning external recognition. Berners-Lee was convinced that the way to achieve this was to present his project at a key conference, due to be held in 1991 in San Antonio, USA, where all the people who mattered in the computer science world would be present. He and his colleague Robert Cailliau submitted to the conference one of the most important scientific papers in the last thirty years, outlining the web, only for it to be rejected on the pedantic grounds that it had failed to situate its arguments adequately within the relevant literature. However, they were given permission to present their project in the second-division form of a demonstration.

The two young scientists flew to San Antonio, only to discover that the hotel where the conference was due to be held had no direct internet access. They persuaded the hotel to extend a phone line to the demonstration room, and charmed staff in the neighbouring university (identified by a local taxi driver) into allowing use of its dial-in service to their home computer. They had then to hunt down, at the last moment, a soldering iron in their hotel in order to bypass an American plug that did not fit their Swiss modem. The demonstration was a triumph. 'At the same conference two years later', Tim Berners-Lee recalls with justifiable pride, 'every project on display would have something to do with the Web'.[3]

Political economy of invention

If scientific advance often takes the form of a logical or associative progression of thought, it is also crucially shaped by the wider context of society. A number of societal factors affect *when* and also *where* scientific progress takes place. One of these – money – was especially important in the case of the development of the internet.

The internet is an offspring of the Pentagon. When the USSR launched the first space satellite in 1957, the US Department of Defense responded by establishing the Advanced Research Projects Agency (ARPA), with the aim of mobilizing American universities and research laboratories more fully behind the country's Cold War effort. Among the new agency's many projects was a scheme to promote interactive computing through the creation of ARPANET, the world's first advanced computer network. Although the network was conceived originally as a way of sharing expensive computer time, it subsequently acquired a more important rationale. Computer networking would facilitate, it was argued, the development of a sophisticated military command and control system. It would also provide a means of sustaining communications channels in the event of a nuclear attack from the Soviet Union.

When ARPANET was identified as part of America's last line of defence against the 'evil empire', it became a spending priority. The development of packet-switching technology and the creation of a rapidly expanding computer network – both central to the birth of the internet – received major funding from the US Department of Defense.

Military spending also indirectly assisted the internet by fostering external conditions favourable to its development. The army funded the first American computer in 1946. So great was the armed forces' subsequent support of 'the nascent computer industry' that it became, in the words of a leading analyst, 'virtually a military subsidiary'.[4] This financial backing helped to establish the USA as the world's leading computer manufacturer and producer of computer software. The American state also sponsored the American space programme, whose by-product − satellite communications − facilitated the functioning of the global internet.

In effect, the American state underwrote a major part of the research and development process that gave birth to the modern internet. This was not something that the private sector was willing to undertake because it was not immediately apparent that computer networking between academics, linked to the defence programme, had any commercial future. Indeed, the giant corporation AT&T was actually invited in 1972 to take over ARPANET, the forerunner of the internet, and declined. It was the American state that picked up the bills in a context of limited commercial interest. Yet, after underwriting the cost of technological development, and also the creation of a significant user base, the American state then proceeded to shepherd the internet to market. The lifting of the prohibition on commercial use of the public internet in 1991 was followed by privatization of the public backbone of the internet in 1995. In effect, the internet became a state-sponsored commercial system.

The actual developmental role of the American state in funding, managing and then commercially floating the internet did not accord with the minimalist, 'night-watchman' conception of government in American neo-liberal ideology. Its interventionism corresponded more closely to the social democratic vision of the state as 'capitalist entrepreneur', with an important role in creating good jobs.[5] American political reality deviated from political rhetoric because of the spending priorities of the Cold War, and also the strong influence exerted by business on American telecommunications policy.

Similar levels of public investment were not available elsewhere, even in countries where the conditions for early internet development were promising. Britain built the first modern computer in the 1940s; developed a significant computer industry in the 1950s; and developed packet-switching, in proto-type, in 1968. But this auspicious start did not gain extensive state financial support, especially in relation to computer projects that offered only a long-term return.[6] It was not until 1981 that the Post Office launched a full-scale packet-switching service − using, after this long delay, expensively licensed American technology.

Military−scientific complex

The internet was the product not only of human ingenuity and state money, but also of the values of the people who first developed it. Data-processing systems do not have fixed forms determined by some inner technological logic but are influenced by the concerns and goals of their inventors, and by the contexts in which they work. For example, IBM developed a highly centralized communication system for business organisations, in which the main computer had a master–slave position to terminals, and the relationship of users to the production and consumption of the data system depended on their position within the corporation. The IBM system both reflected and reproduced, Patrice Flichy argues, the hierarchical culture of the firm.[7]

By contrast, the internet came out of a very different world. Jane Abbate's pioneering history shows that the role of the American military was not confined to paying the bills. On the contrary, she concludes, 'networking techniques were shaped in many ways by military priorities and concerns'.[8] One overwhelming military priority was 'survivability'; in other words, a communication system that would be invulnerable to devastating attack. This led the military to sponsor a decentralized system without a vulnerable command centre that could be destroyed by the enemy. It also led to the development of network technology that would enable the system to function if parts of it were destroyed – a key attraction of packet-switching that dispensed with dedicated, open lines between sender and receiver. Another military priority was to secure a diverse networking system, since this was best suited to different, specialized military tasks. This gave rise to the net's modular structure in which different networks could be added on easily, once minimum requirements were met. It also resulted in the addition of satellite and wireless for internetworking, since these were well adapted to communicating with jeeps, ships and aeroplanes.

However, if the military strongly influenced design objectives, academic computer scientists actually conceived and implemented the net's design. Academics working for ARPA had a significant degree of autonomy, helped by the fact that military objectives largely coincided with scientific ones. Thus the military concern for survivability dovetailed with the desire of the different university departments, which constituted the early internet, to have an unrestricted system of peer-to-peer communication. Similarly, military endorsement of network diversity accorded with the academic goal of making the internet a better research tool by incorporating more networks. When there was a serious clash between paymasters and scientists over the issue of security, it was resolved amicably through the division of the internet into military and civilian networks in 1983.

Partly as a consequence of this harmonious relationship (sustained, seemingly, even during the Vietnam War), scientists were in a position to impose their values on the general development of the net. The ideology of science is committed strongly to the open disclosure of information and, in principle, to intellectual co-operation in order to further the shared goal of scientific advance. This was manifested in the co-operative way in which internet protocols were developed. It was also reflected in the open release of these protocols, since the internet's builders were seeking to promote good science, not to make money. The culture of science also fosters interaction and discussion, and this influenced the way in which the early internet came to be used. Emailing soon eclipsed remote computing as the early internet's principal function.

However, the culture of academic life is, in largely unconscious ways, exclusionary. Academic work is seldom addressed to people outside the relevant knowledge community, which is why so much of it is buried in obscure publications and self-referential vocabulary. This exclusionary tradition was also a feature of the early internet. Considerable computer expertise was needed for people to go online, and academic computer scientists showed little interest in changing this.

Counterculture

The other formative influence shaping the early internet was the American counterculture of the 1980s. This was constituted primarily by three overlapping (and not always harmonious) subcultures: a hippy subculture centred on individual self-realization through the development of self-knowledge and freedom from repressive convention; a communitarian subculture seeking to rebuild a sense of togetherness through new forms of social organisation and collective consciousness; and a radical subculture committed to giving 'power to the people'. While this counterculture was very much in decline by the Reaganite 1980s, it directed considerable energy towards redefining the online world – partly out of disappointment with how things had turned out offline.

The countercultural movement redefined the meaning and purpose of the internet. Even in the early days of ARPANET, computer use was not confined solely to work, since some of its users had emailed each other about science fiction. Commercial online services also developed in the early 1980s. However, the counterculture helped to create new uses for the net. There was a long-running collaboration between computer scientists (who were gratified to be hailed as 'cool' by hipsters) and the graduates of flower power (looking for a way of hanging on to their dreams). This creative relationship was facilitated by techie journalists and cultural entrepreneurs. Through this alliance, the uses of computers were reimagined as an aid to personal liberation, the enabler of virtual communities and an instrument of political struggle.[9]

It was often local area networks, run usually as co-operatives heavily dependent on volunteer labour, which proved to be the most inventive. For example, the WELL (Whole Earth Lectronic Link), set up in the San Francisco area in 1985, was the brainchild of Stewart Brand, then a radical rock concert impresario, and Larry Brilliant, a left-wing doctor and Third World campaigner.[10] Brilliant enrolled numerous fellow former members of Hog Farm, a large, self-sufficient agricultural commune in Tennessee. They created an electronic commune that grew into 300 computer-mediated 'conferences' which brought together social and political activists, as well as enthusiasts of all kinds. One of its largest subgroups was composed of followers of the radical rock group the Grateful Dead. Deadheads (as they were inevitably called) spent hours online discussing the Grateful Dead's enigmatic lyrics and exchanging music recorded at live gigs – something the group supported as part of its public stand in favour of the 'pirating' of its music. Electronic communes like this later surfaced in Europe, most notably in Amsterdam's Digital City founded in 1994.

There also developed geographically dispersed grassroots networks, usually set up by students in university campuses. These included Usenet (1979), BITNET (1981), FidoNet (1983) and PeaceNet (1985). The most important of these were Usenet news groups built around the UNIX system. They were set up initially to discuss issues to do with UNIX software and troubleshooting. They proliferated to cover a wide range of issues, growing from three sites in 1979 to 11,000 by 1988. During these early years, Usenet created a significant space for the expression of radical political (and other minority) views, and recognized the global potential of the internet for building extensive international links.

The counterculture also contributed to the emergence of radical computer capitalism. Thus Steve Jobs and Steve Wozniak, who launched Apple in 1980, came out of the alternative movement. Jobs had travelled to India in a quest for personal enlightenment, while Wozniak was heavily involved in the radical rock scene. In 1982, Wozniak personally funded the organisation of a rock festival dedicated to the Information Age. At the festival, attracting more people than Woodstock, there was a giant videoscreen on which was projected a simple message:

> There is an explosion of information dispersal in the technology and we think this information has to be shared. All great thinkers about democracy said that the key to democracy is access to information. And now we have a chance to get information into people's hands like never before.[11]

In addition, the counterculture influenced American university computer science departments during the 1970s and 1980s. This reinforced the stress on freedom, open disclosure and interaction as formative influences on the technical evolution of the net. It also created a milieu that sustained a determined defence of the pioneer traditions of the internet.

Public service tradition

A further cultural influence shaping cyberspace was a tradition of public service. If the internet was incubated primarily in the United States, the world wide web was a European invention and came out of a legacy which bequeathed mass public service television and radio, parks in the hearts of cities, public libraries and art galleries, and a subsidized art-house film industry throughout much of Europe. The web's principal architect, Tim Berners-Lee, was inspired by two public service precepts: the need to create *free* public access to shared cultural resources (in this case, the storehouse of knowledge contained in the world's computer system), and the need to bring people into communion with each other (in this instance, through the connective potential of the computer). Underpinning Berners-Lee's approach was a strong public service orientation opposed to the exaltation of market values above all else. A frequently asked question, he says, in the United States (though less so in Europe) is: does he regret not making money out of the world wide web?

> What is maddening is the terrible notion [implied in this question] that a person's value depends on how important and financially successful they are, and that this is measured in terms of money . . . Core in my upbringing was a value system that put monetary gain well in its place.[12]

Berners-Lee's decision not to promote the web through a private company was prompted by a concern that it could trigger competition, and lead to the subdivision of the web into private domains. This would have subverted his conception of 'a universal medium for sharing information'. Instead, in 1991 he persuaded CERN to release the world wide web code as a free gift. He subsequently became the head of a public service agency regulating the web (World Wide Web Consortium (W3C)), since this enabled him to 'think about what was best for the world, as opposed to what would be best for one commercial internet'.[13]

Commercial honeymoon

Another influence shaping the net was the values of the market. At first, these seemed benign and progressive. Their initial effect was to counter the exclusionary norms of academic life by democratizing the web. In 1993, a commercial web browser (Netscape) was launched that used colour images, and made the web more accessible. It was followed by the creation of commercial websites that were fun to visit.

In the mid-1990s, all aspects of the internet seemed enormously positive. Even if the internet was a product of a superpower war-machine, its military legacy was terminated in 1990 when ARPANET handed over control of the public internet backbone to the National Science Foundation. A combination of academic, counter-cultural and public service values had created an open public space which was decentralized and seemingly uncontrolled. It had established a tradition of co-operation in which software codes were freely disclosed, and it had greatly extended the uses made of the net, not least through the creation of the world wide web. The growing influence of commerce seemed merely to be extending the benefits of this new medium to more people, without detracting from its fundamental nature.

The largely uncritical reception given to the increasing commercialisation of the net during the mid-1990s accorded with the ethos of the period. This was a time when deregulated capitalism was trumpeted as the only way to organise an efficient economy, and when capitalism's victory over communism was hailed as the 'end of history', following the fall of the Berlin Wall in 1989. The mood music of the time was reinforced by the outpourings of net experts. The MIT guru Nicholas Negroponte set the tone in a celebrated book, published in 1995, which portrayed the internet as the centrepiece of a democratizing digital revolution. 'The information industry', he declared, 'will become more of a boutique business . . . the customers will be people and their computers agents'. The public, he predicted, will *pull* what it wants from the internet and digital media, rather than accept what is *pushed* at it by media giants. Fundamental change was already upon us. Media consumption, he claimed, is becoming 'customized' according to individual taste, and 'the monolithic empires of mass media are dissolving into an army of cottage industries', making obsolete 'industrial-age cross-ownership laws'.[14] Similarly Mark Poster, another revered net expert, also concluded in 1995 that we are entering the 'second media age', in which monopoly is being replaced by choice, the distinction between senders and receivers is coming to an end, and the ruled are being transformed into rulers.[15] In these, and numerous other commentaries, the market was not viewed as a limitation in any way.

The coalition that had created the pre-market internet fractured during the mid-1990s. Some academic computer scientists set up internet companies and became millionaires. Others quietly acquiesced to software licensing restrictions. University administrators looked for ways to make money out of their computer science departments. A new generation of computer industry managers emerged whose informality and populism seemed to set them apart from the stuffy corporate culture of their predecessors. In this changed environment, capitalism seemed hip: the way to make money, express individuality and prevent the state from taking control. The language used to discuss new media changed. The metaphor of the 'information superhighway', with its 1950s' association of statist modernism, gave way to the romantic image of 'cyberspace', derived from science fiction.[16] Everything seemed wondrous, transformative, positive.

Increasing commercialisation

Commercialisation extended the legacy of innovation initiated by public investment. The San Francisco Bay Area, with multiple links to Stanford University, became an incubator of new net enterprises from the launch of Google in 1998 through to the creation of Instagram in 2010.

However, commercialisation also changed the character of the internet. The adoption in 1997 of a standard protocol for credit card transactions gave an important boost to online sales. The internet became in part a shopping mall: a place where virtual shops did business, and where products and services were sold. The internet transformed shopping on a national basis, though it had less impact on international sales.[17]

Online content proved more difficult to sell than offline products and services. One category of content that did sell was pornography. By 2006, the adult entertainment industry in the US – in which online porn came to play a significant part – made $2.8 billion in 2006.[18]

Commercialisation also led to the growth of online advertising. While some advertising sites like craigslist and gumtree proved to be immensely popular, online advertising could also be intrusive. The advertising industry introduced first of all the banner advertisement (a horizontal strip, reminiscent of early press display advertisements). This was followed by advertisements of different shapes such as 'button', 'skyscraper' and pop-up 'interstitials' and, later, audio-visual advertisements (more like television commercials).

The growth of advertising was accompanied by the proliferation of spam. The first recorded example of spam occurred in 1978. It proliferated to the point when, according to John Naughton, it accounted for well over half of global email traffic in 2009.[19] The technically proficient were able to filter out this tidal wave of mostly unwanted information.

Advancing market influence also introduced unobtrusive controls. Internet corporations lobbied government for changes in the law that served their interests. In particular, they pressed for the legal protection of intellectual property rights in a way that threatened to undermine the open, collaborative tradition on which the internet had been built.[20] In 1976, the United States passed a Copyright Act which extended copyright to software. This was buttressed in 1998 by the Digital Millennium Act, which greatly strengthened legal provision against piracy that threatened digital media companies. It overprotected intellectual property rights at the expense of legitimate 'fair use' of web content,[21] but in so restrictive a form that it was difficult to enforce. More recently, some leading internet and telecommunications companies have pressed for the abandonment of net neutrality – the cornerstone of the open, peer-to-peer design of the internet – in order to optimize revenue, so far without success.

Commercialisation also established more subtle forms of control based on market power. The beguiling vision of boutiques, cottage industries and sovereign consumers, conjured up by Nicholas Negroponte, proved to be a fantasy. At an international level, a small number of corporations established a leading position in different sectors of the internet. Indeed, four of these had in 2015 a level of capitalization that made them among the biggest companies in the world: Apple ($700 billion), Google ($430 billion) Microsoft ($380 billion), and Oracle ($175 billion). A small number of large news organisations dominate online news consumption in their respective countries, with a small elite group of news organisations like the *New York Times* and Globo building an international audience in their respective language markets.[22]

Some leading internet companies used their market power in ways that were exclusionary. For example, Apple iPhones and iPads do not allow the addition of applications that have not been approved beforehand by Apple. Disobey the Apple Way, and your handheld computer is liable not to work. The fact that smartphones are tethered to controlled mobile networks in contrast to the way that freely programmable computers are connected via landline networks has enabled the imposition of this new layer of control.[23]

Digital capitalism turned out to be not very different from other forms of large-scale corporate capitalism, even if the chief executive officers (CEOs) of net companies often wore jeans rather than suits. Their instrumentalist culture was embodied, in an extreme form, by Steve Jobs, the driving force behind Apple. Wondering whether to marry his pregnant, long-term girlfriend, or opt for another woman he currently fancied, he undertook a survey of almost 100 friends. Which, he asked, was the prettier? Who did they like better? Who should he marry?[24] Although capable of inspiring intense loyalty, Jobs was also crassly insensitive. When one candidate droned on in a job interview, Jobs broke in saying: 'Gobble, gobble, gobble, gobble'. The interview panel cracked up with sycophantic laughter, prompting the candidate to get up and leave, saying: 'I guess I'm not the right guy'.[25]

Although Jobs studied under a Zen Master, this did not prevent his company from being exploitative. Apple's elegant products were manufactured partly through Foxconn, a company whose factories in China are notorious for their long hours, low wages, and soulless, crowded dormitories. When a number of Foxconn workers committed suicide in 2010, the company response was not to improve working conditions but to build a safety net around its facilities.[26] While this put Apple in an unwelcome spotlight, Amazon, Google, Microsoft, Cisco and HP also outsourced work to low wage contractors with poor records. Likewise, an undercover investigation into Amazon UK found that workers walk miles every day to fulfil exacting packaging and shipping targets for just above the minimum wage. The company relies heavily on agency and seasonal staff, without the security and higher pay of permanent employees.[27]

Apple, Facebook, Amazon, Microsoft and Google all made strenuous efforts to dodge taxes.[28] Thus, Amazon channelled €15 billion to a subsidiary in Luxembourg in 2013 to evade taxes in countries where it made large amounts of money. Similarly, Google has taken advantage of tax treaties 'to channel more than $8 billion in untaxed profits out of Europe and Asia each year' into a Bermuda tax haven.[29] More recently, internet companies have come under attack from environmentalists. Their profligate use of energy in industrial-scale server warehouses is giving rise, it is argued, to needlessly large carbon emissions.[30] There has also been an explosive growth of non-recyclable e-waste caused by dumped computers, monitors, mobile phones, DVD players, ipods, ipads and microchips, positively encouraged by the way new products are deliberately launched with a short life span.[31] The 'immaterial', it turns out, has a large environmental footprint.

Commercialisation of the internet also gave rise to the development of a new regime of commercial surveillance from the 1990s onwards.[32] One method entailed the monitoring of data and traffic over a network (for example Google searches) in a form that tracks users, gathers information about which websites are visited and what users do on these sites. Another method was to install software that monitored the activities of a specific computer and its user. This software had the potential to enter the 'backdoor' of other computers, enabling the monitoring of their activity. The third approach was to collate data from different sources to compile a social network analysis about the personal interests, friendships, affiliations and consumption habits of users.

Surveillance technology came to be deployed very extensively. In the United States, an estimated 92 per cent of commercial websites aggregated, sorted and used for economic purposes data about people's use of the net.[33] Most people made themselves vulnerable to this monitoring by waiving their rights of privacy in order to gain free access. 'Human rights' protection of privacy was relatively weak in the United States, although stronger in Europe.

This technology came to be used in ways that had not been intended. According to a study released in 2000, 73 per cent of US firms routinely checked on their workforce's use of the net.[34] More importantly, autocratic governments adopted surveillance software in order to monitor and censor the internet. Methods developed to assist marketers and advertisers were deployed to support dictatorship.

It used to be widely thought that general online surveillance was a problem confined to authoritarian states. Monitoring communications in the west was directed, it was assumed, towards specific people and targets, and undertaken solely for legitimate purposes such as preventing serious crime and terrorism. It is now becoming clear that national security agencies are seeking to collect big data streams, and then process them afterwards.[35] There are various ways of collecting this information. The Snowden leaks reveal that the National Security Agency (NSA) can compel private companies like Google, Microsoft, Facebook and Skype to hand over consumer data without users themselves knowing.[36] Another way of collecting information entails placing data interceptors on the global submarine cables that are the primary arteries of the internet. It appears that this is something that the UK's Government Communications Headquarters is doing: other national security agencies in Europe are also routinely tapping internet cables.[37] There is now a growing demand for the public to be told more clearly how extensive this shift towards mass monitoring of communications is; what safeguards are in place to prevent abuse; and what protection is available for public interest whistle-blowers.

In short, the commercialisation of the internet played an important part in popularizing the internet, and making it accessible to a wider public. It also advanced creative innovation. But commercialisation had also strongly negative features. It gave rise to economic concentration and the abuse of market dominance. It led to the creation of global digital giants, some of which dodged tax, exploited workers and lobbied for changes in the law that served their interests rather than the public interest. And it led to a system of commercial surveillance that was adapted in authoritarian countries to repress dissent, and is now being utilised in liberal democracies in ways that potentially threaten civil liberties.

Revolt of the nerds

However, the steady advance of commercialism was resisted. The first people to take a stand were computer scientists who opposed the imposition of 'proprietary software' by large corporations.

The nerds' revolt began in 1984, when Richard Stallman, a radical programmer at MIT, set up the Free Software Foundation. He had been outraged when a colleague had refused to pass on a printer code on the grounds that it was now restricted by licence. This seemed to Stallman an enforced form of private selfishness that violated the norm of co-operation on which his professional life had been based. His outrage turned to anger when AT&T announced its intention to license the widely used and previously unrestricted UNIX operating system. In his view, this amounted to the corporate capture, with the full authority of the law, of a program that had been produced communally.

Richard Stallman, a bearded figure with the appearance of an Apostle, gave up his secure job and set about building almost single-handedly a free alternative to the UNIX operating system, called GNU (standing for 'GNU is Not UNIX'). Between 1984 and 1988, Stallman designed an editor and compiler, which were hailed as masterpieces of skill and ingenuity. Then, Stallman developed repetitive strain injury, and slowed down. The GNU project was still some way from completion. A Finnish student, Linus Torvalds, who had heard Stallman give a charismatic talk in Helsinki, filled the breach. With the help of his friends, Torvalds developed in 1990 the missing kernel of the GNU system. The computer community collectively improved the resulting GNU/Linux operating system, making it one of the most reliable in the world. Such was its sustained success that IBM decided in 1998 to hitch its wagon to the protest movement. It officially backed the Linux system, agreeing to invest money in its further development without seeking to exercise any form of proprietary control.

IBM also embraced, on the same terms, the Apache server. This derived from a programme released freely by a publicly funded agency, the National Center for Supercomputing Applications (NCSA) at the University of Illinois. Initially full of bugs, it was transformed by the hacker community through cumulative improvements ('patches') and renamed Apache. It became a widely used free server – its success again accounting for its open source adoption by IBM.

This was followed by the launch of the freely available client software Mozilla Firefox, in 2003–04. By 2011, it had become the second most widely used web browser in the world, having grown against the odds at the expense of Microsoft's Internet Explorer. One of Mozilla Firefox's attractions was that it provided a way of blocking online advertising.

What partly underpinned the effectiveness of this concerted protest was that it enlisted the protection of the state (something that radical libertarians tend to ignore). The Free Software Foundation set up by Stallman released its projects under a General Public Licence (GPL). This contained a 'copyleft' clause (the wordplay is typical computer nerd humour) requiring any subsequent improvement in free software to be made available to the community, under the GPL. Contract and copyright law was thus deployed to prevent companies from modifying free software and then claiming the resulting version as their property. It was also used to ensure that future refinements in free software were 'gifted' back to the community.

The successful Open Source movement kept alive the tradition of the open disclosure of information. It perpetuated the co-operative norms of the scientific community in which people make improvements, or develop new applications (like the world wide web), on the basis of open access to information and then return the favour by making the basis of their discoveries freely available. It also kept faith with the values of academic science, with its belief in co-operation, freedom and open debate in pursuit of scientific advance. The result was the creation of a practical alternative to proprietary software.

The Open Source (OS) movement drew upon highly trained computer scientists as well as skilled hackers. OS activists tended to have a shared belief that the power of the computer should be harnessed to the public good, and were inclined to view any form of authority with suspicion. They also gained satisfaction from the thrill of creativity and recognition from their peers.[38] The OS community was also guided by standards, rules, decision-making procedures and sanctioning mechanisms. It was partly this which made it so effective.[39]

User-generated content

The OS campaign was linked to the drive to participate in the creation of online content. The OS champion, Richard Stallman, had been one of the people who had argued in the 1990s that there should be a web-based online encyclopaedia which could be generated and revised collectively in much the way that OS code is produced. This dream was fulfilled when Jimmy Wales and Larry Sanger launched Wikipedia in 2001.

It became one of the largest collaborative ventures in the world. By 2017, Wikipedia published 5,455,917 articles in multiple languages, and was the fifth most popular website in the world.[40] It established itself as an invaluable (though not always reliable) source of information on a wide range of topics. This achievement was underpinned by the self-correcting mechanism of collective revision, a team of some 70,000 active editors (in 2015), a shared norm of adhering to factual accuracy, unobtrusive safeguards, editorial transparency and an academic tail of footnotes and hypertextual links.[41]

The rise of Wikipedia was followed by the even more spectacular take-off of Facebook. It was set up by Harvard students in 2004, prospered as a young elite social networking site, and then grew exponentially when it became open to all in 2006. It enables users to publish in effect to their friends, while excluding unwanted attention. By 2017, Facebook had 2.2 billion monthly active users.[42] Half its users in 2011 logged in once a day – an indication of its importance in people's lives.[43] Facebook's flotation was accompanied by the launch of numerous other successful social networking sites (SNS), such as LinkedIn (2003), Flickr (2004), Twitter (2007), Gays.com (2008), Jiepang (2010) and Instagram (2010).

Most of these sites were commercial in origin, and were increasingly controlled by major digital groups. But they were free at the point of use, and were sustained by the collective talents, interests and resources of the communities they served. For example YouTube, the video-hosting website (acquired by Google in 2006), offers a space in which users can circulate what they enjoy, and also distribute content they have created, edited or manipulated, often using software tools made available free from OS programmes. The success of this and other similar websites, and the mushrooming of SNS sites in general, marks the renewal of the do-it-yourself, communal tradition initiated by experiments like the WELL and Amsterdam's Digital City.

The radical strand of the early internet also found expression in the founding of WikiLeaks in 2006. A small, non-profit organisation, it receives, processes and makes publicly available information supplied by whistle-blowers and others. It caused a sensation in 2010 when it released footage of an American helicopter gunning down Iraqi civilians and two journalists in Baghdad in 2007, with the chilling combatant comment 'Light 'em all up. Come on, fire!'.[44] This was followed by the mass leaking of US diplomatic cables, which, among other things, provided a revealing insight into America's informal empire. WikiLeaks overcame the potential problem of being buried, and consequently overlooked, in the web's vast emporium, by forming strategic alliances with leading media organisations. In effect, WikiLeaks sought to turn the tables: governments rather than users were to be scrutinised through data stored on computers.

Recalcitrant users

The nerd revolt and the revival of communally-generated content were effective partly because they were backed up by recalcitrant users. The pre-market internet had accustomed people to expect web content and software to be free. For this reason, it proved difficult to re-educate them into becoming paying consumers.

This is illustrated by early attempts to monetise the web. In 1993, the publicly-funded agency NCSA released free its pioneer browser, Mosaic, on the net. Within six months, a million or more copies were downloaded. Members of the Mosaic team then set up a private company and offered an improved, commercial version, Netscape, on a three-month, free-trial basis. However, demands for payment, after the free trial, were widely ignored. Netscape's management then had to decide whether to insist on payment or change tack. It opted to make its service free because it feared – probably rightly – that continued attempts to charge would cause people to migrate to a free alternative. Netscape turned instead to advertising and consultancy as its main source of revenue.[45]

Initially, there was considerable hostility to the idea of net advertising. Indeed, two thirds of Americans said that they did not want any online advertising in a 1995 survey.[46] In the previous year, the US law firm Canter and Siegel had been punished for overstepping the mark. It had posted an advertisement for its immigration law advice service to thousands of newsgroups, only to be inundated the next day with so many abusive replies ('flames') that its internet service provider repeatedly crashed.[47] Over time, resistance to advertising was to some extent overcome, especially after software became available for filtering out emailed spam.

Attempts to persuade consumers to pay for online content met with less success. Companies that charged website fees in the 1990s tended to fail.[48] The music industry, after a long and disastrous delay, found a compromise solution to the online pirating of music: in effect, it opted for charging very much less for online tracks. A growing number of newspaper publishers attempted in 2010–12 to charge for content that they had previously made freely available. This proved to be largely a failure, save in the case of specialized financial journalism.[49]

A tacit détente has been reached. Consumers seem willing to waive their rights to privacy, and put up with a limited quota of advertising, while continuing to resist paying for online content. Meanwhile a growing number of people imposed their own imprint by generating, sharing and commenting on online content.

The rapid diffusion of smartphones in the 2010s deepened people's involvement with the internet. In India, a large survey found in 2016 that 61 per cent of smartphone users check their phones within five minutes of waking up.[50] In the case of the UK, the diffusion of smartphones and tablets appears to have extended people's love affair with the media. Ofcom reported in 2014 that the average adult in the UK now spends more time using media and communications than sleeping.[51] These two countries are part of a wider trend towards mass adoption of new mobile technology linking people to the internet.

Looking back

The history of the internet is thus a chronicle of contradiction. In its predominantly pre-market phase, the internet was powerfully influenced by the values of academic science, American counterculture and European public service. Originating as a research tool linked to a military project, the internet acquired multiple new functions – as the creator of virtual communities, a playground for role-playing and as a platform for interactive political debate. The crowning culmination of this first phase was the gift of the web to the world, creating a storehouse of information freely available to all.

However, this early formation was overlaid by a new commercial regime. A determined attempt was made to charge for software that had previously been free. Major media organisations established well-resourced websites. Search engines, seeking to harvest advertising, signposted visitors to popular destinations. The growth of online entertainment tended to side-line political discourse. New commercial surveillance technology was developed to monitor user behaviour, accompanied by legislation strengthening intellectual property rights. Dominant internet corporations became established, exploited out-sourced workers and evaded taxes in countries where they made large profits. In authoritarian countries, the internet became subject to a significant degree of censorship.[52]

Yet the old order refused to surrender without a fight. Dissenting computer workers collectively developed and made available OS software. Users, conditioned by the norms of the early internet, often refused to pay for online content and shifted to sites that were free. The spirit that had re-imagined the computer and discovered new uses for it in the 1980s was powerfully renewed in the twenty-first century. It led to the creation of the user-generated Wikipedia, social network sites and the whistle-blower website Wikileaks.

This historical account largely leaves out wider questions about the consequences of the net. This is best addressed by sociologists and economists, to whose work we now turn.

Notes

1 Internet World Stats, 2017. Available at: www.internetworldstats.com/stats.htm (accessed 8 August 2017).
2 The best technological histories of the internet are J. Naughton, *From Gutenberg to Zuckerberg* (London, Quercus, 2012) and J. Naughton, *A Brief History of the Future* (London, Phoenix, 2000).
3 T. Berners-Lee, *Weaving the Web* (London, Orion, 2000), p. 56.
4 B. Winston, *Media Technology and Society* (London, Routledge, 1998), p. 218.
5 S. Holland (ed.), *The State as Entrepreneur* (London, Weidenfeld & Nicolson, 1972).
6 J. Gillies and R. Cailliau, *How the Web Was Born* (Oxford, Oxford University Press, 2000).

7 P. Flichy, 'New media history' in L. Lievrouw and S. Livingstone (eds.) *The Handbook of New Media* (London, Sage, 2002).

8 J. Abbate, *Inventing the Internet* (Cambridge, MA, MIT Press, 2000), p. 144.

9 F. Turner, *From Counterculture to Cyberculture* (Chicago, University of Chicago Press, 2006).

10 H. Rheingold, *The Virtual Community*, revised edition (Cambridge, MA, MIT Press, 2000).

11 P. Flichy, 'The construction of new digital media', *New Media and Society*, 1 (1), 1999, p. 37.

12 Berners-Lee, *Weaving the Web*, p. 116.

13 Ibid., p. 91.

14 N. Negroponte, *Being Digital* (London, Hodder & Stoughton, 1996 [1995]), pp. 57–58 and 85.

15 M. Poster, *The Second Media Age* (Cambridge, Polity Press, 1995).

16 T. Streeter, 'Romanticism in business culture: the Internet, the 1990s and the origins of irrational exuberance' in A. Calabrese and C. Sparks (eds.) *Toward a Political Economy of Culture* (Boulder, CO, Rowman & Littlefield, 2003).

17 See next chapter.

18 B. Edelman, 'Red light states: who buys online adult entertainment?', *Journal of Economic Perspectives*, 23 (1), 2009.

19 Naughton, *From Gutenberg*, p. 82.

20 L. Lessig, *Code and Other Laws of Cyberspace* (New York, Basic Books, 1999).

21 L. Lessig, *The Future of Ideas* (New York, Random House, 2001).

22 J. Curran et al., 'Internet revolution revisited: a comparative study', *Media, Culture and Society*, 35 (7), 2013.

23 J. Naughton, 'Smartphones could mean the end of the web as we know it', *Observer*, 17 July 2011.

24 W. Isaacson, *Steve Jobs* (London, Little Brown, 2011) p. 272.

25 Ibid., p. 142.

26 V. Mosco, *To the Cloud: Big Data in a Turbulent World* (Boulder, CO, Paradigm, 2014).

27 C. Cadwalladr, 'My week as an Amazon insider', *Guardian*, 1 December 2013. Available at: www.theguardian.com/technology/2013/dec/01/week-amazon-insider-feature-treatment-employees-work (accessed 29 June 2015).

28 P. Sikka, 'No accounting for tax avoidance', *Political Quarterly*, 2015.

29 T. Bergin, 'OECD unveils proposals to curb corporate tax avoidance', *Reuters*, 16 September 2014. Available at: www.reuters.com/article/2014/09/16/us-oecd-tax-idUSKBN0HB18V20140916 (accessed 6 July 2015).

30 S. Cubitt, *Finite Media* (Durham, Duke University Press, 2017), p. 20.

31 J. Gabrys, *Digital Rubbish: A Natural History of Electronics* (Ann Arbor, MI, University of Michigan Press, 2013).

32 D. Schiller, *How to Think About Information* (Urbana, University of Illinois Press, 2007).

33 Lessig, *Code*, p. 153.

34 M. Castells, *The Internet Galaxy* (Oxford, Oxford University Press, 2001).

35 M. Andrejevic and K. Gates, 'Big data surveillance: introduction', *Surveillance & Society*, 12 (2), 2014.

36 G. Greenwald, *No Place to Hide: Edward Snowden, the NSA, and the U.S. Surveillance State* (New York, Metropolitan Books, 2014).

37 Z. Bauman et al., 'After Snowden: rethinking the impact of surveillance', *International Political Sociology*, 8, 2014.

38 S. Levy, *Hackers* (London, Penguin, 1994).

39 S. Weber, *The Success of Open Source* (Cambridge, MA, Harvard University Press, 2004).

40 'History of Wikipedia'. Available at: www.en.wikipedia.org/wiki/History_of_ Wikipedia#2017. (accessed 8 August 2017). 'Wikipedia statistics'. Available at: www.en.wikipedia.org/wiki/Wikipedia:Statistics (accessed 8 August 2017).

41 J. Dariusz, *Common Knowledge: An Ethnography of Wikipedia* (Palo Alto, CA, Stanford University Press, 2014); J. Zittrain, *The Future of the Internet and How to Stop It* (London, Allen Lane, 2008).

42 Statistica: The Statistics Portal, 4th quarter 2017. Available at: www.statista.com/ statistics/264810/number-of-monthly-active-facebook-users-worldwide/ (accessed 22 February 2018).

43 Naughton, *From Gutenberg*, p. 97.

44 YouTube. Available at: www.youtube.com/watch?v=q1hmPfFDEu8 (accessed 8 August 2017).

45 Berners-Lee, *Weaving*, pp. 107–08.

46 Cited in R. McChesney, *Rich Media, Poor Democracy* (Urbana, University of Illinois Press, 1999), p. 132.

47 G. Goggin, 'Pay per browse? The Web's commercial future' in D. Gauntlett (ed.) *Web Studies* (London, Arnold, 2000), p. 106.

48 D. Schiller, *Digital Capitalism* (Cambridge, MA, MIT Press, 2000); C. Sparks, 'From dead trees to live wires: the Internet's challenge to the traditional newspaper' in J. Curran and M. Gurevitch (eds.) *Mass Media and Society*, 3rd edition (London, Arnold, 2000).

49 M. Myllylahti, 'Newspaper paywalls—the hype and the reality', *Digital Journalism*, 2 (2), 2014; N. Newman and D. Levy, *Reuters Institute Digital News Report 2014: Tracking the Future of News* (Reuters Institute for the Study of Journalism, University of Oxford). Available at: www.reutersinstitute.politics.ox.ac.uk/sites/default/files/ (accessed 10 June 2015).

50 *The Hindu*, 29 December 2016.

51 Ofcom, 'Context, The Communications Market Report: United Kingdom', 2014. Available at: www.stakeholders.ofcom.org.uk/market-data-research/market-data/ communications-market-reports/cmr14/uk/ (accessed 13 July 2015).

52 See next chapter.

Chapter 21

Sociology of the internet

Introduction

There is a very large literature, dubbed 'internetphilia' by Korinna Patelis,[1] which argues that the internet will solve many of our social ills: the decline of community, political apathy, national prejudice, social discrimination, public disempowerment, and much else besides. This tradition argues that the virtual world is free, egalitarian, interactive, self-expressive and global. This virtual world is superior to the physical world which it will redeem.

The counter-argument to this is that the external context shapes the organisation and content of the internet, and filters its impact. In this view, the real world influences the internet more than the other way round.

This is a central debate in net sociology. It also provides a good starting point for assessing the role and influence of the net.

Global understanding

It is often argued that the internet is shrinking the universe and promoting international understanding. For example, the writer Harley Hahn writes: 'I see the Net as being our best hope . . . for the world finally starting to become a global community and everybody just getting along with everyone else'.[2] Frances Cairncross concurs, arguing that the effect of the internet and digitization 'will be to increase understanding, foster tolerance, and ultimately promote worldwide peace'.[3] The central theme of this upbeat commentary is that the internet's international reach, user participation and freedom will assist the world to bond in growing amity.

There is clearly some truth in this argument. For example, YouTube showcases shared experience, taste, music and humour from around the world in a way that promotes a 'we-feeling'.[4] The internet also facilitates the rapid global distribution of arresting images that strengthen a sense of solidarity with beleaguered groups, whether these be victims of natural disasters or protesters facing repression in distant lands. The internet has the potential to assist the building of a more cohesive and understanding world.

But this potential is constrained by the real world in multiple ways. International online dialogue is limited by the fact that most people only speak one language, and are mutually comprehensible to each other. The most widely spoken languages are English, Chinese and Spanish. Only about 15 per cent of the world's population understand English.[5]

The world is also economically unequal, and this inequality is reproduced as a structure of internet access. Thus, in 2015, 87 per cent of North Americans were internet users, compared with 15 per cent of the population in Pakistan, and 6 per cent in impoverished Afghanistan.[6] The dialogue taking place on the internet is between the more affluent, who are unevenly distributed around the globe.

The world is also divided by conflicts of interest and values, and these conflicts can be intensified not lessened by online communication. Thus race hate sites – of which there is a large number[7] – fuel animosity. So does the fundamentalist Islamic group, ISIS (Daesh), whose supporters had 46,000 Twitter accounts in 2014.[8] Yet, ISIS is only the most prominent example of a terrorist organisation using the internet to win converts and exert influence.[9]

Strong national attachments distort news reporting online, not just in traditional media. Popular television channels in seventeen countries devoted an average of only 22 per cent of news items to purely foreign news in 2008.[10] Yet, leading news websites in ten nations proved to be little different, being overwhelmingly preoccupied with domestic affairs, and offering only marginally more foreign news coverage than television and the press.[11]

Lastly, governments in authoritarian states around the world have found effective ways of censoring the internet (something to which we shall return). Communication online is not a space in which citizens can freely communicate with each other because what is permissible can be severely limited.

In brief, the internet is liberating because it is global and interactive. But its ability to build a more tolerant, understanding and empathetic world is constrained by linguistic division, national cultures, authoritarian controls and conflicts of values and beliefs that influence the content of the net and its reception.

Freedom from place

Another frequently invoked claim is that the internet is transforming our relationship to physical location.[12] This is based primarily on inferences derived from the nature of internet technology. Because the net is global, its use is thought to be weakening identification with place ('deterritorialisation'), and in particular with the nation. And since the net enables the formation of virtual communities of like-minded people, unconnected to where they live or work, it is also said to be loosening ties to specific contexts ('disembedding'). Physical and virtual geographies are allegedly de-merging in a form that is weakening national identity and eroding the link between social interaction and locality.

These arguments seem plausible. However, they appear rather less command-ing when they are assessed in the light of actual evidence about internet use. Empirical research shows time and again that the virtual world is best viewed as an extension of the structures and processes of the real world, rather than as a technologically determined space that is profoundly reconfiguring society.

Daniel Miller and Don Slater's classic ethnography of the net in Trinidad illustrates this point. The net, they argue, is absorbed into the everyday life and social practices of its users. For this reason, it promotes, rather than detracts from, a sense of place. A number of Trinidadian websites parade symbols of national identity or express pride in national achievements. Chat rooms celebrate a strong sense of being 'Trini' by enacting through 'ole talk' and 'liming' what are widely perceived to be national traits – the ability to communicate, to be witty about everyday things, to be warm and expressive. Encounters with people of other nations in virtual space heighten rather than diminish a sense of national belonging. Many Trinidadians view themselves as 'virtual' envoys, seek to convey a favourable impression of their country, and are sometimes taken aback by how little other people seem to know about their culture and traditions. Indeed, Miller and Slater conclude (with perhaps a degree of debunking overstatement) that: '"being Trini" and "representing Trinidad" were not always the central or most conscious aspect of internet activities, but we rarely found an internet experience in which they did not feature'.[13] The net also facilitates an idealization of Trinidad among Trinida-dians living in Britain, and provides a concrete way of staying in touch with relatives in Trinidad.

It may be that this case study is untypical. There is, argue Miller and Slater, a widespread desire among Trinidadians to identify with a stable, national community, partly as a consequence of the dislocations caused by slavery, migration and colonial subordination. In some other countries with a less traumatic past, where the tug of national identity is weaker, the net may promote a different relationship to place.

Yet, at the heart of Miller and Slater's account is a core theme that does seem to provide a secure basis for generalization. The virtual world emerges in their analysis not as a featureless space determined by its technology, but as a field of interaction shaped by local contexts. People relate to the net in terms of attitudes, cultural references and concerns derived from *real-world* locations, and this strongly influences in turn what they get out of the net. This insight accords with all that we know about media consumption in general, accu-mulated through two generations of audience research.[14]

This stress on the socially situated basis of net consumption also accords with other studies.[15] The net, and social media in particular, are used as an extension of everyday relationships: they provide a way of staying in touch with relatives, friends and acquaintances. Whether they also support identifi-cation with place depends upon the particular orientations and social contexts of net users.

Thus, Larry Gross reveals the growing importance of the net in providing a source of identity and moral support for isolated, gay teenagers, without links to local gay subcultures, and for gay men in countries where gay sex is illegal.[16] In this case, the net seemingly provides an escape from an oppressive local context to a placeless, global gay village.

By contrast, Madhavi Mallapragada argues that the net helps to sustain an imperilled Indian identity among diasporic Indians living in the United States. The net offers them a channel of communication with friends and relations in India. It disseminates symbols of Indian identity and culture, and provides a forum of discussion on identity themes (such as how to persuade Indian-American teenagers to identify with their Indian heritage). The net also offers a socially acceptable way of searching for eligible Indian life partners.[17] In this case, then, the net fosters identification with a national homeland.

These two case studies, seemingly, point in different directions. One features the net as a portal to a virtual global community, the other as a means of connecting to a physical homeland. But in fact both studies are advancing a similar insight: the varied symbolic uses of the net are shaped by what users bring to their consumption.

Social emancipation

This insistence on the need to contextualize the use of the net in its social setting in order to assess the net's wider influence on society runs counter to another widely canvassed view. This sees the virtual world as a vanguard social space in which a more tolerant, egalitarian and emancipated universe is being forged. This virtual realm of the imagination is supposedly promoting social emancipation in the real world.

The progressive nature of the online world is derived, allegedly, from its postmodern technology. This enables anonymous interaction, in which people are able to escape from the visible markers which proclaim their gender, age and ethnicity, and position them in ascribed social roles. People can assume online whatever identity they want, and also talk about themselves with unaccustomed frankness, in this way exploring fundamental questions about who they are and what they want to be. Role-playing (as in pretending to be a member of the opposite gender) can also be liberating, it is argued, because it enables people to experience at first hand socially conditioned responses, and to acquire new insight into the circumstances of others.

'Virtual disembodiment' – being taken out of one's physical self in the virtual world – is thus said in cybercultural studies to assist the building of emancipated subjectivities and the gaining of enlightenment. This claim is invested with added significance as a consequence of theoretical developments in poststructuralist theory. These stress that there is no fixed and essential self, defined by biology, nature or reason, but rather identities that are always 'performances' enacted in relation to others. Seen in this light, the virtual world is a place for working out: the equivalent of a health club where bodies can be remoulded through relentless exercise. The internet is also, in some accounts, a prefigurative space in which the patterns of the future – in particular fluid, mobile identities freed from the constraints of tradition – can be cultivated.[18]

Online role-playing was a significant feature of the internet in its early experimental phase during the 1980s but became less prominent when net adoption became more widespread, and the uses to which the net was put became more mundane. However, the rise of social media in the 2000s revived the masking of social identities online and gave this research tradition new relevance.

Its central weakness is that it tends to overstate net empowerment by examining role-play in a decontextualized way. Take, for example, Mizuko Ito's acclaimed account of the 'virtually embodied' in which she describes how Melissa assumes the identity of Tenar on entering Multi User Dungeons (MUDs). Tenar is apparently 'a powerful and well-liked figure' who has had virtual sex with, and married, a number of other MUDders. This, we are told, is very strengthening because Melissa is able to import aspects of her dynamic Tenar personality into her everyday world, and her fantasy life 'animates her real life'.[19] Since we are told almost nothing about Melissa's real life, we are forced to take this claim on trust. However, there is one aspect of Melissa's online identity that provokes scepticism. Melissa describes her body online as it used to be when she was a svelte 18-year-old. What, one wonders, are the social pressures and personal anxieties that cause Melissa to present her online self as younger and, by implication, sexier than the person she has become? Does Melissa's wish fulfilment really make her stronger, or does it increase her sense of loss and reluctance to come to terms with her increasing age? It is an entirely characteristic weakness of this celebratory account – and others like it – that such questions are not even addressed.

This 'cyberculture' tradition of research has another recurring flaw. Its underlying notion of empowerment is based on 'self-constitutive strategies of being' – put simply, on individuals taking control through redefining who they are. The virtual world is celebrated because it assists imaginative forms of redefinition and re-enactment. However, this approach tends to neglect the compelling ways in which social roles and identities are superimposed through early socialization and peer-group pressure, and to pay too little attention to underlying structures of power that underpin social regulation.

By focusing attention on the transformative properties of cyberspace, it tends also to downplay the importance of political action in achieving far-reaching change in the real world. Thus, it has taken the collective organisation and networking of the women's movement, sustained over more than a century, to achieve legislative and cultural changes in what is still an incomplete revolution.

Political emancipation

If the internet does not deliver effortless social emancipation through online fun, perhaps it is advancing a progressive politics. After all, it is argued, internet technology converts the desk into a printing press, broadcasting station and place of assembly.[20] It enables 'many-to-many' horizontal communication which cuts across elite, top-down communication by traditional media.[21] In this tradition, the net is also said to be undermining dictatorships by offering a means of bypassing established centres of power and monopolies of communication.[22] Mass self-communication and online networking is building, more generally, a progressive mobilization of popular energy that is changing the world.[23]

Again, this infectious optimism follows a now familiar pattern. It extrapolates from the technological potential of the net the view that a powerful engine of change is at work, and then fastens on to selective evidence to confirm that the net is ushering in a brave new world. What this approach fails repeatedly to grasp is that the impact of the internet is not 'determined' by its technology, and 'programmed' to promote progressive change. Rather, the impact of the net is shaped powerfully by the dynamics of the offline world. This can impede, or it can reinforce, the power of the net to effect progressive change.

In fact, there are many forces in society that act as a brake on the potential empowering role of the internet. Crucially, authoritarian governments have developed effective ways of censoring the net.[24] The most sophisticated is that adopted in China to cope with a large volume of online traffic. In essence, this comes down to three tiers of control. The first, often referred to as the 'the Great Firewall of China', is the blocking of specified websites from operating in the country. The second is the blocking of 'keywords', which prevents users from posting things that contain banned words or phrases. The third is a system of licensed compliance which requires each site to be responsible for monitoring and censoring content, or be shut down. This has generated a legion of site censors, backed up by a large state internet police force. In addition, the state deploys a large number of both paid employees and volunteers to promote official thinking online. This censorship system has evolved into a flexible regime that permits individual criticism of the government but aims to prevent organised protest and collective action. It can lead, when deemed necessary, to draconian measures including the localized disconnection of the internet.[25]

Authoritarian states' internet censorship, though not comprehensive, has been effective enough in normal circumstances to contain online subversion. Indeed, the internet has often been enrolled by authoritarian states to function as agencies supporting the regime rather than challenging it.[26]

A second key brake on the emancipatory power of the internet is the brutalizing effect of poverty. The poor usually have the greatest incentive to upend a system of inequality that places them at the bottom. But to be poor is a demoralizing experience. Those on low incomes tend to be treated with less respect, to be criticized, to be socialized early in life into lower expectations, to have lower self-esteem and sense of political efficacy, lower educational attainments and less internet access.[27] This helps to explain why in most democracies those on low incomes are the least likely to vote and participate in politics, in contrast to the affluent who are most inclined to vote and participate.[28] What happens in the offline world is carried over into the online world. Time and again research shows that the affluent are more politically active *online* – as well as offline – than those on low incomes.[29]

A third brake is that numerous people feel disconnected from politics. A comparative study of eleven nations in four continents found that, in line with other surveys, 35 per cent of respondents overall agreed or agreed strongly with the statement: 'no matter who people vote for, it won't make any difference to what happens'. Others just find politics a turn-off. In the same survey, 54 per cent agreed that 'politics is so complicated a person doesn't understand what is happening'.[30] This level of disengagement helps to explain why the internet is used by many people 'just for fun' or 'to pass the time' (the largest proportion in a Pew survey),[31] to social network, to shop, and to play games but not to access political information, save in passing.[32]

It also helps to explain why blogging has not been the force that was anticipated. A recent comparative survey found that only 1–5 per cent of online users produce a blog, depending on the country.[33] Even in the United States, the country with the highest proportion of bloggers in this survey, only a minority are interested in political blogs. Twelve per cent of Americans regularly read blogs about politics and current affairs, with a further 21 per cent saying that they read them sometimes.[34]

Of course, the internet can be a radicalizing force. In the Arab Spring, the internet and social media played a significant role in micro-blasting dissident ideas and information, feeding images and stories to the satellite TV service, Al Jazeera, and mobilizing people onto the streets in opposition to authoritarian governments in six countries. But these insurgencies had deep-seated underlying causes, and in most cases were preceded by riots and protests over a long period of time.[35] That they were not 'caused' by the internet is underlined by one key fact: the level of internet penetration in five out of the six insurgent states was lower than in neighbouring, stable authoritarian regimes like Saudi Arabia and the United Arab Emirates.[36] The internet did not create the Arab Spring, merely gave it added impetus. In the event, the gun proved mightier than the keyboard: all the insurgencies failed, save in Tunisia.

Whether the internet is a radicalizing force depends on the wider context. In Malaysia, the internet has created a space for growing dissent because the ruling elite is bitterly divided, and opposition to the government is fuelled by ethnic, religious and anti-authoritarian popular forces.[37] By contrast, the internet is largely co-opted in support of the authoritarian government in neighbouring Singapore because the elite is united, and the official ideology is broadly accepted in an economically successful city state.[38]

But if the external context usually provides the key to understanding the net's wider political impact, the internet's technology also makes a difference. It places in the hands of political activists a powerful communication, networking, organising and mobilizing tool, which increases their effectiveness.

The internet enables activists to operate more efficiently on an international level. The first important example of this was when poverty, human rights, environmentalist, trade union, consumer and other civil society organisations used the internet to mount a concerted international campaign in 1997 against the proposed Multilateral Agreement on Investment (MAI) on the grounds that it would lead to a race to the bottom in terms of government regulation. The campaign led to the MAI's abandonment in 1998 (although an attempt is now being made to revive it in a new form).[39]

Net technology also enables the sleeping giant of consumer power to be activated. A minor but intriguing example of this is when a part-time British DJ, Jon Morter, and his friends, decided to launch a protest against the commercial manipulation of pop music. They chose as their target the way in which the winner of the television talent show X *Factor* in the UK regularly headed the Christmas music chart. Through Facebook and Twitter, they launched a counter-campaign for Rage Against the Machine, selecting as their Christmas choice a track which included the line: 'Fuck you, I won't do what you tell me'. The campaign took off, securing celebrity endorsements and extensive media publicity. The protest track secured the No. 1 Christmas spot in 2009, in a collective expression of resentment against commercial control.

The internet also facilitates the mobilization of mass demonstrations. It was central to the activation of mass global justice demonstrations at Seattle (1999), Genoa (2001) and Gleneagles (2005). In this last World Trade Organization (WTO) meeting, debt relief measures for poorer countries were publicly proclaimed (though in fact only partly honoured).

Finally, the smartphone is a powerful witness of official abuse because recorded images can go viral on the net, and be picked up by mainstream media. This was exemplified by the Black Lives Matter campaign, initiated in 2014 which relayed images of unarmed African Americans being killed by the police, the Canadian case of Adam Nobody (who was badly beaten up in Toronto in 2010 by a police officer who thought he was being disrespectful when he gave his real name as Nobody), and a police officer's involvement in the death of a bystander, Ian Tomlinson, caught up in London protests in 2009.[40]

All these examples illustrate progressive campaigns partly because these are the ones that tend to be documented by leftish academics. However, the right in the US was better organised online than the left when the internet first became a powerful campaigning tool.[41] Donald Trump's campaign skilfully used social media, contributing to his election victory in 2016. There is nothing inherently left-wing about the technology of the internet.

Economic transformation

The one area which the internet has seemingly transformed is the economy. The internet's revolutionary impact was hailed from the moment it became a mass medium. In *Wired* (then the bible of the Californian net industry) the magazine's editor, Kevin Kelly, wrote an article which began 'The good news is, you'll be a millionaire soon. The bad news is, so will everybody else'.[42] More soberly, *Business Week* proclaimed in the same year: 'We have entered the Age of the Internet. The result: an explosion of economic and productivity growth first in the U.S., with the rest of the world soon to follow'.[43]

Central to this celebration was the idea that the internet is giving birth to the 'New Economy'. While this concept remains opaque, it is associated with certain recurrent themes. The internet is providing a more efficient means of connecting suppliers, producers and consumers. It is a disruptive technology generating a Schumpeterian wave of innovation, with an accompanying surge of productivity. And it is contributing to the growth of a booming information and communication economy that is compensating for the decline of manufacturing in the deindustrialized West.

At the heart of this theorizing is a mystical core. The internet is supposedly changing the terms of competition by establishing *a level playing field* between corporate giants and small companies. As Steve Jobs asserted in 1996, the internet is an 'incredible democratiser', since 'a small company can look as large as a big company and be accessible . . .'.[44] This is unleashing allegedly a whirlwind force of creativity and growth. The internet is also lowering costs and extending markets, in this way enabling new producers to prosper by catering for newly viable niche markets. More generally, the internet favours, it is argued, horizontal, flexible network enterprise, able to respond rapidly to changes in consumer demand, unlike heavy-footed, top-down, Fordist, giant corporations.[45] 'Small' is not only nimble but empowered and gifted with opportunity in the internet-based New Economy.

This analysis appears plausible only because the internet has led in fact to significant economic change. The internet altered the interactions between suppliers and consumers (as in the case of taxi services); reconfigured some markets (as in the media industries); increased the volume and velocity of global financial transactions; profoundly changed the nature of data processing and communication within business organisations; and gave birth to major new corporations like Microsoft.

But, even so, it is now clear that the transformative economic impact of the internet was overstated. The internet has not been the geyser of wealth, cascading downwards, that was anticipated. In fact the internet age has been one of low economic growth, and flatlining incomes. This was because the economic impact of the internet was overshadowed by the financial crash of 2007–08 and ensuing recession. It was also because the internet has not proved to be the all-powerful engine of wealth-creation that was anticipated. Detailed, authoritative estimates of the internet's contribution to the economy range from 0.8 per cent to 7 per cent of gross domestic product (GDP), depending upon how that contribution is defined.[46] Thus, the McKinsey Report concluded in 2011 that the internet's direct economic input averaged 3.4 per cent of the GDP of the G8 countries and five other major economies.[47]

Even the 'retail revolution' that the internet has inaugurated proves on close inspection to be less spectacular than it is widely thought to be. The 'revolution' is very unevenly distributed between nations. Within the Organisation for Economic Co-operation and Development (OECD) bloc of affluent nations, the British and Danes are the most disposed to shop online: over three quarters did so in 2013. Yet, in the same year, only 10 per cent of people in Turkey and 2 per cent of people in Mexico ordered goods and services online.[48] The volume of online shopping is also not large in relative terms. This is because online sales take place mainly within nations rather than between nations, and are uneven across different retail and service sectors. To put the rise of online selling in perspective, e-commerce sales made up just 6.5 per cent of total retail sales in the United States in 2014.[49]

While this will change, the rise of online retailing will continue to be constrained by the wider context. Some people enjoy shopping, want to try out a product before purchase, or wish to buy without delay. There are also significant obstacles slowing down the pace of international online sales: low internet access in some countries, language difficulties, security fears, differences in broadband speed and in the reliability of postal services, national variations in custom procedures and taxes, local corruption, differences of legislation respecting the cross-border transfer of personal details, the high cost of insurance and much else besides.[50]

Major advances in international online shopping will be engineered in the future through giant retailers like Amazon. However, this underscores the central fallacy in the New Economy thesis, the notion that the internet equalizes competition. Of course, the internet has created new market opportunities that have enabled some start-ups to break through. But in general, large established corporations have had the upper hand. They have bigger budgets, and greater access to capital, than small companies. This gives them a competitive advantage, which they can exploit by lowering prices and increasing promotion. They also have other built-in advantages: large economies of scale, enabling lower unit costs of production; economies of scope, based on the sharing of services and cross-promotion; and concentrations of expertise and resources that facilitate the launch of new products and services. While there can also be diseconomies of scale, large companies have been able to renew themselves through acquiring dynamic young companies.[51] Bigger companies have also been better at exploiting the internet than small ones.[52] Indeed the evidence suggests that there has been a continued trend towards concentration in both the manufacturing and service industries, with enormous gains in some sectors, in the world's leading economy.[53]

The internet itself exemplifies this process. In January, 2011, 73.5 per cent of the world's internet users were reported to have visited either Google or its subsidary, YouTube.[54] In the same month, the iTunes Store accounted for an estimated 71 per cent of worldwide online digital music sales.[55] Facebook gained two billion users, as mentioned earlier, partly due to network effects (the bigger the service, the more useful it becomes). The triumph of these giant corporations illustrates the underlying logic of the capitalist system: the natural processes of competition tend to create oligopolies.

In brief, the economic impact of the internet was filtered through the unequal relations of competition in the marketplace. The prediction that small business would triumph was not fulfilled. Corporate Goliaths continued to squash undersized Davids, armed only with a virtual sling and pebble. The protean power of the internet – its capacity to generate prosperity through increased productivity – was also not as great as was anticipated, and was greatly outweighed by the economic crisis in 2007–08, and its prolonged aftermath. The era of the mass internet proved to be the age of austerity in the west.

Wonders of the net

The limitations of the view that the virtual world is determined by its technology have been highlighted for two reasons. This view has a prominent place in the internet literature, and warrants critical scrutiny in its own right. It also offers misleading solutions to problems for which the real remedy lies in collective action. For this reason its emptiness needs to be exposed.

Yet, if the technological determinist argument is recast as a question – does internet technology make any difference? – the answer is an emphatic yes. Internet technology makes available a treasure trove of information. It offers new sources of pleasure, fulfilment and self-expression. It provides an easy way of staying connected with an extended network of people. It has strengthened civil society, and effected significant changes in the economy. And it offers new hopes and possibilities for the future.[56]

Indeed, further thought needs to be given to how to develop more fully, through public policy, the potential of the internet. Commercialisation will prevail online, unless there is a strong countervailing force. In the twentieth century the democratic state in Britain and elsewhere intervened to limit the commercial takeover of radio and television, and developed a form of organisation and public regulation that empowered and enriched society. The challenge now is to consider how this rich tradition can be re-imagined in relation to the internet; how it can be extended from the national to an international arena; and how it can be funded.[57]

Notes

1 K. Patelis, 'The political economy of the internet' in J. Curran (ed.) *Media Organisations in Society* (London, Arnold, 2000).

2 H. Hahn, 'Voices from the net', 1.3, 27 October 1993. Available at: www.spunk. org/library/comms/sp000317.txt (accessed 7 November 2010).

3 F. Cairncross, *The Death of Distance* (Boston, Harvard Business School Press, 1997), p. xvi.

4 For example, stand-up comedy in Chinese can be very funny, despite the deadening effect of subtitles. It illustrates the way in which humour can cross borders and draw people together. See Dashan, Available at: www.youtube.com/watch?v=iailMSUVenA (accessed 15 August 2011).

5 International Telecommunications Union. 'ITU calls for broadband internet access for half of the world's population by 2015', ITU News, 5 June 2010. Available at: www.itu.int/net/itunews/issues/2010/05/pdf/201005_12.pdf (accessed 10 January 2011).

6 Internet World Stats (2015b). 'Internet world statistics: usage and population statistics'. Available at: www.internetworldstats.com/stats4.htm (accessed 17 May 2015).

7 P. Gerstenfeld, D. Grant, and C. Chiang, 'Hate online: a content analysis of extremist internet sites', *Analyses of Social Issues and Public Policy*, 3 (1), 2003; B. Perry and P. Olsson, 'Cyberhate: the globalization of hate', *Information & Communications Technology Law*, 18 (2), 2009.

8 J. Berger and J. Morgan. 'The ISIS twitter census: defining and describing the population of ISIS supporters on Twitter,' Brookings Center for Middle East Policy. Available at: www.brookings.edu/~/media/research/files/papers/2015/03/isis-twitter-census-berger-morgan/isis_twitter_census_berger_morgan.pdf (accessed 22 May 2015).

9 M. Conway, 'Terrorism and the internet: new media – new threat?', *Parliamentary Affairs*, 59 (2), 2006, pp. 283–98; T. Freiburger and J. Crane, 'A systematic examination of terrorist use of the internet', *International Journal of Cyber Criminology*, 2 (1), 2008.

10 A. Stepinska et al., 'The prevalence of news: domestic, foreign and hybrid' in A. Cohen (ed.) *Foreign News on Television* (New York, Lang, 2013); cf. T. Aalberg et al., 'International TV news, foreign affairs interest and public knowledge', *Journalism Studies*, 14 (3), 2013.

11 J. Curran et al., 'Internet revolution revisited: a comparative study of online news', *Media, Culture and Society*, 35 (7), 2013.

12 J. Stratton, 'Cyberspace and the globalisation of culture' in D. Porter (ed.) *Internet Culture* (New York, Routledge, 1997).

13 D. Miller and D. Slater, *The Internet: An Ethnographic Approach* (Oxford, Berg, 2000), p. 86.

14 J. Curran, *Media and Power* (London, Routledge, 2002).

15 For instance, D. Miller, *Social Media in an English Village* (London, UCL Press, 2016).

16 L. Gross, 'The gay global village in cyberspace' in N. Couldry and J. Curran (eds.) *Contesting Media Power* (Boulder, CO, Rowman & Littlefield, 2003).

17 M. Mallapragada, 'The Indian diaspora in the USA and around the world' in D. Gauntlett (ed.) *Web Studies* (London, Arnold, 2000).

18 D. Bell and B. Kennedy (eds.) *The Cybercultures Reader* (London, Routledge, 2000).

19 M. Ito, 'Virtually embodied: the reality of fantasy in a multi-user dungeon' in D. Porter (ed.) *Internet Culture* (New York, Routledge, 1997), p. 96.

20 H. Rheingold, *The Virtual Community*, revised edition (Cambridge, MA, MIT Press, 2000).

21 M. Poster, 'Cyberdemocracy: internet and the public sphere' in D. Porter (ed.) *Internet Culture* (New York, Routledge, 1997).

22 J. Alexander, *Performative Revolution in Egypt* (London, Bloomsbury, 2011).

23 M. Castells, *Networks of Outrage and Hope*, 2nd edition (Cambridge, Polity, 2015).

24 E. Morozov, *The Net Delusion* (London, Allen Lane, 2011).

25 X. Qiang, 'The battle for the Chinese internet' in L. Diamond and M. Plattner (eds.) *Liberation Technology* (Baltimore, Johns Hopkins University Press, 2012); G. King, J. Pan and M. Roberts, 'How censorship in China allows government criticism but silences collective expression', *American Political Science Review*, 107 (20), 2013.

26 S. Kalathil and T. Boas, *Open Networks, Closed Regimes: The Impact of the Internet on Authoritarian Rule* (Washington, Carnegie Endowment for International Peace, 2003).

27 P. Lister, *Poverty* (Cambridge, Polity, 2003); E. Barry and J. Flint, *Self-Esteem, Comparative Poverty and Neighbourhoods* (York, Joseph Rowntree Foundation, 2010), among others.

28 B. Lancee and H. Werfhorst, 'Income inequality and participation: a comparison of 24 European Countries', *Social Science Research*, 41, 2012; F. Solt, 'Economic inequality and democratic political engagement', *American Journal of Political Science*, 52 (1), 2008.

29 J. Oser, M. Hooghe and S. Marien, 'Is online participation distinct from offline participation? A latent class analysis of participation types and their stratification', *Political Research Quarterly*, 66 (1), 2013; A. Smith, 'Civic engagement in the digital age', Pew Research Center, 2013. Available at: www.pewinter-net.org/Reports/2013/Civic-Engagement.aspx (accessed 1 June 2015), among others.

30 J. Curran et al., 'Reconsidering "virtuous circle" and "media malaise" theories of the media: an 11-nation study', *Journalism*, 15 (7), 2014.

31 Pew, 'State of the news media 2009', 6 March, 2009. Available at: www.stateofthemedia.org/2009/narrative_overview_intro.php?cat=0&media=1> (accessed 10 December 2009).

32 GFK and IAB 'Original digital video consumer study', GFK Media & Entertainment, April 2014. Available at: www.iab.net/media/file/GfKIAB2014OriginalDigitalVideoReport.pdf (accessed 24 May 2015).

33 R. Nielsen and K. Schrøder, 'The relative importance of social media for accessing, finding, and engaging with news', *Digital Journalism*, 2 (4), 2014.

34 A. Kohut et al., 'In changing news landscape, even television is vulnerable', Pew Internet and American Life Project, 2014. Available at: www.people-press.org/2012/09/27/in-changing-news-landscape-even-television-is-vulnerable/ (accessed 30 May 2015).

35 A. Dawisha, *The Second Arab Awakening* (New York, Norton, 2013), among others.

36 Dubai School of Government, 'Civil movements: The impact of Facebook and Twitter', *Arab Social Media Report*, 1 (2), May 2011. Available at: unpan1.un.org/intradoc/groups/public/documents/dsg/unpan050860.pdf (accessed 23 February 2018);

Internet World Stats 'Usage and population statistics: Mid east'. Available at: www.internetworldstats.com/stats5.htm (accessed 4 December 2011).

37 J. Postill, 'A critical history of internet activism and social protest in Malaysia, 1998–2011', *Asiascape: Digital Asia Journal* 1–2, 2014; M. Weiss, 'New media, new activism: trends and trajectories in Malaysia, Singapore and Indonesia', *International Development Planning Review* 36 (1), 2014.

38 Weiss, 'New media'; A. Kenyon, 'Investigating chilling effects: news media and public speech in Malaysia, Singapore and Australia', *International Journal of Communication*, 4, 2010; C. George, *Contentious Journalism and the Internet* (Seattle, University of Washington Press, 2007).

39 P. Smith and E. Smythe, 'Globalization, citizenship and new information technologies: from the MAI to Seattle', in M. Anttiroiko and R. Savolainen (eds.) *eTransformation in Governance* (Hershey, PA, IGI Publishing, 2014).

40 J. Curran, N. Fenton and D. Freedman, *Misunderstanding the Internet*, 2nd edition (Abingdon, Routledge, 2016), pp. 19 ff.

41 K. Hill and J. Hughes, *Cyberpolitics* (Lanham, MD, Rowman & Littlefield, 1998).

42 K. Kelly, 'The roaring zeros', *Wired*, September 1999. Available at: www.wired.com/wired/archive/7.09/zeros.html (accessed 10 December 2010).

43 *Business Week*, October 1999.

44 Cited in J. Ryan, *A History of the Internet and the Digital Future* (London, Reaktion, 2010), p. 179.

45 M. Castells, *The Internet Galaxy* (Oxford, Oxford University Press, 2001).

46 OECD, 'Measuring the internet economy: a contribution to the research agenda', *OECD Digital Economy Papers*, No. 226, 2013, p. 19. Available at: www.dx.doi.org/10.1787/5k43gjg6r8jf-en (accessed 12 May 2015).

47 *Internet Matters: The Net's Sweeping Impact on Growth, Jobs and Prosperity*, McKinsey Global Institute, 2011. Available at: www.mckinsey.com/Insights/MGI/Research/Technology_and_Innovation/Internet_matters (accessed 5 May 2014); cf. J. Deighton and J. Quelch, *Economic Value of the Advertising-Supported Internet Ecosystem* (Cambridge, MA, Hamilton Consultants Inc., 2009); G. Eskelsen, A. Marcus and W. Ferree, *The Digital Economy Fact Book*, 10th edition (The Progress and Freedom Foundation, 2009). Available at: www.pff.org/issues-pubs/books/factbook_10th_Ed.pdf (accessed 2 April 2011).

48 *Measuring the Digital Economy: A New Perspective* (OECD Publishing, 2014). Available at: www.dx.doi.org/10.1787/9789264221796-en (accessed 12 May 2015).

49 P. Bucchioni, X. Liu and D. Weidenhamer, 'Quarterly retail e-commerce sales', 4th Quarter 2014, U.S. Census Bureau News, U.S. Department of Commerce, Washington, D.C., 17 February 2015. Available at: www.census.gov/retail/mrts/www/data/pdf/ec_current.pdf (accessed 12 May 2015).

50 *E-commerce—New Opportunities, New Barriers: A Survey of E-commerce Barriers in Countries Outside the EU* (Swedish National Board of Trade, 2012). Available at: www.wto.org/english/tratop_e/serv_e/wkshop_june13_e/ecom_national_board_e.pdf (accessed 14 May 2015).

51 For introductions to a large literature, see M. Porter, *On Competition* (Boston, Harvard Business School Press, 2008); and H-J. Chang, *Economics* (London, Pelican, 2014).

52 *Measuring the Digital Economy: A New Perspective* (OECD Publishing, 2014). Available at: www.dx.doi.org/10.1787/9789264221796-en (accessed 12 May 2015).

53 J. Foster, R. McChesney and R. Jonna, 'Monopoly and competition in twenty-first century capitalism', *Monthly Review*, 62 (11), 2011.
54 Naughton, *From Gutenberg*, p. 269.
55 Ibid., pp. 277–78.
56 The next chapter explores further the impact of the internet, focusing on social media.
57 See Chapter 28, p. 496 for a modest beginning. This is an area in which we all need to come up with new ideas.

Chapter 22

Social media

Making new societies or polarization merchants?

Great media disruptions change everything: politics, society, psyches. The invention of printing and the emergence of the press, the spread of broadcasting, were each the consequence of social and political upheaval but they also brought about great shifts in society and political systems. So the social media are creating new ways of living and new choices. What feels like and often is, gossip, is shaping how we see the world and profoundly remaking how it is organised.

The social media are reengineering the boundaries between our personal and public lives in a vast sociological and psychological experiment. In *1984* by George Orwell, the first subversive act of Winston Smith, the protagonist, is to buy and begin to keep a secret diary. He is composing his 'self' privately. Indeed he is trying to keep it secret in an audacious and dangerous anti-authoritarian act of defiance. This is because the regime wants to control not only his outward compliance but his inner devotion to it. That seemed dystopian in 1949 – although Orwell based his book on the reality of communist and fascist totalitarianism. Now, beside the willingly shared and lovingly curated 'selves' displayed in the social media, we inadvertently give away such huge amounts of data about our ourselves that our desires, ideas, values and aspirations become data for others, whether we like it or not. Our feelings and sensibilities can be manipulated by algorithms to sell us things and provide us services but also to sell us political messages in ways that feel natural and personal.

In the past we had 'strong' social links to people we knew, institutions we were part of, our close social groups and families: but we had 'weak' links to myriads of institutions, sources of information, professional groups, the places we lived. Poorer, less advantaged groups had fewer 'weak' links and depended for their life chances on other 'strongly' linked personal relationships.[1] The social media are based on maximising personal links. They are 'weak' links as they are institutional and external, but paradoxically have many of the features of 'strong' links because the material viewed comes from personal recommendations. Even those with millions of followers depend on these personal ties. This is an unexpected revolution in social communication. The big five social media companies – Amazon (founded in 1994), Google (1998), Alibaba (1999), Facebook (2004), Twitter (2006), and attendant music and image sharing sites – have changed the way we relate to each other.

Another intriguing feature is that an overwhelming abundance of information and communications are multifaceted and shared multilaterally and multinationally. Political and social power, new interest groups and new problems have international and domestic dimensions: cyber-crime and celebrity brands share the same communication spaces. On the other hand – partly in response to the copious complexity available, partly because of the enhanced tools developed to navigate the variety – narrow 'silos' of information and opinion may develop. Again the weak 'bridging' links to many opinions that the media used to produce may be being replaced by 'strong' personalized links to narrow views.

Having remade diplomacy, upended businesses, churned over power and threatened what states are, this revolution may be altering how we inhabit our own selves. Meanwhile multinational corporations, transnational institutions, celebrities, the accelerated movements of people and goods have diminished the powers of states. Non-state players, such as jihadists and right-wing groups, have media production houses and claim great expertise at using the social media to convert adherents.[2]

Some states, with a will to control their public, also use the increased communication to 'know' ever more about their populations and to enhance their power of surveillance and manipulation. The impact of the previous great media eruptions was the product of social and political forms they existed within. Each was used for good *and* bad ends.

In this way an uploaded and shared video of an atrocity does not just record conflict; it can drive more violence. Although it may move a spectator to pity, produce understanding and lead to engagement and the will to amend, it can equally be a recruiting tool eliciting the desire for revenge or emulation.[3] In a similar way President Trump – elected in 2016 – was perhaps the first post-television president: how he looked and behaved were part of a new script.

Trump's victory, and the Brexit vote in the UK the same year, raised a new problem that mature democracies have not yet addressed. Both campaigns spent millions – in Trump's case, tens of millions of dollars – in tailoring political messages for individual voters on Facebook. These were received without the voters knowing the source of the message. Democratic controls on undue influence, including audits of spending on election campaigning, have no tools to counter this.[4]

And at the same time internet activists, acting either independently or under orders from the Russian state, were clearly also seeking to influence western democratic decisions. Russia's mastery of information warfare, through *maskirovka* over many decades is not well enough understood, but is a central feature of its military success in Crimea and Ukraine. 'The fog of war isn't something which just happens—it's something which can be manufactured', wrote the radio producer Lucy Ash after travelling to Ukraine. 'In this case the Western media were bamboozled, but the compliant Russian media has also worked hard to generate fog'.[5]

In more recent times this capacity has been extended into the non-military sphere. 'The Russian strategy, both at home and abroad, is to say there is no such thing as truth', according to journalist and filmmaker Peter Pomerantsev.[6] More open democratic nations have no solution to this new situation, where fake news has become a policy for those who are constant competitors for strategic and political space, if not actually formal enemies. And far from contesting this, the Trump presidency embraced some of its tactics and techniques, particularly in the spread of fake news. The huge spend on Facebook posts was worth it. Surveys of the 2016 US election showed that the most popular fake news stories were spread more widely than the most popular mainstream (i.e. fact-checked) news stories.[7]

The long policy struggle to shape the impact of the media for democratic ends has raged for decades. Arguments about governance, institutions, market forces, the needs of a well-informed citizenry, battles about freedom of speech and its proper limitations are all part of this struggle. They have just begun to develop around the social media. The problem is we lack the institutional tools to enact policy and the new communities that might produce policy are themselves riven and divisive. But young people are innovative: now they need to be as this is a policy area that will shape their future.

The encouraging news is that however revolutionary the social media are, and however transformative, the problems they pose of trust, finding ways of informing citizens and ensuring that their views are not manipulated, establishing the conditions for varieties of voices to be expressed but also heard, are not new. As Cass Sunstein, the prescient political scientist argued, we need:

> to evaluate any communications technology by asking how they affect us as citizens and not only by asking how they affect us as consumers . . . freedom imposes certain conditions, ensuring not just respect for choices and the satisfaction of preferences, but also the free formation of desires and beliefs.[8]

The message is the community

One of the most resilient findings over nearly seventy years of research into the media has been that society trumped messages. It has been repeatedly shown that the community you are embedded in, the work you do, the family you belong to, the peer group tastes you admire or abhor, all locate you in a social structure that interacts with the media messages you consume and reply to. One aspect of studying the media critically has always been to demonstrate the limits of their influence.

An alternative reforming tradition has argued that the media set public agendas, or that the free market in opinion does not work well in any number of ways, or more simply that propaganda – lies, deceit and the mobilization of public opinion for malign ends – has frequently worked. Nevertheless, comfortingly for democrats, it appeared that the reality of the web of social structures people live within determined their views more than mere images or messages.

The social media are reinventing the significance of those findings, because the online world of the social media offers immediate, real time, warm, personal social support and a community. The social structure that used to be separate from the messages – lives lived in the world of work and home, school and society – has decamped, and become integral to the messaging. The communities that offer individuals support and meaning are frequently online where the social media have personalized communal ties. Communities and messages have merged.

Originally the social media were seen by social theorists like Manuel Castells as offering the first great opportunity for equality and the expression and inclusion of marginalized groups. This is true. However, it also turned out that they were a platform that encouraged and perhaps enhanced marginalized but extreme groups. At one level they are just like any medium – neutral. However they have also provided a particular platform for recruiting more extreme kinds of belief and legitimizing speech and ideas that the original social theorists had no idea might emerge.[9]

Plenty and silos

Yet an over-abundance of communication, messages, information, images, can swamp consumers who have to choose. Their choices (of shoes, music, suppers and beliefs) are then enhanced by algorithms. They are directed towards what they appear to want. This is fantastically useful and occasionally absurd. But accidental or casual choices can dynamically lead in unexpected directions.

Indeed, what people 'choose' as consumers – data impossible not to donate freely – and then massed in vast amounts provides something nearer to prediction than any previous social scientific method. Consuming is now more valuable as an indication of political choices than politics is. Mumsnet, the influential and indeed very useful website for parents, recently offered its interested and engaged users some helpful links to petitions they might *like* to sign – and then it signed them up to them. It was predicting their political preferences and helpfully pushing them to action (even if a minor relatively cost-free kind of action).

Polarization

Amid the proliferation of communication, messages, information and images, and the breakneck pattern of integration and interconnectedness, reliable and important is not easy to distinguish from the insignificant or deliberately misleading. 'Winning' attention is now hard, winning attention for the relatively trustworthy often harder. Winning consideration for the nuanced, the considered, the argued but open-minded, the grey world of uncertainty and 'good enough' is peculiarly tough. The net and social media are rarely deliberative, they are Manichean – most things are black or white.

This overabundance has contributed to a new world of rigid 'silos'. These are sometimes called 'ghettoes' or 'buckets' but silos, 'a system, process, department that works in isolation from others' as the *Oxford English Dictionary* defines them – also resonate with the sense that silos exist in structures but also in ideas, social groups and minds. It might be called the division of labour – specialization after all permits complexity. However, 'silos' can also be a threat because they exclude a wider view, which can be dangerous: the financial crisis of 2008 was at least in part created because almost no one understood aspects of the financial instruments that were being traded.[10]

Cass Sunstein identified the 'growing power of consumers to "filter" what they see' as the 'most profound influence on democracy and free speech'. He argued that the traditional regulatory concerns of the American system – restricted to minimising state power and enhancing individual choice were inadequate to the new environment:

> The phenomenon has conspicuous importance for the communications market, where groups with distinctive identities increasingly engage in within-group discussion . . . as the public becomes balkanised and groups design their own preferred communication packages . . . this is in part one adaption to the online plenty.[11]

It means that opinions and views are reinforced not challenged. Online plenty encourages tunnel vision: it can narrow encounters. Meeting different points of view is harder, not easier.

Helpful and warm

For an example take the interaction between social media and eating disorders: it is not political, it is socially important and embedded in many social and economic developments. But it may also be indicative. One in 150 15-year-old girls, one in 1000 boys, suffer from anorexia in the UK and there is evidence that the whole range of eating disorders from anorexia, bulimia, bingeing and over-eating are increasing.[12]

While any eating disorder is a personal tragedy for sufferers and their families and each individual will have a distinct narrative that explains the emergence of the problem, the diseases are also a social problem. Eating disorders have the highest mortality of any mental disease. Twenty per cent of sufferers go on to have severe medical problems and some die directly or as a result of side effects of the condition.[13] Treating eating disorders is difficult, as eating – or not eating – is a control mechanism people return to when under pressure. Experts now find over-eating far more difficult to treat than anorexia where the prognosis is improving – although the problem is growing.

Evidence shows that the most important factor in improving outcomes is early identification and swift intervention. The management and treatments available have improved. Talking about the experience with other sufferers is often a relief: in this way online forums can be a great support, and young people search for them. Many young people recover.

However, there are aspects of the role of communications in the journey to (and from) eating disorder that seem more widely pertinent. Anorexics have a paradoxical relationship to their condition: 'people with eating disorders often have both positive and negative emotions about anorexia itself and the idea of recovery'.[14] There are a vast number of websites and organisations online dealing with aspects of anorexia and bulimia. Some are outstanding (B-eat is professional, evidence-based, sensitive and supportive of sufferers and their families[15]). Some are financed by adverts from clinics offering treatment for the conditions. Then there are thousands of 'slimming' websites and schemes offering advice on how to lose weight which can be retooled by sufferers as offering advice on how to starve rather than to 'slim'. There are many individual and collective blogs and sites run by those with the condition that can be very helpful in sharing views and problems. Yet discriminating between the values on offer in different sites is not easy.

There are also many, easily discoverable, 'pro-ana' websites which advocate eating disorder as a legitimate individual choice and a way of life.[16] They advance very low calorie intakes, see eating as a 'failure', are disinhibited about bodily functions and express a kind of self-loathing. They are normative in address: typically one exhorts 'RULES, RULES, RULES. This is important you have to set rules for yourself and if you are truly ana, you will have no problem in sticking to them because you are STRONG!' The rules are draconian. Yet such sites also provide direct personal response, warm support to sufferers, many of whom feel dependent but also assisted by them. Many are created by young women.

A European Union (EU) study in 2011 showed that 10 per cent of 11–16-year-olds had seen a 'pro-ana' site. Emma Bond, the author of an authoritative report on 'pro-ana' sites *Virtually Anorexic – Where's the Harm?*[17] observed:

> There are a number of factors that might explain why 'extreme' communities form on the Internet. Online anonymous environments, allow people to express views about their disorder that would be judged negatively in other surroundings. 'Pro-sites' for those with positive beliefs about a stigmatised behaviour exist for other behaviours also such as drug use, self-harm and suicide . . . Cyberspace has emerged as a critical context

for the construction of alternative identities and narratives relating to eating disorders.[18]

Eating disorders emerge against the symbiotic relationship that the media and communications have to food, body image and identity more widely. Advertising, fashion, the food industry, the meaning of food, tastes and society, all have media aspects. It is not that the media *cause* disorders but they are one part of the jigsaw. Changes in the role of meals, the nature of cooking, the availability of fast food are probably more influenced by changes in work patterns than any media campaign. Calorie intake is influenced by what manufacturers put into food: tastes for sweet and salty foods are created and enhanced.

Yet another aspect of the interaction of the media and eating disorders is body image. Images of ideal others, ideas of self-worth, competitive perfection seeking, a kind of misplaced idealism, control, discipline, sacrifice and personal support and the creation of peer groups are all inter-related.

There are flagrantly unrealistic body images of women in the print and online media where images of women are often accompanied by a severe culture of policing – shame and celebration. The *Mail Online*'s news posts, for example, offer a constantly refreshed and never-ending rehearsal of emotional drama expressed in narratives about female weight. Becoming thinner is always seen as a victory and weight gain characterized as disorderly. Post-partem bodies are seen as especially threatening and criticized or praised in a way that is deeply disturbing – and cannot be in the interests of mothers or babies. There is a vigilante scrutiny of deviant female shape, in turn related to soft pornographic images of women with little on: 'The only good thing that comes from heartbreak is weight loss', says Stephanie Davis, 'in nothing but tiny knickers as she flaunts her slimmer figure'.[19] So the wider context of the media images is one context for the emergence of eating disorders.

Although there is a clear media code governing the reporting of eating disorders avoiding 'triggers' detailing minimum calorie intakes, minimum sizes, extreme pictures, all facts which prompt imitative behaviour in sufferers, no such restrictions can be imposed on websites.[20] Although there have been some careful interventions, taking down self-harming websites, they soon re-emerge, and there is no way (and no attempt) to control such triggers.

Anorexia can be 'infectious'. It can sweep through institutions: like a slow moving riot it can run wild within groups. Historically this was observed in schools, which are now alert to the condition. It is about being part of one kind of group at the expense of all other social bonds. Wanting to be an insider not an outsider. Of course, teenagers are especially vulnerable to wanting to belong and may be uncertain: the sites offer one kind of direction and identity.

Now a supportive, warm, online community of sufferers may form such a significant group. Online communities can suffer epidemics as well. To be a popular, active, much-admired member of such a community via notice boards and forums is exciting and there is honour and status to be attained within the community. The eating disorder sites bustle with posts continuously coming in: messages asking for help from new and older users pop up day and night; they are an insistent mixture of despair and display. Pictures are constantly being added. They are clearly a sympathetic space, which provides understanding and without which users may feel bereft (when sites are closed some say they self harm more).[21]

The stated function of almost every pro-ana site however is to help users lose weight: to achieve the inevitably moving target of ever more 'perfect' skeletal, bodies. After a few weeks visiting the sites the extreme images of skeletal bodies stop being shocking and become normal.

If one aspect of eating disorders is that of bonding with a sympathetic community: then another is the retreat from other groups. Rejecting family, friends and indeed everyday contacts is often a part of the eating disorder: and many sites have 'secretive' inner sanctums which are more desirable as you can only join them after a long apprenticeship in starving. Sites are full of 'tips' and cheats – ways of disguising and hiding the disorder from others, deceiving carers about calorie intake and so on. Indeed, the outside world is described as something to be avoided, misled, and is simply irrelevant to the code of behaviour and success within the community of the condition. In this way pro-ana sites do recruit by excluding other realistic interpretations not just of eating – but of the normal life. While online relationships in like-minded groups help people at difficult times, 'support' needs to be understood as a value neutral process. Vulnerable people can be 'supported' in ways that are not in their best interest.

Such 'silos' of opinion (a model for many others) sites are directional, help change an aspiration, (or an accidental encounter) into an implementable programme, 'transforming what might be vague, ill thought out plans into a concrete set of instructions'.[22] They spread information and equip young people with the tools they need to act in the context of a community of sympathetic and like-minded people.

Tone

Why have the social media apparently – among all the other good things they may produce – also encouraged the emergence of more extreme groups? Why do the extreme right and left share such a similar weird, joking, punishing, irony-laden language online?

Partly it is because the media encourage random encounters; people find each other – and then by reinforcing each other's views they auto-legitimize themselves. And once in 'silos', people egg each other on in a competitive spiral. They can choose never to encounter opposed points of view and wage war aggressively against them: finding comfort in being together in a warm familiar group. They can define themselves as 'insiders' by a toxic hostility to outsiders. They groom and recruit members.

'The triumph of the Trumpians' writes Angela Nagle in *Kill all the Normies*:

> was to win in the war against the hated mainstream media . . . we see online the emergence of a new kind of anti-establishment sensibility expressing itself in the kind of DIY culture of jokes and user-generated content that cyberutopians have evangelised for years but had not imagined taking this particular form.

She goes onto argue that, if on the left, 'there is an utterly intellectually shutdown world of Tumblr and trigger warnings and the purging of dissent in which all too many have only learnt to recite jargon', then on the right (in America), 'you will find a deluge of the worst racial smears imaginable, vicious commentary about ethnic communities and women and fantasies of violence against them . . . this may chill critical thought for years as fewer and fewer may have the stomach for it'.[23]

The state, governments and digital territory

The social media are creating new powers: Amazon, Google, Alibaba, Facebook and Twitter have larger revenues and more influence than many mere states. Having parasitically consumed as a right news and content produced by others they have now consumed the advertising that supported that content. But they do not send ambassadors to world conferences, they see 'the state' as an enemy to their uninhibited right to innovate and monetize the public of everywhere. A narrative that started on the right that 'the state' was inefficient and markets better, has in the area of communications been completely swallowed by the left who also sees 'the state' as an enemy. From surveillance to misunderstanding of the role of the BBC, from the response to 'fake news' and the establishment of 'alt' news sites, many of which peddle extreme ideological views, there is a peculiar realignment in which left and right are in agreement. The 'State' is the enemy. The neo-liberals have won. So social democratic reformers have a complex battle on their hands. Yet, as Tony Judt wrote presciently in 2006:

> We may find that a healthy democracy, far from being threatened by the regulatory state, actually depends on it: that in a world increasingly polarised between isolated insecure individuals and unregulated global forces, the legitimate authority of the democratic state may be the best kind of intermediate institution we can devise.[24]

The world is now multipolar and has been remade by the new power of communication and international affairs far more complex than in the bipolar world of the Cold War (although it hardly felt simple at the time). Messaging and interpretations of events swirl around an interconnected world. This is easy to state but demanding to deal with in international affairs. Modern threats are not simple; they are multifaceted and waged at home as well as abroad. They come in unexpected ways and are hard to calibrate. International and national boundaries are porous, threats and opportunities spill from one realm to another. Domestic and international affairs are increasingly shaped by cross-national communities of interest which find expression in communications.

Non-state actors using the social media – from terrorist groups to multinational corporations and entertainment 'brands' – have all been successful at exploiting this new fluidity. Then there is a leaky communication of action, a world in which it is harder for some players (but not others) to restrict or manage who interprets actions. It is, said one alarmed diplomat, like playing 'Eight-dimensional chess'.

Much hostility is extended towards states indiscriminately. They are seen as driving surveillance and developing overweening power. Yet there are contradictions – people want to have clean air and a health service, they want safe streets and to consume, they want not to be attacked by terrorists. So the deal between surveillance and citizen's rights has to be negotiated. Yet just as democratic states everywhere and politics are weakened there is as yet no alternative for governing the social media in the interests of citizens except by policy. We need a Universal Declaration of Digital Rights but the international system that might have produced it is frail. It may be that another newer, cleverer, system will emerge.

Attention

It is irrelevant whether Amazon, Google, Alibaba, Facebook and Twitter are 'well intentioned' or not. It is utterly irrelevant if they claim to want to reform health or 'govern' better. Developing omnipotence is fundamental to how they make money, and their fundamental business model is based on harvesting and feeding attention and understanding it.

The degree of surveillance (voluntarily permitted in exchange for desirable services) has crept up on consumers who are also citizens and who cannot see what is happening but who enjoy the efficiency of enhanced choosing.

Advertisers have always wanted their messages to be seen within or beside sympathetic content – whether in print or on TV they have sought to enhance their messages by putting them in a similar or supportive context. Advertisers have always 'targeted' messages about goods they want to sell at likely audiences. Political movements have done this as well: tailoring messages to different audiences. The media more widely have also always monetized attention: their real economic purpose was to sell audiences. Giving you more of what you want, excluding what you do not want, finding out exactly what your tastes and preferences are, is now so acutely developed that they can predict your political views very quickly from your musical taste.

All of this is potentially enriching. The next generation of health interventions will come from data about how people live. But governance is all and there is no governance in the public interest of any of this new social media landscape.

Fit for purpose institutions

So there is a conundrum: what instruments do we have collectively to address these two entwined problems? There are complex international echo chambers of communication and deep and worrying narrow spaces which may increasingly cordon off the vulnerable?

In the parochial, fussy, sour debate about the future of the BBC around the 2016 White Paper these immediately important issues were hardly recognized. Yet the Corporation, invented in the 1920s, can address both the international multifaceted aspect of communications while having a potential role in enlarging the discussion of the most intimate, personal issues – like eating disorders. It can do both. The BBC's international presence combined with its national role makes it one of the few institutions we have that is fit for purpose in the evolving, interconnected world.

At least this is a policy – not a perfect or adequate one – that can be addressed. We need (and are getting at last) a new generation of social media natives in government. But they need ideas and principles and a progressive tradition and philosophy to call on. The Corporation is a relatively small player in the new international world of communications. Yet this is one institution we have that has the right shape and has the right – public – values at the core of everything it does. When it fails, which it inevitably does, the public can ask it to do better. The new structure of international, national and personal life is being shaped by communications, not borders – and the BBC is in the business of communicating.

If we need to be able to understand what is happening abroad, react to it, we need to understand the domestic consequences and manage those as well. In addition, there are the interconnected problems where unilateral solutions are inadequate. Climate change, the control of epidemics, migration and cyber-crime have thrown up international interest groups and sometimes – at least around epidemics – novel and remarkable forms of organisation. But all of them require complex cross-border, cross-lateral thinking and solutions.

Living together, accepting difference

The twenty-first century's great dividing line, which is not between the East and the West, Christianity and Islam, men and women, or perhaps even haves and have-nots, but between those who want to live together and those who do not, is lived out in practice in the social media. It connects people but it also divides them. Just as most terrorist acts can be seen as a conscious assault on the places and people who are willing to live together, so the social media can bring people together or socialize and normalize intolerance.[25] Much terrorism is directed at the *idea* of co-existence as well as the people who are living together. But it is a broader problem: social media can provide a new communication fuel for people to define themselves as inside some communities and against 'other' groups. This is not least because they provide an apparently uniquely personal space.

But with will and ingenuity policies can be developed. The problem is not quite as new as it seems and the ideals are there. John Stuart Mill – the great nineteenth-century thinker – put the aim best:

> It is hardly possible to overstate the value, in the present low state of human improvement, of placing human beings in contact with persons dissimilar to themselves, and with modes of thought and action unlike those they are familiar . . . Such communication has always been, and is peculiarly in the present age, one of the primary sources of progress.[26]

Notes

1 Mark Granovetter in the 1970s published a series of works that explored these relationships. See *The Strength of Weak Ties – Stanford Sociology*. They have become the basis for a new way of looking at the social media. Available at: https://sociology. stanford.edu/publications/strength-weak-ties.
2 See J. Burke, *The New Threat from Islamic Militancy* (London, Vintage, 2016) for the best and most accessible account of media developments.
3 See J. Seaton, *Carnage and the Media* (London, Penguin, 2005) for a discussion of some of these issues.
4 Available at: www.bbc.com/news/av/magazine-40852227/the-digital-guru-who-helped-donald-trump-to-the-presidency.
5 L. Ash, 'How Russia outfoxes its enemies', BBC News, 29 January 2015. Available at: www.bbc.co.uk/news/magazine-31020283.
6 See Ash, op. cit.
7 Available at: www.web.stanford.edu/~gentzkow/research/fakenews.pdf.
8 C. Sunstein, *Republic.com 2.0* (Oxford, Princeton University Press, 2011), p. 75.
9 See M. Castells, *The Rise of the Network Society*, revised edition (London, Vintage, 2016). And much else.
10 See G. Tett, *The Silo Effect* (New York, Simon & Schuster, 2015).
11 C. Sunstein, *Republic Divided in the Age of Social Media* (Oxford, Princeton University Press, 2017), p. 110.
12 Royal College of Psychiatrists, 2014. Available at: www.rcpsych.ac.uk/healthadvice/problemsdisorders/eatingdisorderskeyfacts.aspx.
13 The costs of eating disorders. Social, health and economic impacts B-eat, 2015. Available at: www.beateatingdisorders.org.uk/.

14 S. Williams and M. Reid, 'Understanding the experience of ambivalence in anorexia nervosa: the maintainer's perspective', *Psychology and Health*, 25 (5), 2010, pp. 551–67.

15 B-eat, the national eating disorder charity, (Youthline).

16 See J. Bartlett, *The Dark Web* (London, Atlantic Books, 2015).

17 E. Bond, *Virtually Anorexic – Where's the Harm? A Research Study on the Risks of Pro-Anorexia Websites* (Beat/Childnet/Nominet Trust, 2012), p. 3.

18 E. Bond, *Virtually Anorexic – Where's the Harm? A Research Study on the Risks of Pro-Anorexia Websites*. Available at: www.thechildrensmediafoundation.org/wp-content/uploads/2014/02/Bond-2012-Research-on-pro-anorexia-websites.pdf.

19 Available at: www.dailymail.co.uk/tvshowbiz/article-3584705/Only-good-thing-comes-heartache-weight-loss-Stephanie-Davis-poses-tiny-knickers-flaunts-weight-loss-Jeremy-McConnell-split.html.

20 Beat Media Guidelines.

21 J. Bartlett, *The Dark Net* (London, Heinemann, 2016), p. 197.

22 Bartlett, *The Dark Net*, p. 207.

23 A. Nagle, *Kill All Normies* (Winchester, Zero Books, 2016), p. 2.

24 T. Judt, *Reappraisals* (London, Vintage Books, 2006), p. 23.

25 See T. Fletcher, *Naked Diplomacy: Power and Statecraft in the Digital Age* (London, William Collins, 2016), pp. 213–33.

26 J. S. Mill, *Principles of Political Economy*. Available at: www.econlib.org/library/Mill/mlp.html.

Part IV

Theories of the media

Chapter 23

Metabolising Britishness[1]

Is there such a thing as 'Britishness'? More than ever, being 'British' is voluntary, not necessary. What is it? Where can we find it? What part do the media play not merely in representing it but in forging changing national realities? Brexit threw the nature of the nation into disarray. It revealed divisions: metropolitan versus old industrial, the south versus the north, the abandoned towns that used to live off the sea versus cosmopolitan centres. But it did not solve the problem of who and what the nation could be. What, indeed, about 'Englishness'? If the nature of the union between the different nations that compromise Britain is a problem – then the meaning of the 'English' nation is even more perplexing. Even raising the subject seems, in one kind of way, indelicate. Is it somehow offensive to even mention the idea of the nation in which we belong but towards which we have complicated allegiances – or which we may feel barely a part of? Surely we are all global citizens, all have multiple identities, which we shuffle and balance? It is quite acceptable, it seems, to assert and celebrate religious and cultural differences, or 'being Scottish' – or any number of the national minorities that so gloriously complicate our communities. In any case, we often like to think of ourselves as rather doughty, beleaguered members of minorities bravely asserting our identity against the nasty (and large) nations, or nasty (and large) majorities. As we are frequently shockingly ignorant of the alternative lives of other people we live in close proximity with, many injustices still occur. But actually, it is quite hard to assert, for example, English working-class identity, without being suspect. Of course, 'nationalism' can be a very dangerous force and typically, in harsh economic times, it is an appallingly destructive one. But does that mean we should abandon any sense of a unique national identity? What part do the media play in relating us to a common predicament?

The media, however inadequately, tell us both much of what we know of others we live with, and even more of what we believe. Images are perhaps one thing; it is when insensitivity turns into acts which alter how people can lead their lives that we need to consider more carefully. Despite many forces dissolving the capacity of nation-states to determine their own future and the nature of the economic and political interconnectedness of international fate, nevertheless we still live in nation-states. We still go to school in them, we get treated by their healthcare systems (or not), are policed within them, walk on national roads and drink national water. But do we live within them in our imaginations?

Perhaps we have, here, a special problem. No one quite knows what it is to be British. 'Britishness', British history, customs and habits seem especially questioned. Indeed, everywhere there is an anxious inspection of national tea leaves for what they might portend (except, of course, we British don't drink as much tea as we used to – perhaps even our auguries have become unreliable?). What is 'Britishness'? This is not the first tentatively anxious enquiry into the mystery. It tends to come up when people are uncertain about it – for if you are clear about what it is and that you feel it, there is no question to be asked. Despite the revolutions in how we live, are there continuing sensibilities and processes that provide a recognizable architecture to what we want to be?

The problem is not that Britain has changed, but rather, whether we need it any more. The national project has, it is argued, been unsettled by colliding forces which play out in confusingly opposite directions. The media have a direct and symbiotic relation to the mystery of the British constitution. Unlike America, or France or indeed Russia, we have no written constitution, no set of legal documents that specify what we are and the nature of the contract we have all made in order to agree to live together. Of course, written constitutions do not guarantee the good life in themselves (the Russians have had a magnificently liberal constitution for nearly a hundred years, but the written rules have had no impact on how Russians have lived during any of that time). The British tradition is unwritten, based on experience and case law and a great, fragile machine of institutions that operate (at their best) according to a flexible interpretation of the duties and rights of individuals and the collective good. The media, in different ways, are central to this – for better and for worse. So in one way the media in Britain, as well as holding local, regional and national political actions to account (or failing to), play an especially important – although informal – part in our collective condition.

Nevertheless, slightly subversively, one might observe that 'Britishness', and certainly the British constitution, have always been a muddle: we just have a new, emerging muddle which has given some power (but by no means all or the most sensible bits) to a new, fairer settlement, recognizing Scottish and Welsh relative autonomy, wanting to include rather than exclude groups and religions and ways of life. Messiness sometimes works rather well. However, the great contemporary priority is tidiness and written-down-ness. The holy grail of 'transparency' has been understood to mean that codifying everything that moves is seen as a solution to abuses of power, when a code is often merely a map of formal relations – when the most deadly of transgressions might still flourish in what people actually do. Many propose that we should write down more of the rules into a more formal constitutional settlement, and in some areas this is just what has happened over the last decade.

Although the worry is that the muddle no longer has any coherence, simply tidying up 'Britishness' will not make it real.

There are a number of things nibbling and gnawing at our sense of our selves. Firstly, there is the most fundamental disappearance of the sense of the physical frontiers of the nation. The British now have almost no grasp of the fact that they are still 'an island nation' (let alone Shakespeare's 'sceptred isle'), as people come and go by air not sea, communicate by internet not mail, when the lives of other lands (India or Turkey) are all so easily accessible through the media, where TV land (even if grasped over the internet) or 'Facebook land' occupy a large space in people's sense of themselves. The vivid apprehension of our coastal edges and what they have meant (and still mean) has almost disappeared, and while we are still more geographically aware than most Americans, and can identify Europe and the continents, we do not have a strong national image of our parameters. Even within these regional limits (perhaps in contrast to the social mixtures of the myriad of national groups from elsewhere that now compromise British society) there is a sense of dissolution.

The most obvious way that 'Britishness' is under strain is the rise and rise of nationalisms within the union. Scotland, and to a lesser extent Wales, bustle with novel institutions and 'feel' no Britishness – on the contrary, they often define themselves in opposition to it. Scotland apparently wants to be shot of 'us'. The political scientist and commentator Anthony King has written a mordant and shrewd assessment of the state of the British constitution. He argues that the devolutionary engine we have landed ourselves with has an in-built friction that will inevitably lead to separation as the 'nations' demand more of the centre and set themselves in opposition to it. Then what about England? (Which, as a child a very long time ago, I just assumed was Britain; the titles seemed interchangeable – as they did to many writers in the late twentieth century.) King's conclusions are marred by a sharp and magnificent glumness, but, despite some acute observations (a reformed House of Lords, the author fears, could wind up comprising 'a miscellaneous assemblage of party hacks, political careerists, clapped-out retired or defeated MPs, has-beens, never-were's and never-could-possibly-be's'[2]), it is perhaps too deterministic. As recent political and economic crises unfold a new sense of the need for the larger union may again emerge. But more profoundly his analysis is limited by a blindness to the shifting nature of power in every aspect of contemporary lives.

In particular, he misses the huge, society-wide shifts in power that are the cultural consequences of media technological change. Power has moved from producers to some aspects of consumer choice. Across all of the media industries there is a real revolution going on, from the music industry to the mutating publishing trade, to news, and from surveillance to consuming, in every aspect of private lives and societies there is a technologically driven Wild West frontier remaking old relationships of authority. This is not the utopia we were promised; there are many aspects that damage common and collective goods.

But it is irreversible and has tremendous unfolding consequences. Constitutional change must mirror a new compact that other forces are making with British citizens. The shape of power is changing, and what a nation is must change with it.

There are many separatist enthusiasts around in the political and intellectual classes. It is nevertheless perhaps worth noting that at least some of the advocates for the 'break up'-of-Britain scenario tend to ignore Northern Ireland, which is far more settled in Ireland and in the European Union (EU) and in the union than it has been for thirty years of bloody, grinding conflict, not least because, as Roy Foster shows in a tour de force of evidence and argument in *Luck and the Irish*, the Irish state has changed out of all recognition – although in fits and starts. He sardonically points out with a certain glee that none of this has happened in any of the ways in which the instigators of the conflict hoped or predicted. Because Ireland has become secular, feminized, venal, successful, vulgar, and the very last thing it wants or is interested in is Northern Ireland. But perhaps Northern Ireland – for so long the most agitated of the nations – has become an inconvenient and complicating reality that many of the protagonists of dissolution prefer to ignore.

While the political geography of the nation is fretfully bothersome (were Scotland to declare independence the political geography of voting would consign England to a one-party state for the foreseeable future), the issue of national identity has been dislocated by many other forces as well. Many other aspects of 'geography', and indeed social and political landscapes, have disappeared. As Robert Colls points out in his troubled interrogation of national spirit, a 'local' and 'regional' map of Britain recognizable since 1840, at which policies were directed and in which people lived, has been replaced since the Thatcher government of the 1980s by a range of uncoordinated, unlocated 'schemes' and agencies driven by a multiplicity of public/private bodies. What they have instead of region or local as a driving force is 'efficiency', and these 'agencies' have measured their achievements in (sometimes invented) 'markets' – not by how they elicit and represent different local interests. Colls observes, 'as forces not entirely of the centre, nor in the centre, yet structured by the centre they came to replace the discourse of "geographical region" or "away from the centre"'. With this new way of talking the periphery ceased to be just geographical. 'At a time when the centre lost the confidence in its power to order things and the metropolis felt less responsible for the rest of the country, the old national shape began to dissolve. This truly odd condition prevails'.[3] Indeed, the whole landscape of Britain has disappeared since the 1970s, as factories became (in a way best captured by the dystopian novels of J. G. Ballard) 'gated communities' and 'lofts', while Methodist chapels – which were the engines of moral and political reform of the industrial revolution and after – have become paint shops. Cities and towns and the British countryside have all mutated, died away and sparked to life under many different pressures. Some cities have been rekindled by government policies which have promoted new kinds of commercial development. Yet, glamorous new areas in Manchester, London, Liverpool, coexist beside enduringly poor areas. However, public spaces in cities have been revitalized in the past decade – money has gone into parks and decent play areas for children as an expression of a common value. But Colls points to a perturbing lack both of locality and of nation in our ideas of ourselves.

There are aspects of 'Britishness' that are above locality, although no doubt also shaped by it. There is certainly uniquely 'British' media ecology. It is altering fast under the pressures that are causing media industries everywhere to adapt or to disappear. Nevertheless it remains a very particular process. It has balanced a partisan press – which, like the press everywhere, is in sharp economic decline, but which is hanging on better here than in many other places – with a broadcasting landscape that is still 'impartial' and non-partisan. It has seen, most catastrophically, an absolute decline in local and regional news vehicles. How can Wales understand itself with only one local newspaper? How can councils operate without the scrutiny that the local media used to bring? We are losing the capacity to think locally.

Yet the business patterns of the British media are distinctive, and so too is the tone. The popular press is far less polite than the American press, and, although often appallingly irresponsible, not corrupted to the extent of the Italian press; religion plays less a part than it does in Holland, and radical news less a part than it does in France – and so on. But the determining difference is the existence of impartial news. The top of the British press has become more intelligent and more comprehensive: the opposite has occurred at the bottom. While individual opinions and views flood the net, those that get megaphoned by broadcasting are still largely managed in the pursuit of representative and balanced views. You may want to swamp the broadcasters with your opposition to a view or a programme, but they will still, in the public interest, interrogate your position, evaluate it and contextualize it. 'Impartiality', objectivity and the fierce contest about the limits of free speech are still features of the complicated media scene here. This has important repercussions for our understanding of international events.

Then there is the class system. It has been very unfashionable to discuss class recently, yet differences still persist. Moreover, class and shifting class images are clearly represented in changing media systems and the changing fortunes of different media, as well as the more obvious symptom of content. The poor (what Orwell called 'the common man', and what we have learnt to call 'the socially excluded' – what, one wonders, will another government call them?), the unhappy, how we talk to our children (or increasingly and horrifying fail to), the elderly, the changed role of women and the extraordinary challenges for young men, these are everywhere and common. How to think of the best nurture for young lives when children and parents have legal rights but there is no way of discussing in court the only thing a child can thrive in – a home with, however it is constituted, a family – is a shared issue. When we

talk and think of the nation, surely we also mean such broad sociological realities that together give us the flavour of the life within it. We also mean literature, plays, art, architecture, design, films, dance, music, humour: we mean
sensibilities and environments. These broader realities are shaped in collaboration with the media.

The next big challenges to 'Britishness' are the Siamese-twinned issues of
the multi-faith, multi-ethnic, multi-ness and the conjoined question of limits
to the elasticity of 'Britishness'. 'Multiculturalism' has been a short-hand way
of talking about the first set of issues, and the very title shows how important
the media have been to this. Finding representative voices, reaching out to
communities, learning sensibilities, has been one side of the task. Discrimina-
tions have been fought with differing degrees of success. Just as the British way
of dealing with these realities has been very different from, for example, the
German way, so our media response has also been different. There are national
differences in how to confront a shared experience of more varied societies.

Yet there is another side to the problem – which was hardly mentionable
until recently. Is there a lowest common denominator of consensus about what
defines belonging, which cannot be breached? Have we worried too much
about diminishing hostility to new pieces in the national jigsaw and not
worried enough about whether there is a shared reality? On the one hand,
there is the problem identified so well by Geoff Dench in his work on the East
End, that thirty years of well-meaning 'triage' in cash-strapped public services,
housing, health and education have, in rationally allocating recourses to the
neediest incomers from abroad, accidentally actively disadvantaged a section
of the British working class, with disastrous political consequences.[4] On
the other hand, there is the problem of including and celebrating many
differences.

Finally, to be a nation, there has to be a sense of exceptionalism, of a unique
inheritance and worldview. Often such a concept of destiny has been forged
through conflict with an outside force. Raphael Samuel argued 'national
sentiment as a historical force can hardly be studied without reference to the
demonisation of enemies both within and without'.[5] Yet the last national
story that we could tell ourselves that had a legitimate and satisfactory 'us and
them' in it – the story of the Second World War – fades and loses purchase.
For several generations, a sense of British 'exceptionalism' had been based on
a myth, but also a powerful reality, and that is now increasingly frail. Nevertheless, this 'us versus them' view of national identity is a fairly conventional
view, and there can be a more generous interpretation of pleasure in a heritage.

The life of nations depends on how the past is lined up with the present.
This seems the great failure and a great opportunity of the moment we are
struggling through. One of the things we need to revitalize is an unembar-
rassed national history once more. 'A nation', claimed Edmund Burke in
1782, 'is not only an idea of local extent, but it is an idea of continuity, which
extends in time as well as numbers and in space'. Terry, a character in *Whatever*

Happened to the Likely Lads on the BBC, commented in 1973, 'Not one of our memories is left intact'. Most people simply don't know what matters about our history any more. Moreover, in a nation which has always used history to explore itself (just as the French have philosophers, and the Americans have political economists and Hollywood, we have history) there is a loss of historical memory and ways of remembering. Indeed, this is more than ever important, as in much of the wider academy, at least, there has been an almost complete abandonment of 'Britishness' as a source of understanding or study. Some universities, turned into businesses, have ducked the challenging task of rethinking a fit-for-purpose way of scrutinising the Britishness of disciplines. Thus, despite being equipped with cohorts of able historians, many of whom still aspire to write stylish, clear English, we have been dreadful at re-inspecting our history collectively. A coy discomfort at aspects of the story has led us to bury it. We have recently failed to tell children any coherent (let alone interesting) national story. While they are taught about Hitler and the Tudors, older students learn little of the nineteenth-century struggle for the franchise; and while it is true that all ten-year-olds learn about an empire in school, it is not ours, of course, it is the Spanish empire and the Incas that they toil over. Who lives where and how on the streets of Britain is shaped by our history. So surely, by now we could confront the awfulness and the admirableness of our own imperial past?

Meanwhile 'globalization', despite being a more peculiar process, with more complex impacts than almost any of the 'theorists' who easily proclaim it have recognized, does mean that we share some cultures internationally — and perhaps lose our own. Yet, conversely, one of the most disturbing aspects of the 'globalization' of the media is that it has led to cross-continental cultural ghettos and silos of narrow interests in which people only encounter the like-minded. 'Nation shall speak peace unto nation' — the BBC's founding mission is far easier than it used to be, but it is far harder to get people to pay attention to anything other than the familiar and comfortable. Moreover, there is a wider sense of tectonic plates moving: Brazil, China and India are storming into the world arena. Where do we fit into this new, emerging map, and does anyone care?

There is another problem: this is not about what we may or may not have lost, but about the dominant way of thinking about 'Britishness'. It has become common to see a sense of the nation as a plastic and fluid construct. Linda Colley's stimulating and influential book *Britons: Forging the Nation 1707–1837*, in itself an attempt by someone who, as she explained, was not clear that she would go on living and working in Britain, was a pioneering example of this. In an authoritative and original account, she demonstrates that a British identity was 'forged' in the eighteenth century out of popular anti-Catholicism and the real threats of French aggression, but also the comfort of watching successes in wars abroad with little direct experience of the reality at home, and out of a reworked monarchy. The British state pre-dated the 'idea' of Britain. However, she also argues that there was a material basis to a sense of nationhood: 'For all classes and both sexes, patriotism was more often than not a rational response and a creative one as well'.[6] She is clear that the contemporary media played a large role in this nation-constructing enterprise. Elsewhere the notion of the constructed nature of nationality gained ground. Benedict Anderson's definition of nations as 'imagined communities' was influential, as were, in a way, a wonderful set of essays edited by Eric Hobsbawm and Terence Ranger, *The Invention of Tradition*,[7] which considered, with a glorious wit, the ways in which ideas of nationality were invented and accepted (I learnt that those kilts I had worn were the late survival of a Highland fantasy). But while Colley was austerely aware that the enterprise of founding a national collective project was precarious and vital, for many of the other writers, as all national sentiment was really little more than a ruling-class trick, there was the sense of the ridiculousness of much national invention, and its ephemeral duplicity. We have ended up with a comforting, moralized version of fluidity in which 'the nation' is seen as endlessly plastic. Indeed, many who have written about the media have persuasively written about the media's capacity to alter and mould: but never asked questions about limits.

These ideas of national remaking were picked up eagerly – and bowdlerized. In a world where advertising can mould desires with such ease, why not remake – or 'rebrand' as it came to be called – the nation? Anthony Giddens, who famously thinks history is irrelevant, as it happened in the past, with his 'Third Way' was, in effect, one such immensely powerful 'rebrander', while Mark Leonard's branding Britain is another version of the same idea. We are in another bout of 'designer' Britishness now. Thus, what started out in the past as an empirical interrogation of collective processes in the hands of accomplished historians has turned into something quite different. It turned into a proposal to 'redesign' Britishness. New, more sellable ways to describe us were advanced with breathy excitement, for it was suggested if you could describe us differently, perhaps, hey-presto, we would be different. It was an essentially propagandistic and certainly ideological view of Britishness, self-consciously shaped for selling us to ourselves and abroad.

The idea was especially attractive because it proposed a way of harnessing the power of the media into a reinvention of our purposes. The media do indeed seep into and chemically alter much of our collective lives, and the mix of outlets that we have ended up with says all sorts of things about the national psyche. The British popular press, gaudy, sentimental, ruthless and dispiriting, is increasingly brutal with ordinary lives as well as with the more powerful (think Sally Clarke, the woman who was wrongly convicted of murdering two babies, on the basis of misleading expert evidence for which the expert has lost his job, and a local and national press campaign, for which no one lost their job – or ever apologised). The press tells us little about the wide world we find ourselves in, and in increasing cash-strapped times is marked by a narrow provincialism. Nevertheless, it is occasionally savagely truth telling, more often hysterical and ruthless – as only a wounded beast can be. Meanwhile, the utopia of better-informed, more intelligent and more deeply contextualized information is provided by a whole range of media – for the stratum of the educated and wealthy. In this way the prospect of 'using' the media to rebrand us looks like a way of managing the media to mould us for more useful ends – nevertheless, you cannot 'remake' Britishness as an advertising campaign. It will not work, because that is not what the 'British' are prepared to put up with. Actually, in such stubborn, prosaic refusals may still lie a national sentiment we can conjure with. Indeed, 'Britishness' can only be a co-production. The public has to collaborate – but will only do so in something that is useful and meaningful to it.

'Britishness' cannot be done to us – it has also to bubble up. This is especially the case in times of crisis – which has often been forgotten by the happy-clappy evangelists of re-engineering national identity. 'Britishness' has to be grounded in the soil of contemporary life, even if that is unsettling. Unfortunately, modern political and academic language is saturated with the easy encomiums of the seminar room, in which people 'negotiate' meanings and 'discourses' are 'contested'. But these words disguise the reality of sharply felt losses and brutish triumphs. It is the real needs and desires of the public, not mythologized or convenient ones, that is the place to start a proper dusting down of Britishness. Being British is more voluntary than it has ever seemed before, but it has to start from realities.

So is there anything 'British' left? Where can we look for our exceptionalism? Actually, there is more of it around than people think: they look for it in the wrong places. But it is not a set of 'things' or 'essences'. George Orwell, whose writing critically (and at times romantically) inquired into the British condition so influentially in the twentieth century once characterized British life as 'Heavy breakfasts and gloomy Sundays'. Although Orwell's essays still resonate with brilliant insights and indeed offer a model of scrutiny and wit, there is no point in trying to pin down 'Britishness' to any such list: Orwell's modesties have been swept away in a blizzard of shopping. The Conservative Prime Minister John Major's attempt to specify Britishness as 'maiden aunts on bicycles and warm beer' certainly never hit the mark, even in the late twentieth century. Early New Labour's 'Cool Britannia' has been spat out. Yet there are qualities which, on closer scrutiny, endure, although some of them we may find deeply unattractive: that surely is part of the British point.

The 'media' play a special role in representing (and at times whipping up) national characteristics. But what is unusual in Britain is that British 'exceptionalism' has been defined and reinforced by a unique media institution which has played a role in metabolising the nation's sense of itself, but which has also represented 'Britishness' abroad: the BBC. The Corporation may, or may not, survive the next decade of rocky problems, with technology, rapacious international businesses – perhaps even more threatening than domestic political vandalism – and a certain capacity for auto-destructiveness posing a set of interrelated looming threats. Nevertheless, inspecting how it has done Britishness is illuminating. The Corporation has an obligation to the nation because it is for the nation – so it has endlessly to try to sort out what the nation is. Mainly, the BBC metabolises the nation by worrying about it. It adds reflective anxiety and creative imagination to the problems it confronts. This is clearly a quality in news and journalism: but it is as much an issue in drama and documentary and in the very administrative principles of the thing. In particular, it is the 'newsiness' of the programming in general – the way in which news provides moral and political climate for other kinds of creativity – and in turn the embedded nature of news in the wider programme-making milieu, that can make for a fertile and sensitive Petri-dish culture. Of course, the BBC cannot and does not survive alone, but that, perhaps, is the point. It is enmeshed in ways of doing things and values elsewhere in other British institutions. So examining what it does tells us something about it, but it may also tell us something more general about the puzzle of us and our present uncertainties.

The Corporation metabolises Britain (when it gets it right) by airing its virtues; by bestowing recognition on groups, issues, achievements, and failures; by including the mad aunts and errant teenagers in the family group; by showcasing and polishing up the crown jewels of culture; by washing as much of the dirty linen as it can find right out there in the street and by taking the mickey out of the whole attempt.

The Corporation has been able to do this because it is part of the British 'unwritten' and informal constitution and, as such, it has related to the British public as citizens, but in a quite different way from any other official body. It consumes an alternative set of data about the British people on the move socially, technologically and aesthetically from any department of state: for it lives in the minds and hearts and imaginations of people at play. People have always had to choose to spend their time with the BBC, and even though the competition for attention has become far more intense, the Corporation has always had to win and woo. So it has never been able to ignore what the people want for long (although it has at some times been out of step with the national mood, and at others it has been able to express and lead it). Yet, at the same time it is enjoined to engage with the public not only as consumers but as members of an evolving society. So the BBC's sense of the nation is at an angle to any government's.

The BBC metabolises the nation materially by distributing recourses according to a political and citizenship map of Britain, not an economic or market one. The media have, over time, been given many privileges: even very broadly defined as the content-producing organisations they still are. They acquired these benefits because, ultimately, they have to serve the public good. The argument for this remains simple: in democracies, electorates need to be recognized and informed; now there is plenty of information available, but navigating it or having attention focused on the things that matter is far more difficult. Distributing resources has meant access to radio, television and now digital technologies, and reshaping the production and ideas map of the country. If the BBC is national, then it has somehow to be part of the wider nation. This is so 'taken for granted' that it is almost invisible in the British mind, yet it has been a powerful engine of integration. A shrewd media regulator, The Office of Communications (Ofcom), which is empowered to try to make sure that the commercial and public roles of the digital and broadcasting industries are properly conducted, observed that the whole of the independence tussle was being played out in Scotland 'through the prism of broadcasting'. Yet there is a devilish paradox in the drama unfolding north of the border: market forces alone would not support an independent production market of any size in Scotland, yet the Corporation is being asked to invest in one. Those campaigning for this are not interested in a better service for any audience, but in developing an economic capacity at home: and yet the decision to invest such resources can only come (and is coming rather generously) from the 'British' BBC: the logic of economic and political decisions is quite different.

Then there is the 'representing the nation' to itself. This is, in part, an issue of representing the bits of the nation to themselves, partly an issue of representing the bits of the nation to the whole and partly a matter of correcting the overall picture by the nuancing that regional perspectives and realities bring. It has done each task variably well over time, at sometimes falling into clichés, but at others creatively harvesting local differences and local contributions to enrich the national brew. Some of this is to do with news, putting the nations and regions on the collective mind-map, as keeping them alert to their own condition is one part of the task. It requires political will.

But metabolising the nation has to be continually reinvented. Take Northern Ireland: the BBC in the 1960s and the early 1970s was part of the problem that was about to erupt. It was staffed solely by members of the Protestant community, failed to 'see' the minority community and was unreflectively 'Unionist'. But slowly it became more responsive, its staff became more representative, the voices it gave access to became more varied, and then, as the troubles gathered venom, it evolved into an admirably pioneering institution. This was a matter both of getting the balance of staff, news stories, plays, documentaries and children's programmes appropriately right to the local audiences and of telling that story into the rest of Britain. Yet at first, when the sensitivity to the variety of Northern Irish voices had improved, another error emerged: an understandable attempt to emphasize the positive distorted the story yet again. The BBC had to learn that it did not exist in order to 'build the peace' or 'build the community'. Later still, visiting journalists from London, hungry for a scoop and some drama but who did not appreciate the local consequences of stories, had to be managed: they were too unresponsive to local meanings. Another corrective lesson: the BBC did not exist to tell exciting stories that were over-dramatised; 'stars' hunting for scoops did damage to the reality on the ground, and that reality was too important to be oversold back on the mainland. Yet, and this is also true, the visiting, observing journalist was also an important part of carrying meanings from community to community. 'Outsiders' brought something to the mix in the province and to the understanding on the mainland. Over time, the BBC learnt how to do it – and on the way produced a world-class news outfit in the region.

Pat Loughrey, the first Catholic to be appointed to a senior position there, and now Head of the Regions and Nations for the BBC, argued that the single most important programme that started the move in Northern Ireland was a phone-in called *Talk Back*, a loud, opinionated, shouting shop at first. There was political pressure to close it down, as it was thought to incite inter-communal violence, but the BBC held steady. After 'about five years of both communities screeching poisonously at each other, they got it out of their system, realised there was a space in which they could be heard, and then they started to listen to each other'.[8] This is one key way the BBC does Britishness: by listening to and allowing an arena for the variety of voices that reflect real communities. But in Northern Ireland the struggle to get it right was part of the bigger solution: there are no easy, quick fixes to attempting to be truthful.[9]

Indeed, one of the things the regions need to do is to correct the metropolitan bias of almost everything in Britain, but the process is more complicated than it appears at first inspection. The BBC has to be part of and let the regions speak their minds on issues and pleasures to themselves. One way is to make programmes about them – another way is to make programmes in them. But devolving to the regions only does its transformative, enlarging work if then the regional insights are brought back to amend and correct the whole picture. This is the trick we have to learn more generally, and it is more complicated than it looks to get this right. In this way, as one ex-BBC mandarin pointed out, putting production capacity out to the regions was not enough: the regional production needs to be able to engage and catch the attention of the centre and the centre needs it to do so. Thus, for example, the whole issue of Europe looked different from the shires and the provinces. In the close Westminster village there is traditionally a good deal of hostility to the whole EU policy, and the BBC political and cultural elites are largely, unavoidably, part of that central mind set – yet reporters working where the EU has brought benefits, out in the valleys of Wales and the Yorkshire Dales, corrected the dominant Westminster-centric view.[10] Indeed, what is true of the regions is true of the world. Going and seeing, bringing back views and understanding, is the single most critical way in which the whole BBC news-gathering and processing machine contributes to our comprehension of our place in all of the worlds that we all live in as a part of.

These dilemmas are merely reproduced when dealing with the increasingly diverse communities that live within Britain. An old BBC problem, that of what constitutes a representative voice, which stands legitimately for a point of view, becomes especially acute when times are dangerous. The

Corporation's determination to represent the Northern Irish 'street' of opinion brought it into conflict with successive governments and took time to get passably right. Yet the inclusion of voices – which does legitimize them – also exposes them to scrutiny. Inclusion is insufficient: every voice must be properly challenged, yet inclusion in the national arena of nation remains one of the most important ways of defining Britishness. Regions, classes, faiths, communities all need recognizing.

Yet what vision of Britishness does the BBC work with? It is perhaps easier to see the kinds of interpretations that have to be balanced in something less contentious than religion, or politics. Take classical music in the BBC as an example of the dilemmas that have to be resolved in practice. The BBC is one of the largest patrons of music in Europe and the world. But working out (and 'balancing') different aspects of Britishness has all sorts of conflicts within it. To render 'British' musical life the best service, what must you do? Well obviously, you must support orchestras in the centre and in the regions – and keep live music performance and performers vitally alive. But that is not enough. You should also play the repertoire of 'British' music, from the great mediaeval choral tradition of Tallis and Bird, through Handel and Purcell, to Elgar, Delius and Walton. However, you ought also to be rediscovering new bits of the repertoire, which at some times the BBC has done almost single-handedly – not just the British repertoire of course, but music in general. However, 'British' music should not just be a heritage trinket, and so, of course, you must commission new work from new composers, John Tavener, Harrison Birtwhistle and the baby avant-garders, even perhaps at times if no one much listens to it, though finding new ways of presenting music is part of the trick. Meanwhile 'British' music must not get out of touch with the world, so you must also get the best foreign performers and conductors to play here, and continually relaunch great music at the audiences. However, then there is the obligation to nurture young British performers and musical life in the schools. 'Young Musician of the Year' was invented brilliantly to do just this, when a BBC producer noted with dismay that there were few young British performers appearing in the international competitions. It worked: and can somebody please un-dumb it down right away? Today's one-size-fits-all populism, with ignorant 'celebrity' presenters asking accomplished young people asinine questions and an interference with the judging system so that the most 'news friendly' performer wins – not the most skilled – gets in the way of the real capacities and interests it is capable of encouraging and displaying. The principle of 'recognition' is one that governments have no purchase on – yet is a powerful, necessary cultural tool. However, occasionally the whole balancing act of allocating money and attention hits the rocks of invention: thus the BBC has always cared obsessively about the quality of sound it has put out, but in the 1970s a new musical kid on the block was the 'early music' movement, with performances on original instruments. Unfortunately, as few had built or played sackbuts for several hundred years, they tended to sound – well – odd. But it was a British movement, and so, after some resistance, the indomitable BBC Producer (a wonderful breed) grasped it – with lots of expensive rehearsal time. But when all of that is sorted into an acceptable division of resources and energy there is another big problem: how do you balance your obligation to interest as many people as possible, and to the music and its development? The answer is all of the above, but in addition replayed in the shifting sands of contemporary musical history and taste. Balancing what is best for 'Britishness' is no easy task. It is a complex business of money and imagination. The problems and perplexities of getting right the 'British' in classical music were just a model for the more commercially pressured issue of somehow getting popular music 'right'. Or of how to commission drama or comedy that was representative, innovative, and spoke to problems yet entertained. Moreover, it never stops all of the lessons having to be re-explored as the parameters and sensitivities alter.

Yet there is another paradox of Britishness: it is often best done when it is not attempted at all. Thus, the BBC World Service wonderfully represents the British interest best, precisely insofar as in not pursuing a 'British' agenda or indeed British 'interests'. It does it by doing impartiality, balance, and when it arrives at them, through hard-won, necessarily imperfect, properly objective judgements. In many ways it (and the 'mother ship of values', the larger BBC) relates to the world on our behalf by setting standards. The receiving audiences will use the World Service because it is useful and accurate for their lives, not because it represents a 'British' voice. Indeed, the perception that it is inflected by our interests damages it. This commitment to trying very hard to describe reality, as opposed to influencing it, has been the basis of the World Service's authority. Perhaps what is true abroad (or indeed increasingly at home, because of the way in which such services now include diaspora audiences scattered throughout Britain), is also true of how we need to see 'Britishness', not as a set of things or values; it is not that 'the beer is bitterer the coins are heavier and the grass is greener, the faces knobblier and mild',[11] but rather a set of processes which engage us in our contemporary reality.

David Hendy's sparkling, thoughtful account of Radio Four, *Life on Air*, makes a similar point. It is 'how' public service broadcasting processes our common life and adds a thoughtful playfulness to content that matters more than the passing scenery of programmes which reflect not only continuities but also changing tastes and agendas. In representing the nation, the 'immense variation in tone', from the warm homeliness of the shipping forecasts to the cerebral investigations of *In Our Time*, has been part of the 'diversification which was embedded as a fundamental goal' in the station's purposes. Radio Four embodied in 'one service a variety of ways with which the nation could view itself. It provides a national kaleidoscope'.[12] The author Lynne Truss put well the odd sense of community it can engender, 'The idea that other listeners, in other kitchens, in other baths, in other traffic jams, are yelling at the same thing is a comforting notion'. Thus, the World Service and Radio Four both show the way to some qualities, of fair representativeness, that are not things or even values, but habits of mind, processes, that are far more pervasive than any of the end-of-Britain doom mongers appreciate. Perhaps the thing is not to 'do' Britishness at all.

One of the last great successful inspections of Britishness was as a consequence of the Second World War, when a series of writers defined national characteristics in ways which critics have spent many years dismissing. Some aspects of these are more relevant to a very much changed Britain than appears at first sight. Not the modesty, or the class structure, let alone the cups of tea or the boiled cabbage. In 1957 Nikolaus Pevsner, the great architectural historian, gave a series of BBC Reith lectures on the 'Englishness of English Art' (by which, being a German, like many of the most anglophile of post-war thinkers, he endearingly claimed he meant, 'just the most commonly acceptable name for that which is the essence of Britishness'). The lectures became a smash hit, selling out by their millions. For Pevsner, whose dry yet utterly comprehensive catalogue of vernacular architecture sought to distil the qualities of national life built in local bricks and mortar, the defining quality of British culture was an emphasis on narrative and preaching. It was, he claimed, epitomized by Hogarth with his great, popular morality tales – criticizing in *Gin Lane* and *The Rake's Progress* the corruption of British society. But, Pevsner notes that the most effective British artistic sermon 'is the recounting of what a sharp eye sees around it'. The hallmark of the British spirit, he claimed was 'Keen observing and quick recording together with an intense interest in the details of the everyday world and a preference for personal experience'.[13] But he also claimed to see (in our great cathedrals, along with extreme length and height) qualities of 'detachment as against passionate single mindedness', although he also argued that the nation's 'rationalism and matter of fact-ness' was matched by an enduring penchant for the 'romantic, weird and the irrational'. Meanwhile George Mikes (a Hungarian this time) observed on a Home Service programme that 'the British will not tell you a lie, but would not dream of telling you the truth'. He also added, that in Britain, 'If you go for a walk with a friend don't say a word. If you go with a dog never stop talking to him . . .'.[14]

Of course this elaboration of empiricism, open mindedness and critical scrutiny was part of an image of Britain widely shared then. Karl Popper's 'Open Society' was an immensely influential underpinning to all of this exploration. Popper's inspiring work provided a stern injunction to keep the arteries of criticism open. It demanded vigilance against the comforts of complacency. Like John Stuart Mill before him, but after the terrible lessons of totalitarian oppression, Popper reminded people that they might fixploratlenging argument very uncomfortable – but that it was always a good thing. The 'Open Society' argument still rages and is what we British still perhaps have as a substitute for the American preoccupation with freedom of speech. In many ways the BBC, at its best, also puts some of these habits of mind into practice: sceptical, evidence driven, committed to the possibility of understanding others and, in as far as it tries to, continually pushing the boundaries of what we might be.

For perhaps there is no easy answer to 'Britishness' – and the recognition is in itself part of the answer. You could invent civic ceremonies. Governments keep proposing them. Yet we have quite good ones around the place: the Queen's Jubilee in 2002 (for example) was not expected by the BBC to be popular, but the people, as far as could be discerned, rather enjoyed it. You could do something with flags, but I, for one, will certainly not be swearing allegiance to any fluttering bit of civic religion. You could make the contract between us and the state more explicit. You certainly ought to do something about interpreting our history again: without polite omissions. You must represent the voices and instincts that exist within the national arena. You absolutely must permit, encourage and develop creative, imaginative energy. Museums, and children reading great books for fun (not dull, pointless reading schemes), artists, theatres and dancers all have much to add to our sense of what matters. But do not try to tidy the 'Britishness' up – after all, one enduring quality is our national hypocrisy. Once one understands that Robespierre energized the murderous Terror in the French Revolution in the eighteenth century by whipping up hatred for hypocrites and demanded that a new 'openness of heart' rule, one begins to see the necessary utility of a quality often associated with the British. Indeed, the contemporary British press seems sometimes to do little else than accuse other people (especially politicians, celebrities, people in public life) of two-faced hypocrisy. It is all of course a wonderfully hypocritical concoction; the British divorce, have affairs, break up marriages, live with each other more than ever before – they just enjoy disapproving of any passing public figure who behaves like they do.

Insofar as the BBC has found ways to be part of a national discussion about our condition, redistributed resources, tried to balance – however inadequately – competing claims, puzzled and questioned whether it is doing the right thing, learnt by trial and error, and above all, attempted to avoid ideological capture for all of the 'purposes' people would like to impose on it, then it has, indeed, most usefully 'metabolised' Britishness. Insofar as the British media more generally remain a place where real vices and virtues are called to our attention, then they do their public work. But do they?

George Orwell, that quintessentially most British of writers, is also the least parochial. His great fables, *1984* and *Animal Farm*, are as relevant to life in oppressive regimes as they ever were – and alert us in more sedate and lucky places to threats all the time. What he wrote in the middle of the last century still resonates and makes readers everywhere more inquiring of their predicament. Perhaps he also provides a way to see the contemporary quandary of our national identity. Writing in the 1930s, he claimed that Britain was 'the most class ridden society under the sun. It is a land of snobbery and privilege, ruled largely by the old and silly'. It was like a family, but one 'with the wrong members in control – and cupboards stuffed with skeletons'. He was pitiless about its double standards, snobbery, pomposity, xenophobia, inability at languages, and the terrible social divisiveness that separated the comfortable from the needy. As Ben Pimlott argued about Orwell, 'Being "British" we have to be reminded, perhaps does not mean that the list is full of things we approve of. Orwell sniffs orthodoxy at a hundred yards and having sniffed it, seeks to upset its adherents'.[15] Yet Orwell also 'refused to scorn qualities of common sense, empiricism and toleration'. Elsewhere, Orwell distinguished between patriotism as 'devotion to a particular place and a particular way of life, which one believes is the best in the world but has no wish to force on other people', and nationalism (which he said could be applied to ideologies like communism and fascism as well as nations):

> which is inseparable from the desire for power. The abiding purpose of every nationalist is to secure more power and more prestige, not for himself but for the nation or other unit in which he has chosen to sink his own individuality.

Orwell was, in short, a critical patriot, and everything he wrote was an extended polemic on the side of seeing the truth – however ugly – in ourselves. It was an embarrassing, awkward intimacy with ourselves that Orwell proposed, but it was above all a state of mind, a way of looking at the world that was fleshed out in his invitation to be critical, find shamefully distasteful – and yet appreciate that which was individual.

Perhaps the only way forward in our current national quandary – and yet one (and that is the delight) that is part of a long history that is distinctly British – is a stroppy-minded, slightly resigned toleration and defence of where we are as a nation. And it is in this slightly bleak describing, recognizing, relishing and laughing at our accurate condition (even if that is a somewhat dissolving condition) where doing 'Britishness' better really lies – because this is the place from which we can hope for better. Orwell wrote of Britain: 'There is something in it that is continuous, it stretches into the future and the past, there is something in it that persists, as in a living creature. It has a flavour of its own'.[16] We may or may not need to go on 'being British', but we do all need to go on being critical, open-minded realists – if we can, and if the media keep us informed, and bring us uncomfortably to face those things about ourselves that we don't want to know. 'Freedom', observed Orwell 'is the right to say what other people do not want to hear'.

Notes

1 L. Colley, 'The significance of the frontier in British History', Harry Ransome Research Centre, University of Texas at Austin, 1995.
2 A. King, *The British Constitution* (Oxford, Oxford University Press, 2007).

3 R. Colls, *Identity of England* (Oxford, Oxford University Press, 2002), p. 333.

4 G. Dench, K. Gavron and M. Young, *The New East End: Kinship, Race and Conflict* (London, Profile Books, 2006).

5 R. Samuel, 'Nationalism and the British', History Workshop (Oxford, 1985), p. 28.

6 L. Colley, *Britons: Forging the Nation 1707–1837* (London, Yale University Press, 1992), p. 15.

7 E. Hobsbawm and T. Ranger, *The Invention of Tradition* (Oxford, Oxford University Press, 1984).

8 P. Loughrey, BBC, author's interview.

9 This is based on interviews in Northern Ireland for the history of the BBC.

10 Interviews with Stephen Whittle about the relocation of religious programmes to Manchester, for the history of the BBC.

11 G. Orwell, 'The Lion and the Unicorn', in *Orwell's England* (London, Penguin, 2001), p. 23.

12 D. Hendy, *Life on Air: A History of Radio Four* (Oxford, Oxford University Press, 2007), p. 395.

13 N. Pevsner, *The Englishness of English Art* (London, Hutchinson, 1957), p. 47.

14 G. Mikes, 'How to be an Alien', BBC Home Service, 1959.

15 B. Pimlott, Introduction, *Orwell's England* (London, Penguin, 2001).

16 *England Your England* (London, Secker and Warburg, 1953), p. 195.

Chapter 24

Global understanding

Gosh, with so much information around, organised in quite new ways and available so easily, surely we are all more knowledgeable than before? A connected world ought to be a more intelligent world. There are thrilling engines of enquiry developing, almost limitless information available, people to relate to, why do we need anything like the news? When worldwide publics can share events as they unfold, send immediate pictures from the hearts of disasters, can more or less communicate with anyone anywhere, who needs story finders, assessors and sellers any more?

In the brave new world of boutique views, grazing media-snackers, bespoke news consumption, when you take your information Indian, American or football style, with auto-didact news producers and content swappers, 'citizen journalists' sending images as events roll, happy connected chatters, posters and eager opinionators all jostling for attention over the net, could it possibly be suggested that there is actually a new problem with ensuring 'news' diversity both nationally and internationally? Don't we have more of the stuff than ever before? Villagers in Africa can text aid agencies to say that the aid has not arrived in their village, and that local officials are corrupt. Pictures from conflicts (well, some conflicts) ricochet about the net, as incendiary as the bullets they show. Anyone can post their view on anything. At least in some societies (like ours) the very detail of political decisions, the documents that drive and make political policy, can be made available for all the public to scrutinise within hours of decisions. The blogosphere bustles with attitude. Like termites, colonies of information workers create huge edifices of knowledge. Isn't all of that teeming life diversity?

But the criteria of judgement remain the same – even in the new world.

For the first condition of a decent society is some kind of common discussion, in public, of the realities of that society. It is a discovery that goes back to the sceptical empiricism of the enlightenment, but it is not 'western', or 'elite', it is just what makes the difference between civilized justice and many graduated degrees of oppression. It is a universal truth and it is what makes 'the media' potentially a public good. The media do this by bringing independent witness to scrutinise events. Many connecting and interactive new conversational forms may do it. Although comedy, drama, the rules and mores of reality shows, radio chat programmes, programmes about animals, children's programmes, interactive games – anything really – play their own creative and vastly important role in elaborating and challenging power – and do some of the vital work of amusing and informing audiences as well as the imperative of delivering their attention and interest – nevertheless they and the news all matter if the apprehending of reality is at the centre of the project. This is not to advocate 'realism' as a style – on the contrary; but satire and absurdity also have to speak to reality if they are to really hit home truths. Art adds its own creative interpretation to new understandings. But, if we are shown verities we recognize (and of course it is a messy, awkward business capturing the zeitgeist and yet moving it on), such realism engages us in a mobile dialogue about who we are, what is happening and what we wish to be. The democratization of the means to communicate globally is a machine transforming knowledge and power. Yet reality is surprisingly hard to recognize. Moreover, it is perplexing enough to understand the conditions of communities we live in close proximity to; appreciating the more distant lives of others is still more challenging. In the past this was a matter of physical distance (which is still more important and complex than people understand – what do you know of the other lives lived in the road you live in?). Now it is as much – perhaps – about psychological and imaginative distance. But the distance is also a material one.

It is quite simply the most exciting period of cultural change for generations. Thus, magnificent opportunities of the new communications order are transforming relationships between traditional power hoarders and some publics. Across all the so-called media industries, all of which are converging but which we recognize, from music, to publishing, to 'broadcasting' (the production of certain kinds of content delivered on any platform), to the news industry, the first great revolution for 200 years, combining new technology, an upturning of creative relationships and unfolding new economic models, is remaking our imagination and understanding. Yet, precisely because of there being so much choice it is easy to ignore anything that we do not agree with or find uncomfortable. We can choose only to consult news and knowledge that fits our view of the world. We can find evidence that supports any prejudice or preference we fancy. We can build a comfortable silo for ourselves. We can also just ignore everything: who needs news about far-away places? The most recent research about the impact of the web on cultural goods (and perhaps, by extension, on cultural products – like news) is that the combination of web and media makes the largest, most popular, most discussed 'celebrity' goods hugely successful, but that smaller, less recognized goods and events disappear. You need a louder, bigger voice to attract attention in the noisy party of the digital world. It is harder to attract attention for things we need to know. It is harder for smaller, less fashionable voices to get heard.[1]

Informed myopia

Indeed, even the most educated publics may follow conventional thinking as unquestioningly as ever. Technological sophistication does not necessarily lead to challenging thought per se. For example, the economic crisis of 2008–09 was often described as a 'credit crunch', because huge economic turbulence was caused by a sudden collapse in the availability of money to lend and this in turn was based, at least in part, on a collapse in confidence. Yet it could also legitimately have been called a 'cognitive crunch'. It was caused by a failure of comprehension. People did not understand the financial instruments that were being used to spread risks, they did not understand the models of finance, they did not understand the consequences of what was in many ways a classic speculative 'bubble' – but one whose impact was swift and global in a quite novel way. It turned out that even those ostensibly wielding the financial tools did not understand them. A priestly caste of experts wielding a formidable set of jargons delivered us all considerable economic benefits: so it was more comfortable for us all to believe that someone else understood the mystery, even if we did not. We delegated understanding. Hard questions requiring simple answers put at earlier stages might have transformed behaviour. It was a lack of comprehension and the assertion that it was all too technically sophisticated for people to comprehend that was one cause of an economic catastrophe. Public understanding is thus not an optional luxury – without it, terrible things happen.

It is also the case that the relationship between the digital world and the 'old' media world is still more interdependent and complex than many assume. The digital world is not 'substituting' for the older media world, but they coexist and amplify messages across each other in different ways. 'Celebrity' events become famous by multiplying their fame across all platforms – old and new.

Yet, despite more interaction we have not arrived at anything like common measures of the scale. For example, wars and conflicts, human suffering of many varieties, caused by natural and man-made disasters, continue to have quite different impacts on the different publics. There is no common register in which they are assessed and attended to. One aspect of this is political. Different public audiences with different political positions interpret conflicts (and are moved often to rage, not compassion) according to their own persuasions.[2] In this way images of suffering still have huge consequences. They agitate and whip up feelings, they are important evidences of injustice, they mobilise action which is sometimes redemptive, sometimes angrily punitive. Yet the relationship between the digital-swapping world of online communication and the news agenda of the apparently more traditional agenda is very close – large movements of engagement and feeling are nearly always amplified through a new co-relationship. Agendas still get set in remarkably traditional ways.

There is another issue – those conflicts, disasters, unfolding catastrophes, issues that get a distorting kind of attention. The world may be inter-connected, but much of what happens is noticed by no one beyond the site of the events. Indeed, it is even more specific and odd: it is pictures of suffering that matter. Without images, events do not have a wide purchase on attention. Thus, take the example of famine. These are usually long-running, slowly gathering emergencies. They take time to develop, there is plenty of evidence that they will occur, they can be reliably predicted, and they are most usually privatized – they happen slowly to people, where they live and only in the very last, absolutely disastrous phases do populations move or end up in relief camps. Indeed, and this is difficult to accept, all famines are essentially political phenomena; they are not caused by absolute failures of food supply but by a political failure to give people access to food. However, such emerging disasters are hard to capture pictorially and governments and relief agencies have spent the last thirty years trying to produce more rational ways of dealing with them. The charities (who get their money in Britain from the public), however, need to catch public attention with dramatic imagery. Thus there is a bizarre concentration on campaigns around visible suffering.

There are also the catastrophes that for various reasons – governmental control, distance, complexity of story, stereotyping, but most usually quite simply because of lack of traditional coverage – simply get no attention. One example would be the cholera outbreak in Zimbabwe in 2009. We had radio reports but, because of the Zimbabwean government's exclusion of journalists, and especially its exclusion of the BBC, which, despite an ingenious attempt to get around the censorship, could get few pictures out of the ravaged country, no one really understood the extent of the social breakdown that such an epidemic represented. Another, different example would be the long-running and horrifically brutal war in Goma, a war with far higher casualties than any other contemporary conflict – but which has had little or no media attention. 'News' still sets our mental map of concern, and if there is no reporting, then we do not notice.[3]

Of course many governments in many places and many cross-national groups are not at all interested in any public understanding at all. Governments have been able to control the description of reality and to restrict the views of dissident voices despite new technological opportunities. Take many of the countries of 'new' Europe. Despite twenty years of development since the collapse of communism and its controls of the media, we need a name for the odd and strangely threatening moment these societies are in. The media are controlled – but in a different way. A report by the Soros Open Society Foundation[4] demonstrates that something novel, yet disconcertingly familiar, was already remaking these societies' capacity to understand themselves long before the economic crisis. Moreover, this engine has been moving fast in the wrong direction: if things were bad in the early 2000s three years later, by 2008, they were definitely worse. When the Cold War ended, democracy was supposed to bloom, a movement towards independent thought and better government to spread through political systems. The chemistry of decency was to go about altering political parties, and these would improve public services, and the economies becoming rule governed would profit and grow in everyone's interests – and all of it to be tested and made better by the power of scrutiny that free media bring to political situations. But it has not happened. A new political malaise – with no precise name – nationalism, nepotism, corruption, clientalism are all part of it, stalks the post-post-cold war. The disease is the repoliticization of broadcasting (and no doubt everything else). It is not an ideologically coherent movement – but it is about the capture of recourses by elites. It is the era of kleptocracy.

This forensic and chilling report by the Open Society Foundation showed how political control of the crudest and most vulgar kind has taken repossession of television, from the Urals to Umbria. Freedom of thought, impartiality of information, wise exploration of the public condition (whether discussed in news, comedy, soap operas or relevant drama), the notion of broadcasting as informing citizens has retreated, not advanced in these countries. Politicians capture regulators, broadcasting is commercialised and bastardized, news is puppetry, drama has all but disappeared. This is a common story all over the former Eastern Europe, but beyond that as well: Italy at the heart of 'old' Europe has a media system in corrupt political control.

Does it matter; does 'television', the main object of the report matter anymore? Don't young people do other things, isn't the internet replacing it, can't people get information from elsewhere? Yet, as the researchers for the Soros report comment, 'reports of the death of television are greatly exaggerated' – it remains the most important window on the world for most people in those societies. Of course the new technologies pose all broadcasters immense and intriguing problems: ones that the political influence largely appearing as commercial exploitation leaves most of these ailing European beasts badly positioned to deal with. Populations still depend on broadcasting for their knowledge and entertainment: they are, however, using it differently. Nor has the 'need' for the engagement that broadcasting can foster (as well as the enjoyment and knowledge) disappeared because of the opportunities of the new technology. The report identifies the more general drivers to the present condition, audiences fragment, ownership consolidates and technology converges. Who, then, represents the public interest or the need for citizens to be informed? Not the weak regulators, certainly not the owners, and barely the broadcasters. The process is not a passive one but an aggressive one. 'Professionals are being replaced by loyal mediocrities', comments the Polish section of the report, managements change in tune to political power, and the rich cultural capacity of the Polish film industry, for example, to create telling fictions is pushed to the very margins of programmes. In Albania, 'Information is neither impartial nor fair. There is almost no media outlet without vested economic or political interests'. In Italy, with Berlusconi back in power, a dark farce plays itself out.

Yet the report in itself was a hopeful thing. You can trust what it shows and you can understand what it tells us. In this way reliable knowledge about advertising revenue, the political manoeuvres, the attempts by some broadcasters to serve their publics better, the impact of the European Union (EU) trying to wrest propriety back into some systems, the report in itself helps to move the situation from dire to remediable. It ought to make the scrutiny and compliance of the media a higher priority in the EU. Political will and action depends on knowledge.

In another continent the story is different – but related. Reporting of African affairs in Africa has, many experts believe, got worse over the last twenty years. Intimidation, politics and the lack of an independent market for the news are problems. While aid agencies have supported local media they have been inexperienced and uneasy with thinking about business models which might give local media in Africa the absolutely vital economic independence they need in order to flourish. It is not a good thing that the 'good' guys in the media world are dependent on aid. Nevertheless, the mobile telephone is a powerful tool in the hands of the communicating citizen. Many of the media organisations and journalists have been heroic – they know witness makes the difference. Meanwhile, the coverage of developing nations back into our world has also declined. We in Britain, for example, feel far less engaged with the story of India than we did even twenty-five years ago. Although this, too, is complex, because it is, of course, very easy for British citizens from the subcontinent to tune into news and information directly themselves – but we do not all share this knowledge any more. Or to be more accurate, although wealthy, information-rich people now can get much more detailed and comprehensive reporting if they pay and look for it, general understanding has been diminished.

However, everywhere the situation is made more complex and far more hopeful by the opportunities of the digital platforms, which provide new spaces for discussion to creep in. In the Middle East a wild west of talk shows, phone-in discussions, music competitions and cooking marathons has produced a vivid, swirling world of opinion. This is combined with new news capacity. Although some believe that the early radical impartiality of Al Jazeera, the news channel, has been captured and tamed, nevertheless there is more and better news available. The media flood across borders. The story is never simple – Egypt imprisons journalists, controls expression and yet the well-off can watch the equivalent of *Newsnight*, a challenging questioning of events on a satellite station. In Saudi Arabia, on the one hand fatwas are issued against opponents, and yet a liberal website has recently been reopened. The American scholar Mark Lynch argues that people are learning to argue, exchange views, question governments, challenge opinion in an exciting new way all over the region.[5]

Yet against this hopeful background there is one stark and growing impediment to knowledge: the acute increase in the threats to journalists and reporting organisations. Telling the truth is no easier than it ever was (even though we are all very sophisticated about what 'the truth' might be). In communist Russia, towards the end of the regime, if the state did not like what you said, you might find it hard to publish what you wanted – but, for the second decade since the end of the communist rule, journalists have been targeted, assaulted and killed, not necessarily directly by the state but by mysteriously opaque interests. It is dangerous to challenge official interpretations of events in many places. This is part of a wider pattern. During the whole of the Second World War, seventy-eight journalists were killed. In 2008 Human Rights Watch listed the names of the 184 journalists killed in that year alone. In the past, independent reporters witnessing conflict had a curious protection: they were the means for both sides in any engagement to get their story out. Yet, as the importance and worldwide nature of propaganda (the significance of mobilising international diaspora has become a vital part in the ambitions of many groups) has grown, those in conflicts have other ways of getting their own version of events out to supporters. Repeatedly, media organisations have been targeted. Al-Jazeera, the BBC, the news agencies Reuters, Associated News, Agence France-Presse have had buildings quite deliberately targeted during conflicts all over the world. Even more threateningly, individual journalists and the local reporters who are often the life-blood of foreign reporting have been threatened, kidnapped attacked and killed – as journalists. Meanwhile journalists in many political systems are threatened, and indeed killed, because they challenge authority. Although this is a romantic version of journalism – under whose mantle many journalistic abuses attempt to hide – nevertheless it is also an important aspect of the power and value of the media. So, in addition to the commercial threats to news making there is a steep rise in the hazards journalists face. Public understanding comes at a cost.

Amoral

What is the commodity that the media carry that makes everything better, without which decency cannot break out, which is under such threat and which people everywhere hunger for (and perhaps find less palatable when they get it)? It is something like objectivity and the stroppy-minded capacity to confront reality. It is not on one side or the other, or at least tries to tell, insofar as it can discern it, what is happening. Journalists are not there to save the world, they are there to report on it. Indeed, news is amoral in the simple sense that it at its best struggles to perceive what is actually happening – it is not there to change the world. Paradoxically, this lack of moral compass is what makes the news useful as a moral guide. Moral news tells us what has happened – that is all it does, and that is everything it does. News does reality, not nice.

Now we need to distinguish more clearly what is actually valuable in the thing we have previously called 'news'. The bits that matter are not necessarily the bits we are familiar with. We believe we live in a world in which 'news' has been made redundant by a super-fecundity of information. However, although the information world seethes with many kinds of plenty, this is not necessarily more original and reliable knowledge. Indeed, the muddle about what news now is has produced a fog of soggy thinking – which, of course, suits some interests very nicely. There is a fatal confusion between news selling (of which there is a great deal more) and news gathering, assessing and making (of which there is a good deal less). The Office of Communications (Ofcom), the British regulator, in its 2007 New News, Future News report, full of state-of-the-art economic analysis of the costs of 'news', committed this fundamental category error – and failed to consider news gathering costs. Sellers commoditize the news for audiences, but few invest in finding out anything that they and we do not already know. Previously, in the old mass world 'news' was just what 'newspapers' and 'news broadcasts' did. It was the heady mixture of (sometimes) novel information and eye-catching sensation – all of the processes were aggregated and were easily recognizable in the end product. But now, to mistake the variety of vehicles that sell news for the news unearthing they depend on is to mistake the wood for the trees. The broadcast news cliché of the female 'blonde in blue' plus 'elder chap in grey' combo – or the even worse smarmy chap in sun tan version – that is a truly global phenomena is a way of selling news, it is not the bit that matters, there is an almost infinite supply of it. We need to take the production of news apart to see what is of consequence to the public interest.

It is the hunter-gatherers of the news ecology who inform our collective lives. Too much news capacity is confined to the back rooms where information is processed and not enough is spent on people on the street. It is often argued that now all we need is news processors directing news, like human traffic lights. But unless you know what you are directing, understand the stories and the background to the stories that have not yet broken, the news directors will be useless. Already news is like a ticking clock, with too much attention focused on the second hand moving around – when the shape of time, the shape of meaning into which an event can be framed is more important and requires a greater, deeper knowledge of what stories mean. Thus, in addition to hunter-gatherers proper news also requires editorial intelligence. It is the integrity of news decision making back on the ranch that also makes news valuable. That editorial sophistication nearly always comes from editors who have been and seen and understand stories directly and personally. They must not (in our interest) just respond to what we are presumed to be interested in, but have to have wider, deeper values. Moreover, news generates creative thought far more than is often recognized – and feeds on culture, in turn. It is the pulling of discussion based on trustworthy judgements (and the resonating of public issues out into comedy and drama and back again) that matters. The diversity that is of public interest is in a variety of news sources and the choice selection of stories.

We may also need rumour squashers just as much as we ever did. One of the things news can do is the opposite of 'whipping up' – it is the proper allaying of fears. The speed of communication has altered everything. The relatives of injured or dead soldiers are now woken, if necessary, in the middle of the night to receive the terrible news – it can no longer be left till the morning, as families might stumble across the news on twenty-four-hour broadcasting. Prime ministers and presidents are expected to react to political events immediately: the time for consideration and assessment has vanished. Indeed, the speed of the news-agenda churn is having profound impacts across a whole terrain of economic and political life. Not following the herd is more than ever vital in breaking stories.

There is another common confusion: innovative audience consumption patterns are also mistaken for 'news' variety. Of course audiences, with their creative exploration of technical opportunities, are remaking all the media industries, from music and art to book publishing and the news. New cultural forms are blossoming. Yet audiences' hunger for experience and the anxious inspection of consumers' new habits has led to another fallacy. People nibble on news from steam television and radio, on the net, on their phones, iPlayers, on bits of paper; at whatever times, for whatever purposes, they pluck news cherries for their own interests and hand them round to their friends. Nevertheless, more and different consumption patterns do not mean there is more newly originated news out there. One change is that audiences are able to avoid what they are not 'interested' in more effectively than ever before. But the news that we have to be concerned about is still the new knowledge, alerting you to your environment and having a collective discussion in public about things that, it turns out, matter.

Another weary old-speak confusion that gets in the way of clear thinking about now: wrong definitions of the freedom of speech problem. In prelapsarian time (a decade ago) the problem was to secure space for a variety of views in the opinion bazaar. The problem was keeping the arteries of opinion open, because there was a shortage of opinion-expressing opportunity. The argument for public service broadcasting, for example, was that it required an enforced variety of opinion to compensate for its powerful position. Yet this negative anxiety evolved into a positive injunction to use impartiality as an instrument that produces better-informed accounts of events and their causes. The idea became a determination to evade ideological, commercial, political and special-interest capture: this value is as relevant as ever.

However, now you can find any opinion you fancy, find somewhere to express any view you want. You can catch Fox News, with its dedicated partisanship, visit evangelical websites, while phone-ins, message boards and chat rooms throb with people all eager to show and tell what they think. Much of the current affairs blogosphere is stridently masculine, and a worrying new gender divide is emerging – leaving half of the human race bored by political discussion. The old argument that there was nowhere to express opinions is surely far less relevant than before. You can find somewhere to parade a view. Nevertheless unfashionable views, ones that challenge orthodoxies of any kind (depending on where you are), still find it far more challenging to attract attention and space. More intriguingly, how we can differentiate between reasonable-looking propaganda, and information that is reliable, accurate, trustworthy is challenging.

'Trust' is itself different now. A fear haunts many modern governments of the democratic kind that the public no longer give public institutions enough 'trust'. Fear of a 'trust' shortage has preoccupied many areas of life, from medical to political, from the game show competitions to official statistics. John Lloyd has argued with elegance and force that the media in liberal democracies have played a malign role in unreasonably denying democratic politics any space to articulate political action – they have deliberately dissolved the trust in the political process.[6] It is an important argument. However, the contemporary map of trust is altering. There is not some Maginot Line of trust, an unmoving wall that has to be defended: the public trusts differently from how it trusted in the past.[7] It is more individualistic, expects a greater intimacy and directness of communication. It is argumentative and, while at some times sceptical, it is also often enchanted with irrational beliefs. Such 'personalisation' may indeed make public attitudes more vulnerable to hysterical media campaigns, particularly in the social media age. However, on balance, it remains very important that the public trust the trustworthy.

Nevertheless, perhaps the problem now is not so much what publics believe, but what they know. People have so many opportunities to have opinions that this is not any longer the scarcity we have to worry about. Now it is evidence that matters. This is why impartiality and objectivity are as salient as they ever were. It is also about the opinion agenda. Nearly seventy years of empirical research has shown that the media do not determine what you think, but do set the agenda of what you think about. People have many ways of forming views, false ideas can be as influential as facts if lots of people believe them and they are not corrected by sceptical reality checkers. Properly funded news polices veracity and stretches public horizons: it also represents and amplifies public concerns. Yet, it is the fertile facts that map reality and form the basis for views that we need to be concerned to preserve.

The other 'opinion' problem is how we are to be brought into relationship with uncongenial views: the 'others' that we may try to avoid. All that opinion expressing is also confused with a variety of opinions: more does not mean wider. More may be a mob. Niche–partisan news selling means that the range of acceptable expression within communities is often a spiralling, narrow one. Both nationally and internationally, great swathes of opinion talk and listen only to other like-minded publics. News can speak across these boundaries if it tells reliable and recognizable accounts of events. People attend when they hear their own reality accounted for justly. It is part of the task of enlarging our collective imagination and attaching our fickle attention to uncomfortable things that we don't understand, that we would often prefer to ignore but which will affect our lives. Proper news is a rationality explorer: it shows you unflinchingly why people, in their circumstances, have the attitudes they have. So the diversity that matters is the diversity of the unexpected and plain reporting.

Moreover, the 'new information' bit of the 'news' is not growing. All over the western world we have lost scrutiny capacity. Startlingly, in a world where everyone says everything is 'global', news values have become more parochial under the intense heat of competition. While simultaneously we are losing genuinely local understanding at an alarming rate, the consequences of the economic collapse of 2008–09 mean that Wales, for example, has been left with very little local reporting. It has political structures of its own, councils, a national assembly – but fewer vehicles to scrutinise what they are doing – except public service broadcasting. The online story of news is one of concentration, not diversity. Thus, more genuinely novel sources of reliable news on the net are difficult to identify because search engines are inadequate. But even so, one recent study showed that the '4,500 news sources updated continuously'[8] from all around the world, about which one search engine boasted, were overwhelmingly lifted and pasted from just four places: three news agencies Agence France-Presse, Associated Press, Reuters and the BBC. The news sellers and opinion strutters were adding their interpretations to a limited set of sources. Another study looked at the decline of 'local' reporting in cities across the world.[9] Yet those who put new things on the collective radar provide an early warning system without which we know that democratic institutions simply fall into weary corruption. This is why a big, well-resourced news organisation like, for example, the BBC's, may be likely to produce more diversity than a small one. Many people are experimenting with ways of assessing news sites so that the public can know which places to turn to for reliable and trustworthy news. But some organisations have a record of appraisal and discovery and a history of reliability: and our own BBC is in this way a potential world resource as well as a national one. Calming news which is accurate needs to be present on the web, and the public have to be able to find their way to it when they need it. News gathering and assessing must be reinvented. Nevertheless, it is the feet on the ground with the Taliban, with the outcast political parties in India or in the back streets of Birmingham that matter. There is no alternative to people witnessing events: reporting is a kind of testimony, and we need more quizzical interrogation of the world. 'Citizen' journalism is a magnificent democratic tool, but it needs situating by people who understand how the world on the ground smells. Variety still depends on independent-minded journalists pursuing stories that are of consequence.

Global institutions: global public

However, being interconnected also means that we need information processors and attention graspers big enough to understand and confront global phenomena. We still need big news organisations – or at least a better way of co-ordinating and testing information so that public understanding has the range to match the institutions we live within. Modern government is large. Global forces impact on individual lives. Huge, international info-tainment businesses often regard news as an expedient political instrument or a branding instrument. Their first concern is not with the quality of information that democratic citizens need. Why should it be? Meanwhile, all of these commercial players seek to translate their interests into politically favourable situations; lobbying is powerful, expensive and rarely sponsored by citizens. The BBC, for example, can bring variety to public discussion because it is large enough and belongs to the public. Moreover, somehow we need to support robust organisations, because the resources devoted to fixing favourable news stories are far larger than those devoted to resisting them.

Some argue that 'partisan' news is the way forward. Yet scandals are exposed by commitment to accuracy, not advocacy. It is not that advocates are not useful – but they also need testing. During combat operations in Afghanistan from 2006–2014, access for independent reporting of British military engagements was very limited, and coverage of some crucial events was restricted to combat camera teams working for the Ministry of Defence. This form of coverage was little more than propaganda, and there were searching questions asked later in NATO about whether things should be done differently in future, with more openness for independent reporting. But the natural tendency of the armed forces is to limit access, rather than recognising the value of independent scrutiny [10]. Meanwhile, aid agencies are paying film-makers to make the documentaries, but who will scrutinise the agencies themselves – now often large, multinational enterprises and remarkably unaccountable? Partisanship is one aspect – but limiting.

Diversity is in the public interest – but modern societies suffer from collective attention deficit disorders. How can people concentrate, when it matters, on things that matter? In the fidgety, non-linear world of the disaggregated attender, how do you mobilize people to notice things? One answer has been sensation, a febrile brew of self-righteous indignation, stirring, shock, salaciousness and attack journalism. Another is to punch a message across all platforms. One of the things democracy needs, that the news can do, is shout and make a fuss about things citizens ought to know. We still need ways of amplify the message across all of the carefully coloured outlets responsive to different audiences. The public interest has to work harder to be noticed, and we need agile but resourceful media to do that.

There is another reason for supporting or creating new vehicles like the big news organisations in the spinal column of our cultural content providers: because news becomes the nervous system of a variety of engagements. News is often considered as a public-service good in its own right (which it is), but there is little discussion of how news seeps into the tissues of an organisation or institutions. The traffic is creatively two-way: comedy, games, drama and children's programmes metabolise news into stories that foster different kinds of discussions of the issues of the day. News alerts programmes to reality, they nurture creative engagement with our predicament. There are a variety of objectivity traders in the world market for knowledge; there are news agencies who are impartial because they sell news to all comers; many news organisations, especially in places that are difficult to work in, fight tenaciously to tell accurate stories. But we need some big, well-resourced and perhaps innovatively organised news producers to test and contextualize stories internationally. But objectivity is hard to do, expensive to produce and more challenging to bring off successfully to the satisfaction of complexly polarized audiences in the contemporary world. Yet the economic model that supports such organisations is under severe economic pressure. On the one hand, we need original models that trade in and test the news that everyone now can produce. It has to be tested because it may, just like old-style news, be accurate but partial. Or it may be a rumour. Or it may be deliberately misleading. The news providers are beginning to get better at handling this material. But it is not enough. We still need news hunters and assessments based on local understanding. We still need the capacity to translate stories from one culture and set of political assumptions into another.

Then there is the really urgent need – a national and an international democratic deficit – to hold international non-governmental organisations (NGOs) to account and to argue about it. After all, charities which are now international big businesses, for example, act in our name, with our money, and what they do influences everyone's future. The world is developing world institutions, they cannot thrive without an international public to address and mould them. Meanwhile, since the 1980s NGOs have boomed. They have become part of a new kind of fifth estate, but they are not all the same. Many critics argue that they are unaccountable; some critics are increasingly cynical about the value of what is called 'aid'. We need to distinguish between those NGOs that are self-interested oligarchies, the ones who, pursuing benign ends, have bad effects, and the ones whose purposes and impacts are valuable, and we really do need to subject them to the kind of scrutiny that tests them. Americans need to know what is done in their name in places they can barely find on a map.

Finally, we need global media with a broad international reach because we have other, invisible and powerful global institutions, and without media scrutiny they will fall into corruption. We need the capacity to make policy in the public interest that matches the size and range of the omnivorously powerful new media institutions. Some of them are global businesses, who operate a good deal more agilely than the media to cover them, some are supragovernmental. Many operate below the radar of any public – let alone the interconnected world audiences to whom they need to be held accountable.

Actually, we at home (wherever that is) need more reporting of distant foreign places for practical issues of self-interested survival – not because it would be nice of us. The first problem is what we understand about our own situation. After all, some of the places we barely bother about have some of the highest economic growth rates and the youngest, most energetic populations and the most difficult economic and political circumstances. Africa, for example. Yet, even the most narrow minded must have noticed that what happens in Britain, down-town Manhattan or Mumbai is hardly a domestic matter any more. Of course there is trade, but there are also bombs. Comprehending what happens in Luton, Walthamstow or Brixton already depends on some kind of understanding of what is happening in Pakistan. The failure to understand foreign places, from their ground up, not out of our preconceived, comfortable stereotypes or sheer blindness, has already had dire consequences in Iraq and Afghanistan, as well as in London and Madrid. But this is two-way. We need to come to terms with unpalatable views. But so does everybody. We need to understand the voices that we do not like and do not agree with even more than those we admire or support. They need to understand us as well. In particular, we have to be concerned about the stories we will need to know about — that at the moment seem distant or trivial. Future stories are as important as or even more so than present ones. Experienced understanding of this kind depends on knowledge and local wisdom. In order to understand the world, not simply interpret it through ideological or info-tainment spectacles, people need to have a historical context within which to place events. Which way things are blowing is only accurately answerable by reference to experience — without it we all too often get the trend of an event (the only thing that matters about it really) quite wrong. Where are the sources of such nuanced, local, deep, long-historical, experienced knowledge of the world in Britain (and indeed in the world)? They are in some government departments, they are in commercial organisations, and they exist in communities. But many of these are woefully incapable of also engaging the public — which they have to learn how to do. Lost local understanding is mirrored by lost international understanding. Indeed, comprehension and explanation requires immersion and local intelligence. It may require friendship. It certainly requires respect and local voices. We need to lay the seeds of our future intelligent knowledge of places now, and we need reporters out, reporting — not editing. Such reporting is expensive, and while much journalism has improved in sympathy and quality — especially the focusing on the voices and views of those who are the subjects of stories, who now increasingly give their own account in their own words — it is also fragile. Just as we all need to know more, we are in danger of making ourselves more stupid. Of course, the cost of ignorance and a loss of knowledge is often catastrophic. In the twenty-first century the front line of every bloody conflict — as well as every commercial endeavour — is in human minds. Fortunes are made and battles won far away from battlefields — in the ideas people have. News making is a knowledge industry: part of the advanced economy of understanding that is remaking the world. Stupid societies make bad decisions. Those that cannot have a common discussion on the realities (both the jolly and the unnerving) of their predicament become tyrannies – either aggressively nasty or myopically stumbling places, replete with trivial comforts but unaware of simmering problems. Getting the thinking around news making right, so that it goes on discovering and alerting us to the unexpected (as well as comforting us with the deliciously shocking familiar), and inventing new ways to tickle the public fancy is important. But the variety that matters is in the hard slog of telling us little stories that we will come to see as important – it is news gathering and news agendas that we have to think about. Keeping information honest is not a luxury: it is a matter of self-interest.

Notes

1 See Ed R. Sambrook, *Global Voice* (London, Premium Publishing, 2007).
2 See J. Seaton, *Carnage and the Media* (London, Penguin, 2005), Chapters 1, 7 and 11 for an extended discussion of these issues.
3 See S. Franks, 'Media, Aid and Disaster', Ph.D. dissertation, University of Westminster, 2007, and in 'Trust and Aid', *Political Quarterly*, 78 (3), 2007.
4 Open Society Foundation, *Television Across Europe: Regulation, Policy and Independence* (EU Open Society Institute, 2008).
5 M. Lynch, *Voices of the New Arab Public* (London, Columbia University Press, 2007). N. Sakr's excellent *Arab Television Today* (London, I. B. Tauris, 2007) also argues for the exciting developments in some media spaces in these societies.
6 J. Lloyd, *What the Media are Doing to Our Politics* (London, Constable and Robinson, 2007).
7 See J. Seaton, 'Trustworthiness: ancient and modern', *Political Quarterly*, 79 (3), 2008, pp. 300–14.
8 C. Patterson, *News Agency Dominance in International News on the Net*, Research Paper (University of Leeds, 2005), p. 47.
9 T. Johnson, 'Young People and City News', Shorenstein Centre, 2007.
10 www.stratcomcoe.org/david-loyn-review-essay-we-have-met-enemy-and-he-us

Chapter 25

Broadcasting and the theory of public service

British broadcasting was started as a public service, and this proved as creative commercially as it was innovative culturally. Indeed, until recently every stage of its development, from the emergence of the BBC, through the introduction of commercial television, to the founding of Channel 4, depended on a set of linked and radical expansions. First, at each stage a novel source of finance was discovered. In turn the growth of broadcasting was financed by the licence fee, advertising revenue and then a tax on the profits of the commercial companies (but one devoted to making programmes). These sources of finance did not compete with each other, and were key to the possibility of political independence. Each stage produced new audiences for broadcasting – the BBC creating an image of its audience as 'participants' in the great affairs of the nation, commercial television popularizing the medium, and Channel 4 decisively registering and enhancing the interests of minority audiences. Finally, of course, at each stage new kinds of programmes and styles of addressing audiences were evolving. Until the 1980s, broadcasting in Britain was not fettered, but liberated for cultural and political expansion by the requirements of public service.

The principle of public service – which has always been fought over and continually reinterpreted – was not the paternalistic and abstract rule which critics have suggested. Nor has it been damaging to entrepreneurial initiative. Indeed, public service regulation has secured the survival of a successful broadcasting industry, one which has become more significant economically and which has become an important exporter of programmes while continuing to discuss and mould national issues. It has, of course, also never been perfect. Broadcasters have often failed to perceive the public interest and, even more frequently, have been too acquiescent to political pressure. Broadcasting has often been used by dominant political actors. Nevertheless, it has provided a flexible means of managing and developing an important utility which has been commercially successful and also served the public.

In the 1980s 'public service' became unfashionable. Yet those who derided it often had a financial interest in weakening it or, alternatively, disliked the political autonomy of broadcasting. However, public service is not a static or dated ideal; it is one we need to redefine and develop. What were the origins of the principle and how did it come to be undermined?

Broadcasting in Britain – monopoly or duopoly – always depended on an assumption of commitment to an undivided public good. This lay beneath all official thinking on radio and television until the 1970s. In 1977 the Annan Report abandoned this assumption, and replaced it with a new principle of liberal pluralism. The ideal ceased to be the broad consensus – the middle ground upon which all men of good sense could agree. Rather, it became, for Annan and those who supported and inspired him, a free marketplace in which balance could be achieved through the competition of multiplicity of independent voices. The result has been confusion and crisis, from which no new received doctrine has yet emerged.

So, by 1982, the Hunt Report on the introduction of cable television could begin to modify the principles of balance and quality even further. These were relegated to a part of the national service in the BBC and ITV. Although both the Hunt Report and the subsequent White Paper advocated some safeguards to protect the British system from the damaging effects of foreign satellite transmissions, and to guarantee the rights of the networks to televise events of national interest, the basis of public service broadcasting was abandoned. Thus cable television, free from constraining ideals, was left to produce programmes that 'were sufficiently attractive for the public to buy'.[1] The 1990 Broadcasting Act suggested that contenders for broadcasting franchises should produce 'sufficient amounts of quality programmes', but not only was this undefined, it only occupied two paragraphs in the Act. By contrast, conditions governing the financial arrangements for the auction of franchises took up fifteen pages.

However, the most obvious long-term symptom of the change in the status of the concept has been a shift in terminology. The concept of public service is elaborated in all broadcasting reports before that of the Annan Committee. As early as 1923 the Sykes Report argued that broadcasting was 'of great national importance as a medium for the performance of a valuable public service'.[2] The next report – that of the Crawford Committee in 1926 – suggested that in view of the scale, significance and potentialities of broadcasting, the duties and status of the Corporation which it had just created 'should correspond with those of a public service, and the directorate should be appointed with the sole object of promoting the utmost utility and development of the enterprise'.[3]

Later reports developed the consequences of this view. 'The influence of broadcasting upon the mind and speech of the nation', commented the Ullswater Report, made it an 'urgent necessity in the national interest that the broadcasting service should at all times be conducted in the best possible manner and to the best possible advantage of the people'.[4] In 1950 the Beveridge Report on broadcasting characterized the ideal of public service more actively. 'Like the work of the universities', Beveridge suggested, 'the work of broadcasting should be regarded as a public service for a social purpose'.[5] The Pilkington Report, which considered both the BBC and the commercial service in 1962, added to this definition: 'The concept of broadcasting has always been of a service, comprehensive in character, with the duty of a public corporation of bringing to public awareness the whole range of . . . activity and expression developed in society'.[6] Indeed the organisation of commercial television was as much a product of the ideal of public service broadcasting as the BBC's had been originally. Thus successive reports developed the idea of broadcasting as a public service – catering for all sections of the community, reaching all parts of the country regardless of cost, seeking to educate, inform and improve, and prepared to lead public opinion rather than follow it.

The Annan Report in many respects broke with this tradition for the first time. This change was noticeable, both in the evidence which was presented to the committee, and in the conclusion of the report. Even the reformers, whether of the left or right, disregarded the public service principle entirely. The BBC referred to it in only the most apologetic tone. The Annan Committee itself took a pluralist view: broadcasting should cater for the full range of groups and interests in society, rather than seek to offer moral leadership. 'For the individual life is a gamble, he is entitled to stake everything, if he desires, on one interpretation of life', it argued. 'But broadcasting organisations have to back the field, and put their money on all the leading horses which line up at the starting gate'.[7] In one elegant metaphor, much of the basis of public service broadcasting had been dismissed, despite the fact that Channel 4 was, in many ways, in practice an extension of it.

Indeed the Annan Report's reinterpretation of public service unintentionally left British broadcasters defenceless against the threats posed by recent technological developments. By so transforming public service it left no grounds on which to manage or control the impact of the inevitable introduction of cable, video or satellite broadcasting. Since 1977, reports and White Papers on the future of these very technologies have not even attempted to assess the impact of unregulated competition for audiences, revenues and programmes on the television system as a whole. Thus it was possible for the Hunt Report to suggest that viewers' willingness to pay for cable television simply constituted a new source of revenue. It was claimed that this would not divert resources from existing channels. (However, it was not apparently thought necessary to support this assertion by either evidence or argument.) By contrast, there was a radical development in the 1986 Peacock Report, which reinterpreted the role of the market in broadcasting.[8] While advocating what Samuel Brittan, a leading monetarist journalist and theorist and member of the Peacock Committee, called 'the goal that British Broadcasting should move towards a sophisticated market system based on consumer sovereignty', the report perceived public service commitments as actually protecting consumer sovereignty. Brittan commented that 'The existence of a tax-financed BBC and the IBA

[Independent Broadcasting Authority] regulation of commercial television were justified by Peacock as a second best, but very successful, attempt to replicate artificially the programme structure of a true broadcasting market'. More than that, the committee took up the elaboration of the public service ideal developed in Channel 4 provision, and suggested that a mature broadcasting service would operate like the publishing industry. 'Pre-publication censorship, whether of printed material, plays, films, broadcasting or other creative activities or expressions of opinion, has no place in a free society', the report argued, and recommended that the government 'embark forthwith on a phased programme for ending it'. Brittan went on to point out not only that the report widened the scope of its enquiries far beyond its original brief of considering the introduction of advertising into the BBC (which it rejected), by assessing the future of broadcasting and how that could be best managed in the context of technological developments, but also that the report demonstrated the fundamental social significance of broadcasting. As Brittan commented:

> Peacock exposed many of the contradictions in the Thatcherite espousal of market forces. In principle, Mrs Thatcher and her supporters are in favour of de-regulation, competition, and choice. But they are distrustful . . . of plans to allow people to listen to and watch what they like, subject only to the law of the land. They espouse the market system but dislike the libertarian value judgements involved in its operation: value judgements which underlie the Peacock Report.[9]

The Peacock Report put public service back on the agenda just at the point when the broadcasting organisations seemed to have abandoned it.

In fact, this abandonment by the broadcasting organisations is a problem, for the authority of British broadcasting has always depended on the pursuit of public service. Indeed, by relinquishing any claim to this, the broadcasting institutions have put into jeopardy a whole set of complex relationships between themselves, the state, their audiences and their programme policy. What caused this crisis? What are its consequences?

The state and broadcasting

One cause of the collapse of the principle of public service broadcasting has been the deterioration in the relationship between the state and broadcasting institutions. In the Sykes Report, Charles Trevelyan argued that 'We consider such a potential power over public opinion and the life of the nation ought to remain with the state'. Because broadcasting was so important it was seen as 'essential that permission to transmit, and the matter to be transmitted should be subject to public authority'.

Air waves were a scarce resource which did not obey national boundaries. Consequently the state was obliged to control the right to broadcast in all societies. In the early British broadcasting reports, however, there is a consensus that state regulation is the best guarantee of broadcasting independence and accountability. As the Crawford Report put it, only the state could license the BBC to be 'a public corporation acting as trustee for the national interest'.

In the 1920s the problem of the relationship of government with broadcasting was dealt with by making new rules and creating new machinery. It was taken for granted that the control over the administration of an organisation could be kept quite separate from whatever the organisation did. Hence it was possible for broadcasting to be politically accountable, and yet remain independent of any political influence. The Sykes Report noted that any detailed control of the work of the Corporation would make a government 'constantly open to suspicion that it was using an opportunity to its own advantage'. It was therefore decided that the minister responsible for the service would be able to answer questions in the House on matters of principle and finance, but he should not be held responsible for the programmes themselves. Later the problem seemed to disappear. Complaints about government intervention were rare, and the issue of excessive interference no longer seemed to exist.

In 1936 the Ullswater Report commented, 'We have no reason to suppose that, in practice, divergent views of public interest have been held by the Corporation and government departments'. Pilkington argued in 1962 that 'The practical resolution of the problem was made easier because the first priority of the department concerned with exercising the government's responsibility (the GPO) is with technical matters'. No conflict had arisen between broadcasters and governments over the definition of public interest. However, by the 1970s this pragmatic argument was felt to be inadequate. Imperceptibly the problem had become one of defending broadcasters against the state. The relationship was increasingly characterized as one of vigilant and stealthy hostility. A cold war had been declared between them. This was partly a consequence of the changing nature of politics in Britain. In a world of increasingly sophisticated news reporting this posed problems for both the BBC and the IBA. 'Politics' and political balance could be treated simply in two- or three-party terms in the 1950s. By the 1970s this was no longer the case. The emergence of centre parties made the work of 'striking a balance' far more difficult for broadcasters. In addition, many fields which had previously been regarded as non-controversial and administrative had moved into the political arena. But also because of a proliferation of parties, interests and pressure groups, because of a widening gap between the major parties and, most of all, because of the rise of issues – of which Northern Ireland was the most critical – for which the gentlemanly and constitutionalist assumptions of the early rule makers could not cater. The problem of providing 'balance' in dealing with treasonable activities in Ulster – when, whether and under what conditions to interview terrorists or members of illegal organisations, how to discuss the issue at all – forced the broadcasting directorates to make new rules and, in effect, to add to the corpus of Britain's unwritten constitution.

The questions which the public asked about broadcasting, the Annan Report claimed, were becoming 'more critical, more hostile and more political'. At the same time, there was a new public mood, 'at once inflationary in the expectation of what political power could achieve, and deflationary towards those in power who failed to give effect to these expectations'.

The interests of governments had come, by the late 1970s, to be seen as inimical to those of broadcasting. The distinction between the broadcasting bureaucracies and what they produced had been challenged. Previously the quality and balance of a company's programmes were believed to be guaranteed by the good order of the administration. This view was now replaced by one of increasingly detailed suspicion. More than that, broadcasters' institutionalized caution about the power of governments had developed into a rejection of all kinds of intervention by the state.

This has had profound consequences for the legitimacy of the public service broadcasting organisations. The Annan Report argued that the authorities have a dual role: on the one hand they exist to ensure that broadcasters operate in the public interest and are responsive to public opinion, particularly as expressed in parliament. On the other hand, they exist 'also to defend broadcasters from undue pressure from whatever quarter'. But these are not complementary obligations; rather they are contradictory. The authorities are supposed both to reflect political pressure and to resist it. It used to be possible for the authorities to perform these two functions when the interests of the state and the broadcasting organisation were seen as similar, if not identical. However, once their interests are opposed, the two aspects of the authorities' role are increasingly difficult to reconcile.

Accountability and broadcasting

This situation would matter less if other mechanisms designed to relate broadcasting institutions to society seemed less perfunctory. Since 1926 they have all suffered from attrition.

Reith rapidly turned the BBC Governors, supposedly 'the trustees of the national interest', into creatures of the Director General. In both commercial television and the BBC, the Boards of Governors depend for their information upon the organisations they were designed to supervise, and they have no independent secretariat or research function. The Governors have remained relatively powerless, and do not see their job as one of representing external interests or views. Similarly, the role of the advisory committees was ingeniously reinterpreted. Reith ensured that these acted as specialists (whether in music, speech or religion) who merely offered their advice over particular policy issues to the Corporation, rather than experts in broadcasting as such.

Indeed the only independent source of power left within these supposedly governing bodies is that of the Chairman of the Board. This power derives from the Chairman's close personal association with the Director General – or the administrative head of the independent service. Yet this intimacy leads to what Heller has called 'the tendency of broadcasting authorities to identify their interests, and by implication the national interest very closely with the survival of the organisation they supervise'.[10]

However, in the 1980s a series of political crises in which the role of broadcasting was crucial – the Falklands War, continuing trouble in Ireland, disputes about the interpretation of foreign events, and profound disagreements about the management of the economy – all exposed the potential vulnerability of the governing body and the Chairman to political influence. Indeed, the Conservative government sought to dominate the governors more directly than any previous administration, by swamping the board with its own supporters. In the 1980s, the problem was not so much the identification of the Chairman with the institution, but rather the identification of the Chairman with the government in power.

Yet the broadcasting organisations had given up so much of the ground themselves. By the 1980s the IBA was to claim that accountability was only a minority interest. The Annan Report had endorsed a system which was little more than a pious rhetoric. 'On balance', the report concluded, '. . . while some improvements could be made, the relations between government and parliament and the broadcasting authorities do not require much adjustment: the chain of accountability is adequate'. Annan apparently believed that accountability was a purely abstract idea – one which includes no reference to the public. But the paragraph nevertheless ends, 'We do not consider, however, that the relations between the broadcasters and the public are satisfactory'. If, as Annan suggested, broadcasting is to abandon the independence of public service, and be based, rather, on a principle of representative pluralism, then the inadequacy of the Governors, and advisory committees, becomes even more serious. By the 1990s accountability had almost been dispensed with as a value. It had, up to a point, been replaced by that of market success.

Independent professionals or men with an interest?

The independence of broadcasting from the state has recently been seen as the most important condition of the service's accountability. This independence has in turn been reduced to the freedom of programme-makers. Yet, as Beveridge once commented, 'To whom is a broadcaster responsible? If it is only to his own conscience the decision might better be described as irresponsible'.

This emphasis on broadcasters' rights is a consequence of focusing the assessment of broadcasting on individual programmes. Pilkington was the last report to elaborate the tradition of public service, and it also argued that 'A service of broadcasting should be judged, not by the stated aims of the broadcasters, but by its achievements'. The Annan Report endorsed this approach.

Nevertheless, broadcasting and broadcasting institutions cannot be understood merely as a collection of separate programme 'texts'. As a report by one of the television unions commented, judging broadcasting organisations by their product 'was like being asked to evaluate the Milk Marketing Board by drinking milk – relevant, but not adequate'.[11]

Broadcasting is a process which cannot be entirely understood from its products. Few would claim that the whole nature of the industrial enterprise can be understood from the shop floor of one factory. Neither can all the pressures which condition broadcasting institutions be revealed by an examination of what Tracey has called 'the world of determination of a television programme'[12] – however important that study might be. The emphasis on programmes as the most important criterion for judging broadcasting reinforces the arbitrary role of professionals at the expense of more general considerations of public service.

The Annan Report claimed that 'Good broadcasting would reflect the competing demands of a society which was increasingly multi-racial and pluralist'. In turn, this variety could be secured only by giving the 'talented broadcasters' greater freedom of expression.

However, broadcasters are not necessarily influenced by a wide variety of interests. Much research has shown how little producers and directors consider their audience. The only information about viewers which seriously affects producers is knowledge of the size of the audience. This is not because audience research is incapable of providing more complex detail, but because to know more would put producers under even greater stress. 'For a sociologist', commented Burns, 'it was rather like watching the whole practice of medicine being reduced to the use of a thermometer'.[13] Producers value the opinion of their colleagues most, but they see very little even of them.

The public interest cannot simply rely on the quality of broadcasters, because to do so is to ignore the pressures which determine broadcasting choices. 'When one stresses the role of individuals manning the system', Garnham argues, 'one is tempted to await a Messiah who will come over – and help transform the system'.[14]

However, the relationship of broadcasters to their organisation has also altered. Burns argued that there had been a considerable change in attitude since the 1960s. Then staff expressed a devotion to public service 'and a belief in the BBC's normative role in the cultural, moral and political life of the country'. By the 1970s this had been replaced by a commitment to professional values. Indeed, as Kumar points out, the emergence of professionalism as the dominating ideology is the product of a particular moment in the evolution of broadcasting organisations. Even the notion of 'lively broadcasting' which determines the professionals' judgements 'expresses a particular stance towards the audience, a judgement of what the audience can and cannot take, which reflects a particular conception of the purposes of broadcasting'.[15]

Indeed the new 'scientific management' of broadcasting organisations has greater power than earlier administrations, whose main concern had been to protect and assist programme-makers who had far higher status within the organisation. 'Because of the need to allocate time and resources economically', Burns argued, 'working relations became impersonally functional'. The steady march of rational managerialism had led to a withering of institutional ardour. Indeed, professionalism is now being superseded in many broadcasting organisations by crude financial managerialism. The pursuit of profit rather than excellence is more likely to dominate decisions in the next decade. Government reforms, culminating in the 1989 Broadcasting Bill,[16] and the auctioning of Channels 3 and 5 to the 'highest bidders' (who in order to bid had to pass a programme quality 'threshold', but who were awarded franchises solely on their ability to raise the largest amounts of capital)[17] will inevitably reduce the power of programme-makers. These pressures are already evident: in the past broadcasting administrators had often been programme-makers first; in a survey of appointments to top posts in television the majority of posts were given to 'accountants, bankers, and financial managers'.[18] Consequently not only were the talented programme-makers upon whom Annan, for instance, rested the future of broadcasting less committed to public service than before, but also they had become less important within broadcasting organisations.

Independence and the theory of broadcasting

The significance of broadcasting independence is also disputed. One side suggests that the independence is functional and must be extended to guarantee accountable broadcasting. The other argues that this same independence poses a serious threat to political institutions, whose control over broadcasting should be strengthened. Working from the same assumptions about the role of the media, Anthony Smith and Colin Seymour-Ure arrived at diametrically opposed diagnoses and solutions.

According to classic liberal theory, the independence of a journalist depended on his ability to follow the uninhibited dictates of his conscience. According to Smith, this is an illusory ideal. In discussing the 1968 crisis in French broadcasting he argues that:

> The ORTF [Office de Radiodiffusion Télévision Francais] strikers had stumbled across the central dilemmas of broadcasting and were demanding in the name of freedom . . . a right which no broadcaster has ever really achieved – the right to be an individual member of a Fourth Estate.

In its place Smith put forward a far more sophisticated and powerful version of the theory, in which the independence of broadcasters is not an individual right – but rather a functional necessity.

Broadcasters are not free, but are 'brokers and megaphones, impresarios and mediators', he suggested. The 'independence' of broadcasting institutions from political control was one solution to a dilemma all broadcasting systems had to solve: namely the necessity not only of regulating the right to broadcast but also of ensuring that broadcasting served the interests of all sections of society. For, Smith suggested, 'The institutions of broadcasting inaugurated a special problem of unlegitimized and unselective power'. Broadcasters are obliged to negotiate political conflict and not take sides in it – precisely because of the immense and dangerous nature of their power. In stable systems, countervailing interests would always be able to enforce damaging sanctions if broadcasters became partisan.

This model implies that all political interests in society can, in practice, be reconciled. It is a logical extension of broadcasting institutions' own view of their role as arbiters that they come to see conflict and opposition as the products of failures in communication. Nevertheless, if there are real differences in interest, incompatible policies, and irreconcilable principles, then the role of the broker becomes untenable.

However, the functional independence of broadcasting institutions has many of the same policy consequences as the older liberal individualism. For, Smith argued, the way to meet recent criticisms is to give broadcasters more independence. The more perfectly broadcasters can do anything they want, the more adequate the service will be. As he is reported as commenting to the Annan Committee:

> If I am free to say anything I want to say except the one thing I want to say then I am not free . . . In broadcasting . . . a single prohibition imposed on a national broadcasting authority or within it tends to corrode the whole output.

Colin Seymour-Ure views the 'independence' of broadcasters rather differently. The independence of the press – no longer the client of political parties – and 'now part of vast corporations who may have very direct interests in the outcomes of policy decisions' is vulnerable because it is compromised by ownership. Broadcasters, moreover, having abandoned the protection of 'public service' ideology are also susceptible to accusations of bias. Seymour- Ure argues that:

> Some Labour politicians used to take comfort in the fact that although the press might be disproportionately conservative, at least broadcasting was balanced. This is no longer true. No doubt broadcasters are not wilfully biased. But the simple fact of deciding their own programme content may in the extreme case lead to a projection of party politicians and leaders that might run entirely counter to the parties' own views.

He suggests that the current interpretation of broadcasting independence has seriously damaged the political system.

The ideal of broadcasting independence – unlimited by any obligation to public service – has become increasingly inadequate. It has contributed to a growing anti-government ethos. It is hostile to many forms of political partisanship. It may inhibit political change and development. It may be that, as Seymour-Ure comments, the period of mass-based party organisation is ending, for one effect of television in many countries seems to be 'the erosion of intervening structures between representatives and electors'. Nevertheless, any increase in the autonomy of broadcasting institutions may have more serious political consequences than had been expected. Rather, it is the democratic processes which need support: not because broadcasters are malign but because of the inexorable pressure of broadcasting independence on the handling of politics. And the devotion of increasing amounts of political energy to managing the media – rather than managing politics.

Choice versus public service?

Double think, according to George Orwell, is the 'power of holding two contradictory beliefs in one's mind simultaneously and accepting both of them'. Through successive regimes, *double think* has nevertheless precisely defined the attitude of politicians towards broadcasting. On the one hand there are people (government ministers, for instance) who tend to believe that the worse excesses of broadcasting, as of the trade unions, should be curbed. There are others (shadow ministers, for instance) who look to broadcasting as a means to correct political bias.

Never, however, have the contradictions been so glaring as in the recent past. The politics of the 1980s and 1990s were orchestrated in a language of freedom, choice, non-intervention, withdrawal of the state: yet they were deformed with successive governmental limitations on the public right to be informed. Where individuals have sought to challenge state manipulation of the news, the government showed neither mercy nor moderation in making an example of offenders. Indeed, the effective range of discussion and investigation is probably narrower here than in most modern democracies – including France, Sweden, West Germany and possibly even the USA. It may not be long before the former Eastern bloc leaves us behind in the matter of broadcasting freedom. Who can imagine the Home Office giving a foreign camera crew *carte blanche* to film what they liked in the Maze Prison – in the way that the Soviet authorities recently provided open access to a western team in one of the USSR's remaining political gaols?

In addition to this, during the 1980s the Conservative government blatantly used television for government propaganda – with a massive increase in public sector advertising. Between 1980 and 1989, commercial television revenues doubled in real terms, and the proportion of advertising revenue generated by the public sector over that period quadrupled; indeed by 1989 it had become the largest single buyer of television advertising. The privatizations of public utilities were the single largest source of television advertising finance between 1990 and 1995.[19] If the ostensible purpose of the advertising was the sale of shares in the shortly-to-be-privatized public sector industries, it also furthered the ideology of privatization.

Throughout the period, public service broadcasting was compared unfavourably with 'the real choice offered to consumers by a more effective market'.[20] Successive reports, government green papers and Bills proposed to 'set free broadcasters from the narrow constraints of control' and it was repeatedly argued that satellite, cable and a deregulated broadcasting system would offer the public a greater choice of programmes more sensitively tailored to their wants by the competitive pressures of the market. In part, of course, government policy was attempting to adapt to a new situation in which cable and satellite would deliver such a multitude of channels and services that the previous regime of regulation would become practically impossible. But more than this, policy was driven by a profound hostility to the principles of public service broadcasting.

Yet the ideology of 'choice' was absurd. Commercial broadcasting is based not on the sale of programmes to audiences, but on the sale of audiences to advertisers. Thus the introduction of more competitors will reduce advertising revenues both by spreading them between a greater number of channels and by splitting potential audiences into even smaller groups. As the main incentive will remain the attraction of the largest possible audience, the competing channels, less constrained by regulation to produce a variety of programmes, will tend to show more of the same or similar programmes.

Indeed, if one contradiction of Thatcherism was that free market rhetoric was accompanied by interventionist practice, another was that talk of the marketplace was accompanied by its virtual eradication. Technological change – with its requirement for long-term investment and large-scale capitalization – has produced a bureaucratic jungle of profit-taking conglomerates which own shares in all the media which the public consumes. The small number of corporate owners is not competitive in a sense that could conceivably be expected to produce an improved product; but their financial rivalry will undoubtedly impose pressure to produce a cheaper one. That means an almost inevitable lowering of standards, since it is cheaper to buy in internationalized soap opera than to make your own drama, and so on. The result is likely to be a lesser variety of the kind of programmes that many of us watch some of the time, and some of us watch most of the time, but which do not attract top audience ratings. We are all, on occasions, members of minorities. Thus the victims of media concentration are variety, creativity and quality, while the proliferation of broadcasting channels in the hands of a small band of operators, 'liberated' by government policy from the obligations of public service variety, is likely to make matters worse. 'Choice', without positive direction, is a myth, for all too often the market will deliver more – but only more of the same.

Conclusion

Broadcasters have come to see the state as their enemy. Yet broadcasting institutions ultimately depend on the state for their legitimation. This authority cannot be replaced by a pluralist ideal of reflecting social and cultural variety. Indeed the adoption of this principle has left broadcasters peculiarly vulnerable to the more general attack on public service broadcasting.

Moreover, arguments with quite different aims from those of the broadcasters, but apparently related, are being used to undermine broadcasting responsibility and independence. Thus neither the emphasis on the authority of the viewers' right to choose from a greater variety of programmes, nor the elaboration of some aspects of the local and regional role of the media, let alone the distinction between a 'service' the public will pay for and a public service, are intended to strengthen the creative autonomy of broadcasters. On the contrary, they are arguments which enhance the power of commercial interests in determining the patterns of broadcasting provision.

Thus, without a commitment to public service, broadcasters are increasingly vulnerable to detailed political interference in the content of programmes. Broadcasting in Britain has in the past had a considerable degree of autonomy from other institutions: it has not in any simple sense been biased. This autonomy is now threatened, partly because the consensus about what constitutes the 'middle ground' of agreed opinion has broken down, partly because the reliance on the skill of professional broadcasters which has replaced it is unjustified, and partly because of the erosion of public service broadcasting. Broadcasting needs to find a new relationship to the state – and a new form of commitment to public service, and indeed a new definition of public service that will work in the conditions of increased competition.

Notes

1 *Report of the Enquiry into Cable Expansion and Broadcasting Policy* (Hunt Report, 1982) [Cmnd 8697].
2 *Broadcasting Committee: Report* (Sykes Report, 1923) [Cmnd 1951], X, 13, para. 21.
3 *Report of the Broadcasting Committee* (Crawford Report, 1926) [Cmnd 2599], VIII, 327, para. 49.
4 *Report of the Broadcasting Committee* (Ullswater Report, 1936) [Cmnd 5091], VII, 617, para. 7.
5 *Report of the Broadcasting Committee* (Beveridge Report, 1951) [Cmnd 8116], IX, 1, para. 217.
6 *Report of the Committee on Broadcasting* (Pilkington Report, 1962) [Cmnd 1755], IV, 259, para. 23.
7 *Report of the Committee on the Future of Broadcasting* (Annan Report, 1977) [Cmnd 6753], XVI, para. 311.
8 *Report of the Committee on Financing the BBC* (Peacock Report, 1986) [Cmnd 9824], II, para. 636.

9 S. Brittan, 'The fight for freedom in broadcasting', *Political Quarterly*, 58 (1), March 1987.

10 C. Heller, *Broadcasters and Accountability*, BFI Television Monograph 3 (London, British Film Institute, 1978), p. 39.

11 ACCT report, quoted in C. Heller, *Broadcasters and Accountability*, BFI Television Monograph 3 (London, British Film Institute, 1978), p. 50.

12 M. Tracey, *The Production of Political Television* (London, Routledge & Kegan Paul, 1978), p. 13.

13 T. Burns, *The BBC: Public Institution and Private World* (London, Macmillan, 1977), p. 137.

14 N. Garnham, *Structures of Television*, BFI Television Monograph 1 (London, British Film Institute, 1973), p. 21.

15 K. Kumar, 'Holding the middle ground: the BBC, the public and the professional broadcaster' in J. Curran, M. Gurevitch, and J. Woollacott (eds.) *Mass Communication and Society* (London, Edward Arnold/Open University, 1977), p. 232.

16 Broadcasting Bill, Bill No. 9, December 1989 (London, HMSO, 300906).

17 See M. Cave, 'The conduct of auctions for broadcasting franchises', *Fiscal Studies*, 10 (1), February 1989, pp. 17–31.

18 'New managers, new talents', *Vision*, December 1989, pp. 15–31.

19 'Television advertising by sector', *Campaign*, July 1989; 'Public utilities flotation advertising spend 1990–95', Hargreaves & Whitticker, Spencer Report, *Adcam*, 1996.

20 S. Velachesky, 'Broadcasting choice', *Hobbart Papers on Liberal Economics*, June 1989, p. 7.

Part V

Politics of the media

Chapter 26

Industrial folklore and press reform

According to Peter Preston, government ministers desire a compliant press, and journalists want a free press. This tension has given rise to '70-year wars' that go back to:

> the Attlee government's surprise at finding a feisty, combative press operating again after years of wartime censorship. Something, ministers thought, had to be done to make it as respectable, as sober-sided, as compliant as the BBC. Thus arose a profusion of commissions and inquiries, of which Leveson is only the most recent, each of them fought off by newspapers crying freedom.[1]

Peter Preston was a distinguished centre-left journalist, who was editor of the *Guardian* for twenty years. He was a progressive Fleet Street voice, and his view of the battle over press reform as a Manichean struggle between the forces of darkness and light, between attempted political control and press freedom, is one shared by most British journalists. It is part of their industrial folklore.

However, the fact that Prime Minister Clement Attlee initially opposed the proposal to set up a Royal Commission on the Press[2] is perhaps an indication that history is more complicated than this folkloric view of the past will allow. As we shall see, different times shaped by different ideas – not the unchanging control-freakery of governments – gave rise to different attempts to reform the press.

Public service moment

In 1949, doctors and nurses had been recently enrolled as public servants in the newly created National Health Service. An enormous investment was being made in university science departments to secure the future. The economy was managed on the basis of public planning. Memories of the sacrifices made by the armed forces during the Second World War were still fresh. Never had public service been more widely recognized as a vocation, nor had the professional class enjoyed in relative terms a higher status.[3]

This encouraged the belief that a professionalizing project would improve the quality of the press. This was interpreted to mean not professionalization in a literal sense – exam-based entry, registered membership and the corporate power to exclude those who transgress professional rules – but something more general and aspirational. Entrenching a public interest culture in the press, it was argued, would increase commitment to truth, accuracy and balance. It would mean elevating the responsibility of journalists to the public above the demands of employers. In this way, the tensions between the needs of society and business would be resolved.

What supporters of this professionalizing project wanted in effect was to change the ethos of Fleet Street. This offered the best route to reform, they argued, because it avoided state intervention that could jeopardize press freedom.

This cultural approach was part of the wider zeitgeist of the time. The Hutchins Commission, set up by the media mogul, Henry Luce, published a report in 1947 which accused the press of failing American society. The remedy, according to the report, was for the press to 'look upon itself as performing a public service of a professional kind'.[4] This could be achieved through the enlightened leadership of owners and managers, through forging an alliance between the press and universities, and through the reform of university journalism education so that its graduates obtained 'the broadest and most liberal training'.[5] The Hutchins report became the Bible of a reform movement that had a profound influence on American journalism.[6]

The movement to 'professionalize' the press in Britain was not only a product of its time but also originated in a journalists' revolt. During the 1930s, the National Union of Journalists (NUJ) became an outspoken critic of propagandistic proprietors, chain ownership and commercialisation.[7] The NUJ's solution was to foster a countervailing culture of professionalism. In 1936, it adopted a 'code of professional conduct', and promised union support for journalists who refused to do things 'incompatible with the honour and interests of the profession'.[8] Promoting a professional culture was championed as a way of creating a space in which journalists would have greater autonomy in which to serve the public. As an NUJ activist complained in 1946, 'a newspaper man is forced to mislead the public or be sacked . . . Staff journalists are marionettes. They cannot be servants of both the public and their employers'.[9]

In 1945, the NUJ called for the appointment of a Royal Commission on the Press. In 1946 NUJ activist MPs moved and seconded a Commons motion authorizing its appointment, and were supported by many other former journalists (though some former journalists spoke against).[10] The motion was carried in a free vote by 270 votes to 157.[11]

The NUJ's support for professionalization, combined with the prevailing public service ethos of the time, shaped the report of the Royal Commission on the Press. The report argued that newspapers were failing to provide the variety, quantity and quality of information which the country needed.[12] The solution was to 'foster those tendencies which make for integrity and for a sense of responsibility to the public'.[13] This could be achieved through the creation of a General Council of the Press whose mission would be to defend press freedom and 'encourage the growth of the sense of public responsibility and public service among all engaged in the profession of journalism'.[14]

One of the General Council's central tasks, according to the Commission, should be to address the deficiencies of recruitment and training in the industry. Too many journalists had only a basic education, while training on the job was too narrow. A better educated workforce would produce better journalism. Another priority entailed 'formulating and upholding a common conception of reputable professional conduct'.[15] The General Council should also adjudicate public complaints, and condemn unprofessional behaviour. Its proselytizing role should be supported by detailed research and monitoring of the press. The overall objective should be to 'interpret the aspirations of a profession', and secure 'the highest professional standards'.[16] This General Council, in short, was to be an agency of cultural change.

The response of most newspapers to these developments was one of mounting horror.[17] Parliament had no right, it was argued, to authorize public scrutiny of the press because Parliament was controlled ultimately by government. 'The appointment of this royal commission', thundered the *Daily Express*, 'is the first step to Government control of the press'.[18] According to a *Daily Mail* columnist, Frank Owen, Parliament's authorization of a public inquiry suggested that 'Hitler won the last war after all'.[19] Other arguments were also mobilized to delegitimate the Royal Commission: it was stuffed full of Liberal Party supporters with an anti-Tory agenda, and it lacked knowledge of popular journalism.[20] However, two national papers cautiously welcomed its appointment.[21]

Most national newspapers reported the final report of the Royal Commission in a highly selective way. The positive things that the Commission said about the press were given prominence, while the negative things were downplayed or omitted altogether.[22] The central theme of press coverage was that the press had been vindicated.[23] And since there was no problem to be fixed – or as the *Daily Mirror* put it, since Britain has 'The Best Newspapers in the World'[24] – there was no need for reform.

Newspaper proprietors obstructed the Commission's professionalizing mission by dragging their feet over the appointment of a self-regulating press body. Eventually, to head off a backbencher's bill with strong cross-party support, they set up reluctantly in 1953 an emasculated General Council of the Press.[25] This body was to be regularly criticized, and reformed, over the next sixty-odd years in ways that will be considered shortly. But the relevant point here is that in all its incarnations – whether as the General Council of the Press, Press Council, Press Complaints Commission (PCC) or the Independent Press Standards Organisation (IPSO) – this self-regulating body was at its core a customer complaints service. It never advanced a professionalizing project in the way that the first Royal Commission on the Press had intended.

The 1949 Commission's championship of broad-based journalism education also fell on stony ground. It had advocated a journalism education curriculum that would include, among other things, knowledge of history and a grounding in economics.[26] But press controllers wanted only narrow journalism training[27] that produced a compliant but competent workforce.[28] Journalism education was organised through the National Council for the Training of Journalists (NCTJ), with a narrow focus on shorthand, media law, knowledge of government and above all reporting and production skills.[29] Even this was pursued in a half-hearted way. In the 1990s, only a minority of journalists had an NCTJ qualification.[30]

The expansion of universities did in fact lead to a more highly educated press workforce,[31] and a growing number of universities offered media studies and journalism degrees from the mid- 1970s onwards. These were mostly broadly based courses, which not only imparted relevant skills but also introduced students to different intellectual disciplines and traditions of thought in much the way that the 1949 Commission had wanted. The response of the British press was to seek to undermine this development in a sustained campaign of denigration.[32] Thus, the *Sunday Times* denounced a media studies degree as 'little more than a state-funded, three-year equivalent of pub chat' symptomatic of 'a dumbed down educational world',[33] while the *Independent* declared that media studies 'students learn nothing of value', and that 'this paper regards a degree in media studies as a disqualification for a career in journalism'.[34] This campaign did not succeed: the more the press attacked media studies, the more teenage student applications rose during the 1990s and 2000s. However, the alliance between universities and the press which supported the professionalizing reform movement in the US never took root in Britain. The British press refused to accept that university media departments were legitimate places to scrutinise its performance, interpret the ideals of journalism and educate new recruits into the industry.

The wider political culture of society also became increasingly hostile to the ethos of public service. This was reflected in the way in which market virtues were extolled, public bodies were privatized and public institutions like the BBC and National Health Service were restructured as internal markets.[35] Hierarchical control was also strengthened in the press industry during the 1980s in ways that further undermined the professionalizing project. Employers fostered a trade identity which celebrated craft skills, in contrast to a professional culture which supported critical autonomy. This trade identity became accepted across the industry. When Andrew Marr, a former editor of the *Independent*, wrote an autobiographical account of journalism, he significantly called it *My Trade*.[36] At the other end of the spectrum, the long serving editor of the *Sun*, Sir Larry Lamb, demanded a

£350 fee as a condition of granting an interview with researchers writing a history of his paper.[37] This was a response from someone steeped in commercial values, utterly at odds with the professional norms of American journalism.

The failure of the professionalizing initiative was further highlighted by what happened. The moral decline of the press after 1980 – reflected in falling editorial standards, declining credibility and the phone hacking scandal[38] – was final confirmation that the 1940s professionalizing project had got nowhere.

Radical Keynesian moment

If the professionalizing project failed, a new initiative was born in the early 1960s. It took press reform in a new direction – economic intervention.

Whereas Conservative governments had presided over the liberalization of the economy during the 1950s, the Conservative administration headed by Harold Macmillan embarked in 1961–62 on an experiment in state planning strongly influenced by 'growth Keynesianism'. It set up the National Economic Development Council, bringing together government, management and unions, to formulate a national economic strategy; created its equivalent in different sectors ('little Neddys'); and developed regional planning policies.[39]

Radical Keynesian thought was also making inroads in economics in a way that was to influence press policy in Europe. In 1959, the American economist Edith Penrose – who had moved to Britain in response to the McCarthyite purges in the US – published *The Theory of the Growth of the Firm*.[40] It illuminated how unequal company competition can lead to market concentration. Her seminal book was an intellectual godparent of the Swedish press subsidies system introduced in 1969–71, fulsomely acknowledged by its principal architect, Karl Erik Gustaffson.[41] More generally, Keynesian analysis of 'imperfect competition' was to be the central intellectual justification for state intervention in press markets (usually in the form of minority newspaper subsidies) in social democratic northern Europe.[42]

Keynesian thought permeated the report of the second Royal Commission on the Press, appointed in 1961 to address the financial difficulties of the British press. Two Cambridge Keynesian economists, Nicholas Kaldor and Robert Neild, submitted influential evidence,[43] and a third Cambridge economist, Brian Reddaway, who was a member of the Royal Commission, championed their analysis,[44] though not their proposed solution. The Commission's report argued that scale economies are especially important in the press industry due to the high cost of producing the first copy of a newspaper. Successful papers can spread their large outlay on the first copy over a large volume of sales, lowering unit costs. This enhances their competitive advantage over smaller rivals, and gives rise to a built-in impetus towards contraction and concentration.[45]

This analysis led the Commission to argue that the state had to intervene. It shied away from recommending selective press subsidies – at least in the short term – because it feared that this would endanger press freedom. But it recommended the establishment of a Press Amalgamations Court to review all proposed newspaper acquisitions and mergers involving large groups. The Court should have the authority to refuse consent, the Commission argued, if it was contrary to the public interest.

After a delay of three years, the Commission's proposal was adopted in an emasculated form. Instead of leaving decisions to an independent court, the Monopolies and Mergers Act 1965 (subsumed into the Fair Trading Act 1973) empowered a politician, the Secretary of State, to have the final say in determining whether a press merger or acquisition should be allowed. This rendered the legislation ineffectual. In response to pressure from powerful press controllers, takeovers were generally waived through – usually on the grounds that it was the only way to save a paper or group.

Between 1973 and 1990, only five out of seventy-five newspaper acquisitions and mergers were disallowed, and these exceptions all involved minor undertakings.[46] All major newspaper acquisitions during this period, such as Murdoch's purchase of Times Newspapers in 1981 following a secret meeting between him and Prime Minister Margaret Thatcher at Chequers,[47] went ahead. And in the period after 1990, no substantial newspaper acquisition or group merger was stopped, even though this was a time when there was a rapid growth of local press consolidation.[48]

The 1962 Commission also recommended that *all* cross-ownership between newspapers and commercial television should be prohibited.[49] Press pressure on government ensured that this recommendation was rejected. Indeed, so effective was press lobbying that the presumption in favour of franchises being awarded to bids backed by a local newspaper group was even retained (until the introduction of franchise auctions following the 1990 Broadcasting Act). The privileging of press groups in the award of franchises was even extended to radio when commercial radio was introduced in the 1970s. Further press pressure resulted in residual controls limiting local cross-media concentration being largely lifted in 2011. Controls on cross-media ownership were thus successfully resisted, bypassed and eroded.

The negation of anti-monopoly controls was not simply a product of press lobbying. Senior politicians were also willing partners in this process. Thus, Prime Minister Margaret Thatcher personally intervened, bypassing the relevant minister, Peter Lloyd, to ensure that Murdoch was allowed to gain control of BskyB, giving Britain's largest press group effective control over Britain's satellite TV monopoly.[50] Similarly, New Labour, in its courtship of Murdoch and other media moguls, attacked in 1996 the Conservative government for being overly restrictive on cross-media ownership.[51] In office, New Labour obligingly withdrew all foreign ownership restrictions on British broadcasting through its 2003 Communication Bill. This Bill also reduced other constraints on media concentration, provoking a cross-party revolt in the Lords led by the film-maker Lord David Puttnam. This revolt resulted in the 2003 Communications Bill being amended to allow 'public interest' grounds for intervention in major media mergers, with the possibility of referral to the Office of Fair Trading (OFT) and The Office of Communications (Ofcom), although the relevant minister still had the final say.

The New Labour government hastened to reassure its press allies that this setback did not matter. The Media and Culture Minister, Tessa Jowell, wrote to the executive chair of News International, Les Hinton, to say that: 'we don't think that the involvement of both OFT and OfCOM in merger decisions should be too onerous'.[52] The Chair of Ofcom, David Currie, was also helpful, telling the Newspaper Society that Ofcom had a 'bias against intervention', and he personally was 'somewhat closer to those who want regulation out of the way'.[53] Murdoch's subsequent bid to consolidate control of BskyB was only days away from being accepted in 2011[54] because the Cameron government wanted the Murdoch empire on side. The bid was withdrawn only when the phone hacking scandal broke, prompting a temporary retreat.

However, anti-monopoly law was only one element of a Keynesian reform approach. In 1974, the Labour Party published a study group plan for re-engineering the newspaper market in order to support press diversity, and in particular to make it easier for new papers to start and survive. Invoking the example of the Norwegian and other European press subsidy schemes, it proposed a production subsidy and launch fund financed through an Advertising Revenue Board.[55]

The press did not usually pay much attention to the musings of party study groups but on this occasion it parked its tanks on the Labour Party's forecourt. A *Sun* editorial warned that the study group's report is 'a sinister and dangerous document'. It concluded about its authors: '<u>BRITAIN BEWARE. THESE PEOPLE ARE DANGEROUS</u>' (original emphasis).[56] *Daily Mail* declared that 'Chairman Mao couldn't have put it better', while the *Daily Telegraph* denounced the pamphlet's 'spectacular dottiness and illogicality'.[57] The *Observer* published a signed denunciation by its proprietor, David Astor, and a subsequent attack by its editor, Donald Trelford.[58] These jeremiads were echoed by similar onslaughts in other papers.[59] The British press made clear that any Keynesian newspaper subsidy/redistribution scheme, imported from abroad, was unacceptable in Britain.

Undeterred, the Labour Party developed over the next twenty years plans to support press diversity, usually combining a launch fund, selective subsidy, advertising redistribution and, latterly, divestment. These Nordic-style schemes were endorsed periodically by the Labour Party's annual conference or national executive, only to be ignored by its parliamentary leadership.[60] But even disregarded policies were a point of contention with the press. Action was finally taken in a decisive way: the Labour Party's media policy committee was closed down in 1996.

Instead, the party's media policy development was outsourced to a corporate-funded think tank, the Institute of Public Policy Research (IPPR), which developed the intellectual case for media deregulation.[61] The central theme of its reappraisal was that the growth of large media corporations enhanced investment, quality and global competitiveness, while old fashioned concerns about media pluralism failed to acknowledge the large expansion in the number of media outlets.[62] This revisionism prevailed in the succeeding period. It was also buttressed by the ascendancy of neo-liberalism which directly confronted Keynesian arguments.[63]

The Keynesian press reform movement thus ended in failure. Anti-monopoly legislation did not prevent a single important press merger. Cross-media ownership restrictions were steadily weakened. Schemes to support greater press diversity were confined to other countries. No effective steps were taken to limit the domination of the British press by a handful of powerful individuals who exercised a disproportionate influence on the news agenda and public life of Britain.[64]

Democratizing moment

The 1970s gave rise to a new approach. This was a time when a growing number of people demanded a say in decision-making, partly as a consequence of a more questioning attitude towards authority prompted by the end of the post-war boom.

Young local politicians argued that local councils should involve people in decision-making.[65] The radical shop stewards movement demanded workers' control,[66] while the Trades Union Congress (TUC) proposed more cautiously that there should be greater employee participation. The Labour government responded by setting up in 1975 an inquiry into industrial democracy, chaired by the Oxford academic, Alan Bullock.

The change in the climate of opinion also impinged directly on the press. In 1971 the Free Communications Group – largely made up of successful, young journalists (with Rowntree funding) – published its clarion call for workplace democracy, *In Place of Management*.[67] In 1972, the NUJ became committed officially to employee participation (although what this actually meant was to be hotly debated in the coming years). In papers as different as *The Times*, *Daily Express* and *Daily Mirror*, journalists were consulted by management in formal meetings. Print workers then demanded that racist and other bigoted content be withdrawn.[68] This culminated in the print unions launching a campaign for victims of press distortion to have a 'right of reply', pursued first through occasional industrial action and subsequently through an unsuccessful parliamentary lobby.[69]

This assertion of shop floor power produced a sharp counter-reaction. The NUJ was accused of trying to censor the press through the power of the closed shop,[70] while print unions were attacked for irresponsibly flexing their industrial muscle.[71] Into this maelstrom of claim and counterclaim stepped the third Royal Commission on the Press, appointed in 1974.

The debate about worker participation forced the Commission to address the issue of who 'owns' press freedom. The tacit assumption (rarely spelt out) is that press freedom is a property right exercised by proprietors as trustees of the public interest. Their freedom is said to be universal since anyone is free to publish. But this was manifestly misleading since, as the Commission pointed out, 'anyone is free to start a daily national newspaper, but few can afford even to contemplate the prospect'.[72] This led the Commission to define press freedom as a collective entity: 'We define freedom of the press as that freedom from restraint which is essential to enable *proprietors, editors and journalists* to advance the public interest . . .' (emphasis added).[73]

This broad-based definition became the basis of its recommended Press Freedom Charter which sought to remove restraints from proprietors, editors and journalists alike. Particular weight was given, in the Charter, to the freedom of editors. In the case of large newspapers, the Commission argued, the editor's contract should specify at least 12 months' notice. The editor should also be free to publish any contribution, regardless of the views of the proprietor, management, union or advertiser. Journalists should be empowered by being 'involved in the appointment of editors' and by being 'free to act, write and speak in accordance with conscience' without the threat of disciplinary action by union or employer.[74] In addition, publishers should be protected through the adoption of detailed rule changes designed to limit the power of the NUJ. The Freedom Charter, the Commission urged, should be introduced on a voluntary basis for three years, and then reviewed by an independent committee. If it was found not to be working, it should be enforced by statute.

The press's response was apoplectic. The *Daily Telegraph* declared that the Commission's report should 'awaken laughter – or tears'.[75] The *Daily Mirror* called it 'a weary wodge of platitudes',[76] while the *Sun* declared that 'the likeliest fate of the report is that it will end up . . . in Whitehall's deepest and darkest pigeon-hole, which is exactly what it deserved'.[77]

The *Sun*'s prediction was correct. The report was lost in an inter-departmental committee, without any political impetus behind it. The report died for much the same reason that the Bullock report, published in the same year and proposing a more radical power-sharing arrangement, also faded.[78] The leaders of industry, including the press, were implacably opposed to any form of internal democracy, and the beleaguered Labour government did not feel that it could impose structural change without consent. And unlike the Bullock report, the Press Commission's report had little support from the left.[79]

The democratic moment passed without achievement. The principal forces behind the demands for workplace representation – trade unions – were hobbled by industrial legislation passed in the 1980s. The 'right to manage' became entrenched: talk of 'co-determination' and 'internal democracy' largely disappeared from public discourse.

Moment of outrage

In 2011, it was revealed that the voicemail of the murdered teenager, Milly Dowler, had been hacked by the *News of the World*, and that a mistaken intercepted phone call had caused her parents to think that she was still alive. These revelations produced a wave of revulsion at a time when the public was already highly critical of the press.[80]

This led to the appointment of the Leveson Inquiry. Its chosen solution for press shortcomings was to strengthen self-regulation. Its chance of succeeding seemed remote. Past enquiries had gone down this route, and all had failed.

Thus, in 1962, the second Press Commission had roundly condemned the shortcomings of the Press Council but concluded that 'the Press should be given another opportunity itself voluntarily to establish an authoritative General Council'.[81] How little was achieved was underscored ten years later, when the Younger Committee investigated the Press Council and found that it was wholly inadequate.[82] However, most of the Committee's recommendations for reforming self-regulation were ignored,[83] so that when the third Press Commission reported in 1977, it once again iterated that the Press Council had failed. Only through extensive reform, the Commission argued, could the Press Council 'fulfil the hopes that were held for it in 1949'.[84]

Yet, so little changed that the Calcutt Committee concluded in 1990 that the Press Council was not working properly largely as a consequence of 'the lack of full commitment by the industry to its aims and objectives'.[85] The press, the Committee continued, 'should be given one final chance to demonstrate that it can put its house in order'.[86] The Home Secretary, David Waddington, told the Commons that 'this is positively the last chance for the industry to establish an effective non-statutory system of regulation'.[87] In 1993, the Calcutt Review concluded that the last chance had passed; the new self-regulatory body, the PCC, 'has not proved itself to be an effective regulator';[88] and it should be replaced by a statutory Press Complaints Tribunal. The report was shelved.

So, when Leveson argued that the press self-regulatory system was not functioning properly, it seemed like Groundhog Day. Indeed, the Leveson report enumerated many of the same shortcomings as previous enquiries. The PCC was not independent, it concluded, and failed to command trust. It lacked the resources, and the will, to do its job properly. It limited the scope of complaints, and its sanctions were inadequate. To this familiar litany of criticism, Leveson added one important, conceptual point. The PCC was not the 'regulator' that it claimed to be but a complaints-handling organisation. It did not monitor compliance with its Code; investigations into systemic abuse were infrequent and inadequate; and remedies were ineffectual.[89] The Leveson report's final verdict was that 'the PCC has failed' and 'a new body is needed'.[90]

Little progress had been made because the press industry had for years obstructed reform. Press controllers had not wanted press self-regulation in the first place.[91] They were determined that it would not develop into a home-grown monster, reprimanding them one moment and telling them to apologise the next. So they had deliberately dragged their feet, only introducing occasional cosmetic changes under duress in order to prevent real change from taking place. Thus, an independent chairperson of the Press Council was appointed for the first time in 1962, and this innovation was followed subsequently by the appointment of an increasing number of public members. But these 'public' representatives were selected through an appointment process controlled by the press. Similarly, after over thirty years of stalling, a Code of Practice was finally adopted in 1989. However, the Code was formulated and modified by serving editors. Likewise, when the Press Council was reconstituted as the PCC in 1991, an inner group composed of senior press executives stayed in control of its finances. They kept the PCC, like the Press Council, short of funds to limit its effectiveness.[92]

Leading this obstruction were those in the press industry who believed that the press regulator was an inherently illegitimate body foisted on the press by a self-serving political elite. In the words of Rupert Murdoch, the Press Council was 'a pussy-footing arm of the Establishment'.[93] If the press regulator was to be tolerated for pragmatic reasons, it should be kept on a tight leash.

This approach was inspired by the belief that freedom of expression is an almost unqualified right, and also concern that the commercial operation of the press should not be constrained. Indeed, freedom of expression and freedom of the market tended to be viewed as an indivisible unity. This mindset generated intense hostility to any attempt to beef up press self-regulation. The suggestion that Press Council adjudications should be given some space on the front page of offending newspapers, the *Sun* guffawed, was 'daft', and deserved a 'raspberry'.[94] 'Short-sighted and smug' was how Sir David English, editor of the *Daily Mail*, described a Press Council report critical of newspapers which paid 'blood money' to friends and family of the Yorkshire Ripper for information. The report showed, English said, that 'the Press Council still does not understand the concept of a Free Press'.[95] In due course, English became the Chair of the 'new broom' PCC Code Committee[96] to make sure it did no harm.

This policy of containment was challenged by doves in the press industry – notably by the NUJ's leadership – and also by some influential figures who wanted self-regulation to be credible.[97] For the most part, these reformers were reined in. The last chair of the Press Council, Sir Louis Blom-Cooper, discovered that 'the industry did not like' his attempts to create a more vigorous body,[98] and increasingly ignored or traduced Press Council adjudications.[99] The last Chair of the PCC, Baroness Buscombe, also complained that her push to 'up our game' encountered resistance from the industry.[100]

Most press controllers thus pursued a policy of passive obstruction. This was backed up by ferocious denunciations of public enquiries which sought to strengthen press self-regulation. For example, the *Daily Mail* inveighed against the first Calcutt Report (1990) as a 'Charter for Hypocrites', while the *Daily Express* called it 'totalitarian' and the *Daily Star* alleged that it would 'turn us into criminals for telling the truth'.[101] The press poured even greater vitriol on the second Calcutt Report (1993). The *Daily Mail* declared that it 'would delight the hearts of latter-day tyrants and totalitarians',[102] while the *Sun* claimed that it will 'stop us telling the TRUTH'.[103]

These public onslaughts were combined with intensive lobbying. Newspaper controllers exerted enormous pressure on the Conservative government, led by John Major, to kill the second Calcutt Report, which recommended statute-based regulation of the press. The government was already, in the words of the National Heritage Minister, Henry Brooke, 'bunkered down' and 'massively on the defensive'.[104] The Labour opposition, intent on improving its relationship with the press, seemed set to side with the press industry.[105] The Major government decided in these circumstances not to add to its woes by having a stand-up fight with the press.[106] It rationalized its decision by hoping that John Wakeham – an esteemed former colleague – would sort out press self-regulation as the first chair of the PCC. In the event, Wakeham merely fronted a dysfunctional system before resigning because of his connection to the Enron financial scandal.

The press once again flexed its muscle when the Leveson report came out. The report was roundly condemned in print, and backchannels to the government were used to block it. These efforts were so successful that Prime Minister David Cameron rejected the report's principal recommendation within 24 hours of its publication. It seemed as if the latest attempt to reform the press would be an instant failure.

Impasse

However, Sir Brian Leveson proved to be an astute politician even if he presented himself as being an aloof judge. He confronted the press's libertarian fundamentalism by arguing that the press was a powerful institution that should not be exempted from 'responsibilities to the public, and to individuals unfairly damaged'. It was wrong that the industry should continue 'marking its homework'[107] – a telling phrase that captured the limitations of the existing system of press self-regulation. His remedy, he stressed, did not entail censorship and should not be misrepresented as statutory regulation.

The Leveson report advanced a hybrid, half-way scheme. Whereas previous enquiries had relied on exhortation or the threat of statutory regulation, Leveson argued that the press industry should organise its own system of self-regulation but that this should be subject to validation by an external body. The new press regulator should no longer be controlled by the industry. To be effective, it should set and enforce standards, and offer a cheap arbitration service in addition to hearing individual complaints. Financial incentives in the form of legal liabilities and exemptions should be established to encourage press groups to join this system of self-regulation.[108]

All media reform groups mobilized behind this report. In the lead was Hacked Off, an offshoot of the Media Standards Trust directed by Martin Moore. Hacked Off proved to be the most effective press reform campaign group in Britain since the 1850s. It had legitimacy because it represented ordinary people who had been victimized by the press. It had access to TV and radio because it was supported by celebrities. It was well resourced, employing at its peak a staff of eight people including a lobbyist, publicist and organiser. It had a talented leadership: an intelligent film star, good at broadcast interviews (Hugh Grant); a former senior journalist, turned journalism professor, who wrote incisively (Brian Cathcart); and a skilled, obsessive organiser, with good Westminster contacts, who was a former Liberal MP (Evan Harris).

Above all, Hacked Off had public support. Poll results varied, depending on the wording of the questions that were asked. But they were broadly consistent in showing support for the Leveson approach. In 2012, 79 per cent agreed that there should be an independent body, established by law, which deals with press complaints and determines sanctions.[109] In 2015, 64 per cent of the public agreed that Leveson's proposals were right or should have gone further.[110] And in 2017, 70 per cent thought that the press should have an independent regulator, with 73 per cent saying that they would most trust a regulator independent both of government and publishers.[111]

Hacked Off organised a political revolt, beginning in the House of Lords where Bills were amended to incorporate Leveson measures. The government blocked these fearing that they would pass in the Commons. This led to a legislative logjam, forcing the government to compromise in order to get its business done.[112] Eventually, the government agreed on a bi-partisan basis that the independent press regulator should be validated not by Ofcom (Leveson's suggestion) but by a 'recognition panel' underpinned by Royal Charter. Section 40 of the Crime and Courts Act (2013) authorized the financial incentives and penalties designed to persuade the press to sign up to the new scheme. In 2016, an independent press regulator, Impress, was validated by the recognition panel. The Leveson scheme was in place.

Newspapers (from the *Daily Mail* to the *Daily Mirror*) unleashed a ferocious editorial campaign against Leveson reform, claiming repeatedly that it would bring to an end '300 proud years of press freedom in Britain'.[113] This campaign traded on historical ignorance, and was based on a cynical lie. Britain, we were led to believe, had a free press in 1750 when to publish fundamental criticism of the social order was a criminal offence, and when even reporting a parliamentary speech was illegal.[114] Britain still had apparently a free press in 1850 when the stamp, advertisement and papers duties sought to price newspapers beyond the reach of ordinary people.[115] Yet this embedded press freedom, hallowed by time, was supposedly coming to an end because an independent panel, underpinned by Royal Charter, would determine whether the press's self-regulation system was autonomous and independent.

The major press groups mounted a highly effective boycott of Impress, ensuring that its regulatory role was confined to a small number of minor publications. Instead they set up IPSO, a regulator they funded and controlled. This new body did not offer an arbitration service. It has not used its much vaunted power to fine newspapers. However, some IPSO adjudications were flagged on the front page of offending newspapers.

The Conservative government had only failed to kill off the Leveson report in 2012 because it lacked a Commons majority to do so following the inconclusive 2010 general election. This enabled Hacked Off to build a Commons majority in favour of Leveson reform by winning over the Liberal Democrats, Labour (under new leader, Ed Miliband) and a small number of backbench Conservative MPs. The press attempted to build a counter-coalition through David Cameron and the veteran New Labour politician, David Blunkett, but was unable to muster enough support.[116] But the political arithmetic changed in 2015 when the Conservatives won the general election with a small majority. The new government refused to 'commence' section 40 of the Crime and Courts Act, activating financial inducements for newspapers to sign up to Impress. In 2017, the Conservative Party promised in its election manifesto to repeal the financial incentive scheme altogether. It also undertook to cancel the next phase of the Leveson Inquiry due to examine newspaper corporate governance and the press's relationship to the police.[117] Uncomfortable revelations arising from official scrutiny of the press were to be annulled in response to newspaper pressure.

All that was needed to deliver the final coup de gras was for the Conservatives to win the 2017 general election. But while they won the largest number of seats, they failed to secure a majority in the Commons. This inconclusive result means that the battle over Leveson reform is not yet fully resolved.

Capture of the political class

This was the first time that the press had a serious fight on its hands. Always before, the press had been able to see off, with effortless ease, attempts to reform it.

Thus, the professionalizing project championed by the first Press Commission had been comprehensively defeated. Diluted anti-monopoly controls, adopted in the wake of the second Press Commission, failed to stop a single major press merger between 1965 and 2017. The democratizing measures advocated by the third Press Commission never got off the ground. And the attempts of five public enquiries to strengthen press self-regulation culminated in the creation of the PCC, a body that always lacked authority and became discredited when it denied that phone hacking had become extensive.

The press prevailed partly because it was a powerful and determined institution that was unashamedly self-serving. It regularly exploited informal contacts with ministers and officials to lobby over decades for legislative changes that were to its advantage.[118] The press was embedded in the matrix of power, and had accumulated expertise in pulling political levers. These were pulled to deadly effect whenever press reform loomed on the horizon.

The press also presented a relatively united front, even though it has multiple subdivisions: tabloids and broadsheets, left-wing and right-wing papers, national and local newspapers, managers and staff. But the only forces within the industry that consistently supported press reform were the press unions. However the NUJ was weakened, and the print unions destroyed, during the 1980s. Leftish and centrist papers did not fill the void this created. The nearest they came to backing press reform was when the *Guardian*, *Independent* and *Financial Times* joined the boycott of Impress, but did not sign up to its rival, IPSO, because the latter was so obviously a reincarnation of a failed system. Qualified abstention was as far as they were willing to go.

This relative press unity was sustained by a creed of righteous libertarianism. Any press reform that involved the state, even in an independent, arm-lengths way, was denounced as paving the way to state control. The logic of this libertarian approach, if pursued consistently, was a media counter-revolution: the BBC, after all, is established by Royal Charter, while British commercial TV is licensed and regulated.[119] But these complexities were not explored in a press whose freedom did not extend to having a free debate about itself.

However, the implacable opposition of a powerful, united institution only partly accounts for the barren record of press reform. Another part of the explanation has to do with the wider political environment. In the early post-war period, there was little pressure for press reform: in the later period, little opportunity.

In the post-war era, the political parties happily co-existed with the press because they were part of the same liberal corporatist system of power. There was no great desire to change things: indeed, the Labour Party did not even set up a study group to think about press policy until 1972. And there were always political costs involved in upsetting the press. Thus, Hugh Gaitskell, leader of the Labour Opposition, refrained from campaigning in 1960–61 against the merger of two giant press corporations, Odhams and the Mirror group, because they were press allies he did not want to alienate.[120] The post-war press also attracted less public criticism than was to be the case later.

But in the post-1979 neo-liberal area, the shortcomings of the press became more pronounced. A press reform group, with extensive trade union backing, was established in 1979, and was followed by others.[121] The public became increasingly critical of the press, the key shift taking place in the 1980s. But although pressure built up for press reform, the democratic system was not responsive to this pressure because the political class – or at least its leadership – was increasingly 'captured' by the press.

Press reform was effectively off the political agenda during 1979–90 because the press was a key ally of the Thatcher government in a shared mission to 'regenerate' Britain. The period of New Labour government (1997–2010) brought to an end any further prospect of press reform. This was not just because Tony Blair and Gordon Brown went to enormous lengths to court the press. It was also because press reform entailed a high opportunity cost. As Tony Blair explained, it would have meant that 'you would have to clear the decks' and there 'would have been an absolute confrontation' with the press. 'The price you would pay for that', he continued, 'would actually push out a lot of things I cared more about.'[122]

Blair and Brown brought press leaders into their social and family life as part of their wooing of newspapers. This had a knock-on effect on David Cameron who did the same thing as part of his mission to wean the press from New Labour when he became leader of the Opposition (2005–10) and Conservative Prime Minister (2010–16). The social integration of press and politicians, at the highest level, became the norm.[123]

Underlying this shift was a realignment of political power. It has become the convention to describe the relationship between politicians and journalists as a tug of war in which each side moves backwards and forwards in a perpetual struggle for advantage. Politicians, it is explained, need publicity; journalists need access to well-placed political sources. Both need each other in a relationship that is both fraught but beneficial for democracy.[124] But what this received wisdom fails to take into account is the way in which politicians lost power during the last thirty years. This explains their increasingly ingratiating relationship to the press.

Politicians ceased to be in charge of effective party machines (until the Corbyn insurgency). Between 1951 and 2011, membership of the Conservative party plummeted from 2.9 million to 177,000, while that of the Labour party decreased from 876,000 to 190,000 during the same period.[125]

Politicians had also diminished cultural capital. In the post-war period, party leaders were able to invoke stable party allegiances, often linked to salient class identities. However, party and class attachments declined from the 1960s onwards. By 2014, 63 per cent of the electorate said that they had only a weak party allegiance or none at all.[126] Once dependable electoral blocs became unstable. Whereas in the 1951 general election, the Labour and Conservative parties commanded 97 per cent of the vote, this was down to 67 per cent in 2015.[127]

Politicians also lost prestige in the neo-liberal era. The global re-division of labour gave rise to industrial rustbelts in Britain. This contributed to electoral disaffection, reflected in falling turn-out. In the 1950 general election, turnout had been 84 per cent: by 2015, it was down to 66 per cent.[128] The reputation of politicians was also badly tarnished by the 2009 expenses scandal. As noted earlier, the large majority of the British public in 2016 did not trust politicians to tell the truth.[129]

One response of politicians to this loss of power was to spend more money on public relations and electoral marketing. Another was to redouble efforts in squaring the press. Even though circulations were in decline, newspapers acquired sharper teeth. Tony Blair, and his close allies, had been shocked by the press mauling of the Labour Leader, Neil Kinnock, in the early 1990s, and consciously resolved to never let the same thing happen to them.[130] Press attacks on the Conservative administration, led by John Major, were a similar cautionary experience for David Cameron and his entourage. As New Labour's principal strategist, Peter Mandelson, acknowledged, politicians on all sides became 'cowed' by the press.[131]

In short, a new generation of politicians – lacking the prestige of post-war leaders, unable to command dependable partisan loyalty as before, no longer at the head of an army of activists – needed press support to offset their diminished power and prestige. But in their Faustian pact with press controllers, one thing became impossible. It was untenable to both seek press support, and at the same time to antagonize the press by seeking to reform it.

Yet, there are indications that the dysfunctional relationship between the press and senior politicians is beginning to change. Ed Miliband, the Labour Opposition leader elected in 2010, was a transitional figure. On the one hand, he recruited a journalist, Tom Baldwin, from Murdoch's empire to head his publicity, and did a sycophantic photo-opportunity holding up a copy of the *Sun*, in the style of New Labour.[132] On the other hand, he displayed new found political courage in pressing for a public inquiry into the phone-hacking scandal.

He was followed by Jeremy Corbyn, elected in 2015, whose communications strategy was directed at bypassing rather than courting right-wing newspapers. In vain, the ancient bazookas controlled by Murdoch, Dacre and other press oligarchs were trained on Corbyn and McDonnell during the 2017 general election campaign, portraying them as patrons of terror and fantasists forever shaking a magic money tree. The campaign failed because the British press is more distrusted than any other press in Europe, its circulation is in free fall, and young people in particular get their news and political information from the internet.[133]

This may prove to be a watershed moment in which the press inspires less fear among politicians. The Corbyn-led Labour party seems set to address press concentration.[134] The Liberal Party (like Labour) favours Leveson reform, as do a number of dissident Conservative Party backbenchers. The collusive relationship formed between the Scottish National Party and Murdoch may not hold, following the eclipse of its architect, Alex Salmond.[135] Meanwhile, the public has become impatient with fawning politicians. In 2017, 67 per cent of people said that Murdoch has too much influence in British politics.[136]

The last seventy years suggest that the press is an institution so powerful that it cannot be reformed. It is now possible – just possible – that in the next decade this could change.

Notes

1 P. Preston, 'Phone hacking is yesterday's news. We should focus on greater threats', *Observer*, 8 January 2017.

2 Herbert Morrison made the case in 1946 that since there had been public enquiries into broadcasting, it was legitimate to have a press enquiry. This gave rise to a long drawn out debate within the Attlee Government, culminating in the decision to allow a free vote in the Commons. See T. O'Malley, 'Labour and the 1947 royal commission on the press' in M. Bromley and T. O'Malley (eds.) *A Journalism Reader* (London, Routledge, 1997).

3 H. Perkin, *The Rise of Professional Society*, revised edition (Abingdon, Routledge, 2002).

4 *A Free and Responsible Press* (Hutchins Report) (Chicago, University of Chicago Press, 1947), p. 92.

5 Ibid., p. 99.

6 J. Curran, *Media and Democracy* (Abingdon, Routledge, 2011).

7 F. J. Mansfield, *Gentlemen, the Press!* (London, W. H. Allen, 1943).

8 T. O'Malley and C. Soley, *Regulating the Press* (London, Pluto, 2000), p. 43.

9 Cited in ibid., p. 44.

10 H. P. Levy, *The Press Council* (London, Macmillan, 1967), pp. 3–4.

11 *Royal Commission on the Press 1947–9 Report (RCP1)* (London, Stationery Office, 1949), p. 4.

12 *RCP1*, Chapters 11–13.

13 *RCP1*, p. 26

14 *RCP1*, p. 165.

15 *RCP1*, p. 174.

16 *RCP1*, p. 169.

17 My grateful thanks go to Eleftheria Lekakis who examined press responses to public enquiries into the press.

18 *Daily Express*, 29 October 1946.

19 *Daily Mail*, 28 March 1947.

20 *Sunday Express*, 30 March 1947, et al.

21 *Manchester Guardian*, 27 March 1947 and *Sunday Times*, 30 March 1947.

22 *Daily Sketch*, 30 June 1949, et al.

23 *Daily Telegraph*, 30 June 1949, cf. *News Chronicle*, 30 June 1949, among others.

24 *Daily Mirror*, 30 June 1949.

25 Levy, *Press Council*; O'Malley and Soley, *Regulating the Press*.

26 *RCP1*, p. 166.

27 A. McBarnet, 'Disciplining the journalist: an investigation of training methods', *Media, Culture and Society*, 1 (2), 1979.

28 O. Boyd-Barrett, 'The politics of socialisation: recruitment and training for journalists' in H. Christian (ed.) *The Sociology of Journalism and the Press*, Sociological Review Monograph 29 (Keele, University of Keele Press, 1980).

29 Little has changed. See NCTJ website. Available at: www.nctj.com/journalism-qualifications (accessed 20 February 2017).

30 A. Delano and J. Henningham, *The News Breed: British Journalists in the 1990s* (London, London Institute, 1996).

31 Ibid.

32 This campaign is described in J. Curran, 'Mickey Mouse Squeaks Back' (Derry, MeCCSA Conference keynote address, 2013). Available at: www.meccsa.org.uk/news/mickey-mouse-squeaks-back-defending-media-studies/ (accessed 20 February 2017).

33 *Sunday Times*, 12 December 1998.

34 *Independent*, 31 October 1996.

35 C. Leys, *Market-Driven Politics* (London, Verso, 2001).

36 P. Chippendale and C. Horrie, *Stick It Up Your Punter*, revised edition (London, Pocket Books, 1999), 'Acknowledgements' [no page number].

37 A. Marr, *My Trade* (Basingstoke, Macmillan, 2004).

38 See Chapter 10.

39 For overviews, taking account of more ambitious attempt to plan the economy in the later 1960s, see A. Cairncross, *Managing the British Economy in the 1960s* (Basingstoke, Macmillan, 1996) and for a more sceptical account, G. O'Hara, 'British Economic and Social Planning', unpublished Ph.D. thesis (University College, University of London, 2002).

40 E. Penrose, *The Theory of the Growth of the Firm* (Oxford, Blackwell, 1959).

41 K. E. Gustafsson, 'Origins and dynamics of concentration' in K. E. Gufstafsson (ed.) *Media Structure and the State* (Gothenburg, Gothenburg University, 1995), pp. 80–81.

42 See P. Murschetz, 'State support for the daily press in Europe: a critical appraisal', *European Journal of Communication*, 13 (3), 1998; E. Skogerbo, 'The press subsidy system in Norway', *European Journal of Communication*, 12 (1), 1997; P. Humphreys, *Mass Media and Media Policy in Western Europe* (Manchester, Manchester University Press, 1996); P. Murschetz (ed.), *State Aid for Newspapers* (Heidelberg, Springer, 2014); R. K. Nielsen with G. Linnebank, *Public Support for the Media* (Oxford, Reuters Institute for the Study of Journalism, 2011). And for the underlying thinking informing this approach, see in particular G. Doyle, *Media Ownership* (London, Sage, 2002) and G. Doyle, *Understanding Media Economics*, 2nd edition (Los Angeles, Sage, 2013).

43 N. Kaldor and R. Neild, Documentary Evidence, Vol. 6, *Royal Commission on the Press* (London, HMSO, 1962), pp. 52–57; and extended cross-examination, Minutes of Oral Evidence, Vol. 3, *Royal Commission on the Press* (London, HMSO, 1962), pp. 25–36. Their proposal for an advertising levy and selective subsidy – but not its rationale – was rejected.

44 W. B. Reddaway, 'The economics of newspapers', *Economic Journal*, 73 (290), 1963, 201–218.

45 *Royal Commission on the Press 1961–1962 Report* [RCP2] (London, Stationery Office, 1962).

46 C. Parkinson, Secretary of State for Trade, *Parliamentary Debates*, 19 December 1980, p. 548, covering 1973–1980; and written answer from John Redwood, Secretary of State, Department of Trade and Industry to Mark Fisher, MP, 29 January 1990, covering 1980–1990.

47 *An Inquiry into the Culture, Practices and Ethics of the Press* (Leveson) (London, Stationery Office, 2012), Vol. 3, p. 1244.

48 For local press concentration, see Media Reform Coalition (MRC), *Who Owns the UK Media?* (London, MRC, 2015), pp. 8–10; and M. Moore, 'Plurality and local media' in S. Barnett and J. Townend (eds.) *Media Power and Plurality* (Basingstoke, Palgrave Macmillan, 2015).

49 *RCP2*, 1962, p. 116.
50 R. Tiffen, *Rupert Murdoch* (Sydney, NewSouth, 2014), pp. 165–67.
51 S. Tunney, *Labour and the Press* (Brighton, Sussex Academic Press), p. 118.
52 Tunney, *Labour and the Press*, p. 135.
53 Ibid., p. 135.
54 Leveson, Vol. 3, Part 1, Chapter 6.
55 Labour Party, *The People and the Media* (London, Labour Party, 1974).
56 *Sun*, 12 July 1974.
57 *Daily Mail*, 8 July 1974; *Daily Telegraph*, 8 July 1974.
58 *Observer*, 14 July 1974 and 24 November 1974.
59 *The Times*, 8 July 1974; *Sunday Times* (Peter Wilsher), 14 July 1974, among others. While the pamphlet contained radical proposals for broadcasting, newspapers focused on its plan for the press.
60 This is well described in Tunney, *Labour and the Press*.
61 D. Freedman, *Television Policies of the Labour Party 1951–2001* (London, Cass, 2003).
62 This is presented eloquently in R. Collins and C. Murroni, *New Media, New Policies* (Cambridge, Polity, 1996). Another researcher on the IPPR project, James Purnell, became subsequently a Blairite Minister of Culture, Media and Sport (2007–08).
63 The battle between economists was continued in the next *Royal Commission on the Press Final Report* [*RCP3*] (London, HMSO, 1977) which emphasized countervailing factors mitigating economies of scale, in an implicit rejoinder to its predecessor.
64 However, Chapter 9 makes the case that the press has influenced public discourse more than public thought.
65 J. Curran, I. Gaber and J. Petley, *Culture Wars* (Edinburgh, Edinburgh University Press, 2005).
66 K. Coates and T. Topham, *The New Unionism: The Case for Workers Control* (Harmondsworth, Penguin, 1974).
67 Free Communications Group (FCG), *In Place of Management* (London, FCG, 1971).
68 P. Wintour, *Pressures on the Press* (London, Deutsch, 1972), Chapter 8.
69 M. Power, 'Right of reply' in J. Curran, J. Ecclestone, G. Oakley and J. Richardson (eds.) *Bending Reality* (London, Pluto, 1986); and O'Malley and Soley, *Regulating the Press*.
70 N. Beloff, *Freedom Under Foot* (London, Temple Smith, 1976).
71 E. Jacobs, *Stop Press* (London, Deutsch, 1980).
72 *RCP3*, p. 3
73 *RCP3*, p. 4.
74 *RCP3*, p. 233.
75 *Daily Telegraph*, 8 July 1977.
76 *Daily Mirror*, 8 July 1977.
77 *Sun*, 8 July 1977.
78 A. Williamson, 'The Bullock Report on industrial democracy and the post-war consensus', *Contemporary British History*, 30 (1), 2016.
79 It was attacked by the left because of its opposition to Keynesian reform of the press, and because of its seeming hostility towards press trade unions. The Report

ended up almost friendless, with critics on both left and right. See for example the numerous hostile references to the report in J. Curran (ed.), *The British Press* (Basingstoke, Macmillan, 1978).

80 Chapter 10, p. 187–188.

81 *RCP2*, p. 102.

82 *Report of Committee on Privacy* (London, Stationery Office, 1972).

83 O'Malley and Soley, *Regulating the Press*, pp. 69–70; *Report of the Committee on Privacy and Related Matters* (London, HMSO, 1990), p. 59.

84 *RCP3*, p. 215.

85 *Committee on Privacy* (1990), p. 65.

86 Ibid., p. 77.

87 A. Bingham, 'Drinking in the last chance saloon', *Media History*, 13 (1), 2007, p. 84.

88 *Review of Press Self-Regulation* (London, HMSO, 1993), p. 63.

89 Leveson, Vol. 4, Chapter 4.

90 Leveson, *Executive Summary*, p. 12.

91 Levy, *Press Council*, pp. 9–10.

92 This assessment is based on Levy, *Press Council; RCP2* and *3*; G. Robertson, *People Against the Press* (London, Quartet, 1983); O'Malley and Soley, *Regulating the Press; Committee on Privacy* (1972); *Committee on Privacy and Related Matters* (1990); *Review of Press Self-Regulation* (1990); R. Shannon, *A Press Free and Responsible* (London, Murray, 2001); Bingham, 'Last chance saloon'; C. Frost, *Journalism Ethics and Regulation*, 4th edition (London, Routledge, 2016); and above all the devastating analysis of the Leveson Report, especially Vol. 1, Part D, Chapters 1 and 2; Vol. 4, Part J, Chapter 4 and Part K, Chapters 2 and 3.

93 Cited in O'Malley and Soley, *Regulating the Press*, p. 68.

94 *Sun*, 8 July 1977.

95 Shannon, *Press Free*, p. 16.

96 Shannon, *Press Free*, p. 127.

97 The most significant of these were Lord Thomson and Cecil King. No one of equivalent importance followed in their footsteps.

98 Bingham, 'Last chance saloon', p. 82.

99 Ibid.; and Leveson, Vol. 1, p. 207.

100 Leveson, Vol. 1, p. 1539.

101 *Daily Mail*, 22 June 1990; *Daily Express*, 22 June 1990; *Daily Star*, 22 June 1990.

102 *Daily Mail*, 15 January 1993.

103 *Sun*, 15 January 1993.

104 Bingham, 'Last chance saloon', p. 86.

105 Bingham 'Last chance saloon', pp. 88–89; Leveson, Vol. 3, p. 1258; O'Malley and Soley, *Regulating the Press*, pp. 93–94.

106 Leveson, Vol. 3, pp. 1246–62.

107 'Full statements of Leveson and Cameron'. Available at: www.holdthefrontpage.co.uk/2012/news/full-texts-of-leveson-and-cameron-statements/ (accessed 26 May 2017).

108 Leveson, *Executive Summary*, pp. 12–18.

109 P. Kellner, 'Leveson: what the public really want', 28 November 2012. Available at: www.yougov.co.uk/news/2012/11/28/leveson-what-public-really-want/ (accessed 26 May 2017).

110 YouGov poll, April 2015. Available at: www.hackinginquiry.org/comment/ new-poll-shows-the-public-want-legislation-to-implement-leveson-if-the-press-continue-to-reject-it/ (accessed 26 May 2017).

111 YouGov poll, November 2016. Available at: www.impress.press/news/yougov-poll.html (accessed 26 May 2017).

112 A fuller narrative is provided by Frost, *Journalism Ethics and Regulation*, pp. 301 ff.

113 *Daily Mail*, 20 October 2016 (cf. *Daily Telegraph*, 15 October 2013); *Daily Mirror*, 31 October 2013; *Daily Express*, 31 October 2013; *Sun*, 27 October 2013; *Daily Mail*, 8 January 2017.

114 Still the best account is provided by J. Brewer, *Party Ideology and Popular Politics at the Accession of George 111* (Cambridge, Cambridge University Press, 1976).

115 See Chapter 2.

116 Interview with Lord [Guy] Black, 10 May 2017.

117 *Forward Together: The Conservative Manifesto* (London, Conservative Party, 2017).

118 Leveson, Vol. 3, Part I, Chapters 5 and 6.

119 See Chapter 27.

120 H. Cudlipp, *At Your Peril* (London, Weidenfeld & Nicolson, 1962), pp. 233 ff.

121 A. Richardson and M. Power, 'Media freedom and the CPBF' in J. Curran et al. (eds.) *Bending Reality* (London, Pluto, 1986); R. Hackett and W. Caroll, *Media Reform* (Abingdon, Routledge, 2006), Chapter 6.

122 Leveson, Vol. 3, p. 1144.

123 See Chapter 9.

124 A. Marr, *My Trade* (Basingstoke, Macmillan, 2004), among others.

125 B. Wheeler, 'Can UK political parties be saved from extinction?', BBC News website, 19 August 2011. Available at: www.bbc.co.uk/news/uk-politics-12934148 (accessed 8 October 2016).

126 M. Phillips and I. Simpson, 'Politics: disengaged and disconnected? Trends in attitudes towards politics' in R. Ormiston and J. Curtice (eds.) *British Social Attitudes 32* (London, NatCen Social Research, 2015), Table 10, p. 137.

127 D. Butler and G. Butler, *Twentieth-Century British Political Facts* (Basingstoke, Macmillan, 2000); P. Cowley and D. Kavanagh, *The British General Election of 2015* (Basingstoke, Palgrave Macmillan, 2016).

128 UK Political Info, General Election Turnout 1945–2017. Available at: www.ukpolitical.Info/Turnout45.htm (accessed 18 July 2017).

129 See p. 158.

130 Leveson, Vol. 3, pp. 1135 ff.

131 Leveson, Vol. 3, p. 1416.

132 *Daily Telegraph*, 13 June 2014. Available at: www.telegraph.co.uk/news/politics/ ed-miliband/10897655/Ed-Miliband-apologises-after-posing-with-The-Sun. html (accessed 18 July 2017).

133 See Chapter 9.

134 *For the Many, Not the Few: Labour Party Manifesto 2017* (London, The Labour Party, 2017).

135 Leveson, Vol. 3, pp. 1407–13. Salmond lost his seat in the 2017 general election.

136 R. Wood, '67% think Rupert Murdoch has too much influence in British politics',
(YouGov survey), HITC Politics, 17 July 2017. Available at: www.hitc.com/
en-gb/2017/07/15/67-think-rupert-murdoch-has-too-much-influence-in-british-politi/
?utm_medium=share%2Bbutton&utm_campaign=social%2Bmedia&
utm_content=/en-gb/2017/07/15/67-think-rupert-murdoch-has-too-much-
influence-in-british-politi/&utm_source=Twitter (accessed 18 July 2017).

Chapter 27

Contradictions in media policy

Introduction

To inform, to discuss, to mirror, to bind, to campaign, to challenge, to entertain and to judge – these are the important functions of the media in any free country.[1] The purpose of public policy should be to enable the media to perform them more effectively. Yet historically, very different traditions of promoting these ideals, or indeed pursuing no ideals at all, have developed in relation to different media. Traditionally, press policy has taken the form of having no policy, and the functioning of newspapers has been left largely to market forces. By contrast, television and radio have been required to pursue objectives set by parliament, and have been subject to regulation.

However, during the Conservative ascendancy of the 1980s and early 1990s, there appeared to be a revolution in official thinking about the media. It was argued that broadcasting should be shaped more by the market, and less by public bureaucracy. The state was portrayed as a threat to media freedom, and regulation was attacked as an obstacle to satisfying the consumer. These themes were invoked, for example, by supporters of the deregulatory Broadcasting Acts of 1990 and 1996. The clear implication was that the gap between press and broadcasting policy should diminish, and the market should be allowed to reign.

A new version of policy consistency was pursued under New Labour, in power between 1997 and 2010. The formerly separate worlds of broadcasting, telephones, computers and print were coming together, it was proclaimed, as a consequence of technological convergence, and this necessitated the development of a common approach for all communications. 'Sectoral policies' for separate media, of a kind pursued by previous administrations, needed to be replaced by a single, coherent vision for the communications industry as a whole.

A new, unifying theme was also advanced by New Labour. 'Communications industries', declared a 2001 government consultation document, 'constitute a large and growing part of our national income'. Their continued growth will promote investment, employment, innovation, choice, diversity and lower consumer prices. However, Britain's communications industry is also faced with intensified competition in a more globally integrated market. Consequently, a key objective of communication policy must be, in the words of the government's 1998 Green Paper, 'not only to defend the domestic position, but also to attract a share of global revenues and jobs to the UK'.

A new ministry was also created to brush away the cobwebs of the past, and impose a new sense of direction and purpose. In 1992, the John Major government established the Department of National Heritage (the nearest synonym to 'Culture' that conservative sensibilities would then allow). It was renamed the Department of Culture, Media and Sport (DCMS) by the incoming New Labour government in 1997, and was rededicated to the task of developing an 'integrated' communications policy.

Yet, New Labour still failed to fulfil its promise of 'coherent regulation in a converging environment'. Like the New Right Conservative administrations that preceded it, New Labour merely added another layer of piecemeal reform. This added to, rather than detracted from, the confusion at the heart of British media policy. This confusion deepened further under the 'modernizing' administrations led by David Cameron (2010–16).

Efficiency

The incoherence of media policy has survived repeated attempts to inject order and clarity. Superficially, official reports on media industries over the past eighty years appear to have much in common. One recurrent theme has been the emphasis on greater efficiency. Thus, in 1949 the Gater Report on the British Film Industry called for more effective financial planning, while the second (1962) Press Commission urged that better machinery for negotiation should be established. In the same way the Annan Report (1977) concluded that 'clear lines of decision making, fewer chieftains, better communications' were needed, and the Peacock Report on the BBC (1986) argued that 'the assessment of efficiency is one of our Committee's chief aims'. Such comments, few of which have ever had any significant effect, have become part of the ritual of investigation.

Most official reports have also taken an optimistic view of the independence of journalists and programme-makers, and their capacity for autonomous reform. Thus two Royal Commissions on the press stressed in identical words that:

> on the quality of the individual journalist depends not only the status of the whole profession of journalism but the possibility of bridging the gap between what society needs from the press and what the press is at present giving it.

Similarly, the Annan Report argued that 'the strength of British broadcasting lies in the creativity of people who make programmes'.

Hence successive reports have suggested better recruitment policies, improved training and education, greater integrity and responsibility among communicators, and new opportunities for independent producers. Annan (1977) proposed an Open Broadcasting Authority which would show minority programmes made by 'small independent production groups', a term which is reminiscent of the 'small independent producer' which film policy has been trying unsuccessfully to help since the Moyne Report in 1936, and which Peacock (1986) championed for mainstream television. In the same way, three Royal Commissions put their faith in individual entrepreneurs as the best way of sustaining a varied press. Even the Calcutt Report (1990) on privacy suggested that newspaper ethics depended 'on the calibre of the individual conscience' – a profoundly innocent view of the solution to tabloid abuses.

This emphasis on individuals as the mainspring of improvement has resulted in economic and institutional constraints being neglected. Repeated attempts to boost film production have foundered because they have not been combined with reform of film distribution and exhibition. Public funding of films swelled the profits of large production companies when there was a buoyant film industry, and led to some films being made that were never shown in commercial cinemas, when the film industry went into decline. Similarly, the Annan Committee proposed an Open Broadcasting Authority (Channel 4, as it became known) to introduce more adventurous minority programmes, yet failed to suggest how its finance could be arranged to protect it from the economic pressures which inhibited experimental programming on the other channels. In the event, an ingenious cross-subsidy scheme was introduced, initially in a form which insulated Channel 4 from conformist market pressure, but this owed nothing to Annan's vague advice on funding. In much the same way, the Peacock Committee hoped that by forcing the BBC and ITV to take a fixed quota of programmes from production companies, a new legion of fearless, creative, independent producers would spring up to create more diverse, popular content. What the Committee did not anticipate was that the independent production quota (first introduced in 1986 and extended in 1990) would expand a vulnerable, casualized, low-paid sector of the television workforce that lacked either the power or the autonomous resources to fulfil what was expected of it, and that it would eventually become subject to a high degree of concentration. Yet the Peacock Committee (chaired by a noted neo-liberal economist) was in fact more alert to economic structures than most such committees. Although appointed by a government hostile to the BBC, it nevertheless protected the BBC, because for the first time its main object was to consider the financial structures that underlay cultural considerations. If the BBC was funded by advertising, Peacock warned, the result would be reduced choice and worse programmes.

However, this inattention to economic constraints occasionally had positive outcomes, though more by accident than by design. When the Annan Committee recommended a minority television channel, it did not anticipate that this would provide a shot in the arm of the ailing film industry. By giving individual, one-off British art movies a secure, predictable audience on television, Channel 4 initially improved film-makers' capacity to raise film finance. By offering an additional distribution system, Channel 4 (and, subsequently, its offshoot Film4) also gave new opportunities for people to see the work of a network of creative and important film-makers. However, this failed to solve the financial difficulties of creative British film-making. In France, where the film industry was relatively more successful, state-generated funding was more readily and consistently available – a crucial factor in artistic and commercial success.

Government and lame ducks

Government intervention has sometimes been justified as an exceptional measure that will make subsequent interference unnecessary and restore a stable and competitive market. This has been particularly true of British film policy, which has been shaped by a combination of crisis-driven expediency and unfulfilled optimism. Thus, in 1927, a Board of Trade inquiry into the film industry advocated special measures to deal with 'unfair, devious and improper trading' by American competitors. This report resulted in the Cinematograph Act, 1927, which obliged distributors and exhibitors to purchase and show quotas of British films. But this was intended to only be a short-term measure, to promote 'free and equitable trade'. In 1949 the National Film Finance Corporation was set up to provide loans for film production. It was seen as a response to a temporary inability of British film producers to obtain private investment capital. The Eady Levy, introduced during the same period, was designed to promote national film production through a tax on box-office takings, which was supposed to fall most heavily on successful foreign imports. Similarly, the last Royal Commission on the press recommended that newspapers should be offered cheap loans in order to pay for the introduction of new printing technology during a period of financial crisis. Its advice was sensibly ignored.

Most of these measures, though advocated as temporary expedients, became settled features of public policy. The 'temporary' import quota introduced in 1927 was strengthened in 1938, supplemented during the 1940s, and abandoned only in 1983. The National Film Finance Corporation, set up as a self-financing agency, was forced to write off many loans and so became a continuing source of state finance for the film industry. It was closed in 1986, subsequently replaced by the anorexic British Screen Finance (with some public money), and then revived, with infusions of lottery funds, as the Film Council in 2000 until its closure in 2011. The Eady Levy survived until 1984 even though it reinforced American domination of the British film industry by subsidizing American-backed films which were only nominally British. The rationale for the levy had changed, and it came to be seen as a way of maintaining employment rather than supporting national culture. All these one-off interventions proved more long-lasting or served different purposes than were originally intended. They might all have been more successful if they had been designed to address long-term problems rather than short-term crises.

Thus, official media reports display over the years many of the same shortcomings and engage in the same ritual responses, while glossing over problems which their recommendations failed to solve. Yet the essential conservatism of official policy is less important than its contradictions. Good policy is not necessarily consistent policy, but one of the most curious features of government relations with the media has been the way in which reports on the press, broadcasting and film industries have often conflicted sharply with one another.

Divergent policy goals

Thus, broadcasting regulation has long sought to preserve a space for national collective expression. As late as the 1970s, no more than 14 per cent of television programmes on BBC or ITV were allowed to be foreign (excluding Commonwealth countries). 'Foreign' was changed to mean non-European Economic Community (EEC) countries in the 1981 Broadcasting Act, but strict rationing of foreign programmes continued. The foreign allowance was set in 1993 at 35 per cent of commercial, terrestrial TV programmes, and at a higher level for Channels 4 and 5 in 1998. It was increased again in the subsequent period. However, in response to the increasing Hollywood domination, Ofcom announced in 2017 that public service commercial broadcasters and the BBC would be compelled to spend more on British-made children's programmes.

This protectionist policy was backed up by limitations on foreign ownership of broadcasting. Until 2003, non-European Union (EU) corporations were not allowed to acquire ITV and Channel 5, though the restriction on majority holding of cable TV companies was lifted in 1990.

However, what was thought desirable in television was not deemed important in the press. There has never been any restriction on foreign ownership of British newspapers. Official inquiries into the press, unlike those into broadcasting, have never seen this as an issue. In film policy, by contrast, cultural autonomy has been believed to be important but it has been eclipsed as an objective by the need to sustain a film industry underwritten by American money. This was acknowledged tacitly by the 1968 review of film legislation when it argued that the National Film Finance Corporation should be maintained not to defend British cultural production, but because 'it constitutes a real attraction for foreign investment'.

The competing claims of the economy, 'culture' and the political system are negotiated in media policy, and resolved in divergent ways in different industries. In film policy, priority has come to be given to maintaining jobs; in television, more attention has been given to cultural concerns. This has resulted in films being conceived and regulated in quite different ways, depending upon whether they are watched in the cinema or on 'live' television.

In the case of television, resources have been redistributed in order to promote quality and diversity. The obligation imposed by the Independent Television Commission (ITC), and later Ofcom, on ITV companies to provide a mixed schedule ensures that some of the revenue generated by programmes (including films) reaching large audiences is invested in more demanding or more minority-oriented programmes watched by smaller audiences. Yet the same principle was never applied to the allocation of film funds through the Eady Levy. This tax on cinema takings was paid to production companies in proportion to the box-office revenue for their films. It constituted a bounty distributed according to market demand. 'The levy', concluded the 1968 Board of Trade review, 'should not be used to breed indifference to economic reality'. Underlying this argument was a concern that cultural or qualitative concerns should not encroach upon market efficiency and the survival of British film-making. By contrast, there has never been a policy in relation to videos and DVDs, apart from a prohibition against objectionable sex and violence.

State as threat

One reason for these underlying tensions and contradictions is that media policy has been shaped by different philosophies. A common feature of much official thinking about the working of the media has been a liberal suspicion of the state. However, this suspicion assumed such evangelical proportions in the case of successive Royal Commissions on the press that it led them into an implicit confrontation with other media inquiries.

Thus, the last Royal Commission on the Press (1977) advanced a sweeping definition of what was acceptable:

> We are strongly against any scheme which would make the press, or any section of it, dependent on government through reliance on continuing subsidies from public funds. We are also opposed absolutely to the estab-lishment of any body which could, or might have to, discriminate among publications in such a way as to amount to censorship in the sense of preferring to support some publications and not others.

Selective subsidies targeted towards weak publications were rejected on the grounds that this could lead to pro-government favouritism. Yet nonselective subsidies were repudiated because they failed to offer special help to the vulnerable. The first approach was found wanting because it might lead to political partiality, the second because it was ineffectual. This catch-22 formula in effect ruled out most forms of market intervention.

Yet the political dangers that successive public inquiries into the press detected in allocating public resources seemed less of a problem in other sectors of the media. 'No public body', thundered the third Press Commission, 'should ever be put in a position of discriminating like a censor between one applicant and another'. This is exactly what the Independent Broadcasting Authority, among other public agencies, did when this advice was given. It is what the ITC, Radio Authority and Film Council did subsequently – and what Ofcom, the British Film Institute and Arts Council do now. The processes of public selection that press inquiries, steeped in a tradition of anti-statism, found so alarming have long been common practice.

The Press Commissions' objection to all policies that can lead potentially to state dependence is no less maverick. If this precept were introduced into the broadcasting sector, it would lead to the immediate privatization of the BBC and Channel 4, the deregulation of all channels, and the free trading of their shares on the open market. Yet not even the most right-wing broadcasting inquiry – chaired by Sir Alan Peacock – was willing to go this far.

Press Commissions' negative view of the state contrasts with their positive view of the market. This is seen as the sheet-anchor of press independence, a view that coloured their opinion of market processes in general. Having rejected public subsidies that induce economic dependence or involve a process of choice, they perceived no difficulty in another kind of subsidy – advertising – that induces economic dependence, involves a process of choice and indeed tends to favour Conservative papers because of their more affluent readerships. In the Commissions' view, public subsidies are fraught with dangers; private ones are not. Similarly, successive Press Commissions failed to make an explicit connection between the high costs of market entry and the predominantly right-wing character of the national press. To have done so would have meant questioning their idealized view of the market as neutral, in contrast to the partiality they perceived to be lurking in the actions of state-linked agencies.

This antagonism towards the state has continued to shape official thinking about the press, and given rise to the same contradictions as before. David Cameron rejected in 2012 the Leveson Report's recommendation that Ofcom should validate a new self-regulation system set up by the press. This meant, he said, 'crossing the Rubicon', taking an unacceptable step towards state involvement in the affairs of the press. But he saw no problem in Ofcom having much more extensive regulatory powers over ITV, Channel 4 and 5. Indeed, it was due to his government that Ofcom regulation was extended to the BBC in 2017.

Benign state

By contrast, public reports on broadcasting generally view the state in a more positive light. Conservative paternalism and an Arnoldian concern with moral and cultural values originally contributed to this view. A liberal corporatist tradition also played a part, equating central planning with the rational and scientific use of resources, as did a radical commitment to redistributing power and democratizing cultural access through the state. Broadcasting was also viewed as being so powerful an influence that it needed to be harnessed to the general good.

All nine major reports on British broadcasting argued that a publicly-appointed agency could act in the public interest, if it was established by the state for this purpose. As the Crawford Committee (1926) put it, 'The actual commission should be persons of judgement and independence, free of commitments, and . . . they will inspire confidence by having no other interests to promote than those of public service'.

Broadcasting has been repeatedly presented in reports as serving the public interest as a consequence of being subject to regulations framed for the public good and controlled by people committed to the best interests of the entire community. The BBC was financed from licence revenue and was therefore, in the words of the Pilkington Report (1962), under 'no obligation, express or implied, to pursue any objective other than that of public service'. Public regulation was seen as both necessary and desirable even after the introduction of commercial television.

This conception of state-sponsored public service has depended on a number of principles. First, that broadcasting services should be made available to everyone in the UK, and not merely developed in areas where it was easy or cheap to do so, or restricted to those who could pay for them. Second, that public service broadcasting should produce a wide variety of high-quality programmes because it is not controlled by the forces that make for low standards and uniformity. Finally, that public regulation should ensure broadcasters' accountability through the relationship of the broadcasting authority with parliament.

Whereas press inquiries are in general pro-market, the opposite is generally the case with broadcasting inquiries. Indeed, public service is deemed necessary in order to make up for the deficiencies of free enterprise. The Crawford Committee (1926) argued that 'no company or body constituted on trade lines for profit . . . can be regarded as adequate . . . in view of the broader considerations which now begin to emerge'. The Ullswater Committee (1936) regarded commercial advertising as incompatible with 'the intellectual and ethical integrity which the broadcasting system in this country has attained'. Much of this opposition was based on the belief that what the Beveridge Committee (1951) called 'competition for numbers' results in standardized programming. This view was justified by references to the deplorable condition of commercial broadcasting in the USA. 'Experience in other countries', concluded the Pilkington Report in 1962, 'is that this kind of competition, so far from promoting the purposes of broadcasting, or extending the range of programmes, or helping to realise the potential of the medium, serves rather to restrict them'.

The necessity of extensive public regulation was never questioned in official reports on television or radio until the Thatcher era. There were signs of unease before that, most notably a concern about the relationship between government (and in particular, party politicians) and broadcasting. But this gave rise to reform, not repudiation, of the public service system. There was also a gradual weakening of the sense of cultural purpose associated with Lord Reith. As the Annan Report commented, 'the ideals of middle-class culture, so felicitously expressed by Matthew Arnold a century ago . . . found it ever more difficult to accommodate . . . the variety of expression of what is good'. The Annan Committee found it harder to define what 'good' broadcasting was in 1977 than did Pilkington in 1962. Nevertheless, Annan did make qualitative judgements, finding the BBC's output, on balance, superior to that of ITV. Annan was opposed to the unrestricted commercial control of broadcasting, and saw the fact that ITV made 'some programmes which both stimulate and entertain, and are not concocted in order to drug their audience into an uncritical stupor' as a product of public regulation. Even the Peacock Committee, which in certain important respects broke with the broadcasting consensus, nevertheless clung to a conception of public service broadcasting as 'a commitment to produce a wide range of high quality programmes to maximise consumer appreciation'. Collective provision and public regulation was producing, in its judgement, a 'mixed diet' of programmes 'at a low cost' that 'has broadened the horizon of a great number of viewers'. While it favoured long-term deregulation, it still made the case for a residual public service system which would secure 'programmes of merit which would not survive in a market where audience ratings was the sole criterion'. These were, it added, not just minority programmes but included ones that attract 'medium sized audiences of which virtually all the population at some stage form a part'.

Broadcasting and press reports do not each constitute a single unity. The second Press Commission was more critical of the market than other Press Commissions, while the Peacock Committee was more anti-statist than the broadcasting inquiries that had preceded it. But in general broadcasting policy has been framed within a pro-state, anti-market framework, while press policy has been formulated within a framework that is anti-state and pro-market. This has produced recurrent inconsistencies that cannot be explained away in terms of technological differences between the two media. For example, the idea that government should give money to a publishing corporation, even one with a publicly-appointed managing authority, would have been anathema to all Press Commissions, which could not countenance even selective subsidies. Yet this is what the Annan Committee proposed when it suggested that a government grant could be given to start an Open Broadcasting Authority, and what the Peacock Committee recommended when it suggested that its proposed Public Service Broadcasting Council could be financed by the taxpayer.

Divergent histories

Differences of perspective are rooted partly in different histories. The press began as an agency of news and political comment. It was also organised as a free market system from 1695 onwards. Traditionally, it has been viewed within a taken-for-granted market framework, and evaluated primarily in terms of its functioning within the democratic system. A 'politics of information', neo-liberal approach coloured the work of all major public inquiries into the press.

By contrast, during the 1920s, radio was not allowed to compete fully with the news service of the press, and was organised as a public service monopoly. It was evaluated primarily in terms of its contribution to culture, education and entertainment, defined by formative Victorian debates. This legacy had an enduring influence on how broadcasting was viewed by subsequent public inquiries.

From the outset, it was also accepted that broadcasting had to be regulated by the state because spectrum frequency was a scarce public resource which needed to be managed in the public interest. This was always an ideological argument, masquerading as a technical one, since it presupposed that public interest management of spectrum scarcity was best entrusted to the state rather than to the marketplace. But it powerfully influenced the approach of all public investigations into broadcasting, even that of the Peacock Committee which sought to challenge and renegotiate this statist legacy.

Consequently, press and broadcasting reports have tended to approach their work in different ways. While Royal Commissions on the press have focused generally on the quality of news and political comment, and formulated their conclusions within a free market system of thought, broadcasting inquiries have concerned themselves generally with the full range of programmes, and promoted reform from a public service viewpoint. This has regularly produced divergent or incommensurate conclusions. Thus, in 1960 the Pilkington Committee recommended a ban on television advertisements 'appealing to human weakness'; yet two years later the second Royal Commission on the press did not even consider the content of newspaper and magazine advertising, let alone recommend its reform. Similarly, the Annan Committee recommended that the joint ownership of commercial broadcasting companies and record or music publishing companies should be banned, on the grounds that there was bound to be a conflict of interest between them. The third Royal Commission on the press, also reporting in 1977, did not propose (or even discuss) a similar measure in relation to the music press and record production.

These discrepancies merely illustrate the different intellectual frameworks in which press and broadcasting policy are conceived. However, these frameworks no longer make sense. Popular newspapers devote less than a quarter of their editorial content to public affairs. Indeed, television has usurped the role of the press as the principal source of news. The distinction between media of 'information' and those of 'culture and entertainment' has completely broken down. The spectrum-scarcity justification for public service broadcasting has also been undermined by the development of cable and satellite television, and more recently by on-demand subscription services like Netflix and Amazon Prime operating within a global computer network. Hence the different policy approaches which have been developed to deal with broadcasting and the press are completely inadequate.

Pressure groups and policy

Another source of inconsistency in media policy derives from the fact that it is shaped by public inquiries confined to one media industry. These have not been given common terms of reference, and they have not been set to work within an integrated framework of communications policy.

The inevitable consequence has been that public inquiries have responded to the divergent pressure groups and economic interests at work in different media industries. Broadcasting inquiries have been powerfully influenced by the BBC, and for this reason have tended to uphold the principles of public service. Press inquiries have been shaped by publishers – who have invested large resources to influence them – and have tended to champion their *laissez-faire* approach.

This sectoral narrowness has also tended to nurture self-interested inconsistency. To take but one example, the 1977 Press Commission favoured limited press holdings in profitable television and radio franchises because, following press lobbying, it came around to the view that these were a valuable, potential source of cross-subsidy for vulnerable newspapers. Similarly the Prime Minister's Working Party on the Film Industry (1977), influenced closely by the views of the industry, proposed that television should finance film-making. On the other hand, the Annan Committee (1977) was exposed to broadcasters who were hostile to the idea that broadcasting should subsidize less profitable media. It consequently opposed the view that 'like an aged parent, the film industry has a right to look to television to support it in its old age'. It rejected the proposal (already endorsed by the Working Party on the Film Industry) for money for film investment to come out of the television levy. It was also much more hostile than the 1977 Press Commission to cross-ownership between press and broadcasting.

A second consequence of the uncoordinated way in which communications policy has evolved is that reforms, proposed and implemented for one industry, have had unforeseen consequences for other media. For example, the decision to establish commercial television in 1955–56, in the wake of Selwyn Lloyd's minority report, contributed almost certainly to the epidemic of newspaper and magazine closures that the second Press Commission was then appointed to investigate in 1961.

This source of inconsistency has yet to be rectified. New Labour and the Cameron governments initiated policy consultations covering more than one medium, and invited comment. But they never set up a full-blown public inquiry into the communications industry which critically scrutinised divergent media policy and proposed a coherent alternative.

Continuing confusion

Of course, a degree of variation in approach to different media could reasonably be justified in terms of their contrasting characteristics. In practice, policy differences are rooted in the histories of different media, and the polarized politics of communication that these have produced. Policy divergence is not the product of rational differentiation between media, nor is it presented in these terms.

However, during the 1980s and 1990s, the rise of the New Right held out the promise of greater policy consistency, at least on its impoverished terms. It sought to reorganise broadcasting on the free market lines of the press. However, while it made policy inroads, and while market values were strengthened within the broadcasting system, its project failed ultimately through lack of political and public support. The BBC and Channel 4 were not privatized. Although a 'light touch' regulator of commercial TV (ITC) was established in 1990, it had a much heavier hand than its press counterpart, the Press Council/Complaints Commission. The ITC licensed the right to 'publish' on domestic airwaves; it excluded television companies which failed to submit adequate public service programme plans; and it was able to impose fines – a power that it used. Unlike the supine Press Complaints Commission, and its successor IPSO, the ITC exerted a significant and positive influence on the industry it regulated.

Indeed, the New Right phase of media reform introduced new contradictions. The ostensible purpose behind rolling back public bureaucracy was to enlarge freedom. However, the Conservative government did not approve of the uses to which this freedom was put. In 1984, it introduced legislation to outlaw video 'nasties'. In 1988, it established the Broadcasting Standards Council (BSC) to monitor levels of sex and violence on television. In 1990, it required broadcasting bodies to reflect BSC codes in relation to sex and violence. During the later 1980s, the Conservative government also unsuccessfully lobbied other European governments to take a tough stand against television sex in the Television without Frontiers Directive (1989). Although committed ostensibly to increasing freedom of expression, the Thatcher government also introduced in 1988 a ban on broadcasting the voices of supporters of terrorist organisations (including democratically-elected Sinn Fein politicians). This conflict between the pursuit of market freedom and the increase of state censorship reflected an underlying tension, at the heart of modern conservatism, between market liberalism and social authoritarianism.

However, New Labour proved to be no more successful than its predecessors in rationalizing media policy. One reason for this was that the Department of Trade and Industry (now, after numerous re-brandings, the Department for Business, Energy and Industrial Strategy) in effect continued to be a second 'media ministry', and promoted a market brief, while the DCMS was more oriented towards public service policies. A second reason was that New Labour's promotion of global media competitiveness as a central objective tended to clash with its aims of promoting media quality, diversity and access. A third reason is that its reappraisal focused on telecommunications, broadcasting and print, but side-lined film (even though film is now funded and distributed partly by television, and the two media are inextricably linked). Nothing that Ofcom has done since during its watch has significantly diminished these inconsistencies (though this is partly a consequence of the legislative framework within which it works).

Incommensurate media policies that have arisen out of different cultural traditions and the impact of different industrial lobbies could be represented as a triumph of organic pluralism, or at least rationalized in some way. But this has yet to happen. In New Labour's green, white and consultation papers on communications, public service broadcasting is defended, without any equivalent attempt being made to justify an entirely different approach to the press. The latter is just assumed to be right, without any argument or reason being given. In this way, the contradiction at the heart of media policy persisted – unacknowledged, unexplained and unjustified – as it has done for over eighty years. All that New Labour's rhetoric about the need for an integrated communications policy achieved was to expose how incoherent it was.

The contradictions at the heart of media policy persisted under the 'modernizing' Conservative governments headed by David Cameron (2010–16) and Theresa May (2016–). Committed to deregulation and free trade, they propped up the film industry through UK tax breaks that subsidized Hollywood, and was a form of British job protectionism in an unofficial global trade war. Pledged to shield the press from any state oversight in however vestigial and distanced a way, the Cameron government supported in 2016 the charter renewal of the BBC, the largest public broadcasting corporation in the world. Abhorring the thought of a Nordic subsidy scheme, the May government was happy for the BBC, in 2017, to sneak in subsidies for ailing local newspapers – stricken by the internet – in the form of an £8 million a year grant for 150 local reporters to be shared.

The entire media landscape is being transformed by the internet, and will be profoundly changed by the rise of on-demand providers like Netflix and Amazon Prime. Demands are now being made for the vast profits harvested by the net leviathans like Google and Facebook to be subject to a levy that will enhance quality and diversity in the rest of the media system. If ever there was a time for a major public enquiry into the full spectrum of media and communication to sort out the legacy of past muddle, and plot a positive policy for the future, it is now.

Note

1 The reports cited in this chapter are listed in the extended bibliography at the end of the book.

Chapter 28

Media reform

Democratic choices

Introduction

The media absorb over thirty hours a week in the average person's life. They are central to the democratic life of Britain. They are vehicles through which different social groups connect to each other, and join in the shared conversations of society. They are also major sources of pleasure and cultural fulfilment. How the media are organised and regulated matters.

Yet public policy about the media is often presented as an arcane subject to do with regulators, 'governance' and 'externalities'. It seems to belong to a rarefied world where only experts are qualified to speak, and where complex issues are susceptible solely to technocratic solutions.

But in essence the debate about how best to organise and manage Britain's media is exceedingly simple. It also involves choices that affect everyone. It is not something that can be left safely to politicians — if unexposed to public pressure — will tend to curry favour with media magnates.

What follows is a summary of public discussion about media policy. It reports not only the principal policy alternatives that are available, but also the thinking behind these. The aim is to provide a map that marks clearly the main points of entry into the democratic politics of the media.

Free market

Free market ideas have been the main driving force shaping media policy since the early 1980s. The starting point of this approach is that consumers are the best judges of what is in their best interests. Media policy should seek therefore to create the conditions of greatest possible competition, thus enabling consumers to exercise sovereign control. This produces media that people want, a wide range of choice, and media independence from government. There is no conflict between the needs of society and the functioning of the market system. On the contrary, 'all provision for the consumer on a competitive basis in a non-distorted [media] market', according to the *Financial Times* journalist Samuel Brittan, 'is a public service'.[1]

The market not only empowers the consumer and fosters freedom but also makes for efficiency. It follows from this that there is very little need to reform the press, since it is organised along free market lines. The opposite is true of public service broadcasting, which is indicted on four main counts. It is controlled by an unrepresentative elite who foist their cultural values on the public. It is vulnerable to government pressure because it is dependent on state-sponsored privileges. It is run by bureaucracies prone to waste and profligacy. And, according to some critics, the BBC and Channel 4 are unaccountable havens for radicals. This is in marked contrast to the competitive environment of the press, where the consumer is in control and where, consequently, unpopular radical views get short shrift.

The case for deregulation, argue neo-liberals, has been further reinforced by technological change. It was once maintained plausibly that broadcasting channels had to be managed in the public interest because the scarcity of air-wave frequencies produced a natural oligopoly. But cable, satellite and digital technologies have multiplied the number of television channels, and these have been supplemented by DVDs, the web and on-demand services. The technical justification for public service broadcasting, based on the need to manage spectrum scarcity, has been undermined.

The world is also changing, it is argued, in a way that makes media competitiveness a key objective of communications policy. The media are part of the expanding creative industries sector, and generate both jobs and exports. But British media are now exposed to increased competition as a consequence of the growing integration of the world's audio-visual markets. Leading British media companies should be free to accumulate increased economies of scope through mergers and acquisitions if they are to compete successfully against heavyweights in the international market. 'Some concentration of [media] ownership', declared New Labour's Green Paper on *Regulating Communications*, 'has been regarded as inevitable, and possibly desirable, since it confers advantage in terms of global competitiveness'.[2]

These different arguments contributed to a cumulative policy of deregulation that began with cable TV in the 1980s, speeded up with the 1990 Broadcasting Act which partly deregulated ITV, and continued with the 1996 Broadcasting Act and 2003 Communications Act that relaxed restrictions on media ownership. A new regulator, Ofcom, was also established with a brief to 'roll back regulation promptly when regulation becomes unnecessary'.[3] Critics argue that Ofcom has been more oriented towards serving the consumer than the citizen.[4]

Yet the pace of deregulation has still not been fast enough for committed neo-liberals. The Adam Smith Institute believes that the BBC should be broken up into 'an association of independent and separately financed stations' funded partly by advertising. It argues that the market should prevail, since 'the only fair criterion of judging a programme is by how many people like it'.[5] Similarly, Rupert Murdoch holds that increased cross-media ownership should be actively encouraged, since it increases investment and is therefore 'a force for diversity'.[6] His son James Murdoch called for the lifting of the impartiality requirement on broadcasters on the grounds it limits their freedom of expression and independence.[7] Some like David Elstein press for the BBC's licence fee to be replaced by a private subscription.[8] Others in this tradition are adamant that the BBC should be scrapped entirely, at least within the next ten years.[9]

Pressure for deregulation comes not only from neo-liberals in Britain but also from their allies abroad. An attempt has been made to advance deregulation through the European Court of Justice, European Commission and in particular the Commission's Competition Directorate. This last even proposed in 1998 that public service broadcasters should be prevented from making programmes of a kind made by commercial broadcasters.[10] European state legislation made it more difficult for national governments to regulate satellite television, if they are uplinked from deregulatory countries in the European Union (EU) like the UK and Luxembourg.[11] In 2010, a European directive eased rules restricting product placement – a hidden form of advertising in films and TV drama. In 2016, the European Commission proposed a further relaxation of these rules. Even so, the neo-liberal push in the audio-visual sector has been only partly successful due to opposition from national governments: Europe remains a relative bastion of public service broadcasting.[12]

Neo-liberals have also sought to advance their aims through international trade negotiation, conducted under the auspices of the World Trade Organization (WTO).[13] The United States tried to impose global free market media policies during the Uruguay round of negotiations (1986–94), only to encounter strong opposition from European and other countries. A fresh attempt was made to outlaw subsidies for media production (including the television licence fee) and eliminate programme quotas during the subsequent Doha round of trade negotiations, which stalled. The neo-liberal strategy of multi-lateral negotiation – although still being pursued – has encountered strong political headwinds.

It is now probable that the US state, with a long history of being strongly influenced by Hollywood, will place greater emphasis on making bilateral agreements with individual countries, where it is able to exert greater leverage to secure a neo-liberal media settlement. This is likely to feature on the trade agenda of post-Brexit Britain.

Public service approach

Whereas the neo-liberal approach focuses on satisfying the wants of the individual consumer, the public service approach is concerned with serving the needs of society. In essence, this comes down to three things: serving democracy, generating content that has cultural value and promoting social inclusion.

Public service broadcasting is not confined to the BBC. It also includes regulated commercial broadcasting (principally Channel 3 and 5) and Channel 4 (a public trust). It comprises that part of the broadcasting system which has a legal obligation to serve the welfare of society.

While the general justification for public service broadcasting has been referred to in different places in this book, it may be helpful to summarize here its main themes. First, public service broadcasting is committed to reporting the news impartially and to giving due prominence to coverage of public affairs. It thus ensures that people are briefed properly as citizens, and contributes to the healthy functioning of the democratic system. In contrast, market-driven media tend to marginalize news in favour of entertainment, offer 'info-tainment' instead of informative analysis, and can follow partisan agendas (like Fox News in the US). Comparative research shows that the level of public affairs knowledge is high in countries where public service broadcasting is strong, and low in countries where it is weak.[14]

Second, *publicly owned* broadcasting is committed to making quality programmes rather than merely offering what is profitable. It seeks to democratize culture by making widely available the best works of literature, drama, art and music. It aims to renew the culture of society by supporting innovation and experiment. It is also seeks to cater for the diversity of the public and the enthusiasms of minorities, as well as of the majority.

Third, public service broadcasting binds together and integrates an increasingly privatized and fragmented society. It ensures that everyone has access to a shared, unifying experience, because it does not discriminate against outlying areas or low-income groups on the grounds of cost or profitability. Its approach is inclusive, seeking to draw together society in its diversity and to frame public discussion in terms of what serves the general good. In addition, because it invests in making programmes rather than relying, like BSkyB, on imports, public service broadcasting maintains a cultural space through which society can express itself and define its collective identity.

Public service broadcasting enjoys widespread public support. Public service TV channels are still very popular, accounting for the majority of viewing in 2015.[15] And because public ownership and regulation ensures a high level of investment in programme-making, Britain is one of the largest exporters of programmes around the world. The prestige of the BBC also enhances the country's soft power.

Yet public service broadcasting is coming under increasing attack not just from the radical right but also from the radical left. One left-wing charge is that the BBC is not truly independent of the state.[16] Another is that the combination of deregulation and marketization has caused public service broadcasting to lose its way.[17] A third accusation is that broadcasters over-represent the political centre at the expense of both left and right. This last accusation was also widely aired during the polarized 1970s when the left and right – mediated by people in the critical centre – came together to demand a new form of public service broadcasting, culminating in the creation of Channel 4 in 1982.[18] If these different elements were to coalesce again, this would significantly weaken political support for existing broad-casting arrangements.

The reformist response is to say that problems – once identified – have concrete solutions. Thus, steps should be taken to limit the ability of govern-ment to 'lean on' the BBC.[19] The BBC should cease to be subject to periodic Charter renewal, and be established as a statutory body like Channel 4. The government should hand over decision-making about the funding of the BBC to an independent body. Above all, appointments to the BBC's new unitary board should be entirely independent from government, and overseen by a new independent appointments body.

Insufficient diversity is emerging as a weakness of public service broadcast-ing, and this too can be fixed. British TV news (ITN as well as BBC) is more inclined to interview and cite people from the world of authority (state and experts), more oriented towards government than opposition, and less disposed to use civil society organisations and ordinary people as news sources, than television news in some other democratic countries with a strong public service TV tradition.[20] British TV is better at costume drama (which can be readily sold abroad) than drama that connects to contemporary issues and concerns. In some respects, the range of TV public service content is also shrinking despite, paradoxically, the expansion in the number of public service channels.

The answer, it is suggested, is that the objectives of public service broadcasting should be amended to include: representing a due diversity of viewpoints in news, current affairs and drama. Ofcom regulation should require higher levels of investment in staple PSB programme genres – current affairs, arts and children's programmes. The BBC should be encouraged to be a more confident, risk-taking organisation by being shielded through new arrangements from the salami-top slicing of its funds. More power should be delegated, with defined budgets, to producers – the key to the BBC2's golden age of the 1960s and the outstanding output of HBO in recent years. And more vigorous steps should be taken to have a more diverse workforce, off-screen as well as on-screen.

The major deregulated parts of the system – BSkyB and Virgin – should be brought into the public service orbit. In particular, they should be subject to a requirement to invest in original production, bringing to an end their largely parasitic existence as rights management rather than programme-making organisations. The list of reserved sporting events – available for broadcast – should be expanded after a period of contraction so that less televised sport is behind a pay wall.

Social market

Situated between the free market and public service approaches – and overlap-ping these – is the social market approach. This sees the market as being, in general, the best way of organising the media. But while being pro-market, this approach frequently identifies shortcomings in the market's actual operation. This leads to advocacy of state regulation or intervention to ensure that the market functions in the public interest.

Thus social market reformers have called, at various times, for intervention to strengthen *pluralism of media control* through curbing media concentration or by fertilizing green shoots of new media enterprise (via tax breaks and quotas for independent production). They have also urged action to support greater *media content diversity* (through selective production subsidies and quotas for particular categories of programme). And they have advocated *national protectionist* measures to support Britain's media industries (through quotas on imported programmes, restrictions on foreign ownership, and requirements for domestic content investment).

This approach is the wild card of media politics, since it draws support from both left and right. The social market tradition often generates inconvenient arguments for its own side, upsetting the left by being market-friendly and upsetting the right by calling for state intervention. We will illustrate the nature of this tradition with two brief historical examples.

Exhibit one is the White Paper on *Media Ownership* (1995), published by the one-nation Conservative National Heritage Minister, Stephen Dorrell, which put the case for retaining significant controls on media concentration. Its starting point is that the media are not a standard commodity:

> A free and diverse media are an indispensable part of the democratic process. They provide the multiplicity of voices and opinions that informs the public, influences opinion and engenders political debate. They promote the culture of dissent which any democracy must have. In so doing, they contribute to the cultural fabric of the nation and help define our sense of identity and purpose. If one voice becomes too powerful, this process is placed in jeopardy and democracy is damaged. Special media ownership rules . . . are needed therefore to provide safeguards necessary to maintain diversity and plurality.[21]

The White Paper then went on to argue that general competition legislation is not an adequate basis for regulating the media because it is framed primarily with economic objectives in mind, and permits levels of media concentration that are too high, given the media's central role in the democratic process. In the event, the White Paper was attacked by both the media and New Labour; Dorrell was moved to another job; and the 1986 Broadcasting Act went further down the path of market liberalization than the White Paper had signposted. Nevertheless, it is a classic social market text that expresses with great eloquence the case for curbing media concentration.

Exhibit 2 is a still more maverick document, written by two Keynesian economists, Andrew Graham and Gavyn Davies. It makes the case for the BBC within the framework of market theory. Television, they argue, has 'public good' characteristics: its programmes can be consumed – unlike a Mars bar – by an infinite number of people without additional cost. Public ownership is a way of enabling this public good advantage to be retained by the public rather than exploited for private profit.

Their second key contention is that extensive intervention is needed to cope with a built-in tendency for a small number of companies to dominate the broadcasting market. 'Thus, while one source of monopoly, spectrum scarcity, has gone, it has been replaced by another – the natural monopoly of economies of scale and of scope'.[22] Economic advantages of size foster oligopoly, and limit real choice. Regulation alone is not a sufficient response to this problem because regulators tend to be influenced unduly by the industries they oversee. Publicly owned organisations such as the BBC are also needed because they produce 'merit goods' that set standards, and influence both the wider broadcasting industry and public demand. This social market justification for public ownership influenced the thinking of the New Labour government which was embracing the free market but had a soft spot for the BBC.[23]

Social market reformers' greatest impact has been fostering national media protection (introduced in the 1920s and sustained in different forms ever since).[24] Their contention is that support for domestic media is needed to fend off the overwhelming economic power of American media corporations, which command much greater revenue and scale economies than British media companies. Protection, they argue, extends competition and choice. It is not xenophobic but simply recognizes that the nation state is where democracy is primarily organised. There needs to be a buoyant national media system, if it is to function as effective intermediary between the government and British public. There also needs to be an autonomous communication space where national concerns, issues and solutions can be debated, not one that is colonized and eviscerated.

Reformers in the social market tradition continue to press for market interventions. For example, the Media Reform Coalition advocates an 'ownership cap', with no single media company being allowed to control more than 20 or 30 per cent of a designated media market. In addition, they argue that any media company with a 15 per cent share in a designated market should be subject to a Public Interest test in respect of any merger or takeover. The acquisition may be permitted only if the media owner meets certain obligations, such as making a cast-iron commitment to upholding media independence or investing in specified amounts of original content.[25]

The social market approach generally takes the form of very specific, detailed proposals. By contrast, there are other traditions which offer sweeping blueprints for change.

Radical visions

If the most formative media vision in the first half of the twentieth century was that of the public broadcasting corporation serving the nation, the most formative in the second half of the century was that of the internet, shaped by the values of openness, user engagement and collaboration in serving the world.[26]

Just as many people have sought to defend, update and improve public service broadcasting, so others have sought to do the same thing in relation to the internet. Activists have defended 'net neutrality' – the principle that the net does not discriminate between any content, application or website – against the self-interested lobbying of giant net corporations. Hacktivists have sought to sustain internet freedom by aiding people in authoritarian countries to evade state censorship. User engagement has been extended by the development of social media, while the public, collaborative nature of the internet has been defended by the Open Source movement.

The two traditions of public service broadcasting and the internet meshed in the creation of public service news websites and programme playback systems. The BBC website (which British newspaper publishers wanted to impoverish or suppress) became one of the most used news websites in the world. The Corporation's iPlayer was a pioneer of streamed, public programme-on-demand.

There is a need for further innovation. One big gap is the absence of a search engine that prioritizes information on the basis of public interest rather than popular 'ratings' criteria: a global public service rival to Google. Another is action to assist journalism start-ups to battle more successfully against media conglomerates, offering heavily subsidized free content. A third is to supplement crowd-funded initiatives with collective public support for new digital projects.

A levy should be imposed, it is argued, on the revenue of high-profit social media, pay-television and 'digital intermediary' organisations to finance a 'public interest content fund' and an 'innovative digital fund' to be dispensed by public trusts.[27] In this way, some of the enormous profits of net and digital oligopolies would be redistributed to support greater media diversity. The political wind is now shifting. In an attempt to disarm public criticism, Google donated US\$450 million in 2016 to cultural industries in Europe.[28] In 2015, 51 per cent in Britain said that they supported a levy on the revenue of social media and pay TV companies to fund new providers of journalism, with only 9 per cent dissenting.[29]

But if public service broadcasting and the internet are the most successful instances of visionary thinking, there are also other examples. One is the radical democratic approach exemplified by Raymond Williams. He argued that collective control over the means of mass communication was needed to further a 'cultural revolution', based on a universal right to transmit and receive information. This would enable people to grow in the power to direct their own lives, extend collective understanding through the exchange of experience, and develop the capacity for independent response and choice.[30]

Broadcasting, according to Williams, has been stunted by authoritarian, commercial and paternalistic forms of organisation. The untried alternative is a 'democratic' one. The BBC and commercial broadcasting should be replaced by public trusts which would own production and transmission facilities on behalf of society and lease these, on long-term contracts, to independent companies which would control programme-making. These companies would be run by broadcasters in a democratic way: administrators would be required to work within the framework of 'elected policy'.

Similarly, newspapers should be acquired by newspaper trusts and leased to their editors and journalists. Newsprint companies should be in separate public ownership, and provide supplies at a 'fair and open price'. Within this system, working journalists would determine editorial policy.

The underlying principle behind this proposed reorganisation is that 'the active contributors [should] have control over their own means of expression'.[31] When the means of expression are so costly that they are beyond media professionals' financial resources to own, society should step in to enable them to exercise control over their own work. This form of public intervention is enabling, since it secures the freedom of journalists and creative staff and protects them 'alike from the bureaucrat and the speculator'.

Raymond Williams' conception raises the issue of why professional communicators, who are unrepresentative of society and often surprisingly uninformed about their audiences, should be established as a communications elite with exclusive rights of control over the media. Different people within the radical democratic tradition offer alternatives. Some favour workers' control in different spheres, with media staff controlling the editorial process, and other workers controlling production, distribution and sales. Others want to vest control in the editor, whose autonomy would be protected by law. Others, still, argue for consumer, party, social group, professional, local community or directly elected public representatives in the direction of the media, to balance media workers' power.

This begs the issue of what form workers' rights should take within media organisations. The basic options, in ascending order of significance, are: staff entitlement to information; the right to be consulted about major decisions; participation in senior appointments; representation on decision-making committees (editorial committees, boards of management or supervisory boards); regular staff elections to senior management posts; and full workers' control.

An alternative vision is the liberal pluralist one, exemplified by the work of John Keane. His starting point is to doubt 'whether any one person, group, committee, party or organisation can be trusted to make superior choices on matters of concern to citizens'.[32] What is needed, in his view, is a media system constituted by different forms of organisation and control. Only some media, he suggests, should be subject to what he calls 'the time-consuming and unwieldy procedures of direct democracy'. Alternatives should include timeshare and common carrier arrangements with private media corporations; the funding of local independent cinemas, recording studios and lease-back broadcasting facilities; subsidized political newspapers; co-operatively run publishers and distributors; a reformed BBC and privately owned media.

The central conception informing his approach is that varied forms of organisation and control give rise to media diversity and multifaceted media oversight of the exercise of power in society.[33]

Legal debate

So far, we have focused mainly on policy discussion concerned with media organisation. Overlaying this discussion is another, related debate concerned with media law.

Libertarians in this legal debate stress the importance of freedom of expression, and the public's right to know the basis on which all decisions affecting the common good are made. Interventionists tend to emphasize other concerns, principally the right to a fair trial (contempt), national security (official secrets), a good reputation (defamation), intellectual property (copyright), public decency (obscenity), and group safety (incitement to racial hatred) and privacy. The main dispute between these two groups is about where the balance should be struck between these competing rights. Their different conclusions are also informed by divergent perceptions of the public. Interventionists tend to emphasize the susceptibility of vulnerable members of society to media influence, whereas libertarians tend to argue that audiences are critical and capable of making up their own minds.

There is also another axis of contention. Some interventionists argue that the media should be prevented from violating the norms and moral values of society, or from disrespecting women, religious, ethnic or disabled groups. This goes beyond the standard case for limited censorship, based on preventing serious harm from being done to others, and potentially constitutes a rationale for a broad measure of control directed against anything that is deemed offensive.

Libertarians respond to this argument in different ways. Some fundamentally reject it, like George Orwell who argued that 'freedom . . . is the right to tell people what they do not want to hear'.[34] Others negotiate its implication by saying that restriction should only apply to content judged offensive by 'reasonable people'. Others, still, negotiate its implementation by distinguishing between minors (who need protection) and adults (who do not need to be cosseted). In general, they suggest, it is better to restrict access to communications (through, for example, under age restriction to internet porn or limitations on what can be broadcast before 9pm) than to suppress them entirely. The final buffer against a major extension of the law in regulating public thought is, it is argued, a credible form of media self-regulation.[35]

Shifting currents

In general, the tide flowed in a more interventionist direction during the 1980s when increased controls were imposed in defence of public decency and national security. The tide shifted in a more libertarian direction in the subsequent period, most notably with the landmark Freedom of Information Act (2000) which extended the right to know. But in the 2010s this movement was reversed, most notably through enhanced surveillance of communications and the prevention of terrorism programme.

Imprinted in the DNA of media politics is a fundamental tension. The political right tends to be non-interventionist in relation to the market, and interventionist in the area of public morality and national security. They are 'liberal' in one area and 'illiberal' in another. By contrast, the left is disposed to be interventionist in the market, and non-interventionist in relation to moral regulation. They want the state to interfere more in one area, and less in another.

However, this is only a rule of thumb guide. There are influential liberals on the right, who want less state involvement in all spheres. There are also interventionists on the left who want stricter controls over both the media economy and public thought.

How the left, centre and right split also varies in relation to specific issues. Thus, in the Leveson debate, the right opted for less regulation of the press, and the centre and left opted for more. But on state surveillance of communications, this was reversed.

Out of this confusing matrix of tensions and conflicting impulses will emerge, it is possible to hope, a better media system: one with power and responsibility exercised on behalf of the public.

Notes

1 S. Brittan, 'The case for the consumer market' in C. Veljanovski (ed.) *Freedom in Broadcasting* (London, Institute of Economic Affairs, 1989), p. 35.

2 *Regulating Communications* (London, Stationery Office, 1998), p. 16.

3 *A New Future for Communications* (London, Stationery Office, 2000), p. 95.

4 P. Lunt and S. Livingstone, *Media Regulation* (London, Sage, 2012).

5 Adam Smith Institute, *Omega Report: Communications Policy* (London, Adam Smith Institute, 1984); Adam Smith Institute, *Funding the BBC* (London, Adam Smith Institute, 1985).

6 R. Murdoch, *Freedom in Broadcasting* (London, News International, 1989), p. 9.

7 J. Murdoch, 'The Absence of Trust', McTaggart Lecture, 2009. Available at: www.theguardian.com/media/2009/aug/28/james-murdoch-bbc-mactaggart-edinburgh-tv-festival (accessed July 2017).

8 *Daily Telegraph*, 2 March 2015.

9 R. North, *'Scrap the BBC!'* (London, Social Affairs Unit, 2007).

10 C. Leys, *Market-Driven Politics* (London, Verso, 2001), p. 148.

11 A. Harcourt, 'Institution-driven competition: the regulation of cross-border broadcasting in the EU', *Journal of Public Policy*, 27 (3), 2007.

12 T. Gibbons and P. Humphreys, *Audiovisual Regulation under Pressure* (Abingdon, Routledge, 2012).

13 M. Puppis, 'National media regulation in the era of free trade: the role of global media governance', *European Journal of Communication*, 23 (4), 2008.

14 J. Curran, S. Iyengar, A. Lund and I. Salovaara-Moring, 'Media system, public knowledge and democracy: A comparative study', *European Journal of Communication*, 24 (1), 2009; T. Aalberg and J. Curran (eds.) *How Media Inform Democracy* (New York, Routledge, 2012).

15 *A Future for Public Service Television: Content and Platforms in a Digital World* (London, Goldsmiths, University of London, 2016), p. 11.

16 T. Mills, *The BBC* (London, Verso, 2016).

17 Leys, *Market-Driven*.

18 S. Harvey, 'Channel 4 and the redefining of public service broadcasting' in M. Hilmes (ed.) *Television History Book* (London, British Film Institute, 2003).

19 *Future for Public Service Television*, p. 156.

20 J. Curran et al., 'Reconsidering "virtuous circle" and "media malaise" theories of the media: An 11-nation study', *Journalism*, 15 (7), 2013, Table 4, p. 826; R. Tiffen et al., 'Sources in the news', *Journalism Studies*, 15 (4), 2014, Table 8, p. 383 and Table 10b, p. 386.

21 *Media Ownership* (London, HMSO, 1995), p. 3.

22 A. Graham and G. Davies, *Broadcasting, Society and Policy in the Multimedia Age* (Luton, University of Luton Press, 1997), p. 1. Their arguments were also presented in multiple, shorter versions.

23 Its influence can be seen in the New Labour government's *A New Future for Communications* (London, Stationery Office, 2000), p. 50.

24 See previous chapter.

25 Media Reform Coalition, 'A Manifesto for Media Reform', 2015. Available at: www.mediareform.org.uk/get-involved/a-manifesto-for-media-reform   (accessed 2 August 2017).

26 See Chapter 20.

27 *Future for Public Service Television*, pp. 100 ff.

28 *New York Times*, 19 July 2016.

29 Cited in *Future for Public Service Television*, p. 100.

30 R. Williams, *Communications*, revised edition (London, Chatto and Windus, 1966), pp. 134 ff.

31 Ibid., p. 163.

32 J. Keane, *Media and Democracy* (Cambridge, Polity Press, 1991).

33 For a radical pluralist version of this argument, see J. Curran, *Media and Power* (London, Routledge, 2002), Chapter 8, in which I piece together actually existing media polices implemented in different parts of Europe to present a model media system.

34 G. Orwell, 'The freedom of the press' [(Orwell's proposed preface to *Animal Farm* which was never printed]. It first appeared posthumously in the *Times Literary Supplement*, 15 September 1972. In this preface, he did not suggest that press freedom was an unqualified right.

35 Useful further reading on these issues includes M. Hanna and M. Dodd, *McNae's Essential Law for Journalists* (Oxford, Oxford University Press, 2016); T. Crook, *UK Media Law Pocketbook* (Abingdon, Routledge, 2013); J. Rowbottom, *Democracy Distorted* (Cambridge, Cambridge University Press, 2010); E. Barendt and L. Hitchens, *Media Law: Cases and Materials* (Harlow, Longman, 2000); and G. Robertson and A. Nicol, *Media Law* (London, Penguin, 1992).

Bibliography

Public reports and papers

Broadcasting

Broadcasting Committee: Report (Sykes Report, 1923) [Cmd 1951].
Report of the Broadcasting Committee (Crawford Report, 1926) [Cmd 2599].
Report of the Television Committee (Selsdon Report, 1935) [Cmd 3703].
Report of the Broadcasting Committee (Ullswater Report, 1936) [Cmd 5091].
Report of the Television Committee (Hankey Report, 1944) (Privy Council Office).
Broadcasting Policy (1946) [Cmd 6852].
Report of the Broadcasting Committee (Beveridge Report, 1951) [Cmd 8116].
Report of the Broadcasting Committee 1949 (1951/2) [Cmd 8117].
Broadcasting, Memorandum on the Report of the Broadcasting Committee (1951) [Cmd 8291].
Broadcasting, Memorandum on the Report of the Broadcasting Committee, 1949 (1952) [Cmd 8550].
The Television Act 1954, 2 & 3 Eliz. II, c. 55.
Report of the Committee on Broadcasting (Pilkington Report, 1962) [Cmnd 1753].
The Television Act 1964, 12 & 13 Eliz. II, c. 21.
The University of the Air (1966) [Cmnd 2992].
An Alternative Service of Radio Broadcasting (1971) [Cmnd 4636].
Sound Broadcasting Act 1972, 19 & 20 Eliz. II, c. 31.
Session 1971–2 Independent Broadcasting Authority, Sub-Committee B, House of Commons Paper 465 (1972).
Observations on the Second Report of the Select Committee of the Nationalized Industries (1973) [Cmnd 5244].
Report of the Committee on the Future of Broadcasting (Annan Report, 1977) [Cmnd 6753].
Broadcasting without Frontiers, EEC paper, No. 9 (1984).
Report of the Committee on Financing the BBC (Peacock Report, 1986) [Cmnd 9824].
Subscription Television: A Study for the Home Office (London, HMSO, 1987).
Broadcasting in the '90s: Competition, Choice and Quality (1987) [Cm 517].
The Future of Broadcasting, Home Affairs Committee (1988).
The Future of Broadcasting, House of Commons Home Affairs Committee 1987–88 (London, HMSO, 1988).
Broadcasting Bill, House of Commons (1989).

Broadcasting Act 1990 (London, HMSO, 1990).

The Future of the BBC (Department of National Heritage, London, HMSO, 1992) [Cm 2098].

Broadcasting Act 1996 (London, HMSO, 1996).

Independent Television Commission Annual Report (London, Independent Television Commission, 2001).

European Audiovisual Observatory Yearbook 2002 (Strasbourg, Council of Europe, 2002), Vol. 2.

Television Audience Share Figures (London, Independent Television Commission, 2002).

Second Public Service Broadcasting Review, Phase 1 and 2 (London, Office of Communications, 2008).

The press

An Inquiry into the Culture, Practices and Ethics of the Press (Leveson) (London, Stationery Office, 2012).

Annual Report of the Press Council (London, Press Council, 1985).

Competition Commission, *Johnson Press plc and Trinity Mirror plc: A Report into the Proposed Merger* (London, Stationery Office, 2002) [Cm 5495].

Department for Culture, Media and Sport (DCMS), *Consultation on Media Ownership Rules* (London, DCMS, 2001).

Monopolies Commission (1965–66), The Times *Newspaper and* Sunday Times (London, HMSO, 1966).

Monopolies Commission (1967–68), *Thomson Newspapers and Crusha and Son Ltd*, House of Commons Paper 66 (London, HMSO, 1968).

Monopolies Commission (1969–70), *George Outram and Company Ltd and* Hamilton Advertiser *Ltd and Baird and Hamilton Ltd*, House of Commons Paper 76 (London, HMSO, 1970).

Monopolies Commission (1971–72), *The Berrows Organisation Ltd and the County Express Group*, House of Commons Paper 224 (London, HMSO, 1972).

Monopolies Commission (1972–73), Westminster Press *Ltd and* Kentish Times *Ltd, Gravesend and Dartford Reporter Ltd and F. J. Parsons Ltd, Subsidiaries of Morgan-Grampian Ltd*, House of Commons Paper 460 (London, HMSO, 1973).

Monopolies Commission (1973–74), *Courier Printing and Publishing Company Ltd and Associated Newspapers Group Ltd*, House of Commons Paper 108 (London, HMSO, 1974).

Monopolies Commission (1974–75), *G. and A. N. Scott Ltd and the* Guardian *and* Manchester Evening News *Ltd*, House of Commons Paper 349 (London, HMSO, 1975).

Monopolies and Mergers Commission, *Wholesaling of Newspapers and Periodicals* (London, HMSO, 1978).

Monopolies and Mergers Commission, *The* Observer *and George Outram* (London, HMSO, 1981).

Monopolies and Mergers Commission, *The Supply of National Newspapers* (London, HMSO, 1993).

Monopolies and Mergers Commission, Daily Mail *and General Trust Plc. and T. Bailey Forman Limited* (London, HMSO, 1994).

Monopolies and Mergers Commission, *Northcliffe Newspapers and Aberdeen Journals Ltd* (London, HMSO, 1996).

National Board for Prices and Incomes, *Wages, Costs and Prices in the Printing Industry* (1965) [Cmnd 2750].

National Board for Prices and Incomes, *Costs and Revenue of National Daily Newspapers* (1967) [Cmnd 3435].

National Board for Prices and Incomes, *Journalists' Pay* (1969) [Cmnd 4077].

National Board for Prices and Incomes, *Costs and Revenue of National Newspapers* (1970) [Cmnd 4277].

Privacy and Media Intrusion (National Heritage Committee, House of Commons, 1992–93, HMSO, 1993).

Privacy and Media Intrusion: The Government's Response (London, HMSO, 1995).

Report of the Committee on Contempt of Court (1975) [Cmnd 5794].

Report of the Committee on Data Protection (Lindop Committee, 1978) [Cmnd 7341].

Report of the Committee on Defamation (Faulks Committee, 1975) [Cmnd 5571].

Report of the Committee on the Official Secrets Act (1972) [Cmnd 7140].

Report of the Committee on Privacy and Related Matters (Calcutt Committee, 1990) [Cm 1102].

Report of a Court of Inquiry into the Problems Caused by the Introduction of Web-offset Machines (1967) [Cmnd 3184].

Review of Press Self-Regulation (1993) [Cm 2135].

Royal Commission on the Press 1947–9 Report (1949) [Cmnd 7700].

Royal Commission on the Press 1961–2 Report (1962) [Cmnd 1811].

Royal Commission on the Press Interim Report (1976) [Cmnd 6553].

Royal Commission on the Press 1974–7 Final Report (1977) [Cmnd 6810].

Royal Commission on the Press Final Report Appendices (1977) [Cmnd 6810-11-6].

Select Committee of the House of Commons on Newspaper Stamps, *Parliamentary Papers*, xvii (1851).

Film

Cinematograph Films Act (1927) [Cmnd 2053].

Report of the Committee Appointed by the Board of Trade (Moyne Report, 1936) [Cmnd 2053].

Report on Tendencies to Monopoly in the Cinematograph Film Industry (Palache Report, 1944) [Cmnd 4059].

Report of the Working Party on Film Production Costs (Gater Report, 1949) [Cmnd 7837].

Report of the Committee on the Distribution and Exhibition of Cinematograph Films (Plant Report, 1949) [Cmnd 7837].

Cinematograph Films Council, Distribution and Exhibition of Cinematograph Films (London, HMSO, Board of Trade, 1950).

Cinematograph Films Bill 1960, 8 & 9 Eliz. II.

The Films Act, House of Commons Paper 206 (1960).

Board of Trade Review of Films Legislation (1968) [Cmnd 3584].

The Prime Minister's Working Party on the Future of the Film Industry (Wilson Report, 1976) [Cmnd 6372].

Report of the Committee on Film Finance (1985) [Cmnd 7610].

Monopolies and Mergers Commission, *Report on the Supply of Films for Exhibition* (London, HMSO, 1994).

The British Film Industry (National Heritage Select Committee, House of Commons, 1995) (London, HMSO, 1995).

Media and information

A New Future for Communications (London, Stationery Office, 2000) [Cm 5010].

Commission of the European Communities (1994) *The EU and the Globalisation of Technology* (Forecasting in Science and Technology Report) (EUR 15150, Brussels).

Commission of the European Communities (1996) *Culture, Homes and the use of Information Technology* (EC EUR 174011, Brussels).

Consumers' Use of the Internet, Oftel Residential Survey, May (Office of Telecommunications, London, 2002).

Europe and the Global Information Society (Bangemann Report) (Brussels, European Council, 1994).

Follow-up to the Consultative Process Relating to the Green Paper on 'Pluralism and Media Concentration in the Internal Market' (Brussels, Commission of the European Communities, 1994).

Globalization of the Mass Media (Washington, United States Department of Commerce, 1993).

Liberalising Trade in Services: A New Consultation on the World Trade Organisation GATS Negotiations (London, Department of Trade and Industry, 2002).

Media Ownership: The Government's Proposals (Department of National Heritage, London, HMSO, 1995).

New News, Future News (London, Office of Communications, 2007).

Pluralism and Media Concentration in the Internal Market (Brussels, Commission of the European Communities Green Paper, 1992).

Regulating Communications: Approaching Convergence in the Information Age (London, Stationery Office, 1998) [Cm 4022].

Report by the Think-Tank on the Audiovisual Policy in the European Union (Vasconcelos Report) (Luxembourg, Commission of the European Communities, 1994).

Strategy Options to Strengthen the European Programme Industry in the Context of the Audiovisual Policy of the European Union (Brussels, European Commission Green Paper, 1994).

Miscellaneous public reports referred to in the book

Parliamentary Debates (1918–60; 1940–43) (London, Hansard).

Machinery of Government Report (1918) [Cmnd 9230].

Board of Education, Inspectors' Report (1932) [Cmnd 4068].

Board of Education Consultative Committee on Secondary Education (Spens Report, 1938), 10/119.

Report of the Department Committee on Curriculum and Examinations in Secondary Schools (Norwood Report, 1943).

The Nation's Schools: Their Plans and Purposes, Ministry of Education Pamphlet 1 (London, HMSO, 1945).

Royal Commission on Local Government (1969) (Redcliffe Maud Report), Research Paper 9, Community Attitudes Survey [Cmnd 3409].

Civil Service Department, Computers in Central Government: The Year Ahead (London, HMSO, 1971).

Report of the Committee on Privacy (1972) [Cmnd 5012].

Royal Commission on the Distribution of Income and Wealth, Report 4 (1976) [Cmnd 6626].

Report of the Committee on Standards in Public Life (1996) (Nolan Report) [Cmnd 1028].

The press

General historical perspectives

R. D. Altick, *The English Common Reader* (Chicago, IL, University of Chicago Press, 1957; London, Phoenix, 1963).

A. Andrews, *The History of British Journalism*, 2 vols (London, Richard Bentley, 1859).

G. Boyce, 'The fourth estate: the reappraisal of a concept', in G. Boyce, J. Curran and P. Wingate (eds), *Newspaper History* (London, Constable, 1978).

P. Brendon, *The Life and Death of the Press Barons* (London, Secker & Warburg, 1982).

C. J. Bundock, *The National Union of Journalists: A Jubilee History, 1907–1957* (London, Oxford University Press, 1957).

J. Chalaby, *The Invention of Journalism* (London, Macmillan, 1998).

D. Chaney, *Processes of Mass Communication* (London, Macmillan, 1972).

M. Conboy, *The Press and Popular Culture* (London, Sage, 2002).

G. A. Cranfield, *The Press and Society* (Harlow, Longman, 1978).

J. Curran, 'Capitalism and control of the press 1800–1975', in J. Curran, M. Gurevitch and J. Woollacott (eds), *Mass Communication and Society* (London, Edward Arnold/ Open University, 1977).

J. Curran, 'The press as an agency of social control: an historical perspective', in G. Boyce, J. Curran and P. Wingate (eds), *Newspaper History* (London, Constable, 1978).

J. Curran, 'Communications, power and social order', in T. Bennett, J. Curran, M. Gurevitch and J. Woollacott (eds), *Culture, Media and Society* (London, Methuen, 1981).

K. Drotner, *English Children and their Magazines, 1751–1945* (New Haven, Yale University Press, 1989).

M. Engel, *Tickle the Public* (London, Gollancz, 1996).

H. R. Fox Bourne, *English Newspapers* (London, Chatto & Windus, 1887; London, Russell & Russell, 1966).

J. Grant, *The Newspaper Press*, 3 vols (London, Tinsley Brothers, 1871–72).

D. Griffiths (ed.), *The Encyclopedia of the British Press, 1422–1992* (London, Macmillan, 1992).

M. Harris and A. Lee (eds), *The Press in English Society from the Seventeenth to Nineteenth Centuries* (London and Toronto, Associated University Presses, 1986).

R. Harrison, G. Woolven and R. Duncan, *The Warwick Guide to British Labour Periodicals 1790–1970* (Brighton, Harvester Press, 1977).

S. Harrison, *Poor Men's Guardians: A Record of the Struggles for a Democratic Newspaper Press 1763–1973* (London, Lawrence & Wishart, 1974).

P. Hennessy, *Whitehall* (London, HarperCollins, 1989).

P. Hennessy, *Never Again* (London, HarperCollins, 1992).

H. Herd, *The March of Journalism* (London, Allen & Unwin, 1952).

F. Knight Hunt, *The Fourth Estate* (London, David Bogue, 1850).

P. Knightley, *The First Casualty: The War Correspondent as Hero, Propagandist and Myth Maker from the Crimea to Vietnam* (London, Deutsch, 1975).

S. Koss, *The Rise and Fall of the Political Press in Britain*, 2 vols (London, Hamish Hamilton, 1981 and 1984).

A. Marshall, *Changing the Word: The Printing Industry in Transition* (London, Comedia, 1983).

M. Milne, *Newspapers of Northumberland and Durham* (Newcastle, Frank Graham, 1972).

S. Morison, *The English Newspaper* (Cambridge, Cambridge University Press, 1932).

A. E. Musson, *The Typographical Association: Origins and History up to 1949* (London, Oxford University Press, 1954).

C. Pebody, *English Journalism* (London, Cassell, Petter & Galpin, 1882).

D. Read, *The Power of News: The History of Reuters* (Oxford, Oxford University Press, 1992).

G. Scott, *Reporters Anonymous: The Story of the Press Association* (London, Hutchinson, 1968).

F. S. Siebert, T. Peterson and W. Schramm, *Four Theories of the Press* (Urbana, University of Illinois Press, 1956; New York, Books for Libraries Press, 1973).

A. Smith, *The Newspaper: An International History* (London, Thames & Hudson, 1979).

A. Smith, 'Technology and control: the interactive dimensions of journalism', in J. Curran, M. Gurevitch and J. Woollacott (eds), *Mass Communication and Society* (London, Edward Arnold/Open University Press, 1977).

G. Storey, *Reuter's Century 1851–1951* (London, Parrish, 1951).

K. von Stutterheim, *The Press in England* (London, Allen & Unwin, 1934).

H. A. Taylor, *The British Press* (London, Arthur Barker, 1961).

J. Tunstall, 'Editorial sovereignty in the British press: its past and present', in *Studies on the Press*, Royal Commission on the Press 1974–77, Working Paper 3 (London, HMSO, 1977).

M. Tusan, *Women Making News* (Urbana, University of Illinois Press, 2005).

A. P. Wadsworth, 'Newspaper circulations 1800–1954', *Transactions of the Manchester Statistical Society*, iv (1955).

C. White, *Women's Magazines, 1693–1968* (London, Michael Joseph, 1970).

F. Williams, *Dangerous Estate* (Harlow, Longman Green, 1959; London, Arrow, 1959).

R. Williams, *The Long Revolution* (Harmondsworth, Pelican, 1965).

R. Williams, 'The press and popular culture: an historical perspective', in G. Boyce, J. Curran and P. Wingate (eds), *Newspaper History* (London, Constable, 1978).

C. Wilson, *First with the News: The History of W. H. Smith 1792–1972* (London, Cape, 1985).

Newspaper histories

Anon, *The History of the* Times, vols 1–6 (London, Times Publishing Company, 1935, 1939, 1947, 1952, 1982, and 1993).

D. Ayerst, *The* Guardian: *Biography of a Newspaper* (London, Collins, 1971).

Lord Burnham, *Peterborough Court: Story of the* Daily Telegraph (London, Cassell, 1955).

P. Chippendale and C. Horrie, *Disaster! The Rise and Fall of the* News on Sunday (London, Sphere, 1988).

P. Chippendale and C. Horrie, *Stick it Up Your Punter! The Rise and Fall of the* Sun (London, Heinemann, 1990).

A. Christiansen, *Headlines All My Life* (London, Heinemann, 1961).

P. Cockburn, *The Years of the* Week (Harmondsworth, Penguin, 1971).

H. Cudlipp, *Publish and be Damned* (London, Andrew Dakers, 1953).

M. Edelman, *The* Mirror *– A Political History* (London, Hamish Hamilton, 1966).

W. Fienburgh, *25 Momentous Years: A 25th Anniversary in the History of the* Daily Herald (London, Odhams Press, 1955).

G. Fraser and K. Peters, *The Northern Lights* (London, Hamish Hamilton, 1978).

M. A. Gibb and F. Beckwith, *The* Yorkshire Post: *Two Centuries* (Leeds, Yorkshire Conservative Newspaper Co, 1954).

S. Glover, *Paper Dreams* (Harmondsworth, Penguin, 1994).

B. Hagerty, *Read All About It!* (Lydney, First Stone, 2003).

P. M. Handover, *History of the* London Gazette, *1665–1965* (London, HMSO, 1965).

D. Hart-Davis, *The House the Berrys Built* (London, Coronet, 1991).

A. Hetherington, Guardian *Years* (London, Chatto & Windus, 1981).

D. Hill, *Tribune 40* (London, Quartet, 1977).

W. Hindle, *The* Morning Post, *1772–1937* (London, Routledge & Kegan Paul, 1937).

H. Hobson, P. Knightley and L. Russell, *The Pearl of Days: An Intimate Memoir of the* Sunday Times, *1822–1972* (London, Hamish Hamilton, 1972).

D. Kynaston, *The* Financial Times (London, Viking, 1988).

L. Lamb, *Sunrise* (London, Macmillan, 1989).

R. J. Lucas, *Lord Glenesk and the* Morning Post (London, Alston Rivers, 1910).

I. McDonald, *History of* The Times *1939–66*, vol. 5 (London, Times Books, 1984).

R. McKay and B. Barr, *The Story of the* Scottish Daily News (Edinburgh, Canongate, 1976).

H. Richards, *The Bloody Circus: The* Daily Herald *and the Left* (London, Pluto, 1997).

J. W. Robertson Scott, *The Story of the* Pall Mall Gazette (London, Oxford University Press, 1950).

G. Stewart, *The History of* The Times, vol. 7 (London, HarperCollins, 2005).

H. R. G. Whates, *The* Birmingham Post, *1857–1957* (Birmingham Post and Mail, 1957).

O. Woods and J. Bishop, *The Story of* The Times (London, Michael Joseph, 1983).

Nineteenth-century press history

W. E. Adams, *Memoirs of a Social Atom*, 2 vols (London, Hutchinson, 1903).

Anon, *Guide to Advertisers* (London, 1851).

A. Aspinall, 'Statistical accounts of London newspapers 1800–1836', *English Historical Review*, lxv (1950).

A. Aspinall, *Politics and the Press, 1780–1850* (London, Home & Van Thal, 1949; Brighton, Harvester Press, 1973).

I. Asquith, 'Advertising and the press in the late eighteenth and early nineteenth centuries: James Perry and the *Morning Chronicle*, 1790–1821', *Historical Journal*, xvii (1975).

P. Bailey, *Leisure and Class in Victorian England* (London, Routledge & Kegan Paul, 1978).

V. Berridge, 'Popular Sunday papers and mid-Victorian society', in G. Boyce, J. Curran and P. Wingate (eds), *Newspaper History* (London, Constable, 1978).

T. Boyle, *Black Swine in the Sewers of Hampstead* (London, Hodder & Stoughton, 1989).

L. Brake, A. Jones and L. Madden (eds), *Investigating Victorian Journalism* (London, Macmillan, 1990).

L. Brown, *Victorian News and Newspapers* (Oxford, Clarendon, 1985).

T. Catling, *My Life's Pilgrimage* (London, John Murray, 1911).

P. Catterall, C. Seymour-Ure and A. Smith (eds), *Northcliffe's Legacy* (Basingstoke, Macmillan, 2000).

I. R. Christie, 'British newspapers in the late Georgian age', in *Myth and Reality in Late 18th Century British Politics* (London, Macmillan, 1970).

C. D. Collet, *History of the Taxes on Knowledge* (London, T. Fisher Unwin, 1899).

S. Coltham, 'The *Bee-Hive* newspaper: its origins and early struggle', in A. Briggs and J. Saville (eds), *Essays in Labour History* (London, Macmillan, 1960).

S. Coltham, 'The British working-class press in 1867', *Bulletin for the Society for the Study of Labour History* (Autumn 1967).

F. Dilnot, *Adventures of a Newspaper Man* (London, Smith, Elder, 1913).

J. A. Epstein, 'Feargus O'Connor and the *Northern Star*', *International Review of Social History*, xxi (1976).

T. H. S. Escott, *Masters of English Journalism* (London, T. Fisher Unwin, 1911).

K. Flint, *The Woman Reader 1836–1914* (Oxford, Clarendon Press, 1993).

J. Foster, *Class Struggle and the Industrial Revolution: Early Industrial Capitalism in Three English Towns* (London, Weidenfeld & Nicolson, 1974).

M. D. George, *English Political Caricature, 1792–1832* (London, Oxford University Press, 1959).

E. Glasgow, 'The establishment of the *Northern Star* newspaper', *History*, xxxix (1954).

B. Harrison, 'A world of which we had no conception: liberalism and the temperance press, 1830–72', *Victorian Studies*, xiii (December 1969).

J. Hatton, *Journalistic London* (London, Sampson Low, 1882).

A. F. Havighurst, *Radical Journalist: H. W. Massingham* (Cambridge, Cambridge University Press, 1974).

P. Hollis, *The Pauper Press* (London, Oxford University Press, 1970).

D. Hopkin, 'The socialist press in Britain 1890–1910', in G. Boyce, J. Curran and P. Wingate (eds), *Newspaper History* (London, Constable, 1978).

D. Hudson, *Thomas Barnes of* The Times (Cambridge, Cambridge University Press, 1943).

L. James (ed.), *Print and the People, 1819–1851* (London, Allen Lane, 1976).

E. E. Kellett, 'The press', in G. M. Young (ed.), *Early Victorian England* (London, Oxford University Press, 1934).

C. Kent, 'Higher journalism and the mid-Victorian clerisy', *Victorian Studies*, xiii (December 1969).

S. Koss, *Fleet Street Radical: A. G. Gardiner and the* Daily News (London, Allen Lane, 1973).

A. J. Lee, 'The management of a Victorian local newspaper: the *Manchester City News*, 1864–1900', *Business History*, xv (1973).

A. J. Lee, 'The radical press', in A. Morris (ed.), *Edwardian Radicalism, 1900–1914* (London, Routledge & Kegan Paul, 1974).

A. J. Lee, *The Origins of the Popular Press, 1855–1914* (London, Croom Helm, 1976).

J. R. McCulloch, *Dictionary of Commerce and Commercial Navigation* (London, Longman, Brown & Green, 1854).

Mitchell's Newspaper Press Directory (Mitchell).

P. Mountjoy, 'The working-class press and working-class conservatism', in G. Boyce, J. Curran and P. Wingate (eds), *Newspaper History* (London, Constable, 1978).

A. E. Musson, 'Newspaper printing in the Industrial Revolution', *Economic History Review*, x, 2nd series (1957–58).

V. Neuberg, 'The literature of the streets', in H. J. Dyos and M. Wolff (eds), *The Victorian City* (London, Routledge & Kegan Paul, 1973).

T. Nevett, 'Advertising and editorial integrity in the nineteenth century', in M. Harris and A. Lee (eds), *The Press in English Society from the Seventeenth to Nineteenth Centuries* (London and Toronto, Associated University Presses, 1986).

L. O'Boyle, 'The image of the journalist in England, France and Germany, 1815–48', *Comparative Studies in Society and History*, x (1968).

P. O'Malley, 'Capital accumulation and press freedom, 1800–1850', *Media, Culture and Society*, 3, 1 (1981).

H. J. Perkin, 'The origins of the popular press', *History Today*, vii (1957).

R. Pound and G. Harmsworth, *Northcliffe* (London, Cassell, 1959).

R. Price, *An Imperial War and the British Working Class: Working-class Attitudes and Reactions to the Boer War 1899–1902* (London, Routledge & Kegan Paul, 1972).

D. Read, *Press and People 1790–1850* (London, Edward Arnold, 1961).

J. Roach, 'Education and public opinion', in C. Crawley (ed.), *War and Peace in an Age of Upheaval* (Cambridge, Cambridge University Press, 1965).

F. G. Salmon, 'What the working class read', *Nineteenth Century*, cxiii (1886).

M. Sanderson, 'Literacy and social mobility in the industrial revolution', *Past and Present*, 5, 6 (1972).

A. R. Schoyen, *The Chartist Challenge: A Portrait of George Julian Harney* (London, Heinemann, 1956).

J. Shattock and M. Wolff (eds), *The Victorian Periodical Press: Samplings and Soundings* (Leicester, University of Leicester Press, 1982).

H. Simonis, *The Street of Ink* (London, Cassell, 1917).

J. A. Spender, *Life, Journalism and Politics*, 2 vols (London, Cassell, 1927).

J. F. Stephen, 'Journalism', *Cornhill Magazine*, 6 (1862).

L. Stone, 'Literacy and education in England 1640–1900', *Past and Present*, 42 (1969).

J. D. Symon, *The Press and its Story* (London, Seeley Service, 1914).

T. Tholfsen, *Working-Class Radicalism in Mid-Victorian Britain* (London, Croom Helm, 1976).

D. Thompson, *The Chartists* (London, Maurice Temple Smith, 1984).

E. P. Thompson, *The Making of the English Working Class* (London, Gollancz, 1963).

R. K. Webb, *The British Working-Class Reader, 1790–1848* (London, Allen & Unwin, 1955).

W. H. Wickwar, *The Struggle for the Freedom of the Press, 1819–1832* (London, Allen & Unwin, 1928).

J. Wiener (ed.), *Millions for the Millions* (New York, Greenwood, 1992).

J. H. Wiener, *The War of the Unstamped* (New York, Cornell University Press, 1969).

Twentieth-century press history

J. R. Adams, *Media Planning* (London, Business Books, 1971).

A. Angell, *The Press and the Organisation of Society* (London, Labour Publishing Co, 1922).

D. Ayerst, *Garvin of the* Observer (London, Croom Helm, 1985).

Lord Beaverbrook, *Men and Power* (London, Hutchinson, 1956).

W. Belson, *The British Press* (London, London Press Exchange, 1959).

A. Bingham, *Gender, Modernity and the Popular Press in Inter-war Britain* (Oxford, Clarendon, 2004).

T. Bower, *Maxwell: The Outsider* (London, Mandarin, 1991).

O. Boyd-Barrett, C. Seymour-Ure and J. Tunstall, *Studies on the Press*, Royal Commission on the Press, Working Paper 3 (London, HMSO, 1977).

R. Braddon, *Roy Thomson* (London, Fontana, 1968).

P. Brendon, *Eminent Edwardians* (London, Secker & Warburg, 1979).

T. B. Browne, *Advertisers' ABC* (London, Browne, 1927).

A. Calder, *The People's War: Britain, 1939–1945* (London, Panther, 1971).

S. Chibnall, *Law-and-Order News* (London, Tavistock, 1977).

C. Chisholm, *Marketing and Merchandising* (London, Modern Business Institute, 1924).

A. Chisolm and M. Davie, *Beaverbrook* (London, Hutchinson, 1992).

H. Christian (ed.), *The Sociology of Journalism and the Press*, Sociological Review Monograph 29 (Keele, University of Keele, 1980).

A. Christiansen, *Headlines All My Life* (London, Heinemann, 1961).

T. Clarke, *My Northcliffe Diary* (London, Gollancz, 1931).

T. Clarke, *Northcliffe in History* (London, Hutchinson, 1950).

G. Cleverley, *The Fleet Street Disaster* (London, Constable, 1976).

C. Cockburn, *Brothers: Male Dominance and Technological Change* (London, Pluto, 1983).

M. Cockerell, P. Hennessy and D. Walker, *Sources Close to the Prime Minister* (London, Macmillan, 1984).

R. Cockett, *Twilight of Truth* (London, Weidenfeld & Nicolson, 1989).

S. Cohen and J. Young (eds), *The Manufacture of News* (London, Constable, 1973).

H. Cox and D. Morgan, *City Politics and the Press* (Cambridge, Cambridge University Press, 1973).

R. Critchley, *UK Advertising Statistics* (London, Advertising Association, 1974).

H. Cudlipp, *At Your Peril* (London, Weidenfeld & Nicolson, 1962).

H. Cudlipp, *Walking on the Water* (London, Bodley Head, 1976).

J. Curran, 'The impact of TV on the audience for national newspapers, 1945–68', in J. Tunstall (ed.), *Media Sociology* (London, Constable, 1970).

J. Curran, (ed.), *The British Press: A Manifesto* (London, Macmillan, 1978).

J. Curran, 'Advertising and the press', in J. Curran (ed.), *The British Press: A Manifesto* (London, Macmillan, 1978).

T. Driberg, *Beaverbrook* (London, Weidenfeld & Nicolson, 1956).

H. W. Eley, *Advertising Media* (London, Butterworth, 1932).

H. Evans, *Good Times, Bad Times* (London, Weidenfeld & Nicolson, 1983).

B. Falk, *He Laughed in Fleet Street* (London, Hutchinson, 1933).

M. Ferguson, *Forever Feminine* (London, Heinemann Educational, 1983).

P. Ferris, *The House of Northcliffe* (London, Weidenfeld & Nicolson, 1971).

C. Freer, *The Inner Side of Advertising: A Practical Handbook for Advertisers* (London, Library Press, 1921).

H. Fyfe, *Sixty Years of Fleet Street* (London, W. H. Allen, 1949).

F. R. Gannon, *The British Press and Germany, 1936–1939* (London, Oxford University Press, 1971).

N. Garland, *Not Many Dead* (London, Hutchinson, 1990).

J. E. Gerald, *The British Press under Government Economic Controls* (Minneapolis, University of Minnesota Press, 1956).

P. Gibbs, *Adventures in Journalism* (London, Harper, 1923).

F. Giles, *Sundry Times* (London, Murray, 1986).

G. Glenton and W. Pattinson, *The Last Chronicle of Bouverie Street* (London, Allen & Unwin, 1963).

P. Golding and S. Middleton, *Images of Welfare* (Oxford, Martin Robertson, 1982).

D. Goodhart and P. Wintour, *Eddie Shah and the Newspaper Revolution* (London, Coronet, 1986).

R. Greenslade, *Press Gang* (Basingstoke, Macmillan, 2003).

J. Haines, *Maxwell* (London, Macdonald, 1989).

S. Hall, 'The social eye of *Picture Post*', *Cultural Studies*, ii (1971).

S. Hall, 'Deviancy, politics and the media', in M. McIntosh and P. Rock (eds), *Deviancy and Social Control* (London, Tavistock, 1973).

S. Hall, C. Critcher, T. Jefferson, J. Clarke and B. Roberts, *Policing the Crisis: Mugging, the State, and Law and Order* (London, Macmillan, 1978).

J. Halloran, P. Elliott and G. Murdock (eds), *Demonstrations and Communication* (Harmondsworth, Penguin, 1970).

D. Hamilton, *Who is to Own the British Press?* (London, Birkbeck College, 1976).

R. Harris, *Gotcha: The Media, The Government and The Falklands War* (London, Faber, 1983).

W. Harris, *J. A. Spender* (London, Cassell, 1946).

G. Harrison and F. C. Mitchell, *The Home Market: A Handbook of Statistics* (London, Allen & Unwin, 1936).

N. Hartley, P. Gudgeon and R. Crafts, *Concentration of Ownership in the Provincial Press*, Royal Commission on the Press 1974–77, Research Series 5 (London, HMSO, 1977).

P. Hartmann, 'Industrial relations in the news media', *Industrial Relations Journal*, 6, 4 (London, HMSO, 1977).

P. Hartmann, 'News and public perceptions of industrial relations', *Media, Culture and Society*, 1, 3 (1979).

P. Hartmann and C. Husband, *Racism and the Mass Media* (London, Davis-Poynter, 1974).

Lord Hartwell, *William Camrose* (London, Weidenfeld & Nicolson, 1992).

J. Harvey (ed.), *The War Diaries of Oliver Harvey 1941–5* (London, Collins, 1978).

M. Hastings, *Editor* (ed.), (Basingstoke, Macmillan, 2002).

H. Henry (ed.), *Behind the Headlines* (London, Associated Business Press, 1978).

H. Henry (ed.), *The Dynamics of the British Press 1961–1984* (London, Advertising Association, 1986).

A. Hetherington, *News, Newspapers and Television* (London, Macmillan, 1985).

C. Higham, *Advertising* (London, Williams & Norgate, 1925).

F. Hirsch and D. Gordon, *Newspaper Money: Fleet Street and the Search for the Affluent Reader* (London, Hutchinson, 1975).

P. Hoch, *The Newspaper Game* (London, Calder & Boyars, 1974).

R. Hoggart (ed.), *Your Sunday Paper* (London, University of London Press, 1967).

M. Hollingsworth, *The Press and Political Dissent* (London, Pluto Press, 1986).

D. Hubback, *No Ordinary Press Baron* (London, Weidenfeld & Nicolson, 1985).

Hulton Readership Surveys (London, Hulton, 1947–55).

N. Hunter, *Advertising Through the Press* (London, Pitman, 1925).

Institute of Incorporated Practitioners in Advertising, *An Analysis of Press Circulations 1934* (London, IIPA, 1934).

Institute of Incorporated Practitioners in Advertising, *Survey of Press Readership* (London, IIPA, 1939).

Institute of Incorporated Practitioners in Advertising, *National Readership Surveys* (London, IIPA, 1956–67).

Institute of Incorporated Practitioners in Advertising, *Joint Industry Committee for National Readership Surveys* (London, IIPA, 1968–84).

S. Inwood, 'The Press in the First World War, 1914–16'. Unpublished Ph.D. thesis (University of Oxford, 1971).

I. Jackson, *The Provincial Press and the Community* (Manchester, Manchester University Press, 1971).

S. Jenkins, *Market for Glory* (London, Faber, 1986).

N. Kaldor and R. Silverman, *A Statistical Analysis of Advertising Expenditure and of the Revenue of the Press* (Cambridge, Cambridge University Press, 1948).

P. Kimble, *Newspaper Reading in the Third Year of the War* (London, Allen & Unwin, 1942).

C. King, *The Future of the Press* (London, MacGibbon & Kee, 1967).

C. King, *Strictly Personal* (London, Weidenfeld & Nicolson, 1969).

C. King, *With Malice Towards None: A War Diary* (ed. W. Armstrong) (London, Sidgwick & Jackson, 1970).

C. King, *Without Fear or Favour* (London, Sidgwick & Jackson, 1971).

C. King, *The Cecil King Diary 1965–70* (London, Cape, 1972).

S. Koss, *Fleet Street Radical: A. G. Gardiner and the* Daily News (London, Allen Lane, 1973).

G. Lansbury, *The Miracle of Fleet Street* (London, Victoria House, 1925).

M. Leapman, *Barefaced Cheek* (London, Hodder & Stoughton, 1983).

H. P. Levy, *The Press Council* (London, Macmillan, 1967).

L. London, *Whitehall and the Jews, 1933–48* (Cambridge, Cambridge University Press, 2000).

London Research Bureau, *Press Circulations Analysed 1928* (London Research Bureau, 1928).

A. G. Lyall, *Market Research: A Practical Handbook* (London Research Bureau, 1933).

D. McLachlan, *In the Chair, Barrington-Ward of* The Times, *1927–48* (London, Weidenfeld & Nicolson, 1971).

S. McLachlan and P. Golding, 'Tabloidization in the British press: a quantitative investigation into changes in British newspapers, 1952–97', in C. Sparks and J. Tulloch (eds), *Tabloid Tales* (Lanham, Rowman & Littlefield, 2000).

I. McLaine, *Ministry of Morale* (London, Allen & Unwin, 1979).

D. McQuail, *Analysis of Newspaper Content*, Royal Commission on the Press 1974–77, Research Series 4 (London, HMSO, 1977).

Mass Observation, *The Press and its Readers* (London, Art & Technics, 1949).

T. S. Mathews, *The Sugar Pill: An Essay on Newspapers* (London, Gollancz, 1957).

R. J. Minney, *Viscount Southwood* (London, Odhams Press, 1954).

S. Mulvern, *The End of the Street* (London, Methuen, 1986).

G. Munster, *Rupert Murdoch* (Victoria, Viking Press, 1985).

G. Murdock, 'Class, power and the press: problems of conceptualisation and evidence', in H. Christian (ed.), *The Sociology of Journalism and the Press*, Sociological Review Monograph 29 (Keele, University of Keele, 1981).

D. Murphy, *The Silent Watchdog: The Press in Local Politics* (London, Constable, 1976).

D. Murphy, *The Stalker Affair and the Press* (London, Unwin Hyman, 1991).

A. Neil, *Full Disclosure* (London, Macmillan, 1996).

News Chronicle: *A Survey of Reader Interest* (London, News Chronicle, 1934).

H. Nicolson, *Diaries and Letters* (London, Collins, 1967).

Lord Northcliffe, *Newspapers and their Millionaires* (London, Associated Newspapers, 1922).

L. Owen, *Northcliffe: The Facts* (privately published, 1931).

B. Page, *The Murdoch Archipelago* (London, Simon & Schuster, 2003).

W. Parsons, *The Power of the Financial Press* (Aldershot, Elgar, 1989).

Periodicals and the Alternative Press, Royal Commission on the Press 1974–77, Research Series 6 (London, HMSO, 1977).

F. Pethick-Lawrence, *Fate Has Been Kind* (London, Hutchinson, 1943).

H. Porter, *Lies, Damned Lies and Some Exclusives* (London, Chatto & Windus, 1984).

R. Pound and G. Harmsworth, *Northcliffe* (London, Cassell, 1959).

A. Rappaport, *The British Press and Wilsonian Neutrality* (London, Oxford University Press, 1951).

Report on the British Press (London, Political & Economic Planning, 1938).

G. Robertson, *People Against the Press* (London, Quartet, 1983).

D. Rooney, 'Thirty years of competition in the British tabloid press: the *Mirror* and the *Sun* 1968–98', in C. Sparks and J. Tulloch (eds), *Tabloid Tales* (Lanham, Rowman & Littlefield, 2000).

T. Russell, *Commercial Advertising* (London, Putnam, 1919).

A. P. Ryan, *Lord Northcliffe* (London, Collins, 1953).

M. Scammell and M. Harrop, 'The press: still for Labour, despite Blair', in D. Kavanagh and D. Butler (eds), *The British General Election of 2005* (Basingstoke, Palgrave Macmillan, 2005).

C. Seymour-Ure, *The Press, Politics and the Public* (London, Methuen, 1968).

C. Seymour-Ure, 'Policy-making in the press', *Government and Opposition*, iv, 4 (1969).

C. Seymour-Ure, *The Political Impact of the Mass Media* (London, Constable, 1974).

C. Seymour-Ure, 'The press and the party system between the wars', in G. Peele and C. Cook (eds), *The Politics of Reappraisal, 1918–1939* (London, Macmillan, 1976).

C. Seymour-Ure, *The British Press and Broadcasting Since 1945* (2nd edn) (Oxford, Blackwell, 1996).

R. Shannon, *A Press Free and Responsible* (London, John Murray, 2001).

A. Sharf, *The British Press and Jews Under Nazi Rule* (London, Oxford University Press, 1964).

W. Shawcross, *Rupert Murdoch* (London, Chatto & Windus, 1992).

K. Sisson, *Industrial Relations in Fleet Street* (Oxford, Blackwell, 1975).

A. Smith, *The British Press Since the War* (Newton Abbot, David & Charles, 1974).

A. C. H. Smith, E. Immirzi and T. Blackwell, *Paper Voices: The Popular Press and Social Change, 1933–1965* (London, Chatto & Windus, 1975).

Social and Community Planning, *Attitudes to the Press*, Royal Commission on the Press 1974–77, Research Series 3 (London, HMSO, 1977).

J. A. Spender, *Life, Journalism and Politics*, 2 vols (London, Cassell, 1927).

R. Stannard, *With the Dictators of Fleet Street* (London, Hutchinson, 1934).
Survey of the National Newspaper Industry (London, Economist Intelligence Unit, 1965).
A. J. P. Taylor, *English History 1914–1945* (Harmondsworth, Pelican, 1970).
A. J. P. Taylor, *Beaverbrook* (London, Hamish Hamilton, 1972).
A. J. P. Taylor (ed.), *Off the Record: W. P. Crozier, Political Interviews 1933–1943* (London, Hutchinson, 1973).
S. J. Taylor, *Shock! Horror! The Tabloids in Action* (London, Bantam, 1991).
Lord Thomson of Fleet, *After I Was Sixty* (London, Hamish Hamilton, 1975).
The Times, The History of The Times, *iv: The 150th Anniversary and Beyond, 1912–1948,* 2 vols (London, The Times Publishing Co, 1952).
J. Tunstall, *The Westminster Lobby Correspondents* (London, Routledge & Kegan Paul, 1970).
J. Tunstall, *Journalists at Work* (London, Constable, 1971).
J. Tunstall, 'The problem of industrial relations news in the press', in *Studies on the Press*, Royal Commission on the Press 1974–77, Working Paper 3 (London, HMSO, 1977).
J. Tunstall, *The Media in Britain* (London, Constable, 1983).
J. Tunstall, *Newspaper Power* (Oxford, Oxford University Press, 1996).
J. Whale, *Journalism and Government* (London, Macmillan, 1972).
C. White, *The Women's Periodical Press in Britain 1946–1976*, Royal Commission on the Press, Working Paper 4 (London, HMSO, 1977).
H. Wickham Steed, *The Press* (Harmondsworth, Penguin, 1938).
T. Wilson (ed.), *The Political Diaries of C. P. Scott* (London, Collins, 1970).
R. Winsbury, *New Technology and the Press*, Royal Commission on the Press and Acton Society Press Group (London, HMSO, 1975).
C. Wintour, *Pressures on the Press: An Editor Looks at Fleet Street* (London, Deutsch, 1972).
J. E. Wrench, *Geoffrey Dawson and Our Times* (London, Hutchinson, 1955).

Broadcasting

Memoirs and biographies

R. Baker, *Here is the News* (London, Leslie Frewin, 1966).
G. Beadle, *Television, A Critical Review* (London, Allen & Unwin, 1963).
M. Bell, *In Harm's Way: Reflection of a War Zone* (London, Hamish Hamilton, 1994).
M. Bose, *Michael Grade: Screening the Image* (London, Virgin, 1992).
J. Birt, *John Birt the Autobiography* (London, Little, Brown, 2002).
A. Boyle, *Only the Wind Will Listen: Reith of the BBC* (London, Hutchinson, 1972).
C. Brewer, *The Spice of Variety* (London, Muller, 1948).
D. G. Bridson, *Prospero and Ariel: The Rise and Fall of Radio* (London, Gollancz, 1971).
H. Brittain, *The ABC of the BBC* (London, Pearson, 1932).
J. C. Cassell, *In Town Tonight* (London, Harrap, 1935).
S. Chesmore, *Behind the Microphone* (London, Nelson, 1935).
Sir Kenneth Clark, *The Other Half: A Self-Portrait* (London, Murray, 1977).
Sir Alfred D. Cooper, *Old Men Forget* (London, Hart-Davis, 1953).
N. Davenport, *Memoirs of a City Radical* (London, Methuen, 1959).
R. Day, *Television – A Personal Report* (London, Hutchinson, 1961).
R. Day, *Day by Day* (London, William Kimber, 1975).

B. Deane, *Seven Ages, An Autobiography, 1927–72* (London, Hutchinson, 1973).

J. Dimbleby, *Richard Dimbleby: A Biography* (London, Hodder & Stoughton, 1975).

R. Dimbleby, *The Waiting Year* (London, Hodder & Stoughton, 1944).

P. P. Eckersley, *The Power Behind the Microphone* (London, Cape, 1941).

R. Eckersley, *The BBC and All That* (London, Sampson, Low, Marston, 1946).

L. Fielden, *The Natural Bent* (London, Deutsch, 1960).

V. Gielgud, *Years of the Locust* (London, Nicholson & Watson, 1947).

G. W. Goldie, *Facing the Nation: Television and Politics, 1936–76* (London, Bodley Head, 1977).

M. Gorham, *Sound and Fury* (London, Percival-Maskell, 1948).

F. Grisewood, *The World Goes By* (London, Secker & Warburg, 1952).

F. Grisewood, *Years in the* Mirror (London, Gollancz, 1967).

H. Grisewood, *One Thing at a Time* (London, Hutchinson, 1968).

H. Hall, *Here's to the Next Time* (London, Deutsch, 1935).

L. Henry, *My Laugh Story* (Edinburgh, Simon Paul, 1937).

A. S. Hibberd, *This is London* (Plymouth, Macdonald & Evans, 1950).

Lord Hill of Luton (C. Hill), *Both Sides of the Hill* (London, Heinemann, 1967).

Lord Hill of Luton (C. Hill), *Behind the Screen* (London, Sidgwick & Jackson, 1974).

J. Hilton, *This and That* (London, Allen & Unwin, 1938).

J. Isaacs, *Storm over Four: A Personal Account* (London, Weidenfeld & Nicolson, 1989).

P. J. Kavanagh, *The ITMA YEARS* (London, Heinemann, 1974).

T. Kavanagh, *Tommy Handley* (London, Hodder & Stoughton, 1949).

F. Keane, *Rivers of Blood; Reporting Rwanda* (London, Hamish Hamilton, 1995).

L. Kennedy, *Ludo: A Life* (London, Macmillan, 1989).

R. S. Lambert, *Ariel and All His Quality* (London, Gollancz, 1940).

C. A. Lewis, *Broadcasting from Within* (London, George Newnes, 1924).

E. Maschwitz, *No Chip on My Shoulder* (London, Jenkins, 1957).

A. Milne, *DG: The Memoirs of a British Broadcaster* (London, Hodder & Stoughton, 1988).

S. A. Moseley, *Broadcasting in my Time* (London, Rich & Cowan, 1935).

S. A. Moseley, *Private Diaries* (London, Parrish, 1960).

E. Nixon, *John Hilton* (London, Allen & Unwin, 1946).

J. Payne, *This is Jack Payne* (London, Marston, 1932).

J. Payne, *Signature Tune* (Edinburgh, Simon Paul, 1947).

W. Pickles, *Between You and Me* (London, Heinemann, 1949).

J. B. Priestley, *Margin Released* (London, Mercury, 1966).

J. C. W. Reith, *Into the Wind* (London, Hodder & Stoughton, 1949).

R. Silvey, *Who's Listening?* (London, Allen & Unwin, 1974).

C. Stuart, *The Reith Diaries* (London, Collins, 1975).

Sir Stephen Tallents, *Man and Boy* (London, Faber, 1943).

H. Thomas, *With an Independent Air* (London, Weidenfeld & Nicolson, 1977).

M. Tracey, *A Variety of Lives: A Biography of Sir Hugh Greene* (London, Bodley Head, 1982).

M. Whitehouse, *Who Does She Think She Is?* (London, New English Library, 1971).

The history of broadcasting

M. Abrams, *Granada Viewership Survey* (1959).

R. Alston, *Taking the Air* (London, Hodder & Stoughton, 1951).

G. L. Archer, *A History of Broadcasting to 1926* (London, Allen & Unwin, 1938).

J. Bakewell and N. Garnham, *The New Priesthood: British Television Today* (Harmondsworth, Allen Lane, 1970).

S. Barnett (ed.), *Funding the BBC's Future* (London, BFI, 1988).

S. Barnett and A. Curry, *The Battle for the BBC* (London, Aurum Press, 1993).

S. Barnett and E. Seymour, *'A Shrinking Iceberg Travelling South': Changing Trends in British Television: a Case Study of Drama and Current Affairs* (London, Campaign for Quality Television, 1999).

E. Barnouw, *A Tower in Babel: The History of Broadcasting in the United States* (London, Oxford University Press, 1966).

BBC Handbook (London, BBC, annually).

BBC, 'Comparative European programming', *BBC Handbook* (London, BBC, 1934).

BBC, *The Third Programme: Plans for October–December 1944* (London, BBC, 1944).

BBC, *The Public and their Programmes* (London, BBC, 1959).

J. Bennett, *British Broadcasting and the Danish Resistance Movement 1940–1945* (Cambridge, Cambridge University Press, 1965).

P. Black, *The Biggest Aspidistra in the World* (London, BBC, 1972).

P. Black, *The Mirror in the Corner* (London, Hutchinson, 1972).

P. Bloomfield, *BBC* (London, Eyre & Spottiswoode, 1941).

G. Brandt (ed.), *Television Drama* (Cambridge, Cambridge University Press, 1981).

A. Briggs, *The History of Broadcasting in the United Kingdom*: Vol. I, *The Birth of Broadcasting*; Vol. II, *The Golden Age of Wireless*; Vol. III, *The War of Words*; Vol. IV, *Sound and Vision* (London, Oxford University Press, 1961, 1965, 1970 and 1979).

A. Briggs, 'The rise of the mass entertainment industry' (Fisher Lecture, University of Adelaide, 1961).

A. Briggs, *The BBC Governors* (London, BBC, 1979).

A. Briggs, *The BBC: The First Fifty Years* (Oxford, Oxford University Press, 1985).

P. J. Brown, 'Broadcasting in Britain', *London Quarterly Review*, 145, 1 (January 1926).

A. R. Burrows, *The Story of Broadcasting* (London, Cassell, 1924).

Sir Cyril Burt, 'The psychology of listeners', *BBC Quarterly*, 4, 2 (April 1949).

H. L. Childs and J. B. Whitton (eds), *Propaganda by Shortwave* (London, Oxford University Press, 1943).

J. A. Cole, *Lord Haw Haw – and William Joyce* (London, Collins, 1964).

C. A. R. Crosland, 'The mass media', *Encounter* (November 1962).

R. H. S. Crossman, 'The politics of viewing', *New Statesman* (25 October 1968).

R. H. S. Crossman, 'The BBC, Labour and the public', *New Statesman* (17 July 1971).

C. Curran, *Code or Conscience* (London, BBC, 1970).

C. Curran, *A Maturing Democracy* (London, BBC, 1973).

C. Curran, *The Seamless Robe* (London, Bodley Head, 1979).

C. Curran, 'Television journalism: theory and practice, the case of *Newsnight*', in P. Holland (ed.), *Television Handbook* (2nd edn) (London, Routledge, 2000).

R. Day, 'Troubled reflections of a TV journalist', *Encounter* (May 1970).

B. Deane, *The Theatre At War* (London, Harrap, 1956).

S. Delmer, *Black Boomerang* (London, Secker & Warburg, 1962).

D. Docherty, D. E. Morrison and M. Tracey, *Keeping Faith? Channel Four and its Audience* (London, Libbey, 1988).

L. W. Doob, 'Goebbels' principles of propaganda', *Public Opinion Quarterly*, 21, 2 (1950).

P. P. Eckersley, *Captain Eckersley Explains* (London, Hodder & Stoughton, 1924).

P. P. Eckersley, *All About your Microphone* (London, BBC Broadcast Library, 1925).

P. P. Eckersley, *The Power Behind the Microphone* (London, Cape, 1941).

H. Fairlie, 'TV, idiot box', *Encounter* (August 1959).

H. Fairlie, 'The BBC', in H. S. Thomas (ed.), *The Establishment: A Symposium* (London, New English Library, 1962).

Sir Robert Fraser, *The Coming of Independent Television* (London, Hutchinson, 1955).

Sir Robert Fraser, *ITA Notes* (October 1970).

V. Gielgud, *British Radio Drama 1922–1956* (London, Harrap, 1957).

P. Goodwin, *Television Under the Tories* (London, British Film Institute, 1998).

G. W. Goldie, 'The new attraction', *Listener* (26 December 1940).

G. W. Goldie, 'TV report', *Listener* (23 October 1968).

G. W. Goldie, *Facing the Nation: Television and Politics 1936–1976* (London, The Bodley Head, 1977).

M. Gorham, *Broadcasting and Television Since 1900* (London, Collins, 1952).

T. Green, *The Universal Eye: World Television in the Seventies* (London, The Bodley Head, 1972).

T. Green, 'The future of broadcasting in Britain', Granada Guildhall Lecture (1972).

H. C. Greene, 'The BBC since 1958', *BBC Handbook* (1969).

H. C. Greene, *The Third Floor Front: A View of Broadcasting in the Sixties* (London, The Bodley Head, 1969).

T. Harrisson, 'War books', *Horizon* (December 1941).

D. Hawkins and D. Boyd (eds), *BBC War Report* (London, Oxford University Press, 1946).

Sir William Hayley, *The Central Problem of Broadcasting* (London, BBC, 1948).

C. Horrie and S. Clarke, *Fear and Loathing at the BBC* (London, Heinemann, 1993).

IBA, Annual Reports.

ITV, *The Annan Report: An ITV View* (London, ITV, 1977).

E. T. Lean, *Voices in the Darkness* (London, Allen & Unwin, 1943).

M. Leapman, *The Last Days of the Beeb* (London, Coronet, 1987).

D. McLachlan, *Room 39* (London, Weidenfeld & Nicolson, 1968).

Mass Observation, *The War Begins at Home* (London, Chatto & Windus, 1940).

H. Matheson, *Broadcasting* (London, Butterworth, 1933).

H. Matheson, 'Listener research in broadcasting', *Sociological Review*, 27, 3 (1935).

A. Mitchell, 'The decline of current affairs television', *Political Quarterly*, 44, 1 (1973).

S. Nicholas, *The Echo of War: Home Front Propaganda 1939–45* (Manchester, Manchester University Press, 1995).

H. Nicolson, *The Third Programme: A Symposium of Opinions and Plans* (London, BBC, 1947).

S. Orwell and I. Angus (eds), *The Collected Essays, Letters and Journalism of George Orwell* (Harmondsworth, Penguin, 1971).

B. Paulu, *British Broadcasting: Radio and Television in the United Kingdom* (Oxford, Oxford University Press, 1957).

G. Pedrich, *Battledress Broadcasters* (London, Marston, 1964).

R. Postgate, *What to Do with the BBC?* (London, Hogarth, 1935).

J. B. Priestley, *Postscripts* (London, Heinemann, 1940).

J. C. W. Reith, *Broadcast over Britain* (London, Hodder & Stoughton, 1924).

N. Riley, *999* (London, Gollancz, 1943).

C. J. Rolo, *Radio Goes to War* (London, Hutchinson, 1943).

G. Ross, *T.V. Jubilee* (London, W. H. Allen, 1961).

P. Rotha (ed.), *Television in the Making* (London, The Bodley Head, 1956).

P. Scannell, 'The social eye of television, 1946–55', *Media, Culture, and Society*, 1, 1 (1979).

P. Scannell, *Radio, Television and Modern Life* (Oxford, Blackwell, 1996).

P. Scannell and D. Cardiff, 'The social foundations of British broadcasting', in J. Curran, M. Gurevitch and J. Woollacott (eds), *Mass Communication and Society* (London, Edward Arnold/Open University Press, 1977).

J. Seaton, 'The BBC and the Holocaust', *European Journal of Communication*, 2, 1 (1987).

J. Seaton, 'Reporting atrocities', in J. Seaton and B. Pimlott (eds), *The Media in British Politics* (Aldershot, Gower, 1987).

J. Seaton, *The Media and the Constitution* (London, Charter 88, 1993).

J. Seaton, 'Broadcasting in the 1980s: is it possible to under-estimate public taste?', *Political Quarterly*, Special issue on broadcasting, 47, 1 (1993), pp. 50–76.

J. Seaton, 'Yesterday's men: deception or mistake?', together with edited transcript of 1994 ICBH Witness Seminar, *Contemporary British History*, 10, 3 (1996).

J. Seaton, 'Misery and the media: the media and ethnic violence', *Contemporary Politics*, 2, 2 (1996).

G. Seldes, *The Great Audience* (London, Oxford University Press, 1950).

T. Shaw, *Eden, Suez and the Mass Media* (Birmingham, I. B. Tauris, 1995).

R. Silvey, 'Some recent trends in listening', *BBC Handbook* (London, BBC, 1946).

R. Silvey, 'TV viewing in Britain', *Public Opinion Quarterly*, 25, 2 (1950).

R. Silvey, *Whose Listening?* (London, The Bodley Head, 1974).

Lord Simon of Wythenshawe, *The BBC from Within* (London, Gollancz, 1953).

A. Smith, *The Shadow in the Cave* (London, Allen & Unwin, 1973).

A. Smith, *British Broadcasting* (Newton Abbot, David & Charles, 1974).

S. W. Smithers, *Broadcasting from Within* (London, Pitmans, 1938).

N. Swallow, *Factual Television* (London, Focal Press, 1966).

J. Swift, *Adventures in Vision* (London, Lehmann, 1950).

I. Thomas, *Warfare By Words* (London, Gollancz, 1942).

The Times, special broadcasting number (14 August 1934).

P. Todd, 'Scarcity of TV time', *Campaign* (26 January 1979).

M. Tracey, *Whitehouse* (London, Constable, 1979).

R. West, *The Meaning of Treason* (London, Macmillan, 1948).

H. Wheldon, 'Competition in television', Address to the Royal Society of Arts (1971).

H. Wheldon, *Tastes and Standards in BBC Programmes* (London, BBC, 1973).

H. H. Wilson, *Pressure Group* (London, Secker & Warburg, 1961).

F. Worsley, *ITMA* (London, Collins, 1948).

The background to broadcasting

M. Abrams, 'Advertising', *Listener* (15 December 1956).

M. Abrams, 'Motivation research', *Advertising Quarterly* (November 1959).

P. Addison, *The Road to 1945* (London, Cape, 1975).

K. Allsop, *The Angry Decade* (London, Owen, 1958).

N. Annan, 'Love among the moralists', *Encounter* (February 1960).

E. Barendt and L. Hitchens, *Media Law* (Harlow, Longman, 2000).

D. Bell, 'Advertising: is it worth it?', *Listener* (13 December 1956).

W. H. Beveridge, *Unemployment: A Problem of Industry* (London, Longman Green, 1910).

W. H. Beveridge, *Public Service in War and Peace* (London, Constable, 1920).

W. H. Beveridge, *Constructive Democracy* (London, Allen & Unwin, 1937).

W. H. Beveridge, *Power and Influence* (London, Hodder & Stoughton, 1953).

V. Bogdanor and R. Skidelsky, *The Age of Affluence* (Harmondsworth, Penguin, 1970).

E. Bowen, *The Heart of the Matter* (London, Faber, 1944).

V. Brittain, *Testament of Friendship* (London, Macmillan, 1940).

G. Bruntz, *Allied Propaganda and the Collapse of the German Empire in 1918* (Stanford, Calif., Stanford University Press, 1938).

Sir Cyril Burt, *The Distribution and Relations of Educational Abilities* (London, London County Council, 1917).

Sir Cyril Burt, 'The measurement of mental capacities', Henderson Trust Lecture 7, Edinburgh (1927).

Sir Cyril Burt (ed.), *How The Mind Works* (London, Allen & Unwin, 1933).

Sir Cyril Burt, *Intelligence and Fertility* (London, Cassell, 1952).

D. Butler and R. Rose, *The British General Election of 1959* (London, Macmillan, 1960).

Lord Butler, *The Education Act of 1944 and After*, First Noel Buxton Lecture, University of Essex (Harlow, Longman, 1965).

Lord Butler, *The Art of the Possible* (London, Hamish Hamilton, 1971).

A. Calder, *The People's War: Britain, 1939-45* (London, Panther, 1971).

H. Cantril, *Public Opinion 1935-46* (Princeton, NJ, Princeton University Press, 1951).

C. Cockburn, *I Claud* (Harmondsworth, Penguin, 1967).

C. A. R. Crosland, *The Future of Socialism* (London, Cape, 1956).

R. H. S. Crossman, 'Psychological warfare', *Journal of the Royal United Services Institution* (August 1952).

R. H. S. Crossman, 'The lessons of 1945', in P. Anderson and R. Blackburn (eds), *Towards Socialism* (London, Fontana, 1965).

H. Dalton, 'The "popular front"', *Political Quarterly*, 4, 7 (1936).

M. E. Dimmock, *British Public Utilities and National Development* (London, Allen & Unwin, 1933).

C. H. Dobinson (ed.), *Education in a Changing World* (Oxford, Oxford University Press, 1951).

T. Driberg, *The Best of Both Worlds* (London, Phoenix House, 1958).

M. R. D. Foot, *Resistance: An Analysis of European Resistance to Fascism* (London, Methuen, 1976).

P. Foot, *The Politics of Harold Wilson* (Harmondsworth, Penguin, 1968).

Fougasse (pseud. C. K. Bird), *The Changing Face of Britain* (London, Methuen, 1950).

B. Gates, *The Road Ahead* (Boston, Viking, 1995).

M. Gilbert, *Churchill*, Vol. 5 (London, Heinemann, 1976).

M. Gilbert and R. Gott, *The Appeasers* (London, Weidenfeld & Nicolson, 1963).

D. Gordan, 'Ten points about the crisis in the British film industry', *Sight and Sound*, 43, 2 (1974).

L. Gorden, *The Public Corporation in Great Britain* (Oxford, Oxford University Press, 1938).

P. H. J. H. Gosden, *Education in the Second World War* (London, Methuen, 1972).

C. Handy, *The Age of Unreason* (Boston, MA, Harvard University Press, 1989).

C. Handy, 'The New Federalist Papers', *Harvard University Business Review*, 3 (Autumn 1992).

C. Handy, *The Empty Raincoat* (London, HarperCollins, 1993).

J. Harris, *William Beveridge* (Oxford, Clarendon Press, 1977).

N. Harris, *Competition and the Corporate State* (London, Methuen, 1972).

R. Harris, *Politics Without Prejudice* (Tonbridge, Staples, 1956).

T. Harrisson, 'Who'll win?', *Political Quarterly*, 15, 4 (1944).

T. Harrisson, *Living Through the Blitz* (Harmondsworth, Penguin, 1978).

J. Harvey-Jones, *Making it Happen* (London, BBC Books, 1994).

E. Hobsbawm, *Nations and Nationalism since 1780* (Cambridge, Cambridge University Press, 1992).

E. Hobsbawm, *The Age of Extremities* (London, Allen Lane, 1994).

J. A. Hodson, *Somewhere in France ... B.E.F.* (London, Whithey Grove, 1940).

J. A. Hodson, *War Diary* (London, Gollancz, 1941).

J. A. Hodson, *The Home Front* (London, Gollancz, 1944).

W. Hutton, *The State We Are In* (London, Cape, 1996).

L. J. Kamin, *The Science and Politics of IQ* (Harmondsworth, Penguin, 1977).

P. Kennedy, *Preparing for the 21st Century* (London, HarperCollins, 1993).

Labour Party, *Twelve Wasted Years* (London, Labour Party, 1963).

D. Low, *Low's Autobiography* (London, Michael Joseph, 1956).

R. Low, *The History of the British Film*, Vol. 1 (London, Allen & Unwin, 1948).

I. McLaine, 'The Ministry of Information'. Unpublished D.Phil. thesis (University of Oxford, 1976).

I. McLaine, *The Ministry of Morale* (London, Allen & Unwin, 1978).

F. Marquis (ed.), *The Memoirs of the Rt Hon. the Earl of Woolton* (London, Cassell, 1959).

A. Marr, *Ruling Britannia* (London, Penguin, 1996).

A. Marwick, 'Middle opinion in the thirties', *English Historical Review*, 79, 2 (1964).

Mass Observation, *The War Begins at Home* (London, Chatto & Windus, 1940).

Mass Observation, *Home Propaganda* (London, Chatto & Windus, 1941).

Mass Observation, *War Factory* (London, Gollancz, 1943).

Mass Observation, *The Journey Home* (London, Murray, 1944).

Mass Observation, *The Press and Its Readers* (London, Art & Technics, 1949).

Ministry of Pensions, *Neuroses in War Time* (London, HMSO, 1940).

J. Montgomery, *The Fifties* (London, Collins, 1965).

H. Morrison, *Socialization and Transport* (London, Constable, 1933).

G. Mulgan, *Politics in an Anti-Political Age* (Cambridge, Polity Press, 1995).

H. Nicolson, *Diaries and Letters 1930–45* (London, Collins, 1967).

T. H. O'Brien, *British Experiments in Public Ownership and Control* (London, Allen & Unwin, 1937).

F. Owen, 'This war', *Horizon* (February 1940).

V. Packard, *The Hidden Persuaders* (London, Longman, 1957).

S. Papathanassopoulos, *European Television in the Digital Age* (London, Sage, 2002).

H. Pelling, *Britain and the Second World War* (London, Collins, 1970).

B. Pimlott, *Labour and the Left in the 1930s* (Cambridge, Cambridge University Press, 1977).

B. Pimlott, *Hugh Dalton* (London, Cape, 1985).

B. Pimlott, *Harold Wilson* (London, HarperCollins, 1993).

B. Pimlott, *The Queen: A Biography of Queen Elizabeth II* (London, HarperCollins, 1996).

J. W. C. Reith, *Personality and Career* (London, George Newnes, 1925).

J. W. C. Reith, *Winning Spurs* (London, Hutchinson, 1966).

P. Renshaw, *The General Strike* (London, Methuen, 1975).

W. A. Robson, *Public Enterprise* (London, New Fabian Research Bureau, 1937).

W. A. Robson, *Nationalized Industry and Public Ownership* (London, Allen & Unwin, 1960).

R. J. W. Selleck, 'The scientific educationalist', *British Journal of Educational Studies*, 15, 3 (June 1967).

B. Simon, *Education and the Labour Movement, 1870–1920* (London, Lawrence & Wishart, 1965).

B. Simon, *The Politics of Educational Reform, 1920–1940* (London, Lawrence & Wishart, 1971).

B. Simon, *Intelligence, Psychology and Education* (London, Lawrence & Wishart, 1978).

P. Sissons and R. French (eds), *The Age of Austerity* (Harmondsworth, Penguin, 1962).

R. Skidelsky, *Politicians and the Slump* (London, Macmillan, 1967).

R. Skidelsky, 'Keynes and the reconstruction of liberalism', *Encounter* (April 1979).

R. Skidelsky, *Maynard Keynes: A Biography – The World After Communism* (London, Macmillan, 1995).

J. Strachey, *Post D* (London, Gollancz, 1940).

B. Sweet-Escott, *Baker Street Irregular* (London, Collins, 1966).

J. Symons, *The General Strike* (London, Cressett, 1957).

S. Tallents, *The Projection of England* (London, Empire Marketing Board, 1932).

A. J. P. Taylor, *English History 1914–1945* (London, Allen & Unwin, 1965).

A. J. P. Taylor, *Beaverbrook* (London, Hamish Hamilton, 1972).

M. Thatcher, *The Downing Street Years* (London, HarperCollins, 1995).

R. Titmuss, *Problems of Social Policy* (London, Longman/HMSO, 1950).

Sir Robert Vansittart, *Black Record: Germans Past and Present* (London, Hamish Hamilton, 1941).

P. E. Vernon and J. B. Barry, *Personnel Selection in the British Forces* (London, University of London Press, 1949).

Beatrice Webb's Diaries, 1924–32, ed. M. Cole (London, Longman Green, 1956).

W. Whitelaw, *The Whitelaw Memoirs* (London, Aurum Press, 1989).

N. S. Wilson, *Education in the Forces, 1939–1946: The Civilian Contribution* (London, Allen & Unwin, 1949).

S. W. L. Woodward, *British Foreign Policy in the Second World War* (London, HMSO, 1970/1).

H. Young, *One of Us: A Biography of Margaret Thatcher* (London, Cape, 1993).

Sociology

T. W. Adorno, *Prisms* (Sudbury, Spearman, 1967).

T. W. Adorno, *The Jargon of Authenticity* (London, Routledge & Kegan Paul, 1973).

T. W. Adorno, E. F. Brunswick, D. J. Levinson and R. N. Sandford, *The Authoritarian Personality* (London, Harper & Row, 1950).

M. Alvarado and E. Buscombe, *Hazell: The Making of a Television Series* (London, British Film Institute, 1978).

H. Arendt, *The Burden of Our Time* (London, Secker & Warburg, 1950).

H. Arendt, *The Life of the Mind*, Vol. 2, Thinking (London, Secker & Warburg, 1978).

U. Beck, *The Risk Society* (London, Sage, 1995).

P. Becker and M. McCombs, 'The development of political cognition', in S. H. Chaffee (ed.), *Political Communication: Issues and Strategies* (Beverly Hills, CA, Sage, 1975).

B. Berelson, 'The state of communication research', *Public Opinion Quarterly*, 31, 2 (1959).

S. Blanchard, *What's This Channel Four?* (London, Comedia, 1983).

J. G. Blumler, 'The audience', in *The Political Effects of Mass Communication* (Milton Keynes, Open University Press, DE 353, 1977).

J. G. Blumler, 'The intervention of television in British politics', *Report of the Committee on the Future of Broadcasting* (Annan Report) (1977) [Cmnd 6753, Appendix E].

J. G. Blumler, 'An overview of recent research into the impact of broadcasting in democratic politics', in M. J. Clark (ed.), *Politics and the Media* (Oxford, Pergamon Press, 1979).

J. G. Blumler and M. Gurevitch, 'Towards a comparative framework for political communication', in S. H. Chaffee (ed.), *Political Communication: Issues and Strategies* (London, Sage, 1975).

J. G. Blumler and D. McQuail, *Television in Politics: Its Uses and Influences* (London, Faber, 1968).

J. G. Blumler and J. Madge, *Citizenship and Television* (London, Political & Economic Planning, 1965).

D. Boorstin, *The Image, Or What Happened to the American Dream* (Harmondsworth, Penguin, 1963).

P. Bourdieu, *Outline of a Theory of Practice* (Cambridge, Cambridge University Press, 1977).

T. Boyce, *Health, Risk and News* (New York, Lang, 2007).

O. Boyd-Barrett, D. Seymour-Ure and J. Tunstall, *Studies on the Press*, Royal Commission on the Press 1974–77, Working Paper 3 (London, HMSO, 1977).

B. Brown, 'An interview with the film censor', *Screen*, 23, 5 (1982).

B. Brown, 'Pornography: some modest proposals', *M/F* (January 1982).

S. Bryant, *The Television Heritage* (London, British Film Institute, 1990).

M. Bulmer, *Working-Class Images of Society* (London, Routledge & Kegan Paul, 1975).

T. Burns, *The BBC, Public Institutions and Private World* (London, Macmillan, 1977).

H. Cantril, *The Invasion From Mars: A Study in the Psychology of Panic* (Princeton, NJ, Princeton University Press, 1940).

D. Chaney, *Processes of Mass Communication* (London, Macmillan, 1972).

M. Cockerell, P. Hennessy and D. Walker, *Sources Close to the Prime Minister* (London, Macmillan, 1984).

S. Cohen, *Images of Deviance* (Harmondsworth, Penguin, 1971).

S. Cohen and J. Young (eds), *The Manufacture of News* (London, Constable, 1973).

Conference of Socialist Economics Microelectronics Group, *Microelectronics: Capitalist Technology and the Working Class* (London, CSE Books, 1980).

I. Connell, 'Commercial broadcasting and the British left', *Screen*, 24, 6 (1983).

G. Cumberbatch and D. Howitt, *A Measure of Uncertainty: The Effects of the Mass Media* (London, Libbey, 1989).

J. Curran, 'The boomerang effect: the press and the battle for London 1981–86', in J. Curran and A. Smith (eds), *Impacts and Influences* (London, Methuen, 1986).

J. Curran, 'Culturalist perspectives of news organisations: a reappraisal and a case study', in M. Ferguson (ed.), *Public Communication* (London, Sage, 1990).

J. Curran, 'The new revisionism in mass communication research: a reappraisal', *European Journal of Communications*, 5, 2–3 (1990).

J. Curran, I. Gaber and J. Petley, *Culture Wars* (Edinburgh, Edinburgh University Press, 2005).

J. H. Dunning, *Multinational Corporations and the Global Economy* (Wokingham, Addison-Wesley, 1993).

R. Dyer, *Light Entertainment*, BFI Television Monograph 2 (London, British Film Institute, 1973).

M. Edelmann, *The Symbolic Uses of Politics* (Urbana, University of Illinois Press, 1964).

P. Elliot, *The Making of a Television Series* (London, Constable, 1972).

P. Elliot, 'Intellectuals and "The information society" and the disappearance of the public sphere', *Media, Culture and Society*, 6, 4 (1982).

P. Elliot, G. Murdock and P. Schlesinger, 'Terrorism and the state: a case study in the discourse of television', *Media, Culture and Society*, 5, 2 (1983).

J. Ellis, *Visible Fiction: Cinema, TV, Video* (London, Routledge & Kegan Paul, 1982).

E. J. Epstein, *News from Nowhere* (New York, Random House, 1973).

R. Ericson, P. Baranec and J. Chan, *Visualizing Deviance* (Milton Keynes, Open University Press, 1987).

J. Fiske, *Television Culture* (London, Methuen, 1987).

S. Frith, *The Sociology of Rock* (London, Constable, 1979).

S. Frith, *The Aesthetics of Rock* (London, Macmillan, 1997).

P. Fussell, *The Great War in Modern Memory* (London, Oxford University Press, 1975).

N. Garnham, *Structures of Television*, BFI Television Monograph 1 (London, British Film Institute, 1973).

N. Garnham, 'Contribution to a political economy of mass communications', *Media, Culture and Society*, 1, 2 (April 1979).

N. Garnham, 'Public service versus the market', *Screen*, 24, 1 (1983).

E. Gellner, *Nations and Nation Building* (Cambridge, Cambridge University Press, 1984).

A. Giddens, *The Transformations of Intimacy: Sexuality, Love and Eroticism in Modern Societies* (Cambridge, Polity Press, 1992).

A. Giddens, *Post-Modernity* (Cambridge, Polity Press, 1994).

A. Giddens, *Beyond Left and Right* (Cambridge, Polity Press, 1995).

T. Gitlin, *The Whole World is Watching* (Berkeley, CA, University of California Press, 1982).

Glasgow University Media Group, *Bad News* (London, Routledge & Kegan Paul, 1976).

Glasgow University Media Group, 'Prime time ideology: the hegemonic process in television entertainment', *Social Problems*, 25, 3 (1979).

Glasgow University Media Group, *More Bad News* (London, Routledge & Kegan Paul, 1980).

P. Golding, *The Mass Media* (Harlow, Longman, 1974).

P. Golding and P. Elliot, *Making the News* (Harlow, Longman, 1979).

P. Golding and S. Middleton, *Images of Welfare* (London, Macmillan, 1980).

J. H. Goldthorpe and D. Lockwood, *The Affluent Worker: Political Attitudes and Behaviour* (Cambridge, Cambridge University Press, 1968).

K. Hafez, *The Myth of Media Globalization* (Cambridge, Polity, 2007).

S. Hall, 'The external/internal dialectic on broadcasting', *4th Symposium on British Broadcasting Policy*, February 1972.

S. Hall, 'The determination of news photographs', in S. Cohen and J. Young (eds), *The Manufacture of News* (London, Constable, 1973).

S. Hall, 'The hinterland of science: ideology', in Centre for Contemporary Cultural Studies, *On Ideology* (London, Hutchinson, 1977).

S. Hall, 'Culture, the media and the ideological effect', in J. Curran, M. Gurevitch and J. Woollacott (eds), *Mass Communication and Society* (London, Edward Arnold/Open University, 1977).

S. Hall, 'Newspapers, parties and classes', in J. Curran (ed.), *The British Press: A Manifesto* (London, Macmillan, 1978).

S. Hall, C. Critcher, T. Jefferson, J. Clarke and B. Roberts, *Policing the Crisis: Mugging, the State, and Law and Order* (London, Macmillan, 1978).

S. Hall, C. Curtis and I. Connell, 'The unity of current events TV', in Centre for Contemporary Cultural Studies, *Working Papers in Cultural Studies*, 9 (Spring 1976).

J. D. Halloran and G. Murdock, *Demonstrations and Communications* (Harmondsworth, Penguin, 1970).

P. Halmos (ed.), *Sociology of Mass Media Communicators*, Sociological Review Monograph 13 (Keele, University of Keele, 1969).

R. Harris, *Gotcha! The Media and the Falklands War* (London, Faber, 1983).

M. Harrop, 'Voters and the media', in J. Seaton and B. Pimlott (eds), *The Media in British Politics* (Aldershot, Gower, 1987).

M. Harrop and R. Worcester (eds), *Political Communication: The 1979 General Election* (London, Macmillan, 1981).

P. Hartmann and C. Husband, *Racism and the Mass Media* (London, Davis-Poynter, 1973).

B. Harvey, *The Condition of Post-Modernity* (Oxford, Oxford University Press, 1992).

F. Hayek, *The Road to Serfdom* (London, Routledge & Kegan Paul, 1944).

D. Held, *Democracy and the New International Order* (Cambridge, Polity Press, 1993).

D. Held (ed.), *Prospects for Democracy* (Cambridge, Polity Press, 1994).

C. Heller, *Broadcasters and Accountability*, BFI Television Monograph 3 (London, British Film Institute, 1978).

E. Herman and N. Chomsky, *Manufacturing Consent* (New York, Pantheon, 1988).

P. M. Hirsch, 'Processing fads and fashions', *American Journal of Sociology*, 46, 1 (1977).

P. Hirst, *After Thatcher* (London, Hutchinson, 1991).

P. Hirst and S. Khilnani, *Re-Inventing Democracy* (London, Political Quarterly, 1996).

P. Hirst and G. Thompson, *Globalisation in Question* (Cambridge, Polity Press, 1996).

D. Hobson, *Crossroads* (London, Methuen, 1983).

P. Hoch, *The Newspaper Game* (London, Calder & Boyars, 1974).

R. Hoggart, *The Uses of Literacy* (London, Chatto & Windus, 1957).

A. Hooper, *The Military and the Media* (London, Routledge & Kegan Paul, 1981).

M. Horkheimer, *The Eclipse of Reason* (Oxford, Oxford University Press, 1947).

C. I. Hovland, *Experiments in Mass Communication* (Princeton, NJ, Princeton University Press, 1949).

C. I. Hovland, 'Reconciling conflicting results derived from experimental and survey studies of attitude change', *American Psychologist*, 14, 3 (1959).

J. Howkins, *New Technologies, New Policies* (London, British Film Institute, 1982).

G. A. Huaco, *The Sociology of Film Art* (New York, Basic Books, 1965).

C. Husband (ed.), *White Media and Black Britain* (London, Routledge & Kegan Paul, 1962).

B. Jackson and D. Marsden, *Education and the Working Class* (London, Routledge & Kegan Paul, 1962).

M. Jay, *The Dialectical Imagination* (London, Heinemann, 1973).

E. Katz and P. Lazarsfeld, *Personal Influence: The Part Played by People in the Flow of Mass Communication* (West Drayton, Free Press, 1955).

T. Klapper, *The Effects of Mass Communication* (West Drayton, Free Press, 1960).

F. G. Kline and P. J. Tichenor, *Current Perspectives in Mass Communications Research* (London, Sage, 1972).

W. Kornhauser, *The Politics of Mass Society* (London, Routledge & Kegan Paul, 1959).

R. Kuhn, 'Government broadcasting in the 1980s: cross channel perspective', *Political Quarterly*, 53, 4 (1982).

R. Kuhn, 'Ballot box', *Stills* (May–June 1983).

K. Kumar, 'Holding the middle ground: the BBC, the public and the professional broadcaster', in J. Curran, M. Gurevitch and J. Woollacott (eds), *Mass Communication and Society* (London, Edward Arnold/Open University Press, 1977).

K. Kumar, *Policy and Progress* (Harmondsworth, Penguin, 1978).

K. Kumar, *Utopia and Anti-Utopianism in Modern Times* (Oxford, Blackwell, 1991).

S. Lambert, *Channel 4* (London, British Film Institute, 1982).

K. Lang, 'Images of society, media research in Germany', *Public Opinion Quarterly*, 22, 3 (1974).

K. Lang and G. Lang, *Politics and Television* (New York, Quadrangle, 1968).

K. Lang and G. Lang, *The Battle For Public Opinion: Watergate and the Media* (Westport, CT, Greenwood Press, 1982).

S. Lasch and J. Urry, *The End of Organised Capital* (Cambridge, Polity Press, 1990).

H. D. Lasswell, *Psychopathology and Politics* (Chicago, IL, University of Chicago Press, 1930).

H. D. Lasswell, 'The garrison state', *American Journal of Sociology*, 46, 2 (1941).

P. Lazarsfeld and R. Merton, 'Mass communication, popular taste and organised social action', in B. Rosenberg and D. White (eds), *Mass Culture* (West Drayton, Free Press, 1957).

P. Lazarsfeld and F. Stanton, *Radio Research 1942–3* (Boston, MA, Duell Sloan Pearce, 1944).

P. Lazarsfeld, B. Berelson and H. Gaudet, *The People's Choice* (New York, Columbia University Press, 1944).

M. Leapman, *Treachery? The Power Struggle at TVAM* (London, Allen & Unwin, 1984).

F. R. Leavis, *Mass Civilisation and Minority Culture* (London, Minority Press, 1930).

F. R. Leavis, *The Common Pursuit* (London, Chatto & Windus, 1952).

F. R. Leavis, *Scrutiny: A Retrospect* (Cambridge, Cambridge University Press, 1962).

F. R. Leavis, *A Selection From Scrutiny*, 2 vols (Cambridge, Cambridge University Press, 1968).

F. R. Leavis and D. Thompson, *Culture and Environment* (London, Chatto & Windus, 1933).

Q. D. Leavis, *Fiction and the Reading Public* (London, Chatto & Windus, 1932).

T. Lovell, 'Sociology of aesthetic structures', in D. McQuail (ed.), *Sociology of Mass Communications* (Harmondsworth, Penguin, 1972).

L. Lowenthal, *Prophets of Deceit* (New York, Harper & Row, 1949).

R. S. Lynd and H. M. Lynd, *Middletown: A Study on Contemporary American Culture* (London, Constable, 1929).

R. S. Lynd and H. M. Lynd, *Middletown: In Transition* (London, Constable, 1935).

A. McBarnett, 'The North Sea oil story', *Scottish Journal of Sociology*, 3, 1 (1977).

D. McQuail, *Towards a Sociology of Mass Communication* (West Drayton, Collier Macmillan, 1969).

D. McQuail, *Sociology of Mass Communications* (Harmondsworth, Penguin, 1972).

D. McQuail, 'Review of sociological writings on the press', Royal Commission on the Press 1974–77, Working Paper 2 (London, HMSO, 1977).

D. McQuail, *Mass Communication Theory: An Introduction* (2nd edn) (London, Sage, 1987).

H. Marcuse, *'The End of Utopia', Five Lectures* (Harmondsworth, Allen Lane, 1970).

H. Marcuse, *One Dimensional Man* (London, Routledge & Kegan Paul, 1974).

M. Mendelsohn and I. Crespi, *Polls, Television and the New Politics* (New York, Harper & Row, 1970).

R. K. Merton, *Social Theory and Social Structure* (West Drayton, Free Press, 1957).

F. Mulhearn, *The Moment of Scrutiny* (London, New Left Books, 1979).

K. Ohmae, *The Borderless World* (London, Collins, 1993).

K. Ohmae, *The End of the Nation State* (London, HarperCollins, 1996).

E. Ostrom, *Governing the Commons* (Oxford, Oxford University Press, 1994).

T. Pateman, *Language, Truth and Politics* (Brighton, Southern Books, 1974).

T. Pateman, *Television and the February 1974 General Election* (London, British Film Institute, 1976).

J. A. R. Pimlott, *Public Relations and American Democracy* (Princeton, NJ, Princeton University Press, 1951; repr. 1974).

A. Ray and K. Rowan (eds), *Inside Information: British Government and the Media* (London, Constable, 1982).

D. Reisman, *The Lonely Crowd* (New Haven, CT, Yale University Press, 1950).

J. P. Robinson, 'The press as king-maker', *Journalism Quarterly*, 41, 4 (1974).

B. Rosenberg and D. White (eds), *Mass Culture* (West Drayton, Free Press, 1957).

P. Schlesinger, *Putting 'Reality' Together* (London, Constable, 1974).

P. Schlesinger, 'Rethinking the sociology of journalism: source strategies and the limits of mediacentrism', in M. Ferguson (ed.), *Public Communication* (London, Sage, 1990).

P. Schlesinger, G. Murdoch and P. Elliot, *Televising Terrorism* (London, Comedia, 1984).

J. Seaton, 'The image of trade unions in the media', in B. Pimlott and C. Cook (eds), *Trade Unions in British Politics* (Harlow, Longman, 1982).

J. Seaton, 'The media and the politics of unemployment', in S. Allen, S. Waton and S. Wood (eds), *Unemployment* (London, Macmillan, 1985).

J. Seaton, 'Politics and the media in Britain', *Journal of Western European Politics*, special broadcasting issue (London, Summer 1985).

J. Seaton and B. Pimlott, 'The role of the media in the Portuguese Revolution', in A. Smith (ed.), *Newspapers and Democracy* (Cambridge, MA, MIT Press, 1980).

J. Seaton and B. Pimlott, 'The Portuguese media in transition', in K. Maxwell (ed.), *The Press and the Rebirth of Iberian Democracy* (Westport, CT, Greenwood Press, 1983).

J. Seaton and B. Pimlott, 'Political power and the Portuguese media', in L. Graham (ed.), *In Search of Modern Portugal: The Revolution and its Consequences* (Madison, University of Wisconsin Press, 1983).

C. Seymour-Ure, *The Press, Politics and Public* (London, Methuen, 1968).

C. Seymour-Ure, *The Political Impact of the Mass Media* (London, Constable, 1974).

C. Seymour-Ure, *The American President: Power and Communication* (London, Macmillan, 1982).

C. Seymour-Ure, 'The SDP and the media', *Political Quarterly*, 53, 4 (1982).

E. Shils, *The Intellectuals and the Powers* (Chicago, IL, University of Chicago Press, 1972).

E. Shils and M. Janowitz, 'Cohesion and disintegration in the Wehrmacht in World War II', *Public Opinion Quarterly*, 12, 3 (London, 1948).

P. Siegelhart (ed.), *Chips with Everything* (London, Comedia, 1982).

P. Slater, *The Origin and Significance of the Frankfurt School* (London, Routledge & Kegan Paul, 1977).

A. Smith, *The Politics of Information* (London, Macmillan, 1968).

A. Smith, *The Shadow in the Cave* (London, Allen & Unwin, 1973).

A. Smith, (ed.), *Television and Political Life* (London, Macmillan, 1979).

A. Smith, 'The fading of the industrial age', *Political Quarterly*, 53, 3 (June 1983).

A. Smith, *From Books to Bytes* (London, BFI, 1993).

B. L. Smith, H. D. Lasswell and R. Casey, *Propaganda Communication and Public Opinion* (Princeton, NJ, Princeton University Press, 1946).

A. Swingewood, *The Myth of Mass Culture* (London, Macmillan, 1977).

M. Tracey, *The Production of Political Television* (London, Routledge & Kegan Paul, 1978).

J. Trenaman, *Communications and Comprehension* (London, Collins, 1967).

J. Trenaman and D. McQuail, *Television and the Political Image* (London, Methuen, 1961).

G. Tuchman, 'Making news by doing work', *American Journal of Sociology*, 79, 1 (1973).

G. Tuchman (ed.), *The TV Establishment* (New York, Random House, 1975).

J. Tulloch, *Watching Television Audiences* (London, Arnold, 2000).

J. Tunstall, *Advertising Man* (London, Constable, 1969).

J. Tunstall, *The Westminster Lobby Correspondents* (London, Routledge & Kegan Paul, 1970).

J. Tunstall, *Journalists at Work* (London, Constable, 1971).

J. Tunstall, *The Media in Britain* (London, Constable, 1983).

F. Webster, *The Information Society* (Cambridge, Polity Press, 1996).

E. G. Wedell, *Broadcasting and Public Policy* (London, Michael Joseph, 1968).

E. G. Wedell, *Structures of Broadcasting* (Manchester, Manchester University Press, 1970).

J. Whale, *The Half Shut Eye* (London, Macmillan, 1969).

J. Whale, *The Politics of the Media* (London, Fontana, 1977).

R. Williams, *The Long Revolution* (Harmondsworth, Pelican, 1965).

R. Williams, *Communications* (London, Chatto & Windus, 1966).

R. Williams, *Television: Technology and Cultural Form* (London, Fontana, 1974).

R. Williams, *Drama from Ibsen to Brecht* (Harmondsworth, Penguin, 1976).

R. Williams, *Keywords* (London, Fontana, 1976).

R. Williams, *Marxism and Literature* (Oxford, Oxford University Press, 1977).

R. Williams, *Politics and Letters: Interviews with the* New Left Review (London, New Left Books, 1979).

J. Willis and T. Wollen (eds), *The Neglected Audience* (London, British Film Institute, 1990).

P. Willis, *Learning to Labour* (Farnborough, Saxon House, 1977).
P. Willis, *Sacred and Profane Culture* (London, Routledge & Kegan Paul, 1978).
P. Willmott and M. D. Young, *Family and Class in a London Suburb* (London, Routledge & Kegan Paul, 1960).
P. Willmott and M. D. Young, *The Symmetrical Family* (London, Routledge & Kegan Paul, 1973).

Mass communications readers

O. Boyd Barrett and C. Newbold (eds), *Approaches to Media* (London, Arnold, 1995).
R. Collins, J. Curran, N. Garnham, P. Scannell, P. Schlesinger and C. Sparks (eds), *Media, Culture and Society: A Critical Reader* (London, Sage, 1986).
J. Curran and M. Gurevitch (eds), *Mass Media and Society* (4th edn) (London, Arnold, 2005).
J. Curran and A. Smith (eds), *Impacts and Influences* (London, Methuen, 1987).
J. Curran, M. Gurevitch and J. Woollacott (eds), *Mass Communication and Society* (London, Edward Arnold/Open University, 1977).
J. Curran, D. Morley and V. Walkerdine (eds), *Cultural Studies and Communications* (London, Arnold, 1996).
J. Downing, A. Mohammadi and A. Sreberny-Mohammadi (eds), *Questioning the Media* (2nd edn) (London, Sage, 1995).
J. Eldridge (ed.), *Getting the Message* (London, Routledge, 1993).
M. Ferguson (ed.), *Public Communication* (London, Sage, 1990).
M. Gurevitch, T. Bennett, J. Curran and J. Woollacott (eds), *Culture, Society and the Media* (London, Methuen, 1982).
M. Levy and M. Gurevitch (eds), *Defining Media Studies* (New York, Oxford University Press, 1994).
D. McQuail (ed.), *Sociology of Mass Communication: Selected Reading* (Harmondsworth, Penguin, 1972).
R. Manoff and M. Schudson (eds), *Reading the News* (New York, Pantheon, 1987).
P. Marris and S. Thornham (eds), *Media Studies* (Edinburgh, Edinburgh University Press, 1996).
J. Munns, *A Cultural Studies Reader* (London, Longman, 1996).
E. Seiter, H. Borchers, G. Kreutzner and E.-M. Warth (eds), *Remote Control* (London, Routledge, 1989).

Economic approaches to the media

T. P. Barwise, A. S. C. Ehrenberg and G. J. Goodhart, 'Audience appreciation and audience size', *Journal of the Market Research Society*, 21, 4 (October 1979).
L. Brown, *Television: The Business Behind the Box* (New York, Harcourt Brace Jovanovich, 1971).
M. Cave, 'The conduct of auctions for broadcasting franchises', *Fiscal Studies*, 10, 1 (February 1989).
R. H. Coase, *British Broadcasting: A Study in Monopoly* (London, Longman Green, 1950).
R. H. Coase, 'The market for goods and the market for ideas', *American Economic Review* (1974), p. 384.

R. Collins, N. Garnham and G. Locksley, *The Economics of Television: The UK Case* (London, Sage, 1987).

R. Collins, N. Garnham and G. Locksley, *The Economics of Television* (London, Sage, 1988).

T. Congdon, B. Sturgess, W. Shaw, A. Graham and G. Davies, *Paying for Broadcasting* (London, Routledge, 1992).

J. Curran, 'Advertising and the press', in J. Curran (ed.), *The British Press: A Manifesto* (London, Macmillan, 1978).

J. Curran, 'Press freedom as a property right', *Media, Culture and Society*, 1, 1 (1979).

J. Curran, 'Advertising as a patronage system', *Sociological Review Monograph*, 29 (1980).

J. Curran, 'The impact of advertising on the British mass media', in R. Collins et al. (eds), *Media Culture and Society: A Critical Reader* (London, Sage, 1986).

J. Curran, A. Douglas and G. Whannel, 'The political economy of the human interest story', in A. Smith (ed.), *Newspapers and Democracy* (Cambridge, MA, MIT Press, 1981).

R. Darlington, 'Telecoms: the broadband revolution', *Information Technology and Public Policy*, 8, 1 (Winter 1989).

E. Epstein, *Broadcast Journalism. The Ratings Game* (London and New York, Vintage, 1975).

D. Freedman, 'The political economy of the new news environment', in N. Fenton (ed.), *New Media, Old News* (London, Sage, 2009).

J. E. Gerald, *The British Press under Government Economic Controls* (Minneapolis, University of Minnesota Press, 1956).

T. Gitlin, *Inside Prime Time* (New York, Pantheon, 1983).

P. Golding and G. Murdock, 'Culture, communications and political economy', in J. Curran and M. Gurevitch (eds), *Mass Media and Society* (2nd edn) (London, Arnold, 1996).

G. J. Goodhart, A. S. C. Ehrenberg and M. A. Collins, *The Television Audience: Patterns of Viewing* (Farnborough, Saxon House, 1975).

N. Gowing, 'Real time television and political crises' (Shorenstein Centre Paper, Kennedy School of Government, 1994).

T. H. Gubach, *The International Film Industry* (Indiana, University of Indiana Press, 1971).

A. Henney, 'Regulating public and privatized monopolies: a radical approach', *Policy Journal for the Public Finance Corporation* (February 1986).

F. Hirsch and D. Gordan, *Newspaper Money* (London, Hutchinson, 1975).

P. M. Hirsch, 'Processing fads and fashions', *American Journal of Sociology*, 77 (1972).

S. Hoyer, S. Hadenius and I. Weibull, *The Politics and Economics of the Press: A Developmental Perspective* (Beverly Hills, CA, Sage, 1975).

R. E. Jackson, 'Satellite business systems and the concept of the dispersed enterprise', *Media, Culture and Society*, 1, 3 (1979).

F. D. Klingender and S. Legg, *Money Behind the Screen* (London, Lawrence & Wishart, 1937).

M. Matson, 'Telecoms: the broadband revolution', Parliamentary Information Technology Committee 2 (22 November 1989).

A. Mattelart (trans. M. Chanan), *Multinational Corporations and the Control of Culture* (Brighton, Harvester Press, 1979).

K. Morgan and A. Sayer, *Microcircuits of Capital: Sunrise Industry and Uneven Development* (London, Polity Press, 1987).

V. Mosco, *The Political Economy of Information* (Madison, Wisconsin University Press, 1988).

G. Mulgan, *Communication and Control* (London, Polity Press, 1990).

G. Murdock, 'Redrawing the map of the communications industries: concentration and ownership in the era of privatization', in M. Ferguson (ed.), *Public Communication* (London, Sage, 1990).

G. Murdock and P. Golding, 'For a political economy of mass communication', in J. Saville and R. Miliband (eds), *The Socialist Register 1973* (London, Merlin, 1974).

G. Murdock and P. Golding, 'Capitalism, communication and class relations', in J. Curran, M. Gurevitch and J. Woollacott (eds), *Mass Communication and Society* (London, Edward Arnold/Open University Press, 1977).

Political and Economic Planning, *The British Press* (London, PEP, 1938).

Political and Economic Planning, *The Factual Film* (London, Arts Enquiry, PEP, 1947).

Political and Economic Planning, *The British Film Industry* (London, PEP, 1952).

R. Putnam, *Hanging Together: Cooperation and Conflict in Seven Power Summits* (Cambridge, MA, Harvard University Press, 1987).

K. Robins and F. Webster, 'Mass communications and information technology', in R. Miliband and J. Saville (eds), *The Socialist Register 1979* (London, Merlin, 1979).

H. Schiller, *Who Knows: Information in the Age of Fortune 500* (New Jersey, Ablex, 1981).

H. Schiller, *Mass Communications and the American Empire* (Boulder, CO, Westview Press, 1993).

M. Sharp (ed.), *Europe and New Technologies* (London, Pinter, 1989).

A. Smith, 'Subsidies and the press in Europe', *Political and Economic Planning*, 43, 569 (1977).

A. Smith, *The Geopolitics of Information* (London, Faber, 1980).

A. Smith, *Goodbye Gutenburg: The Newspaper Revolution of the 1980s* (London, Oxford University Press, 1980).

S. G. Sturmey, *The Economic Development of Radio* (London, Duckworth, 1958).

J. Taylor, 'The broadband revolution: implications for major networks', *Information Technology and Public Policy*, 8, 1 (Winter 1990).

J. Tunstall, *The Media are American* (London, Constable, 1977).

T. Varis, 'The international flow of television programmes', *Journal of Communication*, 34 (1984).

F. Wolf, *Television Programming for News and Current Affairs* (New York, Praeger, 1972).

Politics of mass media

Adam Smith Institute, *Omega Report: Communications Policy* (London, Adam Smith Institute, 1984).

Adam Smith Institute, *Funding the BBC* (London, Adam Smith Institute, 1985).

M. Aldridge and N. Hewitt (eds), *Controlling Broadcasting* (Manchester, Manchester University Press, 1994).

N. Ascherson, 'Newspapers and internal democracy', in J. Curran (ed.), *The British Press: A Manifesto* (London, Macmillan, 1978).

T. Austin and T. Haines (eds), The Times *Guide to the House of Commons June 2001* (London, Times Books, 2001).

R. Avery (ed.), *Public Service Broadcasting in a Multichannel Environment* (New York, Longman, 1993).

T. Baistow, *Fourth-Rate Estate* (London, Comedia, 1985).

E. Barendt, *Broadcasting Law* (Oxford, Oxford University Press, 1993).

J. Barron, *Freedom of the Press for Whom?* (Ontario, Midland, 1975).

D. Berry, L. Cooper and C. Landry, *Where is the Other News?* (London, Comedia, 1980).

J. Blumler and M. Gurevitch, *The Crisis of Public Communication* (London, Routledge, 1995).

S. Brittan, 'The fight for freedom in broadcasting', *Political Quarterly*, 58 (1987).

S. Brittan, 'The case for the consumer market', in C. Veljanovski (ed.), *Freedom in Broadcasting* (London, Institute of Economic Affairs, 1989).

Broadcasting Research Unit, *The Public Service Idea* (London, Broadcasting Research Unit, 1985).

D. Butler and G. Butler, *Twentieth-Century British Political Facts, 1900–2000* (8th edn) (Basingstoke, Macmillan, 2000).

V. Cable, *The World's New Fissure* (London, Demos, 1994).

M. Cockerell, *Live from No. 10* (London, Faber and Faber, 1988).

R. Collins, *Television: Culture and Policy* (London, Unwin Hyman, 1990).

R. Collins, *Satellite Television in Western Europe* (revised edn) (London, Libbey, 1992).

R. Collins, *Broadcasting and Audio-visual Policy in the European Single Market* (London, Libbey, 1994).

R. Collins and C. Murroni, *New Media, New Policies* (Cambridge, Polity Press, 1996).

L. Cooper, C. Landry and D. Berry, *The Other Secret Service* (London, Comedia, 1980).

G. Cumberbatch and D. Howitt, *A Measure of Uncertainty* (London, Libbey, 1989).

J. Curran (ed.), *The British Press: A Manifesto* (London, Macmillan, 1978).

J. Curran (ed.), 'Rethinking the media as a public sphere', in P. Dahlgren and C. Sparks (eds), *Communication and Citizenship* (London, Routledge, 1991).

J. Curran (ed.), 'Regulation and deregulation of the British media', in K. E. Gustafsson (ed.), *Media Structure and the State* (Gothenburg, University of Gothenburg, 1995).

J. Curran (ed.), 'Mass media and democracy revisited', in J. Curran and M. Gurevitch (eds), *Mass Media and Democracy* (2nd edn) (London, Arnold, 1996).

J. Curran (ed.), 'Media and democracy: the third route', in M. Andersen (ed.), *Media and Democracy* (Oslo, University of Oslo, 1996).

J. Curran (ed.), 'Television journalism: theory and practice. The case of *Newsnight*', in P. Holland (ed.), *Television Handbook* (London, Routledge, 1997).

J. Curran (ed.), 'Press reformism 1918–98: a study of failure', in H. Tumber (ed.), *Media Power, Professionals and Policies* (London, Routledge, 2000).

J. Curran (ed.), *Media and Power* (London, Routledge, 2002).

J. Curran (ed.), 'Global journalism: a case study of the internet', in N. Couldry and J. Curran (eds), *Contesting Media Power* (Boulder, CO, Rowman & Littlefield, 2003).

J. Curran, J. Ecclestone, G. Oakley and A. Richardson (eds), *Bending Reality: The State of the Media* (London, Pluto Press, 1986).

J. Curran, S. Iyengar, A. B. Lund and A. Salovaara-Moring, 'Media system, public knowledge and democracy: A comparative study', *European Journal of Communication*, 24, 1 (2009).

P. Dahlgren, *Television and the Public Sphere* (London, Sage, 1995).

P. Dahlgren and C. Sparks (eds), *Communication and Citizenship* (London, Routledge, 1991).

P. Dahlgren and C. Sparks (eds), *Journalism and Popular Culture* (London, Sage, 1992).

M. Dickinson and S. Street (eds), *Cinema and the State* (London, British Film Institute, 1985).

B. Franklin, *Packaging Politics* (London, Arnold, 1994).

C. Frost, 'The Press Complaints Commission: a study of ten years of adjudications on press complaints', *Journalism Studies*, 5, 1 (2004).

C. Gardiner and J. Sheppard, 'Transforming TV: the limits of left policy', *Screen*, 25, 2 (1984).

N. Garnham, 'Public service versus the market', *Screen*, 24, 1 (1983).

N. Garnham, 'Telecommunications policy in the United Kingdom', *Media, Culture and Society*, 7, 1 (1985).

N. Garnham, *Communications and Capitalism* (London, Sage, 1990).

T. Gitlin, 'Public sphere or sphericules?', in T. Liebes and J. Curran (eds), *Media, Ritual and Identity* (London, Routledge, 1998).

Glasgow University Media Group, *Really Bad News* (London, Writers & Readers, 1982).

D. Goldberg, T. Prosser and S. Verhulst, *Regulating the Changing Media* (Oxford, Clarendon Press, 1998).

P. Golding and G. Murdock, 'Confronting the market: public intervention and press diversity', in J. Curran (ed.), *The British Press: A Manifesto* (London, Macmillan, 1978).

P. Golding and G. Murdock, 'The new communications revolution', in J. Curran, J. Ecclestone, G. Oakley and A. Richardson (eds), *Bending Reality: The State of the Media* (London, Pluto Press, 1986).

A. Graham and G. Davies, *Broadcasting, Society and Policy in the Multimedia Age* (Luton, University of Luton Press, 1997).

J. Gray, *After Social Democracy* (London, Demos, 1996).

K. E. Gustafsson, 'Government policies to reduce newspaper entry barriers', *Journal of Economics*, 6, 1 (1993).

A. Harcourt, 'Institution-driven competition: the regulation of cross-border broadcasting in the EU', *Journal of Public Policy*, 27, 3 (2007).

I. Hargreaves, *A Sharper Vision: The BBC and the Communication Revolution* (London, Demos, 1993).

S. Harvey (ed.), *The Regions, the Nation, the BBC* (London, BFI, 1993).

S. Harvey and K. Robins, 'Voices and places: the BBC and regional policy', *Political Quarterly*, 65, 1 (1994).

S. Hearst, 'The development of cable systems and services', *Political Quarterly*, 54, 3 (1983).

P. Hennessy, D. Walker and M. Cockerell, *Sources Close to the Prime Minister* (London, Macmillan, 1985).

D. Hesmondhaulgh, *The Cultural Industries* (London, Sage, 2002).

S. Holland, 'Countervailing press power', in J. Curran (ed.), *The British Press: A Manifesto* (London, Macmillan, 1978).

S. Hood (ed.), *Behind the Scenes* (London, Lawrence & Wishart, 1994).

S. Hood and G. O'Leary, *Questions of Broadcasting* (London, Methuen, 1990).

R. Horwitz, 'The First Amendment meets some new technologies: broadcasting, common carriers and free speech in the 1990s', *Theory and Society*, 20 (1991).

P. Humphreys, *Mass Media and Media Policy in Western Europe* (Manchester, Manchester University Press, 1996).

P. Humphreys, 'The EU, communications liberalization and the future of public service broadcasting', in K. Sarikakis (ed.), *Media and Cultural Policy in the European Union* (Amsterdam, Rodopi, 2007).

N. Jones, *Soundbites and Spin Doctors* (London, Cassell, 1995).

E. Katz, 'And deliver us from segmentation', *Annals of the American Academy of Political and Social Science*, 546 (1996).

J. Keane, *The Media and Democracy* (Cambridge, Polity Press, 1991).

S. K. Kent, *Gender and Power in Britain, 1640–1990* (London, Routledge, 1999).

A. Knight, *A British Success Story* (London, News International, 1993).

R. Kuhn, *Politics and the Media in Britain* (Basingstoke, Palgrave Macmillan, 2007).

Labour Party, *People and the Media* (London, Labour Party, 1974).

C. Landry, D. Morley, R. Southwood and P. Write, *What a Way to Run a Railroad* (London, Comedia, 1985).

C. Leys, *Market-Driven Politics* (London, Verso, 2001).

L. Lichtenberg, 'The Dutch model of press policy', in K. E. Gustafsson (ed.), *Media Structure and the State* (Gothenberg, University of Gothenberg, 1995).

S. Livingstone and P. Lunt, *Talk on Television* (London, Routledge, 1994).

C. MacCabe and O. Stewart (eds), *The BBC and Public Service Broadcasting* (Manchester, Manchester University Press, 1986).

P. McDonald, 'The music industry', in J. Stokes and A. Reading (eds), *The Media in Britain* (Basingstoke, Macmillan, 1999).

B. McNair, *Mediated Sex* (London, Arnold, 1996).

B. McNair, *News and Journalism in the UK* (5th edn) (London, Routledge, 2009).

D. McQuail and K. Siane (eds), *New Media Politics* (London, Sage, 1986).

T. Madge, *Beyond the BBC* (London, Macmillan, 1989).

W. Melody, 'Communication policy in the global information economy: whither the public interest', in M. Ferguson (ed.), *Public Communication* (London, Sage, 1990).

Militant, *What We Stand For* (London, Militant, 1985).

T. Miller, N. Govil, J. McMurria, R. Maxwell and T. Wang, *Global Hollywood 2* (London, British Film Institute, 2004).

E. Moonman (ed.), *The Press: A Case for Commitment* (London, Fabian Society Trust, 391, 1969).

G. Mulgan and K. Worpole, *Saturday Night or Sunday Morning* (London, Comedia, 1986).

R. Murdoch, 'Freedom in broadcasting', MacTaggart Lecture 1989 (London, News International, 1989).

P. Murschetz, 'State support for the daily press in Europe: a critical appraisal', *European Journal of Communication*, 13, 3 (1998).

R. Negrine, *Politics and the Mass Media in Britain* (2nd edn) (London, Routledge, 1994).

T. O'Malley and C. Soley, *Regulating the Press* (London, Pluto Press, 2000).

R. Picard, *Ravens of Odin* (Ames, Iowa State University Press, 1988).

V. Porter, 'The Janus character of television', in G. Locksley (ed.), *Integration: The Single European Market and the Information Communication Technologies* (London, Pinter, 1990).

M. Puppis, 'National media regulation in the era of free trade: the role of global media governance', *European Journal of Communication*, 23, 4 (2008).

G. Robertson, *People Against the Press* (London, Quartet, 1983).

G. Robertson and A. Nicol, *Media Law* (3rd edn) (Harmondsworth, Penguin, 1992).

J. Rowbottom, 'Media freedom and political debate in the digital era', *Modern Law Review*, 69 (4), 2006.

L. Sabato, *Feeding Frenzy: Attack Journalism and Politics* (New York, Free Press, 1995).

P. Scannell, 'Public service broadcasting and modern public life', in P. Scannell, P. Schlesinger and C. Sparks (eds), *Culture and Power* (London, Sage, 1992).

P. Schlesinger, 'From public service to commodity: the political economy of teletext in the UK', *Media, Culture and Society*, 7, 4 (1984).

J. Seaton, 'Government policy and the mass media', in J. Curran (ed.), *The British Press: A Manifesto* (London, Macmillan, 1978).

J. Seaton, 'Broadcasting and politics in Britain', in R. Kuhn (ed.), *Broadcasting and Politics in Western Europe* (London, Sage, 1985).

J. Seaton, 'The media and politics in Britain', *Journal of Western European Politics*, 6, 3 (June 1985).

J. Seaton, 'Pornography annoys', in J. Curran (ed.), *Bending Reality: The State of the Media* (London, Pluto Press, 1986).

J. Seaton, 'The media and the politics of unemployment', in S. Allen (ed.), *The Experience of Unemployment* (London, Macmillan, 1986).

J. Seaton, 'Atrocities and the media', *European Journal of Communications*, 2, 1 (January 1987).

J. Seaton, 'The Holocaust: a case study of atrocities and the media', in J. Seaton and B. Pimlott (eds), *The Media in British Politics* (Aldershot, Gower, 1987).

J. Seaton, 'Down with Aunt Tabitha: a modest media proposal', in B. Pimlott and T. Wright (eds), *The Alternative: Politics for a Change* (London, W. H. Allen, 1990).

J. Seaton (ed.), *The Media of Conflict* (London, Zed Books, 1998).

J. Seaton, *Politics and the Media in the New Millennium* (London, Blackwell, 1998).

J. Seaton and B. Pimlott, 'The struggle for balance: the BBC and the politicians 1926–45', in J. Seaton and B. Pimlott (eds), *The Media in British Politics* (Aldershot, Gower, 1987).

C. Seymour-Ure, 'Leaders and the media', in J. Seaton and B. Pimlott (eds), *The Media in British Politics* (Aldershot, Gower, 1987).

J. Sinclair, E. Jacka and S. Cunningham (eds), *New Patterns in Global Television* (Oxford, Oxford University Press, 1996).

E. Skogerbo, 'The press subsidy system in Norway', *European Journal of Communication*, 12, 1, (1997).

A. Smith, *Subsidies and the Press in Europe* (London, Political & Economic Planning, 1977).

R. Sparks and I. Taylor, 'Mass communications', in P. Brown and R. Sparks (eds), *Beyond Thatcherism* (Milton Keynes, Open University Press, 1989).

W. Stevenson (ed.), *All our Futures* (London, BFI, 1993).

S. Tunney, *Labour and the Press* (Brighton, Sussex University Press, 2007).

C. Veljanovski (ed.), *Freedom in Broadcasting* (London, Institute of Economic Affairs, 1989).

J. Whale, *The Politics of the Media* (London, Fontana, 1980).

P. Whitehead, 'Reconstructing broadcasting', in J. Curran, J. Ecclestone, G. Oakley and A. Richardson (eds), *Bending Reality: The State of the Media* (London, Pluto Press, 1986).

R. Worcester, 'Demographics and values: what the British public reads and what it thinks about its newspapers', in H. Stephenson and M. Bromley (eds), *Sex, Lies and Democracy* (London, Longman, 1998).

New media

J. Abbate, *Inventing the Internet* (Cambridge, MA, MIT Press, 2000).

Advertising Statistics Yearbook 2002 (London, Advertising Association, 2002).

N. Baym, 'Interpersonal life online', in L. Lievrouw and S. Livingstone (eds), *The Handbook of New Media* (London, Sage, 2002).

D. Bell and B. Kennedy (eds), *The Cybercultures Reader* (London, Routledge, 2000).

C. Bellamy and J. Taylor, *Governing in the Information Age* (Milton Keynes, Open University Press, 1998).

T. Berners-Lee, *Weaving the Web* (London, Orion, 2000).

A. Briggs and P. Burke, *A Social History of the Media* (Cambridge, Polity Press, 2002).

M. Cassells, *The Internet Galaxy* (Oxford, Oxford University Press, 2001).

J. Cassidy, *Dot.Con* (London, Penguin Books, 2003).

N. Chenoweth, *Virtual Murdoch* (London, Secker Warburg, 2001).

S. Coleman, 'New media and democratic politics', *New Media and Society*, 1, 1 (1999).

J. Cornford and K. Robins, 'New media', in J. Stokes and A. Reading (eds), *The Media in Britain* (Basingstoke, Macmillan, 1999).

J. Curran, 'Global journalism: a case study of the internet', in N. Couldry and J. Curran (eds), *Contesting Media Power* (New York, Rowman & Littlefield, 2003).

J. Curran and T. Witschge, 'Liberal dreams and the internet', in N. Fenton (ed.), *New Media, Old News* (London, Sage, 2009).

D. Elstein, 'The politics of digital TV'. Available at: www.openDemocracy.net/forum, 2002.

P. Evans and T. Wurster, *Blown to Bits* (Boston, MA, Harvard Business School Press, 2000).

N. Fenton (ed.), *New Media, Old News* (London, Sage, 2009).

P. Flichy, 'New media history', in L. Lievrouw and S. Livingstone (eds), *The Handbook of New Media* (London, Sage, 2002).

C. George, 'The Internet's political impact and the penetration/participation paradox in Malaysia and Singapore', *Media, Culture and Society*, 27, 6, 2005.

J. Gillies and R. Cailliau, *How the Web Was Born* (Oxford, Oxford University Press, 2000).

G. Goggin, 'Pay per browse? The Web's commercial future', in D. Gauntlett (ed.), *Web Studies* (London, Arnold, 2000).

L. Gross, 'The gay global village in cyberspace', in N. Couldry and J. Curran (eds), *Contesting Media Power* (Boulder, CO, Rowman & Littlefield, 2003).

D. Held, A. McGrew, D. Goldblatt and J. Perraton, *Global Transformations* (Cambridge, Polity Press, 1999).

K. Hill and J. Hughes, *Cyberpolitics* (Lanham, MD, Rowman & Littlefield, 1998).

M. Hindman, *The Myth of Digital Democracy* (Princeton, Princeton University Press, 2009).

M. Ito, 'Virtually embodied: the reality of fantasy in a multi-user dungeon', in D. Porter (ed.), *Internet Culture* (New York, Routledge, 1997).

N. Klein, *No Logo* (London, Flamingo, 2001).

C. Kramarae, 'The language and the nature of the Internet: the meaning of global', *New Media and Society*, 1, 1 (1999).

S. Lax, 'The Internet and democracy', in D. Gauntlet (ed.), *Web Studies* (London, Arnold, 2000).

T. Lennon, 'Digital TV: a phoenix risen from the ashes', *Free Press*, 129, 2002.

L. Lessig, *Code and Other Laws of Cyberspace* (New York, Basic Books, 1999).

L. Lessig, *The Future of Ideas* (New York, Random House, 2001).

S. Levy, *Hackers* (London, Penguin, 1994).

M. Lim, 'The internet, social networks and reform in Indonesia', in N. Couldry and J. Curran (eds), *Contesting Media Power* (Boulder, CO, Rowman & Littlefield, 2003).

S. Ling, 'The alternative media in Malaysia: their potential and limitations', in N. Couldry and J. Curran (eds), *Contesting Media Power* (Boulder, CO, Rowman & Littlefield, 2003).

S. Livingstone and M. Bovill, *Young People: New Media* (London, London School of Economics and Political Science, 1999).

P. Lovelock and J. Ure, 'The new economy: internet, telecommunications and electronic commerce?', in L. Lievrouw and S. Livingstone (eds), *The Handbook of New Media* (London, Sage, 2002).

R. McChesney, *Rich Media, Poor Democracy* (Urbana, University of Illinois Press, 1999).

M. Mallapragada, 'The Indian diaspora in the USA and around the world', in D. Gauntlett (ed.), *Web Studies* (London, Arnold, 2000).

R. Mansell, 'New media and the power of networks' (London, London School of Economics and Political Science, Inaugural Professorial Lecture, 2001).

D. Miller and D. Slater, *The Internet: An Ethnographic Approach* (Oxford, Berg, 2000).

V. Miller, 'Search engines, portals and global capitalism', in D. Gauntlett (ed.), *Web Studies* (London, Arnold, 2000).

G. Murdock and P. Golding, 'Digital possibilities, market realities: the contradictions of communications convergence', in L. Panitch and C. Leys (eds), *A World of Contradictions: Socialist Register 2002* (London, Merlin Press, 2001).

J. Naughton, *A Brief History of the Future* (London, Phoenix, 2000).

N. Negroponte, *Being Digital* (London, Hodder & Stoughton, 1996 [1995]).

K. Patelis, 'The political economy of the Internet', in J. Curran (ed.), *Media Organisations in Society* (London, Arnold, 2000).

M. Poster, *The Second Media Age* (Cambridge, Polity Press, 1995).

M. Poster, 'Cyberdemocracy: Internet and the public sphere', in D. Porter (ed.), *Internet Culture* (New York, Routledge, 1997).

M. Price, *Media and Sovereignty* (Cambridge, MA, MIT Press, 2002).

H. Rheingold, *The Virtual Community* (rev. edn) (Cambridge, MA, MIT Press, 2000).

G. Rodan, *Transparency and Authoritarian Rule in Southeast Asia* (London, Curzon Routledge, 2004).

D. Schiller, *Digital Capitalism* (Cambridge, MA, MIT Press, 2000).

D. Slater, 'Social relationships and identity online and offline', in L. Lievrouw and S. Livingstone (eds), *The Handbook of New Media* (London, Sage, 2002).

J. Slevin, *The Internet and Society* (Cambridge, Polity Press, 2000).

C. Sparks, 'From dead trees to live wires: the Internet's challenge to the traditional newspaper', in J. Curran and M. Gurevitch (eds), *Mass Media and Society* (3rd edn) (London, Arnold, 2000).

C. Sparks, 'The internet and the global public sphere', in W. Lance Bennett and R. Entman (eds), *Mediated Politics* (New York, Cambridge University Press, 2001).

L. Stein and N. Sinha, 'New global media and communication policy: the role of the state in the twenty-first century', in L. Lievrouw and S. Livingstone (eds), *The Handbook of New Media* (London, Sage, 2001).

J. Stratton, 'Cyberspace and the globalisation of culture', in D. Porter (ed.), *Internet Culture* (New York, Routledge, 1997).

T. Streeter, 'Romanticism in business culture: the Internet, the 1990s, and the origins of irrational exuberance', in A. Calabrese and C. Sparks (eds), *Toward a Political Economy of Culture* (Boulder, CO, Rowman & Littlefield, 2003).

F. Turner, *From Counterculture to Cyberculture* (Chicago, University of Chicago Press, 2006).

A. Willheim, *Democracy and the Digital Age* (New York, Routledge, 2000).

S. Williams, *Free as in Freedom* (Sebastopol, CA, O'Reilly, 2002).

B. Winston, *Media Technology and Society* (London, Routledge, 1998).

Y. Zhao, 'Falun Gong, identity, the struggle over meaning in and out of reformed China', in N. Couldry and J. Curran (eds), *Contesting Media Power* (Boulder, CO, Rowman & Littlefield, 2003).

Index

Page numbers in **bold** indicate tables.